The Haynes

GM □ FORD □ CHRYSLER

Engine Performance Manual

by Jay Storer
and John H Haynes
Member of the Guild of Motoring Writers

The Haynes Manual
for understanding, planning and
building high-performance engines

ABCDE
FGHIJ
KLMNO
PQRST

Haynes®

APA AUTOMOTIVE PARTS & ACCESSORIES ASSOCIATION MEMBER

Haynes Publishing Group
Sparkford Nr Yeovil
Somerset BA22 7JJ England

Haynes Publishing Group
861 Lawrence Drive
Newbury Park
California 91320 USA

Acknowledgements

Thanks are due to the following people whose extraordinary efforts helped make this book possible:

Ben Smeding of Smeding Performance
Tony Mamo of Airflow Research
Matt Sadler of the Comp Performance Group
Robert Loftis of Eagle Specialty Products

Technical authors who contributed to this project are Mike Forsythe and Mike Stubblefield.

A book in the Haynes Automotive Repair Manual Series

Printed in the U.S.A.

ISBN-13: 978-1-56392-693-8

ISBN-10: 1-56392-693-8

Library of Congress Catalog Card Number 2007938629

07-288

Contents

Chapter 1
Power Planning:
Matching Goals, Budget and Driving Needs

Torque versus horsepower 1-4
Mistake number one 1-5

Chapter 2
Choosing Speed:
Sourcing Performance Equipment and Services

Why you need help 2-1
What is a "speed shop?" 2-2
There's more than one kind of speed shop 2-2
Pick the right people 2-4
Dynamometers: The Ultimate Tuning Tool 2-5
The Flow Bench: The Tuner's Wind Tunnel 2-7

Chapter 3
The Look of Speed

Clean and detail your engine compartment first 3-3
Engine washing 3-4
Painting and final details on a Ford small-block engine compartment 3-5
Dressing up a Chevy big-block engine compartment 3-10

Chapter 4
Computers and Chips

A brief history 4-1
Engine management basics 4-2
Information sensors 4-2
The computer 4-9
Output actuators 4-9
Computer codes keep track 4-11
Add-on chips and performance upgrades for computers 4-11
Piggyback modules 4-11
Flashing or replacing chips 4-12
What to expect from piggybacks and reflashed chips 4-13
Stand-alone aftermarket systems 4-13
What about turbos and blowers? 4-13
Hand-held programmers 4-14
Tuning Tool Test 4-15

Chapter 5
High-performance Ignition Systems

High-performance ignition coils ... 5-1
Where to put the ignition control module and ignition coil ... 5-2
Performance plug wires ... 5-4
Ignition timing controls ... 5-4
Spark plugs ... 5-6
Reading the plugs ... 5-6

Chapter 6
Induction: The Science of Deep Breathing

Short-ram and cold-air intakes ... 6-2
Throttle bodies ... 6-4
Intake manifolds ... 6-5
Carburetion ... 6-8

Chapter 7
Cylinder Heads and Valves

Valve jobs ... 7-7

Chapter 8
Camshafts and Valvetrain

Rocker arms ... 8-1
Camshafts ... 8-2
Lifters ... 8-6
How to degree a camshaft ... 8-8
Valve springs ... 8-9
Blueprinting and valvetrain ... 8-11

Chapter 9
The Fuel System

Carburetors ... 9-1
Finding the right carburetor ... 9-1
Carburetor modifications ... 9-2
Main body ... 9-3
Throttle body ... 9-3
Metering block (Holley carburetors) ... 9-5
Main body and air horn (Rochester carburetors) ... 9-6
Float bowl ... 9-7
Accelerator pump(s) and controls ... 9-7
Secondary circuit ... 9-8
Heat ... 9-9
Fuel lines and filters ... 9-10
Do you need a high-performance fuel pump? ... 9-11
Carburetor modification kits ... 9-11
Fuel injection systems ... 9-12
Why fuel injection? ... 9-12

What is fuel injection?.......... 9-12
Throttle body injection (TBI) 9-12
Multiport electronic fuel injection 9-13
Input: Information sensors.......... 9-20
Procession: The computer.......... 9-23
Output: System actuators 9-23
Modifying a fuel injection system.......... 9-25
What about Throttle Body Injection (TBI) systems? 9-25
High-performance fuel pressure regulators and gauges 9-25
Bigger fuel rails and high-flow injectors.......... 9-26
High-performance fuel pumps 9-27

Chapter 10
The Exhaust System

Stock exhaust manifolds.......... 10-1
Backpressure and flow 10-1
Modifying the exhaust system 10-2
Exhaust systems 10-4
Mufflers.......... 10-5
Conclusion.......... 10-6
Installing and typical cat-back system 10-6

Chapter 11
Power Adders: Juice and Boost

Part A Nitrous Oxide 11-2
Part B Supercharging.......... 11-7
Part C Turbocharging 11-15

Chapter 12
The Bottom End: Building it to Last

Blueprinting.......... 12-3
Crankshaft work.......... 12-5
Connecting rods 12-9
Pistons.......... 12-11
Engine block.......... 12-14
Stroker engines 12-17
Balancing.......... 12-19

Chapter 13
Engine Builds:
How the Pros Make Big Power with Reliability

Part A Building the GM LS1 for Extreme Street Duty 13-2
Part B Pro-building a 427-inch Ford Small-block.......... 13-17
Part C Blown 572 Big-block Chevrolet build 13-29

Chapter 14
Crates and Swaps

Crate motors.......... 14-2
Choosing a crate motor 14-11

Engine swaps 14-13

Chapter 15
High-performance Cooling Systems

Coolant additives 15-1
Radiators 15-2
Radiator cooling fans 15-3
Water pumps 15-4
Under-drive pulleys 15-4
Electric water pumps 15-4
Deep sump oil pans and engine oil coolers 15-4
Transmission oil coolers 15-5

Chapter 16
Monitoring Engine Performance

How much will it cost? 16-2
What kind of gauges do you want? 16-2
Where do I put the gauges? 16-3
Typical gauges 16-4
G-Tech tuning tools 16-5
G-Tech/Pro 16-5
G-Tech/Pro COMPETITION 16-6
Scan tools: Spend some quality time with your car's computer 16-6
Installing a Tachometer 16-8
Installing pillar pod gauges 16-12
Installing a wideband air/fuel ratio gauge 16-16
Innovate LM-1 wide-band air-fuel ratio meter 16-19
Innovate LMA-3 Multi-sensor Device (AuxBox) 16-21

1 Power Planning: Matching Goals, Budget and Driving Needs

The sign on the wall in many old speed shops used to read "*Speed Costs Money . . . How Fast Do You Want To Go?*" Money doesn't grow on trees and neither does vehicle performance. It's almost a tradition for a young man to enthusiastically start a hot rod project, get in way over his head, and be unable to complete it due to lack of money. Eventually, he winds up selling his dream vehicle for half of what he's put into it, just to afford the most basic of vehicles for daily transportation. This scenario has been repeated through every generation of Americans for the last six or seven decades.

You want more performance, or you wouldn't be reading this book, but how much do you need and how much can you afford? Is the best plan for you a streetable car/truck that can be used on the weekends for fun at the drags, or an all-out race car with a maxi-motor? Plan ahead for the end results

Youth can be forgiven for heady enthusiasm, but performance fans of all ages need to begin any project with a dose of reality and common sense. The foremost consideration is how much you really have to spend, followed closely by a realistic look at what performance equipment and shop work really costs. When you add up your wish list of parts you've seen in a mail-order catalog, you may be overlooking all the little incidentals that are part of the true cost. For instance, you see a new aluminum intake manifold for $250. Before you enter this on your proposed list of engine mods, add the cost of a set of intake gaskets ($22.50), a tube of RTV sealant ($6.95), 4-barrel carburetor ($350), phenolic carburetor spacer ($29.95), linkage brackets ($30-$50), fuel line and inline filter ($15-$20), and a new air cleaner ($39.95). As you can see, what you envisioned as a $250 expense is really closer to $800. The little things are the ones that add up a bit at a time until you're talking real money. For each modification you'd like to make, investigate the real costs, including hardware, and any machine work that needs to be done at a shop, etc.

Making smart performance choices isn't just about the money, either. You must consider what is practical for your driving needs. Is this project vehicle something that has to double as transportation, or will it be only be used on weekends? When you do drive it, will it see a lot of slow cruising time? Do you plan on spending any serious time on the dragstrip or participating in some other kind

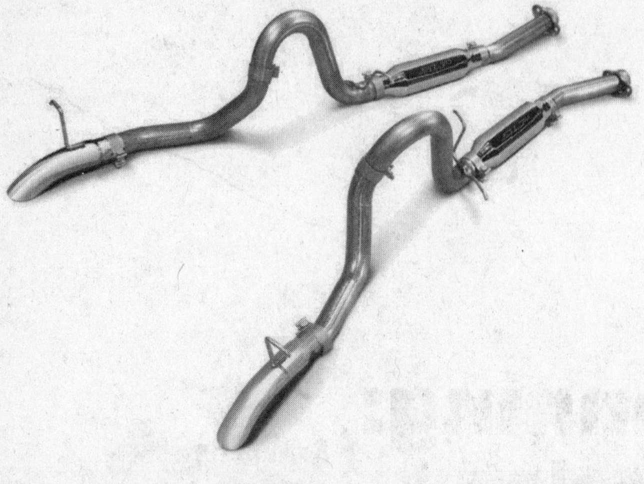

One of your best investments in improved performance and economy is a free-flowing exhaust system. A cat-back system like this SLP "loudmouth" dual set for '86-'93 Mustangs will give you improved sound and performance, even if you do nothing else to the car

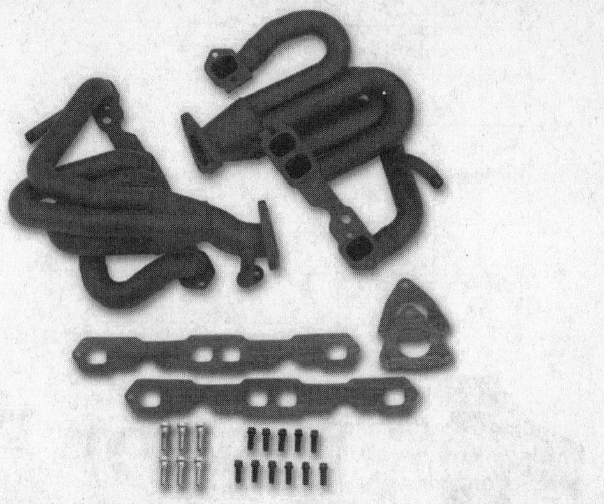

A set of exhaust headers would be the next step in exhaust improvement, to complement the dual exhausts and also to provide the free-breathing required for engine mods to come later. These are 50-state-legal Hooker Headers for '94-'96 Impala SS models with 350 LT1 engines, shown with ceramic coating

of motorsports? These factors will have a lot of influence on how you build your performance engine. If you plan on some runs down the 1320, you'll also have to invest in other aspects of the car, like safety equipment (helmet, scattershield, driveshaft safety loop, etc.). Plus, you'll have to make needed clutch/transmission/rear axle improvements to handle the punishment your modified engine can deliver to the drivetrain with slicks hooked up on a sticky track. If your car is realistically going to do a lot of cruising, then you need an engine with a reasonable idle and good bottom-end torque. Be aware that too much camshaft will leave you with low intake manifold vacuum, so your power brakes may not work very effectively. Considering these kinds of side-effects first will allow you to make educated choices in engine mods.

An engine built to make 600 horsepower at the racetrack is not going to idle smoothly, get good gas mileage or go 200,000 miles between overhauls as a stock engine would. Performance modifications are frequently called "upgrades," but we need to keep in mind that the performance end of the operational spectrum is what's being upgraded, not necessarily the driveability. Often you'll have to give up some of the smooth, reliable and economical operation you've come to expect from your vehicle.

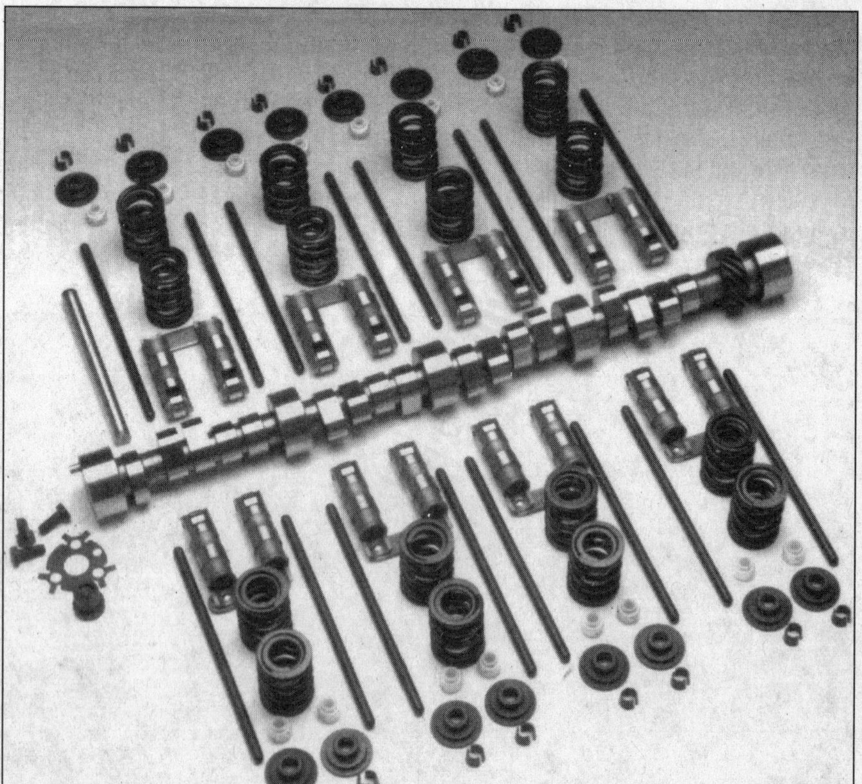

Some would say the camshaft profile is the heart of a performance engine, and although it takes some tools and skills to install a new cam, the right one can make or break the personality of the engine. Cams kits aren't hugely expensive, and often come with lifters and other valvetrain components

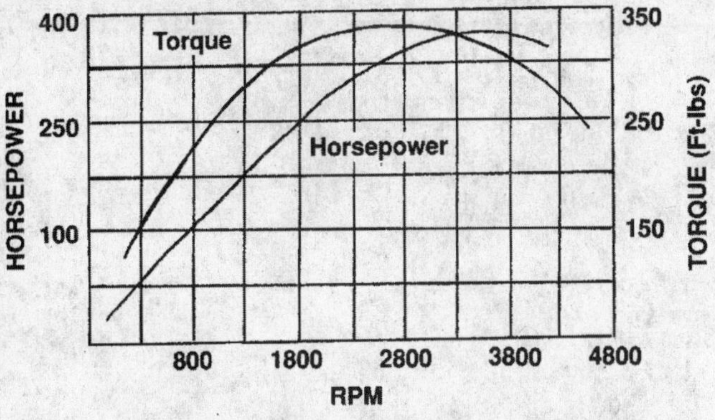

An engine's "personality" is often judged by its dyno sheet, indicating the where and how much of torque and horsepower production. For a street vehicle, don't always look for the highest horsepower alone when comparing modifications or replacement engines. For tractable street use, and especially for towing, *torque* rules. Build or buy an engine that makes lots of low-end torque "under the curve"

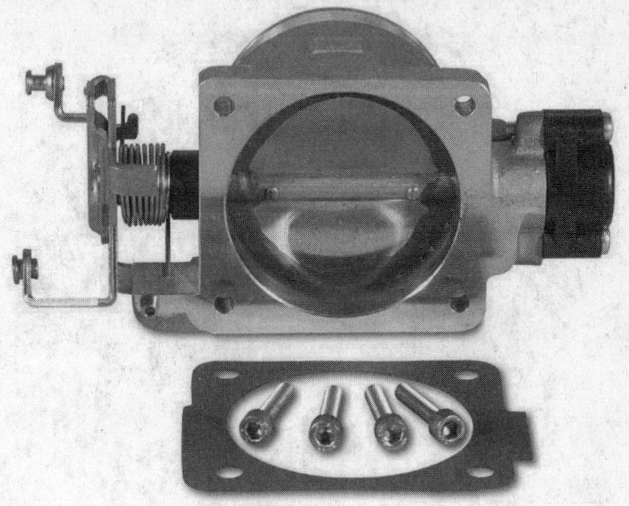

Once you've improved the exhaust system and added a cold-air intake and/or a performance cam swap, you might look into taking in more intake air via a somewhat larger-diameter throttle body (EFI engines) or a bigger carburetor. Don't go too big on the throttle body unless you have big heads or a power adder

So it's best to have a plan for your project, even if you don't have all the money to do everything right away. Don't plan on having a 9-second car that you can still loan to your mom on grocery day - neither one of you will be happy. Most of us will want to build a vehicle that is a compromise: a car that has the power we want, but is also fun to drive. It should have some sauce to it when we hit the throttle, but still be practical to drive to work every day. Many upgrades, such as an exhaust header, cat-back system, and cold-air-intake tube give free horsepower, with the only compromise being more noise (or as we like to call it, engine music). These upgrades are one-time installs, easy to do, don't require future upgrades and are no-brainers for any performance project, since they come with no harmful side-effects.

When you get into stroker rotating assemblies, nitrous oxide, turbos and superchargers, you'll be spending more money and, unless you make changes to your engine management system, you're also more at risk of engine damage. High-rpm camshafts and big-port/valve cylinder head work will reduce your car's low-speed driveability and frequently decrease your gas mileage. Often, when these modifications are designed to increase high-rpm horsepower, you'll actually lose some low-rpm power, and for most if us, that's where our street vehicles need power the most.

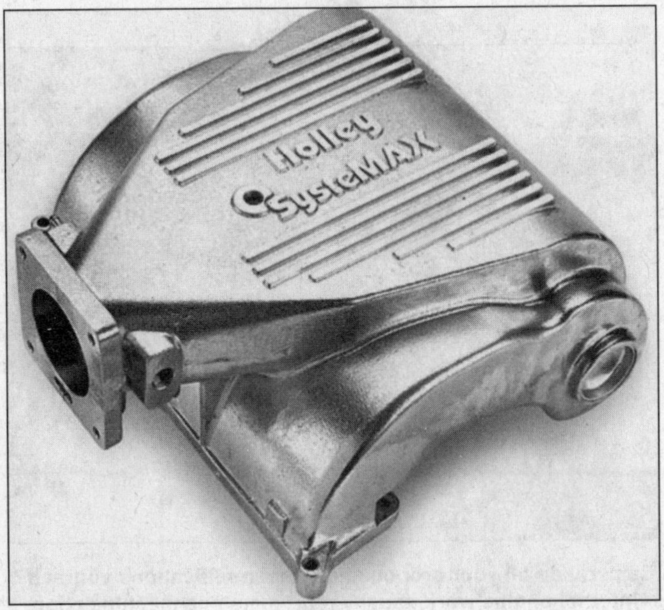

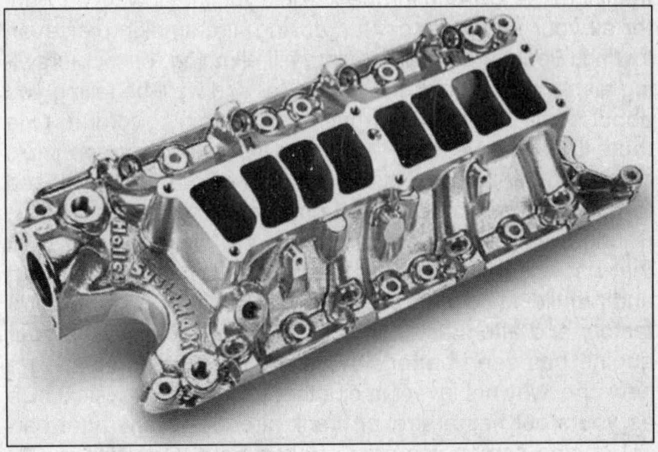

An engine that's had a displacement increase - as with a stroker kit - or is going to have nitrous or forced induction can stand to gain more power with a larger, free-flowing intake manifold. This is a Holley SysteMax upper and lower intake set for 5.0L Ford Windsor engines

Because speed parts have an interrelated effect on an engine, some manufacturers offer their parts as a "suite" with cam, intake and heads, all designed to work together. This Holley small-block Chevy package makes 425 hp on a 10:1 350 with a 750-cfm carb, and features a 0.488 (intake) Lunati cam, double-roller timing chain set, dual-plane Holley intake manifold, aluminum heads, ARP head bolts and hardened pushrods

With enough mods or a displacement increase, your newly-pumped-up engine is going to need more air/fuel mix. Increased carburetion, here in the form of a progressive dual-quad (two four-barrel carbs) setup, complete with larger braided stainless hose, fuel pressure regulator and fuel pressure gauge fills that bill for this engine swap

Torque vs. horsepower

These two terms are perhaps the most used and misunderstood measures of an engine's power. Torque is the twisting force exerted on the crankshaft, while horsepower indicates how quickly the engine makes power. Most enthusiasts read about how much horsepower a racing engine makes and they want the same for their vehicle, but power in a useable range is what we need off-track. Torque is what pushes you back in your seat when launching across an intersection. You could say that horsepower rules the track, while torque rules the street! Making engine modifications that increase low-end torque will give you the power you want for all your street needs: fun driving, tire-smoking, or even towing. Serious off-road driving, hill-climbing, or rock-crawling all require lots of low-end torque, and we'll be telling you about some of the proven methods of gaining torque. One route that we cover here in detail is increasing your engine's displacement. This is the time-honored path to increased torque, but this is not a bolt-on operation by any means. Boring the cylinders and/or installing a "stroker" crankshaft that has a longer-than-stock stroke both require removing and rebuilding your engine. However, there are a number of factory and aftermarket sources for "crate" engines. If your engine has seen better days and you're contemplating a new one, why not invest in one that's the same physical size as yours but has a stroker crank already? Many aftermarket engine companies offer stroked Ford, Chrysler or GM engines that directly replace the small-block or big-block engine you already have, with varying power levels available from mild to wild. The Big Three automakers all have full catalogs of performance equipment and powerful crate engines for all budgets and goals, and most come with a warranty (see Chapter 14). Compared to making one improvement at a time to your existing engine, you can get almost instant satisfaction by dropping in a new performance engine, *if* you have the budget!

Can you do all your proposed engine modifications yourself? Internal engine work usually requires some machine shop procedures, or at least specialized measuring tools and experience. You may have to pay a qualified shop for this kind of work. Use a shop familiar with performance engines

Specialty engine shops can provide high-performance engines for popular Ford and Chevrolet combinations that you can just oil up and drop in. Compare the costs of the machine work and aftermarket parts it would take you to duplicate such an engine, and you may decide this turn-key engine approach would work better for you. Aftermarket crate engines often come with a good warranty, too

The Detroit automakers, Ford GM and Chrysler, also offer brand-new performance engines you can order right at your local dealership! Mopar fans can answer "Yes!" to the question *"That thing got a Hemi?"* by installing this new-age 5.7L Hemi, set up for either carburetion or fuel injection.

Mistake number one

The most common mistake when enthusiasts start to modify their cars, is getting dazzled by those seen at shows or in magazines. This leaves the temptation to just start throwing parts at your car in an effort to be as cool as those show vehicles. That isn't the best plan, because every level of performance for your vehicle should be a coordinated effort.

Many enthusiasts start out buying parts that really don't help their engine at the performance level they're seeking. For instance, an aftermarket ignition system will add nothing to your relatively-stock engine except looks. The stock ignition works fine for most purposes, so unless you're building your engine to a higher level, you don't absolutely need the hot coil and amplifier. However, when you get to the bigger modifications like a supercharger or turbocharger, that performance ignition system will be *required* in order to fire the engine with the increased cylinder pressure of a power adder like nitrous or a turbo.

Planning ahead means you won't have a garage full of expensive parts you bought, then later took off when you changed to higher or lower-level parts, because things didn't perform the way you expected.

Depending on how much performance you want to have in your street-driven vehicle, you could be better off with another vehicle. Before you get irate, we're only proposing you trade your base-model car for a factory-customized or performance version. A lot has already been done to models like these at the factory, such as the addition of wheels, performance suspension, brakes, special trans programming and performance engine mods. If you did all of this to your existing car or truck, it would probably cost you close to what it might cost to trade up. It's something to think about, especially for those who hesitate to take on a major project themselves. You must ackowledge your limitations when it comes to hands-on work, whether it's engine, transmission or chassis work. Weigh installation costs and complexity of each of the steps you propose to make on your vehicle before making any decisions.

Operations that are normally done on a lift, such as exhaust system or suspension work, will be difficult at best to perform at home, even if you have a set of four sturdy jackstands and a good floor jack. Unless you know someone who has a vehicle lift you can use, these jobs may have to be farmed out, and if so, you must consider this in your budget plans. It doesn't make budget sense to buy $500 worth of new tools to do a job that could have been finished in a shop for the same price, including the parts!

Don't build your dream car up to a level of virtual race car unless you are prepared to trailer it to and from the dragstrip. Be sure you can handle all the associated costs of running a race car, such as a tow vehicle, trailer, fuel jugs, tie-downs, extra wheels/tires, air tank, safety equipoment, etc. Driving a car at high speed with open headers is certainly a thrill, one the average person will never experience, but thrills in the automotive world are costly. Just to put our thoughts in perspective, though, count yourself lucky your absorbing interest is automotive. People who get into racing either boats or airplanes have enough money tied up in just spare engines that would cover our car plans ten times over!

Whatever you do to your dream project vehicle, you can safely enjoy its true performance by running it at your nearest dragstrip when they have "street drags" or "test and tune" days. For checking the effect of various mods you make, it's cheaper than a dyno and way more fun! Your buddy says his car is faster? Check it out here with real timing equipment, and get the timeslip to prove who's boss

Let's hope we don't see any of our readers in gory newspaper photos of street racing aftermath. The traction is poor, safety is non-existent, and there are no timing slips in street racing. It's not worth arrest, loss of your car or worse

Once you get your hot-rodded vehicle finished, and you're enjoying the adrenaline kick that stepping down with your right foot brings you, don't be tempted to start challenging others on the street, or engaging in reckless driving. It just isn't worth taking chances with your life or others. Most dragstrips across the country have "test and tune" track days where true street cars can run under safe conditions, and with accurate timing slips to clip to your dashboard for bragging rights. At the track, you can choose to race another entrant and see who comes out on top - it's all in fun.

Pre-armed with some of the advice of this Chapter to calm your unbridled enthusiasm a little, the rest of this book will open many doors on the path to greater engine power. Enjoy the journey as much as the destination!

2 Choosing Speed: Sourcing Performance Equipment and Services

Why you need help

Let's say that you've decided to pump up your engine, but you're new to this game and now you're concerned, maybe a little worried. You've never tackled something like this before, and now the magnitude and expense of what you're about to do is beginning to sink in. Relax. Even someone who's never turned a wrench can install simple bolt-on components like headers or a cold-air intake. If you're more mechanically inclined, you probably already know how to measure valve clearances, adjust the idle, things like that.

But before you get too deep into any engine mods, ask yourself just one question: Do I understand how each subsystem under the hood is interdependent with, and therefore affects the performance of, every other engine sub-system? It's the sheer complexity of all this interrelatedness that makes raising performance - without impairing drivability - so challenging. It would be nice if performance modifications were Plug 'n Play, like desktop computer systems. But the reality is that high performance components like radical cams, computer chips, nitrous systems, superchargers and turbochargers are going to require some recalibration. Whether you've tweaked every bicycle, lawn mower, motorcycle and car that you've ever owned or this is your first foray into modifying anything, you're going to make some mistakes. Some of them could be costly, so proceed cautiously and methodically, and get some help!

Let's face it: there is always going to be someone out there who knows more than you do about the pitfalls of transforming a stock street motor into a high performance engine. Why? Because he's standing on top of a bigger pile of broken parts, which means that he's already tried stuff - some of which worked out, some of which didn't. But each time something broke, he learned from his mistake, and moved on until eventually, from the summit of that mountain of broken parts, he saw how it all works together. Some Big Picture Guys open speed shops. These are the shops you want. They'll help you bypass that mountain of broken parts, saving you lots of money and grief.

Maybe you're already peppering a local speed shop owner with questions about your project engine. But even if you already have a shop that you can work with, the following information will help you determine whether it's right for you, or whether you should move on. Maybe you're still looking for the right shop. If so, this Chapter will help you choose a good one.

Performance engine building has a long and storied history, as evidenced in this early picture of So Cal speed shop

What IS a "speed shop?"

Practically since the automobile was invented, enthusiasts who wanted more sporty performance or hill-climbing ability gravitated to neighborhood garages and automotive machine shops to kick tires, trade ideas and admire each other's work. There was no aftermarket high performance industry. These early shops and their hot rod customers were strictly do-it-yourselfers. The dominant form of pre-WW II racing was dirt circle tracks, which by the Twenties, were operating all over the country, particularly on the East Coast and in the Midwest. During those decades, racing was a rich man's sport. The grassroots racing that developed for the average guy was based on modified Ford Model T engines and chassis with cut-down or aftermarket "speedster" bodies that emulated what was running at Indianapolis Motor Speedway during that period. In California, racers had access to a number of flat, hard-surfaced dry lakebeds to play on. They would drive out to these lakes by the hundreds every weekend, strip off the windshields and fenders, put taller rear tires on to gain higher speeds and run, sometimes five or six abreast. The pioneering speed equipment companies developed and tested their products every week on the dry lakebeds. But the coming of World War II put a halt to racing activities all over the country, as fuel, rubber and other materials were rationed.

Then in 1946 everything changed. On the very day that he was discharged from the Army Air Corps, young B-29 mechanic Alex Xydias opened the doors of So Cal Speed Shop. So Cal became famous for its hot rods, which set many high-speed records on the dry lake beds of Southern California. Xydias was one of the first shop owners to actually market and sell a wide array of purpose-built speed parts, mainly for flathead V8s. His formula was simple: Race on Sunday, sell on Monday. His cars and crews were on the cover of *Hot Rod Magazine* five times in the early '50s. By the time So Cal Speed Shop closed its doors in 1961, the aftermarket high performance industry was rolling. Today you can find speed shops everywhere on the planet. Do an Internet search for "speed shops" and you will get well over 6 million hits in less than 1/10 of a second! Obviously there is no shortage of speed shops. But not all firms that think of themselves as speed shops are the same thing. And even when they appear to be similar, they're not necessarily equal.

Whether you're just adding a few bolt-ons or building a 1,000 horsepower screamer, you'll want to find a speed shop that understands your needs

There's more than one kind of "speed shop"

Retail speed shops

Speed shops come in all sizes and specialties. Most shops are in business to sell high-performance hop-up hardware. The staff often knows something about the speed equipment that they sell (some guys at these shops actually know *quite* a lot). Some shops, for a fee, will also install the speed products you buy from them. During the initial stages of a project, a retail-only speed shop might be perfectly satisfactory if you already have the requisite automotive mechanical experience and the right tools to do the job. But be realistic about your own skills. Some modifications are expensive, and could be damaged or ruined, or could damage or ruin something expensive (like the engine!) if installed incorrectly.

All retail speed shops sell high performance parts. Mail-order outfits usually offer the best deals on most parts because of their lower overhead. Seasoned, serious enthusiasts like mail order because they know exactly what they want and where to get it for the lowest possible price. But if you're new to this game, you might want to stay away from mail-order emporiums until you know what you're doing. It's remarkably easy to get in over your head when you're dazzled by colorful photos of cool-looking equipment. Besides, by the time you factor in shipping costs, the risk of damaging or losing parts in the mail and the hassle of returning the wrong parts, you might decide that's it better to pay a little more for customer service.

Most retail speed shops provide advice on what to buy based on your budget and your goals. Often the only real difference between these shops is the quality of the advice that they offer to their customers. So look for a shop with

Retail speed shops provide a wide variety of performance hardware, and knowledgeable counter-people are an excellent resource

It's good to work with a speed shop that keeps a substantial parts inventory - that way you can get those little last-minute parts without a wait

a technically savvy staff whose advice you can take to the bank (so that you don't take yourself to the cleaners). You want a staff that gives good, honest advice even more than you want competitive prices. Knowledge is power.

But speed shops do have to make a living - who doesn't? - so keep in mind that this is first and foremost a *business* relationship. Running a speed shop is a balancing act: a good shop dispenses advice about how to pump up horsepower, and it sells the products you need to make it happen. You want a shop that's going to help you improve your engine's performance and tell you how to get there. Sure, the staff wants to have fun with fast cars and hang out with other enthusiasts, but they *do* have a bottom line.

Besides affordability, honesty and knowledge, what else should you look for in a speed shop? One that will help you prioritize your modification plans, starting with the most cost-effective modifications, then progressing upward from there. And one that will step up and do the job for you when it's over your head but will also willingly step aside when it thinks you can handle the job yourself.

Many shops now sell complete engines for reasonable prices

Obviously, you can get pretty far into a project using a retail-only speed shop. Still, there are a lot of things that these establishments don't offer. They don't generally provide custom services such as machining, welding, fabricating, flow benches and dynamometers. For those types of services you will have to move on to more specialized speed shops.

Performance-oriented automotive machine shops

Unless you're blessed with the skills of a machinist, welder and fabricator, be prepared to find a good machine shop at some point. Although general automotive machine shops are as ubiquitous as speed shops, performance machine shops aren't. For many routine machining procedures, general automotive machine shops will be able to help you with the machine work that you need. Boring a block for higher performance is almost the same procedure for any engine.

But what if you want to port the heads or get a really trick four-angle valve job? Then you must farm out the work to a machine shop that specializes in high-performance engines. Besides custom machining services, many performance machine shops also offer aerospace-grade welding, custom fabrication and other services that you won't find at a regular machine shop. These shops might sell speed products, or they might not. They can often provide the parts needed to do the job; some shops require you to provide the parts. Sometimes shops actually make the parts that you need. These kinds of shops can order the equipment you need and modify or install it for you, but they don't have a big stockroom in back filled with every possible part a customer would want.

Dynamometers: The Ultimate Tuning Tool

Horsepower talk is cheap when you're sitting around, kicking tires and telling lies with your buddies. If a friend claims a certain amount of horsepower for his engine, there's no way to verify such a claim without subjecting it to the ultimate tuning tool: the dynamometer. A dynamometer is a device that can accurately measure horsepower. There are two kinds of automotive dynamometers: engine dynos and chassis dynos.

The dyno is the ultimate tool in evaluating an engine's performance potential. Here an engine dyno is in use (with the engine safely in a test-cell)

Engine dynamometers

Engine development work is easier with the engine removed from the vehicle and installed on an engine dynamometer. An engine dyno is capable of loading the engine as if it were being run while installed in the vehicle. Engine dynos can provide a very accurate picture of an engine's power output because they measure power at the flywheel, with no power losses through the transmission/transaxle or driveline. This means, of course, that the engine must be removed from the vehicle and installed on the dyno. Then all the auxiliary systems - fuel supply, electrical supply, exhaust extraction, intake air for combustion, air flow for cooling, coolant temperature control, throttle actuation, etc. - must be provided. Because of these requirements, engine dynos are usually installed in enclosed, soundproof test cells that can provide the engine with these auxiliary systems. Despite the complexity of setting up an engine dyno/test cell site, engine dynos are popular with automobile manufacturers and OEM engine developers because of the degree of control over the test parameters made possible by isolating the engine from the vehicle. Serious developers and researchers want repeatability (consistent results from test to test) unaffected by factors that can't be controlled by the tester. They also want the capability to install special testing sensors and to make easy adjustments and changes to the test engine. For these reasons, engine dynamometers are used extensively by automobile manufacturers to develop new engines, and to test them for reliability and endurance. Engine dynos are not always used by speed shops because testing an engine out of the vehicle isn't practical for most shops, or affordable for most customers.

Chassis dynamometers

If a shop owner proudly shows off his dynamometer when you take the tour of his shop, chances are it will be a chassis dyno. The chassis dynamometer is the dyno of choice for most shops because it allows them to test an engine's performance without removing it from the vehicle. The typical chassis dyno uses a series of big rollers that are connected to some type of power absorber capable of controlling the load that's applied to the rollers. To measure horsepower, you simply position the drive wheels on the rollers, start the engine, put it in gear and record the data. The chassis dyno operator can dial a specific amount of load into the rollers to simulate acceleration, passing or going up a steep hill. The main advantage of a chassis dyno is that you don't have to remove the engine to dyno it. This, of course, simplifies both the testing procedure itself and the setup for the testing. Another advantage is that the chassis dyno delivers "real world" numbers, that is, it reflects the actual horsepower at the drive wheels, not the horsepower at the crankshaft. The disadvantage of a chassis dyno is that the results aren't that consistent or repeatable because of the factors - driveline losses, and tire wear, pressure and temperature - that influence each dyno run.

The chassis dyno measures the power that's actually delivered to the wheels and is a more accurate indicator of your vehicles's potential

The quality of consulting at a performance machine shop is often more specific and more technical than the advice dispensed by retail speed shops. The owner of this type of establishment usually has vast hands-on experience building all sorts of wild high-power engines. He really knows what works, and what doesn't, because he's the first one to hear about it when something blows up. So think of his advice as the gold standard.

For your machining work, be sure to pick a shop that has experience building high-performance engines

Tuning shops

Novices often waste thousands of dollars on inappropriate modifications because they don't yet understand how some modifications affect drivability. For example, you might run out and buy an expensive exhaust system for your project engine only to discover that, when you fire it up, it actually produces less torque down low than the stock system, or it's too loud to use on the street in your area. You might install a carburetor or fuel injection system that doesn't really match the flow characteristics of your engine, or install a radical cam that is so lumpy at idle that it will never pass a smog test. These types of screw-ups can get expensive in a hurry.

To avoid these types of dilemmas, you might have to seek help from a third type of speed shop. These days, performance V8 enthusiasts are turning to tuning shops for help because modern V8s are equipped with the same engine management computers, information sensors and output actuators as Asian and European four-cylinder motors. When you add serious power to a V8 by dropping in a radical cam or bolting on a blower or a turbo, the engine management system needs recalibration to operate seamlessly.

A good tuner is part computer geek and part rocket scientist. Think of him as the automotive equivalent of a corporate information systems guy. His job is to make sure that everything under the hood is working together happily and harmoniously. He can also recalibrate the engine management system when you add nitrous, a turbo or a blower. He does this by burning a new chip for your engine management computer or swapping it out for a programmable aftermarket chip, then putting the finished project on a chassis dyno to see what she'll do. All without ever turning a wrench! But perhaps the most important thing he can do is keep your performance engine smog legal, if yours is to remain in street usage.

Good tuning shops that cater to fuel-injected, high performance engines are well-stocked with highly specialized tools such as wide band air/fuel ratio meters, exhaust gas analyzers, electronic diagnostic equipment like scan tools and oscilloscopes, flow benches and dynamometers. When looking for a good tuning shop, make sure that it has this type of equipment and knows how to use it, or the "tuner" is just blowing' smoke. Other tuning shops may be more well-versed in carburetion, and help you choose the right carburetor, then tune the ignition timing, carb jetting and secondary opening timing on four-barrel carburetors.

Pick the right people

Perhaps the most critical step in bringing your engine project to a successful conclusion is picking the right people to work with. Maybe you can't judge a book by its cover, but you can evaluate a prospective speed shop by answering the following questions.

Does the staff know what it's talking about?

If you're looking for a good machine shop/engine builder, bear in mind that there are no shortcuts to becoming a good machinist or engine builder. Remember that the best ones are standing on top of the tallest piles of broken parts. Basically, all engine building knowledge springs from the same well. Breakthroughs are rare. Nobody gets to the top in this game unless he's willing to take chances, try out new ideas, add what works to his performance repertoire and eliminate what doesn't. Before establishing a business relationship with a shop that offers machine shop or performance engine building services, try to get a sense of whether your engine is just another rung on the ladder for the shop's learning curve. Make *sure* that its broken-parts-phase is behind it. Don't become an unwitting guinea pig for someone who's still learning. Ideally, you are looking for one of the Enlightened Ones, the elite inner circle of guys who pretty much know *everything* about how to build your dream engine. Settling for less could actually prove to be more expensive in the long run.

For the real deal performance engine builder, there are two just kinds of experiences: good experiences and . . . *learning* experiences. When a modification works the way it's supposed to, that's a good experience. When it doesn't, that's a learning experience. A good engine man isn't afraid to make mistakes, but he doesn't *repeat* those mistakes. He learns from them and moves on. And good shops use their own engines, not customers' motors, to research and develop new ideas. If you decide to work with someone who intends to use your engine as a test-bed for new ideas and/or products, make sure that you get paid somehow for this service, perhaps in the form of free or discounted parts and labor.

When asked about his background, an inexperienced builder looking for new customers might fudge the truth a bit. An experienced guy who has been in business for awhile won't need to. If his shop is neat, clean and filled with hand, power and machine tools and clean and craftsmanlike vehicles, and if his office is filled with trophies from the track and photos of smiling customers standing proudly next to their project vehicles, then stick around and ask him some questions. A good engine man has nothing to hide (except his most closely held speed secrets!) and he'll be happy to tell you how he got to where he is.

Ask a prospective engine builder about his educational background and his experience and training. Some builder/tuners might bristle when asked this question, but if you're going to spend thousands of dollars at this establishment, you need to judge for yourself whether the guy standing before you is really qualified to modify your engine, or tell you how to do it. Did he start out taking auto shop classes at a local high school? Did he study auto mechanics at a local community college? Is he a certified ASE (Automotive Service Excellence) technician? Is he an ASE-certified *Master* Automotive Technician (CMAT)? Does he have dealership experience? Did he work for or own an independent garage? Did he ever work for a professional big-time drag racing or stock car racing team? His answers to these questions will tell you whether this guy has devoted a chunk of his life to cars, or whether he's simply out to make a buck.

Some of the best builders gained their special knowledge and skills while working for an automotive manufacturer as an engineer, technician, mechanic, machinist, technical consultant or crew chief for a factory race team. Many people in performance engine shops have their own race cars and have learned by experience at the dragstrip.

A former factory employee not only has vast experience with the engine you want to modify, but he might also maintain some connection to the factory, even if it's an unofficial relationship. Someone connected in this manner often has insights into the inner workings of, say, the engine management system, unavailable to his competitors. While engine builders with factory connections aren't really necessary in the initial stages of a project, their special knowledge can be invaluable once you start pumping up the horsepower of your engine, especially if you're planning to keep it street legal.

Some people will tell you that building a performance engine is art, some will tell you that it's science, some will tell you it's both - but it's neither. Engine building is *engineering*. That's not to say that one must have a degree in mechanical engineering to build engines. Most engine guys are probably not engineers, but the good ones think like engineers. They understand enough physics, mechanics, hydraulics,

The Flow Bench: the Tuner's Wind Tunnel

If you're looking for a speed shop to re-work your cylinder heads for optimum airflow, look for one that owns and knows how to use a flow bench. Since the power output of an engine is directly proportional to the amount of air it can inhale, a good tuner will try to remove all resistance to airflow in the induction system so that the engine can pack as much mixture into the combustion chambers as possible. In order to do so, he must be able to measure the volume of air flowing through the intake manifold and the cylinder head so that he can quantify the results of his modifications. The device that he uses to measure airflow through the intake manifold and the cylinder head(s) is known as a flowbench. For tuners, the flow bench is an essential tool. Think of the flow bench as the tuner's wind tunnel. Engineers use the wind tunnel to measure how well air passes over and around a stationary vehicle placed inside the tunnel. A flow bench measures how well air flows through the intake system itself.

During the intake stroke, the volume of the cylinder increases as the piston travels down. But the mass of the air in the chamber is the same, so its density has decreased and so has its pressure. The result is known as a pressure drop, or pressure differential, between the air inside the combustion chamber and the ambient air outside the engine, which is at barometric pressure. It's this pressure differential, produced by the piston on the intake stroke, that initiates the flow of air from outside the engine through the induction system and into the combustion chamber. It would be difficult to measure flow through a running engine; that's why we have flow benches.

A flow bench consists of a series of vacuum motors that produce a pressure differential on one side of the passage being tested. The pressure drop causes air to flow through the passage, and the flow bench measures that flow. Each time a tuner removes or reshapes a restriction to flow inside a passage, he uses the flow bench to measure the airflow through the passage to verify that his modification has increased, rather than decreased, flow. Thus the flow bench enables the tuner to quantify the results of his modifications.

pneumatics, electricity, etc. to define a problem in engineering terms, then solve it the way an engineer would.

Look for a full-service machine shop with experience in machining, welding and fabricating. A shop that offers these services will be able to do a three- or four-angle valve job, weld up a cracked block or head or make you that special bracket without relying on subcontractors or sending you to a shop that you're not familiar with.

Are the customers happy?

Look for a speed shop with satisfied customers. If your friends drive vehicles with engines similar to yours, and if they're having success at the strip or the track with modifications made by a particular shop, then that shop is probably a good place to start. If you're forced to seek help from a shop that's farther from home, ask around at the strip or at car club or social gatherings. A speed shop owner's reputation for knowing - or not knowing - what he's doing gets around pretty quickly. Word-of-mouth advertising should be part of your search, but don't make it the only part. People pleased with the work done by their shop might be tempted to exaggerate somewhat. But people *displeased* with work recently done might also exaggerate, so you've got to take this anecdotal advice for what it is - hearsay. However, there's no question that people vote with their dollars. Speed shops with happy customers will probably provide more good advice than will shops with unhappy customers. Performance enthusiasts who live outside a major metropolitan area sometimes have to travel two or three hours to reach a good tuning shop, but a shop with many recommendations will be worth it in the end.

Can the speed shop deliver what it's promising?

Most speed shop owners start out as self-employed small businessmen who do it all with a small or nonexistent staff. But as they become established and successful, smart shop owners usually hire skilled and knowledgeable technicians to remedy any gaps in their capabilities, thereby enabling them to become full-service shops. (Some shop owners, however, simply surround themselves with yes-men who just try to keep the boss happy; stay away from these establishments.) If possible, try to get to know some of the key people who work at the prospective shop with whom you are considering doing business. Are they happy and excited about their work and about working at this particular shop? If they're not, then you might be less than happy here as a long-term customer. Ask employees the same kinds of general questions you've asked their boss about their education and training. This isn't as hard as it might sound. Employees are usually hired for their expertise in one area, such as engine assembly, welding, fabrication or machining, so it's not that difficult to assess their qualifications. A speed shop owner who's really proud of his staff will probably brag a little about their accomplishments *before* he hired them.

Good shops get results; bad ones don't. So look at a prospective speed shop's track record. If more straight-line performance is what you want, then look for a shop with drag racing experience. Most horsepower specialists have (or sponsor) a drag racing vehicle that they use to try out new ideas and develop new products in competition. If a shop's dragster has already earned a championship or two using its own homegrown speed products or tuning services, then the proprietor of the shop probably knows his stuff. Of course if his customers have achieved similar successes, then what works for them will probably work for you.

Is the shop affordable?

Affordability is a relative term, when you're contemplating spending perfectly good money on an engine that's probably basically okay the way it is. Affordability is relative to how much money you make, but also to how much of it you're actually free to spend on your engine. And it's relative to what you intend to do to your engine. Some modifications are more cost effective than others. There are people with $20,000 in their engines. Are those engines twice as powerful as a $10,000 engine? Probably not, but you'd be amazed how many people spend megabucks on their engine, then ignore the rest of their car because they're broke! An experienced shop owner will sit you down before you spend a penny and have you do a "build sheet," which is an overview of what you want to do to your engine, and how much each modification is going to cost. The total cost of some projects can get into five figures pretty quickly, so it's imperative that you shop hard when you're purchasing parts. If you're buying a stock part, always compare its original equipment (OEM) price to its aftermarket price, which could mean a local shop or mail order. If it's an aftermarket or performance part, always compare the price that you'll pay for it at your local speed shop versus its mail order price.

Always be straight up with a speed shop owner about where you want to go with your project and let him know what you can really, *really* afford. This is your *hobby* (okay, maybe it's your obsession!), so don't let it snowball to the point that it interferes with essential living expenses such as rent or mortgage payments, car payments, credit card debt, etc. Figure out how much money a month you can realistically afford to spend on your project, then divide that into the total estimated cost of the project and you'll know roughly how long it's going to take to get there. And you'll know the true meaning of affordability!

Is the shop local?

Some speed shops sell their parts nationwide. These mail order emporiums usually take phone orders and have websites you can browse before ordering. When you're buying tune-up parts or bolt-on performance goodies, mail order prices can be hard to beat. But, if you're planning to do modifications that require machining, welding, fabrication or actual *tuning*, a long-distance relationship will be difficult at best. Even if a mail order outfit's reputation is sterling, you don't want to get involved in lengthy phone calls, e-mails, and rewrapping and returning custom parts that don't fit or don't work.

Does the shop do the work on time?

Project engines are like new buildings. In the building trade, the progress of a new home or office building proceeds in spurts, with long intervals of waiting for the building code inspector to sign off the most recently completed phase of the project, punctuated by brief bursts of activity. Project engines progress in a similar fashion, with long intervals of waiting - for parts, machine work, custom fabrication, etc. - punctuated by feverish bursts of activity assembling or installing things once they're ready. So be patient - or expect to develop patience - when you enlist any speed shops to help you build a high performance engine.

But patience-as-a-virtue notwithstanding, nobody wants to do business with a speed shop that is unable, or unwilling, to deliver goods or services in a timely manner, particularly if the project engine powers a daily driver. Be realistic. If you can't afford to be without your car for lengthy periods of time, either obtain a back-up car, or look for a shop that's willing to work on your engine when you don't need the car, like evenings, or weekends, or holidays. More complex projects like complete engine builds are unavoidably time-consuming, so find a shop that will take the time it needs to do the job right, but no longer. Timeliness is not something you can always determine up front, but if you've hooked up with a procrastinator, it will become apparent soon enough.

Is the shop owner easy to get along with?

Most speed shop owners are helpful and supportive. And some can be a little eccentric, which is probably unavoidable in a field filled with self-made, self-promoting small businessmen whose success is tied to their accomplishments. These are guys trying to make a living in a very competitive business, so they're usually not shy about touting their capabilities. And some of them don't suffer fools or stupid questions lightly. But if you find a shop owner who's good at what he does you will probably be able to overlook his idiosyncrasies.

However, if you find that a speed shop owner is persistently patronizing or talking down to you, lecturing you or grumbling about the stupidity of other customers and/or his competitors, get rid of him. You want results, not therapy. A truly hard-working professional doesn't have the time to talk trash about his customers or fellow tuners. He's too busy taking care of business.

3 The Look of Speed

Stock engine compartments aren't generally designed to be good looking. And unfortunately, most components are usually black. Open the hood on a car and what do you see? Black plastic air filter housing, black air intake duct, black battery, black radiator, black heater hoses, black vacuum hoses, black fuse box, black electrical harnesses, black accelerator and cruise control cables, black valve cover (with, of course, a black oil filler cap), black . . . well, black everything. Black, black, black everywhere! A sea of black! It's as if the engine compartment was dressed for a funeral.

For stunning visual impact, nothing beats the classic gleam of chrome and highly polished aluminum. Although upkeep can be challenging, many consider this to be the ultimate look

Of course, if you were like most drivers, you would never personally open your hood anyway; your mechanic would handle that! Which is why the manufacturers spend no extra money on making your engine compartment pretty. They assume that you'll never look at it anyway. So why not have a black engine compartment that will help hide the filth? That's practical for the manufacturer. But pleasing to look at? Hardly.

In more recent years, color-coordinated engine compartments have become popular. By painting the engine and engine-compartment accessories the same color as the rest of the vehicle, a more coordinated custom look is achieved. However, if the car is driven regularly, the engine heat will ultimately cause areas of the paint to discolor and peel, and repainting can cause a "patchy" look

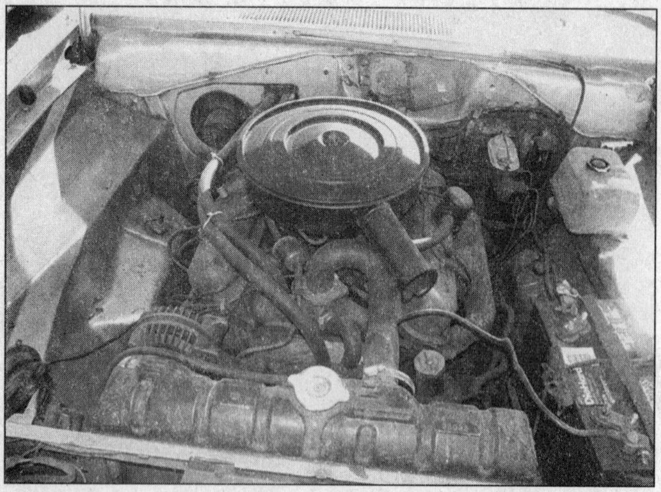

A counter-trend in engine compartment design is toward a more stock look. Whether your show car is trying to compete in a stock class, or you simply like a more original look, basic clean up, chrome accents and painting can turn an engine compartment like this . . .

. . . into a beautiful resto-mod showpiece that will attract attention every time you "need" to pop the hood at the local gas station!

Here's another gorgeous resto-mod engine compartment. This owner spent a great deal of time and money staying true to the original look. The OEM details include original-type hoses, clamps and fittings

If you drive your car daily, don't expect your engine compartment to look this nice for very long. With open wheel-wells, the engine compartment of this show-only car would be ruined in daily service

Chrome and billet-machined accessories are available for most popular engines. Although expensive, billet pulleys and brackets give a high-tech look to this big-block Chevy

It's becoming more popular to chrome firewall components, such as this brake booster. But if you want to stay with a more original look . . .

. . . there is paint available from companies like Eastwood that simulates the original cadmium plating

But you aren't like most drivers, so your engine compartment doesn't have to look like it's in mourning. You like to work on your engine and show it off to your friends. Your engine is the heart of your car, so why not make it the visual centerpiece as well? Unlike high-performance modifications, engine compartment dress-up is one area where you can really let your creativity and originality run wild, without spending a lot of money. Most of the mods you'll see in this Chapter are a hundred bucks or less. So check it out! And have fun with it!

Clean and detail your engine compartment first

Before we talk about things you can do to dress up your engine compartment, let's take a few minutes to discuss engine compartment detailing, which is a good thing to do even if you never spend a penny to trick out the engine bay. After 20,000 or 30,000 miles, an engine usually begins to leak a little coolant or engine oil. Brake fluid, power-steering fluid and transmission fluid leaks might also appear. As the miles click through the odometer, these little leaks slowly spread out, dirt and road grime start sticking to the areas covered by oil and the engine gets dirty. Some of the leaking fluids, if they're not regularly removed, can degrade paint, plastic and rubber. Batteries can also be messy. A bad voltage regulator can allow the alternator to overcharge the battery, which can spit highly corrosive sulfuric acid onto painted surfaces. Battery connections must also be cleaned regularly, or one day you'll hear that dreaded "click-click," which means that you're not playing with a full 12 volts.

Underhood cleanup isn't difficult, and no real mechanical knowledge is necessary (although extensive detailing can involve removing and painting various engine parts and accessories, if you carry the process all the way). You can do it at home in the driveway or at a coin-operated carwash, or you can have the engine detailed by a professional the first time, then maintain it yourself with very simple regular cleanups thereafter. You might only detail what is immediately visible when the hood is open, things like the top of the air cleaner and the battery, and maybe radiator and heater hoses and vacuum lines. If you own a car that you race or show on a regular basis, you are probably already a true "motorhead" who simply loves engines. You may already have devoted more time, money and accessories to the engine than the outside of the car, and your engine sparkles like a jewel at all times. You're never reluctant to open your hood to show off your engine, either!

Your auto supply store has a variety of degreasers, most of which are biodegradable and non-toxic, though you should observe common-sense precautions about eye and skin protection when using any cleaners

Pressure washers and steam cleaners give the best results when cleaning an engine. Be sure to soak the greasy areas before spraying

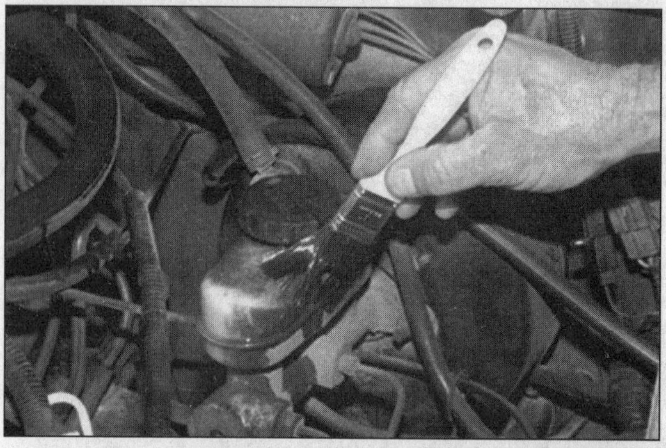

Greasy areas will take second or third applications of spray degreaser, and you should use a parts-wash brush or old paintbrush to work it in and loosen stubborn deposits. With a little elbow-grease . . .

Engine washing

The first step in detailing the underhood area is washing, which can be as simple as squirting soapy water on and around the engine, then rinsing it off. If a simple soap-and-water wash doesn't do the job, the next step is to work with the kinds of chemical cleaners, such as Gunk, that you can buy at automotive parts retailers. If *that* doesn't work, the next step is to have everything professionally steam-cleaned. Regardless of the method, the idea is to rid the engine of all grease and accumulated dirt. Which way you decide to go depends on how dirty your engine compartment is and how clean you'd like it to be. Each method has its advantages and drawbacks.

In a basic wash and detail, a clean engine might need nothing more than a simple soaping up and hosing down. If you can't remove the accumulated dirt and grime this easily, stronger measures are called for. Chemical cleaners for degreasing engines are available at your local auto parts store, and there are even some effective household cleaners. Most oven cleaners work well on heavy grease deposits on your engine. And many household liquid or spray cleaners, like 409 or Simple Green, will also work in most cases.

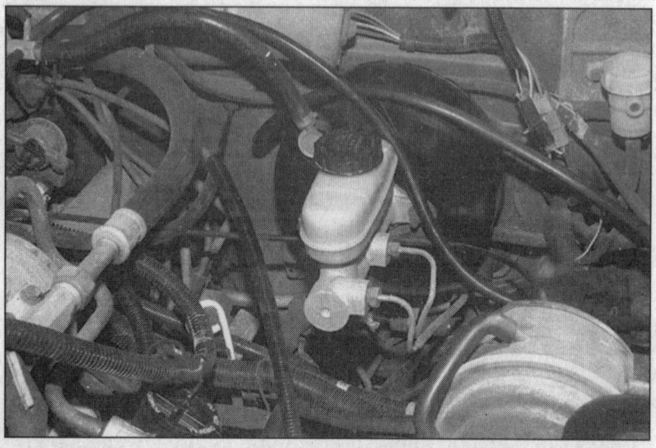

. . . your engine compartment will start looking like new!

Pressure washing

On engines with heavy grease deposits, it's helpful to have some kind of pressure to help loosen the deposits. If you don't want to spend a lot of money, try doing the job in your driveway with a pressurized metal spray container filled with liquid cleaner (or with a siphon-type solvent gun that uses your air compressor). Buy a pressure-sprayer that you can charge up with up to 100 psi of air or, if you have a particularly big job, rent or purchase a pressure-washer, which will remove gunk much more efficiently than solvents and water alone.

Moisture

One problem with pressure washing is moisture, which isn't good for ignition and fuel system components. Try to avoid spraying directly onto the ignition coil(s), wiring, distributor cap (if you've got one), spark plugs, and carburetor or throttle body. Keeping critical components dry during engine cleaning is a precaution that should be taken no matter what wash method you use. In spite of your best efforts, your engine might start but run poorly after a steam bath, or it might not start at all. So have some electronic parts cleaner and some clean rags handy. You might have to dry out the distributor cap or the boots at the ends of the coil wire and each spark plug wire.

Don't detail a hot engine

In most cases it's not a good idea to detail a hot engine. Some enthusiasts like to clean an engine while it's still hot because the heat makes the chemicals work faster at loosening dirt. But some normally-hot components such as the exhaust system (and turbocharger, if you have one) can crack if they're exposed to a sudden bath of cold water when the part is really hot.

1 Pulleys, brackets and other small parts can be removed and painted to accent your now-clean engine

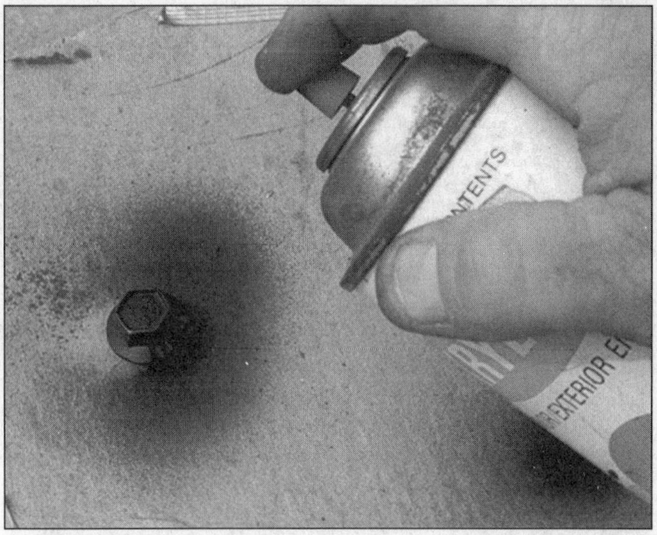

2 Even fasteners can be renewed with cleaning and some semi-flat black spray paint. Use a piece of cardboard with pencil holes punched into it to hold the bolts conveniently for spraying just the heads

3 A Valve cover is a prominent upper-engine feature, and along with the air cleaner housing, are the most commonly and easily painted engine parts. We will follow the process of detail painting with a neglected aluminum valve cover. You may have stamped steel covers that need cleaning, fine sanding and painting only

Painting and final details on a Ford small-block engine compartment

Follow along as we freshen up this Ford small-block engine compartment that's been neglected for years.

4 The valve cover has been removed from the engine and the gaskets surfaces scraped clean. Now it is doused liberally with degreaser, which is worked in and out of the details with a scrub brush

5 Put on another application of degreaser and let it sit according to the product's directions, in this case about five minutes. On aluminum parts, don't let the cleaner sit on the part too long; it can dull the finish

6 A thorough rinsing is necessary to remove the grime and all traces of the chemical cleaner

7 Before any painting, the old paint must be prepped. On a steel cover, the original paint would be wet-sanded smooth with #320 or #400 paper. On the details in this finned cover, fine steel wool is used to remove any loose paint or remaining dirt

8 This is where some of the elbow grease is required: polishing. We're using Mother's Mag & Aluminum Polish. Compare the already-polished right side to the untouched areas at left. The tops of all of the fins must be polished too

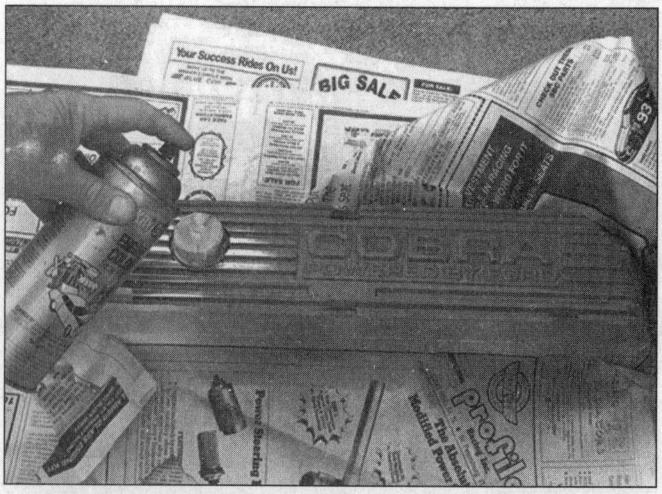

9 With newspaper and masking tape, the areas not to be painted are masked off and the cover can be painted with engine-specific spray paint. Several light coats are better than one heavy coat

10 When the paint is dry, at least an hour later, peel away the masking and begin wiping paint off the highlights with lacquer thinner and a rag wrapped around your fingertip

11 A light touch with the rag and thinner is all that is needed. Be patient and go slowly. Using too much thinner on the rag will put wet thinner down into the painted valleys and dull the paint, or even remove it. Get the worst of the paint off in the first pass; then let it dry a few minutes before lightly going over the remaining traces of paint on the fin tops

12 The rewards speak for themselves when you compare the rejuvenated valve cover with the one yet to be cleaned. The accent color is the color of the rest of the engine and will look great in place

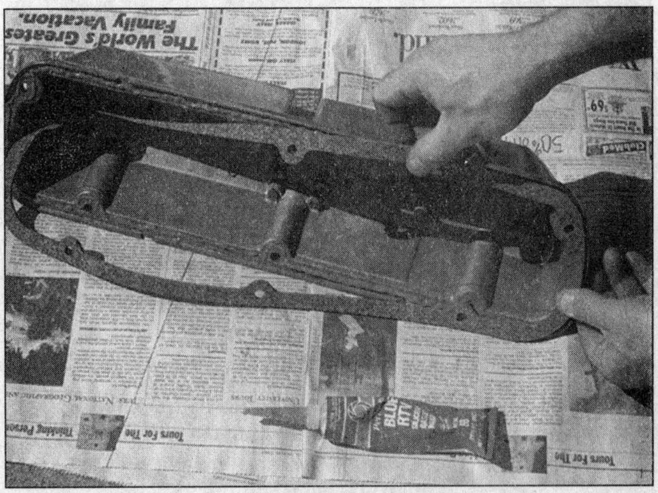

13 Of course, the valve covers must be reinstalled on the engine with new gaskets and RTV sealant. It's a small detail, but we used blue silicone to match the blue of the Ford engine

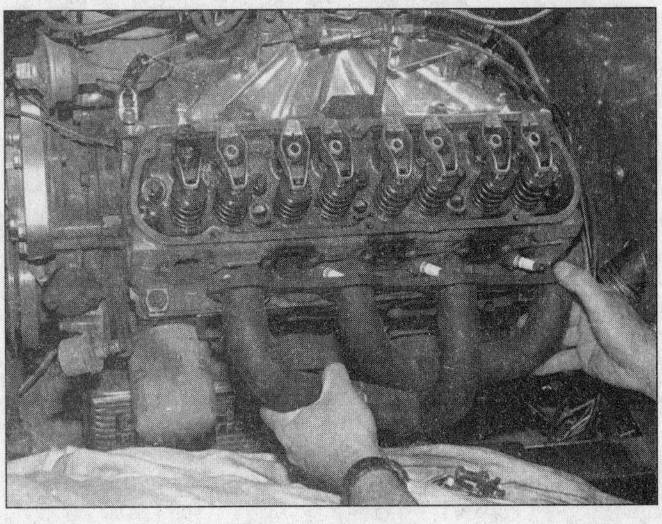

14 Once the air cleaner housing and valve covers have been detailed, the exhaust manifolds are usually the next to tackle because they usually are quite rusty. This tubular header is being removed for coating with high-temperature aluminum-chrome-look finish. Several sources for this kind of coating are listed in the Sourcelist at the end of this book

15 The simplest treatment for standard cast-iron exhaust manifolds is to clean them thoroughly of rust, using chemical rust-removers, sandblasting or using a wire-brush attachment in your electric drill

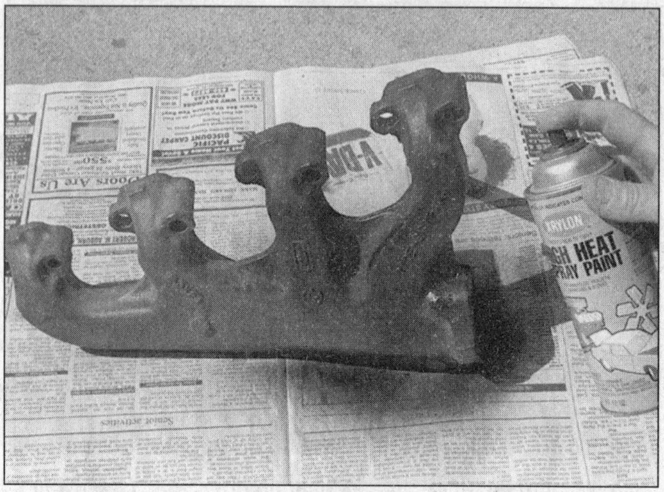

16 There are special paints available that give manifolds a new cast-iron look, yet protect the parts from rust. Or, you can use readily-available high-heat exhaust paint (sometimes also called barbecue paint). There are several colors of this paint, but most enthusiasts use flat black

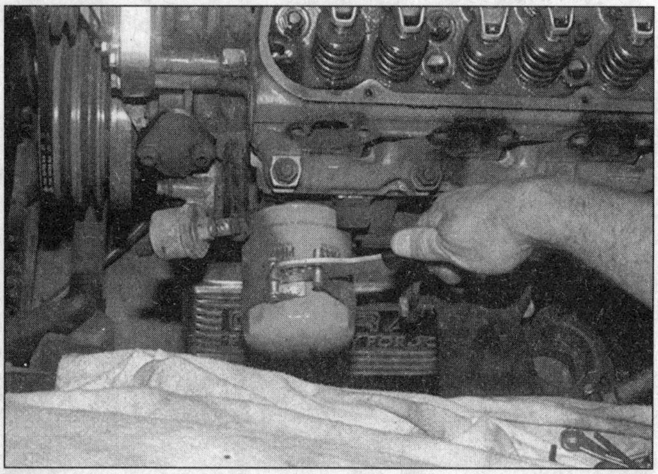

17 With the exhaust removed, this engine will be a lot easier to repaint and detail. Next the oil filter is removed, so that painting can be more thorough. The filter pad area itself will be masked off

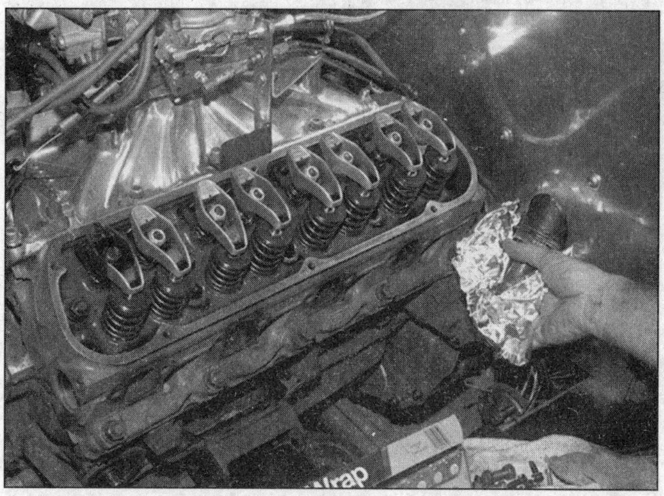

18 Household aluminum foil makes a great masking tool because it can be formed to go around most anything, like this steering joint. All of the engine surfaces that are going to be painted must be thoroughly cleaned before masking

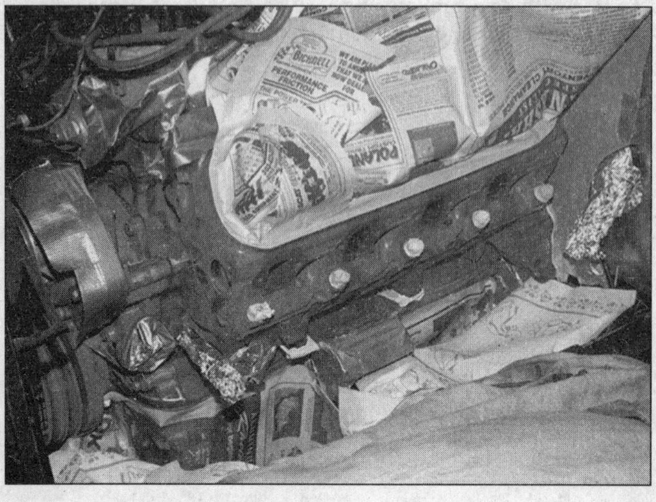

19 Here the valve cover area, firewall, steering, oil pan, water pump and other areas have been masked off, using foil, duct tape and newspaper with masking tape. Even the tops of the head studs have been masked, so their black color will contrast better with the engine color. The finished product will look less like it was hastily painted, and more like it had been rebuilt

20 Several light coats of Ford blue engine paint are bringing this engine back to fresh-looking status with only an hour or two of prep work

21 The finished engine, with the headers Ceramachrome coated, the valve cover detailed with fresh paint, new oil filter and cleaned-up wires and distributor cap is something to be proud of

22 Spark plug wires can become grimy with time, but a little vinyl cleaner on a rag run over the length of the wires puts them right back into shape

23 The top of the distributor cap and the spark plug boots can all be treated to a little protectant to make them look like new again

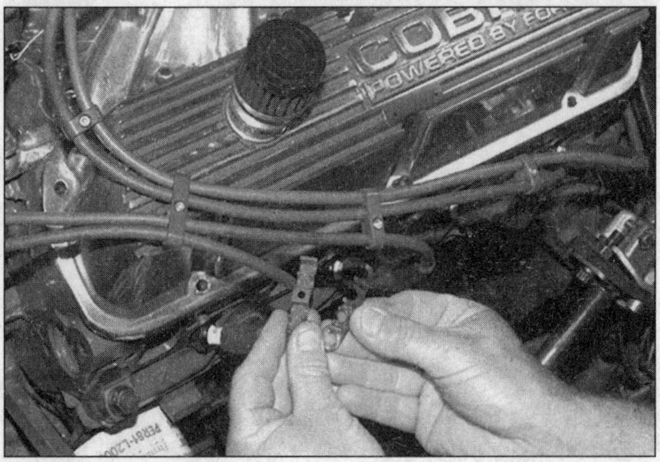

24 This is in the realm of accessorizing, but most auto supply stores have special spark plug wire separators that dress up the wires and also prevent crossfiring

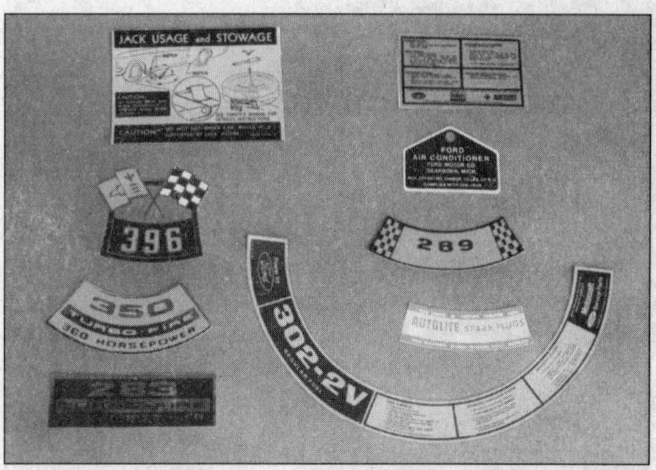

25 New air cleaner and valve cover decals can be obtained from restoration sources and really put a finishing touch on repainted engine components

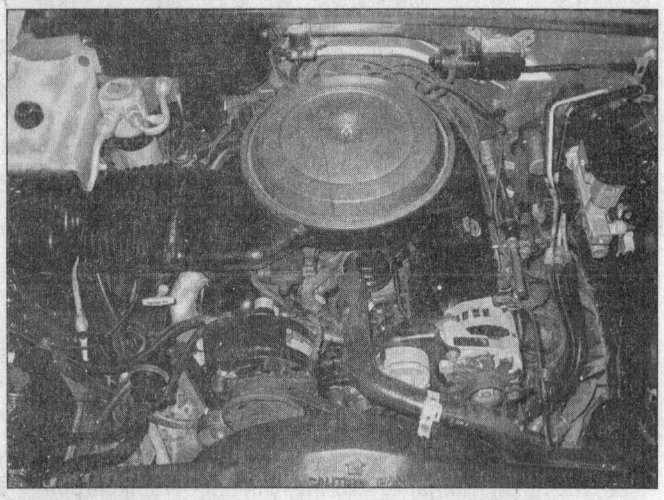

1 Although the stock engine compartment is clean, you really wouldn't want to show it off . . .

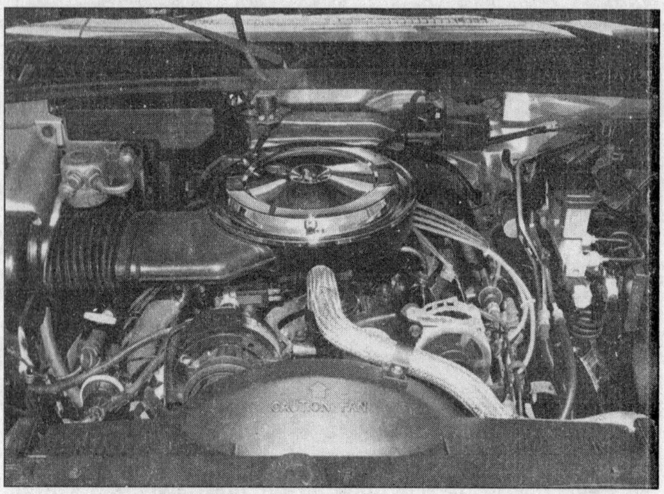

2 . . . but, with inexpensive parts and a day's work, it starts looking like it's from a show car

3 We'll start by replacing the spark plug wires with brightly colored high-performance ones. The most important thing to remember here is to do only one wire at a time to avoid mixing them up. Twist and pull on the boot to remove it from the spark plug . . .

Dressing up a Chevy big-block engine compartment

We added some inexpensive parts to this Chevy engine compartment. If looks improve performance, we just added 100 horsepower!

4 . . . disengage it from the cable guides . . .

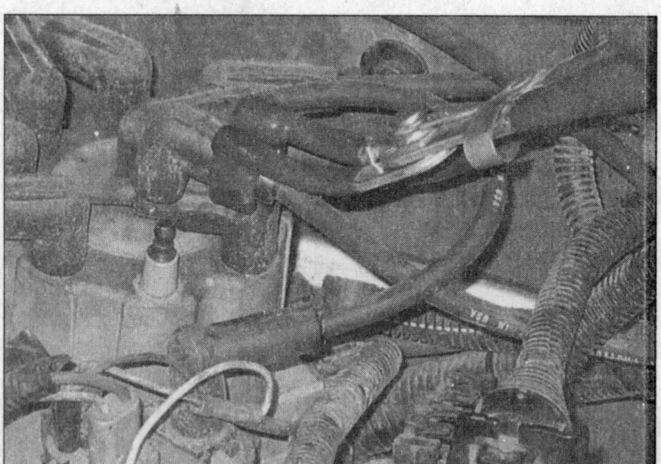

5 . . . and pull it off the tower on the distributor cap. We're using a special plier-like tool that's designed for spark plug wire removal. They're commonly available at auto parts stores

6 Each spark plug wire is a specific length, so, before installing the new wire, make sure the cable lengths are similar and that the boots at both ends are identical

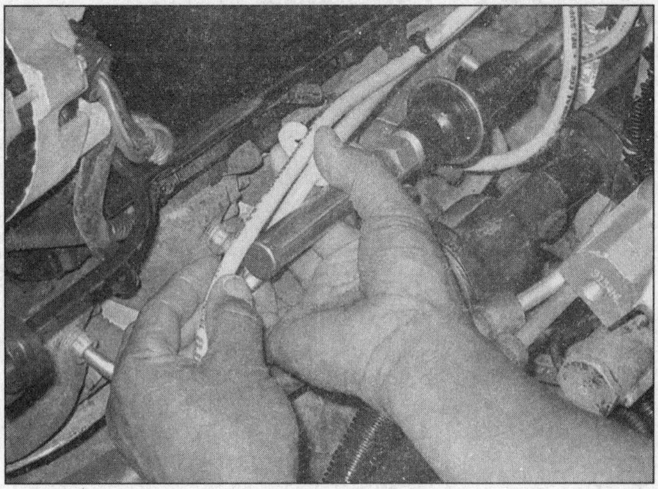

7 If you're using thicker wires like we are, you'll need thicker cable guides as well

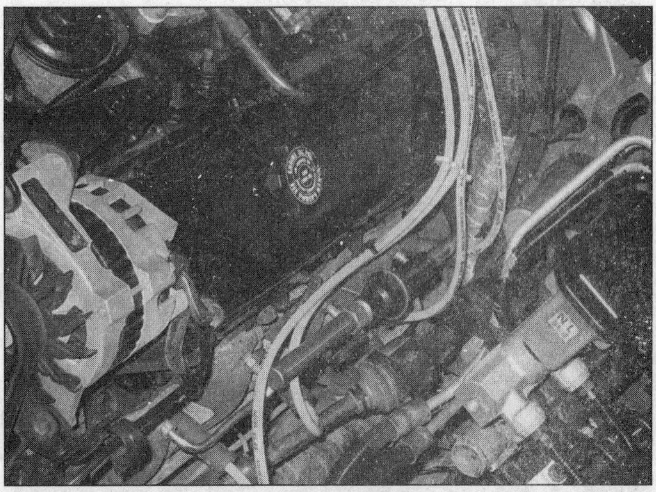

8 Doing one wire at a time, work carefully and route the wires away from hot components. When you're done, it should look something like this

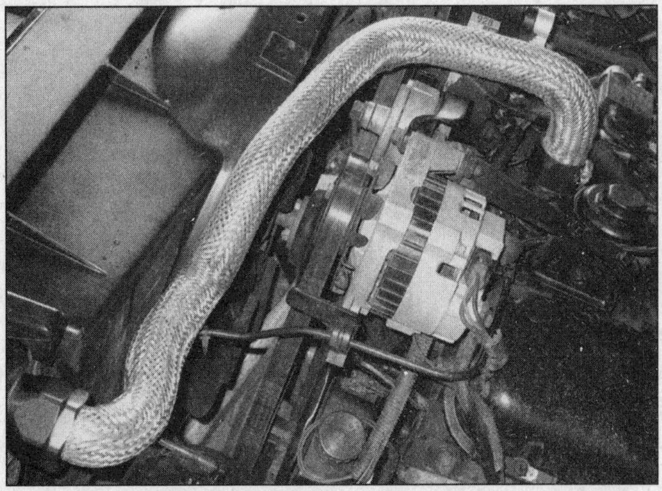

9 You've probably seen braided metal hoses on show cars. But did you know you could add this look with inexpensive kits from your auto parts store? Kits typically include sheathing to cover your radiator, heater and vacuum hoses

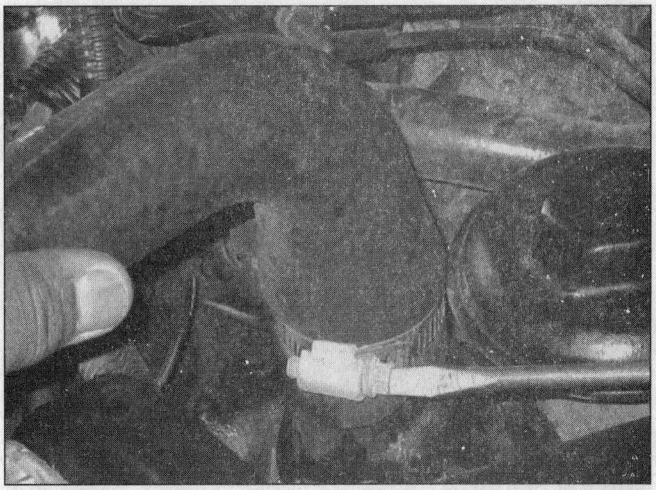

10 The first step in covering the cooling system hoses is to drain the coolant and remove the hoses. Be sure your engine is cooled down before you start

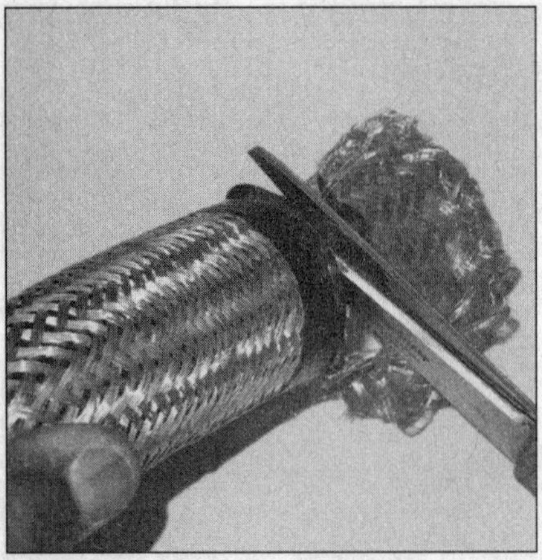

11 Insert a short section of PVC pipe (usually included in the kit) into one end of the cover to hold it in a rigid tubular shape. Now wrap the end of the cover with electrical tape (to reduce fraying) and trim the cover to length

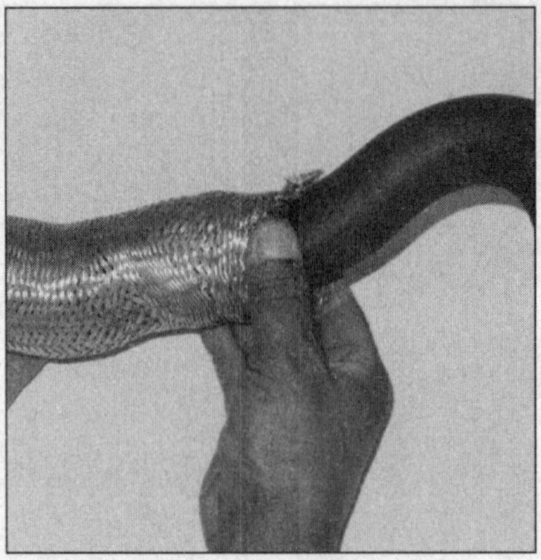

12 Pull the hose through the cover . . .

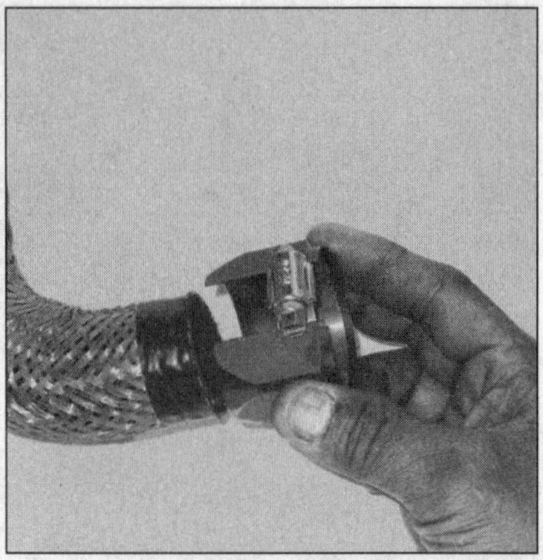

13 . . . install the clamp end over the cover . . .

14 . . . and reinstall the hose. Tighten the worm-gear-type clamps securely

15 A quick way to spruce up the look of your engine compartment is to replace that boring old valve cover with something a little flashier. First, get everything out of the way and unscrew the valve cover bolts. The Haynes manual on your particular vehicle will give you further details

16 Lift off the valve cover. If it's stuck, tap it loose with a rubber mallet. Do not pry it off with a sharp object, or you may damage the mating surface

17 Install your new gasket on a clean surface, or you won't get a good seal

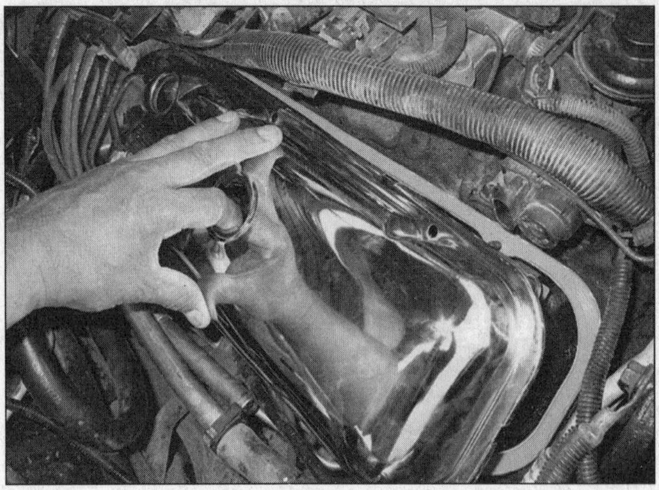

18 With the valve cover in place, tighten the bolts, being careful not to overtighten them

19 Buff off any fingerprints and smudges so your valve covers are nice and shiny

20 Replacing the air cleaner cover is an easy way to add a large chrome accent to the engine compartment. Just unscrew the wing nut, remove the old cover (you might want to replace the filter while you're at it) . . .

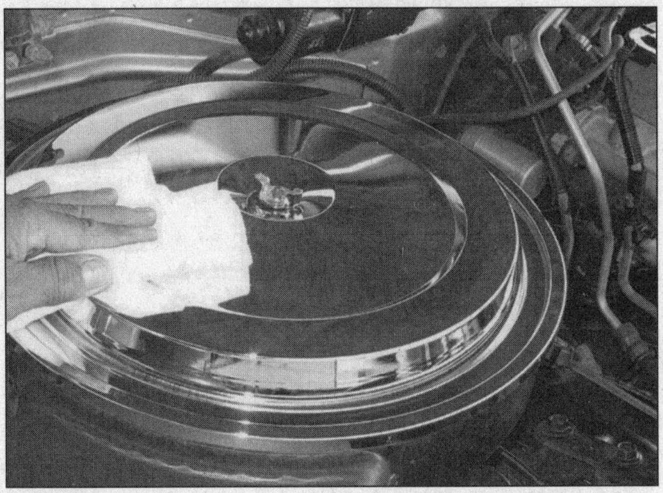

21 . . . put on the new cover, polish it and you're ready to show it off!

Notes

4 Computers and Chips

In addition to better fuel economy, improved reliability, cleaner air and self-diagnostic capabilities, computerized engine management systems also offer a simple means of gaining more performance from your vehicle without even getting your hands dirty.

The "brain" of the electronically-controlled engine management system is a powerful onboard microprocessor that's calibrated to optimize the emissions, fuel economy and drivability of the vehicle. Its programming is 90% generic (common to all vehicles), and the other 10% is very specific to the vehicle/engine/transaxle/accessory package used in each make/model/year of the vehicle. Parameters such as ignition timing and fuel calibration play a big role in how a vehicle drives. Factory programming is designed to keep the emissions in compliance with State and Federal standards, yet provide a fuel curve appropriate for all kinds of driving conditions and climates.

Obviously, factory programming is a compromise, and maximum performance isn't the vehicle manufacturer's mandate. Because enthusiasts focus more on high-performance, their programming needs differ significantly from an OEM.

A brief history

When emissions equipment began appearing on cars in the Seventies, most car enthusiasts looked at these developments as the end of performance cars as we knew them. The average car enthusiast at that time was old school, meaning they were used to carburetors (and non-electronic ones at that) and ignition points. The first generation of cars with emission controls offered unimpressive performance was and plagued by drivability problems. Early emissions systems were seen as - and in many cases actually were - nothing more than clumsy Band-Aids.

Later, when onboard computers and electronically controlled fuel injection were finally integrated with an array of information sensors and output actuators, cars started getting better. Fuel economy improved, starting was better and there was automatic compensation for altitude - reasonable performance began to creep back in. All of this was great for

consumers, car manufacturers and the air that we breathe, but performance enthusiasts were marginalized for awhile. Remember that few people were computer savvy until personal computers began finding their way into the average home in the mid-Eighties. Old school hot rodders were still behind the curve at first because they initially resisted the application of computer functions to cars and were resistant to modifying cars with those newfangled onboard computers.

Fast forward to today - computers are now common in everyday life. We use computers for online banking, investments, communications, video games and shopping. And we design everything from buildings to cars to books like this with computers. And certainly, nobody even considers improving engine performance nowadays without some sort of computer.

Though information sampling was somewhat rudimentary at first, automotive engineers just kept finding more and more new uses for computers as they realized the power and potential of comprehensive engine management systems. For example, they began taking into account non-emission factors like power steering, air conditioning and transmission performance, all of which affect drivability and performance. Over time, engine management systems acquired more and better information sensors, faster and smarter computers with more sophisticated maps (programs) and faster and more reliable output actuators. In the car world of today, the computer has become a useful, reliable and sophisticated tool that a car cannot do without, and with which you must acquaint yourself if you want to have access to all your performance options.

Federal emissions and fuel economy standards were the impetus for much of this development, and there is much to learn about how your car's engine management system works before you can make informed decisions about performance modifications to your engine.

Engine management basics

At the heart of every automotive computer system is an onboard computer, referred to by OEMs as the Engine Control Unit (ECU), the Engine Control Module (ECM) or the Powertrain Control Module (PCM). In this book we're just going to call it the computer. An array of sophisticated information sensors monitor various functions of the engine and send data to the computer. The computer compares this incoming data to its map (program), makes operational decisions at lightning speed generates output control signals to various output actuators - coils, injectors, motors, relays, solenoids, etc. - all of which keep the engine running smoothly and efficiently.

The computer is the "brain" of the electronically controlled fuel and emissions system, and is specifically calibrated to optimize the performance, emissions, fuel economy and driveability of one specific vehicle/engine/transaxle/accessory package in one make/model/year of vehicle. The following list includes the types of sensors and actuators on most late-model vehicles.

The Accelerator Pedal Position (APP) sensor, which replaces the accelerator cable, has begun to appear on many cars in this decade. If your vehicle has an APP sensor, you'll find it at the top of the accelerator pedal (Mustang shown)

Information sensors

Note: *The following list includes all of the principal information sensors that you will find on your vehicle, but it is by no means comprehensive. For a complete list of the sensors used on your vehicle and their exact locations, refer to your Haynes repair manual.*

Accelerator Pedal Position Sensor (APPS) - The APPS provides the computer with a variable voltage signal that's proportional to the position (angle) of the accelerator pedal. The computer uses this data to control the position of the throttle plate inside the electronically controlled throttle body. Earlier APPS units were located somewhere on the firewall and were connected to the accelerator pedal by an accelerator cable (even though the connection between the APPS and the throttle body was electrical). All current APPS units are located at the upper end of and are an integral component of the accelerator pedal assembly, i.e. there is no accelerator cable at all.

Ambient temperature sensor - The ambient temperature sensor, which is usually located somewhere on the front of the vehicle like the front bumper (*not* the bumper *cover*), monitors the ambient temperature. The computer uses this data, along with data from monitored line voltage, to control the battery's charging rate. The computer keeps system voltage at a higher level in colder temperatures and at a lower level in warmer temperatures.

Camshaft Position (CMP) sensor - The CMP sensor generates a signal that the computer uses to monitor the position of the camshaft. In a typical design, the CMP sensor is positioned adjacent to the circumference of a "tone wheel" mounted on the front end of the camshaft. The tone wheel

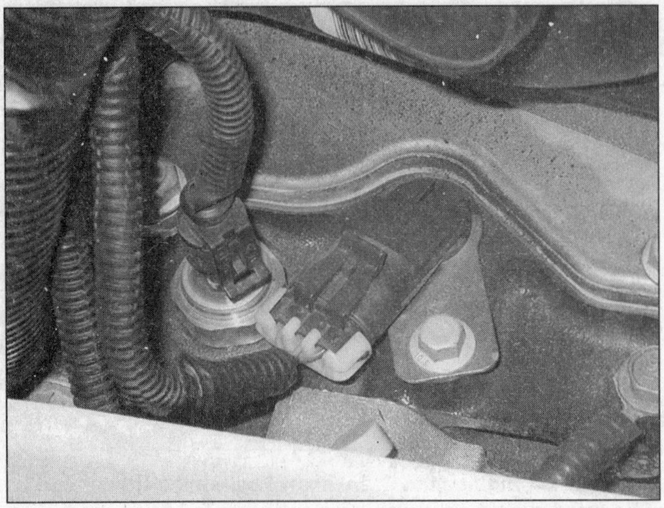

On pushrod engines, the Camshaft Position (CMP) sensor is usually located at the front or rear end of the valley (Chevy small block shown) . . .

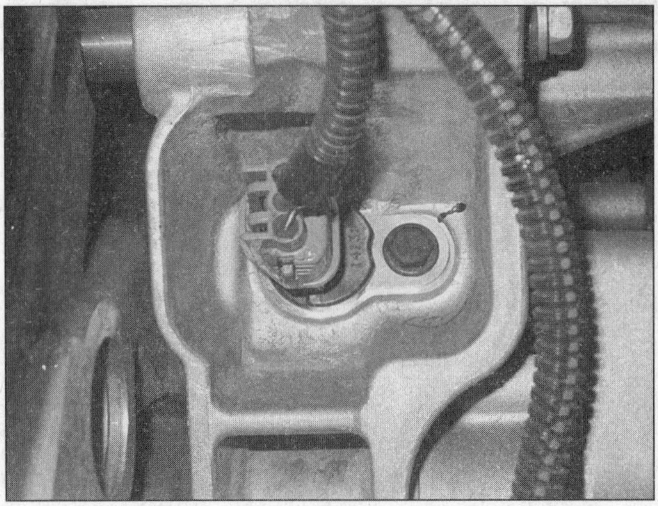

. . . or on the upper part of the timing chain cover (Hemi shown)

has notches machined into it. When the engine is operating, the CMP sensor receives a 5-volt signal from the computer, then switches back and forth from a high (5-volt) to a low (0.3-volt) signal every time one of the notches in the tone wheel passes by it. This data enables the computer to determine the position of the camshaft (and therefore the valve train) so that it can time the firing sequence of the fuel injectors. The computer also uses the signal from the CMP sensor and the signal from the Crankshaft Position (CKP) sensor to distinguish between fuel injection and spark timing.

On pushrod engines, the CMP sensor is usually located at one end of the valley between the heads or the timing chain cover. On overhead cam engines, it's usually located on the front end of one of the cylinder heads or on the timing belt or timing chain cover. On some engines, there are two CMP sensors, one for each cylinder head.

Crankshaft Position (CKP) sensor -The CKP sensor generates a signal that the computer uses to calculate engine speed and crankshaft position, which enables it to synchronize ignition timing with fuel injector timing, to control spark knock and to detect misfires.

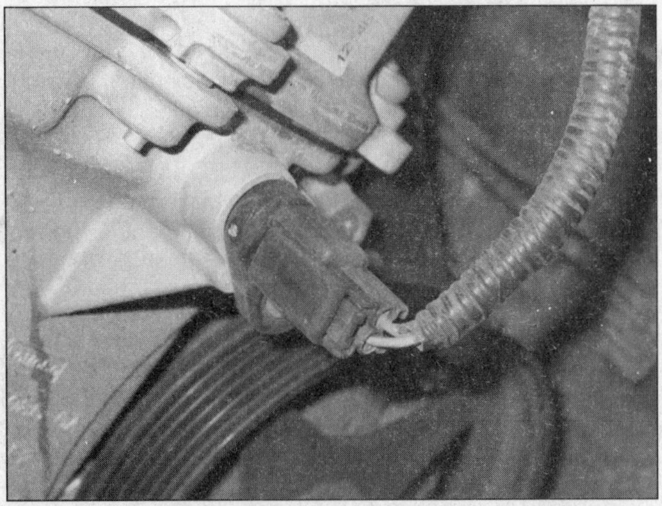

On overhead cam engines, the Camshaft Position (CMP) sensor is usually located at the front end of one of the cylinder heads. Some of the newer engines, like this Ford 5.4L V8, have two CMP sensors. This is the CMP sensor for the left cylinder head . . .

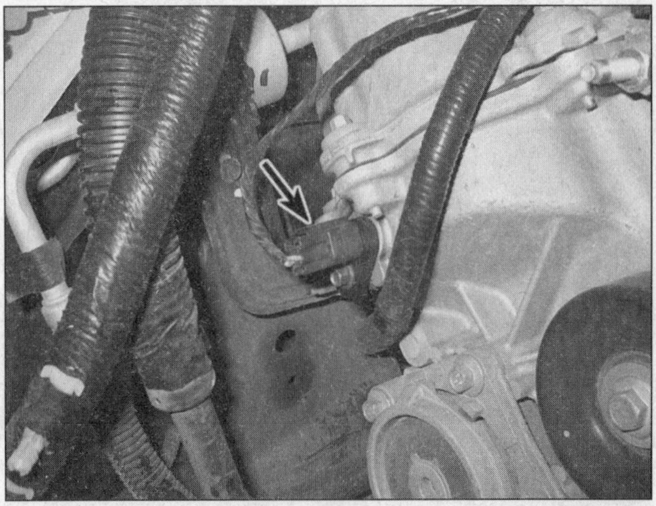

. . . and this is the CMP sensor for the right cylinder head

On some engines the Crankshaft Position (CKP) sensor is located on the timing chain cover, somewhere near the crankshaft pulley (Mustang 4.6L V8 shown)

On other engines the Crankshaft Position (CKP) sensor is located on the side of the block, near the transmission end of the engine (Chevy 5.3L V8 shown, starter motor removed for clarity)

On some engines, the CKP sensor is located near the crankshaft pulley. On other engines the CKP sensor is located on the rear side of the block, where its tip is positioned adjacent to a tone wheel on the crankshaft. On a few engines it's even on the transmission bellhousing, adjacent to a tone wheel on the flywheel/driveplate. Regardless of the location of the CKP sensor on your engine, you'll usually have to raise the front of the vehicle to access it.

Cylinder Head Temperature (CHT) sensor - The CHT sensor, which is used on some engines, is located on the cylinder head. Unlike a conventional ECT sensor (see below) the CHT sensor measures the temperature of the cylinder head, not the temperature of the engine coolant. But the computer is able to infer the temperature of the coolant from the CHT sensor signal nonetheless. If the CHT sensor indicates a temperature above a certain threshold (say, for example,

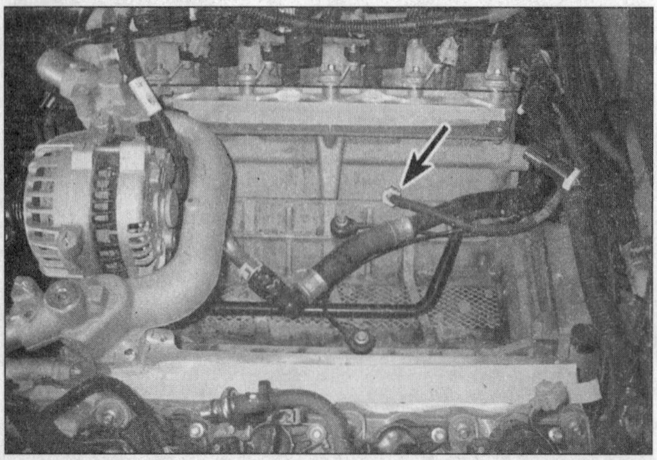

On Ford 4.6L V8s, the Cylinder Head Temperature (CHT) sensor is located on the inner wall of the right (passenger's side) cylinder head, so you'd have to remove the intake manifold to access it. On other modern engines with a CHT sensor, access isn't this difficult

250-degrees F), the computer initiates a fail-safe cooling strategy that allows you to drive home in "limp-home" mode. For example, on Ford's 4.6L V8, the computer disables half of the fuel injectors, and alternates which half of the injectors is disabled every 32 engine cycles. The cylinders that are not injected act as air pumps to help cool down the engine. In the Ford system, if the CHT sensor indicates a temperature of 330-degree F or higher, the computer shuts down all of the injectors until the temperature goes below about 310-degrees F.

Engine Coolant Temperature (ECT) sensor - The ECT sensor is a Negative Temperature Coefficient (NTC) "thermistor" (temperature-sensitive variable resistor). In an NTC-type thermistor, the resistance of the thermistor decreases as the coolant temperature increases, so the voltage output of the ECT sensor increases. Conversely, the resistance of the thermistor increases as the coolant temperature decreases, so the voltage of the ECT sensor decreases. The computer uses this variable voltage signal to calculate the temperature of the engine coolant. The ECT sensor tells the computer when the engine is sufficiently warmed up to go into closed-loop operation and helps the computer control the air/fuel mixture ratio and ignition timing. The ECT sensor can be located on the intake manifold, a cylinder head or the engine block.

Exhaust Gas Recirculation (EGR) valve position sensor - When the temperature of the combustion chambers reaches about 2500-degrees F, oxides of nitrogen (NOx) are produced and released into the exhaust system, out the tailpipe and into the atmosphere. NOx is a precursor of ground level ozone and photochemical smog. Two emission components on every vehicle are designed to reduce NOx; one of them is the Exhaust Gas Recirculation (EGR) system (the other is the catalytic converter). When commanded to do so by the computer, the EGR system recirculates spent exhaust gases back into the combustion chambers to dilute

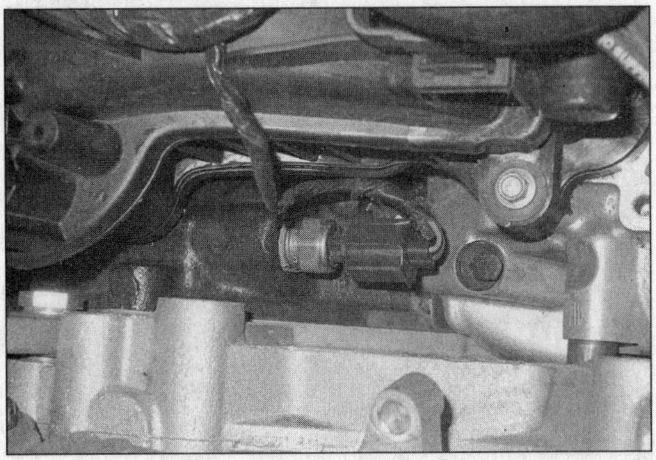

On late-model Hemis, the Engine Coolant Temperature (ECT) sensor is located on front part of the intake manifold, right behind the timing chain cover

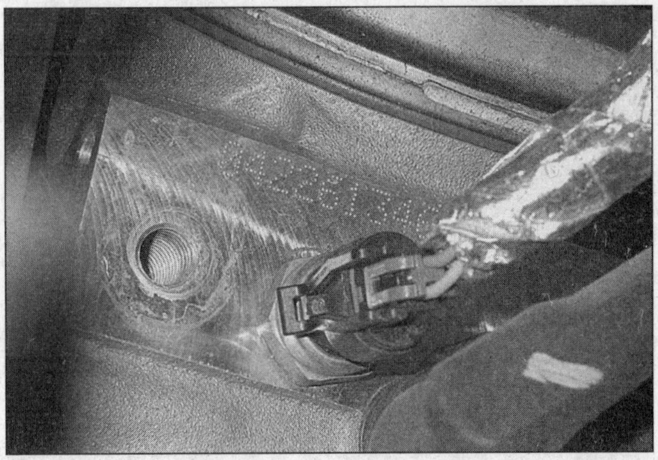

On some Chevy V8s (4.8L, 5.0L, 6.0L) the Engine Coolant Temperature (ECT) sensor is located on the outside wall of the left cylinder head

the incoming air-fuel mixture, which lowers the combustion chamber temperature. A computer-controlled pintle valve inside the EGR varies the amount of spent gases being reintroduced into the intake manifold. The EGR valve position sensor monitors the position of the pintle valve in relation to the operating conditions of the EGR system, and sends a variable voltage signal back to the computer, which uses this feedback loop to control the "duty cycle" of the EGR valve. The EGR valve position sensor is usually an integral component of the EGR valve assembly and cannot be removed.

Fuel tank pressure sensor - The fuel tank pressure sensor is a component of the Evaporative Emission Control (EVAP) system. It's located on top of or near the fuel tank. The fuel tank pressure sensor monitors the pressure of fuel vapors inside the tank. When the vapor pressure exceeds the upper threshold, the fuel tank pressure sensor signals the computer, which opens a valve, allowing the fuel vapors

The Intake Air Temperature (IAT) sensor is located on the resonator on a Hemi (the resonator is the cold air box between the air intake duct and the throttle body, so it's the perfect location for measuring the temperature of incoming intake air)

to migrate to the EVAP canister, where they are stored until they're purged. The fuel tank pressure sensor is also referred to as the vapor pressure sensor by some manufacturers. The fuel tank pressure sensor is located on top of the fuel tank or somewhere on the EVAP canister assembly.

Intake Air Temperature (IAT) sensor - The IAT sensor is a Negative Temperature Coefficient (NTC) "thermistor" (temperature-sensitive variable resistor) that monitors the temperature of the air entering the engine and sends a variable voltage signal to the computer. The voltage signal from the IAT sensor is one of the parameters used by the computer to determine injector pulse-width (the duration of each injector's "on-time") and to adjust spark timing (to prevent spark knock). The IAT sensor is always located on the air filter housing, the air intake duct, the resonator or the intake manifold. And on many of the newer fuel injection systems the IAT sensor is an integral part of the Mass Air Flow (MAF) sensor. See *Mass Air Flow (MAF) sensor* for more information.

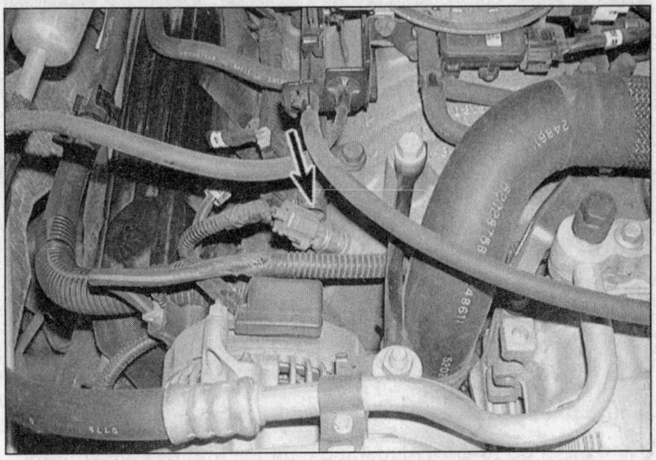

On some engines like this Dodge 5.9L, the Intake Air Temperature (IAT) sensor is located on the intake manifold

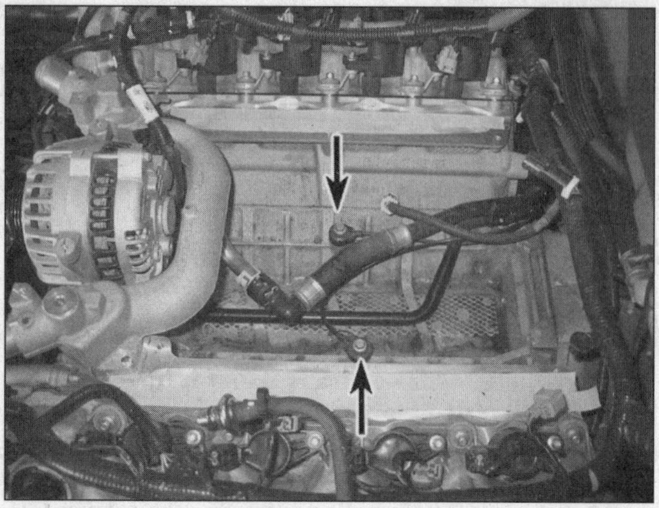

On some engines, like this Ford Mustang 4.6L V8, there are two knock sensors located in the valley between the cylinder heads. On other engines, there is only one knock sensor, but it's located in the same area. In either case, you have to remove the intake manifold to access either sensor

On other engines, such as this Hemi, the two knock sensors are located on each side of the engine block. This is the left side knock sensor, which is located just below the exhaust manifold and just ahead of the starter motor

Knock sensor - The knock sensor is a "piezoelectric" crystal that oscillates in proportion to engine vibration. (The term piezoelectric refers to the property of certain crystals that produce a voltage when subjected to a mechanical stress.) The oscillation of the piezoelectric crystal produces a voltage output that is monitored by the computer, which retards the ignition timing when the oscillation exceeds a certain threshold. When the engine is operating normally, the knock sensor oscillates consistently and its voltage signal is steady. When detonation occurs, engine vibration increases, and the oscillation of the knock sensor exceeds a design threshold. If allowed to continue, the engine could be damaged.

On most popular fuel injected engines that use a Manifold Absolute Pressure (MAP) sensor, the sensor is located on the intake manifold (small-block Chevy shown)

Manifold Absolute Pressure (MAP) sensor - As the altitude increases, the air becomes thinner. Because the air density changes with altitude, the computer needs to know whether the vehicle is at sea level or at some higher elevation. Altitude and barometric pressure are inversely proportional: as the altitude increases, the barometric pressure decreases. The MAP sensor monitors the pressure or vacuum downstream from the throttle plate, inside the intake manifold. A MAP sensor measures intake manifold pressure and vacuum on the absolute scale (from zero psi, not from sea-level atmospheric pressure [14.7 psi]). The MAP sensor converts the absolute pressure into a variable voltage signal that changes with the pressure or vacuum. The computer uses this signal to calculate intake manifold pressure or vacuum, barometric pressure, engine load, injector pulse-width, spark advance, shift points, idle speed and deceleration fuel shut-off.

Mass Airflow (MAF) sensor - A MAF sensor is another means by which an engine management computer can measure the amount of intake air drawn into the engine. It uses a hot-wire sensing element, which is constantly maintained at a specified temperature above the ambient temperature of the incoming air by electrical current. As intake air passes through the MAF sensor and over the hot wire, it cools the wire, and the control system immediately corrects the temperature back to its constant value. The current required to maintain the constant value is used by the PCM to determine the amount of air flowing through the MAF sensor.

Oxygen sensors - An oxygen sensor is a galvanic battery that generates a small variable voltage signal in proportion to the difference between the oxygen content in the exhaust stream and the oxygen content in the ambient air. The com-

The Mass Air Flow (MAF) sensor is always mounted inside the air filter housing, at the air intake duct end of the filter housing (as on this Mustang V8) or as a separate component between the air filter housing and the air intake duct

Upstream oxygen sensors are located right on the exhaust manifolds (like this Mustang V8) . . .

puter uses the voltage signal from the upstream oxygen sensor to maintain a "stoichiometric" air/fuel ratio of 14.7:1 by constantly adjusting the "on-time" of the fuel injectors.

On OBD-II vehicles with a single exhaust pipe, there are usually three oxygen sensors. The two upstream oxygen sensors, each of which is located somewhere north of the catalytic converter, are either screwed into the exhaust manifolds or they're located somewhere below the manifold flange, on the pipe that connects the manifold to the catalyst. The downstream oxygen sensor is located right behind the catalytic converter.

On OBD-II vehicles with dual exhaust pipes, there are four oxygen sensors: two upstream and two downstream. The upstream sensors are located in the same place as the upstream sensors on single-exhaust-pipe vehicles. The downstream sensors are located right behind the catalytic converters (there are two catalysts on dual pipe models).

Power Steering Pressure (PSP) switch - The PSP switch is located somewhere on the high pressure power steering fluid line between the power steering pump and the steering gear or steering rack, or it's installed on the pump itself. The PSP switch monitors the fluid pressure inside the power steering system. The pressure is proportional to the drag imposed on the engine by the power steering pump. When the PSP switch indicates that the pressure has exceeded a specified threshold, usually during low-speed vehicle maneuvers, the computer increases engine idle speed.

. . . or they're located somewhere below the manifold flange, on the down pipe that connects the manifold to the catalytic converter (like this Chevy)

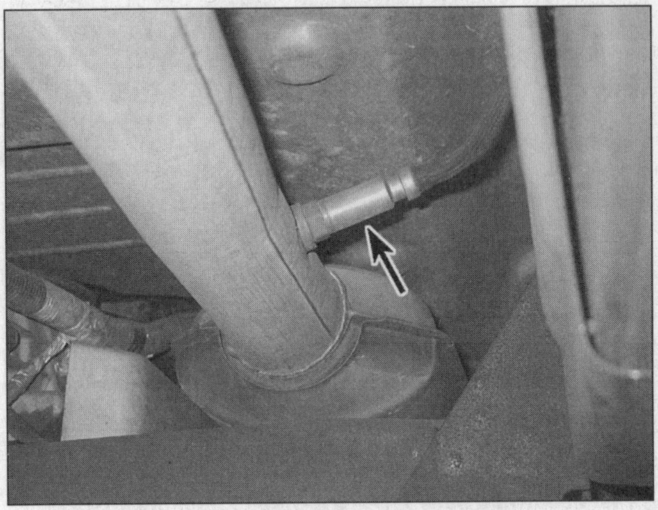

The downstream oxygen sensor is always behind the catalytic converter

The Throttle Position (TP) sensor is mounted on the side of the throttle body, on the end of the throttle plate shaft (Ford Mustang V8 shown)

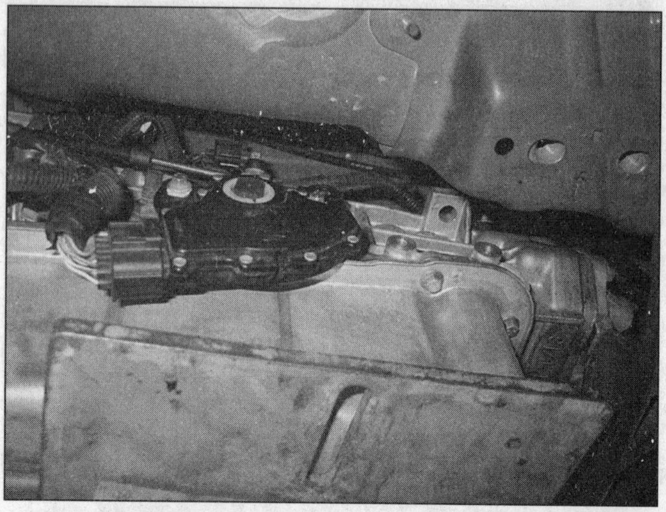

The Transmission Range (TR) sensor, which is the space-age version of the old Park Neutral Position (PNP) switch, is almost always located on the left of the transmission (Ford Mustang shown)

Throttle Position (TP) sensor - The TP sensor is a potentiometer that receives constant voltage input from the computer and sends back a voltage signal that varies in relation to the opening angle of the throttle plate inside the throttle body. This voltage signal tells the computer when the throttle is closed, half-open, wide open or anywhere in between. The computer uses this data, along with information from other sensors, to calculate injector "pulse width" (the interval of time during which an injector solenoid is energized by the computer).

The transmission speed sensors are located on the side of the transmission and both of them look identical. How do you know which one is which? The Input Shaft Speed (ISS) sensor is the forward sensor and the Output Shaft Speed (OSS) sensor is the rear unit (Dodge automatic shown)

Transmission Range (TR) sensor - The TR sensor performs the same functions as a Park/Neutral Position (PNP) switch: it prevents the engine from starting in any gear other than Park or Neutral, and it closes the circuit for the back-up lights when the shift lever is moved to REVERSE. But the TR switch is also connected to the computer, which sends a voltage signal to the TR switch, which uses a series of step-down resistors that act as a voltage divider. The computer monitors the voltage output signal from the switch, which corresponds to the position of the manual lever. Thus the computer is able to determine the gear selected and is able to determine the correct pressure for the electronic pressure control system of the transaxle.

Transmission speed sensors - There are usually two transmission speeds sensors on modern electronically-controlled automatic transmissions, the **Input Shaft Speed (ISS) sensor** and the **Output Shaft Speed (OSS) sensor**. The ISS is a magnetic pick-up coil that generates an alternating current (AC) signal output to the computer (sometimes the Powertrain Control Module, sometimes the Transmission Control Module) that's proportional to the speed of rotation of the input shaft. The OSS is also a magnetic pick-up coil that generates an AC signal output to the PCM or TCM that's proportional to the speed of rotation of the rear planetary carrier lugs (the computer interprets this data as output shaft rpm). The computer compares the ISS and OSS signals to determine the correct transmission gear ratio, to detect a speed ratio error or Torque Converter Clutch (TCC) slippage and to calculate parameters such as the torque converter element speed ratio. The computer uses this information to detect slippage inside the transmission and to estimate probable future failure.

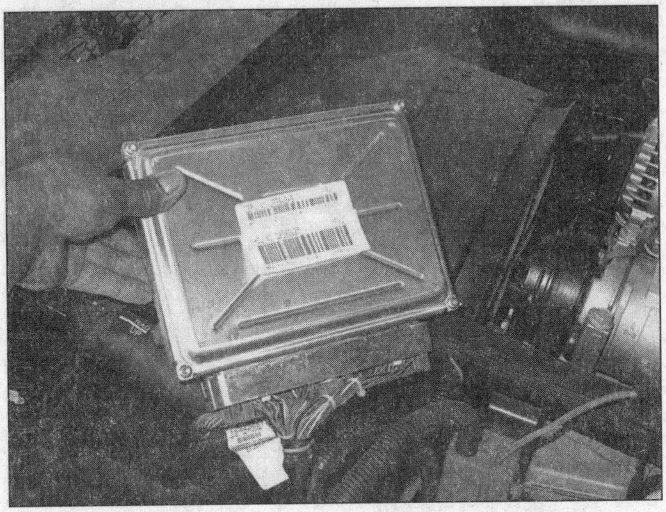

The Powertrain Control Module (PCM), which is the SAE-approved terminology and which is also a fancy name for the engine management computer . . .

. . . is located somewhere in the engine compartment (Ford Mustang shown), or somewhere inside the vehicle, usually behind one of the kick panels or under the dash (for the specific location of the computer on your vehicle, refer to your Haynes manual)

Vehicle Speed Sensor (VSS) - The VSS, which is used on manual transmissions, is a magnetic pick-up coil or Hall Effect switch that is located somewhere on the extension housing or, on 4WD vehicles, on the transfer case. The computer uses the VSS signal to calculate vehicle speed.

The computer

The computer receives data inputs, processes the data and outputs commands. The computer receives data from all of the information sensors described above (input), compares the data to its program and calculates the appropriate responses (processing), then turns the output actuators on or off, or changes their *pulse width* or *duty cycle* (output) to keep everything running smoothly, cleanly and efficiently. The computer can be located in the engine compartment or inside the vehicle, usually somewhere inside or below the dash. The computer is referred to by some manufacturers as the Engine Control Unit (ECU), the Engine Control Module (ECM), the Powertrain Control Module (PCM), etc. Though PCM is the current SAE-recommended terminology, some manufacturers still use one of the other terms above or some other term. In this book we simply refer to it as "the computer."

Output actuators

Electronic Throttle Body - Some of the newest vehicles are equipped with an electronic throttle control system. These vehicles do not have a conventional accelerator cable-actuated throttle body. Instead, they use an electronic throttle body that is controlled by the computer. The throttle plate inside the throttle body is opened and closed by a computer-controlled throttle motor. There is no cruise control cable and no idle air control valve either. Both functions are handled electronically by the computer. The computer determines the correct throttle plate angle by processing the input signal from the Accelerator Pedal Position (APP) sensor, which is located at the upper end of the accelerator pedal.

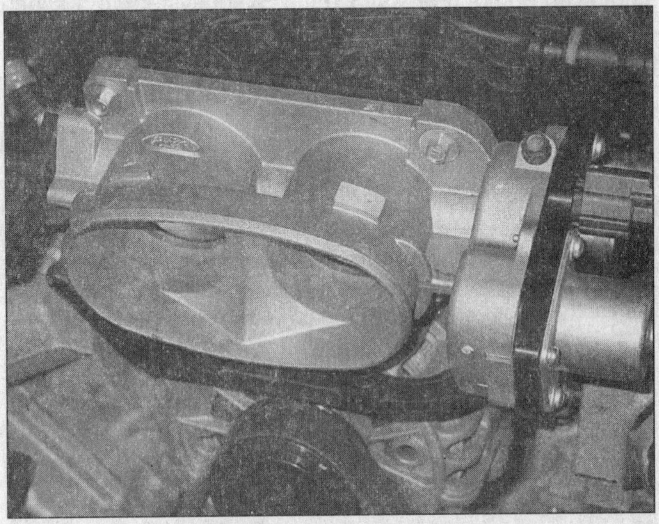

Electronic throttle bodies have no accelerator cable. Instead they're controlled by the engine management computer via an Accelerator Pedal Position (APP) sensor, which tells the computer where your right foot is at, then commands a solenoid inside the throttle body to open or close the throttle plate(s) accordingly (Mustang V8 shown)

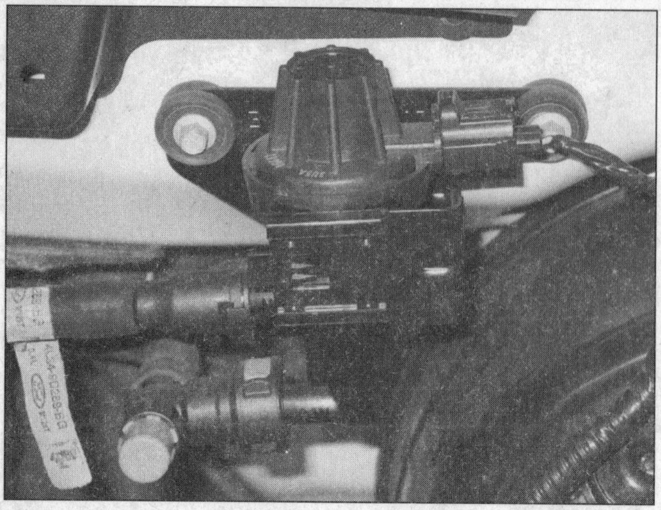

A typical Evaporative Emissions Control (EVAP) canister purge valve, mounted on the firewall (Ford)

A typical Exhaust Gas Recirculation (EGR) valve (Chevy)

EVAP canister purge valve - The EVAP canister purge valve is a computer-controlled solenoid that controls the purging of evaporative emissions from the EVAP canister to the intake manifold. The EVAP purge valve is never turned on during cold start warm-ups or during hot start time delays. But once the engine reaches a specified temperature and enters closed-loop operation the computer energizes the valve between 5 and 10 times a second.

EVAP leak detection systems - EVAP leak detection systems are complex (and probably of little interest to most performance enthusiasts!). Earlier systems use a computer-controlled pump to pressurize the EVAP system to a specified pressure, then monitor whether it can hold the pressure. If it can't, it's leaking. Current systems impose a (relative) vacuum inside the system, then monitor whether it can maintain that vacuum. If it can't, it's leaking. Both systems are able to discriminate between a small leak and a large leak. When the computer detects a leak in the EVAP system, it displays a diagnostic trouble code.

Exhaust Gas Recirculation (EGR) valve - When the engine is put under a load (hard acceleration, passing, going up a steep hill, pulling a trailer, etc.), combustion chamber temperature increases. When combustion chamber temperature exceeds 2500-degrees F, excessive amounts of oxides of nitrogen (NOx) are produced. NOx is a precursor of photochemical smog. The EGR valve allows a portion of the exhaust gases to be recirculated back to the intake manifold where they dilute the incoming air/fuel mixture, which lowers the combustion chamber temperature and decreases the amount of NOx produced during high-load conditions.

Fuel injectors - Each fuel injector has a computer-controlled inductive coil that opens and closes a tiny pintle valve at the lower end of the injector. When its coil is energized by the computer, the pintle valve is pulled open against spring pressure and the injector sprays a fine mist of fuel through one or more tiny orifices into the intake port, where it mixes with incoming air. On modern engines, fuel injection systems are referred to as Sequential Fuel Injection (SFI) systems because the injectors are fired *sequentially*, in the same firing order as the spark plugs. The computer also controls the injector "pulse width," which is the interval of time during which each injector is open. The pulse width of the injector (measured in milliseconds) determines the amount of fuel delivered.

Idle air control (IAC) valve - On mechanically actuated throttle bodies, the IAC valve controls the amount of air that bypasses the throttle plate when the throttle valve is closed or at idle position. The IAC valve opening and the resulting airflow is controlled by the computer. (On electronic throttle bodies, there is no IAC valve; this function is handled by the computer.)

A typical Idle Air Control (IAC) valve (Chevy)

Computer codes keep track

In the years between the Clean Air Act Extension of 1970 and the emergence of OBD-II in 1996, earlier engine management systems were characterized by an increasingly sophisticated array of self-diagnostic capabilities. After OBD-II became the law in 1996, these earlier On Board Diagnostics came to be known as OBD-I. The diagnostic part of the OBD-I and OBD-II acronyms refers to the ability to retrieve information from the computer about the performance characteristics and running condition of all the sensors and actuators in the engine management system. This is invaluable information in diagnosing engine problems.

The computer will illuminate the CHECK ENGINE, SERVICE ENGINE SOON or MALFUNCTION INDICATOR LIGHT on the dash if it recognizes a component fault for two consecutive drive cycles. It will continue to set the light until the computer does not detect any malfunction for three or more consecutive drive cycles.

The diagnostic codes for an OBD-II system can only be extracted from the computer by plugging a OBD-II code reader or scan tool into the computer's data link connector (DLC), which is usually located under the left end of the dash. Your Haynes repair manual will show you the location of the data link connector, list the diagnostic codes that apply to your vehicle and tell you a lot more about the engine management system of your specific make and model. Aftermarket generic scanners are available for all makes and models. But before buying a generic scan tool, contact the manufacturer of the code reader or scanner you're planning to buy and verify that it will work properly with the OBD system you want to scan.

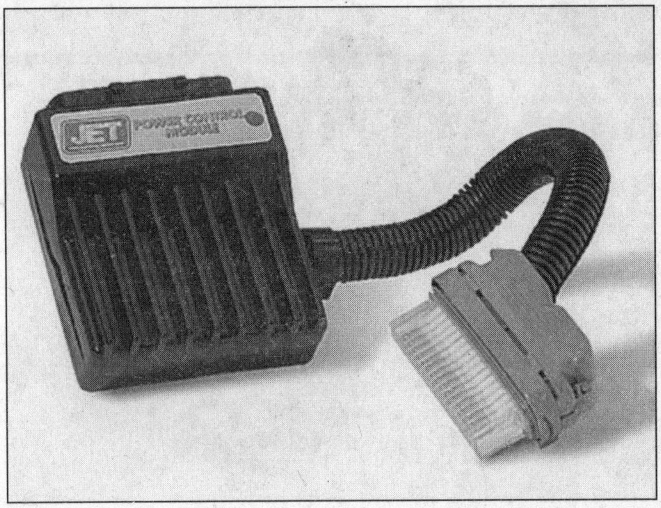

This JET Performance Power Control Module is an add-on computer module that upgrades the performance of your stock computer. Add-on modules are easy to install and can add 20 to 30 horsepower to a stock engine!

Add-on chips and performance upgrades for computers

Many enthusiasts upgrade their engine management system with aftermarket modules to improve the performance of their engines. These new black boxes offer advantages such as increased fuel flow, a better ignition advance curve and a higher redline. When combined with other engine upgrades, replacing or tuning computer components can provide substantial performance gains. But this strategy does have its downside. Replacing any original-equipment computer components can void your warranty or cause you to fail an emissions inspection. Nonetheless, despite these obstacles, if you're going to modify your engine beyond a certain point you will have to consider dealing with the computer.

The factory programming in your car's computer is highly developed, extensively-tested software that works perfectly for your engine in stock condition. But the goal of the factory engineers is maximum fuel economy, drivability, longevity and efficiency. Your goal as a performance enthusiast is higher performance, so your programming needs are slightly different. The average driver will never see 6000 rpm in the car's lifetime, but the typical enthusiast wants to visit the upper power band as often as possible.

When you're looking for better performance, the factory computer programming needs some help with the ignition timing and the fuel curve. Virtually all new cars are designed to run on the lowest grade of unleaded pump gas, with an 87-octane rating. To get more performance, the ignition curve can be given more timing and the fuel curve adjusted for more fuel at higher rpms, but the octane rating of the gas now becomes a problem. When the timing is advanced, the engine may have more of a tendency to exhibit detonation or ping, both of which are signs of an improper burn in the combustion chamber and potentially dangerous to the lifespan of the engine. Thus, if you want more timing in your computer for more power, you'll probably have to up the grade of gasoline you buy. In fact, the more serious engine modifications you make, the more you will probably have to reprogram your computer. One of the first strategies that you should consider is an add-on performance module that can be plugged into the computer system without actually replacing the stock computer.

Piggyback modules

JET Performance and other firms offer a wide range of add-on modules that can be wired right into the existing engine management system without actually removing or replacing your stock computer. JET's Performance Control Modules monitor certain information sensors (MAP, ECT, TP and CKP), then adjust the spark timing and air/fuel ratio. The result is improved horsepower and torque. One of these little black boxes can produce gains of 20 to 30 horsepower!

When shopping for an add-on module, read the specifications and intended use very carefully. These modules are

A typical removable, plug-in type Programmable Read-Only Memory (PROM) chip

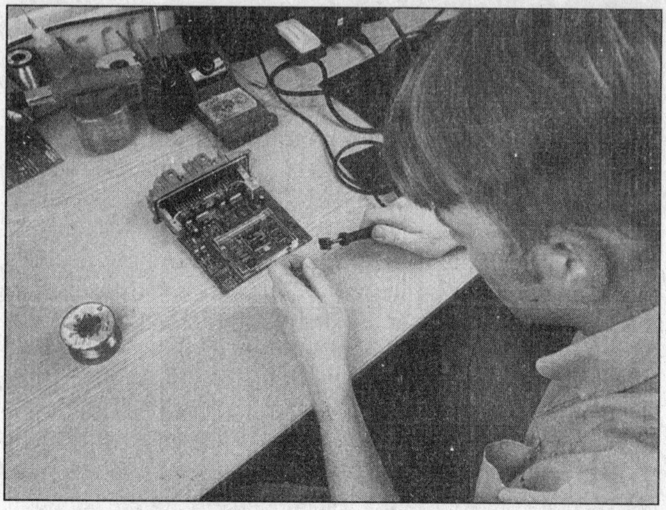

Non-serviceable chips must be carefully unsoldered from the motherboard, which is why this procedure is usually carried out by a specialized company or tuning shop with the right tools and reprogramming equipment

often sold in increasingly radical configurations: Stage 1 is usually for street engines with no other modifications; Stage 2 is for modified engines. Both of these stages are usually street legal in most states (check your local laws). Stage 3 and higher stages are for all-out racers and are probably NOT legal.

Flashing or replacing chips

As your modifications progress, your programming needs will change. For example, while most bolt-on engine modifications will work well with increased timing, the serious power adders like nitrous oxide, superchargers, turbochargers and even just high-compression pistons will require *less* ignition advance. The big gains in horsepower come from modifications that increase the cylinder pressure in the engine, the force pushing the pistons down. Increases in cylinder pressure really raise the octane requirement in a hurry. The best you can get at most gas stations won't be enough to stave off detonation, unless you're lucky enough to live near one of the few stations that sell 100-octane unleaded racing gas, and that gets pricey.

So as you make more and different changes, your computer will need brain surgery. If you've already read Chapter 2, then you may already have located a trustworthy speed shop near you. They'll be able to help you with computer upgrades.

In many new cars, the programming that affects the areas you want to modify is part of a "chip" on the motherboard of the computer. The chip is a very small piece of silicon semiconductor material carrying many integrated circuits. These are usually called Programmable Read Only Memory (PROM) chips. In some cases, the PROM chip is a "plug-in" which can be easily removed from the computer and replaced with a custom chip. Other chips are factory-soldered to the board. Computers with plug-in chips are the easiest to modify, but not all vehicle computers have replaceable chips.

We don't recommend removing a soldered chip from the motherboard at home. Your factory computer is very expensive to replace and just a minute mistake with the solder or the heat source could ruin it. Aftermarket companies offer reprogramming services for these kinds of computer's, and some tuning shops also have equipment to do this.

Your car is going to be out of service a few days, either parked at the tuning shop that is doing the upgrade, or parked at home while you wait for your modified computer to come back from a computer upgrade company. How it works in the latter case is that you order and pay for the upgrade service from a reputable company, and they send you instructions, forms to fill out, and special packaging for the computer. You remove the factory computer from your car (we recommend, of course, that you use a Haynes repair manual for your make and model to locate and properly disconnect the computer), and send it via overnight service to the company, where they will either replace the chip or reprogram it. Based on the information you have given them about your vehicle, driving needs, and modifications you have made to the engine, they will custom-program the timing, fuel and even the transmission shifting information if the vehicle has a computer-controlled electronic automatic transmission. They can even change the factory-set rev limiter and/or top speed limiter! They ship it back the same or next day and you reinstall it with their instructions. **Note:** *A performance chip generally will not void your warranty, but you might want to remove it if you bring your vehicle in to a dealer for diagnostic work, in case the dealership downloads an updated factory program as part of your service. If there is a warranty problem with your vehicle, and the dealer determines that an aftermarket part such as a programmer was installed and was responsible for the problem, the* *dealer will most likely not cover the problem under warranty. Read the fine print in your warranty for the exact wording.*

What to expect from piggybacks and reflashed chips

By themselves, engine management changes can result in some improvement in power, but results will vary with make and model, and how far off the factory programming was from a performance standpoint. As with any aftermarket product, be wary of power gains cited in advertisements and manufacturer literature. Exaggerated claims by overzealous marketing departments have been known to creep into print. Not that it's "untrue," mind you, but the advertised power increase is probably referring to a modified engine that is still using the stock programming. In that situation, such an engine benefits more from the addition of a new aftermarket computer than does a stock engine.

That's the thing about aftermarket chips and computers - they make only modest gains by themselves, but they'll produce even better results in conjunction with other engine modifications. Conversely, mechanical engine changes alone won't make *their* advertised power increases either, unless you *also* do some reprogramming or replace the computer. A stock vehicle with reprogrammed spark and fuel might gain only seven or eight horsepower, although it may affect torque enough at lower rpms to improve the "feel" of the car. Now take the same stock engine with an OEM computer and add a bigger carburetor or throttle body, an improved intake manifold, a new camshaft and exhaust headers. When you reprogram the computer, the same chip could be worth 20 horsepower this time. The extra airflow, improved breathing and increased fuel flow all need more timing to achieve their best numbers. If there's one lesson to learn about modifying automobile drivetrains, it's that all your modifications must work together in a planned, integrated way to achieve the results you're looking for.

Stand-alone aftermarket systems

When an engine reaches the upper levels of its performance potential, a factory computer is no longer flexible enough to allow the maximum performance gain from your modifications. We're talking about a full-built machine that is as comfortable on a racetrack as it is on the street. Indeed, many highly modified machines operate in both environments. The aftermarket offers complete, stand-alone engine management systems for such machines. Just take a stroll through the pits at any drag strip and you'll see such systems under the hoods of the serious players.

These systems are very expensive, but allow the most freedom in controlling an engine for maximum performance. They come with Windows-based software for your laptop or desk PC, and allow control of not only the fuel and timing curves but also for nitrous oxide systems and boost adders like turbochargers and superchargers. Some systems are "plug and play" units, which means they're a direct replacement for the factory computer. Others have more features for the true racer and require some wiring to integrate with your factory harness. If you're already computer knowledgeable, working with these systems will be interesting, but they can be intimidating for the PC-challenged. Most stand-alone systems are designed for racing, and may not have 50-state street-legal status. Once installed, the typical stand-alone system that controls ignition and fuel injection may require 10 or more hours of programming time to achieve the optimum setup for a particular modified vehicle. Unless you're very technically minded, such programming might best be left in the hands of an expert tuning shop that already knows the basics of setting up a stand-alone system.

What about turbos and blowers?

In the case of some modifications, particularly turbocharging and supercharging, you need a way to control ignition timing and fuel based on a parameter that the factory never considered: boost. Instead of the engine gulping fuel and air under atmospheric pressure like a normally-aspirated engine, a blown engine is being force-fed. The more pounds of boost applied to the engine, the more the ignition timing needs to be retarded, and in some cases the more fuel needs to be injected. Aftermarket companies offer a variety of add-on electronic controllers that connect to a manifold vacuum port on your engine and send varying signals to the computer based on how much boost is applied. Some even have a dashboard control so that you can select the timing you need based on the quality of fuel available to you. When you have your engine set up for best results on 93-octane and you're stuck somewhere that only has 91 or 89-octane, you'll need to make a timing adjustment or risk engine damage.

Other electronic controllers can be used to allow the factory Manifold Absolute Pressure (MAP) sensor to regulate boosted conditions as well as normal vacuum. If you have annual emissions inspections in your state, check with your local authorities. Find out if aftermarket controllers are legal, and ask the manufacturer of the controller if they have a C.A.R.B. (California Air Resources Board) exemption number. Aftermarket products with an Exemption Order (E.O.) number are legal in all 50 states. Some products have the E.O. number stamped right into the part; other products come with a sticker or a form-letter that describes the products approval status.

When more control is needed, there are aftermarket computers that work in conjunction with the stock computer. The factory computer and its programming is retained to do all the closed-loop emissions and efficiency programming (closed-loop means that the computer is in charge of

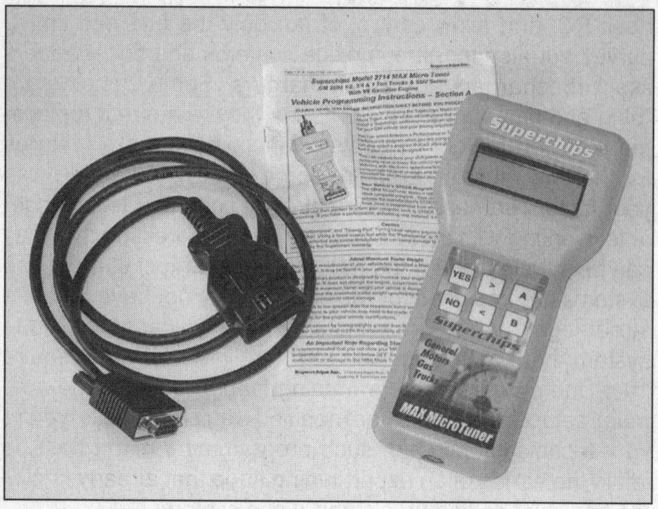

The Superchips MAX MicroTuner is capable of saving a version of your stock computer's data, then downloading one several performance-level programs into your vehicle's engine management system, including a conservative 87-octane rated program and a 91-octane performance program. You can switch programs or back to stock with the tool anytime

With most hand-held programmers, simply hook the cable to the programmer at one end and the other to the diagnostic port of your vehicle, and the instructions walk you through a simple step-by-step procedure for the programming that best suits your needs

all functions), while a secondary box attaches next to the stock computer and handles the functions of controlling timing, fuel and boost. Such boxes are called "piggyback" units. The advantage of piggybacks is that they are user-programmable for the functions that you're interested in. They can be connected to a PC, which will display the fuel and timing maps and let you make changes appropriate to the modifications you've made. Some piggybacks include a fallback map with the stock settings. Once you have dialed-in exactly what you need, you save that map. If you make new modifications to the engine, you can go back to that map and experiment some more. At least one aftermarket unit allows you to switch, at the dashboard, between any of four maps you have created. For example, you could save your "street use with 93-octane" map, your race day with 100-octane map, etc.

Hand-held programmers

The advent of the standardization that came with OBD-II, including the diagnostic trouble codes and diagnostic connector, has given rise to the popularity of hand-held programmers that you can use at home to do what the chip companies have been doing. The nature of computer tweakers is such that they constantly seek new challenges, and some of these data-stream wizards went from PCs to vehicle computers.

The latest hand-held units pack a lot of computing information in a package that looks like a controller for a video game. The programmer cable plugs into your diagnostic test port, just like a scan tool. You follow the manufacturer's instructions and, with the engine off, push buttons on the programmer to alter the programming in your vehicle computer. Most programmers include everything that you need: the cable to hook up the tool to the diagnostic link, connection instructions and operational instructions. Many of these programmers can also be used as a scan tool.

Some programmer units can copy and store the stock programming of your specific vehicle computer; all you have to do is punch in the VIN code! On most units, you can select and install any of several levels of performance programming, depending on what you want. The programs usually vary in intensity and octane rating. A mild program will tolerate 87 octane, a step up requires 89 octane and the killer program requires 91 octane. Depending on the engine, one of these hand-held programmers can find an extra 15 to 30 horsepower inside that computer program!

An advantage of hand-held programmers over reflashed chips is that you can switch programs or go back to stock anytime that you want - or have to. If you carry the tool in your glove box when you're out on the road, you can change the engine's state of tune, should you need to. Let's say that you're out in the boonies, you run low on gas, pull into a station and the only fuel available is 87 octane, except that you're running a state of tune that requires 91 octane. In five minutes, you can switch to a program that's compatible with the lower octane fuel, fill 'er up and you're on your way!

Another nice feature of some hand-held programmers is that they give you the option of adjusting your engine's rev limiter and the transmission shift points. And you can change any of these parameters back and forth as necessary. And did we mention that you can use your hand-held programmer as a scan tool?

Tuning Tool Test

1 For our test case, we used a Predator tuning tool on a stock 1999 Ford F-150 Lightning. Like Hypertech and other brands, the Predator installs its software quickly and allows the user to easily return the vehicle to stock tune if the need should arise.

Hand-held tuning tools have become very popular for their ease of use and relatively low price compared to having your PCM custom tuned by a professional. Some performance enthusiasts question whether a "generic" tune is really the best way to go. In general, if your vehicle is staying pretty close to stock, these tools are an excellent way to add some power without affecting overall driveability. If you're building a wild motor where you're adding 50-percent more power, you're more than likely going to want custom tuning where the air-fuel ratio and spark curve can be tailored specifically to your engine.

But our question was: Do these tools really deliver what they promise? Can you really add significant horsepower without bolting on any parts or even opening the hood? Here's what we found:

2 With "before" and "after" runs on the same chassis dyno, we were able eliminate the variables and show what the tool could really do

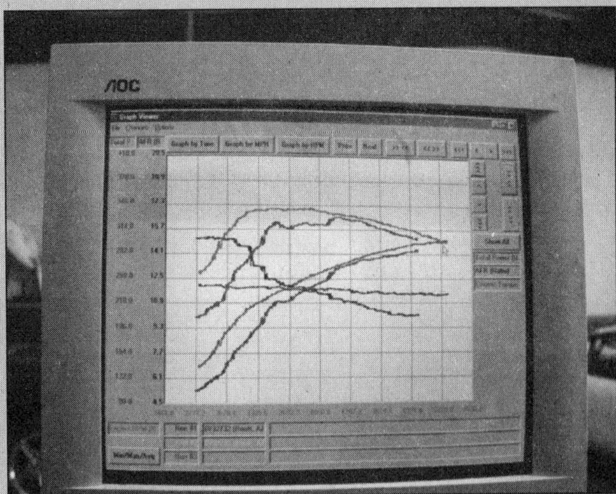

3 After tuning with the Predator (the manufacturer tweaked the tune a bit for our vehicle), the truck made 305 horsepower @ 5350 rpm, which was a 21 horsepower improvement (torque improved an equal amount). ¼-mile E/T improved from 14.26 to 13.81. That's pretty impressive for not picking up a wrench through the entire process!

Notes

5 High-performance Ignition Systems

Higher engine speeds can strain your stock ignition system, and modifications that increase cylinder pressure (superchargers, turbochargers, nitrous) can totally put out the fire. Major power-adders such as high-compression pistons, nitrous oxide, supercharging and turbocharging mandate ignition system upgrades to handle the higher cylinder pressures that these types of modifications produce. Ignition coils need to induce a lot more zap to light off an air/fuel ratio that's significantly denser than the stock mixture. The denser the mixture, the harder it is for the spark to jump the gap between the plug's electrodes.

High-performance ignition coils

An automotive ignition coil is a fairly simple device. It consists of two coils of insulated copper wire wound around a common iron core. One coil is referred to as the *primary* winding and the other coil is known as the *secondary* winding. The primary winding consists of a larger gauge wire wound in several hundred turns. The secondary winding consists of a smaller gauge wire wound in many thousands of turns. When current passes through the primary winding it creates a magnetic field. Because of the common iron core, most of the primary winding's magnetic field also couples to the secondary winding.

The primary winding functions as an inductor that stores energy in the magnetic field surrounding it. Inductance is an effect caused by this magnetic field that's formed around the primary winding conductor. Electrical current flowing through this conductor produces a magnetic flux that's proportional to the amount of current flow. Any change in this current produces a change in magnetic flux that generates an electromotive force that acts to oppose this change in current. Inductance is a measure of the amount of electromagnetic field generated by the change in current.

When this primary current is suddenly interrupted, the magnetic field surrounding the primary winding quickly collapses, which causes a high-voltage pulse across the secondary terminals through *electromagnetic induction* (the production of voltage across a conductor located in a changing magnetic field). Because of the thousands of turns in the secondary winding, the secondary voltage pulse is usually several thousand volts, which is strong enough to jump the gap between a spark plug's electrodes as the voltage grounds to the engine.

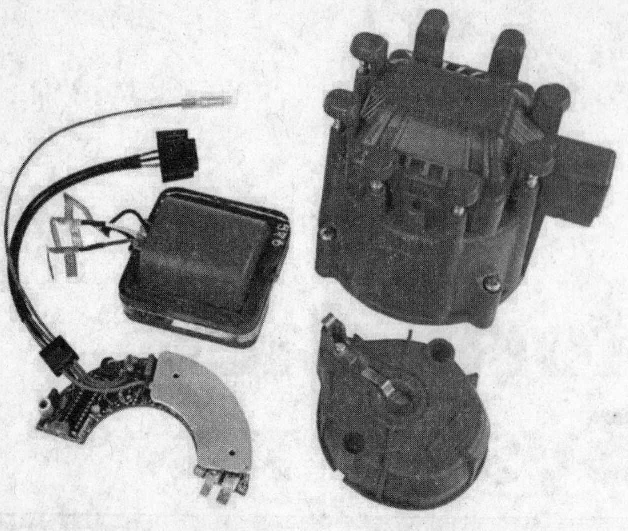

If you've modified your engine for increased performance, you may consider an ignition upgrade like this "ultimate HEI" kit from MSD that transforms any Chevy HEI distributor system

An aftermarket coil with more windings and a heavy-duty case can lower resistance and up your secondary voltage to the spark plugs

That's basically how a coil works. There's little difference between the design of an OEM coil and a high-performance coil aside from the number of turns in the primary and secondary windings. By itself, an aftermarket coil won't add any horsepower and won't improve your fuel economy, but it can produce a smoother idle and improve throttle response. But the real advantage of a performance coil is what it can do for spark in a high-performance environment. The typical aftermarket high-performance coil is capable of inducing quite a bit more secondary voltage (as much as 40,000 or more volts) than a stock unit. This means that the spark can jump the gap between electrodes even at elevated cylinder pressures (the higher the compression pressure, the higher the resistance across that gap between the electrodes). And it can eliminate certain types of misfire problems in the upper rpm range, which is critical as your modifications become more extreme.

Most Ford and Mopar engines are already equipped with a very good OEM coil, but when subjected to the types of performance modifications mentioned at the beginning of this section, they will need a more robust coil. Many GM vehicles also have a very good high-energy coil, which is an integral component of the High Energy Ignition (HEI) distributor, but they too will eventually require a higher performance coil as the modifications become more extreme. Some HEI-style performance coils and ignition control modules are drop-in replacements for the stock units inside the distributor. Other GM replacement coils and control modules are designed to be mounted outside the distributor. If you're an old school enthusiast, you'll be happy to know that you can find performance coils that look exactly like stock vintage units, even though they're up-to-the-minute modern electronic designs under the skin. The same firms that produce these coils also sell distributors that look old school on the outside but are really modern electronic distributors inside.

Later model vehicles don't use a conventional ignition system setup (a stand-alone ignition control module and a distributor, to divvy out the spark to each cylinder). Instead, they're equipped with a small ignition coil/control module unit located on top of and connected directly to each spark plug. There are no spark plug wires on these vehicles. Each coil is controlled and timed by the engine management computer. These individual coils add up to very good ignition performance overall. Don't invest in a competition aftermarket ignition system (with large box and harness) on a late-model vehicle unless you are really planning a lot of engine mods or drag racing.

Where to put the ignition control module and ignition coil

The stock ignition coil is usually located on the engine, probably to keep the secondary cable to the distributor as short as possible. But, this isn't necessarily the optimal location for the coil on a high-performance engine because heat isn't good for the coil. Ditto for the ignition control module, which is often located in a hot part of the engine compartment. Engine vibration is also rough on electronic components. So, when you replace your coil and/or ignition control module with high-performance components, try to put them somewhere besides the engine, preferably in a spot that isn't subjected to heat and/or vibration.

This ignition coil installation is neat and nice, but it's going to absorb serious heat and a good deal of vibration. The builder was obviously trying to put the coil in close proximity to the distributor to keep the secondary cable as short as possible, but this is not a great location

This coil installation is better. It's also near the distributor to minimize the length of the secondary cable, but it's mounted slightly above the engine on a small bracket bolted to the water pump housing where it will absorb less heat

On this engine the spark plug wires are artfully wrapped around the front of the head, but the lower end of the ignition control module might be a little close to the front exhaust header

If the distributor is mounted at the rear of the engine, the firewall is a good location for the coil and the control module. The coil is close to the distributor, and both the coil and control module are isolated from engine vibration and heat

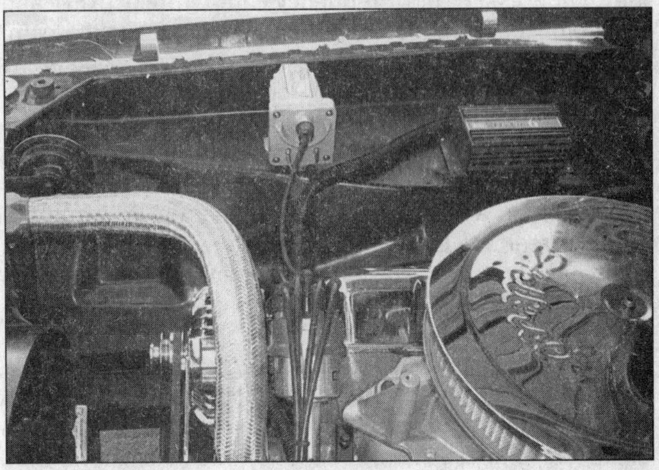

This Mallory ignition control module and Accel coil are in the ideal location, on the cowl behind the engine, where they're isolated from engine heat and vibration, yet very close to the Mallory distributor

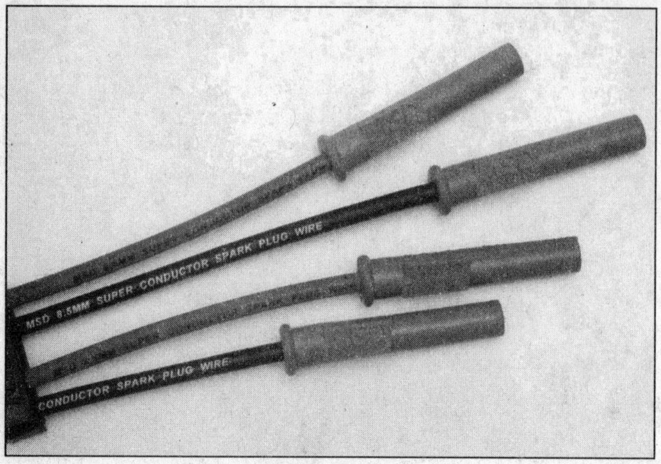

Your engine is probably already in need of new plug wires, so go for a set of fatter and more colorful performance wires that look good and can handle your high-rpm usage without voltage leaks (these are from MSD)

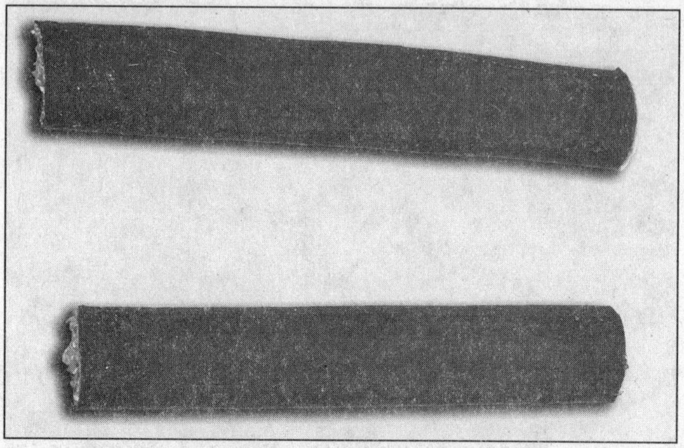

If you have to route your high-performance plug wires near the exhaust manifolds or headers, heat-resistant fire sleeves will protect them from the intense heat radiating off the manifolds or headers

Performance plug wires

Once you've upgraded to a high-performance ignition coil, better quality spark plug wires are the inevitable next step. Spark plug wires consist of a conducting material surrounded by several layers of insulation. The conductor carries the current to the plugs, while the insulation (or shielding) prevents high secondary voltage from leaking out. If you keep your stock plug wires after installing a high-performance coil, you are asking for trouble. Voltage seeks the path of least resistance (any good ground close enough to a plug wire), and will leak from insufficiently insulated wires during high rpm or high boost conditions.

The typical factory plug wire has a core of carbon-impregnated material surrounded by fiberglass and rubber insulation. Carbon-conductor wires are inexpensive and they suppress Radio Frequency Interference (RFI) and Electromagnetic Interference (EMI), which affects the computer. Unfortunately, they have a limited life span, and aren't capable of handling high-energy ignition components.

Race cars use solid metal conductor wires, which provide a high-capacity, low-resistance current path for high-energy ignition systems. However, if you're as much into music as you are into performance, metal-core wires are out for street use because they cause serious interference issues for your audio system. They can also interfere with the engine management computer, which will cause driveability problems.

Most aftermarket performance plug wires use a very fine spiral wire wound around a magnetic core, covered with silicone jacketing. Wire sets are available in thicker-than-stock diameters to handle more current flow. Some small vehicles have stock plug wires as skinny as 5 or 6 mm, while aftermarket wires are offered in 8 mm, 8.5 mm and, for racing applications, 9 mm. The 8 and 8.5 mm wires are big enough to handle the voltage of most ignition systems for high-performance street vehicles, but there's no such thing as having too much insulation on your plug wires. Finally, there's the cosmetic factor: performance plug wires are available in lots of hot colors, not just boring black.

Good aftermarket wires also have thicker plug boots, because the boot-to-plug contact area is a frequent source of voltage leaking to ground. Look for plug boots that fit tightly to the spark plug; if the boot fits tightly only at the bottom, air can become trapped between the plug and the boot. This trapped air can be heated when the engine is running hard, expanding enough to pop the boot and plug wire off the plug. **Caution:** *With any boot, remember to use a spark plug boot tool whenever you install or remove the boots from the plugs. Never pull on the plug wire itself. The plug wire's core is fragile and can be broken by careless stretching.*

The heat coming off exhaust manifolds, header pipes and turbochargers can be as high as 1500-degrees F. Unfortunately, on some engines the spark plug boots and wires are dangerously close to the intense heat pouring off these components. If you're going to install high-performance plug wires that are routed close to these hot spots, protect them with heat resistant fire sleeves. Most fire sleeves can continuously withstand 500-degrees F, and can intermittently withstand up to 3000-degrees F. Some fire sleeves (such as MSD) use a layered woven fiberglass-quartz fiber; others (such as Accel) use a heat reflective wire.

Ignition timing controls

Ignition timing - when the spark ignites each cylinder's air/fuel mixture - is critical in any engine. The air/fuel mixture doesn't explode in an instantaneous flash - it actually takes a period of time. The flame front from the point of ignition travels through the mixture, slowly at first, then building speed. This is good, because what is needed is a gradual build of pressure, not a sharp spike, which can be destructive to pistons, rods and crankshafts. Since the mixture takes time to

If your engine starts pinging on gasoline that's too low in octane rating for the load that you're putting on it, a timing control box like this unit allows you to adjust the ignition timing from inside the car

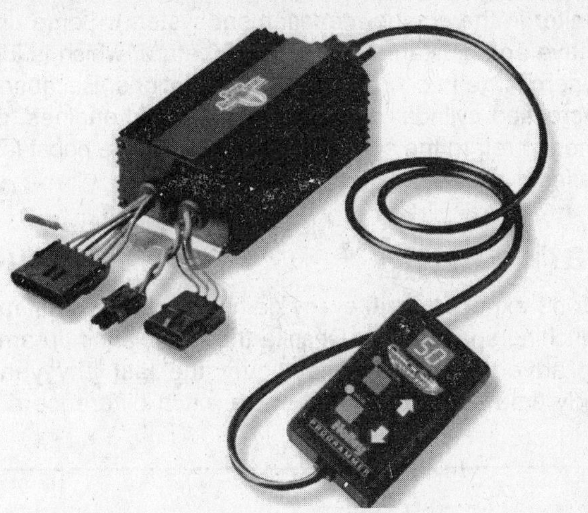

A CDI ignition control box can provide multi-fire capability, user-settable control of rev-limit and retard control for boosted engines and nitrous. This Holley kit even has a "soft-touch" handheld programmer for adjustments

burn, the spark is timed to trigger some time before the piston reaches Top Dead Center (TDC). So the initial timing is some degrees Before Top Dead Center (BTDC).

Firing with too much advance (too soon before the piston reaches TDC) builds pressure in the cylinder before the piston reaches TDC, so that the piston and the rising pressure are fighting each other. On the other hand, if the timing is not advanced enough (not soon enough before the piston reaches TDC) the engine can't make the most of the gas expansion, which decreases efficiency and wastes power.

What complicates any discussion of ignition timing is that the spark event must be timed differently at different engine speeds. As engine speed goes up, there is less time available for the combustion event, so spark must occur sooner. Other factors also influence the correct ignition timing, such as engine load, temperature and fuel mixture. If you map out the ignition advance on a graph related to rpm, you get what's called an ignition advance curve, an important factor in performance tuning.

Once you start modifying the engine, you have changed the ignition parameters, so you must adjust the timing. If you're building up a modern engine, installing an aftermarket chip or reprogramming your computer will advance the timing and adjust for other parameters, but you'll probably have to use higher-octane gas.

On older vehicles, a Capacitive Discharge Ignition (CDI) system is the hot setup. A CDI system consists of a module that you mount in the engine compartment and a wiring harness to connect the module to your ignition system. The typical module consists of a transformer, a charging circuit, a triggering circuit and a capacitor. Battery voltage is bumped up to 400 to 600 volts by the transformer, then the current flows through the charging circuit and charges the capacitor. A capacitor is an electrical device that can store energy in an electric field between two conductors known as plates. When current is applied to the capacitor, electric charges of equal magnitude - but opposite polarity - build up on each plate. A rectifier in the charging circuit prevents the capacitor from discharging prematurely. When the triggering circuit receives a signal from the ignition control module (a stand-alone module or a circuit inside the ignition coil or the computer), the triggering circuit opens the charging circuit and disables the rectifier. This allows the capacitor to discharge its 400 to 600 volts to the ignition coil primary winding. When the typical stock coil primary winding is fed 12 volts, the secondary winding outputs several thousand volts, which is sufficient to fire the plugs on a stock engine. When a high-performance primary coil winding is fed 400 to 600 volts, the secondary winding can put out as much as 40,000 volts.

The amount of time that it takes for the primary winding in a coil to build up voltage is known as its "rise time." The rise time is determined by engine speed. As rpm goes up, rise time goes down because the primary winding has less and less time to reach saturation before the voltage supply is interrupted. The advantage of a CDI system is that it gives the coil primary winding a much bigger voltage boost to begin with, which means that the secondary winding gets a much bigger induced boost from the primary winding, so that it in turn induces a much higher secondary voltage. It's this ability to put out a hot spark very quickly that enables a CDI system to provide good spark even during high load, high rpm conditions.

CDI systems also provide improved throttle response at lower speeds and keep the spark plugs cleaner in engines with some miles on them (though a CDI system is by no means a substitute for a properly maintained engine). CDI systems have been used on high-performance engines for decades and are well proven. Today you can buy CDI systems with all kinds of features. One of the most common is a rev control (later model vehicles already have a rev limiter in the engine management system). Some units also have an adjustable spark retard feature, which is ideal for supercharged or turbocharged applications. Because of the increased cylinder pressure with boosted engines, it is common to retard the spark progressively as the boost level increases.

Spark plugs

Don't expect to make any gains in power or mileage by switching spark plugs. Despite the wild claims dreamed up by advertising copywriters over the last fifty years, the only time spark plugs will make much difference on a street-driven engine is when the engine is really in need of a tune-up and you install fresh plugs. In that instance, the spark plugs could bring back 5 or 10 lost horsepower, but most aftermarket plugs can't really *make* new horsepower the engine didn't already have.

Nonetheless, there are a wide variety of spark plugs out there to choose from. If your engine is only mildly modified, stick with the factory recommended spark plugs, gapped to factory specs. If you add an increasing number of performance modifications to your engine, you may have to reconsider what type of plugs to run, and even what size electrode gap is best. Most engines with above-average level of modifications can utilize a plug that is one heat range colder than stock. Examine your plugs regularly and carefully with a magnifying glass to look for signs of beginning detonation or other problems.

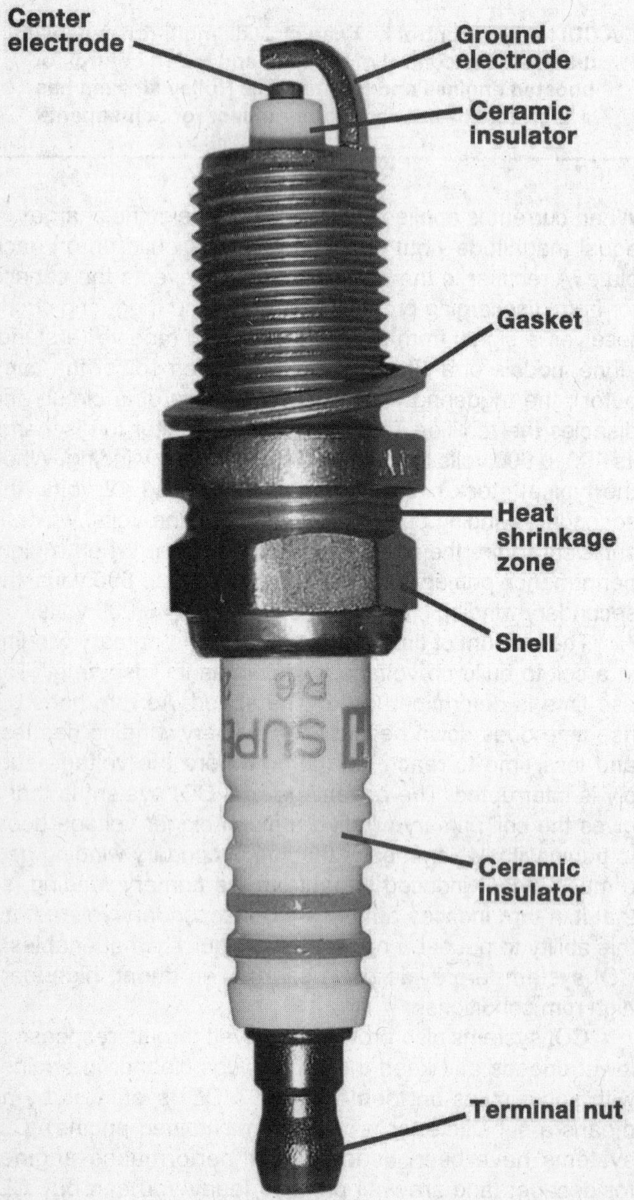

Spark plug nomenclature

Reading the plugs

Without a lot of complicated and expensive test equipment, you can tell a great deal about the operating conditions inside your engine just by examining its spark plugs. Of course, scan tools and other electronic gear are very helpful, but they tell you all about the outside conditions and whether there's a problem with the computer or one of its information sensors. This is all good information, but diagnosis of the true internal operating conditions of an engine, stock or high-performance, begins with a very close look at the spark plugs.

This may seem like a primitive tuning tool, but watch the pit activity at any professional-level race and you'll see the top mechanics looking at spark plugs with a magnifying glass. A spark plug tells a story, and it can save you an entire engine by giving early warning signs of detonation. The color, uniformity, cleanliness and even smell of a freshly pulled spark plug can tell you a lot, if you know what to look

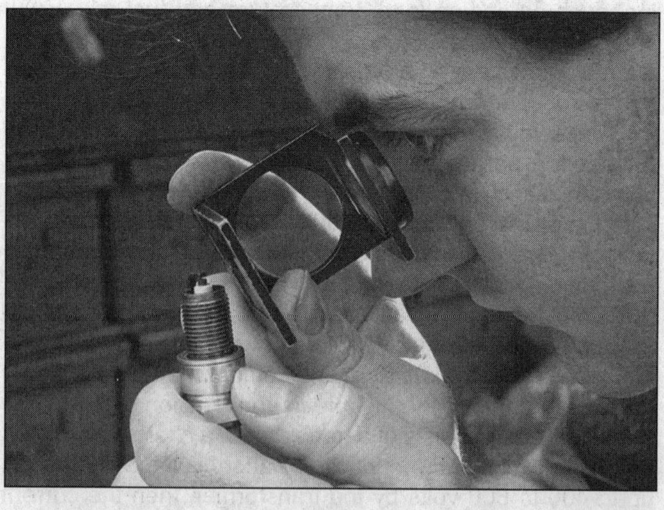

A really good magnifying glass will let you see every tiny detail. Special spark plug examining tools, equipped with a built-in light, are also available.

for. On the inside of the back cover of this manual you'll find a chart of various spark plug conditions, close-up and in color.

When you pull the plugs on your street-driven vehicle, you're looking at long-term conditions - the plugs can tell you if the engine is too rich, too lean, if it's burning oil, if the electrodes are worn from too many miles, etc. Whenever you make important changes on your state of tune, like adding more performance equipment, double-check the part's influence by doing a plug check.

Pay particular attention for signs of detonation. This can appear as metallic flecks on the spark plug insulators - the result of tiny bits of aluminum being blasted off the piston crowns. Another sign of detonation could show up as little black flecks - the result of detonation upsetting the oil rings, allowing oil to sneak by and get into the combustion chambers. Black spots can also be the result of the two colliding flame fronts burning fuel deposits onto the insulator. Severe detonation can also crack the spark plug insulators.

Any sign of detonation means a either a higher octane fuel is needed, a colder spark plug is needed, a richer air/fuel mixture is needed, the ignition timing is too far advanced and/or, on engines equipped with a power adder, too much boost is being made. Whatever the cause, if it isn't dealt with and corrected, severe engine damage will be the result.

The method used to get the most accurate plug reading for wide-open-throttle operation is to perform what is known as a "plug cut." This is where the engine is shut down at the end of a run, then the plugs are inspected immediately, or at least before the engine is started again. When the plugs are removed, the area on which you'll want to concentrate is the part of the insulator way inside of the plug (where it attaches to the metal body of the plug). For this, you'll need a magnifying glass and a penlight. If the air/fuel mixture was in the correct range, the insulator in that area should be a light tan or, if a very high octane fuel is being used, a grayish color.

The middle area of the insulator indicates the richness or leanness of the air/fuel mixture under cruising or half-throttle conditions. The tip of the plug is the area that reveals what's going on at idle. When you do a plug cut after a high-speed pass, however, these two regions will probably be white, as the result of all deposits being cleaned off the insulators during high-rpm operation.

The ground electrode (or strap, as it's sometimes called) is also a valuable source of information, indicating the general amount of timing advance attained during a run. When inspecting the plug, look for a change in color somewhere on the electrode. If all is well, it should be found somewhere near the middle of the curved part of the electrode. If the color change is closer to the threaded part of the spark plug, the timing is too far advanced. If it's closer to the tip of the electrode, the timing isn't advancing enough. If there's no color band at all, try switching to a plug with a higher heat range.

Being able to read the plugs after various modes of operation (idle, cruise, and wide-open-throttle) will help you understand what needs to be done, in terms of carburetion or fuel mapping, to dial in the right air fuel mixture under all conditions. Just keep in mind that the plugs will reflect the last operating conditions before the engine was shut down.

Notes

6 Induction: The Science of Deep Breathing

Induction is one of the more important aspects of building big engine power, for several reasons. First, the intake path is external, meaning changes in induction are basically all bolt-on procedures, and easy to change back if you want to try something different. Swapping carburetors or throttle bodies are simple jobs. Second, the intake path, if left stock, will limit the effectiveness of other modifications. Third, when you open the hood, the stuff on top of the engine is what everyone sees first, and a racy, aftermarket intake on your engine gives a certain street "credibility."

Nothing sets off a performance engine like a specialty induction system, but this small-block Ford may be over-carbureted with a tunnel-ram manifold and dual-quad Holley setup, and a blower-type scoop. Your intake has to be matched to the rest of the engine mods.

On those trains you see in old westerns, the combustion, in this case burning wood or coal to heat a boiler that makes steam, is outside the cylinders, which are the horizontal "drivers" that make the wheels go. The difference in our kind of engine is that the fire and the production of pressure takes place right inside the engine, hence the term internal combustion engine. A combustible mixture of fuel and air comes into the combustion chamber, which is the area above the piston and the area surrounding the valves in the cylinder head. The mix is ignited at just the right time and the resultant rapid expansion of gasses forces the piston down, turning the crankshaft.

That's the most basic description of how your engine works, but the relevance of these basics to this Chapter is that your car's engine can be described as simply an air pump. Gasses travel in and out of the engine at all times. The incoming gasoline is vaporized due to the carburetor or high-pressure (fuel injection) system and the operating heat of the intake manifold and heads. These fuel vapors are mixed with the incoming air from the induction system, sucked into the combustion chamber to make power, and the hot gasses that remain go out the exhaust port and through your exhaust system.

This should all sound pretty basic and simple, and what should also seem simple is that the path to increased power in an internal-combustion engine is to get more air and fuel into the engine. That's the job of the induction system.

A cold-air intake for your ride may be the simplest induction improvement you can make. This late-Mustang package from Roush Performance features a lifetime filter element and a formed air-dam to keep underhood hot air away from the intake

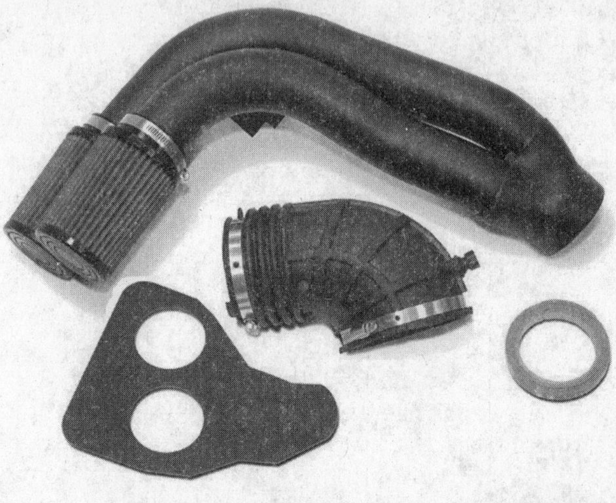

This cold-air kit for '94-'97 Camaros and Firebirds from SLP has two filters and is 50-state legal

Short-ram and cold-air intakes

The OEM manufacturer of you car has spent considerable time developing the intake and exhaust system. In the intake tract, the OEM engineers have their first priority to develop smooth, reliable power with maximum fuel economy and driveability. The high-rpm horsepower needed for drag racing is far from their minds. Even if the factory engineers were performance minded, their dreams would be quashed by in-house numbers-crunchers, insurance consultants, environmentalists, and government-mandated fuel economy standards. So it is up to us, the hot rodders of the 21st century, to extract the performance potential we know is waiting to be unlocked in our engines.

A further priority faced by factory engineers - and this applies to engineering on all aspects of production car design - is NVH, which stands for Noise, Vibration and Harshness. As car consumers want even economy cars to be as quiet and smooth as what we used to expect only from luxury cars, the engineers are increasingly challenged. How does this affect our induction system? Take a look at the stock induction path on any modern car. If you follow the airflow from outside the car to where the intake manifold bolts to the cylinder head, you'll see a sometimes-tortuous roadmap full of more twists and turns than a rat-maze experiment at the high-school science fair.

The stock inlet bringing air into the air filter housing (the beginning of the stock airflow system) usually attempts to get some sort of cool air in, but the factory plays it very safe in locating this pipe, hoping to fend off customer problems if any dirt or water were to get into the airbox. Once inside the air filter housing, the air may have to pass by plastic baffles and other devices designed to limit the noise produced by air rushing into the engine. Once past the air filter, the airflow usually goes through a "corrugated" flexible tube and connects to the throttle body. If you're lucky, that tube has only one bend in it, but some vehicles have several. The flexible tubing used is designed more for noise-reduction than smooth, unrestricted airflow. The ribs inside the plastic tubing may dampen noise, but they disrupt high-rpm airflow.

Your first and simplest improvement to your induction is to step up and pay the price for an aftermarket air filter. The "lifetime" aftermarket filters are made of pleated cotton in a wire mesh frame and treated with a special oil to trap dirt. According to the aftermarket filter manufacturers, this style of filter will flow more air when dirty than a stock paper element will when brand new. The aftermarket filters can be washed and re-oiled on a regular basis, while the stock paper filters have to be replaced every 10-15,000 miles. If you drove your car for 150,000 miles, what you would have spent for those 10 factory filter elements would be far more than the cost of one aftermarket filter, and the aftermarket unit flows better. If the vehicle has a decent filter box design, just changing to a quality aftermarket air filter can be worth a few horsepower.

In the case of some vehicles with a bad original design, tuners installing an aftermarket filter will often disconnect the car's battery for an hour, then reconnect it after the new filter is in place. The tuners feel that the filter makes enough difference that the best results are obtained when the vehicle's engine management system has to "relearn" and adapt to this change in airflow, even if it isn't a drastic change.

An aftermarket filter is a good idea for a vehicle you plan to keep for many years, even if you never modify the engine. However, if you are going further (and this book is betting you will), don't get an aftermarket filter for your stock airbox. You're going to be using a new air induction system that comes with its own pleated-cotton, high-flow filter, and this filter will have a different configuration than the stock filter. So if you even think you might modify your engine, don't install a replacement aftermarket filter, but put that money towards a new cold-air intake.

Performance air intakes are available in two basic forms, the "short-ram" and the "cold-air" intake. In each type, the aftermarket manufacturer has tried to design a free-flowing intake without regard to engine noise. Virtually all are made of metal tubing (generally aluminum) or ABS plastic, with the smoothest possible bends and an interior that has a larger cross-section than the stock system. All types are fitted with a high-flow filter, usually in a conical configuration. The best designs are not only capable of flowing more air volume, but maintain a higher air velocity than a stock system.

The least expensive and easiest intakes to install are the short-ram types. You'll spend longer getting the stock air filter box and inlet tube out than installing the short-ram. If you have any doubts about removing the stock components, consult the Haynes repair manual for your car (the airbox mounting bolt locations are shown in Chapter 4). On some vehicles, the MAF sensor is located on the air intake and must be removed, then reinstalled on the aftermarket intake. Most cars also have a hose connecting the crankcase (usually at the valve cover) to the air intake, and the stock hose may need to be shortened to connect to the aftermarket pipe, or a new, longer hose must be used. Short-ram intakes place the new filter relatively close to the engine, and modifications to the engine or body are rarely necessary. Most short-ram installations take only a half-hour to install and may be good for 4 to 8 horsepower, depending on the application.

If you can isolate the filter end of your short-ram system, you can reduce the temperature of the incoming air, which is worth horsepower on any engine. If the short-ram's filter is right over hot engine components and near the radiator, it's going to pick up hot air, which can negate the gains you make in increased airflow. Try to build a sheetmetal or plastic "dam" around the filter end of your intake, so that only air from an outside source gets into the filter. Several aftermarket companies make either a short-ram intake that comes with a model-specific dam, or they make a dam that is model specific and can be used with most air intakes.

Did we say colder air was important? For purposes of performance, the colder the air the more power you make. For every drop of 10-degrees F in the intake air fed to your engine, your power goes up about 1%. That may not sound like much, but if you have a 300 hp engine now, and you manage to reduce your intake air temperature by 100 degrees, you could gain 30 horsepower! That's more than you probably gain with a "stage 1" set of aftermarket cams or a header and full aftermarket exhaust. Air gets denser as it gets colder, so more air is packed into the engine, even with the same volume of airflow.

Having said this, you must realize that a drop of 100 degrees isn't that easy to achieve in a street-driven car, but the point is made that any drop in air temperature you make is worth the effort, and such modifications do not affect fuel economy or driveability at all, something that can't be said for all engine modifications.

Cold-air intake systems are one of the most-widely-installed bolt-on performance improvements in the high-performance world. They are usually the first modification made to an engine, and have become so common that people want one on their car whether it makes any more power or not.

Aside from the "look" of the intake, the true cold-air package is important because it is longer, reaching down to pick up colder air from below the grille or in the car's fenderwell, rather than the hotter engine compartment air. Typical engine compartment air temperature could be 30 to 50 degrees F higher than the ambient outside air, even when the vehicle is at speed and cooler ambient air is presumably flowing through the engine compartment. When you're talking about trying to make performance in a hot environment as found in the Southwestern states (or anyplace in July), the problem is that much worse. High outside temperature combined with high engine compartment temperature means your engine is being fed some pretty thin air.

Aftermarket cold-air intake systems can be worth 8 to 20 horsepower, depending on the design and the quality of the air filter included with it. Obviously, a cold-air intake is going to need some bends in order to reach the cold-air, but if there are too many bends or bends made too sharp, the horsepower gain from the colder air could be offset by a reduction in airflow. The longer the pipe, the more friction there will be for the incoming air, even on a straight length of pipe. A few bends and the air is further restricted.

An aftermarket air intake must, of necessity, be a compromise between performance goals and the installation environment. If there is a problem with cold-air intakes, it is the location of the filter. Of course, we want it to be in the cold-air stream, but this is usually in the fenderwell where the filter can be at the mercy of dirt and water. In some weather conditions, the filter could become blocked by snow or mud, or water could actually be ingested by the engine. There are several ways to avoid the hydro-lock disadvantage of the cold-air intake. The intake and filter companies have wraps and protective plastic or sheetmetal pieces that protect the filter from most water and dirt. Lots of enthusiasts take the front pipe off their cold-air intake during the winter. There are some models of two-piece cold-air intakes where the fenderwell pipe can be removed and the filter attached to the pipe still on the engine, effectively making a long-ram into a short-ram. Perhaps the best solution if you want to keep the cold-air intake on all year is an air bypass valve. The bypass valve opens if the air filter is submerged in or blocked by water, and lets engine compartment air (filtered by a foam element) feed the engine instead of from the fenderwell air filter.

One additional note about aftermarket air intakes - they are noisier than a stock system. Since you are eliminating the carefully engineered sound baffles and plastic dams in the stock intake tract, you're going to be much more aware of the sound of air rushing through to feed your engine. However to most enthusiasts, this is the sound of increased engine power, and that's considered a good thing.

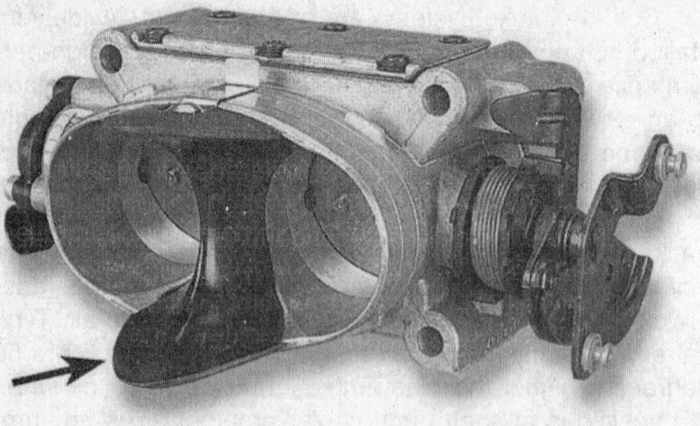

Even if your EFI engine isn't modified enough to need a bigger throttle body, Holley makes this plastic "airfoil" divider that straightens the air path to smooth out turbulence on 5.7L GM TPI and LT1 engines. It installs in minutes and is said to be worth about 5 horsepower

With the extra airflow required for interior engine mods, a bigger aftermarket throttle body should be on your to-do list. This billet-aluminum throttle body should wake up your 5.0L EFI Ford, but requires recalibration of your MAF sensor to work best. Most engine mods on computer-controlled engines require retuning the software

Throttle bodies

Once you have an improved aftermarket intake system installed, there are other improvements you can make to the intake system to flow more air. Everything that is between the cold-air pipe and the intake port on your cylinder head also controls the airflow. Once you start modifying your engine and need more airflow, theses other parts become the still-restricted limitation on how much air you can get into the engine.

Engine building experts will tell you that the final limit to an engine's breathing capabilities is the cylinder head and its valves, ports and camshaft design (see Chapter 8). Changing these elements involves tearing into the engine for more serious and expensive modifications, and is the line that some budget-minded enthusiast are saving up to cross. Some tuning experts will also tell you that unless you have made such internal changes or are planning to add a major power-adder like nitrous or a turbocharger, the aftermarket intake you have installed is about all you need on the induction side of your engine.

However, if you have changed the cam or ported the heads, etc. on your late-model computer-managed engine, then you may need to increase the airflow allowed by your stock throttle body. As we have mentioned in previous Chapters, all of your engine modifications have to be chosen to work with each other as a system. You don't want only one or two parts that make high-rpm horsepower if the rest of the components are going to restrict that effort. Conversely, it does no good to install a high-flow component in one area of the engine, such as a big throttle body, unless you can run at higher rpm. Don't even think about changing throttle bodies until you have removed all restrictions in the exhaust side of the vehicle first (see Chapter 11).

Throttle bodies are available in various sizes, usually differing from stock units in the main throttle bore diameter. Using a throttle body that is too big will just compromise your low-end power. Correct sizing of the large pipes used in aftermarket cold-air intakes is important, because if the pipe is too small it restricts air volume, too big and it slows the air velocity. The same goes for the throttle body bore. Installing an aftermarket cam could mean that a slightly-larger-than-stock throttle body could help, along with some changes in the fuel and exhaust systems to increase fuel flow to match the airflow. Know the exact bore diameter of your stock throttle body before shopping for an aftermarket unit.

Most aftermarket manufacturers have good technical support people who can help you select performance components that perform well with their own parts. You can contact them by phone (most companies have a tech-support line) or check their web site for FAQ's, or E-mail the specifics of your vehicle to find out what their experience has told them works best. For instance, if you install a particular aftermarket cam, the cam manufacturer can tell you what other components are needed (or not) to take full advantage of their camshaft. The fine print in most cam manufacturer's catalogs/ads tells you the other equipment used in conjunction with their cam to achieve the hp numbers advertised. In other words, a particular cam may make 40 horsepower, but that's with a particular size header and a certain cfm of intake airflow. Your research ahead of time - looking at magazine articles, catalogs and web sites - can save you from making a misguided purchase of a part that won't help your particular application.

If yours is a mild engine and there are several steps in throttle body size available, don't just buy the biggest one made, even if it is red-anodized aluminum. Play it safe and buy the smallest increase over stock, unless you install a big throttle body at the same time that you make other major engine changes. If you install a too-big throttle body now,

This 78mm throttle body from F.A.S.T. is destined for our stroker LS-1 engine with a high-lift cam and high-flowing AFR heads. With these mods to the airflow, more fuel is also required, so we added F.A.S.T 36 pounds-per-hour units. You can check out the results of these upgrades in Chapter 13

and don't make your other modifications until much later, the interim period will find you with a low-rpm dog that won't be much fun to drive. **Note:** *If you do install a larger throttle body, remove your intake manifold and have the throttle body opening in the manifold enlarged to the same size. It does no good to install an expensive new throttle body if it's restricted by a smaller, stock-sized hole at the intake.*

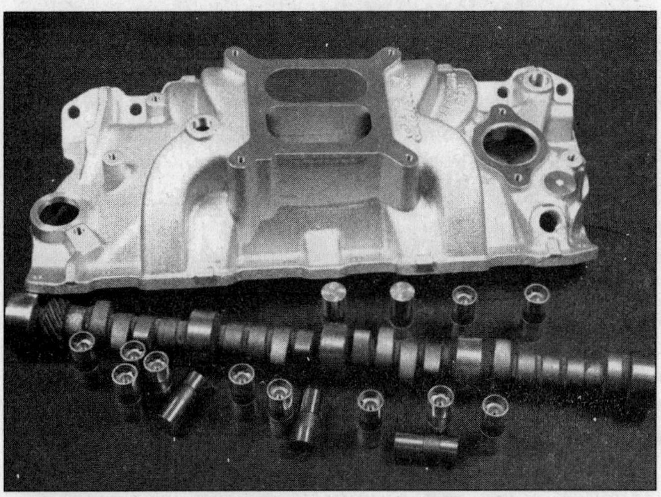

The basic hi-rise four-barrel intake manifold is the mainstay of carbureted aftermarket performance. A number of manufacturers offer them with a matching camshaft kit, so you know they will work together

Throttle body installation isn't too complicated. A good aftermarket unit will come with clear instructions. Carefully mark all the hoses and wires on your stock throttle body with masking tape and a marking pen so you can connect them all to the right places on the new throttle body. Some cars have hot water hoses connected to the throttle body, in which case you'll have to wait until the engine is completely cool before starting work. You'll also have to clamp-off these hoses or drain the radiator before disconnecting them to prevent coolant from spilling all over the place. You also have to disconnect the throttle linkage, and on some cars, the cruise control or transmission linkage as well. On most cars, the throttle body is attached to the intake manifold with four bolts, although sometimes it isn't easy to get at all the bolts. Take your time, and if necessary, refer to a Haynes repair manual for your car (throttle body removal and installation is covered in Chapter 4 in Haynes repair manuals).

Intake manifolds

As we follow this "weakest link" discussion of the engine's intake breathing, the final component in your intake system is the intake manifold that connects the throttle body to the cylinder head. This is that last section of the exterior intake path. If you have made the kind of camshaft, boring/stroking and exhaust mods that necessitate a larger throttle body, then an improved intake is probably on the agenda also. If you have added a supercharger or turbocharger and the boost level is going to exceed 8-10psi, then your system could certainly use a more free-flowing intake manifold.

Intake manifolds are designed for specific levels of engine performance and rpm range. Your stock manifold was probably a good design for its intended application - normal driving. To design a performance intake manifold, increased airflow volume and velocity are the goals, just as with the big throttle bodies. The perfect manifold would be one that combined the right size ports, the right length of runners and the internal shapes to make maximum power. As with throttle

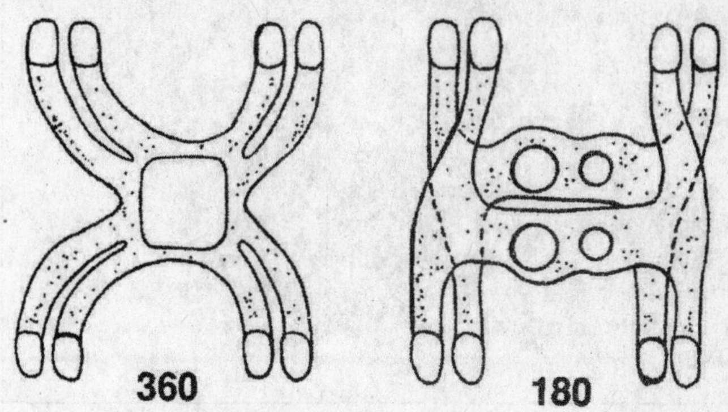

Two of the basic designs in four-barrel intake manifold runners are represented here. The dual-plane ("180-degree") on the right has two sets of runners routed to the carburetor base, while the single-plane ("360-degree") design on the left has one open plenum feeding all eight cylinders

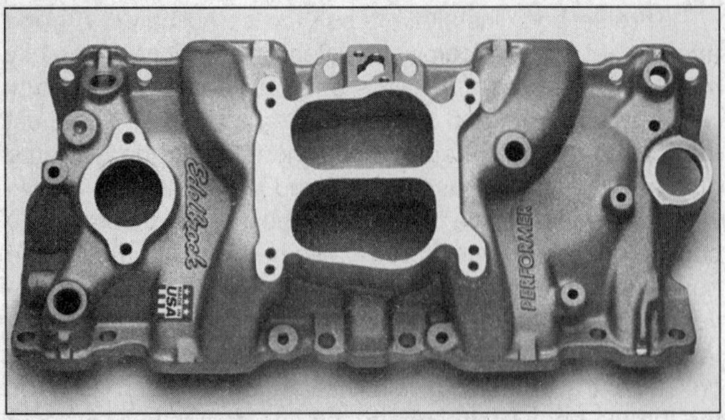

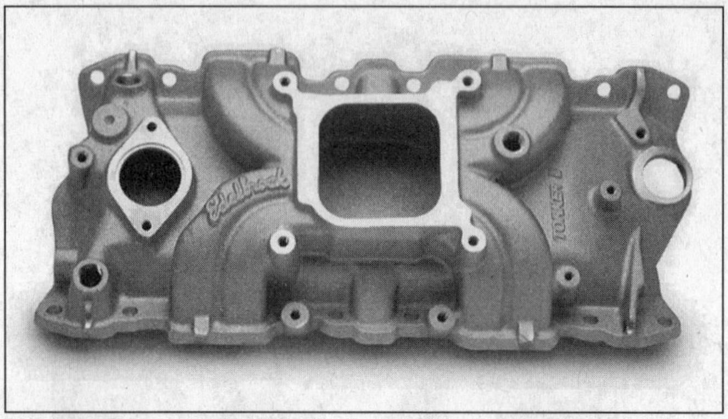

Two Edelbrock manifolds that exemplify the two runner designs: the Performer dual-plane at left, and at right is the higher-performance-level single-plane Torquer manifold. Note the open plenum under the Torquer's carb platform

The next level up in performance four-barrel intakes would be the air-gap type with longer runners that enter the head ports at a better angle. This one is an Edelbrock non-EGR piece for Ford 351 Cleveland engines

bodies, the best manifold for pure high-rpm power is going to be unsuited to normal street driving on a mild engine.

Perhaps because of the level of modification required to best utilize a bigger intake manifold, and the fact that most street enthusiasts don't achieve that level, most aftermarket manifolds, especially ones with huge plenums and/or long runners, are for serious, no-compromise engines with boost and/or nitrous setups.

Old-time hot rodders sometimes make fun of the plastic parts that appear on modern engines. But sometimes change is good, especially when it means more horsepower! Lightweight nylon and polymer intake manifolds do not conduct heat efficiently; therefore, they can actually make more power than a metal manifold, which tends to run hotter. Don't worry too much about the durability of these manifolds. Sure, they may not take a hit from a hammer as well as a cast-iron

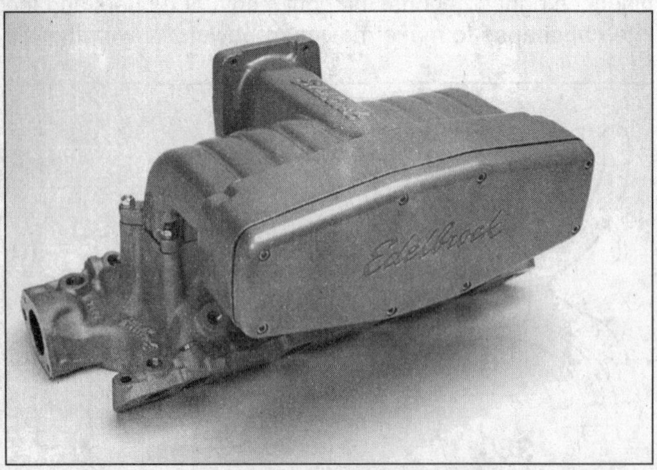

There are performance intake manifolds for late-model EFI engines, too, offering a bigger plenum volume for higher-rpm airflow needs, such as this upper and lower Edelbrock Performer set for 5.0L Fords. It's 50-state-legal for '86-'95 models. They also have a bigger version, The Victor 5.0 for 4000-7000 rpm racing use

The LSX intake manifold from F.A.S.T. has become a performance standard for GM's Gen III and IV V8 engines. Its polymer construction saves weight and also helps it stay cooler than an aluminum piece. Lower intake temperatures equal higher horsepower!

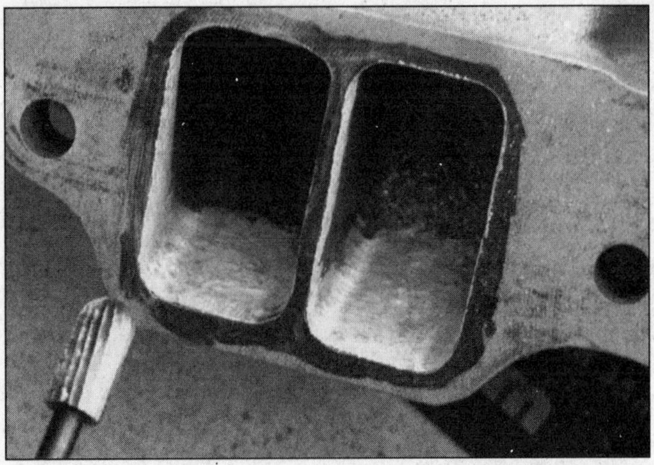

You can usually get a little improvement in airflow by "port matching" your intake manifold to your cylinder head ports. Using a new gasket as a guide, scribe a line to be used as a guide when grinding

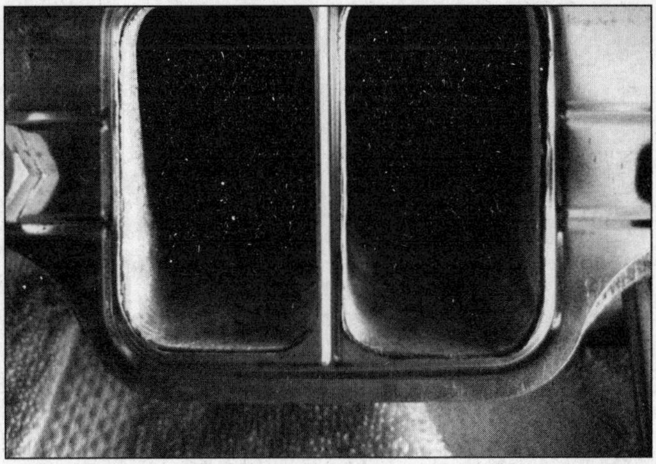

When the grinding is done, the gasket should match the port exactly

manifold, but they have been proven to last for hundreds of thousands of miles in normal driving.

A few modifications can be done to your stock manifold, so you don't always have to rely on what's available in the aftermarket. An old hot rodder's trick is to "port-match" the manifold to the cylinder head. If you look at the cylinder head mounting surface of the manifold and compare its ports to that of the intake manifold gasket, you'll invariably see that the ports in the gasket are slightly bigger than the ports in the manifold or the head. Remove your intake manifold and mount it in a vise with the ports facing up. Clamp a new gasket on the manifold, with the gasket perfectly aligned over the mounting bolt holes. Now scribe a line inside the gasket ports onto the manifold.

Take the gasket off and use a small electric or air-powered die grinder to grind out the manifold ports to the scribed line. Take your time and don't go beyond the scribed line or you could hinder the gasket's job of making a good seal. Try to gently blend the new port size back up into the ports on the manifold as far as you can, to improve the transition for the incoming air. Ideally, the cylinder head should be treated similarly to match the gasket, but you can wait until you have some other reason to pull the head. Performance gains in port-matching aren't large, but it costs you nothing to make the effort.

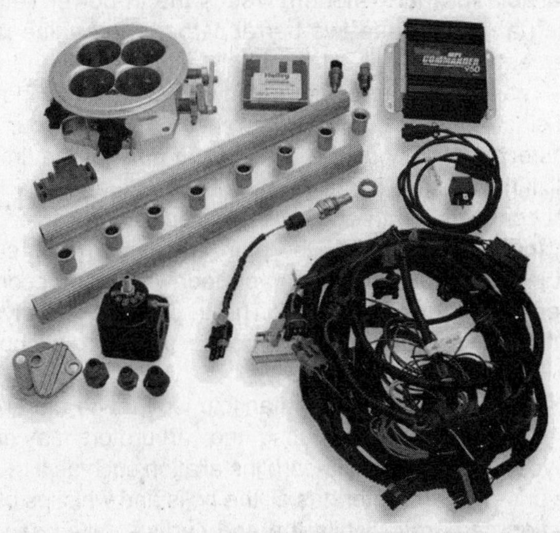

For those of you who have an older engine you'd like to run with the advantages of multi-port fuel injection, kits are available to top off your engine like this Holley package featuring their Commander 950 computer, all the sensors and harness, fuel rails, throttle body and injectors. Software and fuel pressure regulator are included. You just need a machine shop to bore the injector holes in your existing intake manifold

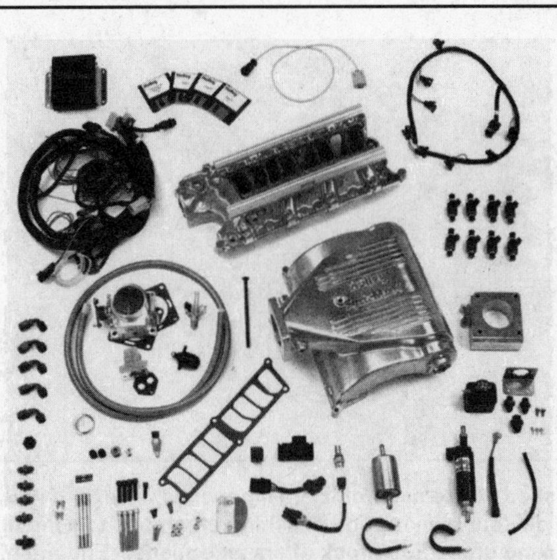

For an even more complete EFI-upgrade installation, Holley offers the same kit with a high-flow SysteMax II intake manifold and 70 mm throttle body of OEM-style, plus plenty of instructions

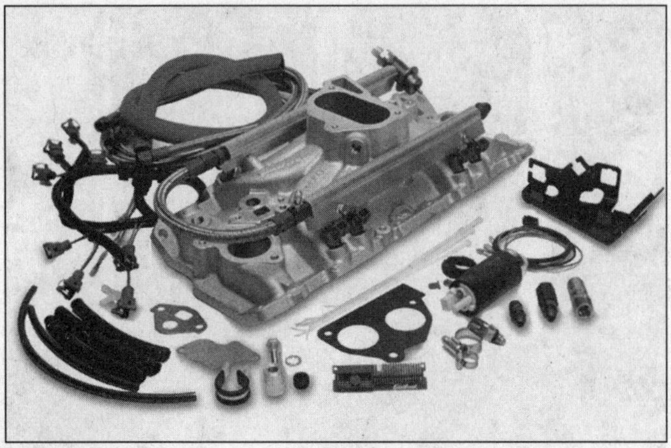

Edelbrock also makes EFI upgrade kits; here's a Performer Multi-Point setup for small-block Chevy trucks that originally had two TBI injectors. There's a new chip for your computer and it's 50-state-legal

If you have made the big modifications to your engine that we have discussed, then all of the intake treatments above will pay off handsomely in higher performance, though anytime you make serious horsepower, it usually means putting your power band higher up the rpm scale. Even if all you ever do to your intake system is add a good aftermarket short or long-ram pipe and filter, this will make some of the cheapest horsepower you stand to gain, and without affecting your driveability beyond a minor increase in engine noise level at speed.

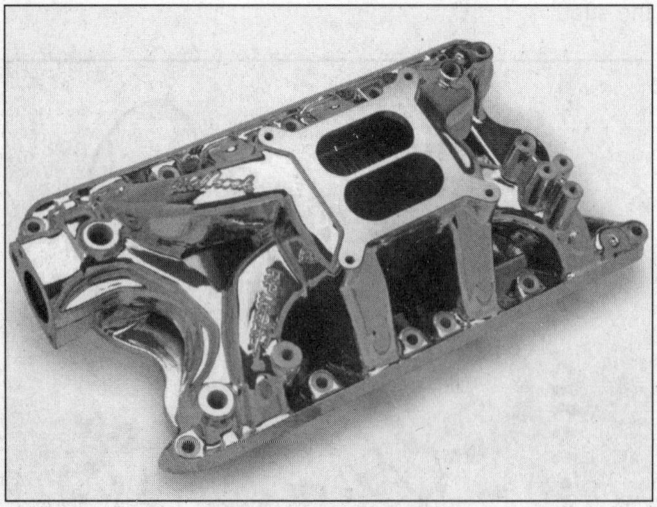

Polished intake manifolds are more expensive, and you have to do your own routine polishing touch-ups to keep them looking great. Edelbrock offers an optional "Endurashine" coating on their manifolds that looks just like chrome and you only have to dust it off with a clean rag. Other companies may offer similar treatments, which are less expensive than ordering a polished manifold

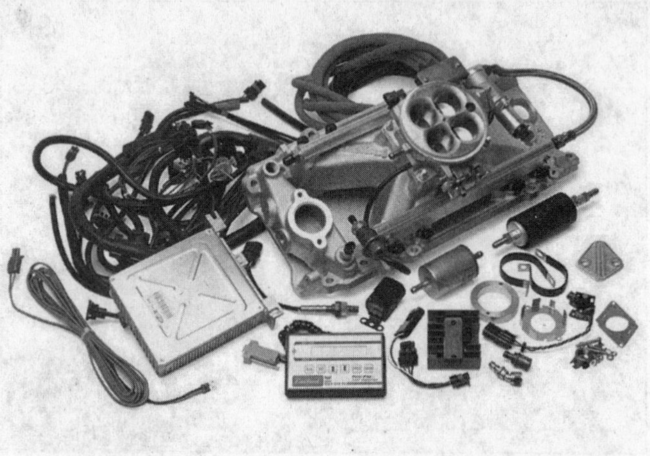

A higher-performance Edelbrock Pro-Flo multi-point EFI setup, this one's for a big-block Chevy, has a 1000-cfm throttle body and a user-friendly digital calibration module that requires no laptop computer to tune. The Pro-Flo system uses a Motorola ECU and the module displays tach, temperature and spark info, plus there's a Rich/Lean light for your dash

Carburetion

In the world of carbureted pre-emissions engines, you have a bewildering variety of intake manifolds to choose from. There are single four-barrel-carb manifolds for every V8, plus dual-quad design for two four-barrel carbs, and even nostalgia-type manifolds that hold three, six or even eight two-barrel carbs!

One of the most popular nostalgia-style intakes still available for many modern V8s is the tri-power setup, utilizing a row of three two-barrel carbs. The engine runs on the center carb until 3/4-throttle is achieved, when the front and rear carbs open up for some serious airflow. The practical side of the 3x2 (three 2-barrel carbs) is that your engine runs economically on the center carb most of the time, only utilizing the extra carbs when you need them. The linkage that connects the three carbs is called "progressive," meaning that you can adjust the point at which the outer carbs cut in. You know the punch you feel when the secondaries open on a four-barrel carb? The tri-power setup gives you that and more, when tuned properly, plus it looks cool when you open the hood.

While a multiple carb manifold isn't much more expensive than a four-barrel casting, the carburetors may gang up on your wallet. In a multi-carb installation such as a tri-power, the primary carburetor has all the bells and whistles of a production carburetor while the end carbs - called secondary carbs to distinguish their function from the center primary carb - are modified. They do not need, and should not have, choke assemblies or idle circuits and are jetted differently as well. They also need longer throttle shafts to accommodate the linkage used for multiple carburetion. There are multiple-carb experts around the country who do a nice business in preparing such setups, often selling the components as a

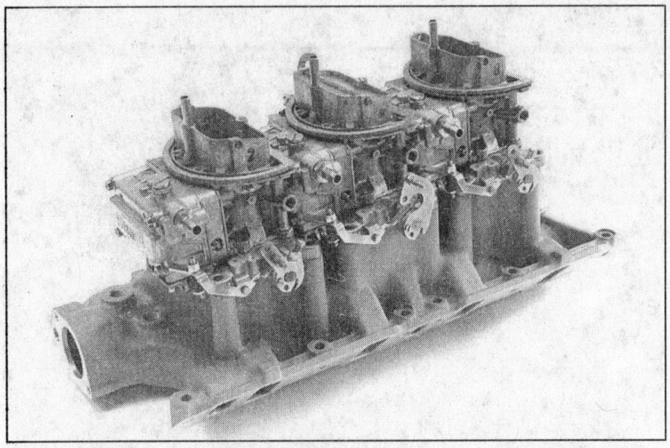

Triples or "tri-power" have a magic appeal among performance engine enthusiasts, and they can run just fine on mild or wild street machines. This is a small-block Ford Blue Thunder 3x2 intake that is offered by Carl's Ford Parts with three matched Holley carburetors and the right linkage. Topped with a Shelby finned, all under-one-roof air cleaner, this is heady stuff for Ford fans!

The current popularity of tri-power induction prompted Barry Grant Fuel Systems to come up with an all-modern design for one, called the "Six-Shooter." Available for small-block and big-block Chevys, small-block Fords and even 326-455 Pontiac V8s, it uses new-design 250-cfm Demon two-barrels, fuel lines and linkage, plus a billet air filter housing and a reusable element

packaged deal, with intake manifold, modified carbs jetted for your particular application and engine size, plus linkage and fuel lines all plumbed.

Dual-quad installations are also nostalgic arrangements that also have a pleasing kick when the right pedal goes to the floor, and a serious visual appeal. In most intakes like this, the rear carburetor is set up as the primary and a modified front carburetor only comes into play only when the linkage is set to employ it. Due to the amount of air/fuel flow that dual-quads can deliver, this is not a configuration that should be used on a mild engine, on which performance could actually decrease with dual quads.

Dual-quads (two four-barrel carbs) have been a performance mainstay for 50 years now. Here's a pair on a 350 Oldsmobile engine in Ron Galligan's sweet 1950 Olds. In most street dual-quad setups, the rear carburetor operates as the primary, while the linkage is set for the front carb to open at 3/4-throttle

There's no question that the most popular induction by far for American V8 performance engines is the classic four-barrel carburetor on an aftermarket manifold. It's the simplest, most bang-for-the-buck setup possible. With the one carburetor sitting in the center of the manifold, air/fuel distribution between the cylinders is more even than with any multiple-carb setup short of exotic 4x2 Weber intakes with a carb throat for every intake port.

Check the length of the intake runners on this design of dual-quad intake, called a "tunnel-Ram," originally developed in the Sixties by an East Coast drag racer with a '55 Chevy gasser, then adopted by the aftermarket. It's designed for racing but some have used them on modified street machines. It's a system designed to endear you to the local gas station owner

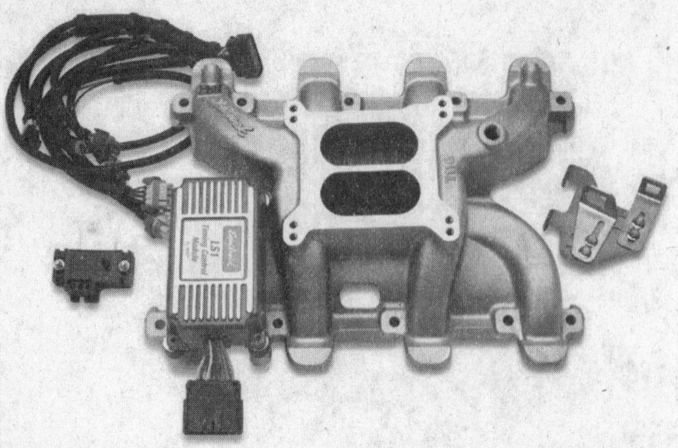

Some modern engines have never been offered with a carburetor, so the aftermarket steps in to fill that need when rodders use a late-model high-tech engine in a non-emissions application. One that is popular today is this Edelbrock four-barrel intake for the LS-series GM V8s. These are normally a problem to run with a carburetor, because the ignition and fuel are controlled by the PCM. The solution here is a kit with a special timing control module that works with OE sensors and offers six different timing curves

Here's that Edelbrock retro-carb kit installed on an LS-1. With an Edelbrock cam and four-barrel carb, the otherwise stock engine made 410 hp and 418 foot-pounds of tire-smokin' torque

Four-barrel carburetors that work well are widely available at competitive prices, in sizes to suit virtually any engine's displacement and level of modification, from mild streeter to monster motors for drag racing. The carb and intake manufacturers are quite good at recommending the right size for your application. The basic comparison scale for carburetors is cfm: cubic-feet of air per minute. While this doesn't indicate every aspect of suitability for an application, it's a starting point. When you have selected the right cfm-size carb for your engine, it can be fine-tuned from there for more specific needs. Four-barrel carbs are available in cfm ratings from 450 to 1000 or more, with the latter being race-only pieces for big engines.

Your driving conditions are an important aspect of choosing a carburetor. Many four-barrel carbs are designed to work well out-of-the-box for the most popular V8, the 350 Chevy. With a mild cam and headers a 600 cfm carb should be perfect. Note though that you may read magazine tests or manufacturer's recommendations that show higher horsepower with a 750-cfm carb, but sometimes perception from the seat of the driver's pants is more "real" than the results on the dyno. In other words, the bigger carb will make more power, but higher up on the curve, while the 600-cfm carb has better throttle response in daily driving due to its higher velocity at the lower engine speeds at which we usually drive. Response is a subjective matter that the dyno doesn't tell you.

Perhaps you have a 302 Ford small-block in an older Mustang. That jetted-for-a-350 carb will work, but you have 50 cubic inches less displacement so response will not be as good as would be provided by a 550 or 570-cfm four-barrel. For advice and direction in choosing a four-barrel carb, look

Today there are only three major aftermarket carburetor companies: Edelbrock, Holley and Demon Carburetion. The Edelbrock Performer four-barrel is a much-improved version of the old Carter AFB/ThermoQuad design, and it fits both square-bore and spread-bore manifolds. Their sizes include 500, 600, 750 and 800 cfm ratings

Holley has a wide range of carburetors for street and racing. This is the single-feed Model 1850, a 600-cfm street carburetor with vacuum-operated secondaries, and it's a very popular model for mild engines

The larger performance Holley four-barrels have a separate fuel inlet for the primaries and secondaries, called the "dual-feed" design. This basic performance carb has electric choke, adjustable vacuum secondaries, built-in fuel filters, and are sized from 570, 670 and 770 to 870-cfm. Even bigger Holleys are available for racing

On Holley four-barrels of the dual-feed design, you will need a special dual fuel line like this to connect the two float bowls to your fuel system. A kit with a flexible center section like this one makes aligning the two fittings to the carb a snap

at all the carburetor catalogs and websites for their recommendations.

Intake manifold selection for a four-barrel carb installation is another choice you'll have to make. The runner arrangement and size, even the "elevation" of the carburetor are factors in the manifold design. There are four-barrel manifolds for every V8, with the "low-rise" design for vehicles that have tight hood clearance, because you will have to allow for the extra engine height of a large, aftermarket air cleaner too. The generic term "hi-rise" in manifolds, for vehicles that have the room, feature a taller carb platform, which allows longer runners for developing more volume and higher-rpm capacity. Perhaps hundreds of thousands of V8s are running around with a four-barrel carb and hi-rise intake, so if the carb size choice is right, there are few driveability problems with this common setup.

A few features (generally indicated in a manifold company's catalog as footnotes) to look at are the exhaust-heat crossover under the center of the plenum, and whether the manifold is EGR-capable. Exhaust heat for better fuel atomization and faster warm-ups is important for daily drivers, especially in areas with cold weather, but a cooler intake (without the exhaust passage) will provide a denser air/fuel charge to the engine for performance. **Note:** *If you have a manifold with a crossover passage, you can easily eliminate*

The OEM GM four-barrel in the carbureted days was a Rochester QuadraJet, which featured secondary bores larger than the primaries. This design is referred to as the "spread-bore" design. Today spread-bore carbs, like this Holley, are offered by aftermarket companies for those engines. The smaller primaries are said to be good for economy in normal driving

Hot rodders seem to be constantly swapping carburetors around, hence the availability of aftermarket carburetor adapters such as this Holley model to mount a spread-bore carb to a square (Holley) base on your intake manifold

There's a performance four-barrel carb to fit just about any application, from mild to wild. These three Holleys run from the mild 600-cfm 1850 (left) to the 750-cfm dual-feed to the racing 1050-cfm Dominator for drag racing

Here's the underside look of those same three carbs. Notice the difference in the bore sizes! The race carburetors also have many other design features that keep them from being what we would call "streetable." The Dominator (upper right) has an accelerator pump for the secondaries as well as the primaries, called a "double-pumper" design

that function and have a cooler charge by gluing a thin piece of stainless-steel sheetmetal to the crossover port on each side of the manifold before installation.

If your vehicle is equipped with an EGR valve (exhaust gas recirculation) for emissions purposes, then you should use an intake manifold with a mounting boss for EGR to be legal. Besides the legal part, your engine will run better and cleaner with the EGR than without, since the EGR function is tied into whatever engine management system you have.

Besides the low-rise/hi-rise decision, there are single-plane and dual-plane designs. In the dual-plane design, two of the four bores in the carburetor are over a section of the manifold that feeds four cylinders, and the other bores connect to the other four cylinders, usually with one set of passages over the others. The single-plane design is open on the inside, where all four bores are over a common plenum space that feeds all cylinders. For most street applications that will never see more than 5000 rpm, the dual-plane is much better for low-end torque and driveability, while the single-plane will make more horsepower at higher rpm.

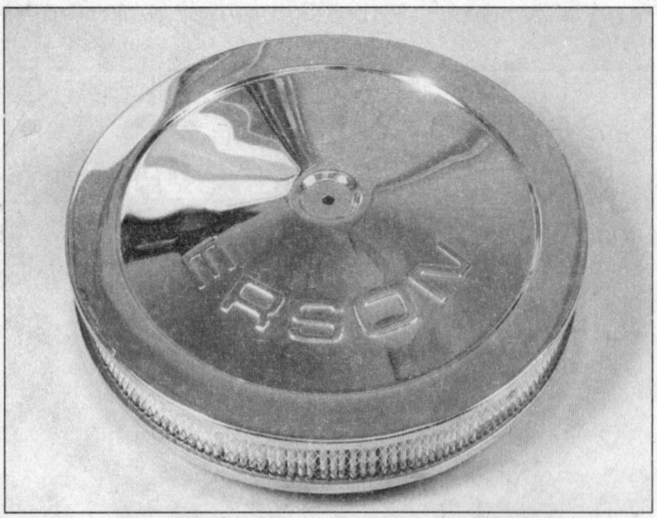

If you run a four-barrel carb, you'll also want to have as large a diameter air cleaner as possible for low restriction. Depending on hood clearance, this typical aftermarket air cleaner could use filter elements of 1-4 inches in height. Obviously, taller elements allow more air in

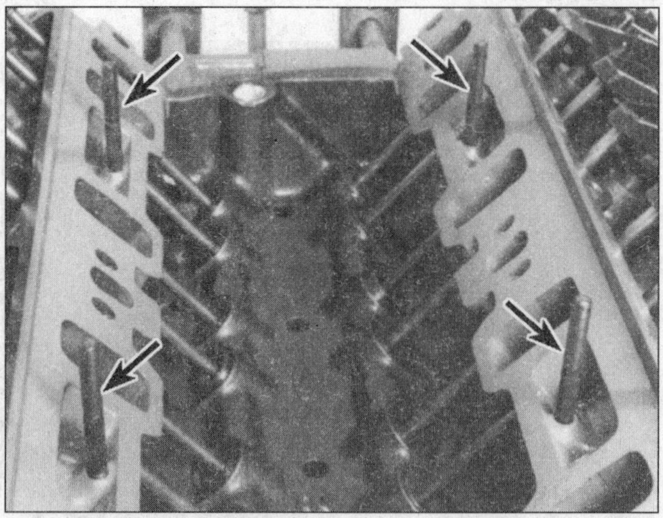

Here's a tip for perfect gasket alignment when installing an intake manifold. Take four long bolts of the same size as your intake bolts, cut the heads off and cut a screwdriver slot in the tops with a hacksaw (double-up on the blades to achieve a wider cut). Hand-thread these on your heads at the four corners, install the gaskets and manifold, leaving the studs to align everything as the other bolts are installed

If the higher position of the carburetor in the hi-rise manifold is good for performance, then even higher should be better, right? You will find several choices available, including taller manifolds where the carb base is high enough that it is separate from the bottom of the casting that seals against the engine's valley. These are called "air-gap" single-plane manifolds and are common on serious performance engines, because raising the plenum and carburetor not only allows for longer and straighter runners, but also keeps the charge cooler because air flows under the plenum and the hot-oil-splashed valley heat is separated from the bottom of the manifold. They look cool too, but are recommended only for fully-modified engines.

Check the recommended rpm ranges listed by the manifold manufacturers. A dual-plane "street" intake manifold with a 600-cfm carburetor may be listed as having good performance from idle to 5000 rpm, while a tall air-gap single-plane design with a larger carburetor may run its best from 3000-7000 rpm, supporting a higher horsepower engine. Talk to your local speed shop or dyno shop for their recommendations. One route to take where driveability and budget are concerned is to start with a typical hi-rise, dual-plane manifold and small four-barrel, then swap on a bigger four-barrel as you make other engine modifications. Most four-barrel manifolds can accept several different cfm-rated carburetors without modification.

Notes

7 Cylinder Heads and Valves

Flow of the air/fuel mixture gasses into and out of the combustion chambers of your engine is what makes an engine mild, moderate or asphalt-ripping in power level. We've discussed the induction system in the previous Chapter, and the next extension of the intake path is from the mounting flange of the intake manifold down to the combustion chamber, that is, the intake port in the head, the valve and the combustion chamber. Likewise, an engine with good flow into and out of the heads needs a full-on performance exhaust system with headers and appropriate-sized pipes and mufflers. Fixing the exhaust is much easier than the intake, and is one of the few mods that can improve fuel economy rather than hurt it. A proper performance exhaust is good for power levels from stock to near-pro-racing level. Since the exhaust is hotter, faster flowing, and nowhere near as dense as the incoming air/fuel charge, the exhaust system doesn't need constant upgrades. A carefully selected exhaust system can keep up with your camshaft, intake, or even cylinder head changes. Install a good exhaust system to start with, then leave it alone so you can concentrate on the intake side of things.

The performance bottleneck in almost any engine is this area, where the ports and valves have the final say on how much volume and velocity of mixture is going to get into and out of the combustion chamber. This display engine cutaway is an inside peek at a high-flow LS engine. Even with great heads and big valves, you can see how air/fuel must still take a sharp turn to enter or exit the chamber

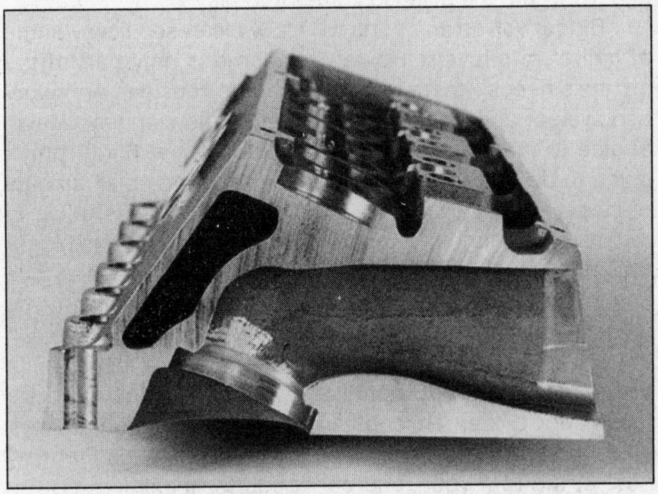

If ports and valves are too big, the velocity will be slow at street engine speeds, hurting performance and response. Note on this aftermarket performance head how the size of the port gradually tapers from the intake manifold side to the valve seat. The gradual slope helps to increase velocity

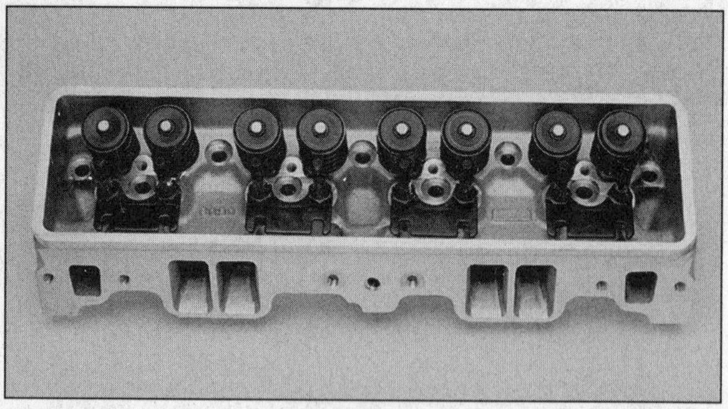

Considerable work and expense in rebuilding used cylinder heads for performance can be avoided by purchasing new aftermarket iron or aluminum heads. This aluminum Performer head from Edelbrock can top off your Windsor small-block Ford with stainless-steel valves, stock compression ratio, performance valve springs and retainers, and it's 50-state legal for emissions

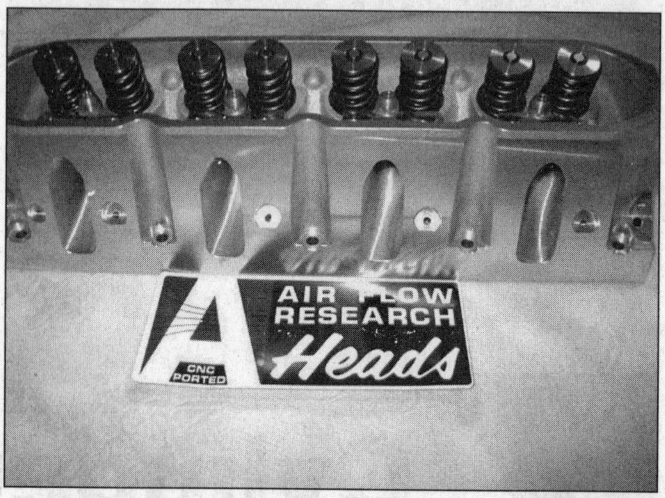

Clean air and big power don't have to be mutually exclusive. The AFR Mongoose street heads we chose for our LS1 engine have an Executive Order from the California Air Resources Board. While making industry-leading power, we're told these heads actually produced less emissions (and better fuel economy) than stock heads during testing

With the intake and exhaust system modified and a performance camshaft in place, the next step in improving your engine's breathing should be modifying the cylinder head. Except for port-matching (see Chapter 6), most cylinder head work is not for the do-it-yourself modifier. Too much experience and expensive equipment is required, so find a well-recommended machine shop in your area that has experience with modifying cylinder heads for street and racing. The basic ways to gain more power from a cylinder head and its valves are no mystery. You'd like to get more air/fuel mix into the combustion chamber, and have it burn fully to extract maximum power from the engine. Bigger ports in the heads and bigger valves will, of course, accomplish that, but the execution of the idea is more important than the idea, and it's where the science comes into play.

Bigger valves and ports will allow increased flow volume at higher rpm levels. However, volume is only part of the engine's needs - there is also velocity to consider. An induction system and cylinder heads that will flow enough for an engine to make a boatload of horsepower at 6500 rpm is going to be somewhat lazy at lower rpm. The small amount of incoming fuel/air mix at lower engine speeds is going to rattle around in those huge ports and slow down. The bigger the ports, the slower the gasses will move at a given engine speed. Imagine a garden hose. With no nozzle in place, you get a certain water speed from the hose, but when you pinch the end down with your fingers to make a smaller opening, the spray speeds up; smaller ports and valves maintain more velocity than big ones. In a racing application, the cylinder head decision is simple - you pick the heads that flow best at the rpm your race car needs for maximum power, while idle and mid-range are not even considered. Choosing cylinder heads for a street-driven vehicle means keeping enough mixture velocity at low and mid-range speeds to maintain good throttle response.

It used to be that performance enthusiasts and racers had few choices in cylinder heads and a number of machine shop and cylinder-head-specialist procedures had to be performed on the stock factory head castings. Ports were enlarged and reshaped, valve sizes were increased, valve head shapes were changed, valves seats were cut differently, and combustion chambers modified and polished, all to gain more flow. The experts who used a flow bench (and on-track results from sponsored race cars) to test the results of their work and kept experimenting laid the groundwork for what we now know about cylinder head work. In those

Stainless steel valves, with a performance shape to the backside of valve head, are found on most aftermarket performance heads. Aluminum heads like these are fitted with high-nickel hardened valve seats that are perfect for unleaded gasoline use. Fitting older (pre-emissions) iron heads with new hardened seats is an expensive proposition, making the new heads often a better buy in the end

days, the reshaping of ports in stock iron heads was a laborious and dirty process of grinding with noisy tools, and a pair of race-ready heads took a long time to deliver to a customer.

Dealing with factory iron heads is a limited proposition for really powerful head flow. The existing ports and chambers don't leave much room for reshaping. Although iron is tough to grind, you can easily grind into water-jacket space or even cut into the valve-spring/guide area if you're not careful. What a cylinder head guru would ultimately love to do is reshape the path of a port, not just make it bigger and smoother. A stock cylinder head is designed to do just one job, and with the least expensive casting that will get the job done. Compromises are always a part of OEM engine design, so if you could see cutaways of the ports in most cylinder heads, you would see that air flows into the intake port for a ways, then takes a sharp dive down toward the valve. The angle of that change in airflow is the problem. Ideally, the intake and exhaust ports would lead to their valves in a straight line, as they do in most Formula One engines. In modifying passenger-car engines for performance, this becomes less practical because the heads would need to be more complex. The intake and exhaust systems would be hard to package for a "V"-type engine in a standard vehicle, due to the angles at which they would mount to the heads. The spark plugs would likely have to be located in the center of the combustion chambers, which is another packaging issue.

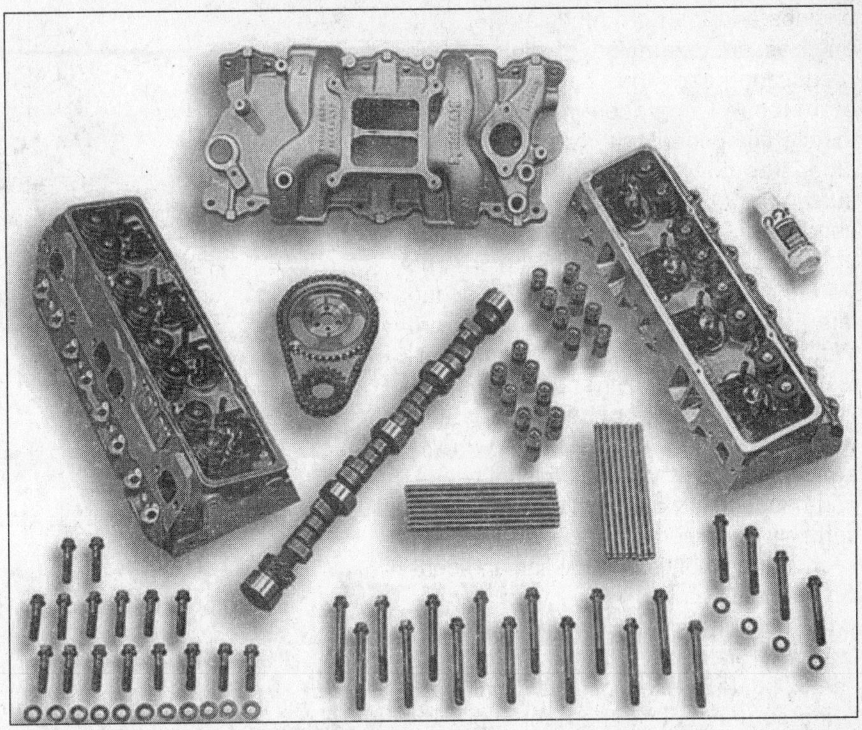

Several manufacturers now offer their cylinder heads as a planned package with other parts, so you know that the intake, heads and cam are all compatible with the same level of performance. This Holley SysteMAX small-block Chevy package makes 425 hp on a 10:1 350 with a 750-cfm carb, and features a .488 (intake) lift Lunati cam, double-roller timing chain set, dual-plane Holley intake manifold, aluminum heads, ARP head bolts and hardened pushrods

For our purposes, however, a great deal can be done with minor port reshaping and other cylinder head work. The latest offerings from Detroit are equipped with ever better cylinder head designs, as the engineers try to extract more efficiency wherever they can for fuel economy. The GM LS

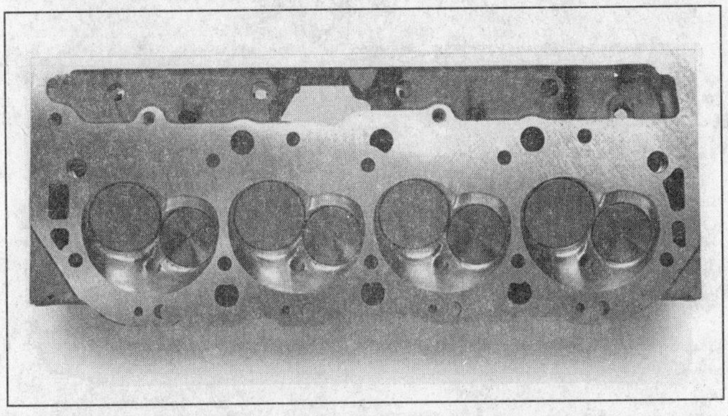

Competition heads are often unsuited for street applications, not only because of overkill port volume, but also due to altered port locations. This is an Edelbrock big-block-Chevy race head designed with famous big-block builder Pat Musi. It's full CNC-ported, and is a 24-degree angled design with raised exhaust ports. With 2.30-inch intake valves (1.90 exhausts) and huge 367cc intake ports, these heads can support a 950 horsepower motor!

Higher horsepower engines, especially when equipped with aluminum heads, require correct and even clamping loads, so many head manufacturers and engine builders utilize high-strength aftermarket head bolts like these from ARP. It's good insurance

engines and the Ford modular 4.6L/5.4L engines are examples of high-flowing production heads than can support several steps of upgrades in other performance components. If your engine is an older iteration of a late-model engine, such as a 302 Ford or a 350 Chevy, you can benefit from using stock later-model iron heads as a budget speed mod. The Vortec heads from GM for 350s or the late Explorer heads for small-block Ford Windsor engines are significantly better than the old Chevy and Ford heads. If you can get a set of such heads at a wrecking yard or from a buddy who is switching to aftermarket aluminum heads, iron heads might be worth using, and will certainly offer more power per dollar than spending a lot of time rebuilding and porting your old heads.

This Chapter offers some advice on the basic elements of rebuilding cylinder heads, but today's economics dictate that doing so may not be the right approach for your performance engine. There are many aspects of an engine that need precision machine work before the motor can be assembled, but the cylinder heads require perhaps the most work to renew. Some of the steps include: installing new valve guides and reaming them to the proper stem-to-guide clearance, fitting the tops of the guides with performance valve stem seals, machining the valves and valve seats with a performance cut, drilling and tapping the heads for screw-in rocker studs and pushrod guide plates, matching the ports to the gasket openings on the intake and exhaust, milling the head surface to perfect flatness, and opening up the bowls beneath the valves for more airflow. Of course, there are other expenses if your heads need crack repair, if new hardened valve seats must be installed for modern unleaded fuel, and/or if you need a few valves replaced. Buying better rocker arms, valves, guide plates, studs, etc. can add even more to the parts bill for rebuilding heads.

The modern alternative to the preceding bad news is to purchase a set of brand new performance heads from one of the many fine aftermarket companies. GM, Ford and Mopar also offer heads through their performance parts programs. There has never been a better time to shop for quality heads. All of the

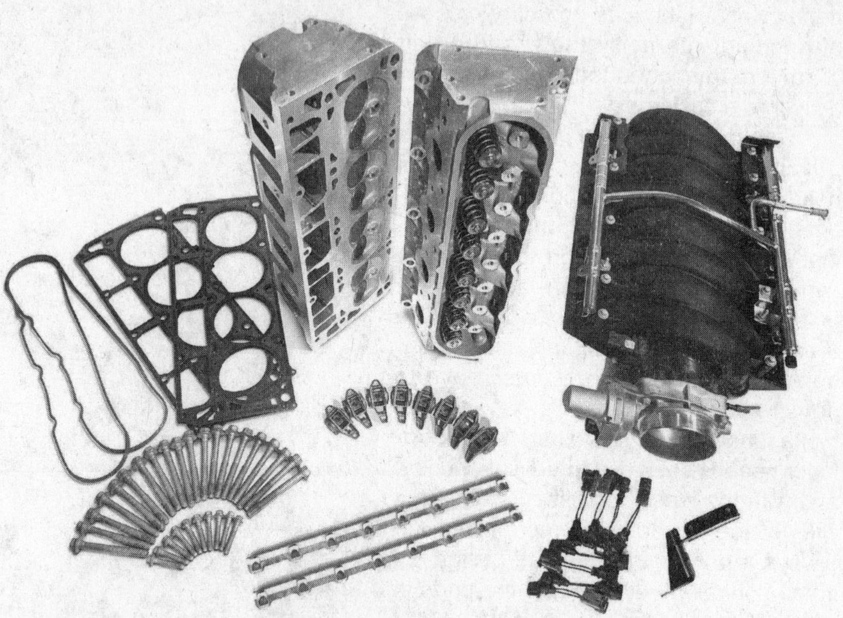

If you have a later-model performance car and you'd like more performance than just a cam swap and headers, but you're not in the market for a new crate motor, an engine top-end kit may be your one-package solution. SLP offers this box of goodies for the LS series GM powerplants. The new heads feature 64cc chambers (raising compression from the stock 70.2cc's), Competition Cams springs and titanium retainers, and included is the L76 intake manifold and new 1.7-ratio rocker arms. The package is available for blocks with 4.00-inch bores or larger

Edelbrock has their "Total Package" top-end kits for most popular V8s. This setup for a small-block Ford Windsor includes aluminum heads, intake manifold, double-roller timing gear set, plus a matched cam/lifter set and all the bolts and gaskets required for installation. On a 302 with 9.5:1 compression ratio, it's said to make 376 hp and 340 ft-lbs of torque

Cubic Inches	Small Bore/Short Stroke Intake Runner Volume	.050" Camshaft Duration
Up to 350 CID	170-180cc	210-225°
302-350 CID	200-210cc	215-235°
347-400+ CID	215-220cc	230-245°
383-421+ CID	235cc	240°+
Cubic Inches	**Large Bore/Long Stroke Intake Runner Volume**	**.050" Camshaft Duration**
Up to 350 CID	180cc	210-225°
302-350 CID	200-210cc	225-235°
347-400+ CID	215-220cc	230-245°
383-421+ CID	235cc	240°+

When choosing aftermarket performance heads, the port and valve sizes need to be tailored to the rest of your engine. Factors such as camshaft and displacement help determine how much port volume your combination can use. This handy chart from Racing Head Service of cam and runner volume choices gives you ballpark guidelines of what will make a good fit. Note that the cam figures are for actual duration at 0.050-inch lift, which is a more standardized measurement than the advertised duration figures listed by cam manufacturers

popular engines are very well covered by a number of companies, and new heads are coming out all the time. At Edelbrock alone, they are making new aluminum heads for many out-of-the-mainstream engines, such as older Oldsmobiles, Pontiacs, Buicks, Ford FE-series engines, AMC V8s, and both small and big-block wedge Chryslers. They still make the intake manifolds and finned aluminum heads for flathead Fords that put them in business back in the 1940's!

The aftermarket heads available today fall into two camps, either street/bracket-race performance or race heads. It wasn't very long ago that aluminum cylinder heads seemed exotic for a street engine, but today they are widely used. The more competition there is among manufacturers in this part of the performance world, the more prices tend to level out, in favor of the consumer. Today, you can buy a ready-to-bolt-on pair of aluminum heads for not much more than the cost of rebuilding and porting a pair of old cast-iron heads. Some companies also offer cast-iron performance heads for a lesser price than their aluminum ones. What's the difference? The iron heads are stronger in some ways, but aluminum heads can handle a little more compression on pump gas because of their greater efficiency in shedding heat. Given the same valves, compression ratio and port sizes/shapes, an engine will generally make about the same power with aluminum or cast-iron heads. Aluminum heads are half the weight of their iron counterparts and look cool on a detailed engine, but some enthusiasts who might like to keep their engine mods less obvious prefer to have painted iron heads so nothing is given away to a casual observer.

If the one perfect cylinder head could be found, it could be copied and cast as is, but with the power of today's CNC machining, one casting can be machined with several programs to serve the needs of several different engine state-of-tune requirements. These are intake ports for a big-block Chevy - note the machining marks

The fantastic strides that have been made by modern CNC machining equipment have resulted in a wider variety of aluminum cylinder heads. A procedure that used to take a professional cylinder head porter 20 hours or more with grinders can now be achieved automatically. A machine that is programmed to do it all, and make every head exactly the same. Aluminum is much easier to machine than cast-iron, so manufacturers can produce them at a lower price then ever before.

The intricacies of port design and airflow physics is really beyond the scope of this book, but the basics of choosing cylinder heads is matching the heads to your particular engine on two main factors: displacement and camshaft profile. For example, a 350 Chevy V8 for performance street use with a relatively mild cam might use heads with 170-180cc of volume in the intake ports, whereas the same

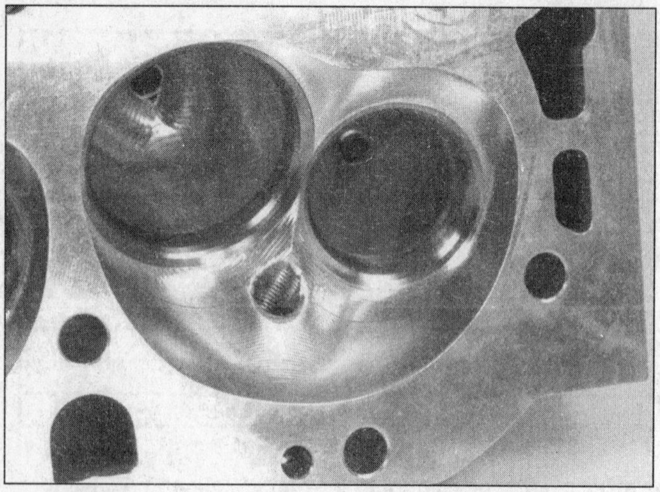

It's amazing how intricate automated machining can be. Note the work around the bowls and chamber on this head

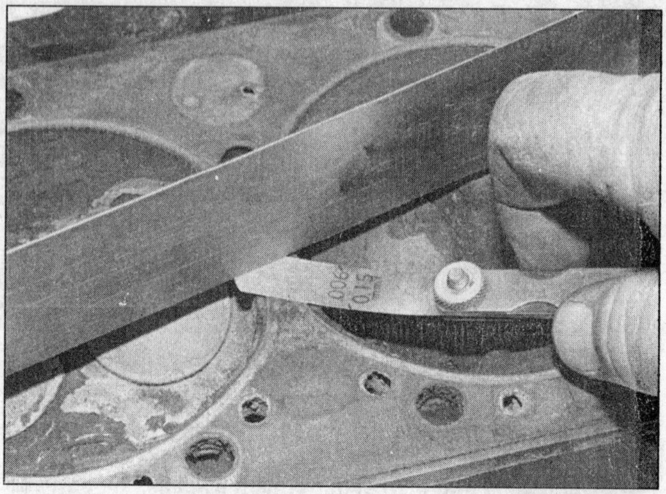

If you are thinking of reworking some older stock heads, take them to the machine shop first for a physical. The machinist will check them for warpage, cracks in the chambers, bad valves, worn guides and other defects. Learning what the potential repair costs could be before you have any work done is the smart avenue to follow

engine with a bigger cam could use intake ports in the 200-210cc range. A racing version of the same engine may use heads with even bigger intake runner volume, but such heads on a street engine will fall flat with a small cam. All engine modifications need to be selected together to make a cohesive plan for the desired performance/driving goal. The manufacturer of the camshaft you select will have good advice for you as to cylinder head and compression ratio selection to match your cam.

One of the areas head porters specialize in is shaping the bowl area, which is just below the valve seat. The sharp turn in the ports just before the combustion chamber gives the port a long side and a short side. The "short side radius" is an area that really slows down the mixture, so this part of the bowl is studied and carefully modified for better performance. On most CNC-ported heads, this area is all done according to the programmed instructions for the machining center.

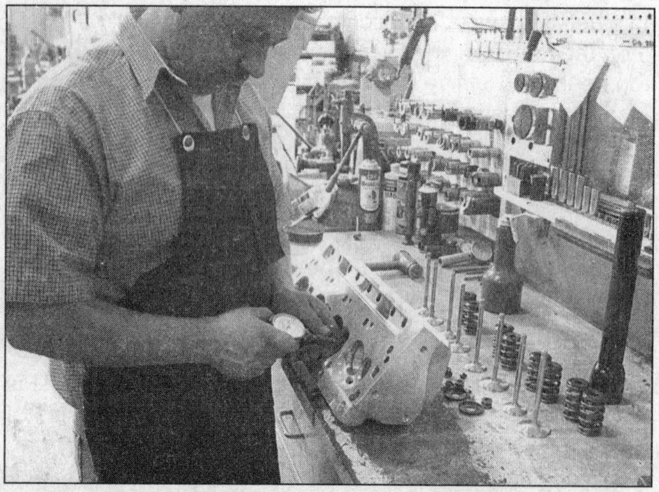

In some engine shops, stem-to-guide clearances are checked, even on brand-new heads. Here Ben Smeding checks the inside diameter of the valve guides with an inside micrometer

Racing heads will differ in other, more subtle areas, too. If you look through the ports of a V8 cylinder head, you can see the valve guide sticking down into the port. In terms of airflow, this "stump" is a direct affront to performance (as is the valve stem itself). In racing heads, the intruding portion of the valve guide is often shortened, and the cylinder head metal around it is ground and shaped to be more streamlined. This is good, but is usually impractical for street heads because valve/valve guide life is probably going to suffer. Since race motors are under a lot of stress anyway, they are subject to frequent teardowns and rebuilds - high-mileage life isn't so much of a factor in these applications. Many racing heads have relocated ports (raised exhaust ports are common) that require special intake manifolds and custom exhausts that may not fit well in a stock engine compartment.

Two important factors when choosing heads are the compression ratio and the legality for your application. Your engine's compression ratio is the biggest factor in the octane it requires, and if you go much above stock in compression ratio, you'll need the middle-grade gas even for normal driving. Consider if the increase in your fuel costs is going to be worth the extra horsepower gained by raising the compression ratio. Many vehicles are still subject to emission regulation and testing, and for them we recommend buying heads that are "50-state legal" for emissions. After the expense and labor of installing aftermarket heads, it would ruin your day to fail a state emissions test and have to take them off.

When selecting cylinder heads for the street, it's easy to go overboard with port volume. Those big, peak horsepower numbers on race heads will seldom be realized in a street engine. In terms of power-per-dollar, a set of good street

An outside micrometer is used to check the stem diameter of the valves in several places. Comparing this to the diameter inside the guides gives you the clearance, which on a typical V8 might be 0.0008 to 0.0027 inch for an intake valve and 0.0018 to 0.0037 inch for an exhaust valve (which needs more expansion room because it runs hotter)

On new guides, slow and careful "touch-up" with a slender hone can bring the tighter guides right to the desired clearance specifications

heads with an inexpensive 50-hp shot of nitrous (that has no effect on mixture velocity when unused) will provide much more seat-of-the-pants response than installing a set of heads that flow way more than your engine can utilize. Keep in mind that well-designed street heads can greatly improve peak horsepower as well. Our AFR Mongoose street heads have the same port volume as stock heads, yet flow 70 more cfm (cubic feet per minute). Figuring approximately 2 horsepower per cfm, that's a whopping 140 horsepower that can be added to a properly built engine - all while keeping high port velocity for low-rpm performance and driveability.

Valve jobs

The most basic of cylinder head work is a valve job, which will assure the valve seats and guides are in good condition. This is very important for an engine running at high rpm, and is essential if your engine has lots of miles. If you're planning to install a performance camshaft with new valve springs and lightweight retainers, make sure you get a good valve job at the same time, preferably a three-angle valve job from a performance machine shop. You won't see much performance gain from this work - it's insurance against damage on an engine that will be pushed to the limits. In the performance valve job, the valve face and valve

Valve jobs used to be done with machines that used rotating cutting stones to grind the various seat and valve angles, so a three-angle valve job was considerably more work than a stock job. Cylinder head and performance engine shops often have a "machining center" that is CNC controlled and can be programmed for any type of work

The cutting head on this Contour Epoch machine can automatically cut any combination of valve seat, throat (lower) and top cuts, all in one operation, with no grinding stones. Traditional grinding stones for cutting seats and valves have to be trued regularly as the stones wear

seat angles in the head are changed from just one angle to three or more. In a three-angle valve job, the center angle is the one where the valve meets the seat, and the upper (70-degree) and lower (30-degree) angles are designed to smooth the flow path from the port, around the valve head, and into the combustion chamber. This improves the flow at low-lift and is not as expensive as porting. The side view of the valve seat will have more of a transitioned slope than a stock port/seat with an abrupt angle.

Bigger changes to the cylinder heads may be detrimental to street performance. If you are planning head work, talk to the machinist first and thoroughly explain everything you've done to the engine so far, and any future mods you plan. He'll make specific recommendations for what aspects of the head he'll modify to work with your specific engine mods or power-adders.

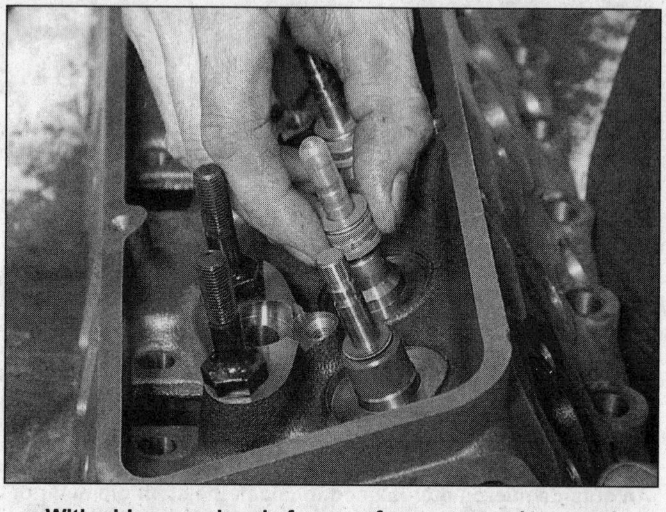

With old or new heads for a performance engine, good valve guide oil seals are very important. Most aftermarket performance seals require some machining of the top of the guides so the seals fit tightly. On this engine, the builder has installed spring-clamp-type Teflon seals on the intake valves, and OEM-style, low-friction umbrella seals on the exhaust valves. Sealing the intakes tight is important to keep oil from diluting the intake mix and causing detonation

8 Camshafts and Valvetrain

So addictive is the need for speed, that once you've made a few mods and have gotten used to the increased performance, you just have to have more! Sooner or later, you will be swapping out the stock camshaft and lifters, as the cam is the key player in a performance engine, often defining the results of other mods and the engine's torque and horsepower curves.

When your body runs fast, you breathe harder, and your vehicle's engine works much the same way. To make more power, an engine must "inhale" more air/fuel and "exhale" more exhaust. To make this happen, you can open the valves more, leave them open longer and/or enlarge the "ports" (passages in the cylinder head where the air and exhaust flow).

The modifications discussed here usually come only after all the other bolt-ons have failed to gain you the power you're after. Most valvetrain modifications require going inside the engine, which is not a place an amateur should go alone. Nevertheless, if you have some engine experience and a copy of the applicable Haynes repair manual for your model and year of vehicle (see your local auto parts store for a copy), you could tackle a rocker arm, cam or cam-and-kit swap that could bring you some new-found power.

After the installation of a good, free-flowing exhaust system and a cold-air induction on top of the engine, plus maybe a a sharper tune on your engine management via a hand-held reprogrammer, your next step up in performance should be new rocker arms and/or a camshaft. In fact, you shouldn't jump into a camshaft swap until these aspects of your engine's breathing have been improved already, as they will limit the new cam's ability to reach its potential.

Rocker arms

The camshaft is the "mechanical computer" inside your engine that times valve events, and has a major infuence on both power and driveability, but not everyone is equipped or ready to install one. An easy alternative is to install higher-ratio rocker arms. You simply remove the valve covers, remove the stock rocker arms, install the aftermarket ones and readjust the valve clearance. Your Haynes repair manual will detail the whole rocker adjustment operation.

The simplest valvetrain upgrade could be the installation of low-friction roller rocker arms. With a slight increase in rocker-arm ratio, you can gain some power with higher valve lift. This style is a stamped-steel design with a roller-tip that offers budget performance

If your stock rocker arms have a 1.5:1 ratio, it means that when the pushrods push up on the rocker at the cam's highest lift, the rocker arm multiplies that movement by one and a half times in relaying the movement to the valves. If your camshaft's lift at the cam lobe is 0.274-inch, then your valve's total lift will be one and half times that, or 0.411-inch.

Aftermarket rocker arms are available for most popular engines that increase the ratio, so our previous example would achieve 0.438-inch lift if equipped with 1.6:1 rockers.

Tough-yet-lightweight aluminum roller rocker arms like this one from Crane Cams are stiffer than stock, have less friction and have rollers at the tip and the pivot

This will give you some performance gain, but it can't change valve timing or duration as a custom camshaft would. There are other benefits to aftermarket rockers, though. Most are made with roller-tips for reduced drag at the point where rocker and valve stem meet, reducing engine frictional losses a little and thereby helping both performance and economy. A number of aftermarket rocker arms are also available with roller-bearings in the center for further friction reduction, and are made of lightweight materials like aluminum. Lighter valvetrain weight allows an engine to rev quicker.

If you decide to upgrade to a performance camshaft later on, you'll have to check that it is compatible with your new rocker-arm ratio. Too much combined lobe and rocker-arm lift could make the valves hit the pistons, so you might have to revert back to stock-ratio rocker arms with the new cam.

Camshafts

The camshaft is one of the key players in the operation of an engine, kind of like a bandleader directing the timing of all the other components. It determines the what, when and how much of anything that goes into and out of the engine. This is another subject a great deal can and has been written about, and we're not going to bore you with heavy theory and formulas. What you need to know for now is that a stock camshaft is designed as a compromise to consider economy, emissions, low-end torque and good idling and driveability. A performance camshaft opens the valves wider (lift), keeps them open longer (duration) and is designed mainly to produce more horsepower. It usually makes its gains at mid-to-higher rpms, but sacrifices some low-end response. The hotter the cam, the more pronounced these attributes become. Stock camshafts are designed as a compromise to consider economy, emissions, low-end torque and good idling and driveability. The performance camshaft lifts the valves higher (lift), keeps them open longer (duration) and is designed mainly to produce more horsepower. A perfor-

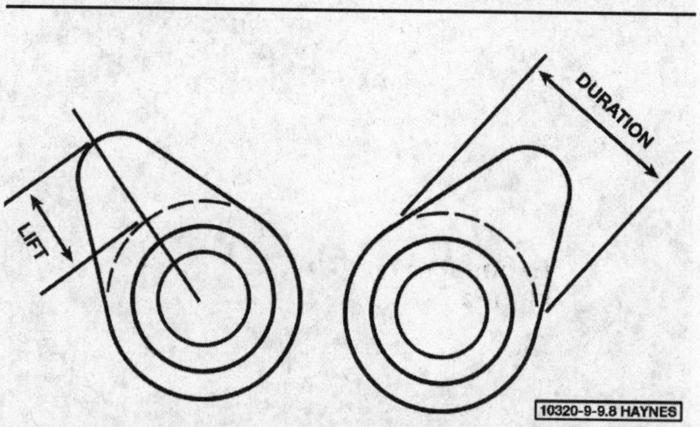

There are many aspects of camshaft profile design, but the two most important are lift (how far the valves are opened) and duration (how long the valves are held open) - together they increase performance by allowing much more flow in and out of the engine

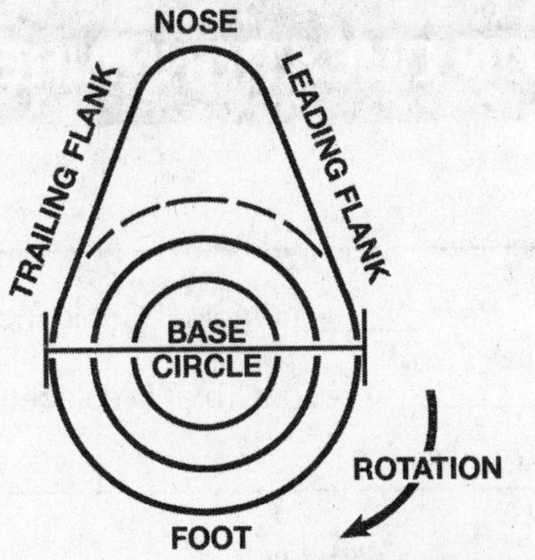

24048-2D-12.11B HAYNES

Here are some more camshaft terms. The difference between the measurement of the base circle and the foot-to-nose measurement is the peak lift of the design. The actual profile of the leading flank and the trailing flank are different, due to the lifter acceleration and deceleration rates the engineer is trying to achieve

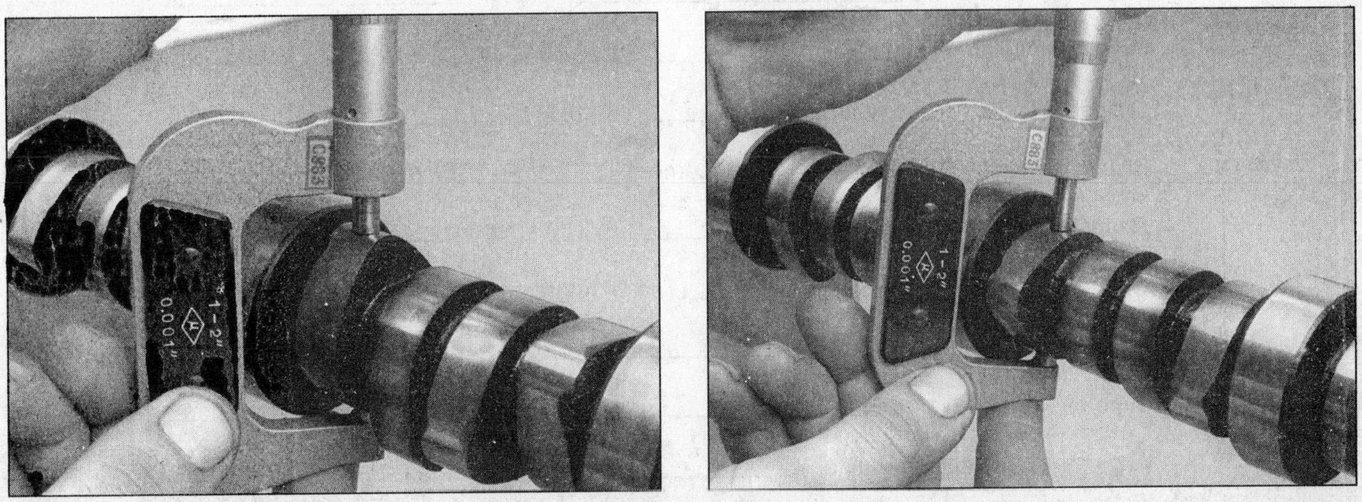

Using a micrometer, you can check the total lift on any camshaft. Measure from the bottom of the base circle to the top of the lobe, then subtract the measured size of the base circle from that. Remember that you need to multiply that figure by the rocker-arm ratio to come up with actual lift at the valve

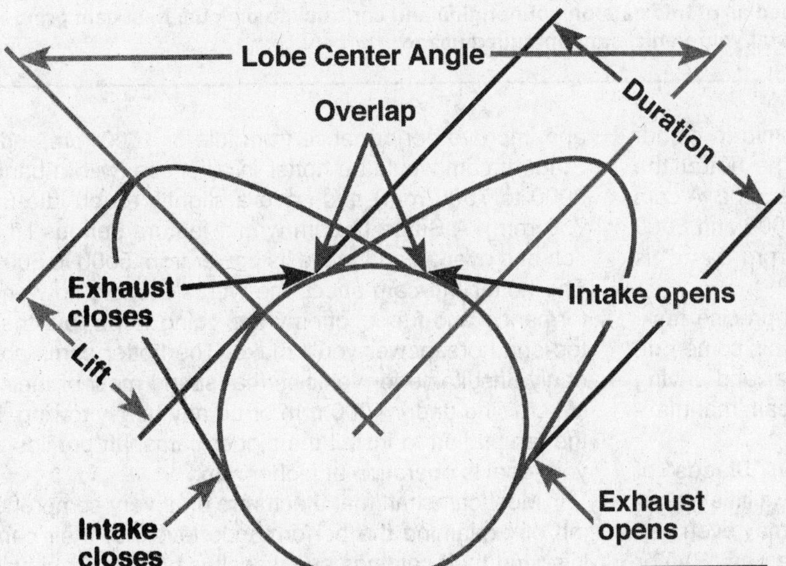

10333-8.3 HAYNES

Here's yet more detail on the terminology of camshaft design. If you have an engine design/simulated dyno program on your computer, you can change some of the cam specs and see just what effect duration, lift, overlap and lobe center angle have on performance. Or you could just ask the manufacturer to choose the best cam for your application

ENGINE SPECIFICATION QUESTIONNAIRE

Type of Use ______

Engine Make/Model ______ Year ______ Original Cubic Inches ______

Cylinder Bore Size ______ Stroke ______ Present Total Displacement ______

Number of Cylinders ______

Valve Size: Intake ______ Exhaust ______

Carburetors: Make ______ Model ______

Intake Manifold: Type ______ Fuel Injection ______

Cylinder Heads: Year/Type ______ Ported? ______ Milled? ______

Pistons: Stock ______ Replacement ______ Compression Ratio ______

Chassis: Make ______ Year ______ Weight ______

Gear Ratio ______ Tire Size ______ Tire Diameter ______ Size of Track ______

RPM Range During Competition: ______ to ______

Type of Transmission ______ Auto Stall Speed ______

Any other pertinent information? ______

______

______

How specialized is the right camshaft profile for your application? Just look at a typical camshaft selection information sheet from a cam manufacturer. They need all of this data on your engine and car/truck to pick the best cam grind to suit your vehicle and intended usage

mance camshaft usually makes its gains at mid-to-higher rpm and sacrifices some low-rpm torque. The hotter the cam, the more pronounced these attributes become. A cam design that is advertised for power between 3000 and 8000 rpm won't start feeling really good until that rpm "band" is reached.

Installing camshafts is an expensive and precise task. The most important work comes before any tools come out. You need to pick out the best cam for your car and driving style by consulting with your speed shop or a cam manufacturer's tech line.

Aftermarket cams are often advertised in "Stages" of performance. A typical Stage 1 cam might have a little higher lift than stock and a little longer duration. You may even see such cams advertised for truck applications as an "RV" or "Torque/Towing" grind. It would still keep an excellent idle and improve performance from idle or 1000 rpm and up. A Stage II cam would be hotter in all specs (with a band from 3000 to 7000 rpm) and have a slightly rough idle (maybe 750 rpm). A Stage III cam would feature serious lift, duration and overlap and make its power from 5000 to 8000 rpm. The hotter the cam specs the worse the idle, low-end performance and fuel economy are going to be, but the more top-end horsepower you'll make. The hotter cams are ordinarily unsuitable for vehicles that spend most of their street life cruising under 4000 rpm or do any heavy towing. Resist the temptation to install the bigger camshaft profiles unless your goal is operation at higher rpm.

Most camshaft manufacturers do a very comprehensive job of explaining the performance levels of their camshaft kits, and their catalogs and websites have lots of invaluable tech tips for selecting and installing camshafts.

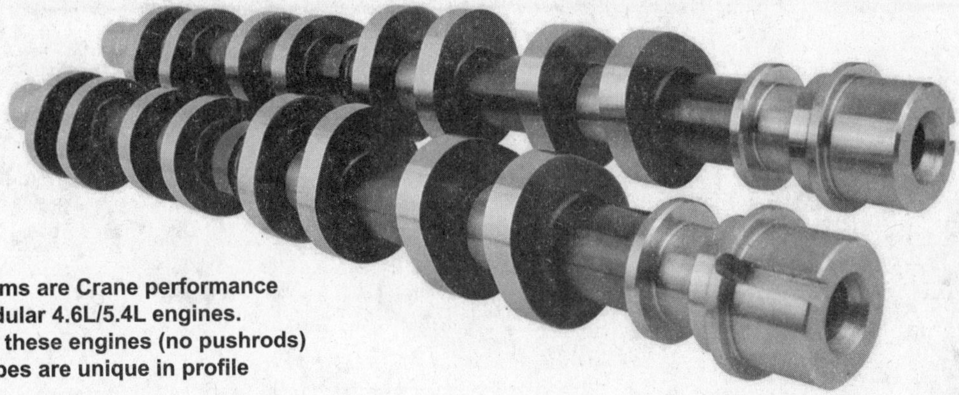

These unusual-looking cams are Crane performance items for the Ford modular 4.6L/5.4L engines. The overhead-cam heads on these engines (no pushrods) are efficient, but the lobes are unique in profile

Everything inside your engine is interrelated. A modification in one place usually requires some adjustment or modification elsewhere. In the case of the camshaft, a big increase in lift may mean that you'll have to check for valve-to-piston clearance to avoid an expensive collision there. For a very high-performance camshaft, the engine must be built to accommodate it, particulary in the piston selection. An engine of this level probably needs aftermarket pistons anyway, to raise the compression ratio and because you'll want stronger hypereutectic or forged pistons for durability at higher rpm. An engine with a hot cam and performance pistons will then require better airflow into the engine and

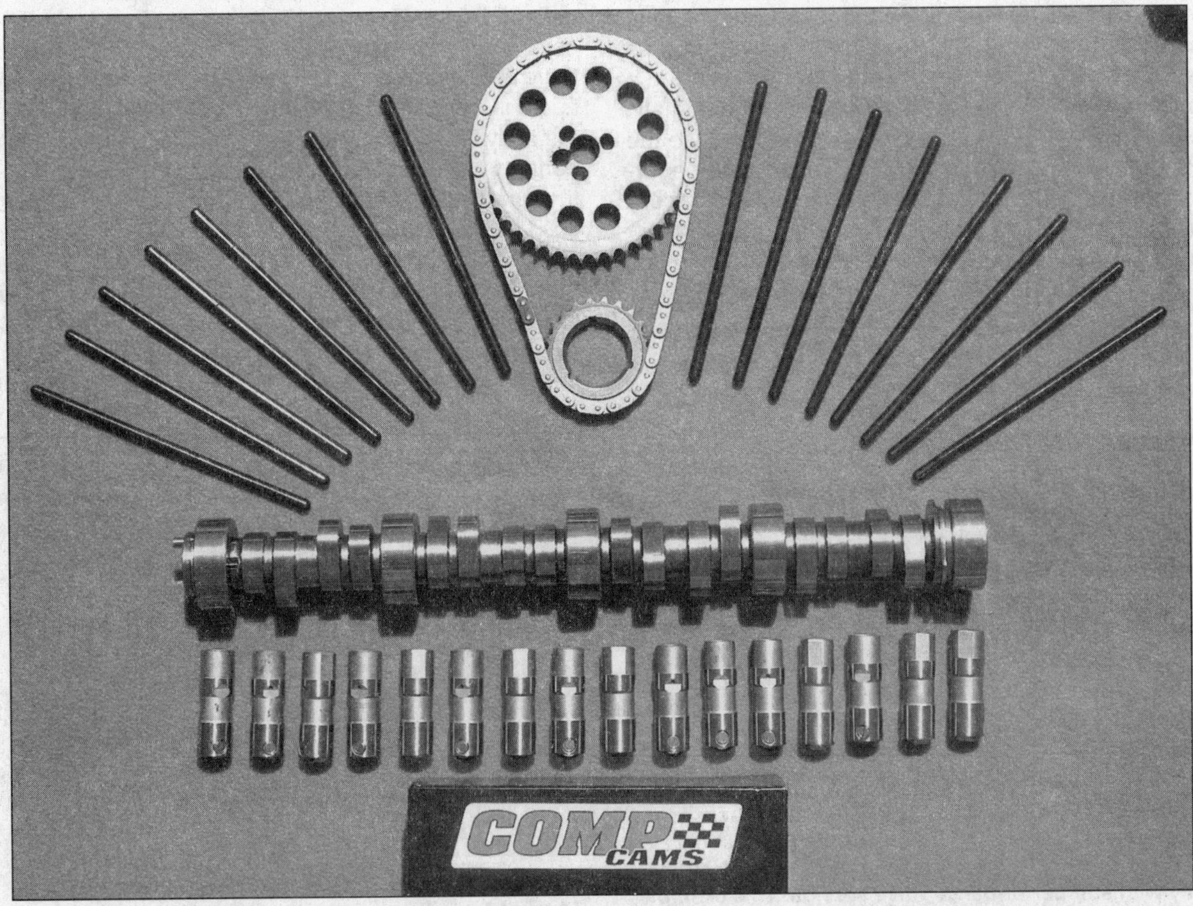

A number of interrelated components go along with the camshaft to make up the valvetrain. New performance camshafts are often sold as a kit with lifters, and some with a package that includes stronger pushrods, springs, and retainers. Major manufacturers like Competition Cams can provide all your valvetrain components. Buying from a single source helps ensure all parts will work together

To see the difference between a performance cam and a stock one takes a micrometer to measure the lobe heights, but the flat-tappet cam lobes (left) and roller cam lobes are hard to confuse. The roller cam profile (right) can have much more area under the curve and smoother ramp acceleration/deceleration

more fuel delivery, so you can see how important it is that engine mods be planned to work together. Other aspects that may make a hot cam grind too much for your everyday driving include a rougher idle and lower engine vacuum, which can mean your power brake booster may not be as effective. The latter problem can be dimished by installing a vacuum storage tank. Vehicles with a late-model automatic transmission may not like a radical cam either, because the converter doesn't have enough stall speed. Serious performance engines will require transmission mods for durability and a higher-stall-speed converter. These are just some of the aspects to consider in camshaft selection.

The flat-tappet (non-roller) lifter is crowned almost flat on the bottom, and has more friction than a roller design, especially with stiff performance valve springs. This example is a hydraulic flat-tappet lifter, as denoted by the clip at the top retaining the hydraulic part of the lifter inside. There are numerous quality aftermarket hydraulic flat-tappet cams that work very well for street/performance use

Lifters

There are several basic types of camshaft design, all defined by the type of lifter they use. There are flat-tappet cams and roller-lifter cams, and within these two categories there are solid lifters and hydraulic lifters. Engines in the past had only solid lifters, then the hydraulic lifter came into use in the early Fifties, offering quieter engine operation without the periodic valve adjustments required with solid lifters. None of the American V8 engines this book is concerned with have solid lifters, but in some racing applications, solid lifters are still used. Improved hydraulic lifters have been developed that work well with most street-performance cams, and are pretty much the norm today.

Roller lifters have a steel roller pinned to the camshaft end, which greatly reduces the friction of the lifter rubbing

Roller lifters may be solid or hydraulic, but all roller lifters need to be retained in the engine in a way that keeps the rollers oriented in full contact with their camshaft lobes. One design uses tie-bars like this to keep the lifters from turning

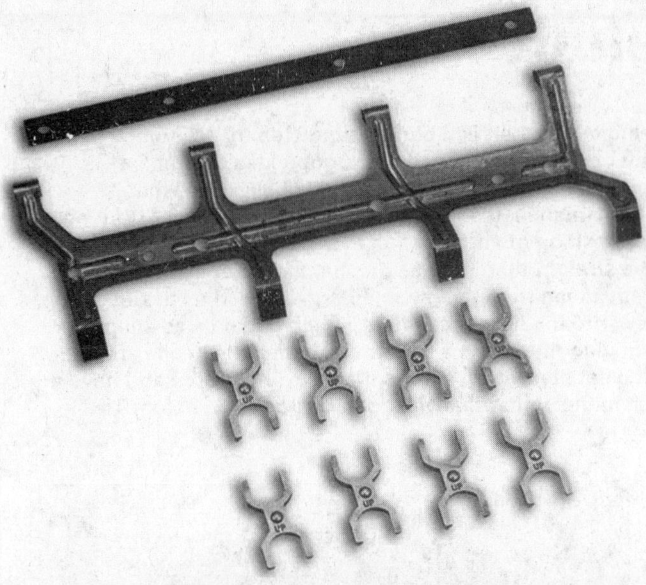

On small-block Ford engines, factory roller lifters are left in the correct orientation by "H-clips" that fit between the flats on a pair of lifters. All of these clips are kept in contact with the lifters by this sheetmetal "crab" that bolts to the valley and puts slight pressure on all the clips

against the camshaft lobes. Originally developed for racing engines, roller cams can be ground to more radical profiles and take much stronger valve spring pressures without wearing out the camshaft lobes. In the past 10 or 15 years, roller camshafts have come to be widely used in late-model

The lifters in GM LS engines live in plastic "cassettes" like this that hold four lifters. When assembling an engine, lubed lifters are installed in the cassette, then the cassette is installed in the engine. There is an aftermarket tool that holds all the lifters up while the camshaft is being replaced, so you don't have to remove the intake or heads when swapping cams

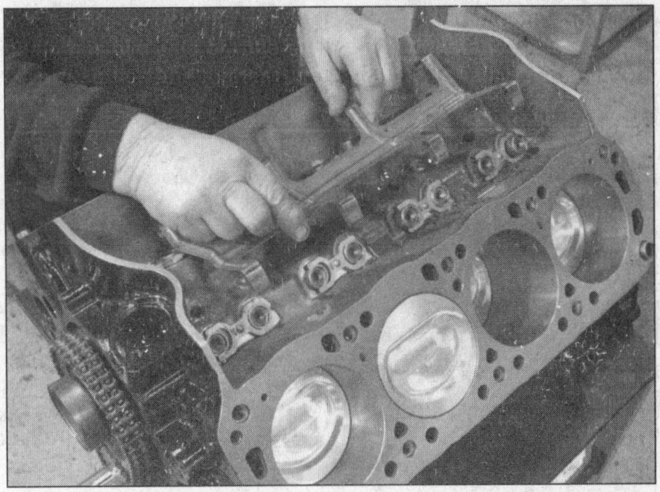

Ford engines not originally equipped with a roller cam (or aftermarket Ford-style blocks) can easily be retrofitted with stock Ford clips and crab. You must drill and tap 2 holes in the valley for the short bolts that hold the crab, so this should be done before you install cam bearings in the block. Bolts must be short enough not to extend into the camshaft bore!

production Detroit engines, as engineers seek to get every last drop of efficiency out of engines to meet corporate fuel economy standards. Since roller lifters do not take on the wear pattern of the camshaft, factory roller lifters can be used with an aftermarket roller cam, making swaps of performance roller cams common in late-model engines modified for performance. One caution with roller cams is that the hardened camshaft and it's integral gear require a matching gear on your distributor. If you buy an aftermarket distributor,

In any performance engine rebuild or new camshaft installation, the timing chain and gears should be replaced with a heavy-duty set that has two rows of rollers, called a "double-roller." The gears have two rows of teeth and the chain has two sets of rollers, to better withstand higher spring pressures and higher rpm without the chain stretching

How to degree a camshaft

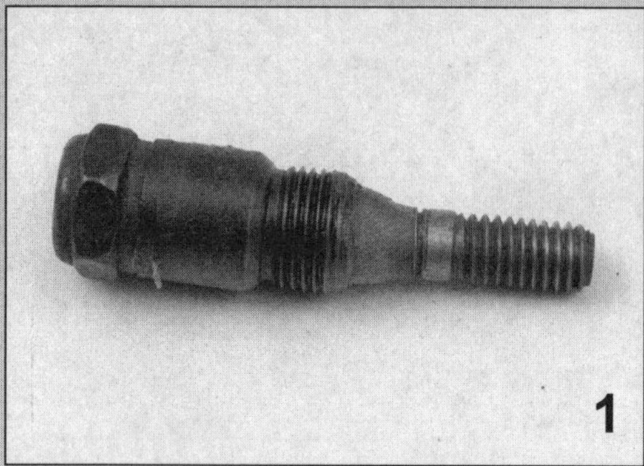

1

1 Degreeing a camshaft is a blueprinting step that is sometimes not done on street engines, but is a good idea any time a camshaft is installed to verify that the cam is delivering what it advertises. In a nutshell, the idea is to find the true, exact TDC (Top Dead Center) position of your engine, then determine if the camshaft is going to be straight up (timed as the manufacturer intended) or is retarded or advanced from that spec. First, you need a "positive-stop tool" to screw into the spark plug hole, which could be as simple as this old spark plug fitted with a bolt epoxied in. If the heads are off, you can bolt a flat steel strap across the #1 cylinder bore and have a threaded bolt in the center that will contact the piston before TDC

2

2 With the piston down in its bore and the stop-tool in place, attach a large degree-wheel with 360 degree-marks. Make a temporary pointer out of stiff rod and secure it to the engine with a bolt. Rotate the engine slowly one direction (turn from the flywheel end, not the bolt holding the degree-wheel) until the piston first hits the stop-tool, and note the relationship of the pointer to the degree-wheel. Now rotate the engine the other direction until the piston once again is stopped, and note the degrees. Halfway between the two places you stopped is exact TDC. Turn the engine to that spot, then loosen the degree-wheel's mounting bolt and rotate the wheel until the pointer is opposite the TDC mark on the wheel

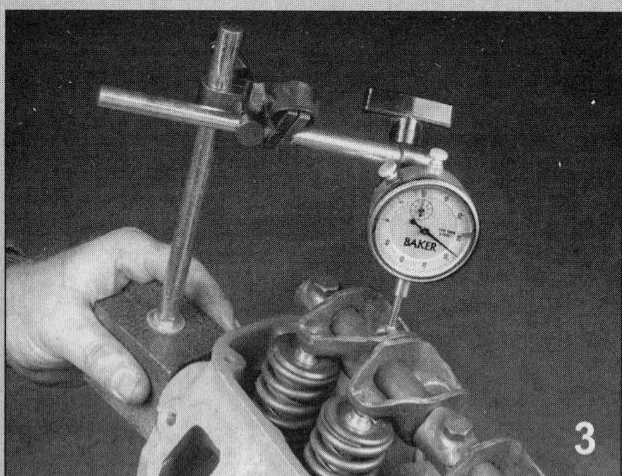

3

3 Mount a dial-indicator in line with the intake pushrod (if the heads are off, put the indicator directly on the solid lifter body). Rotate the engine slowly until the indicator shows 0.050-inch of movement and write down the degree position, then further rotate the engine until you come full circle to where the indicator again shows 0.050-inch movement. This is the extent of intake lobe travel. Do the same for the exhaust lobe and compare your specs to those on the cam manufacturer's instructions

4

4 If your cam specs were off a few degrees from the manufacturer-intended specs, either advanced or retarded, the situation can be corrected with camshaft index bushings like these from Lunati. You drill out the camshaft gear's pin hole to accept a tight fit of the offset bushing. A set includes bushings for several degrees of cam movement, either for retarding or advancing, plus a stock position bushing if you want to go back to what you had originally

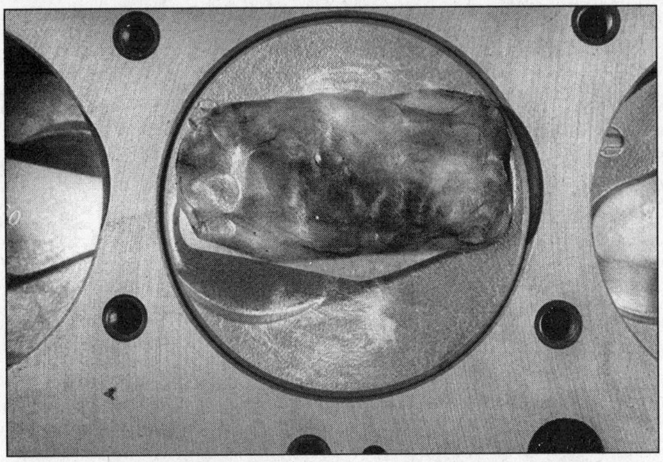

If you are assembling an engine with a bigger cam and/or higher-compression pistons, you should check the valve-to-piston clearances. Apply a wad of modeling clay to the top of the piston, over the area where the valves could hit. Apply over the piston reliefs if applicable. Install one head (with gasket), two solid lifters, and two rocker arms. Rotate the engine through two revolutions

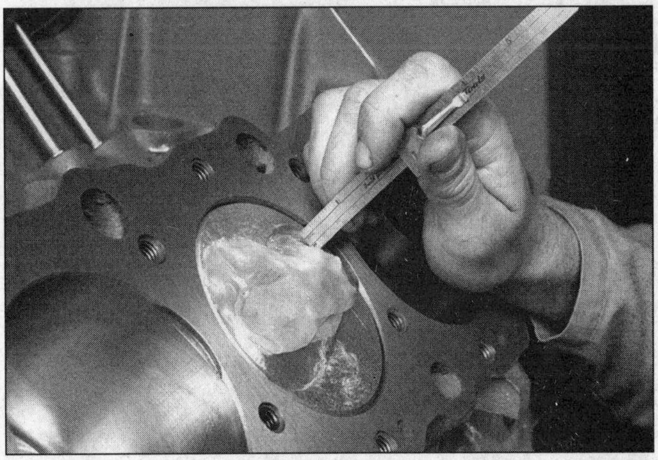

Remove the cylinder head and examine the clay. Slice through the valve-impressed area of the clay and measure the thickness of the clay where the valves imprinted. A safe amount of clearance should be 0.080-inch for the intake valve and 0.100-inch for the exhaust valves. This is an insurance step that could save considerable grief. If clearance is insufficient, machine the piston tops

specify if you are using a roller cam or not. If you are putting a roller cam into an engine that did not come with one, you'll have to buy a new roller-compatible gear and install it on your existing distributor. Of course, if your engine is new enough to not have a distributor, that's one less mod you'll have to make. Hydraulic roller cams have become very popular with the performance-street crowd today, although they are more expensive than an equivalent flat-tappet cam.

Valve springs

When you install a "bigger" camshaft, you'll usually want to install better valve springs. High-performance valve springs allow the valves to open further without the springs binding and also are stronger to prevent valve "float." Valve float occurs when the engine is at high rpm and the inertia of the valve is too much for the spring to handle. So the valves

With GM LS engines many builders find that even a stock engine can be improved by installing better valve springs, which allow the engine to rev 500-600 rpm higher without valve float. This upper-valvetrain package from SLP includes new springs, retainers, keepers and bolts, plus rollerized rockers that offer 1.85 ratio. Compared to stock rocker arms at 1.7 ratio, the SLP parts give 10% more lift and 12 more horsepower without changing the camshaft

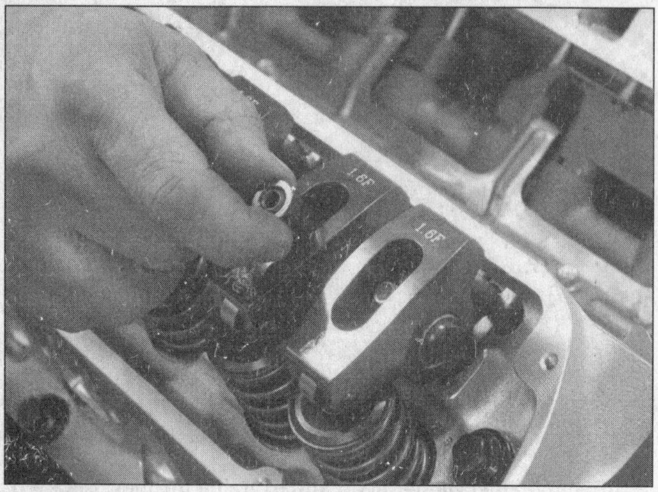

Whether you use stamped-steel or aluminum rocker arms, valve adjustment can be kept right where you want it by using Posy-Lock nuts on the rocker-arm studs. These tall nuts have an internal Allen screw that, when tightened after the big nut is at the right spec, hold the valve adjustment securely. For solid-lifter cams, these are a must

actually lose contact with the lifter or cam follower and can make contact with the piston, bending the valve and/or damaging the piston.

For this reason, high-performance valve springs are recommended whenever you change the camshaft or make other modifications to extend the rpm range beyond stock. Your stock springs will not last long at repeated high-rpm operation, and when springs fail, the valves usually hit the pistons with results that aren't pretty.

Most aftermarket camshafts are sold in a kit, with various other valvetrain components included. New valve springs are almost always included, and often new retainers are part of the package. The aftermarket valve spring retainers are usually made of a material that is lighter than that of the stock retainers, and is often stronger as well. Light weight in valvetrain components means the engine doesn't have to work as hard accelerating these components as rpm rises, and for performance use, everything from valves to springs to retainers and even keepers are made of lighter metals. A lightweight valvetrain makes an engine "sing" easier.

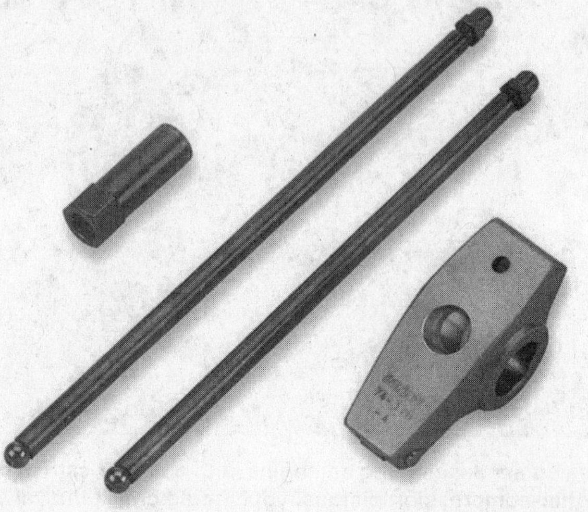

If you have mixed various valvetrain components and/ or changed heads, you may want to check your geometry. This kit from Lunati is an easy way to determine the correct pushrod length for various rocker arms and camshaft lifts. You set the special rocker arm so that it just touches the valve tip, with clearance at the pushrod end. The adjustable end on the pushrod is screwed out until the pushrod clearance is removed. Then you can measure this pushrod length and, using the chart that comes with the tools, determine the exact proper length of pushrods to order for your lift and rocker-arm ratio

Performance valve springs are a key element of your valvetrain. Higher-rated springs get their strength from tougher material, thicker wire and by adding a second coil inside the main spring. The inner coil may be of round wire or flat spring steel, and dampens oscillation of the main spring

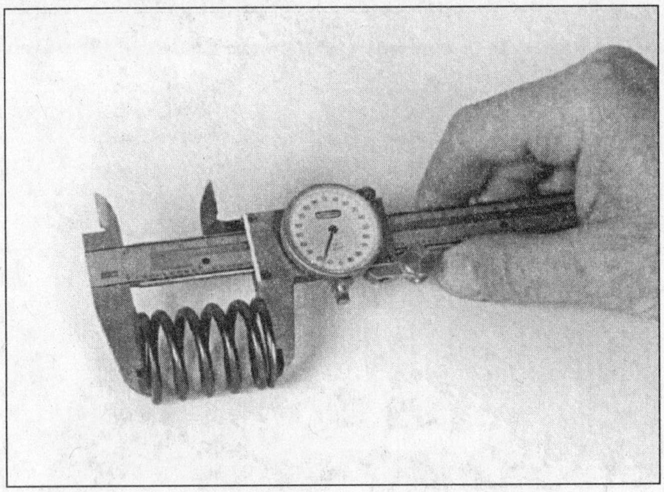

Valve springs have specs, just like any other precision components, and these should be checked on new or used springs. The free length is easy to check with vernier calipers. Make sure all your springs are the same

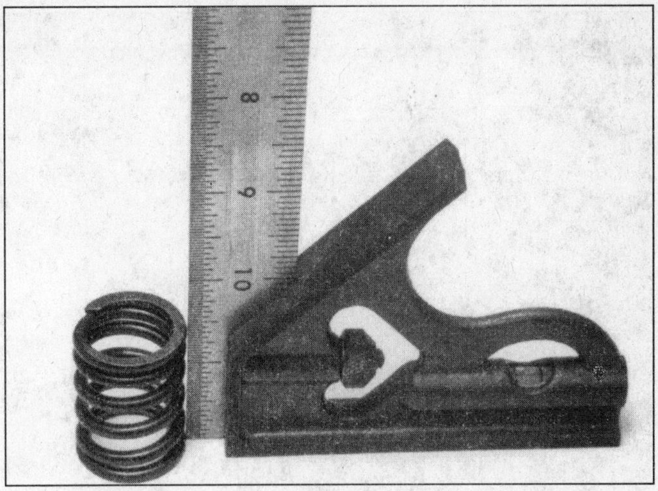

Used springs should always be checked for "squareness" with a square on a very flat surface

Installing aftermarket valve springs can be done two ways. You can remove the cylinder heads and use a valve spring compressor while working on the heads on a bench. This approach is great if you're already going to remove the heads for some other work, like having new guides installed. To just replace the springs and retainers without taking the whole upper half of the engine apart, you'll need a tool to be used with your air compressor. Basically, you turn one cylinder to Top Dead Center and insert the tool (an air hose adapter) into the spark plug hole, connect your air compressor and pump the cylinder with air. Unless your engine sports high mileage and is in need of a serious rebuild, this will keep the valves from falling into the cylinder while you remove the valve springs with the heads still on the engine. Use the spring compressor to remove the old spring, install a new seal on that cylinder's two valve guides, and install the peformance springs and retainers.

The installed height is another critical measurement of a valve spring. You can check all the heights with vernier calipers, measuring from the spring seat in the head to the top of the spring

Blueprinting the valvetrain

There are several specifications to check when installing aftermarket valve springs, to blueprint the valvetrain for even output from every cylinder. New springs are provided with a spec sheet that should list the installed spring pressure with the valve open and closed, as well as the free spring height, and installed height. Measure the length of each spring (free, not installed) with vernier calipers and compare them. All should be very close to equal. You need a special spring pressure gauge to compare the spring pressures, but you could take your new springs to a performance machine shop and they could measure all yours for a nominal fee. In case one or two springs were a little shy of the others, you can correct to a certain degree by installing thin shims between the valve spring and the spring seat in the cylinder head. The instructions that came with your new cam kit should tell you the specs and the limit of how many shims can be used.

Another aspect of the valve springs to consider is the presence of coil-bind. Because your new cam is going to lift the valves higher, the springs will get compressed more. If the valves are lifted too high off their seats, the coils of the valve springs could actually touch each other at maximum lift, which can lead to spring failure or even worse, engine damage. Cranking the engine over by hand with a breaker

Higher spring pressure is why we install aftermarket performance springs, so this important spec must be checked. Machine shops have a tool like this to check spring pressures. They can lower the arm on the press until the spring is at its installed seat pressure or the open-valve pressure at a specified valve lift

A simpler tool, used in a bench vise, can also be used to check spring pressures. Make sure all of your springs meet the manufacturer's specifications

bar, you can observe the clearance between the coils. Also check to see if the stock rocker arms still have adequate room in their slots (at the bottom, around the rocker studs). The higher lift of the cam could push a stamped-steel rocker arm to where it bottoms out against the stud. A paper-clip can be used to check for clearance at the stud/rocker interface, and you can lengthen the slots if needed with a small abrasive cone in a hand-held grinder.

For more radical camshaft applications with their attendant high spring pressures, factory (pressed-in) rocker-arm studs can pull up out of the cylinder head, with clattery results for the valvetrain. When the camshaft manufacturer tells you that it is required for your particular cam application, you should have a machine shop install screw-in studs. They will remove the press-in studs, drill and tap the holes and thread in stronger aftermarket studs. Not a big job, but good insurance.

Sometimes, an aftermarket cam profile with tougher springs will require a different length of pushrod. As the geometry of the pushrod, rocker arm and valve stem tip

When you have installed a higher-lift cam, it's possible for the valve springs to reach their limit and for the coils to touch each other (called "coil-bind"). Rotate your engine to maximum lift and use feeler gauges to check that there is still some clearance between the spring coils. If not, you'll need new springs

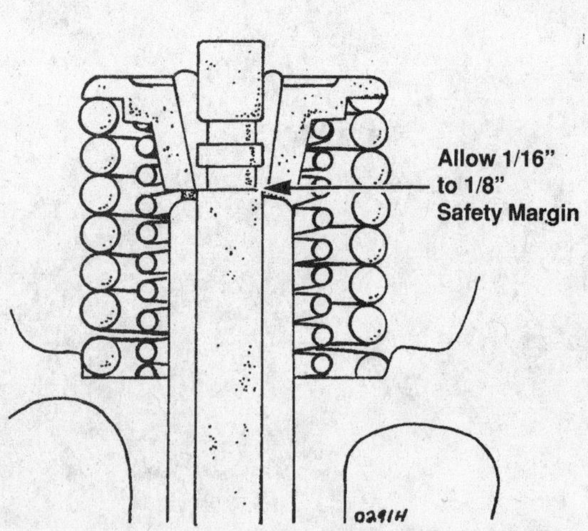

This illustration not only shows the condition of coil-bind, but also an interference between the bottom of the valve spring retainer and the top of the valve guide. If there is interference, machine the top of the guides to achieve 0.075 to 0.125-inch clearance when the spring/retainer is at full lift

changes as the engine rotates, observe the relationship of the components. If the pushrod tip doesn't stay centered under the end of the rocker arm, or the other end isn't sitting right over the valve stem, a shorter or longer pushrod may correct the geometry. You can buy a special pushrod "length checker" which is a pushrod with an adjuster sleeve near the top. You install the tool and adjust its length until the geometry is the best you can achieve, then you remove the tool, measure it and order pushrods of that length. Pushrods are also another aspect of the valvetrain that may need to be updated. Depending on the valve spring pressure you are using, stock pushrods may bend or break under high rpm use. Aftermarket pushrods are made to be much stronger, but their design is sometimes tapered at the ends, leaving strength in the middle where it is needed but keeping overall weight down.

When you do get the camshaft specs right for your engine and your kind of driving, it's a thrill to hear and feel the engine get up "on the cam" and just take off! Some guys love retaining the nearly-stock idle that a mild cam grind provides, while others install a bigger cam just because they don't want their car to sound stock at all. The sound of a cammed engine with tinny exhaust headers is pure music to the ears of the latter crowd!

Notes

9 The Fuel System

It's not inaccurate to think of an internal combustion engine as a big air pump, because it mainly moves a lot of air through the induction system, into the combustion chambers and out the exhaust. Of course, it must also have enough fuel to support combustion, yet it's an engine's ability to pump air that ultimately determines how much power it can produce. But, no matter how much air a motor inhales, no combustion is possible without a proportional increase in fuel.

For the first 80 years of the automobile, nearly all vehicles used carburetors to add fuel to intake air. Today many modified old-school motors still employ high-performance four-barrel carbs. In a carburetor, incoming air passes through a venturi (a tapered funnel that increases air speed), producing a relative vacuum or pressure drop that draws fuel from the float bowl through jets and machined orifices into the incoming air stream. A mechanically driven fuel pump produces about 5 psi of pressure to keep the float bowl filled with fuel. One of the problems with mixing air and fuel in a carburetor is that the fuel is essentially wet as it enters the airstream. After mixing together in the carburetor, the air and fuel mixture passes through the intake manifold and into the combustion chambers. If the intake manifold is cold, some of the wet fuel clings to the walls of the manifold's internal passages, especially if they're angled too sharply. While a carbureted engine is still cold, the choke enriches the air/fuel mixture to compensate for the fuel that sticks to the manifold walls, and hot coolant heats the carburetor and the manifold to improve vaporization. After the Clean Air Act Extension of 1970 mandated lower tailpipe emissions, carburetor cold start systems were deemed unacceptable because a large amount of unburned fuel came out the tailpipe.

So about 35 years ago government and social demands for better fuel efficiency and lower exhaust emissions compelled manufacturers to start phasing out carburetors and replacing them with fuel injection systems. Today, all new vehicles sold in this country are fuel injected.

Nevertheless, many high-performance street engines are still carbureted, so let's look at how to select and modify a typical four-barrel carburetor. (For a detailed description of how Holley carburetors work and how to tune, repair and overhaul all the popular Holley models, refer to Haynes Techbook 10225. For the same information on Rochester carburetors, refer to Haynes Techbook 10230.)

Carburetors

Finding the right carburetor

Carburetor selection

Matching the carburetor to the engine and application is critical for performance and/or economy. Many hot rodders like the look of a huge carburetor, or carburetors, on their engine. They fall into the trap of "bigger is better." This might hold true for cubic inches, but it almost never applies to carburetion.

If an engine is over-carbureted, it will have poor throttle response, will bog and hesitate at low speeds and run poorly until very high rpm. Fuel economy and emissions will also suffer.

Larger displacement engines and engines that run at high rpm need larger capacity carburetors than smaller engines running at lower speeds. The critical factors in selecting the right carburetor size are engine displacement, maximum rpm and volumetric efficiency.

Volumetric efficiency

Volumetric efficiency (VE) is a measure of the engine's ability to fill the cylinder completely, and is generally expressed as a percentage. For example, a 100 cubic inch engine that gets 80 cubic inches of air/fuel mix into the combustion chamber on each intake stroke has a volumetric efficiency of 80-percent.

A volumetric efficiency of about 80 to 85-percent is generally what an average, well built, high-performance street engine will provide. Stock engines achieve approximately 70 to 75-percent volumetric efficiency. You must decide at what rpm range you want your engine to run best.

When selecting a carburetor, use the following formula or chart to estimate the required cubic feet per minute (cfm) rating. Round off all results to the nearest carburetor size. Be realistic; you're only hurting the end result of all your hard work by overestimating.

Put in your specific numbers for cubic inches and the rpm range of the engine. For the accompanying chart, a figure of 80% VE is used but for an engine that is more highly modified a figure of 85% should be used to calculate your actual cfm needs.

Engine displacement (cu. in.)	Engine RPM 4000	4500	5000	5500	6000	6500
250	245	260	290	320	350	380
275	255	290	320	350	380	420
300	280	315	350	380	420	450
325	300	340	380	415	450	490
350	325	365	405	445	490	525
375	350	390	435	480	520	565
400	370	420	465	510	555	600
425	400	450	500	550	600	650
450	420	470	520	580	625	700

As a general rule, high-performance small-block engines will need 400 to 600 cfm carburetors, and big-block engines will need 600 to 800 cfm carburetors (exact size will depend upon the actual engine modifications that have been made). Note: ***The table shown here is for stock street engines. For high-performance models, increase the CFM rating about ten percent***

The formula to use in figuring your own requirement (cfm) is:

(cubic inches ÷ 2) x (maximum rpm ÷ 1728) x VE = cfm

Example:

You have a 350 cubic inch engine that will reach a maximum of 7000 rpm. Let's also say you've built an engine that's well thought out with the right combination of parts, so you're VE is roughly 85%, compared to the 80% used for milder engines. Plug these numbers into the formula:

(350 ÷ 2) x (7000 rpm ÷ 1728) x 85% = 602 cfm

So you would need a 600 cfm carburetor to handle the needs of the engine. **Note:** *As a general rule, high-performance small-block engines will need 400 to 600 cfm carburetors and big-block engines will need between 600 to 800 cfm, depending on actual displacement and level of modification. Smaller carburetors generally give better throttle response but fall off slightly in power at high rpm.*

Carburetor modifications

Most carburetors have seven basic operating systems:

Fuel inlet/float circuit
Idle circuit
Low speed/off idle circuit
High speed/main metering circuit
Power enrichment circuit
Accelerator pump circuit
Choke circuit

The main purpose for modification of one or more of these systems is to increase engine performance.

When engine and other vehicle modifications for performance applications are performed, some carburetor operating characteristics change. These changes necessitate dialing-in the carburetor to achieve peak engine performance.

Anyone having a good basic working knowledge of carburetor systems can dial-in or modify a carburetor. The purpose of this section is to explain and illustrate some of the available parts and methods for modifying carburetor operating characteristics to achieve the best possible performance.

When a carburetor is subjected to heat over a period of time, the heat has a tendency to warp the individual components. This can create a vacuum or fuel leak that just tightening the bolts and screws cannot correct. The arrows indicate the areas that should be checked for warpage (typical Holley carburetor)

All carburetor tuning begins with the disassembly and inspection of the carburetor. This serves to familiarize yourself with the systems and components of the unit. **Note:** *Modifying or tuning a carburetor is usually a trial and error process. If you anticipate disassembling your carburetor frequently, it's a good idea to use special rubber or Teflon gaskets, which can be reused many times before they are replaced. Check with your local speed shop or auto parts store regarding the availability of these gaskets.*

Main body

If the carburetor has been in service for any length of time, inspect the flat surfaces for warpage. If warpage exceeds 0.010-inch in the indicated areas the carburetor must be resurfaced to ensure a good gasket seal. It's usually not necessary to have the surface machined except in extreme cases. To true the surface, we recommend draw filing with a medium-fine flat file. **Caution:** *Don't try to file any surface that has a raised sealing bead on it, such as the top and underside of the main body on some Rochester carbs.*

Throttle body

Many carbureted high-performance engines have a problem maintaining a low, smooth idle. The usual cause is the camshaft. The more extreme the cam profile (the larger the lift and duration), the more difficult it is for the engine to produce vacuum. This makes it necessary to raise the idle speed to compensate. Sometimes, even after the base idle screw has been turned in as far as it will go the engine still has a hard time idling.

Because the vacuum is lower and the idle rpm requirement is higher, the throttle plates must be opened for additional airflow. Unfortunately, since transfer slot exposure is increased, fuel flow is also increased, which usually makes

Check both sides of the throttle plate and the underside of the air horn for flatness (typical Rochester carburetor)

When the base idle screw is adjusted all the way in, it's a good indication of an idle adjustment problem (typical Holley carburetor)

The gap shown here by the arrow is what happens to the throttle plates when the screw is turned as shown in the previous illustration (typical Holley carburetor)

Note how the gap between the throttle plates and the bore exposes too much of the transfer slots. When that happens, you can't get any more adjustment from the idle mixture screws (typical Holley carburetor)

the engine run too rich and makes adjustment difficult. The idle mixture screws are no longer useful because as the throttle plates are opened, you lose vacuum at the idle ports, so the idle mixture screws lose their ability to meter fuel. One way to close the throttle plates back down to partially cover the slots and still provide the extra airflow needed is to drill a 3/32-inch hole in each primary throttle plate. **Note:** *If the engine is radically modified, it might be necessary to drill holes in the secondary throttle plates too.*

On some carbs, idle airflow can be increased *without* drilling holes in the throttle plates by simply increasing the secondary airflow. To do this, turn the secondary throttle stop screw, concealed in the throttle body casting, clockwise about 1-1/2 turns. This opens the secondary throttle plates and increases airflow without a significant increase in fuel flow. Basically it spreads the airflow, which provides a better balance between the primary and secondary throttle bores. As a result, the primary throttle plates can now be lowered into the bore, putting them closer to the proper relationship with the transfer slot, which improves idle mixture screw adjustability.

In some applications where the vacuum is unusually low, drilling holes in the primary throttle plates might still be necessary. The correct idle setting should expose 0.045 to 0.060-inch of the idle transfer slot below the bottom edge of the plate.

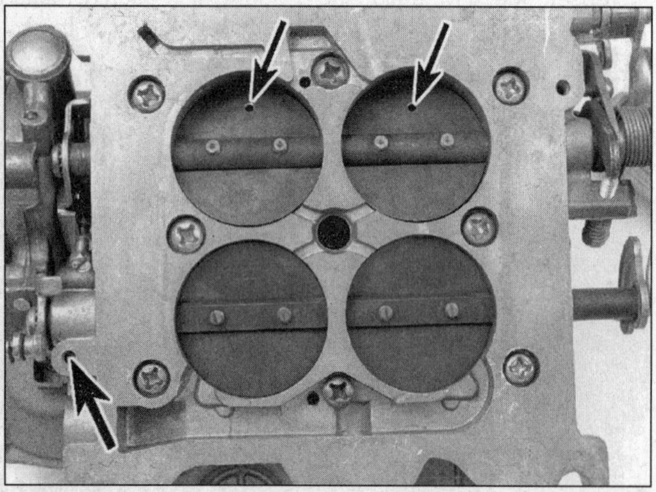

The holes (upper arrows) drilled in the primary throttle plates will allow you to back the base idle screw out to a normal position, and you will regain control of the idle mixture. The lower arrow points to the secondary throttle stop screw (typical Holley carburetor)

The holes drilled in the throttle plates will allow you to back the curb idle screw out to a normal position so that you can regain control of the idle mixture (typical Rochester carburetor)

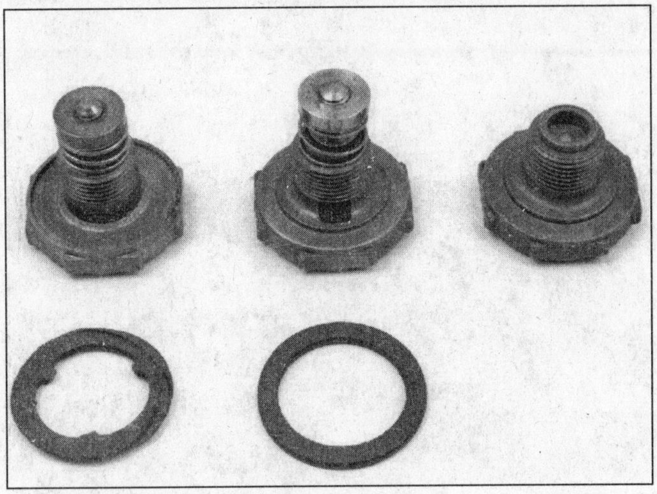

There are many different Holley power valves available to fit the range of manifold vacuum readings that you may get from your specific engine. Choose the power valve that is approximately 1 to 1-1/2 inches of vacuum lower than the reading on your vacuum gauge. (The one on the right isn't a power valve, but a plug to take the place of a power valve in some applications)

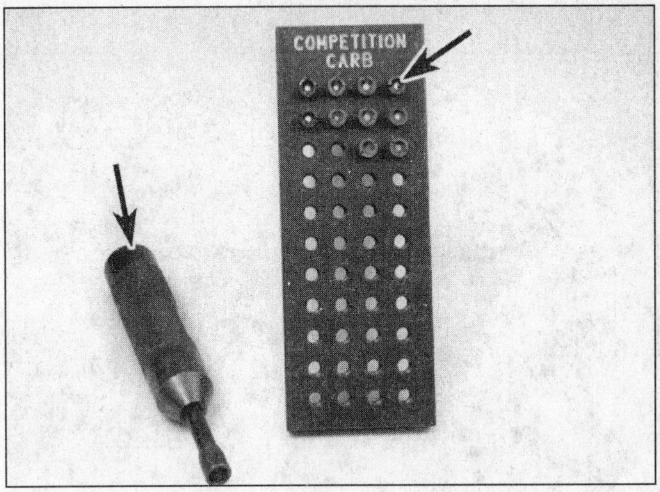

There is a wide range of main metering jets available for all Holley and Rochester models. One of the easiest ways to keep all of them organized and undamaged is to get a pre-drilled and threaded holder from your local auto parts store or speed shop. The tool on the left is a special driver just for jet removal and installation. It captures the jet in the end of the tool so you can get it into or out of tight places without damaging the jet

Metering block (Holley carburetors)

Proper idling characteristics also require fuel metering that's matched to the vacuum levels that your engine produces. Correct power valve timing is helpful in obtaining a clean idle and part throttle. The opening point of the power valve should be 1 to 1-1/ 2 inches less than manifold vacuum at idle. With the camshafts presently in use, a number 65 (or 6.5 inch) power valve is usually sufficient to maintain good control. **Note:** *If you have a really radical cam profile it might be necessary to go all the way to a 3.5 inch power valve; but first you'll have to accurately measure the manifold vacuum at idle on your engine.*

The power valve is designed to supplement the fuel flow through the main jets. During acceleration, low manifold vacuum allows the power valve to open. When the power valve is operating, fuel flow through the valve and channel restrictions effectively increases fuel discharge in the main well about 6 to 10 jet numbers.

The main system in the metering block incorporates the main jet, the main well and the booster venturi. Performance carburetors are designed with more than adequate capacity in the main system passages and therefore do not require modification. The main jets installed by the manufacturer of a performance carburetor are generally in the ballpark for most applications. There is usually no need to modify bleeds, since this changes the system balance and booster venturi pull-over point, which can cause driveability problems. So make any air/fuel ratio changes in the main system with the jets.

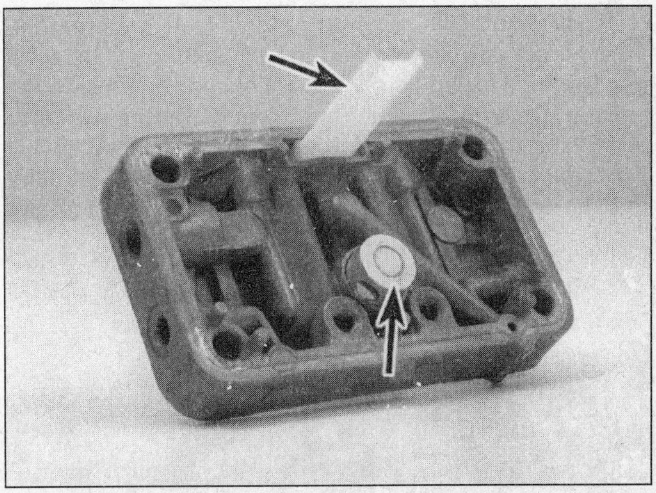

Baffles are used mostly in racing applications where the fuel sloshing around can cause a flooding condition, or a lean condition from fuel moving away from the power valve and opening to nothing but air (typical Holley setup)

The use of various types of baffles is another modification that improves performance, even though it doesn't directly control fuel flow. As fuel sloshes around in the fuel bowl during acceleration, braking and cornering, it can flood over at vent areas or cavitate at the power valve. Neither of these conditions is a desirable situation. Installing these baffles can offset both conditions.

If engine modifications are causing a low-vacuum condition at idle, remove the spring under the power piston and shorten it to prevent the power enrichment circuit from operating when it shouldn't (typical Rochester carburetor)

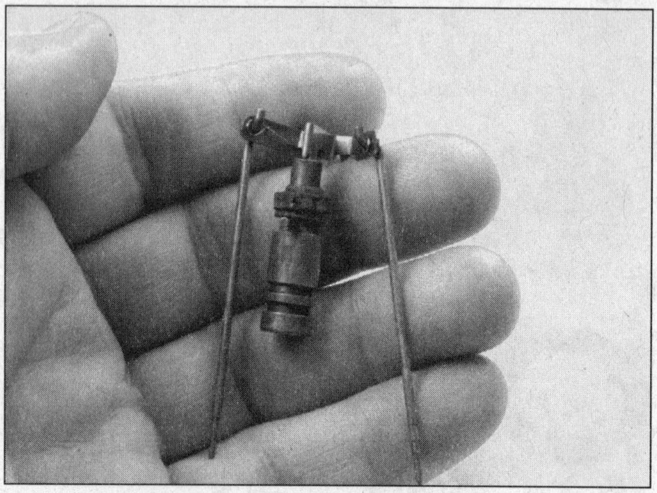

Metering rods are available in different profiles to provide the correct amount of fuel enrichment at the desired point in the power curve (typical Rochester setup)

Main body and air horn (Rochester carburetors)

The power valve or power piston/metering rod assembly is designed to supplement the fuel flow through the main jets. During acceleration, low manifold vacuum allows the power valve to open. Fuel flow through the power valve or past the raised metering rods effectively increases fuel discharge in the main well approximately 6 to 10 jet numbers during the time it's operating. In the case of the power piston/metering rod(s), all of the enrichment takes place in the main circuit, as the metering rod(s) is/are lifted up in the main jet(s).

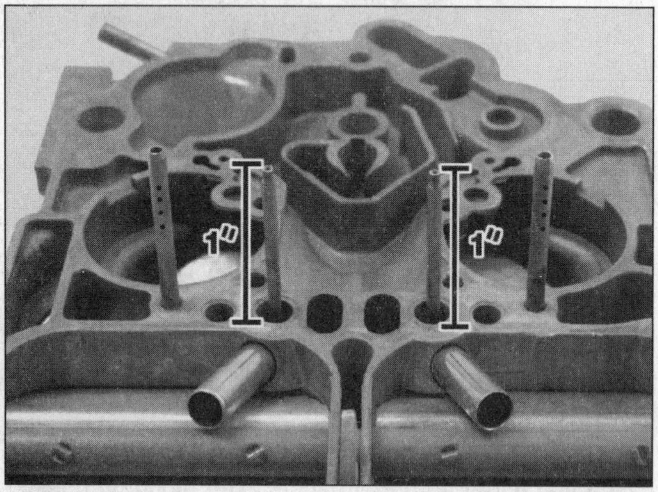

To reduce restrictions in the secondary fuel passages, carefully drive the air bleed tubes in to a height of one-inch. The 0.030-inch holes in the fuel feed tubes help to provide a better transition as the secondary throttles are actuated (typical Rochester carburetor)

If the intake manifold vacuum is extremely low at idle, the spring tension in the power valve or under the power piston may overcome the force of vacuum pulling the piston down (or holding the power valve shut). In an instance such as this, the power valve would open or the power piston would raise up, pulling the metering rods higher up in the main jets. This condition would cause the mixture to be way too rich during idle, off idle and even while cruising. A problem like this would not clear up until wide open throttle had been reached and the spark plug fouling from the over-rich mixture had been blown out. To overcome this problem, the power valve or power piston spring will have to be weakened or shortened. This can be done by clipping coils from the spring. Remove only 1/2 coil at a time so as not to take off too much.

The main jets that come with the carburetors are generally in the ballpark for most applications. Of course, this varies with the extent of engine modification. At any rate, the first changes that should be made to the air/fuel ratio in the main system should be made with the jets, or on models that have metering rods, the jets and metering rods.

To provide a better response as the secondary throttle plates open up, drill a series of four 0.030-inch holes, starting at 1/4-inch from the bottom and about 3/32-inch apart, through the secondary fuel feed tubes. Also, carefully drive the air bleed tubes into the air horn approximately 3/16 of an inch, so they protrude one-inch from the surface of the air horn. This will reduce the restriction in the secondary fuel passages. **Caution:** *Be careful not to distort the orifices at the ends of these tubes.*

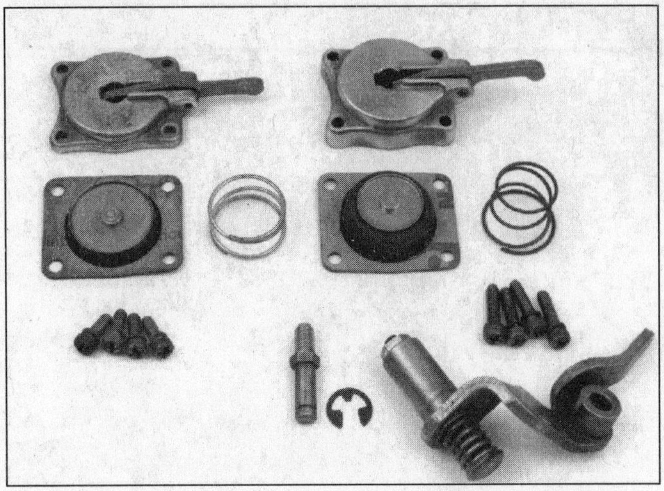

Here's an example of two different capacity accelerator pumps for a typical Holley: The one on the left is a standard 30 cc pump while the one on the right is the 50 cc setup, including pump cover and screws, diaphragm and spring, lever assembly and mounting stud. Note: *Some applications will require a 1/4-inch spacer to get enough clearance to operate properly*

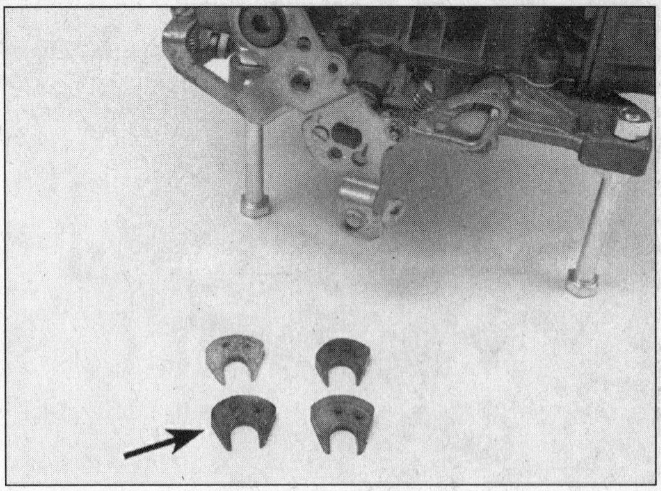

Another way to modify the way the accelerator pump delivers the fuel shot on a Holley is to change the plastic cam that operates the lever. As you can see, the shapes (profiles) are all slightly different and will control fuel discharge differently

Float bowl

The float bowl and float require no modifications, but the fuel pressure affects how the whole system operates. Inlet pressure should be between 7 and 8 psi at idle. A higher pressure might create flooding problems by overpowering the needle and seat assembly. Use Viton-tipped needles unless you're using a racing fuel with a very high octane or are using an octane booster in a proportion that exceeds the booster manufacturer's recommendations. When used in high concentrations, some of these boosters can create problems by attacking the Viton on the needle.

Accelerator pump(s) and controls

Holley

Note: *If the vehicle has an automatic transmission you should increase the size of the shooter over the original size. If increased shooter size exceeds 0.042-inch, use the hollow accelerator pump discharge nozzle screw to ensure that there's enough fuel flow.*

The more mass you have to move and the quicker you want to move it, the more fuel it's going to take. There are three areas in the accelerator pump circuit that you can alter to fit your performance needs.

First, use a 50 cc accelerator pump instead of the standard 30 cc pump. You might even have to use two pumps if your engine consumes that much fuel during acceleration.

Second, change the shape of the plastic cam that determines the type of accelerator pump shot that is delivered.

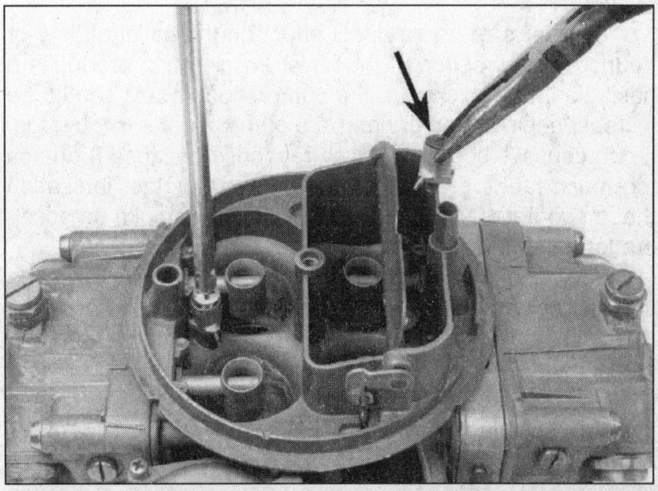

There are either one or two of these discharge nozzles in your Holley carburetor, depending on the model. They're available in a variety of sizes and tip types. The numbering system is similar to the one used on the metering jets, a number stamped in the side indicating orifice size

The height and shape of the cam can change the squirt characteristics to deliver fuel sooner or later, or in longer or shorter bursts during the stroke of the accelerator pump.

Third, use different styles of fuel discharge nozzles, sometimes referred to as "squirters" or "shooters." These nozzles use a numbering system similar to main metering jets, stamped on the side of the nozzle. They also have different types of tips on the nozzles. The performance versions are longer and discharge the fuel farther, out into the air stream in the center of the venturi. Standard shooters don't have these extended tips.

On Holley units with mechanical secondaries, the adjustment for the secondary throttle plates is made by bending the linkage in the middle (arrow). Be sure the secondary plates open fully (perpendicular to the throttle body)

The modification for the vacuum secondary opening speed on a Holley is very simple, since the entire vacuum secondary control assembly can be removed, or just the top can be taken off, to change the diaphragm control spring

Shooter size has a direct effect on the initial off-line or "launch" performance. If the initial acceleration produces a hesitation, then picks up, the pump shooter size should be increased. On the other hand, if a pump shooter is too large, it can cause a bog or sluggish response because it dumps too much fuel too soon into the venturi. Another indication that a shooter is too large is a puff of black smoke on acceleration.

You'll probably need to fine tune your vehicle by some trial and error to get it exactly right. To get back on track, use the stock shooter size recommended by the manufacturer.

Rochester

The accelerator pump shooter size has a direct affect on the initial off-line or "launch" performance. If the initial acceleration produces a hesitation, then picks up, the pump shooter size should be increased. On the other hand, if the pump shooter is too large, it can cause a bog or sluggish response from too much fuel. Another indication that the shooters are too large is a puff of black smoke on acceleration.

To alter the shooter size, you'll have to obtain a set of very small drills (approximately 0.0135 to 0.040-inch) and a pin vise. Make changes only 0.002-inch at a time. When you have a clean, instant throttle response when the throttle is opened up under a no-load condition, you'll know you have the right diameter shooter orifices.

The duration of the pump squirt can be changed by altering the duration spring tension. A weaker spring gives a longer duration, but a weaker shot of fuel. Increasing the tension on the duration spring will give a shorter but harder injection of fuel.

The capacity of the pump can be changed by boring out the pump well and using a larger diameter pump cup, but this modification must be performed by a machinist specializing in carburetor modification.

Secondary circuit

Mechanical and vacuum secondaries (Holley)

All "double-pumpers" are equipped with mechanically actuated secondaries. There isn't much to modify with this type of secondary operation. But be sure to verify that the secondary throttle plates are fully opened at wide-open throttle. If the plates don't open completely, slightly bend the secondary link in the center of the linkage to allow the throttle plates to fully open.

You can modify the performance of the vacuum secondary over a wide range of operation. Modifying the vacuum secondary diaphragm is your best bet for all around driveability and versatility. It can be adjusted for stock or high-performance conditions, for manual or automatic transmissions and for heavy or light vehicles. Changing the spring that controls the timing and speed at which the secondary throttle plates are allowed to open, adjusts the secondary plates for these conditions. Manufacturers' kits give you several choices, from a very lightweight, low resistance spring to a stiffer, slower opening spring. Here again, as in previous modifications, trial and error is still the best way to fine tune your vehicle to reach its maximum performance.

Secondary circuit (Rochester)

To modify the secondary circuit on a Quadrajet, you're pretty much limited to changing the secondary metering rods and the opening point of the air valve. Jet sizes can't be experimented with, since the secondary circuit uses fixed orifices instead of removable jets.

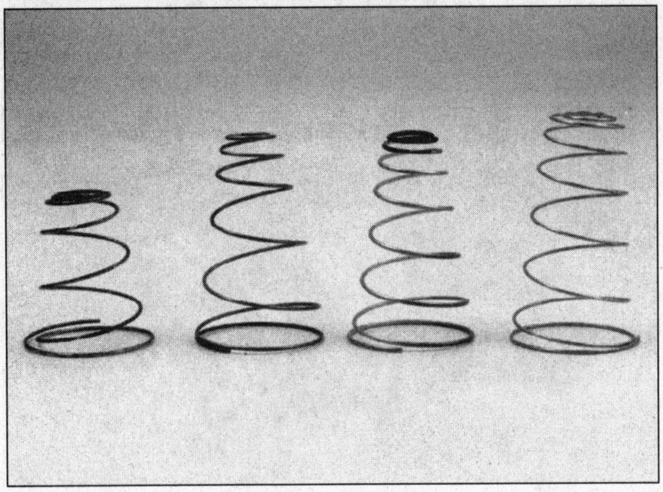

Here are four different springs for the vacuum secondary diaphragm on a Holley (there are actually seven different spring rates available). Each spring is designated by color. The colors for each spring rating and its relative load are as follows:

White - lightest
Pale Yellow - lighter
Darker yellow - light
Purple - medium light
Plain (no color) - medium
Brown - medium heavy
Black - heavy

This Allen screw (lower arrow) on a Rochester Quadrajet locks the adjusting screw (left arrow) that controls the tension on the air valve spring. Reducing the tension on this spring (loosening the adjusting screw) allows the air valve to open sooner, which in many cases is sufficient to improve throttle response and secondary operation without changing the secondary metering rods. The Allen screw must be loosened before the adjusting screw can be turned (and it must be tightened before you let go of the adjusting screw)

Before installing different secondary metering rods, try adjusting the opening point of the air valve. For high-performance applications, you'll want to adjust the air valve to open sooner, so the secondaries are actually effective in metering fuel sooner. There is an adjusting screw on the right side of the air valve shaft which controls the tension on the air valve spring. By reducing the tension on this spring, the air valve will open sooner and secondary fuel metering begins. When making this adjustment, turn the adjusting screw out about 1/8th turn at a time, until a slight bog appears as the throttle is opened, then turn the screw back in 1/8th of a turn, or enough to make the bog disappear. The bog results from a too-lean condition, caused by too much airflow through the secondaries.

There are over 90 different secondary metering rod sizes/tip profiles which will enable you to fine-tune the operating characteristics of the secondary system. Tuning the secondary side will take time and patience. You'll have to experiment with the size and shape of the tips on the rods to achieve the desired fuel metering as the secondary throttle plates begin to open and at wide-open throttle.

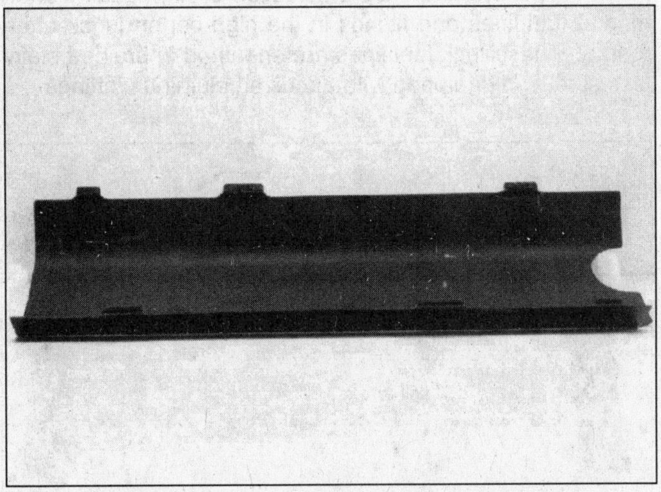

Some types of manifolds don't allow the installation of a windage tray, but most do. The advantage to these is that they keep hot oil from contacting the bottom of the manifold. The cooler you can keep the fuel mixture, the more power your engine will make

Heat

Though heat isn't a modification, if it gets out of control it will certainly modify the way the carburetor performs. The ability to cool the fuel mixture has a direct impact on the way the engine runs. The cooler the fuel mixture, the more power that can be made from that mixture, since it will be denser. There are several ways to insulate the carburetor and fuel from engine heat.

First, an aftermarket windage tray between the heads will prevent hot oil from splashing against the underside of the intake manifold and will keep the air/fuel mixture cooler as it enters the combustion chambers. The next time you remove the intake manifold, check with your local speed shop and ask whether a windage tray can be installed under the manifold on your engine.

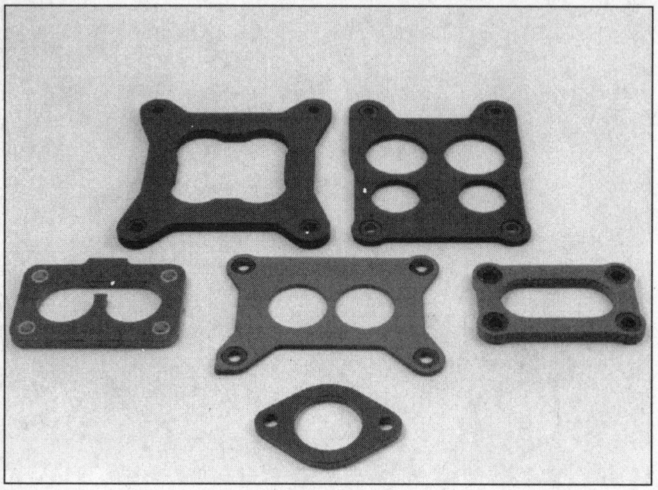

These are a few of the different types of insulator gaskets found in typical carburetor overhaul kits

Some of the insulating spacers now available are made of injection-molded plastic and come in varying thicknesses. You can find insulating spacers for both square bore and spread bore applications

Second, install an aftermarket carburetor insulator base gasket and an insulating spacer between the carburetor and the intake manifold. These are made of different types of heat insulating materials, from paper to a phenolic composite. If space allows the installation of any of these, use them to keep the carburetor (and ultimately the fuel mixture) cooler.

Third, install an aftermarket heat shield between the carburetor and the manifold. Heat shields are made of aluminum and act as a heat sink. The shield absorbs heat from the manifold and, because of its large surface area, quickly dissipates it before it reaches the carburetor.

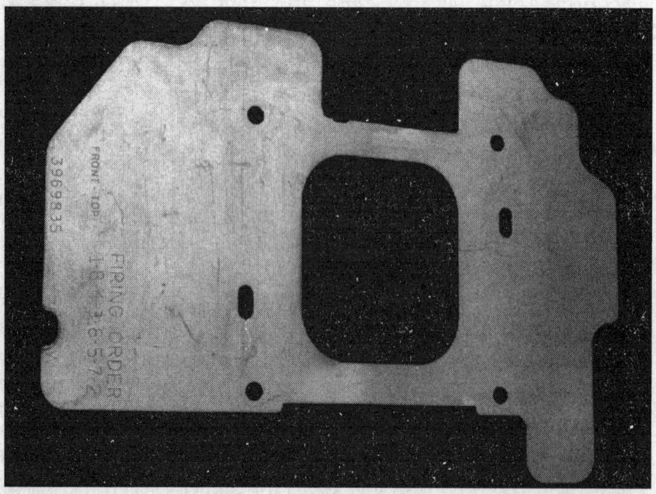

This type of insulator acts more as a cooling fin rather than an insulator. It's made from aluminum, so it absorbs heat quickly and spreads it over the large surface area, where the air passing over the exposed surface can dissipate the heat before it can all get up to the carburetor

Fourth, reroute your fuel lines away from hot components. One of the most overlooked causes of avoidable heat is the routing of the fuel lines and filters. Many people go to great lengths to buy all the right parts, and do all the trick stuff to their engine but overlook the details. Running fuel lines too close to headers or touching the engine block at some point creates a hot spot, which if severe enough can even cause vapor lock.

Fuel lines and filters

Once you have installed a high-performance carburetor, the job won't look complete unless you install new fuel line plumbing. There is a HUGE selection of high quality aftermarket fuel lines and fittings in the high-performance aftermarket. These trick fuel lines are sheathed in braided stainless steel and equipped with anodized aluminum fittings.

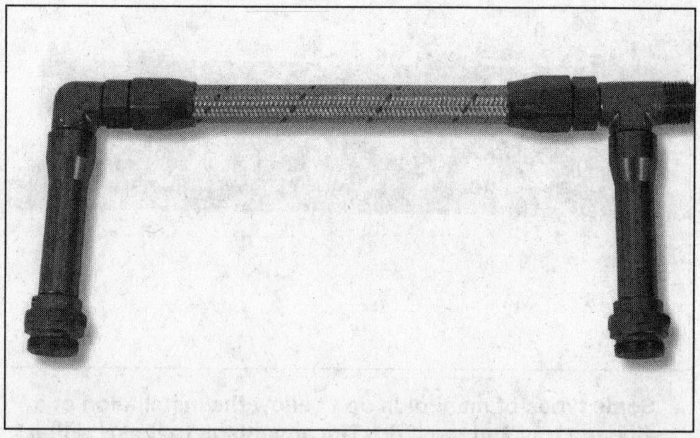

This trick Earl's fuel line plumbing, which is designed to fit a Holley double-pumper, is typical of the sort of fuel line goodies available in the high-performance aftermarket

Earl's anodized inline fuel filter features a removable, cleanable screen. In other words, you don't have to replace the fuel filter ever again

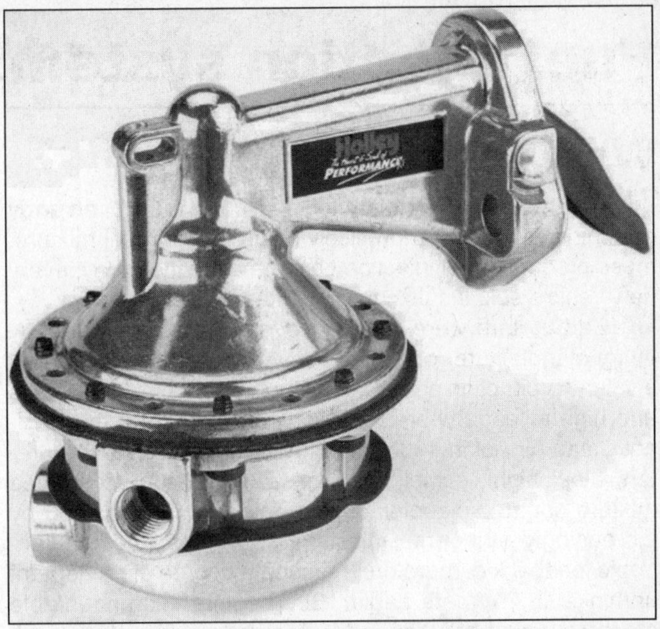

This high-performance Holley pump (this one's for a big block Mopar engine) delivers 110 gallons per hour, a lot more fuel than a stock mechanical pump, and the outlet fittings can be rotated so that the fuel lines are correctly routed

Do you need a high-performance fuel pump?

As the horsepower potential of your engine goes up, so does its need for more carburetor. The problem is that too much carburetor wastes gas, negatively affects driveability at lower engine speeds and doesn't necessarily produce any more horsepower. Once you install the right size carburetor for the modifications that you've made, you might find that the carb is too thirsty for the stock fuel pump. Mechanical fuel pumps for carbureted engines are designed to pump fuel at relatively low pressure, which is created by resistance and/or restrictions inside the fuel delivery plumbing. If you're drag racing on the weekends, your launches can generate from 1.5 to 3 G's, which imposes a hindering force on the fuel in the lines (at the G force times the weight of the fuel in the lines), which might cause the carburetor to temporarily run low on fuel. It probably won't hurt the motor but it will hurt performance. A high-performance pump can make this phenomenon a non-issue. Other factors like gallons per hour (gph) and gear ratios also affect fuel delivery. The easiest way to find out the gph of your engine is to have it professionally calculated on a dyno. This number is critical when selecting a high-performance mechanical fuel pump because aftermarket pumps are rated in terms of how many gallons of fuel per hour they can deliver.

A good way to get most or all of the performance goodies discussed in this section is to obtain a performance overhaul kit like this Holley Trick Kit. Even though these parts can be purchased separately, one of these overhaul kits gives you everything you need

Carburetor modification kits

Many of the parts used for modifications and performance tuning are available in individual kits, or you can get everything in one complete overhaul package, such as Holley's "Trick Kit." You'll find these kits at most local parts stores. So, do it yourself and learn why things really do or don't work, and in the process save yourself some money.

Remember, nothing is so small or simple that it should be overlooked or taken for granted. The details are everything - they distinguish a professional approach to doing a job versus the amateur repair that always seems to have to be done over again because of impatience and/or poor planning. Do it right and do it once.

Fuel injection systems

Why fuel injection?

With the advent of computers that could monitor an array of engine sensors and precisely control the air/fuel mixture, mass produced fuel injection became a reality. Today, every new vehicle sold in this country is fuel injected.

Carburetors were used for over 75 years by virtually every manufacturer on all but a tiny handful of special models. Low production costs and high power, not low emissions and high mileage, were the priorities. Even after the original Clean Air Act in 1963, the Big Three stuck with carburetors, albeit highly complicated units with computer-controlled mixture control solenoids. By the mid-Eighties, pushed by increasingly stringent emissions legislation, these "electronic feedback carburetors" reached a degree of refinement unthinkable 20 years earlier. But, despite this undeniable progress, time finally ran out for the venerable carburetor. It simply couldn't meet Federal or state emissions standards. There were five major problems with carburetors:

1 The venturi constriction limits the amount of mixture available at higher engine speeds, which causes power to fall off. The solutions are twofold: Either multiple carburetors, or progressively linked secondaries. The second solution is the better choice, but the result is a more complicated carburetor.

2 The distance between the carburetor and the combustion chambers results in a poorly distributed and uneven mixture. This problem is compounded by the limited amount of space usually available for the intake manifold. So the shape of the intake manifold is usually less-than-ideal for getting the air-fuel mixture to the combustion chamber.

3 Cold starts can be difficult on a carburetor-equipped vehicle. A choke mechanism helps, but because its opening angle is never a perfectly accurate response to the actual operating conditions of the engine during warm-up, it always wastes fuel and diminishes driveability. The use of a choke mechanism also necessitates the addition of a fast idle cam, which opens the throttle plate slightly while the engine is "on choke." The fast idle cam promotes a slightly faster idle during warm-up, which wastes fuel, but without it, the engine might stall.

4 Transient enrichment during acceleration is poor. When the throttle is opened suddenly, it leans out the mixture because fuel flow doesn't keep up with air velocity. The addition of an accelerator pump alleviates this problem by squirting extra fuel into the throat of the carburetor, but the pump wastes fuel and increases emissions.

5 During hard cornering, the fuel in the float bowl may try to "climb" the walls of the bowl, lowering the fuel level in the bowl, raising the float, closing the float valve and blocking fuel delivery. Properly-designed baffles installed in the float bowl can mitigate this tendency.

Fuel-injection systems have none of these problems. Fuel is metered much more precisely under all operating conditions because it's sprayed out of the injectors under pressure instead of being drawn through carburetor tubes and passages by pressure differential. When fuel is sprayed under pressure, instead of pushed by atmospheric pressure differential, fuel delivery can be increased or decreased much more rapidly and accurately. And it's because of this quick and accurate response to changing operating conditions that fuel injection has replaced the carburetor.

What is fuel injection?

There are many types of fuel injection, and some of the components differ from one system to another, but the principle is always the same: Pressurized fuel is squirted into the bore of a throttle body by one or two injectors, or directly into each intake port by an injector. Besides the injectors, most of the other components used on one injection system are found on all fuel injection systems. We'll look at each of those components in a moment. But first, let's look at what happens in a fuel injected engine: Fuel is pumped from the fuel tank by an electric fuel pump, through the fuel lines and fuel filter, to the throttle body (throttle body injection systems) or the fuel rail (port fuel injection systems), then through the fuel injector(s) into the airstream. Each injector contains a tiny valve that's opened and closed by a small solenoid. A small computer "fires" the injector by turning on this solenoid, which lifts the valve and allows the pressurized fuel to exit the injector through a precisely machined nozzle that "sprays" the fuel in a manner similar to the nozzle on your garden hose. When the computer de-energizes the solenoid, the valve closes, shutting off the spraying fuel. This cycle of operation occurs over and over, many times a second, as long as the engine is running. Injectors are designed - and warranteed - to last a very long time, at least five years or 50,000 miles. Obviously, injectors are manufactured to a very high degree of precision. Now lets look at the basic components in a typical electronic injection system.

Throttle body injection (TBI)

On throttle body injection (TBI) systems, one or two injectors are located inside a carburetor-like casting that's installed in the center of the manifold just like a carburetor. Because the fuel mist sprayed out of an injector into the airstream has better atomization properties than fuel drawn from a float bowl, and because pressurized fuel is sprayed in a consistently uniform pattern, throttle body injection systems offer better fuel economy and lower emissions than carburetors. However, because of the throttle body's centralized location, some of the air-fuel mixture can still drop out of suspension as it travels from the throttle body to the

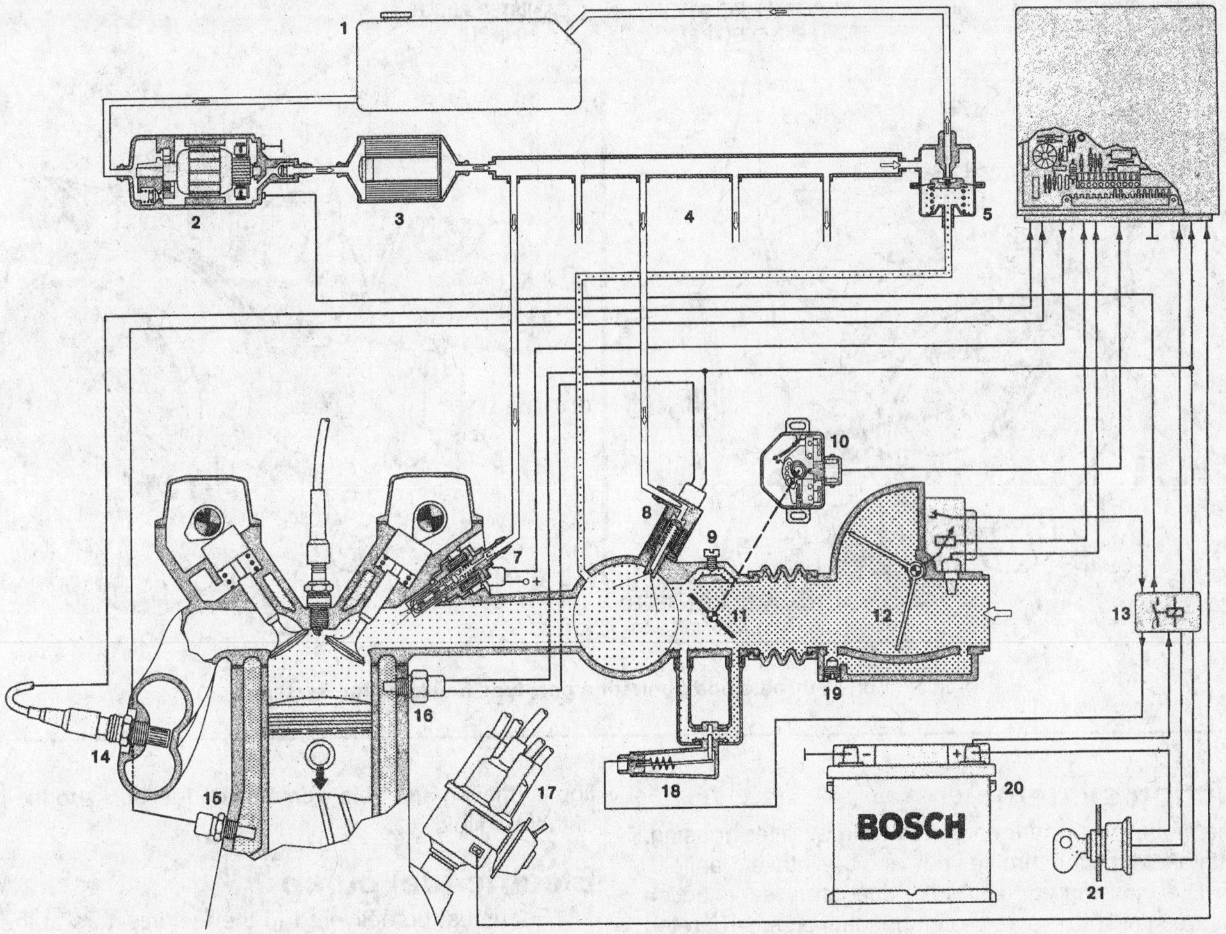

Schematic of a typical electronic port fuel injection system

1 *Fuel tank*
2 *Electric fuel pump*
3 *Fuel filter*
4 *Distributor pipe*
5 *Pressure regulator*
6 *Control unit*
7 *Injector*
8 *Cold start injector*
9 *Idle speed adjusting screw*
10 *Throttle valve switch*
11 *Throttle valve*
12 *Airflow sensor*
13 *Relay combination*
14 *Lambda (oxygen) sensor*
15 *Engine coolant temperature sensor*
16 *Thermo-time switch*
17 *Distributor*
18 *Auxiliary air valve*
19 *Idle mixture adjusting screw*
20 *Battery*
21 *Ignition switch*

intake ports, so in this sense it's not that much better than a carbureted vehicle. Still, fewer fuel droplets fall out of suspension and cling to the walls of the intake manifold, wasting less fuel and resulting in a better-than-carbureted mixture. TBI systems are a popular compromise between carburetors and port fuel injection systems because they're less expensive (they're probably cheaper than most electronic feedback carburetors), they're vastly superior to carburetors for cold starts and they offer better driveability during engine warm-up.

If you're ready to upgrade from a carburetor to fuel injection, a TBI system is far more affordable than a port fuel injection system. Edelbrock, Holley and other firms offer affordable high-quality throttle body injection systems.

Multiport electronic fuel injection

An electronic port fuel injection system uses a common fuel rail, which acts as an accumulator, or reservoir, for pressurized fuel. Eight individual electro-mechanical injectors spray this pressurized fuel directly into each intake port. Because no fuel is lost in the intake manifold, port injection systems offer better cold starts, more power, better mileage and lower emissions than throttle body injection systems.

Now let's look at the typical components found in an electronic fuel injection system.

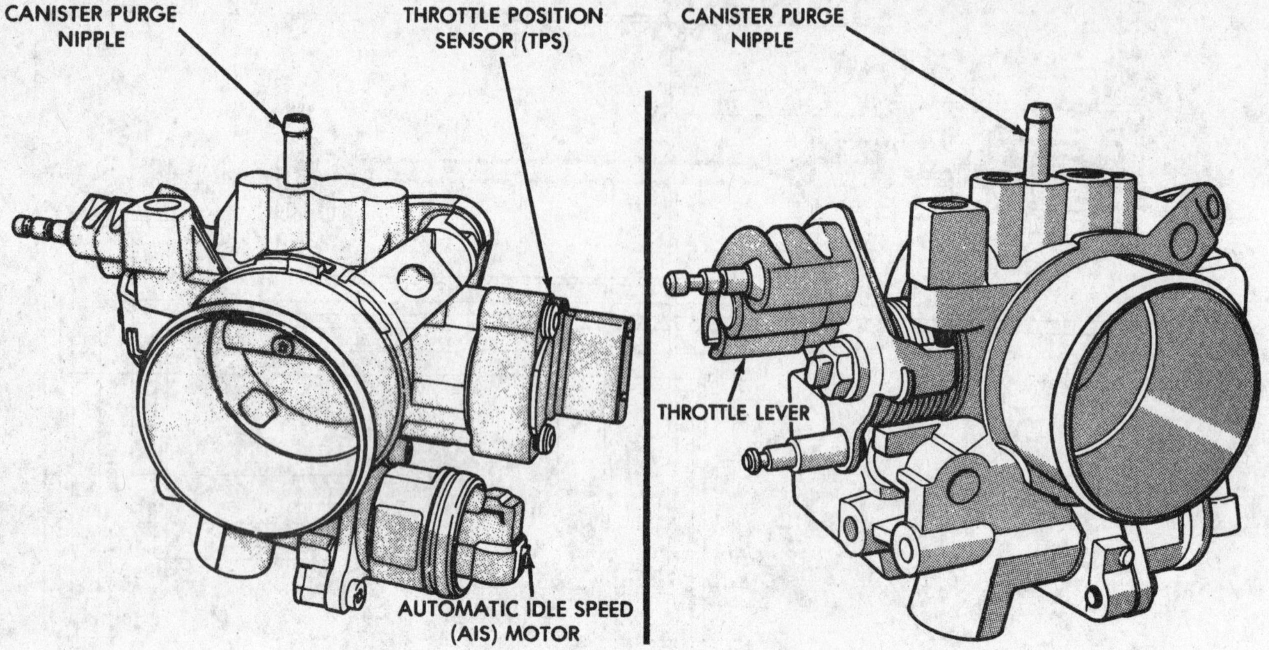

Typical (Mopar) throttle body unit for a port-type fuel injection system

Induction system

The induction system consists of the air filter housing, the air intake duct, the throttle body and the intake manifold. The air filter housing and air intake duct on a fuel injection system are similar to the same components on a carbureted engine. The throttle body, unlike a carburetor, controls only airflow. The throttle body is a relatively simple casting with a large throttle plate inside. Some throttle bodies are a two-barrel design with two throttle plates. On some units the second plate is opened by a progressive linkage in a similar fashion to progressive linkage on a four-barrel carburetor. Typically, the throttle body is also used as a source of intake manifold vacuum, so there are often several vacuum hoses connected to small pipes that are plumbed into the area just downstream from the throttle plate(s). Many other devices, such as the idle air control valve and Manifold Absolute Pressure (MAP) sensor, are also located on the throttle body.

The intake manifold on a fuel injection system is significantly different from the manifold used with a carburetor. The typical fuel injection manifold has a large air reservoir, known as a plenum, between the throttle body and the eight individual intake runners for each cylinder intake port. A fuel injector mounting hole is machined into each of these intake runners so that fuel is sprayed directly into the intake port just upstream from the intake valve. The advantage of this design is that it solves the vaporization problem of carburetors. When fuel is pumped into the injectors at 45 or more psi, then sprayed as a fine mist into the intake ports, the surrounding metal is significantly hotter than the inside of the intake manifold. Vaporization is far superior to the kind of distribution you get with a carburetor, where the fuel distribution is uneven and gets worse when fuel sticks to the inside of the manifold.

Electric fuel pump

Fuel must be delivered to the fuel injectors at the right pressure, in the right volume and within a fairly consistent temperature range. There must be no fuel vapor or air bubbles in the fuel at the point of delivery. The electric fuel pump, with a little help from the fuel pressure regulator, makes all this happen.

Electric fuel pumps have a number of advantages over mechanical pumps:

1 A mechanical pump, because it's driven by the camshaft or crankshaft, must be bolted to the block. An electric fuel pump can be located anywhere.

2 The speed at which a mechanical pump operates is determined by engine speed - it pumps more slowly at idle, more quickly at higher rpm. An electric pump runs at a constant speed.

3 Engine heat is transferred through a mechanical pump to the fuel. This doesn't happen with an electric pump, which is actually cooled and lubricated by the fuel passing through it.

4 A mechanical pump must create a strong enough vacuum to draw the fuel from the tank, through the fuel filter, through the fuel lines, and into the float bowl of the carburetor. An electric pump pushes fuel to the injectors;

5 An electric pump can be insulated to reduce noise; it can also be located inside the fuel tank, for further noise reduction.

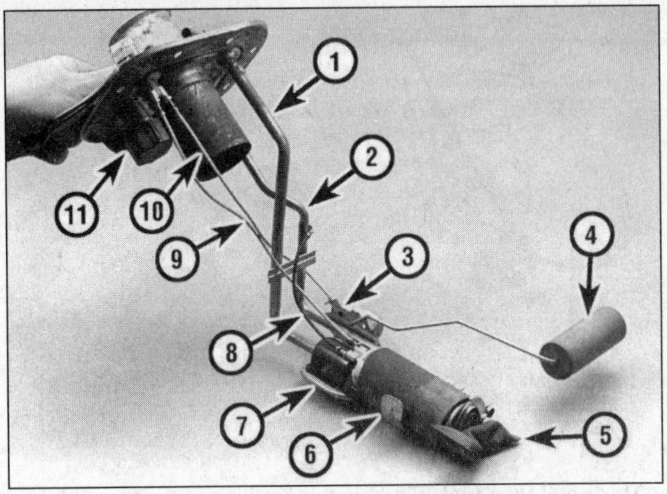

A typical in-tank fuel pump assembly

1 Fuel feed line
2 Fuel return line
3 Fuel level sender
4 Fuel level float
5 Fuel pump intake strainer
6 Fuel pump
7 Pulsation damper
8 Fuel pump ground wire
9 Fuel pump hot wire
10 Fuel level sender hot wire
11 Splash cup liquid vapor separator

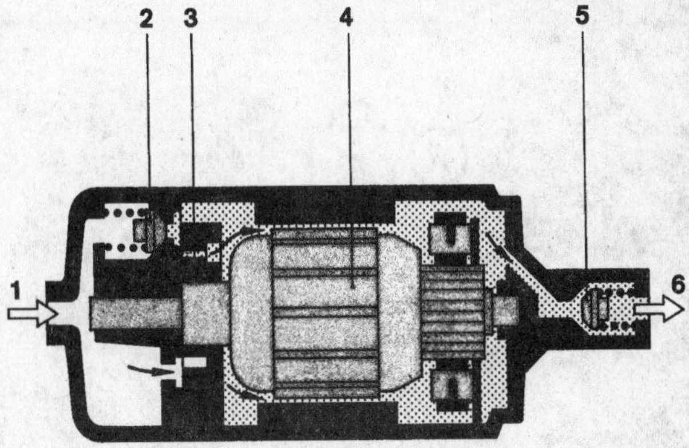

Cutaway of a typical electric fuel pump for a fuel injection system

1 Fuel inlet
2 Pressure relief valve
3 Roller cell pump
4 Electric motor armature
5 Non-return valve
6 Fuel outlet

Now, let's look at how the typical pump works: Most electric fuel pumps are the roller vane type, consisting of an electric motor and a rotor inside an integral housing. The rotor has pockets (slots) machined into its outer circumference. A roller (something like a roller bearing) is installed in each pocket. The diameter of the roller is only a few thousandths of an inch less than the distance between the walls of the pocket. Which means the roller is free to move up and down - but not sideways - in its pocket. As the rotor is turned by the electric motor, the rollers are forced outward by centrifugal force, and roll along the inside wall of the pump housing. Because the bearing surfaces (the sides) of the rollers contact both the pump housing wall and the pocket walls, they create a seal. The rotor itself is round, but the pump housing is an oblong shape which allows the rollers to move out farther from the rotor on the suction side than they do on the pressure side. In other words, the space between the rotor and the pump housing on the suction side is larger than the space between the rotor and the housing on the pressure side. So as the rotor turns, a pressure differential, or vacuum, is created on the suction side of the pump.

Air pressure inside the top of the fuel tank is pushing against the surface of the fuel. This is what forces the fuel into that low-pressure area at the suction side of the pump. As the rotor continues to rotate, fuel is trapped in the space between the two adjacent rollers, the rotor and the housing. As this space moves closer to the pressure side, it gets smaller and smaller, raising the pressure of the fuel, which is finally forced out the pump outlet. Of course, when this little sequence is repeated 3500 to 4500 times per minute (the speed of the typical pump), a good deal of pressure can be created. A spring-loaded check valve near the pump outlet maintains fuel pressure at whatever level it's adjusted for at the factory. The check valve also prevents the fuel pressure from reaching a level so high that it might damage some part of the system.

These pumps can develop a lot of heat. The rollers, which are the hottest parts, are cooled and lubricated by the fuel itself as it travels through the pump. Fuel is even pumped through the electric motor part of the pump, to help cool the motor.

The electric motor uses permanent magnets to create a stationary magnetic field. The armature (the part of the motor that turns) is wound with wire and has a commutator section which gets its current from brushes. The typical pump operates at speeds of 3500 to 4500 rpm. The outlet pressure can be set as low as 10 psi for some throttle body injection systems, to as high as 60 or more psi for some high-performance port-injection systems.

Fuel injection systems are equipped with at least one electric fuel pump. Some systems have two pumps: a transfer pump inside the fuel tank (to prevent cavitation), and a main pump outside the tank. Some GM pumps accomplish the same thing with only one pump by adding an impeller, or centrifugal, pump to the roller vane type described above. The impeller separates vapor out of the fuel before it's delivered to the roller vane pump. And it adds some pressure to the fuel before it enters the roller vane section, thus ensuring a consistent output pressure.

Pressurized fuel is pumped through the fuel filter, fuel lines, fuel rail (port injection) and out the injectors. Because the pump delivers more fuel than the injectors can use, the excess fuel is returned to the fuel tank via the fuel pressure regulator and a return line.

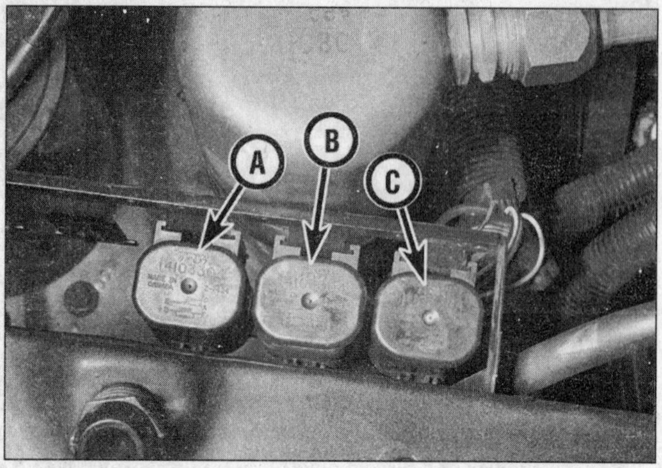

The typical fuel pump relay usually - but not always - looks like a small plastic or metal box. The fuel pump relay (A) shown here, on a GM vehicle, is right next to the cooling fan relay (B) and the air conditioning relay (C). If you have difficulty finding the fuel pump relay, refer to your Haynes Automotive Repair Manual

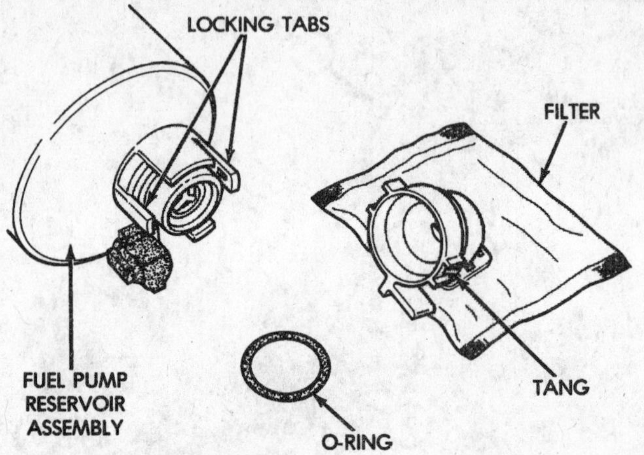

This sock-type fuel "filter" is the first line of defense for the fuel injection system; it protects the pump itself from debris in the bottom of the fuel tank

Fuel pump relay

The electric motor in a fuel pump draws several amperes of current. The pump motor is turned on, controlled and turned off by the fuel injection or engine management computer. The pump current is too high for the circuitry in the computer to handle. So a relay is used for the actual switching. The computer simply controls the relay. A relay is an electrically operated switch with an input magnetic coil, an armature (spring arm) and output switch contacts. Fine wire is wound around the laminated iron core of the input coil. The laminated core increases the coil's magnetic field strength. The armature is a spring-loaded iron bar in close proximity to the electromagnet. The armature arm itself is usually the spring. The armature is electrically insulated from the relay base.

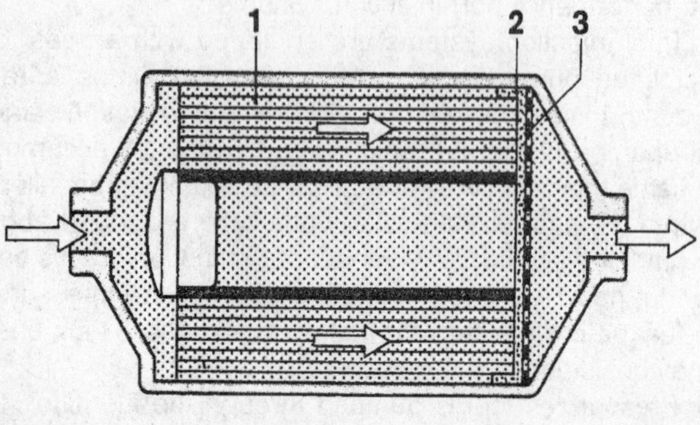

Cutaway of a typical fuel filter

1 *Paper element*
2 *Strainer*
3 *Supporting plate*

One electrical output contact is attached to the armature; the other output contact is mounted on a stationary arm. Power from the battery is always available to the stationary arm contact. When the computer sends a small current through the electromagnet coil, its magnetic field pulls down the armature arm, the two contacts close and the large current needed to run the fuel pump moves through the contacts. The relay allows battery current to go to the fuel pump without going through the ignition switch or computer.

Fuel pump relays can be located almost anywhere in the engine compartment or in the passenger area. If you can't find the fuel pump relay, check the owner's manual, or refer to your Haynes Automotive Repair Manual.

Fuel filter

There are actually two types of fuel filters. The first type is a woven plastic screen, strainer or "sock," located inside the fuel tank at the inlet end of the fuel pump. These filters must have a known, uniform porosity. In other words, they must possess a specified ability to stop materials down to a certain size. That size is usually expressed in microns. A micron is 4/1,000,000 of an inch (0.00000394 inch).The screen/strainer/sock type filter has a porosity of about 70 microns. This type of filter isn't usually replaced as a maintenance item, but should the tank ever be filled with dirty gasoline, it could become clogged. If this happens, the filter must be removed and cleaned, or replaced.

The other type of fuel filter is a replaceable metal canister which must be changed at the interval specified by the manufacturer. This filter contains a porous material that allows fuel - but not solid particles - to pass through. The filter element in a fuel filter is usually a fibrous or paper-like material; some filters even use a porous metal. A filter must be able to do several things. It must let the fuel pass through, yet it must catch all particles of dirt above a certain size, and it must prevent these particles from working their way through the filter for the service life of the filter.

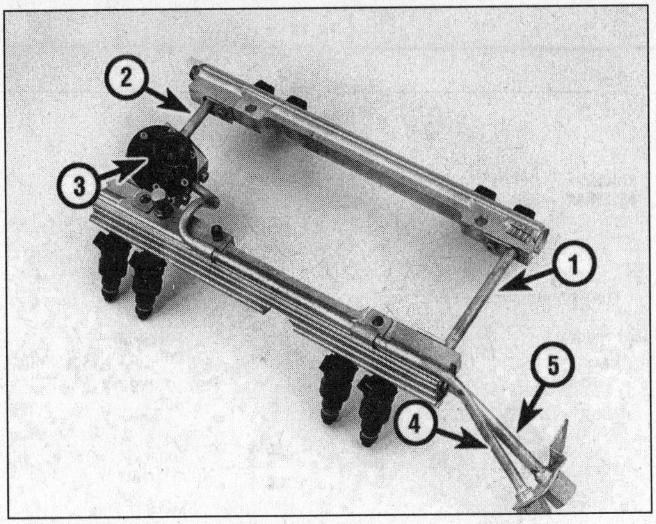

Components of a typical fuel rail assembly (Chevy Corvette)

1 *Front crossover tube*
2 *Rear crossover tube*
3 *Fuel pressure regulator*
4 *Fuel outlet pipe*
5 *Fuel inlet pipe*

The engine can't run without the proper supply of fuel at the right pressure. So the size of the filter pores must be large enough to allow fuel to flow through easily. Yet the pores must be small enough to trap dirt that will damage or clog the fuel injectors. Typically, the best compromise is around 10 to 20 microns.

Filters hold on to the dirt by using a chemically-treated porous paper. The chemical treatment makes the paper sticky. When a particle of dirt contacts the paper, it's unable to break free. The filter element is also folded into an accordion shape to increase the surface area of the filter and help trap dirt particles in the folds so they can't break loose. The increased surface area afforded by the accordion arrangement also means fuel can pass through easily even if part of the filter becomes clogged.

Over the last decade, more and more manufacturers have begun integrating the fuel filter into the fuel pump/fuel level sending unit module. The easiest way to determine the location and type of fuel filter used (and its location) on your fuel injection system is to refer to the Haynes repair manual for your vehicle.

Fuel pulsation damper

This device is similar in appearance to a fuel pressure regulator, except that it has no vacuum pipe. It's usually mounted at the fuel inlet line-to-fuel rail connection. A spring-loaded diaphragm inside the damper smoothes out the rhythmical pressure surges from the fuel pump. Think of it as a shock absorber for fuel pump pulsations. Pulsation dampers were once common on fuel injection systems but have all but disappeared over the last few years.

A typical throttle-body injector; compared to port-type fuel injectors, throttle body injectors are usually shorter and larger in diameter, just like this unit

Fuel rail

The fuel rail serves two purposes. It's a pressurized reservoir for delivering fuel to the injectors, and it stabilizes the fuel pressure at the injectors. The pressure rapidly rises and falls inside the fuel rail as the injectors open and close. If the volume inside the fuel rail is too small, this rapidly fluctuating pressure can affect the amount of fuel injected. On older tubular type fuel rails - they look sort of like big fuel lines - the fuel pressure fluctuates wildly as the injectors open and close because the interior volume of these units is too small. But most manufacturers have responded by installing larger fuel rails with greater volume. On these newer, larger units - usually generously oversized square section aluminum tubing - pressure is steadier at the injectors. If you elect to replace a carburetor or TBI system on your engine with a modern aftermarket port fuel injection system, the fuel rail volume will be even larger than an OEM fuel rail, and more than adequate for whatever modifications you make.

Fuel injectors

A throttle-body type injector is installed in the mouth of the throttle body. Port-type fuel injectors are installed between the fuel rail and the intake port. The upper end of

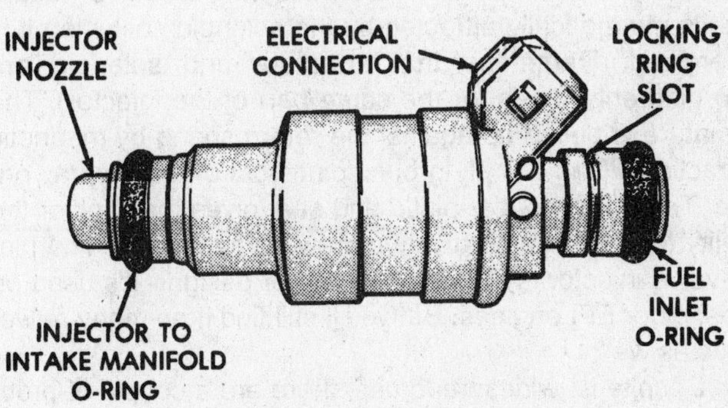

A typical electronic port-type fuel injector

each port injector is press-fitted into the fuel rail; an O-ring forms a seal between the injector and the fuel rail. The lower end is also fitted with some sort of O-ring or sealing ring that's supposed to prevent air leaks and protect the injectors from heat and vibration (if these lower O-rings crack, air leaks into the combustion chamber, leans out the mixture and increases idle rpm). Most injectors are protected internally by an inlet fuel screen or filter in the fitting for the fuel line connection.

An injector is a solenoid valve. Inside the injector, a coil surrounds a metal armature. On signal from the electronic control unit, current flows through the coil, creating a strong magnetic field. This magnetic field pulls the solenoid toward the armature, compressing the return spring. A needle valve is attached to, or is part of, the solenoid. When the solenoid moves up, the needle valve is lifted off its seat, allowing the pressurized fuel inside the injector to spray out through the orifice or nozzle. A pintle on the tip of the needle valve helps to atomize and distribute the fuel; the shape of the needle, the valve seat, the pintle and the nozzle all determine the spray pattern. When the control unit cuts the current to the injector, the field collapses and spring force slams the valve shut. Some older solenoids must lift up about 10 to 30 thousandths of an inch to open the valve; they take about 2 milliseconds to do so. The lift on some newer injectors is as little as 0.006-inch; opening time on these low-lift units is about 1 millisecond. Because the distance it must travel is so short, the valve responds very quickly. An injector may be held open for as long as 20 milliseconds. Fuel is delivered to the injector at a relatively constant pressure, so the longer the valve is open, the more fuel will be sprayed out. Very precise fuel delivery control is possible with injectors.

The injector(s) in throttle body injection systems are somewhat larger in size than the typical port injector. They must deliver more fuel at a given time because they must serve either all of the engine cylinders (single injector) or half of the engine cylinders (dual injector). The spray pattern is usually broader too.

Electronic solenoid injectors all work the same way. Their differences are primarily in the area of valve design, so that's how injectors are usually classified. Three basic types of injector valves have emerged as the most common on modern vehicles.

The pintle-valve injector uses a spring-loaded armature that is magnetically attracted by the solenoid coil when it is energized. (Remember that "armature" and "solenoid" are two different names for the same part of the injector). The armature is pulled up against the return spring by magnetic attraction, lifting a finely-ground pintle out of a tiny spray orifice. The design of the pintle and seat gives the injector the ability to provide a relatively narrow spray pattern. The pintle-valve injector is the original injector design - it's used on most older EFI engines. But you'll still find it on many newer ones as well.

Despite its widespread use, there are a couple of problems with the pintle-valve injector. First, because of the small contact surface area between the needle and the valve seat,

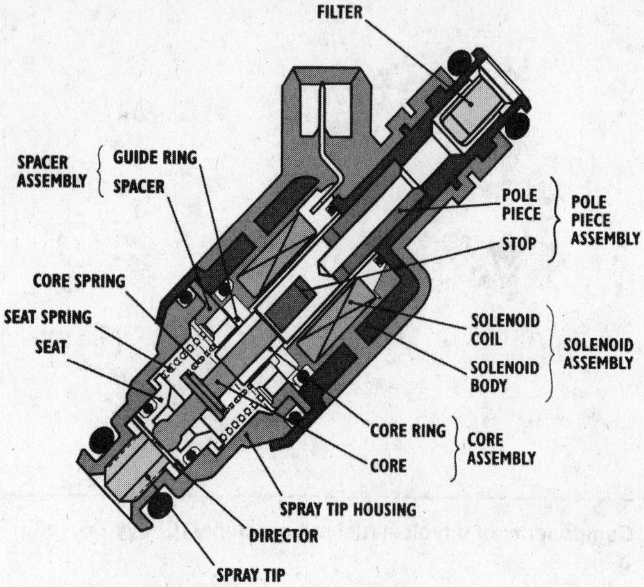

Cutaway view of a typical injector

even modest fuel deposits which build up in those areas can create a major restriction to fuel flow through the orifice, which eventually leads to lean fuel delivery problems. Second, the armatures on pintle-valve injectors are usually heavier and larger than the valves used in other injector designs. So their response time is slower. And wear is greater, so the service life of the typical pintle valve injector is shorter than that of other designs.

The ball-type injector is typically used in throttle body injection systems. The electrical part of a ball-type injector is similar to that of a pintle-valve injector. But its armature (solenoid) is smaller and has a rounded valve tip that mates with a conical seat.

The ball-type injector has several things going for it. The smaller armature design of the ball-type injector allows quicker response time and means less seat wear and fuel fouling. The spray pattern is typically wider. The multiple-orifice design (there are six orifices in the unit shown in the accompanying illustrations) also allows a higher fuel flow rate for a given firing time. And more fuel can be delivered while the valve is open.

The disk-type injector looks similar to pintle-valve and ball-type injectors, except it doesn't have an armature. The magnetic field produced by the coil is directed toward the valve area by the shape of the injector core. The valve itself is a disk-and-seat arrangement with the spray orifice in the center of the seat.

The disk in this type of injector is a much smaller mass to move with a magnetic field, so it's able to respond more quickly. Because of its lighter weight, less spring tension is needed to return the disk to the seat to stop fuel flow. Which means the disk doesn't slam down with as much force when the coil is de-energized. And the greater contact surface

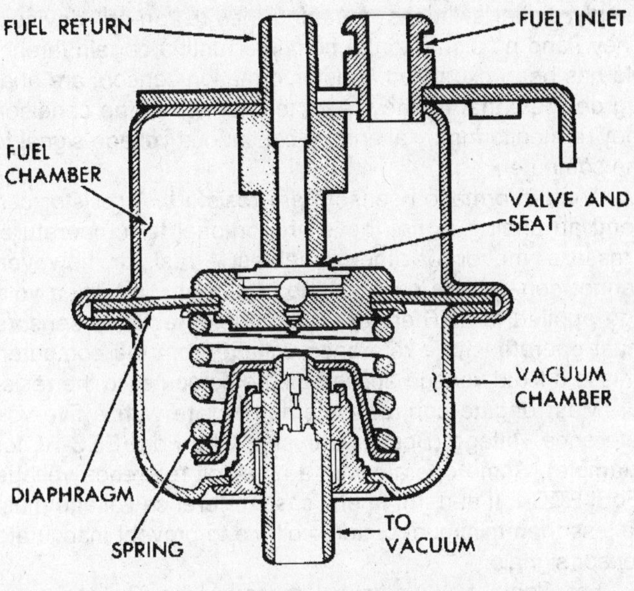

Cutaway of a typical fuel pressure regulator assembly

area between the disk and the seat reduces point-to-point contact pressure. This design seems to resist the build-up of fuel deposits better than other injector designs. And even when such deposits do occur, they don't restrict fuel flow as significantly as in other designs.

If you're shopping for aftermarket high-performance injectors, Edelbrock, FAST and Holley all offer performance injectors that will deliver faster throttle response and better fuel atomization than stock injectors. But make sure that the injectors you're considering are an appropriate drop-in replacement for your stock fuel rail and the engine management computer. For example, the low-impedance injectors offered by some aftermarket manufacturers are intended only for highly modified engines with turbos, blowers, nitrous, etc. They're also incompatible with the stock computer, and will quickly destroy it. If you're going to install low-impedance injectors you must also install a high-performance computer, specially designed to work with these injectors. Besides, do you really need 160 pounds/hour of fuel delivery?! Be realistic. High-impedance injectors can deliver up to 60 pounds/hour and work just fine with the stock computer.

Fuel pressure regulator

The fuel pressure regulator alters the fuel pressure in accordance with engine operating conditions, such as changes in manifold pressure or vacuum.

The fuel pressure regulator on a conventional return-type fuel injection system is a fairly simple device. It consists of a metal housing with a spring-loaded diaphragm and a valve attached to the fuel side of the diaphragm. A fuel inlet tube directs fuel to the valve; the inlet tube and the fuel side of the housing are usually an integral piece. An outlet pipe extends into the fuel side of the housing and serves as the seat for the valve. When the valve is seated, fuel is blocked; when it's open, fuel flows through the outlet pipe. A vacuum hose connects the back (spring) side of the diaphragm housing to the intake manifold.

Here's how it works: Fuel from the pump fills the fuel lines, the fuel rail, the fuel injectors and the fuel side of the pressure regulator. The diaphragm spring, which holds the valve against its seat, is designed to compress when the pressure against the diaphragm reaches the upper limit of the operating range of the system. When fuel pressure exceeds this upper limit, the diaphragm is pushed back against the compressed spring. The valve, which is attached to the diaphragm, is lifted off its seat, and fuel flows through the outlet pipe and returns to the fuel tank. As fuel flows out of the regulator, the fuel pressure in the fuel rail and the regulator drops back within its operating range, and below spring pressure. The spring pushes the diaphragm back to its normal position, seating the valve and blocking fuel flow.

The vacuum or pressure port on the back side of the diaphragm also affects the total force applied against the diaphragm. If pressure from the intake manifold is routed through the port to the back side of the diaphragm, it acts like an extra spring applying additional force to the diaphragm; it will take a higher fuel pressure to open the regulator valve. Until that higher pressure is reached, the fuel pressure at the injector nozzles is higher - so they spray more fuel in a given amount of time, resulting in a richer air-fuel mixture.

Let's look at some typical examples: At low speed, the throttle is only partially open, so there's a vacuum in the intake manifold. A vacuum signal is transmitted to the pressure regulator, lowering the pressure on the spring side of the diaphragm. Less fuel pressure is needed to push the diaphragm against its spring and open the regulator valve, which means less fuel will be sprayed out the injector nozzles. But when you step on the gas, the throttle plates open, intake manifold vacuum drops, the vacuum signal to the regulator vanishes, and there's greater pressure pushing against the diaphragm. Now it takes more pressure to push the diaphragm against its spring, so the valve stays seated until a higher pressure is reached. In the meantime, the injector nozzles have more fuel pressure available, resulting in a richer air-fuel mixture.

The vacuum line between the manifold and the pressure regulator on turbocharged vehicles carry pressure as well as vacuum. When you mash the throttle on a turbo, the engine revs build, the turbo pumps air into the intake manifold and pressure in the manifold goes up to, say, seven pounds of boost. A seven psi pressure signal is transmitted to the pressure regulator through the connecting hose from the intake manifold - so the valve in the regulator has an extra seven pounds psi forcing it closed. Which means more fuel pressure will be needed to overcome the pressure holding the regulator valve closed. So the fuel pressure at the injectors increases, and more fuel is sprayed through the injector nozzles each time they're opened. The result is a richer mixture, which is just what a turbocharged vehicle needs under boost conditions.

On returnless systems the pressure regulator is an integral component of the fuel pump/fuel level sending unit module inside the fuel tank. Anytime the line fuel pressure gets too high, it forces the spring-loaded pressure regulator to open and the excess fuel is dumped back into the tank.

Fuel hoses and lines

Pressurization of the fuel provides a nice spray pattern at each injector nozzle, but it poses special problems for fuel hoses and lines. The pressure in a carbureted system is typically no more than 4 to 6 psi, but a throttle body injection system is typically pressurized to around 9 to 15 psi, and a port fuel injection system to about 30 to 50 psi. This is why fuel injection systems use specially designed fuel hoses and lines to connect components like the fuel pump, fuel filter, accumulator and fuel rail (port systems) or throttle body (TBI systems). Fuel-injected vehicles use rigid steel tubing under the vehicle, which can be securely attached to the frame or pan. Steel lines can withstand high pressure easily. They're also coated or plated to resist corrosion. If you ever have to replace metal fuel lines, don't substitute copper or aluminum - they'll crack.

Flexible synthetic hoses are used for bridging the gap between the rigidly mounted steel fuel lines and the fuel injection system. Because the engine shakes and vibrates, it's not feasible to run metal lines directly to the fuel injection system. Two types of flexible hoses are used. One type has three layers: The inner layer is a fuel-resistant, rubber-like, synthetic material made by DuPont. This material, known commercially as Neoprene, doesn't swell or dissolve when it comes in contact with fuel the way rubber does. The next layer is a woven polyester fabric which gives the hose strength against pressure and flexing. The outer layer of the hose is another synthetic rubber material, such as Hypalon, which allows it to resist abrasion and weathering. The other type of "hose" is really an extruded plastic (nylon) tubing. Nylon tubing is commonly found on fuel-injected vehicles because of its ability to withstand higher pressures.

There are many types of hoses designed for different applications on automobiles. When servicing a fuel-injected vehicle, NEVER substitute hoses or lines designed for use on carbureted vehicles. Fuel hoses designed for low-pressure systems will not stand up to the higher operating pressures of fuel injection systems. Always use the same type and size hose or line specified by the manufacturer.

Input: Information sensors

A sensor is an input device that converts one form of energy to another. Since a computer can only read voltage signals, an information sensor must convert motion, pressure, temperature, light and other forms of energy to voltage. Automobile sensors come in many forms - switches, timers, resistors, transformers and generators. Sensors monitor various engine operating conditions such as air flow, air mass, air temperature, coolant temperature, exhaust oxygen content, manifold absolute pressure, throttle position, etc. and transmit this information to a computer in the form of low-voltage signals. Some information sensors are simply digital switches, meaning they're "on-off" devices. They send no signal to the computer until a certain threshold has been exceeded. Most information sensors are analog devices, that is, they react to changes in the condition they're monitoring by altering a continuous voltage signal to the computer.

Most information sensors are resistors. A resistor can send an analog signal that's proportional to temperature, pressure, motion or other variables. A resistor, however, cannot generate its own voltage. It can only modify a voltage applied to it. Therefore, automobile resistive sensors must operate with a reference voltage from the computer. This is a fixed voltage applied by the computer to the resistor. Most engine control systems operate with a five-volt reference voltage (Bosch, Chrysler, GM, Ford EEC-IV, for example). Some operate with a nine-volt reference voltage (Ford EEC-I, II and III). In any case, reference voltage must be less than minimum battery voltage to prevent inaccurate sensor signals.

Let's look at how a typical sensor works: The computer sends a reference voltage to the sensor. As sensor resistance changes, so does the return voltage. Let's assume that a temperature sensor can be calibrated to send a 0-volt return signal at 0-degrees F, and a 5-volt return signal at 250-degrees F. Every 1-degree temperature change causes a 0.02-volt change in the return voltage. The computer reads these 20-millivolt increments and computes them to "air temperature" or "engine coolant temperature."

Manifold Absolute Pressure (MAP) sensor

The MAP sensor monitors the pressure or vacuum downstream from the throttle plate, inside the intake manifold. The MAP sensor measures intake manifold pressure

A typical (Chevy) MAP sensor

1 MAP sensor
2 Mounting screws
3 MAP sensor vacuum line
4 MAP sensor electrical connector

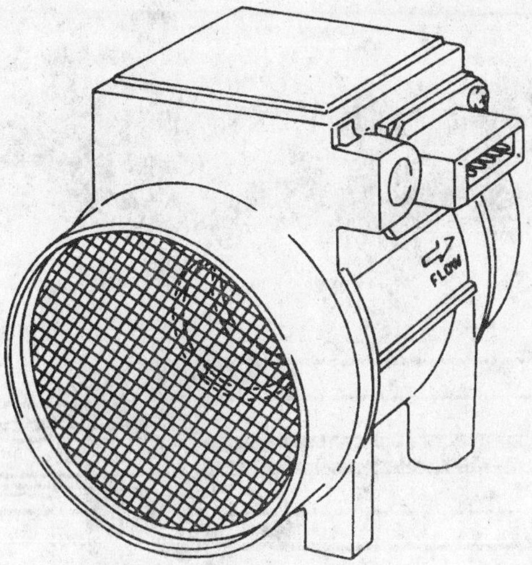

Typical Mass Air Flow (MAF) sensor

and vacuum on the absolute scale (from zero instead of from sea-level atmospheric pressure [14.7 psi]). The MAP sensor converts the absolute pressure into a variable voltage signal that changes with the pressure. The computer uses this data to determine engine load so that it can alter the ignition advance and fuel enrichment.

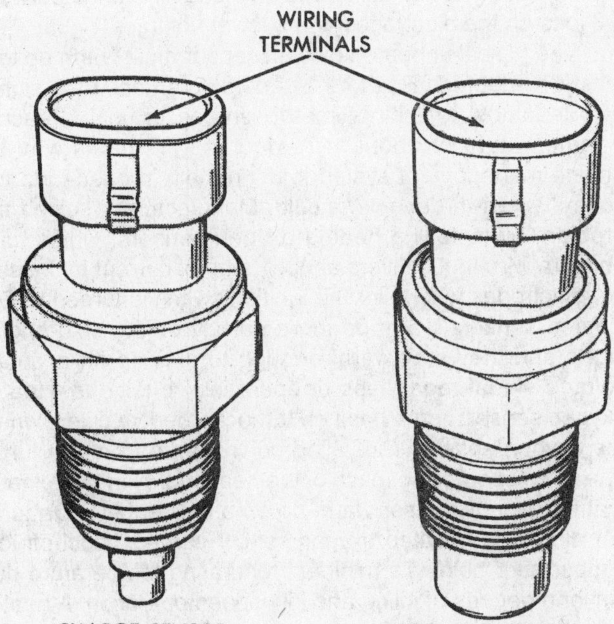

Typical Intake Air Temperature (IAT), or air charge, temperature sensor (left) and Engine Coolant Temperature (ECT) sensor (right). IAT and ECT sensors are used on virtually all fuel-injected vehicles

The manifold pressure sensor has a couple of corrective features to account for differences in temperature and altitude. An air-temperature sensor signals the control unit to correct the injector pulse width for colder, denser air. Altitude compensation is provided by the venting of one cell to the atmosphere. In the part-load range, both manifold pressure and atmospheric pressure are reduced as the altitude increases, so the fuel injection signal must be adjusted for the thinner air.

Most manufacturers no longer regard manifold-pressure sensing as a sufficiently accurate measurement of engine load. Modern systems measure air flow or measure air mass.

Mass Air Flow (MAF) sensor

The MAF sensor is another means by which an engine management computer can measure the amount of intake air drawn into the engine. It uses a hot-wire sensing element, which is constantly maintained at a specified temperature above the ambient temperature of the incoming air by electrical current. As intake air passes through the MAF sensor and over the hot wire, it cools the wire, and the control system immediately corrects the temperature back to its constant value. The current required to maintain the constant value is used by the PCM to determine the amount of air flowing through the MAF sensor.

Air and coolant temperature sensors

All fuel injection systems use temperature sensors to measure air and engine coolant (or cylinder head) temperature because temperature affects intake air density and air-fuel mixture ratio. Most temperature sensors are thermistors. A thermistor is a special kind of variable resistor whose resistance changes with changes in temperature. Most are Negative Temperature Coefficient (NTC) resistors, which means their resistance decreases as the temperature increases.

The bimetal element used in a thermistor has a highly predictable and repeatable property: The amount of current and voltage it conducts at a certain temperature is always the same. This characteristic makes the thermistor an excellent analog temperature sensor. As the temperature increases, the resistance decreases, and the current and voltage increase. The control unit uses this rising voltage signal, along with signals from other sensors, to alter the injector pulse width or the fuel pressure as the engine warms up.

Air temperature sensors are referred to as Intake Air Temperature (IAT) sensors. Coolant temperature sensors are known as Engine Coolant Temperature (ECT) sensors. Cylinder Head Temperature (CHT) sensors are used instead of ECT sensors on some Ford engines. IAT sensors are always located somewhere on the air filter housing, the intake air duct or the intake manifold. ECT sensors are always screwed into a coolant passage, usually near the thermostat or on the intake manifold. CHT sensors are simply screwed into the cylinder heads.

Oxygen sensor

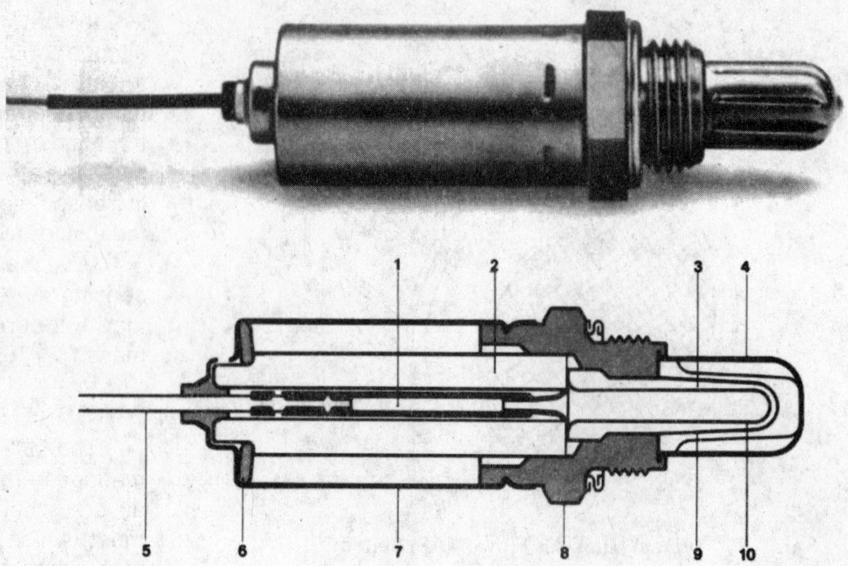

Typical oxygen sensor (also known as a Lambda sensor or simply an O2 sensor)

1 Contact
2 Supporting ceramic
3 Sensor ceramic
4 Protective tube (exhaust side)
5 Electrical connection
6 Disc spring
7 Protective sleeve (air side)
8 Housing (-)
9 Electrode (-)
10 Electrode (+)

The oxygen sensor, or sensors (1996 and later vehicles have two, three or four of them), is the most important information sensor on a fuel-injected vehicle. The oxygen sensor compares the difference between the amount of oxygen in the exhaust and the amount of oxygen in the ambient air, and it expresses the results of this comparison as an analog voltage signal that varies between 0 and 1 volt.

The oxygen sensor is based on the lambda concept pioneered by the Robert Bosch Corporation (Bosch still calls the oxygen sensor a lambda sensor). Lambda is the Greek symbol which engineers use to indicate the ratio of one number to another. When discussing the control of the air-fuel ratio, lambda refers to the ratio of excess air to stoichiometric air quantity.

At the stoichiometric (ideal) air-fuel ratio of 14.7:1, the maximum amount of air available combines with fuel. There's no air left over, and there's no shortage of air. Lambda, therefore, equals 1. But if the mixture ratio is lean, say 15, 16 or 17:1, there's air left over after combustion. The lambda ratio of excess air to the ideal amount of air is now greater than 1, say, 1.05, 1.09, 1.13, etc. And if the mixture is rich, say 12, 13 or 14:1, there's a shortage of air, so the lambda ratio is less than 1, say, 0.95, 0.91, 0.87, etc. If the air-fuel ratio is richer than 11.7:1 or leaner than 18:1 (lambda ratios of less than 0.8 or greater than 1.20, respectively) the engine won't run.

The oxygen sensor is really a galvanic battery which generates a low-voltage signal between 0.1 and 0.9 volt (100 to 900 millivolts). When oxygen content in the exhaust is low (rich mixture), sensor voltage is high (450 to 900 millivolts). When exhaust oxygen content is high (lean mixture), sensor voltage is low (100 to 450 millivolts). The oxygen sensor voltage changes fastest near a lambda ratio of 1 (air-fuel ratio of 14.7:1), making it ideal for maintaining a stoichiometric ratio.

The oxygen sensor consists of two platinum electrodes separated by a zirconium dioxide (ZrO_2) ceramic electrolyte. ZrO_2 attracts free oxygen ions, which are negatively charged. One electrode is exposed to ambient (outside) air through vents in the sensor shell and collects many O_2 ions, becoming a more negative electrode. The other electrode is exposed to exhaust gas and it too collects O_2 ions. But it collects fewer ions and becomes more positive, compared to the other electrode. When there's a large difference between the amount of oxygen in the exhaust and the amount of oxygen in the air (rich mixture), the negative oxygen ions on the outer electrode move to the positive inner electrode, creating a direct current. The sensor then develops a voltage between the two electrodes. When there is more oxygen in the exhaust (lean mixture), there is less difference between O_2 ions on the electrodes and a lower voltage.

The typical unheated oxygen sensor must warm up to at least 572-degrees F before it generates an accurate signal, and its fastest switching time doesn't occur until it reaches a temperature of about 1472-degrees F. This is why the engine management system must remain in open-loop fuel control when the engine is cold. Manufacturers solved this problem by installing heated oxygen sensors, which have an extra wire that delivers about 1 amp of current to the sensor electrodes whenever the ignition switch is turned to ON. Heated sensors warm up more quickly during cold-engine starts and they stay warm enough to provide an accurate voltage signal regardless of operating conditions. Heated oxygen sensors are a must on turbocharged vehicles, where the oxygen sensor is installed downstream from the turbo. The turbo absorbs so much of the heat energy in the exhaust that it prolongs sensor warm-up on a cold engine. On turbo vehicles, an unheated oxygen sensor can also cool off to a temperature below its minimum operating temperature during long periods of idling and low-speed operation. A heated oxygen sensor solves these problems.

Oxygen sensors are always installed in the exhaust manifold(s) or in the exhaust pipe very close to the manifold, but exact locations vary for different engines. Most pre-1996 engines use only a single sensor. 1996 and later engines have a sensor in each manifold.

Throttle Position (TP) sensor

The TP sensor tells the computer whether the engine is at idle, at wide open throttle or at some point in between. An older TP sensor might be nothing more than a simple wide-open throttle (WOT) switch or idle position switch which indicates the extremes of throttle travel with a high or low voltage. However, the typical modern TP sensor is a potentiometer.

A potentiometer is a variable resistor with three terminals. A reference voltage is applied to one end of the resistor, and the other end is grounded. The third terminal is connected to a movable wiper, or contact, that slides across the resistor. Depending on the position of this sliding contact - near the supply end or the ground end of the resistor - return voltage will be high or low. Since the current through the resistor remains constant, so does the temperature - so the resistance doesn't change because of variations in temperature. The result is a constant voltage drop across the resistor so that the return voltage changes only in relation to sliding contact movement. A potentiometer-type TP sensor is both a load and a speed sensor. It tells the control unit not only the position of the throttle, but the speed with which it's being opened or closed.

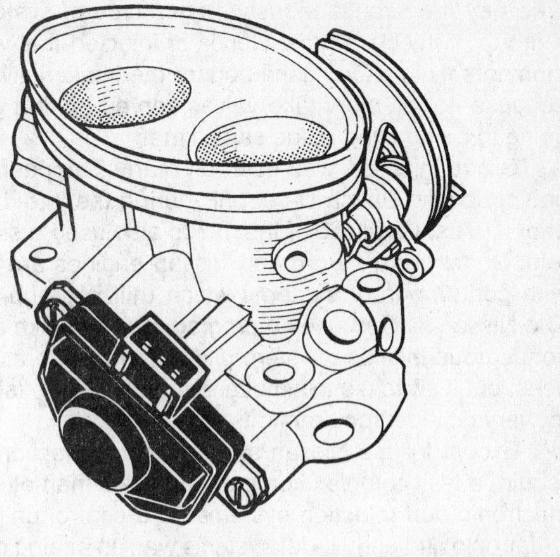

The Throttle Position (TP) sensor is always located on the throttle body, on the end of the throttle valve shaft

Processing: The computer

Also known as the Electronic Control Module (ECM), Electronic Control Unit (ECU) or Powertrain Control Module (PCM), this small microcomputer is the "brain" of the fuel injection system. It receives analog (continuously variable) voltage signals from the information sensors, converts them to digital (on-off signals) and processes this information in accordance with its program or "map." Despite its complexity, the control unit is one of the most reliable components in the entire system. The failure rate of computers is remarkably low. Which means it should be the last component you suspect in the event there's a problem with your fuel injection system.

Output: System actuators

The outputs, or actuators, of the electronic engine management system are those computer-controlled devices - fuel injectors, idle speed motor, EGR solenoid, EVAP canister purge solenoid, etc. - which can be altered in some way to change the operating conditions of the engine. Fuel injectors are the principal actuators in electronic fuel injection systems. Two factors influence the quality and accuracy of their delivery: When they're opened, and how long they're open.

Timing the injection system

Not all electronic fuel injection systems "fire" (open) the injectors in the same sequence. A popular misconception is that injectors open every time the intake valve opens. While it's true that each injector must open every other crankshaft revolution, it doesn't necessarily open at the instant before the intake valve opens on the intake stroke. Three distinct strategies are employed by manufacturers for timing their injectors; of course, there are many more names for these three groups than there are real differences. Figuring out exactly what kind of injector timing a system uses can be tricky.

Group injection - In this type of system, half of the injectors are fired at the same time. For example, on a four-cylinder engine, two injectors are fired during one crankshaft revolution, then the other two injectors are fired during the next crank revolution. On a V8 engine, four injectors fire during the first revolution of the crank; then the other four fire on the next go-round. When a group of two, or four, injectors

The typical automotive computer is a compact rectangular box, usually aluminum or plastic. You'll find it in the engine compartment, usually on or near the firewall or cowl, or inside the vehicle, usually behind the left or right kick panel, under the dash, under a seat or inside the console

fire, they fire simultaneously. In this type of system, when a group of injectors fires, clouds of injected fuel vapor wait momentarily in each intake port for the intake valve to open because not all the intake valves served by that group are going to be opening at the same time.

Group injection was used on many European vehicles equipped with Bosch D-Jetronic during the late 1960s and early 1970s. Cadillacs of the 1970s also used a similar system. Some current Ford and Nissan engines are equipped with contemporary systems which utilize group injection. The Nissan system uses a program that fires like a conventional group injection system under normal operating conditions, but it switches to simultaneous double fire (see below) for very rich fuel requirements.

Except for the Nissan system, group injection systems require a less complex computer program than other pulsed electronic port injection systems. The control unit used on D-Jetronic and early L-Jet systems was an analog computer; simple programs are a must on analog computers. Other components on early group injection systems were similarly rudimentary: D-Jet systems used an injector timing device similar to a pair of mechanical ignition points (!) Crankshaft position sensors are used on modern group injection systems.

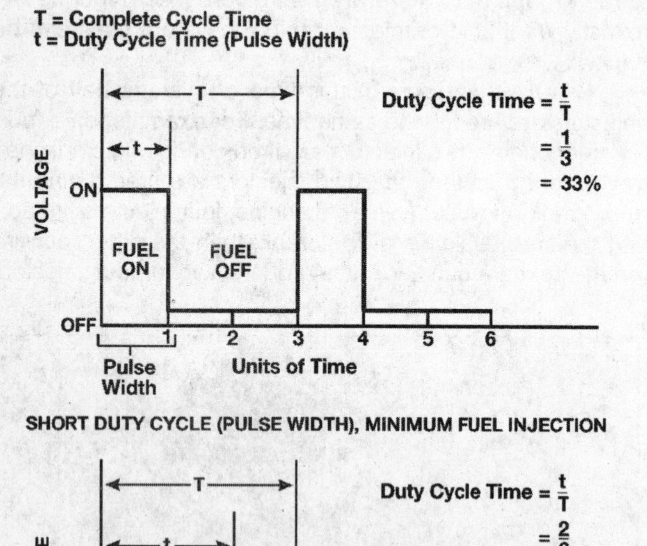

Pulse width is the length of time, measured in milliseconds, that the injector is energized. Pulse width is controlled by the computer

Simultaneous double-fire injection - In a simultaneous double-fire system, all the injectors are fired together as one big group every crankshaft revolution. But only half of the fuel needed by each cylinder is injected each time its injector opens. In other words, each injector fires twice before its corresponding intake valve opens to admit the air/fuel mixture. Again, as in a group injection system, the injected fuel vapors form a cloud behind their respective valve while they wait for it to open.

Sequential fuel injection - In a sequential system, the injectors are fired one at a time, in the same firing order as the cylinders. Each fuel injector delivers fuel just upstream from the intake valve. Fuel delivery is timed to occur immediately before, during or after intake valve opening, depending on engine rpm and intake manifold air velocity. This system currently produces the highest performance and fuel efficiency.

Fuel injector pulse width

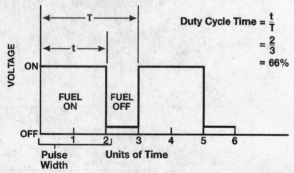

Injector "on-time," known as pulse width, is controlled by the electronic control unit. Pulse width is the length of time - measured in milliseconds - that the injector is energized. The electronic control unit alters injector pulse width in relation to the amount of fuel the engine needs. It takes into account such factors as airflow, air temperature, throttle position, coolant temperature, oxygen content in the exhaust, crankshaft position, vehicle speed, and even fuel temperature. The control unit samples these conditions many times a second, so the pulse width changes constantly. A short pulse width delivers less fuel, a longer pulse width, more. Basically, when the oxygen sensor detects a rich condition in the exhaust gas stream, the electronic control unit shortens the pulse width to lean out the air-fuel mixture; when a lean condition is detected, the control unit lengthens the pulse width to enrichen the mixture. But keep in mind that this basic feedback loop is also influenced by the other variables mentioned above.

This Edelbrock Performer Multiport Electronic Fuel Injection (MEFI) kit is designed to replace a factory TBI injection system

Modifying a fuel injection system

On a modern fuel-injected vehicle your stock engine management system will adapt to the increased airflow of an aftermarket intake pipe or a high-flow air filter. However, the physical limitations of the stock fuel delivery system under wide-open throttle (WOT) conditions can hold back the engine's potential when more aggressive mods are made. Since you are modifying the engine to go faster (to spend more time at WOT), you need to develop the fuel combination that works best for your engine and the modifications you've made. The major mods you can make - cams, head work, power-adders - have all been done before, and high-performance firms have plenty of data on the fuel system upgrades needed to work with their speed parts.

A performance-type, adjustable fuel pressure regulator will be adequate for all your pressure control needs for now, and with any future engine add-ons (this one is made by BBK)

This SLP fuel pressure regulator, which is designed for mid to late-Nineties LT1 fuel injection systems, uses the guts from the stock regulator inside a trick billet housing

What about Throttle Body Injection (TBI) systems?

The best thing that you can do upgrade a TBI system is to replace it with a modern multiport electronic fuel injection system. These kits, which are drop-in replacements, include a new throttle body, intake manifold, fuel rail and injectors, and a new computer. Expensive, yes, but they offer more horsepower, better fuel economy and lower emissions.

High-performance fuel pressure regulators and gauges

An adjustable fuel pressure regulator is probably the first modification that you should consider adding to your fuel system. Most aftermarket units are drop-in replacements for the stock regulator, but they have an adjuster screw on top that allows you to change the fuel system pressure. Once you start playing with your fuel system pressure, you'll need to install an accurate fuel pressure gauge. Most enthusiasts mount their fuel pressure gauge in the engine compartment, where they need to be able to see it when calibrating the fuel system. Some aftermarket gauges are designed to be screwed right into the stock fuel rail in place of the Schrader valve, and some aftermarket fuel rails have a threaded hole just for adding a fuel pressure gauge.

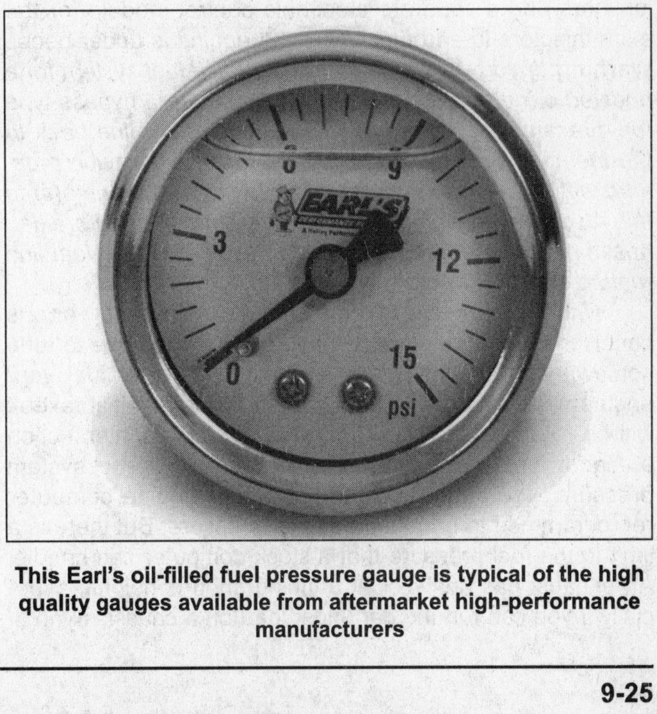

This Earl's oil-filled fuel pressure gauge is typical of the high quality gauges available from aftermarket high-performance manufacturers

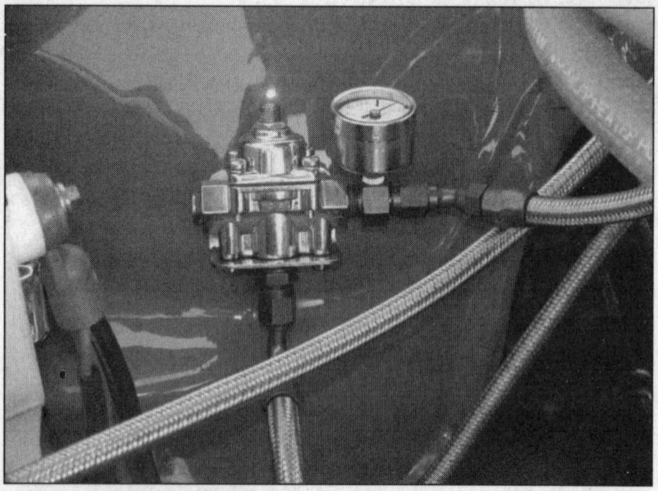

Mount your high-performance fuel pressure regulator and fuel pressure gauge in a convenient spot, so that when tuning the engine the gauge is easy to read and the regulator is easy to adjust. This clean installation is mounted on the inner fender

Some supercharged engines use a couple of extra fuel injectors to ensure adequate fuel flow under boost. This kit for a Whipple blower installation includes a module with electronic management of the extra injectors

When you increase the fuel pressure, you are putting a greater load on the injectors. Too much fuel pressure will shorten the life of the injectors. Experts tell us that for street vehicles with mild bolt-on modifications, you should not increase the factory specified fuel pressure much more than 10%. For example, if your modifications necessitated a fuel pressure increase on a vehicle with a stock pressure of 45 psi, you could safely raise it by 4.5 psi to 49.5 psi. Engines built for all-out racing will require a completely aftermarket fuel system that delivers much higher pressure and volume, with special injectors, fuel pump, regulator, fuel rail and stand-alone engine management. Engines with a power adder like a supercharger will possibly require extra injectors and a separate electronic control module for the extra injectors to add fuel when the engine is under boost. **Warning:** *If you assemble a high-pressure fuel system for a boosted or nitrous application, you must use a bypass-type fuel-pressure regulator with a separate return line back to the fuel tank (see Chapters 9, 10 and 11). Too much pressure without a bypass regulator could cause the pump(s) to fail. Also, use only high-pressure-rated metal or AN braided hoses in a high-pressure system to avoid possible fuel line rupture.*

Without your own dynamometer to simulate various conditions, especially under load at WOT, you have to tune somewhat by feel and by ear. If you have too much fuel, your engine will be "doggy" at the bottom end and initial takeoff will be rough unless you're always leaving an intersection at higher rpms. To manage a minor increase in fuel system pressure, you might need to have your engine computer reprogrammed to handle the higher pressure. But there is a limit to the fuel pressure that a stock computer can handle. An exhaust gas analyzer at a tuning shop is helpful, especially if you can run the car under load on a chassis dyno. If you live near an experienced tuning shop, they can help a lot because they know what has worked on engines similar to yours.

Bigger fuel rails and high-flow injectors

The stock fuel pump should be able to handle fuel demand for a typical engine mildly modified with bolt-on equipment. But if you go beyond these simple additions, upgrade the fuel rails, and maybe the injectors. Aftermarket billet aluminum fuel rails not only look cool, but they deliver more fuel volume because their main internal passage is bigger. The larger volume acts like a plenum in an intake manifold, providing all the injectors with a larger and therefore more stable supply of fuel, especially if you upgrade to larger fuel injectors. Most rails also have extra ports, for attaching a fuel pressure gauge or adding a line to an extra injector for blown or nitrous applications. Most high-performance fuel rails also accept aftermarket AN fittings (sometimes called "aircraft" fittings) for engine builders who want to plumb their fuel system with colorful, custom lines. This feature is handy for radical modifications because you might have to increase the fuel line diameter all the way back to the gas tank to assure adequate supply, and billet fuel rails accept these bigger-than-stock fuel lines easily.

But even bigger fuel rails can't deliver more fuel than the injectors can handle. So at some point you might have to add a set of high-flow injectors. High-performance injectors are capable of opening faster and spraying more fuel than stock injectors. And some of the latest performance injectors have "shower nozzles," multiple orifices in the business end that spray a lot more fuel than a single orifice.

High-performance injectors like these FAST units provide quicker response and spray a lot more fuel into the intake port while they're open

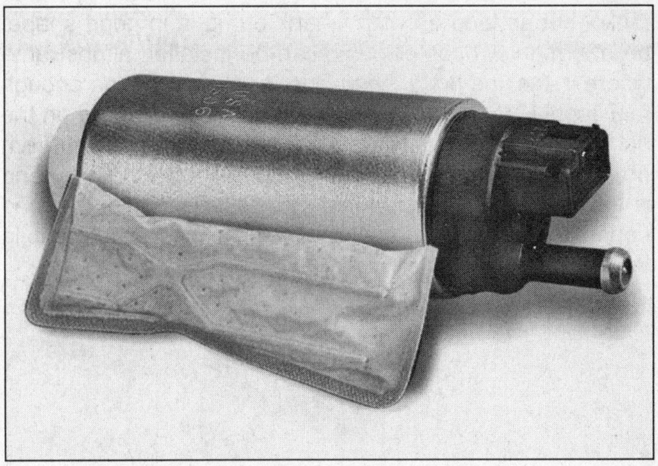

To provide enough fuel for your modified engine, you might need to replace your stock in-tank fuel pump with a high-pressure unit like this Holley

High-performance fuel pumps

Eventually, if you install extreme power-adders like a supercharger, turbo or nitrous, your stock fuel pump may not be able to supply enough volume or pressure under WOT. In most modern cars, the electric fuel pump is mounted in the fuel tank, usually in an assembly that includes a filter and the fuel level sending unit. With these other components connected to the fuel pump, and the number of hoses and electrical connectors attached there at the top of the tank, not everyone wants to substitute another pump for the in-tank unit. Some modifiers have adapted a fuel pump from a larger domestic car to fit their tank, but this is a lot of work, and the aftermarket makes a number of high-flowing pumps that directly replace your stock in-tank pump. So if you find that you eventually need more fuel-pumping capacity, start with a high-performance aftermarket pump that's a drop-in replacement for the stock in-tank unit.

If you increase the volume of the system to the point at which it needs even more pressure, add an extra fuel pump as a booster, leaving the stock pump in the tank as a booster to the in-tank unit.

Racers often use a high-flow, high-volume electric pump located just ahead of the fuel tank. Electric fuel pumps are designed to push fuel rather than pull it, so generally they should be mounted near the rear of the car, close to the fuel

For serious power mods, a second performance pump, like this billet Edelbrock unit, can be installed outside the fuel tank as a booster for the in-tank fuel pump

For all-out drag racing, a high-flow, high-volume electric pump like this Holley Dominator, which can move 350 gallons per hour, is the hot ticket

tank - but as long as your in-tank pump is in good shape, an aftermarket booster pump can be installed almost anywhere in the line up to the engine, and is more than enough fuel supply for a street-driven ride. It can be installed on the underside of the chassis as long as it's safely away from hot exhaust components or moving suspension parts, and is tucked up high enough that it can't be damaged by road debris. Some modified applications install the extra pump in the engine compartment.

Electric pumps can be noisy, another reason manufacturers stick them down in the fuel tank where the sound is dampened. Wherever you mount the pump, make sure you utilize the rubber isolation mounts that should come with the pump. A chassis-mounted pump without rubber mounts can make an annoying hum, audible inside the car if you don't have your stereo on.

10 The Exhaust System

Of all the bolt-on modifications you can make, improving the exhaust system is one that benefits several areas, regardless of the level of performance you're after. Once you have a free-flowing system, it'll work with all future mods.

When you assemble the right package of exhaust components that allow your engine to really breathe, the vehicle's going to sound as good as it performs. It bears repeating here that the exhaust system is one of the few aspects of modifying that gives you the performance you want without any of the drawbacks or compromises that usually come with engine mods. On the contrary, the exhaust work should have no effect on your idling or smooth driveability, and your fuel economy will actually go up, not down! The cool sound is a bonus, too.

Stock exhaust manifolds

The original stock cast iron exhaust manifolds on your engine are quiet, sturdy and compact. *And*, you already own them! If you're just lightly modifying your vehicle, they should work fine. Several good cast iron manifolds were used on high-performance and police models, especially in the 1960s. On small-block engines, the "ram's horn" design used in the 50's and 60's flows very well. Manifolds designed for Corvettes are usually better than others are. These may still be available from your dealer or a salvage yard. If you intend to use these on a different body style than they were originally designed for, be sure there is enough clearance and the outlet is in the right place.

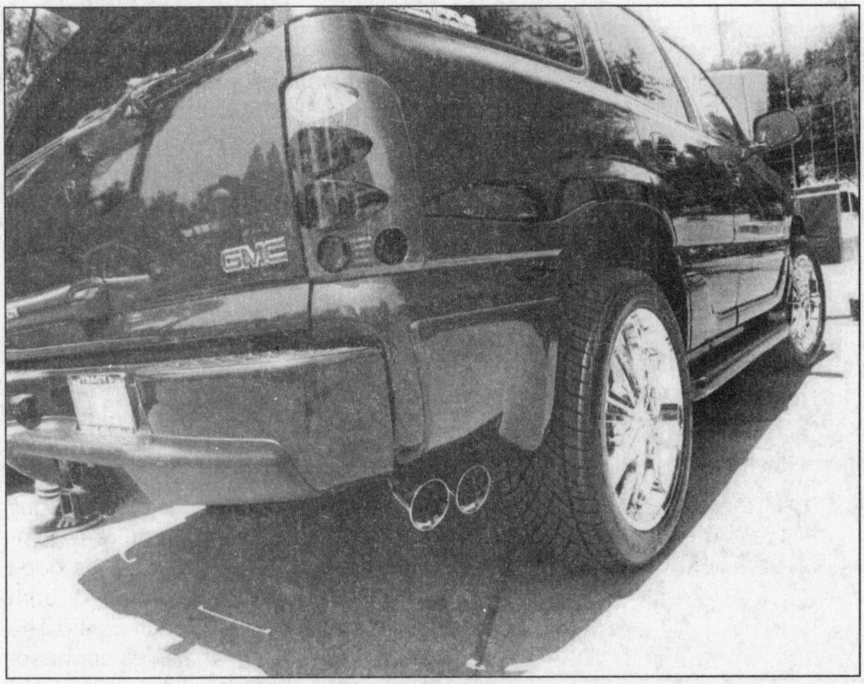

Backpressure and flow

All engines, regardless of how they're used, have to rid themselves of the byproducts of combustion. An exhaust system should facilitate a swift exit path for those gases. An obstruction in the exhaust stream reduces engine efficiency because the pressure waves coming out with the gasses back up, which causes the cylinders to work harder to complete their four-stroke cycle. In exhaust terms, this is called backpressure, and getting rid of it is the chief aim of performance exhaust system designers.

Of course, the right-sized length of straight pipe, with no catalytic converter and no muffler, would offer the least backpressure to the engine, but it's not very practical for a street-driven machine, nor is it legal. For our purposes, we have two main components between the exhaust valves and the tip of the tailpipe: the headers, and everything from the catalytic converter (on vehicles so equipped) on back (which includes the exhaust pipe, silencer, tailpipe and muffler).

Modifying the exhaust system

Aftermarket headers

Like we said, in some OEM vehicle applications the stock exhaust manifolds aren't too bad, at least for the needs of your stock engine. The exhaust flow needs of an engine go up exponentially with the state of performance tune. The flow and backpressure needs of a stock engine aren't excessive, especially when the engine spends the bulk of its driving life under 4000 rpm. But what happens when you modify the engine, then constantly subject the now more powerful engine to the heavy loads of hard acceleration or regularly keep it revved-out in the upper end of its rpm range? The exhaust system that was once adequate is now restrictive to a great degree.

Tubular steel exhaust headers generally provide increases in power without significant changes in fuel economy. They do this by allowing the exhaust gases to flow out of the engine more easily, thereby reducing pumping losses. Headers also "tune" or optimize the engine to run most efficiently in a certain rpm range. They do this by using the inertia of exhaust gases to produce a low-pressure area at the exhaust port just as the valve is opening. This phenomenon, known as scavenging, can be exploited by choosing headers of the correct type, length and diameter to match your engine type, driving style and vehicle.

How much power you make with just the headers depends on several factors. On a vehicle with a really restrictive stock exhaust system, particularly exhaust manifolds full of tight bends and twists, headers will make a bigger improvement than on a vehicle with a decent stock system to start with. What's behind the headers can make a big difference as well. If the stock exhaust system includes restrictive converter and muffler designs, small-diameter exhaust pipes and lots of wrinkle bends, the headers aren't going to have much chance of making a big improvement in performance. Good headers on a typical vehicle engine with few other modifications can be expected to make only 5-10 horsepower, depending on how good or bad the stock manifold had been. That's with a stock exhaust system from the headers back.

A free-flowing path for your engine begins right at the engine with a smooth tubular header and down pipes, like this BBK kit for Ford V8s

That sounds disappointing, but if we take a case where the engine has numerous modifications yet still has a stock exhaust manifold, the same aftermarket headers could release much more than 10 horsepower. Any of the big power-adder modifications, including nitrous oxide and supercharging virtually require headers and a free-flowing exhaust system to take advantage of their power potential.

Installation of performance headers is usually quite easy. Most aftermarket headers are made to use all the factory mounting points. Make sure before buying headers that you give the shop your exact year, model, engine, 2WD or 4WD and other pertinent data. If you can, buy headers with a high-temperature ceramic-type coating. It looks almost as good as chrome, but will not turn color or burn off, and it also has a scientific plus. The coatings will retain heat *inside* your head-

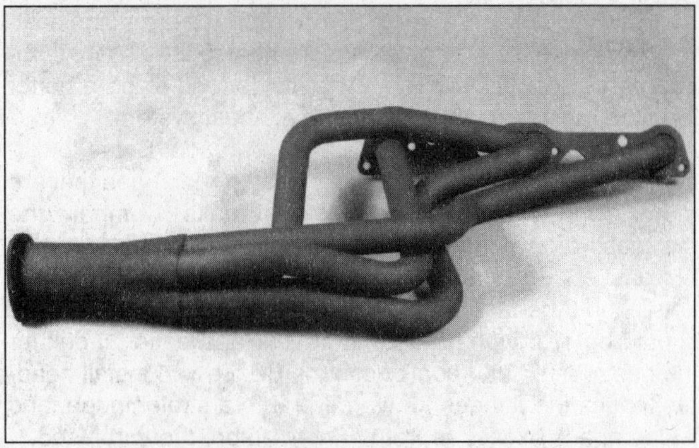

The goal of performance header design is to have the right size and length pipes, and arrange them so that each pipe complements the others in terms of timing the pulses, and having smooth bends that reduce backpressure better than factory cast-iron manifolds. This is a classic four-into-one design

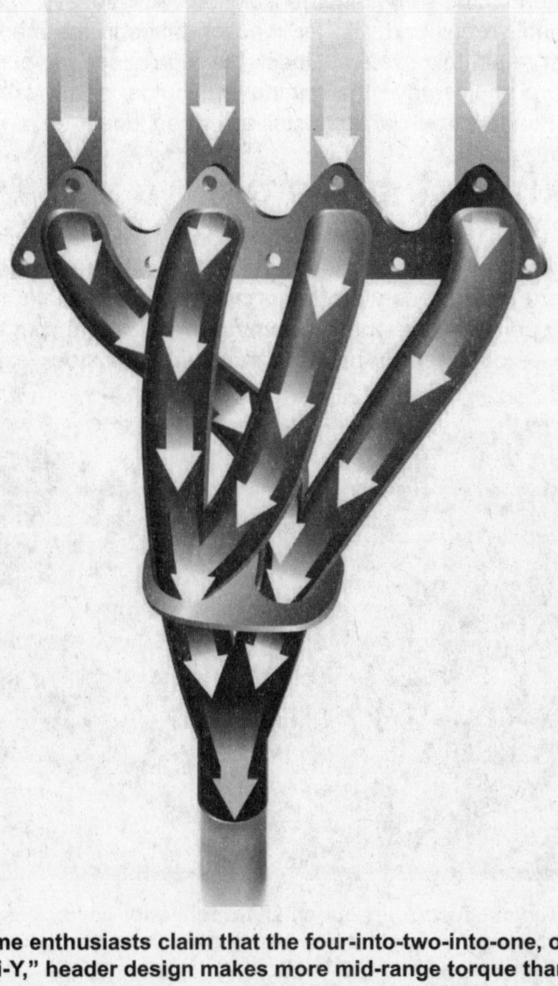

Some enthusiasts claim that the four-into-two-into-one, or "Tri-Y," header design makes more mid-range torque than a four-into-one design. In our experience it simply moves the fat part of the torque band to a different part of the midrange, so research your options carefully before picking a four-into-one or a Tri-Y

ers, and that helps performance in two ways. The coating allows less exhaust heat into the engine compartment, and keeping heat in the exhaust inside the headers means the hotter gasses will move out of the system more quickly.

Header manufacturers produce a large variety of headers designed for different purposes. Most of them provide detailed information, recommendations and specifications on their products to assist you in selecting the right headers for your application. Some companies also have technical hot lines to answer customer questions.

Header designs

Most headers come in a conventional four-into-one design. This means that all four pipes on one side of the engine come together inside a large diameter collector pipe. These four-into-one designs tend to produce more peak power at high rpm at the expense of low and mid-range torque.

Another, less common approach to header design is commonly known as "Tri-Y" because of their appearance. The initial four pipes are paired into two pipes and then these are paired again into one pipe at the collector. This design provides more low and mid-range power, but sacrifices a slight amount of horsepower over about 6,000 rpm compared to the four-into-one design.

One of the more recent developments in exhaust system technology is the Anti-Reversion (or AR) header. They have a small cone inside the pipe near the cylinder head that prevents reflected pressure waves from creating extra backpressure. The AR design also allows the use of larger diameter tubing without sacrificing a lot of low-end torque. Anti-reversion headers broaden and extend the torque curve and improve throttle response.

Length and diameter

Selection is not an exact science, but rather a series of compromises. Generally, long tubing and collector lengths favor low-end torque and shorter lengths produce their power in the higher rpm range. Larger diameter tubing should be used on large displacement engines and smaller cross-section tubing should be used on smaller displacement models.

Most street headers have primary tubes that are 30 to 40-inches long. Primary tube diameter should be about the same as exhaust port diameter. For small-block engines this is about 1-5/8 inch. On big-block engines, 1-7/8 inch is typical. The collectors are usually about 10 to 20-inches long and three to four inches in diameter.

Component matching

It's also important to match the characteristics of the intake and exhaust systems. Keep in mind that heavier vehicles with relatively small engines need more low-end torque and higher numerical gearing to launch them than lighter vehicles with larger engines. Follow the manufacturer's recommendations to ensure that you obtain the correct model for the application.

Open-plenum, single-plane intake manifolds with large, high-CFM carburetors should only be used with four-into-one headers designed for high rpm. This combination should also include a high-performance camshaft matched to the other components and a fairly high numerical gear ratio.

If you want a more tractable street engine, you may want to go for a 180-degree dual-plane manifold with a somewhat smaller carburetor and "Tri-Y" type headers or four-into-one headers with relatively long tubes. A mid-range camshaft would help complete the package.

Buying tips

Be sure to check the manufacturer's literature carefully to determine if the headers will fit your vehicle and allow you to retain accessories such as power steering, air conditioning, power brakes, smog pumps, etc. Note if there is sufficient clearance around the mounting bolts for a wrench. Also, some headers interfere with the clutch linkage on manual transmission models, so check for this, if applicable.

Some applications require the engine to be lifted slightly or even removed to allow header installation. Find out how the mufflers and tailpipes connect to the headers, also. Most installations require some cutting and modifications to the existing exhaust system, which may require a trip to the muffler shop. Check the instructions, ask questions and know what you are getting into before you purchase any components. Don't let poor planning get you stuck with a ticket for driving to the muffler shop with open headers!

Most headers don't come with heat shields like stock manifolds do and tend to melt original spark plug wires and boots. Plan on purchasing a set of heat-resistant silicone spark plug wires and boots, along with the necessary wire holders or looms to keep them away from the headers. You may even have to shield the spark plug ends of the wires with heat-resistant fire sleeves (see Chapter 2).

Also, look for header kits that have adapters for heat riser valves and automatic choke heat tubes. Some models with air pumps need threaded fittings in the headers to mount the air injection rails. If your vehicle has an exhaust gas oxygen sensor, be sure the replacement headers have a provision for mounting the sensor.

After the headers are installed, the fuel mixture may be too lean. The carburetor will usually require re-jetting and may need some other adjustments. Test the vehicle on an engine analyzer after installation and tune the engine as necessary; failure to do so may result in driveability problems and/or burned valves.

Disadvantages

Headers have several disadvantages that should be considered before you run out and buy a set. Because of their thin tubing construction, headers emit more noise than cast-iron exhaust manifolds. Most headers produce a tinny sound in and around the engine compartment and some also produce a resonance inside the vehicle at certain engine speeds. On the other hand, many enthusiasts don't consider this a disadvantage at all!

Tubular headers also have more surface area than cast-iron manifolds, so they give off more heat to the engine compartment. Engines with stock manifolds tend to do a better job of retaining this heat inside the exhaust system.

Another drawback is port flange warpage. Some lower-quality headers have thin cylinder head port flanges that are more prone to warpage and exhaust leaks. Compare the thickness of the flanges on various brands and also check the gaskets and hardware supplied with the kits. The gaskets should be fairly thick and well made and the hardware should be of a high grade and fit your application. Look for the best design and quality control. Before you install headers, check the flanges for warpage with a straightedge, and if warpage is excessive, return them before they are used.

If you aren't installing chromed or coated headers, corrosion can also be a problem. Regular paint will quickly burn off and rusting will begin. Before installation, thoroughly coat the headers with heat-resistant paint, porcelainizing or aluminizing spray.

Some aftermarket tubular exhaust headers are not approved for use on catalytic converter-equipped vehicles in California and some other jurisdictions. Additionally, vehicles originally equipped with air injection tubes in the manifolds must retain this system. Check the regulations in your area before you remove the original manifolds, and make sure the headers you want to install are smog legal.

Exhaust systems

Once the exhaust gases exit your efficient new headers, they still must travel the length of the vehicle's underside before they're pushed out the tailpipe. Substantial gains in both performance and economy throughout the rpm range can be obtained by properly modifying the stock exhaust

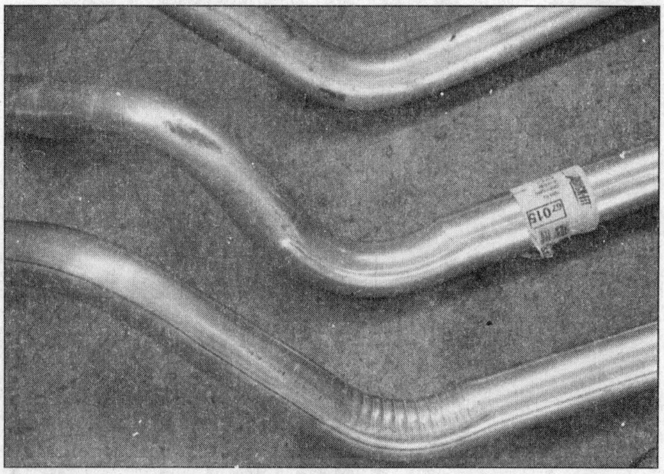

The exhaust from your catalytic converter on back is as important as a good header. Here are three examples of exhaust pipe bends: at bottom, a crinkle-bend, often found on stock pipes, which detracts from good flow; middle, a better bend made with a hydraulic bender at a muffler shop; at top, a smooth mandrel-bent pipe that provides the smoothest exhaust flow

system. The less restriction, the more efficient the engine will be. By increasing the flow capacity, you can unleash the potential horsepower in your engine.

The original mufflers, pipes and catalytic converters on most vehicles have small passages and tight bends. Perhaps the most difficult task when choosing exhaust components for a performance street vehicle is to make the system reasonably quiet while still having low restriction. Also, vehicles originally equipped with catalytic converters won't pass emissions inspections if the catalysts are removed.

Before you purchase a new exhaust system or individual components, you need to know what is available and the pros and cons of various items. Determine what you want your vehicle to be like, what your budget is, then design a balanced system that meets your requirements.

Many special parts and even complete high-performance systems are available for some popular models. If you have a less-common vehicle, you may have to devise a system composed of universal parts or use items originally designed for other vehicles.

If you intend to do the modifications on your vehicle yourself, find a level concrete area to work. Raise the vehicle with a floor jack and support it securely with sturdy jackstands. **Warning:** *Never work under a vehicle supported solely by a jack!*

Most exhaust system work requires only a small number of common hand tools. Sometimes, special equipment such as an acetylene torch, a pipe expander or pipe bender will be necessary. Muffler shops have this equipment and can modify, fabricate and install custom exhaust systems. But remember, the more work you do yourself, the more money you can save.

One of the easiest ways to reduce backpressure and increase flow capability is by adding dual exhaust pipes. This effectively doubles the capacity of the exhaust without making the vehicle appreciably louder. Sometimes you can reuse most of the original parts on one side and install new parts on the other.

If your vehicle is required to use one or more catalytic converters, you can install a "cat-back" system from each catalyst all the way back to the tailpipe. Most aftermarket exhaust systems for modern catalyst-equipped vehicles are called cat-backs because they include everything from the catalyst to the tailpipes. The typical cat-back system is broken down in several pieces to simplify packaging, shipping and installation, but it bolts right up to the rear flange of the catalyst and includes whatever the system requires - intermediate pipe, pre-muffler silencer, rear exhaust pipe, muffler, tailpipe, etc. Cat-back systems are an easier way to source everything you need instead of obtaining all the components separately.

Mufflers

As a general rule, mufflers and pipes with large inlet and outlet openings can handle more flow volume than smaller ones, all other factors being equal. Also, shorter mufflers are usually louder and have less restriction than longer ones, so keep this in mind when choosing mufflers. We all like a good growl or purr from our exhaust system, but a really free-flowing muffler can be annoying to others who might not share our love for a healthy engine exhaust note.

The perfect exhaust would purr at idle, make the hair on your neck stand up when it accelerates and sound like a symphony at full song! Some manufacturers characterize each aftermarket exhaust system anywhere from mellow to aggressive. The perfect sound is such a subjective thing. One way to find a sound that you like is to listen to other people's cars at shows and events. When you hear one that you really like, ask the owner what type of exhaust he's running.

Conventional or original equipment mufflers

This is the type your vehicle came with from the factory. They are usually of reverse flow construction, and are quite heavy and restrictive. The only time you should consider using these is if you are adding dual exhaust and want to match the original muffler to save money.

Glasspack mufflers

Glasspack mufflers are usually less expensive than conventional or "turbo" mufflers, and have less restriction than original equipment types. Unfortunately, most of them are also too loud to meet most noise regulations and they vary greatly in quality and performance.

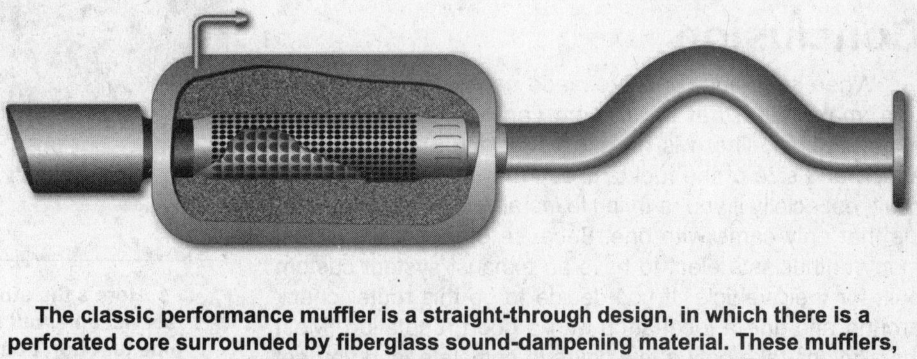

The classic performance muffler is a straight-through design, in which there is a perforated core surrounded by fiberglass sound-dampening material. These mufflers, which were referred to as "glasspacks," were noted for their performance sound. Chambered performance mufflers, which don't use fiberglass, are popular nowadays

Turbo mufflers

Originally, factory engineers designed a large, high flow muffler for use on the turbo Chevrolet Corvair. Hot rodders found out and started using them for all sorts of vehicles. The name "turbo muffler" was first applied to these Corvair parts and gradually became generic, covering all high-flow oval shaped mufflers.

Turbo mufflers offer the best features of stock and glass-pack mufflers. They are simply high-capacity mufflers that have low restriction without making much more noise than the original units. Today, virtually every muffler manufacturer sells a turbo-type muffler. They have expanded coverage to include many models, and there should be one to fit your application.

Exhaust crossover pipes

Every dual exhaust system should have an exhaust crossover pipe located upstream of the mufflers. This tube balances the pulses between the two sides of the engine and allows excess pressure from one side to bleed off into the opposite muffler. This reduces noise and increases capacity. Be sure that any system you purchase incorporates this design, which improves power throughout the rpm range.

Stainless steel

Stainless steel mufflers and pipes are preferable to regular steel ones if you plan to keep your vehicle for a long time and/or do a lot of short-trip driving. Several specialty manufacturers produce ready-made and custom-built exhaust components from stainless steel. These parts are extremely resistant to corrosion and most are warranteed for the life of the vehicle. They usually cost several times more than standard components, so consider that when you make a purchase decision.

Pipe diameter

Exhaust pipe diameter is measured inside the pipe. Small increases in diameter result in large increases in flow capacity. As a general rule, small block engines displacing 5.0 to 5.8 liters run well with 1-7/8 to 2 inch diameter exhaust pipes, with the more powerful ones using 2-1/4 inch. Engines over 6.5 liters almost always use 2-1/4 to 2-1/2 inch pipes.

Conclusion

When shopping for a pre-made cat-back exhaust system, make sure that the system can accommodate your exact vehicle. There is no one kit fits all. Things like the shape and size of the fuel tank can make routing pipes difficult, especially if you're trying to install two pipes on a vehicle that only came with one. Because of these difficulties, many enthusiasts elect to have an exhaust system custom built for their vehicle. If you decide to go this route, check around and find a local shop with a good reputation. Most installations take only a few hours to complete, and you get to pick the kinds of mufflers you want, from mild to raucous, and have the tailpipes exit at the location of your choice.

Turbo mufflers have large passages and high flow capacity

Changing the exhaust of your vehicle for a performance system is one of the modifications with more perks than almost any other. You get increased power, improved fuel economy, the sound that will complement your performance profile, and parts that make your ride look better, too. All that, and there's no real downside or sacrifice as with most engine mods.

Installing a typical cat-back system

Now let's look at how a professional installs a cat-back system (this one's on a 2000 Chevy Silverado truck).

1 Here's the stock exhaust on a typical vehicle. It's serviceable, but the giant muffler and single exhaust pipe just don't cut it for our purposes of performance, sound and appearance. Marco Muffler of Sacramento, CA does these day in and day out for dealers and customers

2 This is important: Before any welding is done on a computer-controlled vehicle, you must disconnect the battery to prevent electrical spikes from smoking your computer! At Marco, they use this surge protector device attached to the Chevy ground and positive lugs underhood; it's easier and you don't lose your radio presets

3 Most factory exhaust systems are welded together on the assembly line, so the only way to remove it is to cut it off. Here the technician has supported the giant stock muffler and uses a Sawzall to liberate it. Telescoping stands likes these are invaluable in exhaust work, as you'll see

4 The stock pipe ahead of the muffler is a 2-1/2 inch. A hydraulic bender is being used to form a new piece of three-inch aluminized pipe to the same shape as the stock pipe. Foot controls operate the bender

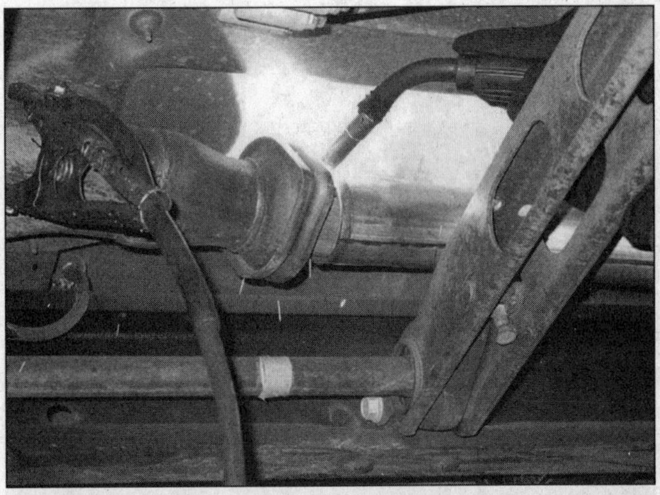

5 The flange is cut off the stock pipe and bolted to the vehicle's cat-back assembly, then the new 3-inch pipe is aligned and tack-welded to the flange

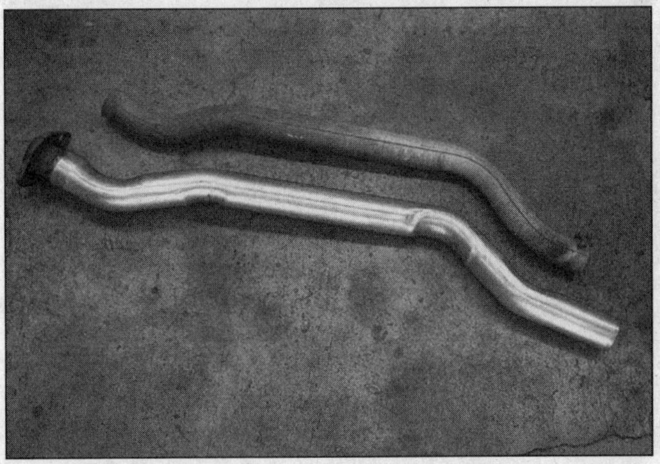

6 Compare the old pipe and the new (here with the stock flange fully welded to the new pipe). The increase in pipe diameter will reduce backpressure in the system

7 The single rear tailpipe has been removed and, with the new front pipe bolted back on the vehicle and supported by a stand, the planning for the performance muffler and two new rear pipes can begin

8 The stock hanger and rubber donut isolator support the back of the 3-inch front pipe. The hanger is being welded to the pipe, after which the excess length of hanger will be trimmed off

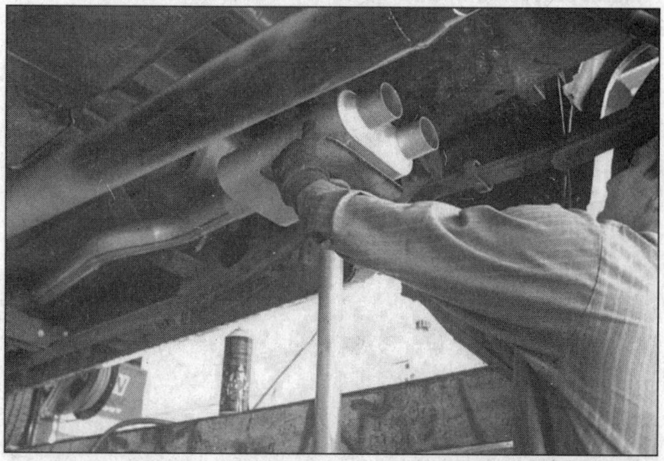

9 The new Flowmaster performance muffler has a large single inlet for applications like this and two 2-1/2 inch outlets for twin tailpipes. This is a 40-series muffler for aggressive sound, but there are quieter 50 and 60-series models

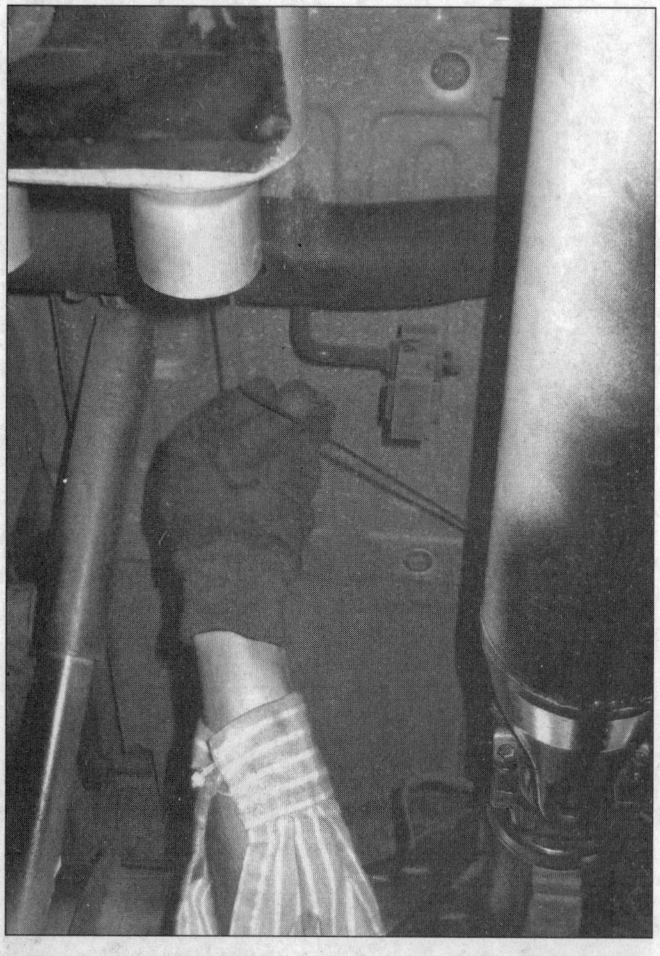

10 Muffler shops very often use a long length of welding wire to make a pattern for a custom pipe they're going to bend. Experience tells them just where to bend the pattern and the new pipe

11 The wire pattern is held next to the hydraulic bender, where the new 2-1/2 inch tailpipes are bent to the same angles

12 Routing pipes requires the installer to check for any possible interference between the proposed pipe and anything on the vehicle like shocks, stabilizer bars, etc. Here, the parking brake cable has been cinched down with three zip-ties to keep it away from the left tailpipe area

13 Not all the bends are made at once. After each bend the pipe is tried on the vehicle again. Here the technician is determining where the last bend will be made. Note that pipes are left long because the bends really shorten the pipe beyond your initial guesstimate

14 The entire system is only tack-welded together until every piece is fitted and the hangers are in place. You can see the routing of the two custom tailpipes in their final shapes

15 All stock or custom hangers must be in place - you can't leave any spot unsupported. The front hanger for the left tailpipe is being welded in position

16 Since they use their fingers, muffler men are never without a measuring device. The tailpipes are located evenly by one-finger distance between them and the bumper, and a three-finger distance to the side from the large flanges on this vehicle's trailer hitch assembly

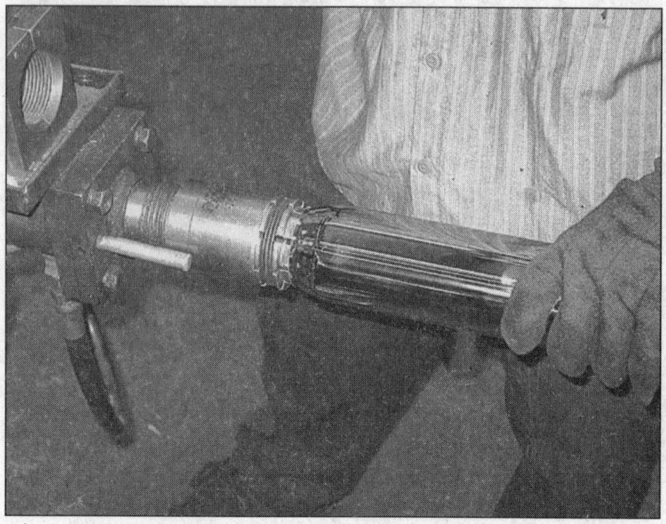

17 The chromed tips can accommodate several sizes of tailpipes - our tips are enlarged on this swaging tool on the hydraulic bending machine, until the tip just fits over a 2-1/2 inch pipe sample, also located on the bending machine for efficiency

18 The new tip is slipped over our extra-long tailpipe until it's lined up in an aesthetically pleasing fashion with the rear bumper. A mark indicates where the pipe and tip should be welded, but the pipe is actually cut off a little ahead of this mark

19 The tall stand supports a large bar used to align the tip with the pipe. After observing the pipe and tip for alignment in all directions, the tip is tack-welded in four places around the tailpipe

21 A nice touch is spraying all the welded seams with high temp silver paint to match the rest of the aluminized tubing's appearance. Overspray is kept to a minimum by holding cardboard behind the area being sprayed

22 The owner is going to be very happy - a muscle-car sound, improved power and economy, and a great pair of chromed tips to show this vehicle hauls!

Notes

11 Power Adders: Juice and Boost

Power adders, as the term is generally used, refers to nitrous oxide, supercharge and turbochargers - the Big Three of bolt-on engine performance. These methods are applied externally to an engine and, while they can be readily used on the street, can produce serious amounts of horsepower. The first of these, nitrous, is a gas that doesn't actually burn, but is an oxidizer, delivering more oxygen through chemical breakdown at high temperatures, allowing your engine to burn extra fuel. When you inject nitrous oxide and gasoline at the same time and in the proper proportions at full throttle, you'll get a kick in the butt as if you were instantly driving a car with an engine twice as big! It's often referred to as the "liquid supercharger."

The other big power-adders, supercharging and turbocharging, take two different approaches to the same end result; they act as air pumps to pack more charge into the engine. Ordinarily, an engine has to suck in all its air and fuel, and can only make so much power at a given rpm with internal engine modifications. Supercharging and turbocharging cram air/fuel into the engine, which is why they're called "forced induction." When you accelerate a supercharged or turbocharged engine, the needle on the boost gauge starts to climb and you get that very satisfying punch - like a horizontal version of the feeling you get when a roller coaster plummets down a steep hill! All three of the power adders we'll be looking at also have the added advantage of easily adjusted power levels, so if you don't need a big boost all the time, you can dial back the power-adder for everyday driving. That's something you can't really do with internal engine-power mods like camshafts, valves, heads and increased engine displacement.

11a Nitrous Oxide

Nitrous oxide as a horsepower source can appear to be a miracle or a curse, depending on your experience. It's a fact that nitrous oxide (N2O) is the simplest, quickest and cheapest way to gain a large horsepower boost in your car. But, just like in children's fairy tales, you court disaster if you don't follow the rules that come with the magic potion.

Not that this musclecar with 426 Hemi power needed a boost - but just in case, the owner has fitted a professionally-plumbed nitrous-oxide system that should pump another 200 horsepower in when the situation demands it! Nitrous kits run the gamut from mild to wild, from less than $500 to several thousands with all the bells and whistles

Done right, a nitrous kit is one of the best horsepower-per-dollar investments you can make, and is the most popular power-adder. The smallest nitrous kits offer at least a 50-horsepower increase for an investment of $500. In other engine bolt-on speed budgeting, that same $500 wouldn't even cover a really nice cat-back exhaust system that may only net you 15 horsepower. Kits are available that add from 50 hp to 300 hp (and more for racing engines). The more nitrous and fuel you add, the more power the engine makes, right up to the point where the engine comes apart. In the end, it is the durability of the engine itself, which is just a pressure vessel to capture the energy of the burning fuel, that determines how much nitrous you can run. As tempting as it is to just keep putting bigger nitrous jets in your engine for more power, you need to do your research first to see what the limits of your engine are and what can be done to protect against damage done by detonation. You may have heard horror stories about engine disasters caused by nitrous oxide, but in most cases the cause is usually a fault in tuning the application. The serious drag racers have done everything possible to their engines to strengthen them to handle big loads of nitrous.

The basic street-use nitrous kit consists of: a nitrous bottle (usually one that holds 10 pounds of liquid nitrous oxide), bottle mounting brackets and hardware, fuel and nitrous jets, high-pressure lines (usually braided-stainless covered AN-type with a Teflon inner liner for the high nitrous pressure), nitrous filter, solenoids, switch and electrical connectors. Kits are always sold without the nitrous in the bottle; you'll have to go to a local speed shop to have the bottle filled.

In a simple dry nitrous system, there may be a plate under the carburetor or a single nozzle like this (or several nozzles), but the nozzle handles only nitrous - extra fuel is added through the regular EFI injectors

The wet system of nitrous distribution is used on bigger systems, and the nozzles supply nitrous at one connection and extra fuel at another. There could be a single nozzle like this on a smaller engine, or one for every cylinder on a bigger engine. Wet applications have a separate fuel delivery system for more capacity to the nozzles

There are two basic types of nitrous kits that deliver both the nitrous and fuel differently. The "dry" systems designed for factory EFI engines have a nozzle and solenoid only for the nitrous, and this nozzle may be almost anywhere in the intake system - behind the MAF sensor (if equipped) and ahead of the throttle body is typical. To deliver the extra fuel to go with the nitrous, the stock system fuel pressure is raised during the WOT (wide-open throttle) period of nitrous usage, and reverts back to the stock fuel pressure in all other driving conditions.

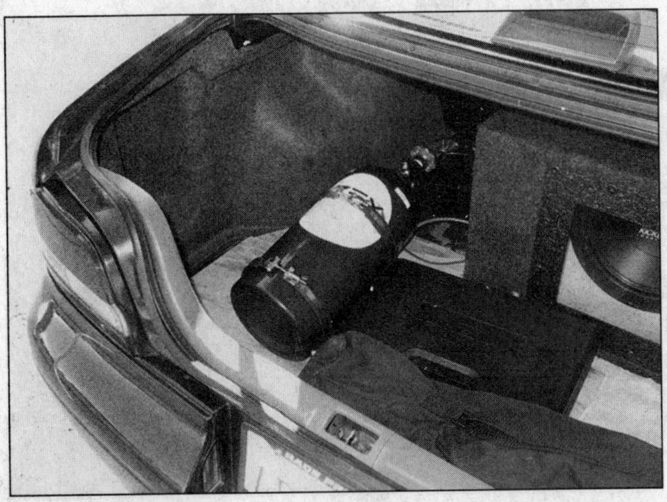

In most vehicles, the typical 10-pound bottle of nitrous oxide is mounted like this in the trunk, with the front end tilted up. The bottle should be protected from sun exposure or the bottle pressure can vary too much. Neither too much pressure or too little is acceptable

This NOS kit for a dry system is designed for easy installation on EFI engines and comes with everything you need for fuel enrichment while juicing the engine

The "wet" system of nitrous will have solenoids for both nitrous and fuel - both of which are turned on when the nitrous system is activated. The fuel and nitrous in a simple system are plumbed into a single injector that merges the two - the gasoline and its oxidizer - as they enter the engine. More sophisticated wet systems may have an N2O nozzle for each cylinder of the engine, and one or more fuel nozzles mounted separately. In high-output racing applications, individually feeding each cylinder allows for tuning each cylinder separately for fine control. The extra nozzles also mean there is ample supply of nitrous and fuel for very high-horsepower installations.

There are all sorts of extra features available for most of the nitrous kits on the market today. There are varying designs of nozzles, different electronic controls that work with your factory computer to control timing and fuel delivery, optional bottle covers, bottle warmers and remote shut-off valves for the bottle. There are also computer mods (see Chapter 4) and external controls that pull back the ignition timing under nitrous use, and staged nitrous kits that deliver a certain amount during launch, then a little more, and the full blast for the top end.

How does it work? In basic terms for a simple nitrous system, the tank or bottle of nitrous oxide is mounted in the trunk and plumbed up to the engine compartment with a high-pressure line. This is connected to an electric solenoid, from which nitrous (still a liquid at this point) can flow to the nozzle attached to your intake system. If you turn on an arming switch in the car, battery voltage is available to a button-type switch that is located on the steering wheel, dash or shifter. When your throttle linkage reaches wide-open, the solenoids are triggered and the flow is a go. The extra fuel admitted at the same time as the N2O is easily oxidized and creates enough cylinder pressure to add 50, 75, 100 or more horsepower in an instant.

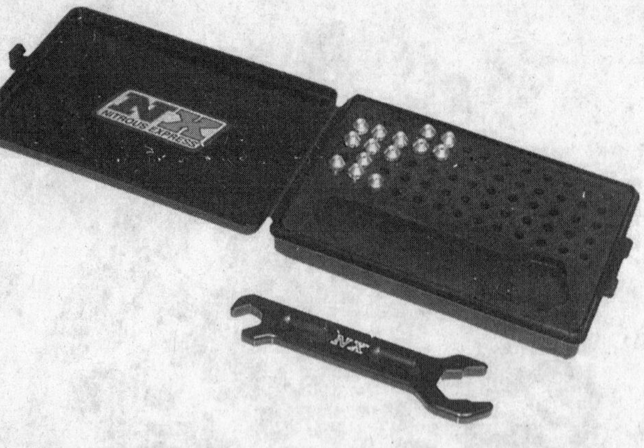

Kits are offered with varying levels of power, like 50-75-100 horsepower. The more nitrous and fuel you flow, the more power. You can change the small jets (as seen in this Nitrous Express kit) to vary the level

Here are some of the things you'll be doing in a typical installation. The bottle of nitrous oxide is mounted in the trunk of the car as the first step. You will have already filled the bottle with nitrous at your local speed shop or tuner. Your kit manufacturer's instructions will tell you how to mount the bottle, which must be oriented a certain way. The high-pressure line is run from the bottle up to the engine compartment, either through the interior under the carpeting and through a hole in the firewall (always have a grommet around the line), or routed under the car. If you take the latter route, secure the line all the way along with tie-wraps and keep it away from hot or moving components and where it won't be subject to abrasion or rock damage. Whatever the route, tape off both ends of the line before routing it through the car, and if you have any nitrous related wires (such as for a bottle warmer, remote gauge or remote bottle opener), route them along with the line.

Next, the solenoid(s) are mounted to the firewall, then the nitrous line for the tank is connected to the nitrous solenoid. If it is a wet system, the stock high-pressure fuel line must be tapped with a "T", and a fuel line run to the gasoline solenoid. Your kit's instructions will be very specific about these safety-related connections. Find the manufacturer-recommended location for the nozzle and install it (usually on the intake tube) with the nozzle oriented towards the throttle body, and install the jet(s) for the horsepower level you've selected. Connect a nitrous line from the solenoid to the nozzle, then do the same with the gasoline from the fuel solenoid to the nozzle. Wet system kits generally have different-colored hose for the fuel and nitrous lines so there is no mix-up.

Follow your kit's instructions carefully about wiring the solenoids and switches, and about purging the fuel and nitrous lines. Having the fuel line empty on your first shot of nitrous will get you off to a bad start. When everything checks out, take your car out to a road with no traffic and put the squeeze on your engine!

Detonation is when the pressure and temperature in the combustion chamber spike up enough to create uncontrolled burning of the fuel/air mix, and is the underlying cause for most of the nitrous horror stories. Improper setup of a nitrous system (otherwise known as "pilot error") is one of the leading causes of detonation damage. Even mild street kits require the highest-octane pump gasoline you can get. If you're in a situation where you're forced to buy a lower-octane gas, either don't use your nitrous until you use up all that gas and get premium again, or carry a few bottles of octane booster in your trunk. Just make sure the booster absolutely does not contain lead. With a 10:1 compression you can get by on the street with 93 octane, but if you add a nitrous kit on top of that compression, you should be using premium *and* an octane booster.

For most carbureted American V8s, the nitrous method of choice is the simple-but-effective plate-style nitrous like this kit from Edelbrock. The 1/2-inch thick plate has a spray bar inside that distributes the nitrous (and fuel, in this case) for 100-250 horsepower. The plate simply bolts in place between the intake manifold and the four-barrel carb

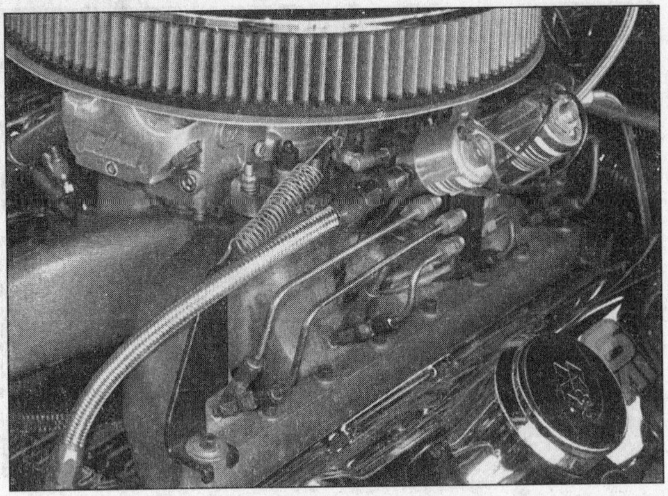

A high-capacity juice system on this street machine has a separate solenoid set for each bank of the engine, feeding fuel and nitrous to all eight of the wet nozzles

On this custom installation, note how the fuel line has been connected to a Y-fitting to split extra fuel to each bank of the engine. Most systems use braided stainless steel hose with anodized AN fittings, and some feature small-diameter stainless hard lines to feed the nozzles

The ignition system is especially important when your engine is on the bottle. You'll need good plug wires, a good cap and rotor (if your car has a distributor), and the right spark plugs. For most street applications you should go one range colder on the spark plugs, and gap them smaller than the stock recommendation. This makes it easier for the spark to jump the gap under high pressure. Do **not** use any kind of projected-tip spark plug. In setups using more than 50 hp jets, plugs two steps colder may be required and an aftermarket ignition with high-output coil, fat wires and ignition amplifier box will be more helpful, as will a header and cat-back exhaust system.

If you have previously added a chip or had your ECU reprogrammed to make a few more horsepower, then you should revert back to stock specs, since most computer upgrades aggressively alter the ignition timing curve. The nitrous more than makes up for a few horsepower, and going back to stock specs can help avoid detonation. In engines that have 10:1 compression or use higher doses of nitrous, you'll want to install an aftermarket timing control that will actually retard timing while the juice is on. Your engine should be in top condition before adding a nitrous kit. The extra cylinder pressure can cause blow-by on worn piston rings and any oil that sneaks into the combustion chamber can create immediate detonation.

Running the engine lean - meaning not adding enough fuel to go along with the nitrous - is one of the biggest tuning mistakes that result in detonation. After you have made your first few runs on your newly-installed nitrous system, you should do what any good race tuner would do - pull all of your spark plugs for a very close examination, looking for discoloration or any of the other signs of overheating that signal detonation. When you make any other modifications or changes to your engine, you should do another plug reading. When you see the early signs of detonation on the spark plugs, you have time to examine the engine and find the cause before any parts are destroyed.

The pressure in your N2O bottle has a definite effect on the richness/leanness of your fuel/nitrous mixture. Consistent bottle pressure is important. Your kit manufacturer will probably give you a recommended bottle pressure or range to work within. Pressure below what is recommended will induce a rich condition, which will hurt power some but won't damage the engine. On the other hand, too high a bottle pressure will cause a lean condition. An additional option you can take to avoid detonation is an adjustable low-fuel-pressure switch, which taps into your fuel system. If your fuel pump slows down or there is a leak that causes the fuel

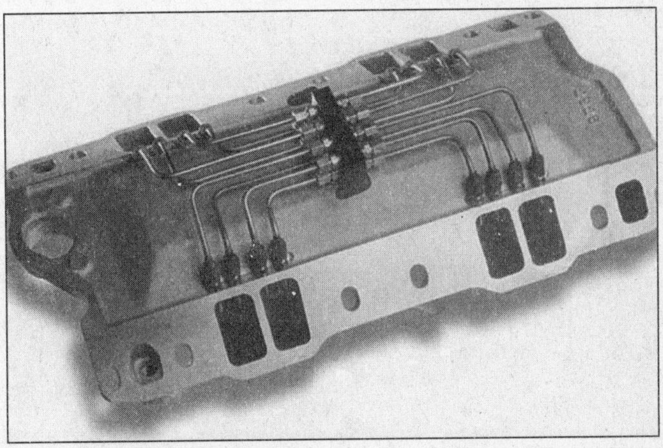

Some enthusiasts would just as soon not have everyone know they are running on the bottle, so as not to give away their actual power potential. For them, NOS (shown) and other suppliers will make up a complete nitrous and fuel plumbing setup under the intake manifold. Only two lines, the fuel and nitrous supply, will come out from under the manifold, usually at the back of the engine where it is inconspicuous

pressure to fall below a threshold you set, the nitrous is shut off to save the engine from a lean burndown.

The bottom line for avoiding detonation is regular checks of your spark plugs. If you start to see any signs of detonation (which could show up as cracked insulators around the center electrodes, or tiny silver or black flecks on the insulators), then use a slightly smaller jet in your nitrous nozzle to richen up the fuel/nitrous ratio. Most systems are set up rich to start off safe. Once you're more familiar with the use of nitrous and you're brave enough to try leaning it out a little for more power, make sure you jet in tiny increments and keep checking those plugs.

For the real performance gluttons, nitrous can be combined with forced induction. Turbos can add tremendous horsepower to an engine, but when a turbo is large enough to flow really well at high rpm, it will usually be too big to spool up quickly at the low end, thus exhibiting what most is known as "turbo lag." With a carefully timed dose of nitrous, the car will have a great launch, then the juice is cut off just when the boost is up and the turbo takes over for the rest of the ride, with no lag!

Obviously, when you have two such amazing power-adders on your engine at once, there's a giant step up in the cylinder pressures. Some of the things we may have mentioned as "options" for a mild N2O system are suddenly mandatory. You might want to add things like free-flowing intake and exhaust components, an all-out ignition system with racing plugs, a pumped-up fuel system with an extra pump, bigger injectors and a fuel management box, and a few other items to prolong the life of the engine (see Chapter 12). Forged pistons, good connecting rods, a forged-steel crank and cylinder head studs may all be necessary. Your car is going to have a serious problem getting all this newfound power to the ground, so you might also look at driveline components. Once you put on the slicks that you'll need to make use of this horsepower, the high loads are going to take their toll.

It doesn't matter if it's in a primered car or a show vehicle, when you've got a big-block with a GMC blower and a dragster-style hat on top, you command the center of attention anyplace you go. This is one mean Camaro!

11b Supercharging

Turbochargers and superchargers both accomplish the same results, but the turbo differs in that its turbine is driven by exhaust gasses, rather than by mechanical means. A supercharger is driven by the engine, either with gears, chains or belts, so there is a direct correlation between the engine speed and the boost produced by the supercharger. While the turbocharger may have the upper hand when you're talking about all-out high-rpm performance on the track, the supercharger shines at improving street performance as soon as you hit the throttle.

Since the supercharger is directly linked to the crankshaft, it starts making its boost right from the basement. This gives you the kind of low-end power you get to enjoy in most normal driving circumstances without hammering the gas pedal to the floor all the time. Driving a supercharged car gives you the sensation that you have a much bigger engine, without the nose-heavy weight and less-acceptable fuel economy. Low-end torque is what we need and that's what a mechanical supercharger does best. By packing in more air, the engine ingests a denser mixture of air and fuel without the effort of having to suck it in with nothing but normal atmospheric pressure.

As heady as all this is, we must be realistic about boost levels. The mere installation of a supercharger doesn't

Showy engines are commonplace in the world of street rods, but when only 5% have a whining blower and a scoop sticking out of the hood, they are the ones that get noticed. More so than with any other type of power-adder, a supercharger wins in the macho appearance department

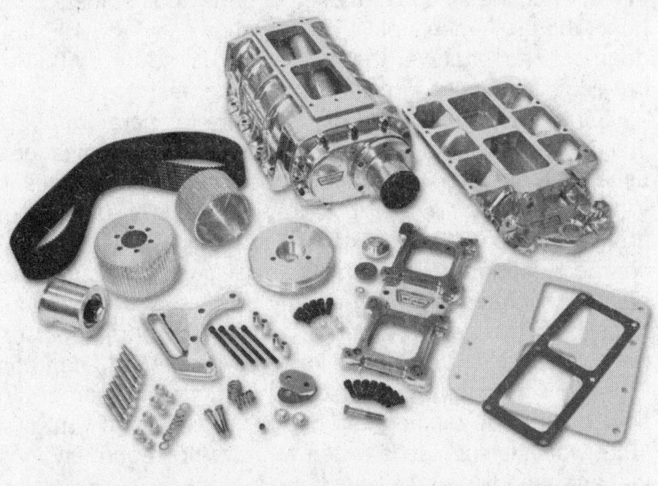

GMC-style Roots mechanical blowers, similar to what you see on dragsters, are still available in kit form from Weiand for small and big-block Chevrolet engines. This package has everything you need except the carbs and fuel line. Big blowers usually use two 500-cfm four-barrel carburetors on top. Make sure you have room for the three-inch-wide belt drive. With a 50% increase in power, this kit makes 10 or more psi on a small-block and 5-7 psi on a big-block

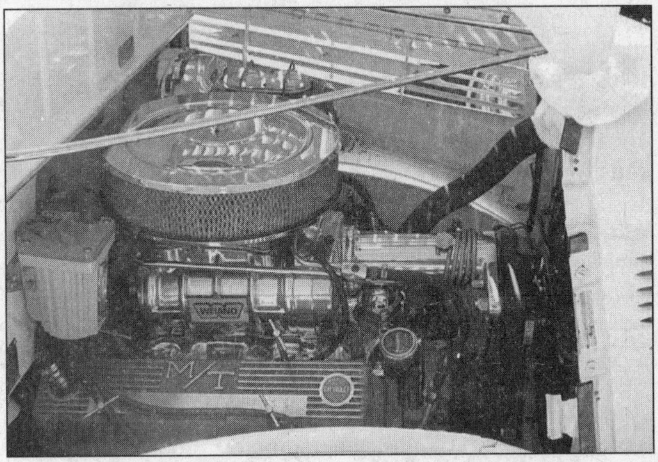

There are a number of lower-profile superchargers that will work in applications with lower hood clearance, and they usually have a smaller belt drive that's better where length is a problem, such as in street rods

Edelbrock offers this E-Force kit that features the new Magnuson MP112 supercharger. A 350 small-block Chevy made 507 hp/500 ft-lbs of torque with this blower kit installed

On EFI engines, a blower with a rear inlet like this can be used with a large throttle body without hitting the hood. Note that the installer used a large diameter cold-air-intake pipe and plumbed it down away from the hot engine compartment

mean the ruination of your engine. Nonetheless, there is a finite limit to the boost your blower can make, and probably a much lower limit of how much boost your engine can take, regardless of how the boost was generated. You'll find most street supercharger kits are limited to 5-7 psi, to make some power while working well on a basically stock engine that sips pump gasoline. Some kits on the market have optional pulleys that will spin the blower faster for more boost, but, as with any power adder, you can only go so far in increasing cylinder pressure before you have to make serious modifications to strengthen the engine (see Chapter 12 for more on engine durability mods). Most mechanical superchargers have a means of changing the relationship of blower speed to engine speed. On most street setups the blower is underdriven, meaning that it turns slower than the crankshaft. If the blower is driven at engine speed, it will make more power. Racecars may have blowers that are overdriven, meaning they turn faster than engine speed.

We discussed the demon that is detonation in the nitrous section. The two main factors in detonation control are heat and timing. Octane is also a factor, but once you have stepped up to using the premium pump gas, there isn't much you can do to get more octane unless you resort to using a can of aftermarket octane booster with every tank of gas. That can get both annoying and expensive. Ignition timing does offer some ways to deal with detonation. Supercharged engines generally like more timing, especially initial advance, but once you are making full boost and the vehicle is under load; too much ignition advance can bring on the death rattle you don't want to hear. Your computer-controlled engine management system incorporates a knock sensor on the block that signals the computer to pull back ignition timing if knock begins. However, things happed more rapidly in a boosted car under heavy acceleration than in a stock application. How much advance your application can handle is a trial-error-experience thing, but if you are using a production blower kit from a known manufacturer, these tests have already been made and some kind of timing control program should be included.

Heat in the blower and intake tract has a major effect on detonation control. A boosted application that can take 8 psi on a cool morning may need some kind of controls to counter detonation on a hot afternoon. Although a supercharger does not put as much heat into the intake tract as an exhaust-driven turbocharger, plenty of heat is still added. When you compress air and force it through the whole intake tract, the friction of these hot parts against the airflow heats the air. A mechanical supercharger may add 100-200 degrees F to whatever the ambient air is, so on a 100-degree day, the intake air could be 300 degrees!

One really effective way to lower the temperature of the intake side is with an intercooler. This is a heat exchanger, usually an air-to-air cooler, which mounts in the intake tract. When boosted air is forced to travel through a cooler (like a small radiator) that is exposed to outside air, the intake charge temperature drops and power goes up. That's the beauty of intercooling - it not only helps avoid detonation, it makes more power. Whether you have a normally-aspirated or forced-induction application, with every 10-degrees F drop in the intake temperature, you gain one percent in power. Drop the temperature by 100-degrees and you gain 10%, which is substantial when we're talking about engines that are already pretty efficient.

The bad news is that most bolt-on supercharger kits don't include an intercooler. In some cases, small mechanical superchargers don't make high levels of boost, especially if they are part of a CARB-approved package, and plumbing the whole thing through more pipes and an intercooler may slow down the air enough to almost negate the positive effect of the cooling.

Big blowers in late-model cars call for some creative induction methods, such as this custom duct that puts the air filters off to the side

A carburetion choice for hood clearance that looks as good as it works is a pair of side-draft Weber carbs mounted on top of a supercharger

Your engine's existing compression ratio has an important effect on the boost level you can hope to utilize with any forced induction system. The higher the static compression ratio, the less boost you can run without detonation. If your compression ratio is too high, the small amount of boost you can reliably use may not be worth the effort and expense of the supercharger system. Systems with an air-to-water intercooler mounted in the intake manifold are quite effective, with coolant circulated by an auxiliary pump through the intercooler.

Roush Performance offers 2005-2007 Mustang owners a chance to gain 115 hp with eight hours of installation work. Their ROUSHcharger features an intercooler and ECM calibration, plus a 3-year, 36,000-mile warranty. Here it is in kit form and installed

The Eaton design positive-displacement blowers from Magnuson feature two rotors that, when turned, grasp the fuel/air mix firmly and compress it into the engine. As engine speed goes up, so does boost

Centrifugal superchargers are sort of like a turbo with a mechanical drive system - the Powerdyne unit shown here has a unique internal belt-drive for quieter operation

Our modified engines generally have higher compression ratios than other vehicles on the road, and that's a good thing for performance, but not so good for supercharging. Just as a guideline, you should be able to use 5-7 psi of boost if your engine's compression ratio is 9:1 or lower. If you are rebuilding your engine before installing the forced induction, it's a good idea to equip it with new forged pistons of 8:1 compression. This will allow (all others factors being equal) 8-12 psi of boost, which is a big difference in performance when your foot goes down. This is just a general guideline, and the design and efficiency of the supercharger you choose will also be a factor.

There are several types of superchargers for street performance. Of course, each manufacturer will tell you that their design is the best, but you should do plenty of research on your own before making a decision to buy a kit that may cost $3000 to $6000. The two main types of supercharger design you will see are the Roots type (or "positive displacement"), and the centrifugal design.

The Roots-type mechanical blower uses a pair of rotors that turn inside a housing. Some may have straight rotors with two or three lobes, and as the rotors turn, they capture a certain amount of air and propel it to the inner circumference

Back in '57 when this Thunderbird was built, Ford offered a special hi-perf 312 engine with a Paxton-McCulloch supercharger. Only a few hundred were built, but this 'Bird owner just added the modern equivalent centrifugal supercharger to this restored and hot-rodded 312 for a resto-mod approach to performance

If you're running a blower on a late-model EFI engine, you'll need a large throttle body and cold air intake duct to feed the supercharged engine's thirst for air and fuel

In smaller-blower applications with a ribbed-belt drive, the diameter of the blower pulley changes the rate at which the blower spins versus the crankshaft speed. This Roush smaller blower pulley for supercharged Fords could net you an extra 25 hp and 25 ft-lbs of torque. When changing blower drive ratios for more boost, you must also adjust the fuel curve, and up the octane level

of the case and out to the intake manifold. Each time they turn around, they capture air, hence the "positive" description. The benefit of this type is that it starts making boost at very low rpm, but some root-type blowers are noisier than other designs, intoduce more heat into the intake tract and take a little more crankshaft horsepower to drive. Most of the blowers used today have proven designs that have been around for years, and in the case of the Eaton blower, have been used by major car manufacturers on OEM-supercharged installations.

A variation of this type of blower is the screw-type. These have two rotors with helically-wound vanes that, as the name implies, look like two giant screws. When the two screws mesh together, the air is actually compressed between the screws. Manufacturers of this design feel that the result is a more effective supercharger, but they are generally more expensive than other types, due to the high cost of materials and manufacturing to produce a close-tolerance blower.

This Powerdyne installation is on a Lincoln Navigator, something akin to a heavyweight boxer in a tuxedo, exhibiting punch and style

Weiand has been making blower kits since the Fifties, but this kit using a 144 blower is strictly modern. It's designed for 1993-1995 TBI GM trucks, which need some serious waking-up. With a calibrated PROM for the computer and Teflon-tipped rotors, these trucks arise with 100 new ponies at only 4-6 psi of boost

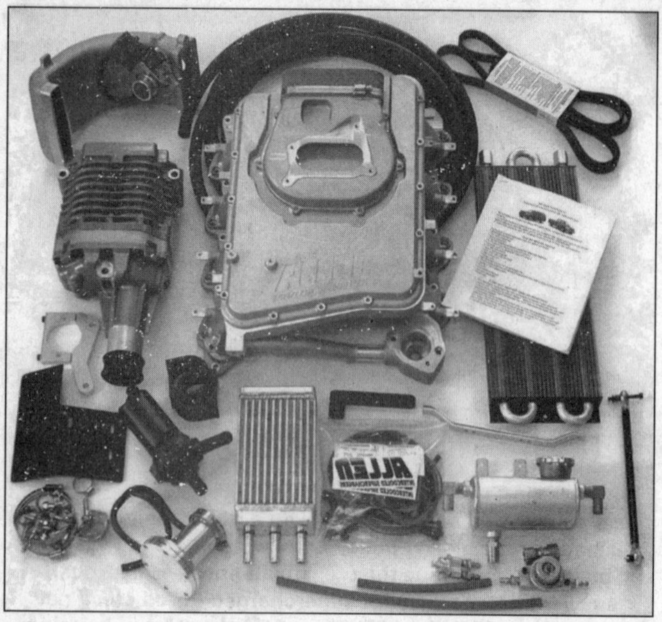

Allen Engine makes a quality kit for Ford 4.6L modular engines. The package comes with an internal air-to-water intercooler, makes 80 more hp and 100 foot-pounds of torque with reliability and smooth operation. Kits are available for Thunderbirds, F-150's and other Ford applications

Old, new or in-between in age or style of vehicle, you'll find mechanical superchargers making horsepower

The other major type of bolt-on supercharger is the centrifugal design. From a quick examination, the centrifugal blower looks just like the compressor half of a turbocharger, being a multi-vaned wheel within a scroll-type housing. Unlike a turbocharger, this type of blower isn't driven by exhaust but by a mechanical drive from the engine, usually a belt. On the back of the compressor, there is a gearbox that speeds the compressor wheel up compared to engine rpm. With a centrifugal design supercharger, you get some of the boost potential of a turbocharger without the added intake heat from the exhaust-driven turbine. These types of blowers are not positive displacement, and thus do not necessarily make their boost down on the low end, but have plenty of air-movement potential when they are spinning rapidly. The centrifugals also do not take as much horsepower to drive as positive-displacement mechanical blowers. In general, centrifugal superchargers will make more power (all other conditions being equal) than a positive-displacement type,

This 2004 Chevy pickup makes a good case for supercharging. With only six pounds of boost and 91-octane gasoline, the truck has tons of bottom-end power and can tow anything the chassis is rated for. The installation used a kit from Whipple with a twin-screw blower and all the necessary hardware

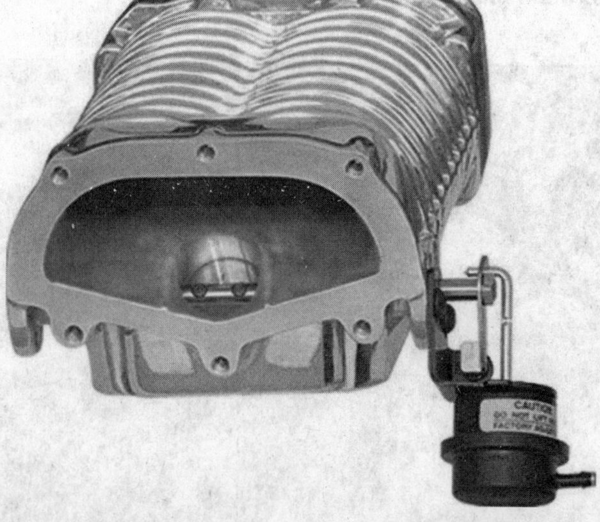

Some superchargers use a bypass valve that reduces losses during idle and cruise conditions - the valve is on the inside on this Magnuson blower and is actuated by the external vacuum control

Today, there are many tuners who are equipping old-school blowers and induction systems with modern EFI injectors, and utilizing an aftermarket engine management program. This setup with the injectors in the hat is by Blower Drive Service

This Radix blower setup from Magnuson is for small-block Chevys and features an internal intercooler in the intake manifold - taking heat out of the intake tract makes power and reduces the chance of detonation under boost

but the power will come at higher rpm. You have to decide what your own performance needs are to decide on the right kit for your application.

Unlike a turbocharger kit, the typical supercharger includes a whole new intake manifold, since the intake must match the outlet configuration of the blower. On most centrifugal blower kits, however, a new intake manifold isn't needed, because the boost can be plumbed to your existing intake.

Most reputable blower kits have everything you need to install the system and use it reliably. Contents include the blower, intake manifold (if needed), belt, mounting hardware, instructions and some type of electronic gear to control fuel delivery and/or ignition timing. Some kits use a larger-than-stock fuel pump that replaces your in-tank pump, and a special fuel pressure regulator that may be boost-sensitive. Other included components could be hoses, wire harnesses, air intake, an intercooler, and parts that relocate items in the engine compartment to provide room for the blower. Some installations may include an oil filter relocation kit that allows for easier oil changes after the supercharger kit is installed. These kinds of extras are installation specific.

Most kits can be installed by a competent mechanic - provided he reads the manufacturer's instructions before rip-

This Weiand blower kit for small-block Chevys uses the 142 Pro-Street supercharger for a 25 to 40% gain in power with only a single four-barrel carburetor. Gaskets, bolts and intake manifold are included. On the photo of the installed kit, notice the simplicity of the ribbed belt-drive and tensioner setup

ping out the stock parts and slapping new parts in. The quality of the instructions varies among manufacturers, but all companies have tech lines to answer your questions about installation or tuning, as well as web sites that explain the typical FAQs (frequently-asked questions). A Haynes repair manual for your specific vehicle will be a big help, especially when dealing with "where did this gasket go?" or "what wire went here?" kinds of questions.

The manufacturer of the kit you utilize has done their homework to make their blower right for your car or truck, but it's your responsibility to see that your engine is ready for the blower. At the relatively low boost levels of most kits, a stock engine in good condition should work fine. The supercharger should not have any serious effect on the engine's longevity, but of course that assumes your engine is in perfect condition to start with. There is an extra load on the crankshaft to drive a mechanical blower, and the boost is not going to be all that effective if your valves are leaky and your piston rings are worn. Leaking valve guides or rings can permit some engine oil to enter the combustion chamber, and this is an invitation for detonation under boost, even if everything else in your installation is done right.

Boost and detonation both put increased loads on pistons, rods, bearings and crankshaft. For applications where you will be drag racing or running high boost on the street, you might consider aftermarket internals such as forged connecting rods and a forged-steel crank.

As far as other mods go, bigger valves and ported cylinder heads won't be as important with forced induction, but camshaft choice can make a difference in your boosted engine. What works best for a no-power-adder engine is not going to be productive for your supercharged engine. Consult with the manufacturer of the kit you're planning to install to see what they recommend. Even if you leave the stock cam in place, at least install high-performance valve springs and lightweight retainers (see Chapter 8).

The two most important engine modifications that can complement your forced induction are the exhaust and ignition system. The supercharger is designed to pack more air into the engine, and your stock exhaust system is going to stifle all that from getting out of the engine. A good header and cat-back exhaust will help reduce backpressure, allowing the supercharger to do a better job. All that boost pressure makes it harder for the spark to jump the plug gaps, so an aftermarket coil and plug wires should be considered a minimum investment here (see Chapter 5).

11C Turbocharging

Of the three major power adders (nitrous oxide, superchargers, and turbochargers), the turbocharger offers the biggest power potential. Its durability and practicality has been proven many times over on production cars and trucks worldwide. At the other end of the performance spectrum, it is responsible for some of the quickest and fastest bullets in racing, and also brings smiles to thousands of street performance tuners whose needs fall somewhere between the OEM crowd and the seven-second scene.

Boost - the increased pressure inside your engine when the turbocharger is working - pumps up both the engine and your heart rate. Unlike nitrous oxide, which only comes on when you arm a switch and hit full throttle, the turbocharger lies under your hood ready and waiting for any opportunity to rocket you forward with a smooth whoosh and a high-speed whine like a small jet engine. The sound and the performance are both addictive.

Do you like high engine speeds, like 8,000 or 9,000 rpm? At speed, a turbocharger is rotating at 100,000 rpm or more! It is very precisely machined and balanced and made of materials that will withstand very high temperatures and operate for many years with little maintenance.

This engine by BanksPower is a beautiful illustration of turbocharging, a small-block Chevy with 700 horsepower - thanks to a turbocharger on each cylinder bank, big wastegates, stainless turbine shields, and all the right internal goodies to withstand the serious heat and cylinder pressures. Packaging for a turbo installation is often more complicated than for a supercharger, but the potential gain is much higher

There are basically three main elements to a turbocharger: the exhaust turbine, the intake air compressor, and the housing/shaft/bearing assembly that ties the two pressure-related sections together. The job of the turbine is to spin the shaft of the turbocharger. The turbine is composed of an iron housing in which a wheel covered with curved vanes or blades rotates. These blades fit precisely within the turbine housing. When the turbine housing is mounted to an engine's exhaust manifold, the escaping hot exhaust gases flow through the housing and over the vanes, causing the shaft to spin rapidly. After the exhaust has passed through the turbine, it exits through a large pipe, called a downpipe, to the rest of the vehicle's exhaust system.

Within the compressor housing is another wheel with vanes. Since both wheels are connected to a common shaft, the intake wheel spins at the same speed as the turbine, so the compressor draws intake air in where the rapidly spinning wheel blows the air into the engine's intake side. The more load there is on the engine, the more the turbocharger works to give the engine horsepower. As the engine goes faster, it makes more hot exhaust, which drives the turbocharger faster, which makes the engine produce more power.

The unit in the center of this turbo sandwich has the important function of reliably passing the power between the two housings. What makes this so difficult is the tremendous heat involved and the high speeds at which the shaft must turn.

Millions of turbochargers have been manufactured using a sleeve-type bearing that relies on a high volume of engine oil to keep it and the shaft cool enough to continue without seizing, but many of today's performance turbochargers feature ball-bearings. The technical name for the center portion of the turbo is the CHRA, for "center housing and rotating assembly." Some turbos are fitted with a water-cooled CHRA, where engine coolant is circulated through the bearing housing to carry away extra heat beyond what the oil can do. The CHRA is also sometimes called a "cartridge."

The limitation for the supercharger-equipped car is in top end performance, and this is where the turbocharger has the distinct advantage. In order to make any more boost with a supercharger, you have to change the pulleys or gearing that drives it, and there is generally nothing you can do to the inside of it to make more boost. The turbocharger is much more customizable, with various wheels and housings available to suit whatever the intended engine or purpose. Boost can be made to come in early, or come in later at a higher boost level. The same basic turbocharger can be used for street use or modified to make more boost than your engine can live with! Such customizing, called sizing, should be done by an experienced turbo shop that can

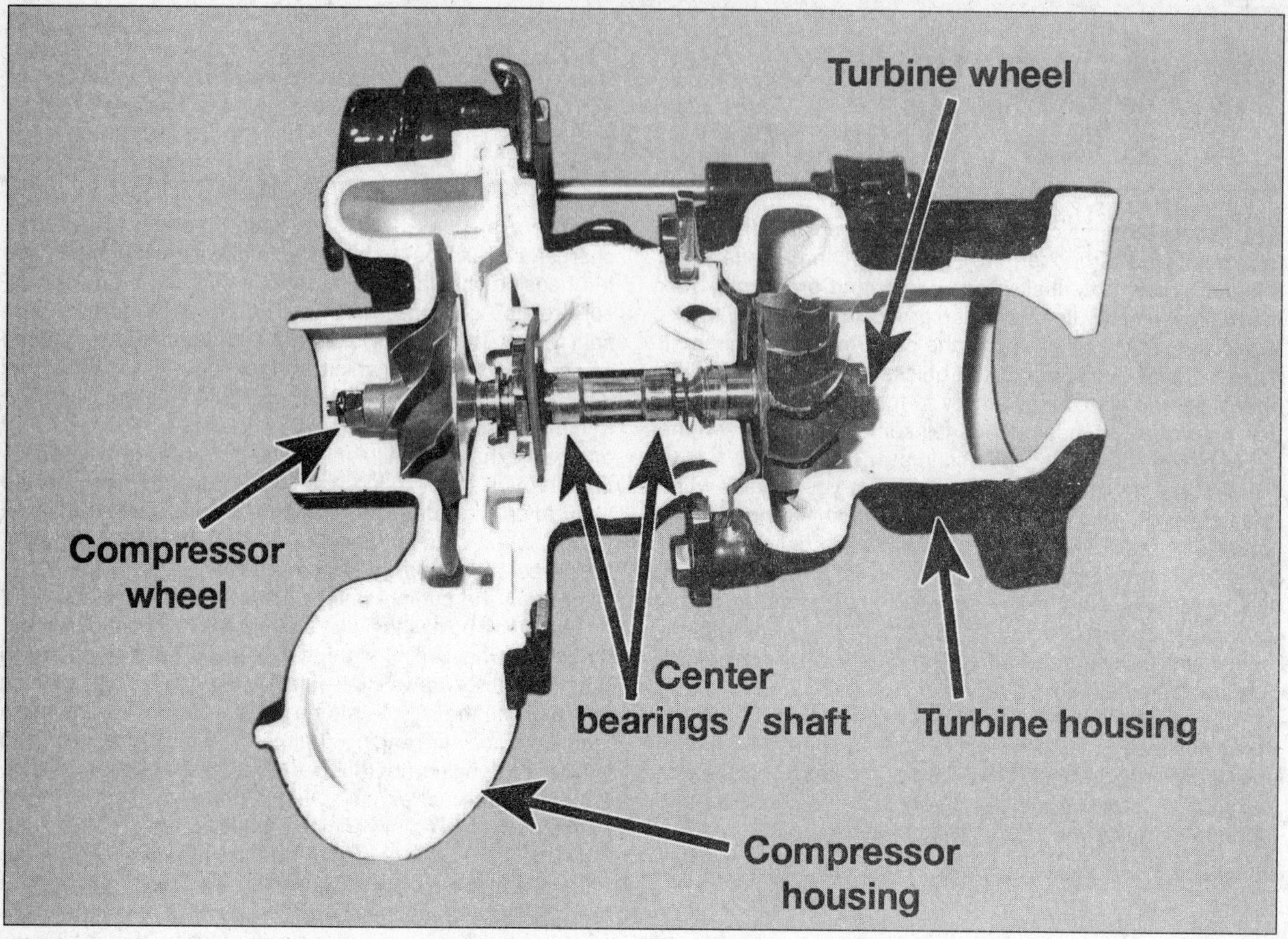

This cutaway of a typical turbocharger graphically shows how the main components work together inside the three housings. The very hot turbine that is driven by exhaust gasses, the compressor wheel/housing that generates the boost to the engine's intake system, and the CHRA housing/shaft/bearing assembly between the other two housings

select the exact right components for your engine size and power requirements. A turbo expert can take your information on the engine modifications, bottom-end strength (see Chapter 12) and projected horsepower goal, figure the airflow required to meet those parameters, and come up with the right-sized turbocharger with the proper compressor and turbine. Too big or too small and you and your engine will be unhappy.

The increased intake tract heat is perhaps the biggest downside to turbocharging, but a number of excellent fixes have been developed over the years. First, improper turbo selection can worsen the heat problem. If the chosen turbo is not running at its proper efficiency, it can overspeed, a condition in which the air is moving too fast for the capacity of the engine, causing it to back up in the intake tract. This hurts the turbocharger and your performance. The proper initial choice of turbocharger and the match of its turbine and compressor to your exact needs should keep you out of that range and make the right amount of boost without excessive shaft speeds.

The standard high-temp coatings used on headers will probably fail on a turbo manifold, but some of the coating companies have a ceramic-based coating that can withstand very high temperatures (up to 2000-degrees F). Further isolation of the exhaust side heat can be realized by using a shield over the turbine housing. Shields are available that are a formed sandwich of thin stainless steel sheetmetal with a core of high-temperature insulation. Some have an exterior that looks like formed tinfoil, but others have a smooth-shaped stainless exterior that has the added benefit of making the whole installation look as cool as it acts.

The most effective and most common method of dealing with air temperature in the intact tract on a turbocharged car is an intercooler. This is a honeycomb affair much like a radiator, usually mounted out in front of the vehicle in an opening below the bumper where cooler air is found. The boosted air from the compressor is ducted through pipes and into the intercooler, and then to the intake of the engine. Thus, the cooler is between the compressor and the engine, so it's called an intercooler.

There are few aftermarket complete kits for turbocharging late-model V8 engines. Specialty shops do most very-high-performance turbo setups. This one has custom headers from each side going forward to feed one good-size turbo, low and at the front of the engine, that blows through the intercooler in front of the radiator and supplies cooled boost to the custom Wilson aluminum intake manifold. Note the detailing in the braided hoses, and the care to heat-wrap wires and hoses, too

Most intercoolers for street-driven machines are of the air-to-air type. Compressed air flows into one end, through the tubes and fins of the cooler just like engine coolant does through a conventional radiator. The outside air, especially at vehicle speeds where the turbo is really working, flows over the intercooler and cools off what's passing inside, making it denser. It then flows out the other end and to the engine. Although the longer piping of the intercooler system does add more frictional area for the air to pass over, the cooling effect and resulting denser air charge makes enough change in horsepower to more than make up for that. In some cases, a good intercooler is taking out more than half of the intake heat.

Of course, you can run a turbo setup without an intercooler, but you can't make optimal horsepower and the dreaded specter of detonation will be haunting you unless you're using high-octane gasoline and a few other tricks. Even factory-built turbocharged cars, like the Subaru WRX and others, have intercoolers designed into the car, both to make more power at a safe level of boost and to cope with the poor quality of gasoline available to us at today's pumps. On some production turbo cars, the intercooler is compactly mounted on top of the engine and is fed cold air through a hood scoop.

Even more efficient than the air-to-air intercooler is a water-cooled design. In this style, all the intake air is forced to pass over a small radiator in an airtight housing. This radiator works in reverse of your engine's radiator, in that the coolant flowing through the core is cold and extracts heat from the air flowing through, rather than vice-versa. Plain water is used as the coolant, and a separate electric water pump is used to circulate cold water from a remote tank through the air-to-water intercooler.

The primary leash on the turbo beast is an exhaust wastegate. The wastegate is a device that senses boost pressure in the engine and releases some exhaust to the atmosphere when needed. If the boost is too high, releasing the exhaust pressure built up causes the turbine wheel to

Another dead-serious turbo installation, this one features two turbos, one near each fenderwell. They pick up outside air from behind the headlights, blow it through the intercooler, then to two big plenums with aftermarket throttle bodies. With the amount of boost that can be produced with two turbos, a small-block race motor can make 1100 or more horsepower. The world's fastest stock-bodied car, a Firebird with a twin-turbo small-block Chevy (less than 372 cubic inches) went 300 mph at Bonneville!

Intercooling is virtually a must for a turbo installation, especially on a V8 with a crowded engine compartment where a lot of heat is generated. Compressed intake air flows through one side of the cooler, gets cooled by outside air flowing over the cooler, then enters the engine. Intercoolers are made in many sizes, to suit applications from turbo'd Hondas to big-rig trucks

slow down, reducing the boost to a safe level. On most production turbocharged cars, the wastegate is integral to the turbocharger and dumps excess exhaust back into the exhaust system downstream of the turbine. In most of these applications, the system is designed for a relatively low level of boost to maintain OEM reliability and when the wastegate actuates, the driver never even notices it. The power simply doesn't increase.

Aftermarket boost controls for wastegates can be operated from the dash, where each turn of the knob may represent one psi of boost. You can set it for the stock boost level when you only have pump gas available, or crank it up when you're at the track and have race gas. Other controls for some cars may be electronic, with several boost levels that you can select with the push of a button.

The main boost control device on a turbocharger is an exhaust wastegate - the more the turbo system is designed to flow, the bigger the wastegate must be to be effective

A second type of control used in most turbo installations is a blow-off valve. Unlike the wastegate, this type installs on the intake system. When a turbocharger is spinning at high speeds and making boost, it can't stop or even slow very easily or quickly. If you happen to quickly back off the throttle when you've been under boost, the intake system is still filled with pressurized air. The plate in your throttle body is closed but the turbo's compressor is still packing in air behind it. Since the pressure has no place to go, a pressure wave backs up into the compressor and tries to make the wheel go the other way, causing a pressure surge that is damaging to the compressor. Another negative effect of the pressure backwave is that the turbo starts to slow down, so when you get back on the throttle again it has to work to catch up to the pressure it had before. These two problems can happen to any turbo car if the throttle is closed, but is particularly prevalent on manual transmission cars where you are on-off-on the throttle for every shift. The solution is the blow-off valve. Mounted on the intake pipe, the valve contains a spring-loaded diaphragm or piston that lifts when it senses a surge. As soon as the air is released for a split-second, you're through with your shift and the boost resumes with hardly a noticeable lapse.

A complete turbocharging kit from most reputable aftermarket companies will include virtually everything you need for your application. The manufacturer will have done the research to size the turbo for your particular engine/vehicle, and will have included the equipment to alter your stock electronics and fuel system to provide the right amount of fuel and timing control.

When you start shopping for a turbo kit you may at first question the expense, but just compare turbocharging to other methods of upping your horsepower. We've seen many enthusiasts who have spent the price of a turbo kit on bolt-on performance parts and didn't get the power increase they could have had with a turbo, not to mention the decent fuel economy, low-end driveability and factory idle quality that are also hallmarks of the turbo.

Although most turbocharging kits have everything you need to actually install the turbo, there are a number of considerations beyond the supplied parts. Is your engine ready for boost? The kit instructions, if they're good ones, will give you recommendations for other modifications you can make to allow the turbo setup to work even better on your engine.

Perhaps no other accessory is more important for a turbo'd car than an accurate boost gauge. Unless you have a way to keep track of actual boost in the engine, you'll never know if the turbo is working at its potential, or if the wastegate is adjusted where you want it - and working. The gauge is also helpful to troubleshoot your system. If you see a lesser amount of boost than normal (under the same conditions of throttle, rpm and load), you should inspect the piping and hoses in your intercooler plumbing to see if there is a leak. The best boost gauges are dampened to give steady needle readings and indicate both vacuum (negative side, in inches of mercury) and boost (positive side, in inches of mercury or psi).

A really good radiator is going to be more important than ever, and you may want to consider an aftermarket heavy-duty radiator with more rows of tubes than stock. Most cars have a radiator that's barely adequate for the stock engine. Aftermarket companies also make some really excellent fan/shroud combinations that allow more air through the radiator than a stock fan.

The other type of boost control is a blow-off valve, which is designed to be mounted on the intake side and prevents pressure surges if you close the throttle very quickly, like when shifting, while the turbo is working hard

Oil is a big issue with a turbo because the oil not only lubricates this very precisely machined and balanced assembly, the oil is also part of the cooling system for a device that gets really, really hot. Keeping the turbo alive and cool means that there must be a steady flow of clean oil, in and out. Most kits supply a braided-steel hose and fittings to plumb the pressurized oil from the engine to the top of the CHRA. The supply line should be free of sharp bends or kinks, but this is even more critical on the much larger drain hose that comes from the bottom of the CHRA. The hose doesn't carry a great deal of pressure like the supply hose, but it must be capable of carrying away an unrestricted volume of oil back to your oil pan. If there is any restriction in this drainback system, oil will back up into the CHRA and slow the cooling/lubricating action.

Most kits don't include this, but you may want to consider a turbo timer as an option. This is an electronic unit that will run your engine for a specified period, say five minutes, after you shut it off with the key. This is a cooling cycle for the turbocharger, and some OEM turbo cars have one. The reason for this is a problem called coking. Nothing illegal here, it's just that when you have been running your turbo hard and then shut off the engine, tremendous heat-soak occurs in the CHRA because oil is no longer flowing through to cool the bearing. The coking happens because the oil that remains sitting in the turbo's hot bearing area may cook into coke, the kind of coal-like material used in steel foundries. These little particles of now-crunchy oil get circulated in the turbo and the rest of your oiling system upon the next startup, which isn't good for engine longevity. The turbo timer gives the turbo a chance to cool down after a run.

A final for your good-to-do list in terms of oiling is using an engine oil cooler. Many import engines have a factory oil cooler sandwiched between the oil filter and the block, with coolant lines connected to the cooling system.

Power adders are heady stuff. You will love the feeling of juice or boost, and for your first month of driving you'll be using it all the time. Eventually, you'll settle down and only use the power-adder's extra horsepower 5-10% of your driving time, and your fuel economy will return to something near stock.

Notes

12 The Bottom End: Building it to Last

Large amounts of horsepower can be obtained in various ways, as this book is dedicated to explaining. You may choose the "external" path to power, with add-ons such as a supercharger, turbocharger or nitrous oxide. These are all proven methods of increasing performance without removing the engine from the vehicle. In some cases there can be a combination of forced induction *and* nitrous oxide for truly serious performance numbers.

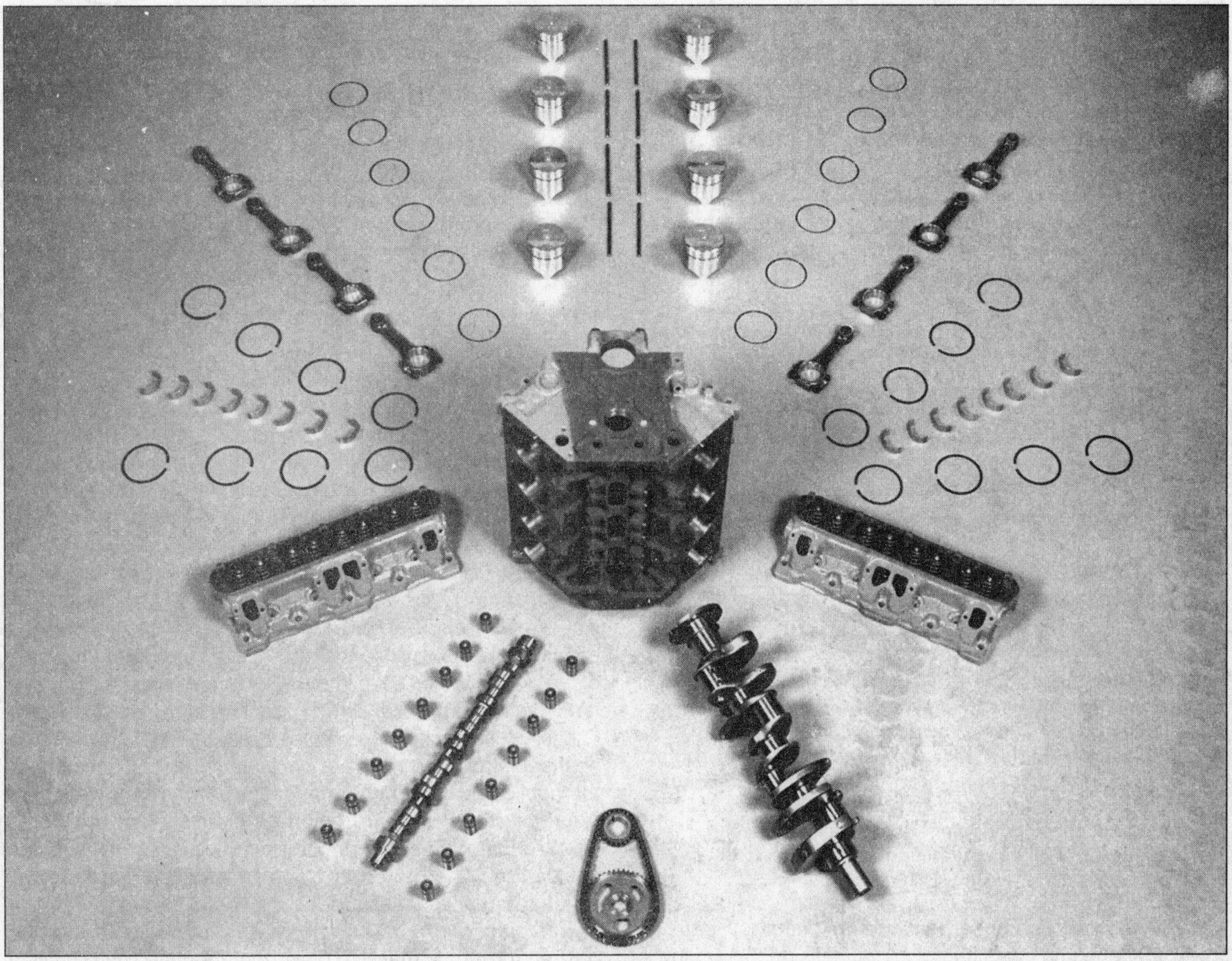

Just like a model car kit without the plastic trees, here are the basic elements of an engine laid out, in this case for a small-block Mopar. The prepped block and heads, plus all the other internals, is from Performance Automotive Warehouse, and is ready for you to clean, lube and assemble. If you have the right Haynes Repair manual or Techbook for your engine and some experience, you can assemble a package like this and save money compared to a ready-built performance engine. You can also have all the machine work done at a local machine shop and just purchase the rotating and reciprocating parts for the assembly

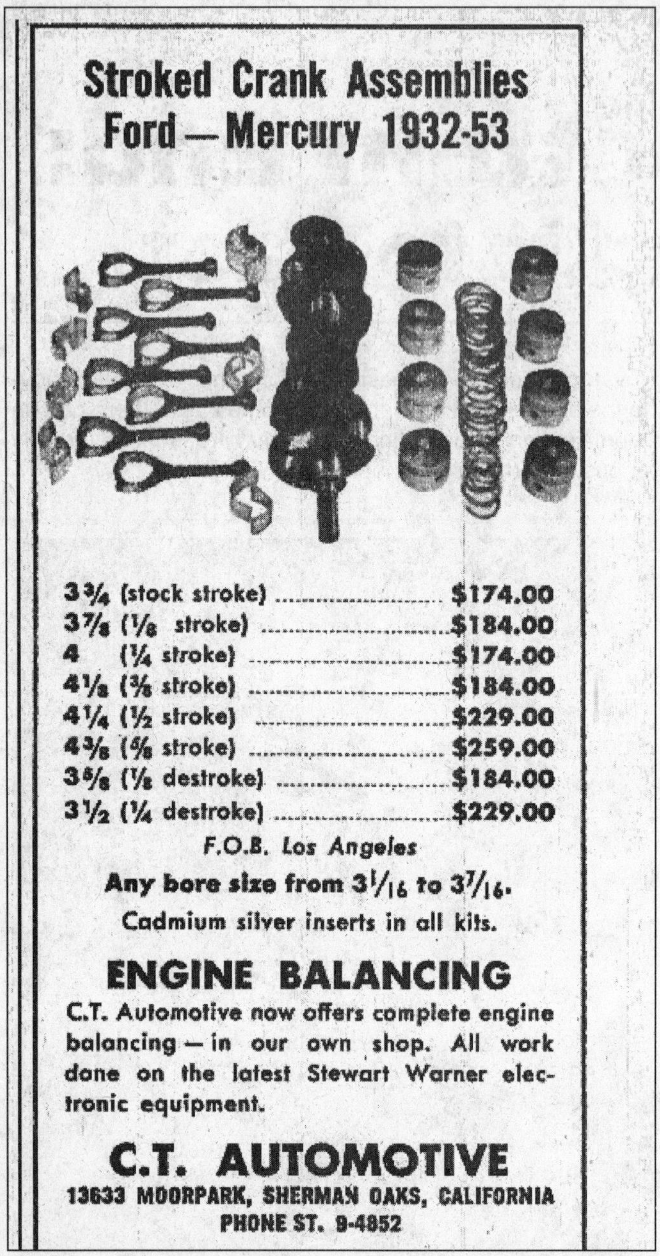

There is nothing new about aftermarket assemblies offered for popular engines being rebuilt for high-performance use. This ad, with all the bottom-end pieces for a Ford flathead V8, was in a 1953 issue of Hop-Up Magazine. The flathead Ford engine was cheap and so popular for hot rodding (until the overhead engines came in during the early Fifties) that it brought aftermarket speed equipment from small manufacturers to the multi-billion-dollar industry we have today

A modern version of the flathead setup would be something like this Sledgehammer kit from Lunati, featuring a nitrided, non-twist 4340 forged steel crankshaft, H-beam forged rods, Wiseco pistons and King Allecular bearings. Packages like this small-block Chevy kit are available for a wide variety of compression ratios and displacements (strokers, too)

This Chapter is concerned with the "internal" path to power that encompasses changes made inside the engine's short-block, all that rotating and reciprocating mass that delivers your engine's power to the flywheel, transmission and ultimately, the rear tires. The internal and external modifications are not necessarily on divergent paths. If you make any serious power with add-ons, heads, valvetrain and induction, you'll have to tear the engine down anyway, because a stock bottom end running higher rpm and loads due to these modifications is going to disassemble itself . . . the hard way.

Modifications to the bottom end of an engine can be those machining steps that ensure your engine is as close to perfect as can be and that there are no flaws that could show up later under high stress, or they could be replacement components that are designed with high-strength and high-performance to start with - usually aftermarket products.

We are looking to either improve the existing bottom-end components to increase their durability in performance use, or we are replacing all the reciprocating and rotating components with aftermarket performance/racing pieces that are especially designed with greater strength. Most stock crankshafts, pistons and rods are *castings* that are machined for the application, and in normal everyday use they work fine. A further step up in durability for a crankshaft or rod would be castings of a better iron than production quality, such as ductile iron. The preferred type of manufacturing for rods, pistons or crankshafts is *forging*, in which the red-hot blank part is placed in a set of huge dies and pounded into the desired form by a massive blow from the machine. This is a method of manufacture that makes the material more dense and resistant to cracks or fractures. The process, through streamlined today by modern equipment, is little different in principle than what was done by blacksmiths of old, who made strong parts by heating the metal in a forge and then condensing it by hammering it repeatedly while the part is on an anvil.

The process of forging is much more expensive than making cast parts, and thus in factory engines, forged rods, pistons and crankshafts are usually found only in performance vehicles or heavy-duty applications such as truck or marine engines. The biggest investment in building a powerful performance engine may be the bottom-end components, since all of the stock pieces are generally replaced with forged aftermarket equivalents. A forged crankshaft or rod that is the dimensionally the same as its stock counterpart won't produce a single extra horsepower, but does provide the insurance that your performance engine will survive the process of adding or modifying components of the engine that *do* increase horsepower.

Blueprinting

When mass-produced engines and components meet with a vehicle on the assembly line, they are the products of an army of highly-skilled engineers, handling the design process and the design-for-manufacturing modifications it takes to build these components and engines. Their concerns for component longevity and stress levels are necessarily tempered with the reality that cost, materials and time are just as important to the company they work for. If the company loses money through cost overruns, many jobs could be at stake. The engineers only have to make the parts good enough to last a normal service life under average conditions. Many Detroit parts are over-engineered to some degree and have proven to be successful in high-performance and even some racing situations, but the "weakest link" will always display itself under sufficient load.

When engineers create the blueprints (computer CAD drawings today) for engines and components, the precise dimensions, tolerances and clearances are spelled out. Making parts to those exact specs can be slow and expensive. Along the way, wider tolerances creep into the manufacturing process and parts, the way pistons, for example, are often sorted into categories of size. Those that are too big or too small are discarded, while others might be a *little* big or a *little* small but are still useable. These parts go into everyday engines in a rapid process of machining and assembly. Likewise, a block has tolerances for the bore size. In some cases, manufacturers designate pistons with size designations of A, B, C etc., and also assign size designations to the cylinder bores. Ideally, pistons are selected and installed to provide the best fit, or closest to the engineered dimension for piston-to-bore clearance. Under normal conditions, such an engine can deliver good service for 200,000 miles or more, and with standard rebuilding practices could live for generations.

Where does performance fit in with this discussion of tolerances? Let's look back at the Sixties. Drag racing was fully established all across the country, with myriad competition classes from "stockers" to Top Fuel dragsters.

That first group encompassed a host of classes for stock-bodied, stock-engine cars. While the speeds and ETs

If blueprinting can be defined, it is the careful measurement of all aspects of the engine, and where possible, to machine components to be consistent and as close to a desired standard that would provide more power or reduced friction

Precision measuring tools, and the experience to take accurate and consistent readings with them, are vital to blueprinting an engine that will serve above-and-beyond stock performance standards. Here an inside micrometer is being used to check the inside diameter of the main bearings for bearing clearance and to check for any slight out-of-round condition that could slow down a spinning crankshaft

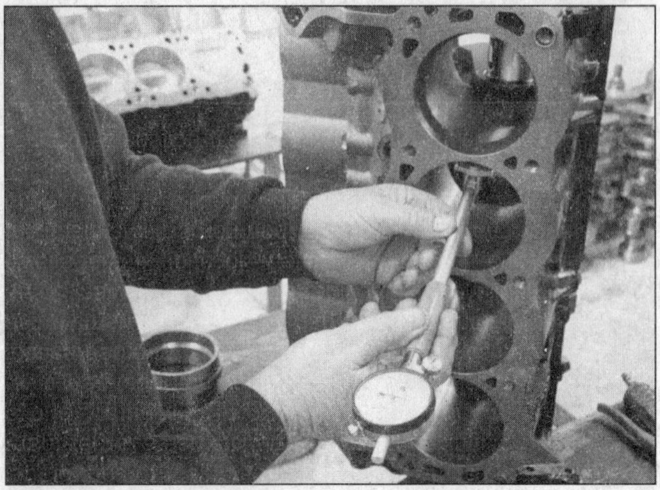

A dial bore-gauge reads the cylinder walls for exact size and any taper or out-of-round conditions. On a finished machined engine, these aspects should be perfect, but the professional engine builder makes a final double-check before picking the piston that best fits that cylinder. The act of double-checking is one of the time-consuming steps in engine-building that separates the professionals from the amateurs

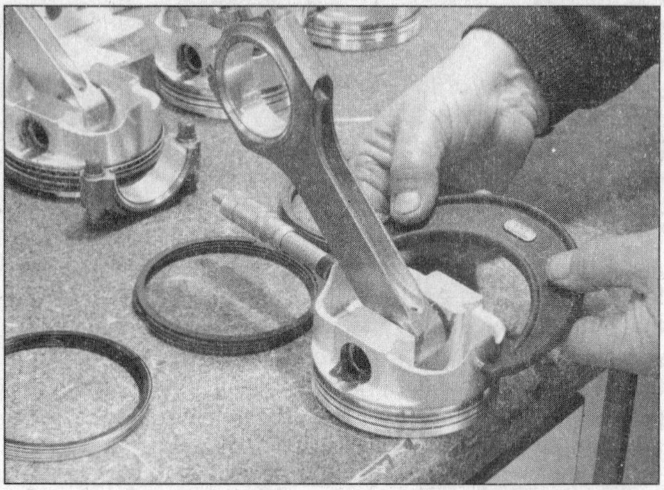

Pistons are usually near-perfect as cast or forged and machined, but they must all be carefully measured for size and roundness if an engine is to be truly blueprinted. All of the pistons could be installed in any cylinder, but the exact-right fit is what blueprinting is all about. Tiny improvements here and there add up to power and reliability

weren't as dramatic as the higher levels of race cars, these were cars the crowd could identify with. For the competitors, the Stock classes offered affordable racing and a training ground for moving up into the faster machinery.

The Stock class racers were in large part responsible for the expression "blueprinting." If the rules required that virtually every part in your engine had to be stock, right down to a specified casting number, how was a racer to get an edge over his competitors? It may have started with camshafts. If you went to a GM warehouse where you may have had an in with a friend that worked there, you could check out a bin full of camshafts. Though all had the correct part number for your application, you carefully measured the lobe lift on all of them and selected the one with the highest lift, since there was a manufacturing tolerance for the lobes.

This may sound extreme, but one little trick like that, combined with similar "improvements" throughout the car, usually resulted in a car with an edge. Besides selecting

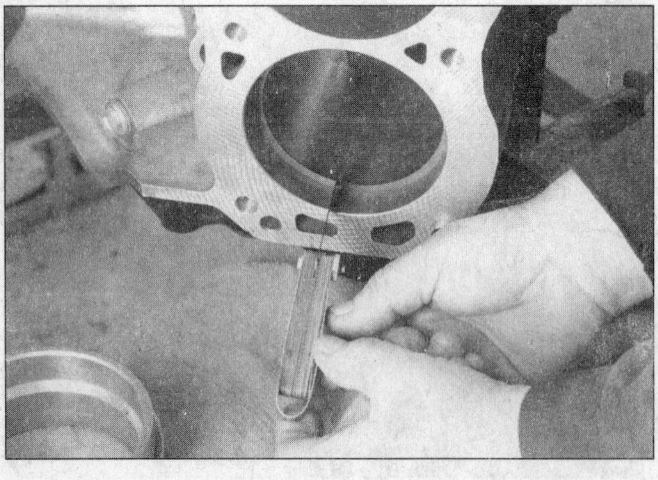

A package of standard rings will fit the engine they are intended for, yet cylinder-to-cylinder variations may mean variances in ring end gaps throughout the engine. Ring seal is vital on a performance engine, and excessive end gaps can cause a loss of compression or variance between cylinders. The gap is measured by feeler gauges, with the ring pushed squarely down into the bore with the top of a piston, or a tool made for this purpose

In the performance world, "standard" rings are never used. Instead, aftermarket performance rings are made slightly oversize, with little or no end gap. These can be tried and the ring ends filed carefully in a tool like this, a little at a time, until the end gaps are perfect on every ring for each cylinder. The three rings for a particular cylinder will be installed on the piston already chosen for that cylinder

The old hot rodder/racer expression has always been "balanced and blueprinted" to describe an engine "put together right." Before the assembly procedure, all the rotating and reciprocating components are weighed and balanced to be the same (such as all eight pistons weighing within a few grams of each other), then the crankshaft is balanced with weights to simulate the loads on the rod throws

the right components to make incremental power changes, the Stock class racers went further by detailing every part, including the block. The deck surfaces, main cap bores, camshaft bores and all other important dimensions were trued to be as close to the original engineers' "blueprints" as possible. When sanctioning bodies allowed a specific combustion chamber volume measured in cc's (cubic centimeters) for a particular engine, the heads would be meticulously massaged so that every chamber had the same volume, hence the maximum legal compression.

Blueprinting for these competitors became an obsession. They were always looking for a new way to improve their engine, and their results sparked interest in other drag racing classes and other motorsports. Soon, everyone was decking blocks parallel to the crankshaft mains, boring cylinders very precisely, and using a torque plate during the cylinder bore honing operations.

The path to power sometimes can be as simple as reducing friction. A piston/rod going up and down in a bore that is slightly out-of-round, tapered or not bored as squarely to the deck as the others, is going to have slightly more friction that the others. At 2500 rpm in a stock vehicle, it'll never be noticed and the engine should live a full life, but in a performance application, any unnecessary drag or resistance to rotating or reciprocating parts is going to cost horsepower. You can't eliminate friction altogether, although racers have dreamed of doing so, but lessening the load on the engine by making everything swing as free as possible will provide results in horsepower and reliability both.

To an engine builder, there is nothing like the sight of a professional-grade crankshaft ready to install. In a performance/racing engine, you may lose a piston once in a while, but losing a crankshaft means the whole bottom end is toast, and probably the block too. All the expense and time invested in the engines' parts and assembly could be negated by an inferior crankshaft. This Lunati crank is as beautiful as engine insurance gets

Crankshaft work

Blueprinting a crankshaft means making every dimension true to its design, even those aspects that a normal rebuilder would just take for granted as being correct. For instance, the throws on a V8 crank are spaced at 90-degrees from each other, such that if you looked at an end-view of a crankshaft from the snout, you would see one throw at each of the four compass points. It is possible for a factory crankshaft to have a throw or two that is not *exactly* 90-degrees, something that could occur through tolerances in casting and machining the crank, or could be due to stresses from overheating or abuse. Whatever the cause, this is a dimension that should be checked by a competent machine shop. If one of the throws is a little off, minor offset grinding of the throw can correct this.

Assuming the crankshaft is found to be straight, and true in terms of offset in the throws, then attention is turned to the dimensions and condition of the main and rod journals. Careful measurements on each journal will indicate if the journal diameter is within the small-range of specs for that type of engine. Production V8 engines in general may have a range of acceptable diameter of about 0.001-inch, which is a pretty precise tolerance. If you're dealing with a new crankshaft, things should be exact, but in a performance engine, everything must be checked thoroughly, with no detail assumed to be correct until it is measured.

On a used crankshaft, you need to find out if the journals are out-of-round or tapered from wear. By measuring with a micrometer at a number of points around each journal's circumference, you'll be able to determine whether or not the journal is out-of-round. A straight journal will measure the same no matter where you place the micrometer. Take measurements at each end of the journal, near the crank throws, to determine if the journal is tapered. The difference from end to end should be no more than 0.0005-inch.

Now the (cleaned) crankshaft can be laid in the block, supported by only the front and rear main bearings. With the

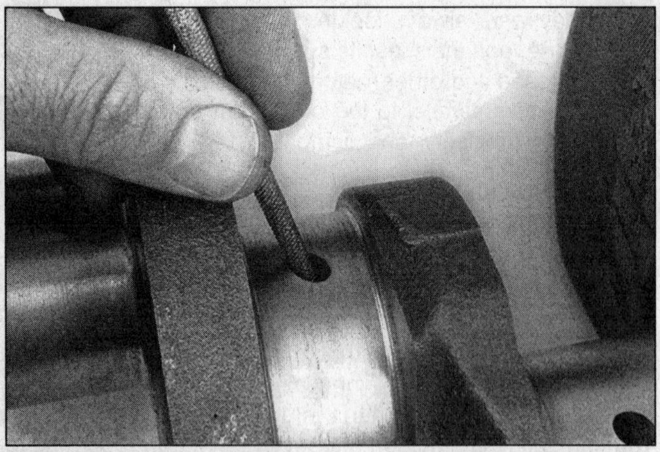

A common step in preparation of an OEM crankshaft is to provide better oiling by filing the oil holes, which creates a radiused entry for better flow, like porting a cylinder head. After performing this procedure, the crankshaft journals should be micro-polished at a machine shop. The polishing is done with very fine abrasive cloth that removes very little metal, just smoothes it

Part of the prep for any crankshaft, new or used, is to clean out the oil galleries in the crank. Most crankshafts are cross-drilled, meaning the oil hole goes all the way through. Small brushes are made just for this purpose

block upside down on an engine stand, position a dial-indicator against the top of the center main bearing journal and slowly make several rotations of the crank, watching the dial indicator. The variation in runout measurement should be no more than 0.004-inch.

With a full set of main bearings in place in the block, install the bearing caps and lower bearings halves and torque the main caps to specifications in several progressive steps. Attach a dial-indicator stand to the front of the block so that the tip of the indicator is against the nose of the crankshaft. Use a large screwdriver to pry between the center main cap and the crank counterweight. Push the crankshaft as far to the rear as it will go and zero the dial indicator. Now push the crankshaft forward while observing the indicator. The measurement here is the crankshaft's end-play, which should be generally no greater than 0.010-inch. If the end-play is greater than this, check the thrust surfaces of the crankshaft for wear. If no wear is evident, and you were using used bearings during the end-play check, new bearings should correct the end-play.

Other work that can be done to the crankshaft at this time should include a thorough cleaning of the crankshaft and particularly the oiling holes. Special brushes are made to fit in the oiling holes, and should be run back and forth with solvent to remove any dirt or particles. The oil holes in factory crankshafts generally have only a very small radius where the hole exits the journal. For performance applications, this hole is usually given a much larger radius to allow for more generous oil flow to the bearings, and to expose a less-sharp opening to the bearings. This can be done with a round file, being very careful not to scratch the surrounding journal surface. A better tool for the job would be an electric drill fitted with a round-stone bit. After doing this, the crankshaft must be cleaned again. Aftermarket performance crankshafts usually have radiused oil holes already.

For racing or performance use, the oil holes in the journals are often cross-drilled. They are drilled all the way through the journals (if not already machined that way from the factory), so that oil can flow from two locations instead of one.

If your used crankshaft had been found to be slightly undersized, and you are sending it out for regrinding, you can have the machine shop radius the oil holes and micro-polish the journals for you. The polishing procedure takes a negligible amount of metal from the surface, but leaves a smoother surface and further smoothes the radiuses at the oil holes. The shop should also be able to grind your jour-

On this aftermarket forged crank for a big-block Chevy, note that the oil holes were flared very nicely during the manufacturing process. Note also that the area where the journal meets the counterweight is not a square edge, but radiused. This requires special bearings that are radiused on the edges, but the lack of a square-cut edge makes for a stronger crankshaft

Specialized equipment is required to grind crankshafts and is seldom a part of a normal automotive machine shop's tooling inventory. Crankshaft specialty shops can not only regrind a crankshaft to straight and even tolerances, but can also offset-grind the rod journals to either blueprint a crank so every throw is at 90-degrees, or even offset-grind enough material to increase the stroke. That used to be common in the early days of hot rodding, but today the wide selection of reasonably-priced stroker crankshafts means this procedure is seldom used except on vintage engines. This is a Berco crankshaft grinder in use at Eagle Specialty Products

nals with a more gradual radius at each end, which is said to make the crankshaft stronger in that area. The increased radius works in conjunction with radiused bearings and a similar radius at the thrust sides of the connecting rods. In

Like any engine specification, crankshaft endplay has a maximum and minimum dimension. Performance builders like to keep this spec on the small side, at 0.004 to 0.006-inch, while OEM specs might allow a 0.012-inch maximum. Endplay is measured with a dial-indicator on the front of the crank, with the main bearing caps tightened to the specified torque. Prying the crank forward and back gives the clearance on the indicator

When oil holes have been radiused or other work done on crankshaft journals, it's common practice for performance applications to micro-polish all the journals. This really doesn't take off metal, but makes the surface of the journals slicker for better oil flow and longer bearing life

general, radiused corners in the bottom end components are better than sharp corners that can concentrate the loads at one point.

Another step for the crankshaft that is often done for performance applications is a surface treatment called Tuff-triding, which surface-hardens the journals for increased resistance to wear. Another surface-hardening treatment is called Nitriding.

If you are assembling a serious performance engine, you will likely be replacing all of the bottom-end components with new aftermarket parts, in which case, the crankshaft will need only minor checking of measurements, not the machine work as outlined above for a stock crankshaft. Aftermarket crankshafts generally have radiused journals, lightening holes through the rod throws, radiused and cross-drilled oil holes, heat-treating, and some even feature spe-

A feature of aftermarket performance crankshafts you'll often find are holes drilled lengthwise through the rod journals. This is said to reduce mass at this critical point, without sacrificing strength. This crank also has radiused journals

cially designed counterweights to reduce mass and avoid crankshaft flexing under stress. When shopping for a crankshaft, manufacturers often rate their array of components in general horsepower levels to make it easy to choose the right parts for your application. For example, one crankshaft may be rated as suitable for power levels up to 500 hp, while others may be rated for 800 hp. The differences will be in the materials and design. If you're realistic about the power level you are building your engine to, the "500 hp" crank may be all you need for your performance street machine. On the other hand, if the engine is for a racecar or very serious street machine with big displacement and/or power adders, get the best components you can.

There is a lot of talk about the differences in manufacturers' products, and of course each manufacturer will tell you that theirs is the better product, citing various features. It can be confusing to the uninitiated. There are both cast-steel and forged steel crankshafts, and one thing that can be said for certain is that forged is always stronger than cast. Many of the less-expensive aftermarket crankshafts available today are being made in Asia, and there seems to be an opinion among some builders that the overseas crankshafts are not quite as strong as the more-expensive US-made counterparts, due to differences in the purity of the steel used. A rough guide for crankshaft selection could be that a cast-steel aftermarket crankshaft is good for mild performance use, a factory-forged steel crank is suitable for heavy-duty truck use and high-performance street use, the imported forged cranks are next highest in durability, and the 4340-steel-forged American crankshafts have the aerospace-quality materials suited for all-out performance and racing applications. There are many grades of steel, from

On engines with distributorless ignitions, another aspect to consider on the crankshaft is the precision placement of the crankshaft trigger wheel. Shown is the trigger on the back of a GM LS-series engine's Eagle stroker crankshaft. If you're using a complete aftermarket fuel/spark EFI system, the trigger is unnecessary, except if the crankshaft and lower end components were balanced to the crank with the stock trigger wheel. Placement of the trigger (or reluctor) is critical when pressed onto the crankshaft, as is run-out, which can be no more than 0.018-inch maximum or the engine could be damaged

1053 (OEM forgings) to 4130 and 4340 chrome-moly steel (aftermarket racing cranks), and a host of heat-treating processes in manufacturing crankshafts. Some would say that even a forged crank is only as good as the material it is pro-

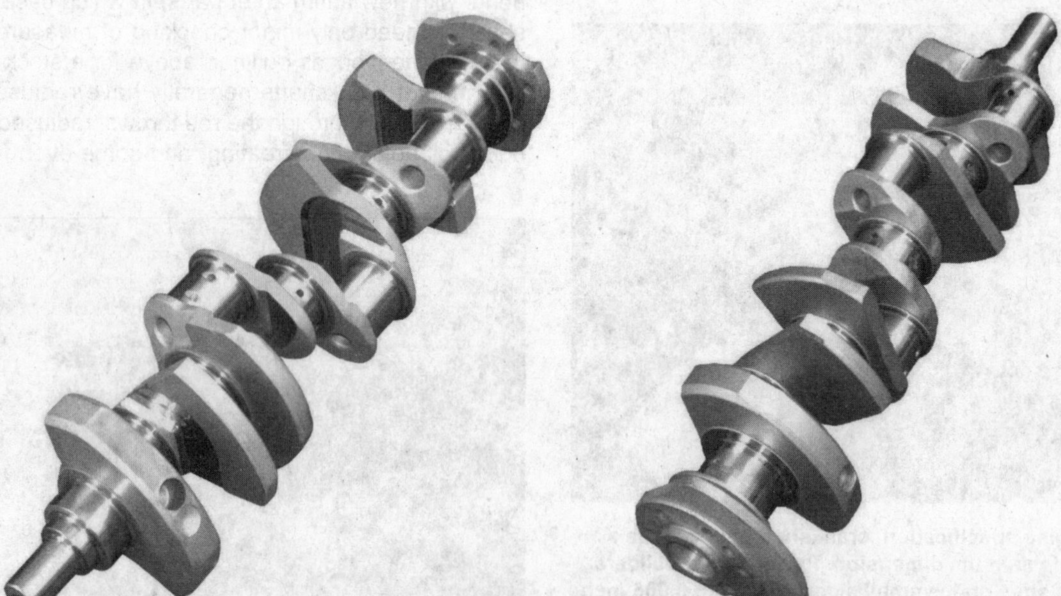

These two Eagle crankshafts illustrate the differences there can be in rotating/reciprocating weight. The extra-light racing crank at left for a small-block Chevy has a bob weight of 1855 grams, while the 4-inch-stroke big-block crank at right has a bob weight of 2350 grams

Aftermarket crankshaft manufacturers can do a lot with the basic forging, machining special counterweights, bigger snouts for blower applications and other features using a CNC lathe, such as this HAAS unit, for precision work

The casting or forging seams on the sides of OEM connecting rods have always been considered likely points for fatigue or cracks to begin under stress. Engine builders used to grind down the seams (rod in foreground is almost finished, compare to the stock rod at rear) and polish, then shot-peen the rods for durability

duced from.

You can't hurt an engine by buying more protection than it needs, just your wallet. Do your research before buying any bottom-end components, and make sure what you're buying is suited to your application. As an example, cast-steel aftermarket crankshafts for a typical 350 small-block Chevy engine may carry a manufacturer's rating of "500 hp," while a 4340 forged crankshaft for the same engine would be roughly twice the price (or more) and rated for "700-1000" hp. Specialized stroker crankshafts will be even more expensive. There is no independent testing body for these parts, and the manufacturer's make their own ratings, so don't take these numbers as a guarantee of any kind.

From here, your reworked or aftermarket crankshaft is ready for the balancing operations discussed at the end of this Chapter.

For most street and semi-racing applications, there are many excellent forged rods in the I-beam design as seen on this Eagle rod. Check the manufacturer's recommendations, but good ones are suitable for 500 or more horsepower engines

Connecting rods

In standard rebuilding practices with used connecting rods, several aspects of the rod are checked, and corrected if they are not within specifications. First and foremost would be the rod straightness, which is checked on a dedicated fixture. Any twist or bend in the beam of the rod can be detrimental in a performance engine, and rods with these problems are replaced. If the rods are straight, they are then checked for center-to-center length, measuring between the pin-end hole and the big-end hole. Minor differences are acceptable in a stock engine, but if two rods in your engine were twenty thousandths shorter that the rest, then those two pistons wouldn't reach TDC at the exact point they are supposed to, and the compression ratio between all cylinders would not be equal.

Luckily, equality in rod length is easily and routinely corrected by standard machine shop work. The small-end of the rod is bored out, square to the rod, and fitted with a pressed-in bronze bushing for the piston pin, while the big-end of the rod is resized. A small amount of material is machined from the mating surfaces of the rod caps, then the caps are reinstalled and torqued on the rods. The big-end hole is then machined to specifications, thus in one operation correcting the rod length as well as making the big-end square to the rod and the hole round and to exact size.

It should be noted at this point if you are installing aftermarket rod bolts (a common practice to make stock rods better equipped to handle higher loads), this should be done

The other profile for a performance connecting rod is the H-beam design. They'll handle lots of horsepower, but they're generally a llittle less expensive than a performance I-beam rod

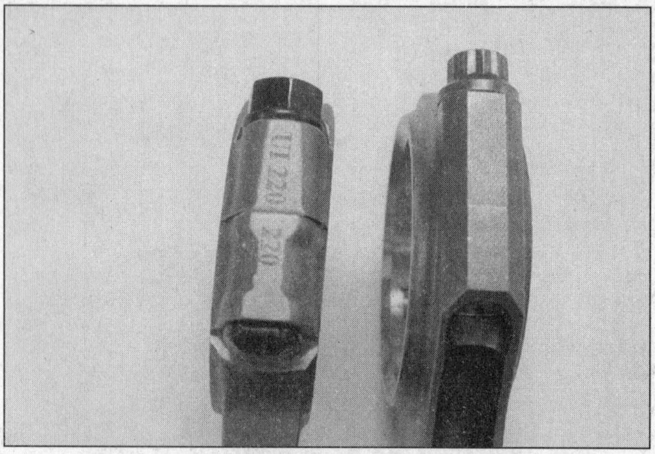

Connecting rod bolts are an important consideration in any performance engine. A good bottom-end is only as good as the weakest link, and even stock rods can be improved in durability by adding stronger aftermarket bolts. You'll find that aftermarket rods all come with high-grade aftermarket bolts, with the strength, diameter and material determined by the horsepower level they can take. At left is a high-strength bolt in an I-beam rod, while a stronger, forged H-beam rod uses aircraft-type 12-point capscrews instead of bolts/nuts

before the rods are resized. New and stronger rod bolts are of tougher material and often of a larger diameter, so they will have a different torque reading than the stock bolts. A different torque spec will slightly alter the shape of the big-end's hole. After fitting the new rod bolts - and in cases of larger bolt diameter - drilling the rods to accept them, you should put the rod in a soft-jawed fixture and torque the new bolts/nuts to the specified torque, then loosen them. Repeat this three times, then after a final torque, they will be ready to be resized. Now the holes will stay round at the new torque spec.

Factory rods can be prepared for better durability with several procedures. The casting or forging lines on the sides of the rods are said to be a stress point where fractures can begin under heavy load. These lines can be ground smooth on both sides of the rod, using a narrow belt on a stationary belt sander. Performance machine shops use a horizontal table with the sanding belt in line with the rod, so that the rod rests flat on the table and the sanding lines will be parallel to the rod's beam. The sanding should always be from the big-end to the small-end.

Removal of the lines may make the rods live longer and serves another purpose as well. The rods will now be lighter, and when it comes to the reciprocating parts of the engine, lighter is better, since it's easier for the crankshaft to push a lighter mass up and down the cylinders. After rods are sanded like this, they are usually shot-peened as well, with the rods placed in a metal cabinet and bombarded with small metal shot pellets. The purpose is to make the rod surface metal more compact, and thus stronger. The big and small holes are protected during this attack by heavy duct tape. The shot-peening procedure further reduces surface irregularities that could lead to fractures under stress.

The economics of the global marketplace have changed things a bit from the previous decades when it comes to bottom end components. Today a wide variety of performance connecting rods are available, and costs have come down to the point where brand-new high-strength rods may be a better bet than reworking stock rods. Unless you have to use stock rods in some particular spec-class racing venue,

When rods are fitted with new bolts, they should be torqued and loosened three times to fully seat them in the rod, for an accurate torque reading during final installation in an engine. Note the fixture being used to secure the rod while doing this; the soft aluminum jaws hold the rod evenly, without marring the surface, where a regular vise could cause marks that could lead to possible fracture points.

A good I-beam rod for power levels up to 550 horsepower might be this Lunati 4340 steel rod with smooth sides, 3/8-inch high-strength rod bolts, and shot-peen treatment. These are sold in matched-weight sets. Aftermarket rods like these are usually a better deal all around than grinding and rebuilding old rods and adding new bolts

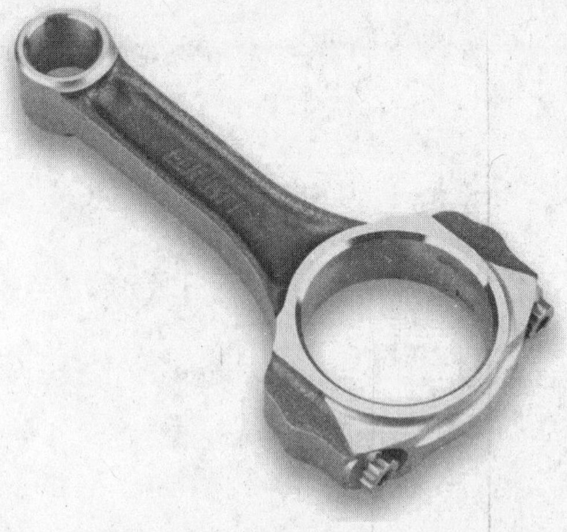

A step up, for engines up to 900 horsepower, could be this Lunati Pro-Mod rod with a noticeably beefier big-end, forged 4340 steel construction and tough aircraft capscrews

a new set of rods today can cost little more than having a set of old rods machined, sanded, balanced, shot-peened and fitted with high-strength bolts. There was a time only a decade or two ago when the famous (and very expensive) Carillo steel rods were one of the few choices in aftermarket rods. Several companies have been making aluminum connecting rods for a long time, but their usage is generally in drag racing applications, not street performance, and they require consistent teardowns for checking.

Steel is the preferred material for most performance and racing purposes, and must be considered an investment in engine longevity. Back in the Fifties when drag racing was growing swiftly, you only had the choice of stock rods, or what were called "boxed" rods. For the latter, stock rods were Magnafluxed (an inspection process that can spot hidden flaws or hairline cracks), then a section of new steel was arc-welded to each side of the rod, filling in the open areas of the typical I-beam connecting rod. After sanding and shot-peening, the boxed rods were stronger than stock, although they were considerably heavier.

Today we have a number of manufacturers making high-strength rods for us to choose from. The two basic types of connecting rods in terms of shape are those with an I-beam and those with an H-beam. The former are typical of factory rods on almost all OEM engines, the latter typical of high-performance and racing rod designs. The designation basically refers to what the shape of the rod would look like from the end view if sawed in half. In the I-beam rod, the open section is towards the front and back of the rods, while the H-beam has the open area at each edge, or side. This sounds like a minor difference, but the H-beam design has been proven in racing for decades as the stronger of the two profiles, having much greater resistance to twisting and high loads. Given this, just because a rod is an H-beam doesn't mean that it's unbreakable. As with all aftermarket bottom-end components, the materials and manufacturing precision used to make the rods are of high importance.

There are a number of economical aftermarket rods, so your selection should be based on your projected power level and the recommendations of your favorite engine-builder or machine shop. Look for features such as X-ray inspection, high-strength bolts, shot-peening, and balancing to within 1-2 grams, for a rod that may weigh 570 grams, for example. That's much closer than any set of factory rods that haven't had careful aftermarket balancing.

H-beam rods will generally cost more than I-beam rods, with more-expensive bolts, many with 12-point aircraft-style nuts, precision machining and testing, consistent weight and other features. Manufacturers rate these rods in the 750-800 hp range at up to 8000 rpm. For all-out racing or endurance engines, custom racing rods can cost three or four times the "production" H-beam price.

One common feature of H-beam rods is that they are bushed for floating pins. The small-end is fitted with a precisely-machined bronze bushing. The floating pin design eliminates some friction losses for that extra tiny bit of horsepower.

Pistons

Next in line is the piston, but unlike the connecting rod, a piston has as much to do with *making power* as making the bottom-end stronger.

The choices in performance pistons are staggering. Typical pistons in OEM applications are of the cast variety, while most performance pistons are forged. You should be sensing by now in this bottom-end Chapter that forged rotating and reciprocation parts are important to building a big-power V8 engine that can run both strong and long. Although all pistons are made of some variety of aluminum, you have three

Compare these two pistons. The flat-top piston on the left is for a relatively low compression ratio, with a positive impact on the chamber volume due to the large relief cut for the intake valve. The Big-block Chevrolet piston on the right subtracts some 48 cc from chamber volume due to the high dome, for a considerably higher compression ratio. Even with the reliefs, the piston-to valve clearance must always be checked to be sure your chosen cam profile will work with this dome

basic material categories: cast, forged and hypereutectic.

Advances in piston materials and design have grown at an incredible rate. Both OEM engineers and race-engine builders continually strive to come up with better and better designs, with the factory engineers trying to gain tiny advantages in fuel-economy, performance and durability while at the same time meeting ever-more stringent emissions regulations. For racing purposes, engineers are always trying to make pistons lighter and yet stronger at the same time. Professional racing such as NASCAR has seen consistently rising horsepower with the same size engines. Where they may have raced at 7000 rpm before, they are now up to 9000 rpm on the big tracks, and this has spurred development of most aspects of performance engine technology.

One of the factors that has accelerated piston design is new technology in rapid prototyping and machining. When CNC (Computer Numerical Control) machining became commonplace, manufacturers of OEM and performance pistons could have a machine automatically follow a computer program to machine a piston blank just about any way they wanted. The same forged-aluminum blank could be machined to suit a variety of applications, with different compression heights, valve reliefs, ring locations, etc. CAD/CAM computer software (Computer-Aided Design/ Computer-Aided Manufacture) allowed engineers to model new designs and then send the program to a CNC machine to make it, in a much shorter time frame than ever before. The same type of new development work was going on with aftermarket cylinder head manufacturers, who could better take advantage of their designs when piston manufacturers could more easily provide custom pistons to accommodate the high-flow heads.

Cast-aluminum pistons have been the norm for many decades. They are cheap to manufacture in mass quantities and serve their purpose well, but performance engines have always used forged pistons for their greater strength, and the ability to better handle higher compression ratios. One of the significant differences between cast and forged pistons is their expansion rate. Cast pistons expand more with heat than forgings, which means that piston-to-bore clearances must be looser to accommodate piston skirt growth. Forged pistons expand less and thus can be run to tighter tolerances, which reduces compression losses and oil consumption. As engineers experimented more with adding more silicon content to the aluminum, the expansion rate of cast pistons was reduced. In the aftermarket performance arena we now have the choice of cast pistons for economy, forged pistons for strength and close tolerance blueprinting, and *hypereutectic* cast pistons that are something in between. With as much as 16% silicon content, hypereutectic pistons have about 15% less expansion that ordinary cast pistons, and with heat-treating can be improved in strength as well.

In the pursuit of light weight, piston skirts today have become much shorter than they were, as new designs use different shapes and under-the-dome reinforcements to retain strength. The shorter pistons obviously have less drag on the cylinder, another plus on the performance side.

For serious performance use, forged pistons are the logical choice, although they do have a minor drawback for everyday street use, in that they tend to take longer to warm up, and can "rattle" a little until the engine is fully warmed. Most performance enthusiasts are willing to live with that to have the benefits of the greater strength.

Since the top of the piston is essentially the bottom floor of the combustion chamber, it has a considerable influence on the emissions and performance of the engine. The right shape on top of the piston determines more than just the compression ratio; it also can direct the flame-front of the combustion process to ensure more complete combustion. The top also serves to determine the final compression ratio and also must be fitted with notches, called valve reliefs, to allow the valves to clear at TDC. If you have a higher-lift cam, you need bigger reliefs.

Special coatings that were once exclusive to very expensive race engines are now available in the broader piston market today. Today's short piston skirts are often coated or impregnated with graphite and moly concoctions to reduce scuffing and drag. At the same time, special coatings have been developed for the tops of pistons, too. Oven-baked ceramic coatings can provide extra protection for the top of the piston, while at the same time making the combustion process more efficient by not allowing as much heat to be drawn off by the pistons.

Rings and piston pins are another important aspect of piston selection. Stock pistons/rods are fitted with press-fit pins that are installed by heating the small-end of the rod then putting the rod and piston in a fixture and pushing in the pin, which is cold. After it cools, the pin is secured in the rod and must be pressed out at a machine shop if the engine is being rebuilt. The alternate method of pin retention used in performance pistons/rods is to hone the bushing in the small-end to accept the pin, then install locking rings in special grooves in the pin holes at the sides of the piston. The spiral locks are thin, flat versions of the rings you put your car keys on, and can be twisted in by hand with a small screwdriver. The result is a floating pin that is free to rotate in both the piston and the rod, so friction is reduced. A side benefit of floating pins is that a piston can be removed from its rod simply by pulling the spiral lockrings out, without need for heat or a press.

Modern pistons are designed with the rings closer to the top of the piston than they used to be, partly because the pistons are getting shorter and the piston pins are located higher up in the piston, but also because the area around the piston and above the top ring is a sort of dead zone that contributes to incomplete combustion. Making this area small reduces emissions and saves fuel. Today's ring packages, for both OEM and performance use, are much thinner than older designs. The biggest single frictional load on an engine is the drag of the piston rings against the cylinder walls. Making the rings thinner reduces that drag, but requires rings that are stronger and more heat resistant, and also requires as round a cylinder as is possible, so expert machine work on the block is essential.

Thinner rings may have less drag, but they must be better able to handle heat, since the contact with the cylinder walls is smaller and there is less heat transfer away from the piston. Aftermarket pistons and rings have to be made of better materials, and some pistons feature anti-galling plating or coatings in the ring grooves. Because the right rings for a particular piston design are so specific, pistons are almost always sold with the matching rings.

When buying pistons for serious performance engines, you need to determine what compression ratio you want first. Without getting into the formulas and math required to compute compression ratio, just be aware that there are several components of the engine that make up the combustion chamber volume, which is the volume above the piston at TDC, compared to the volume above the piston at BDC. For instance, if the volume at BDC is 100 units and the volume at TDC is 10 units, this would be a 10:1 compression ratio, meaning that the air/fuel mix in the cylinder will be compressed 10 times before ignition.

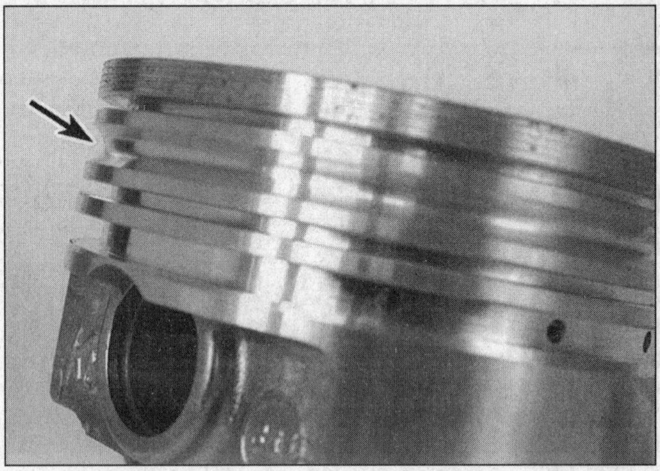

An interesting piston design is this one from Keith Black, for a 392-cubic-inch small-block Ford stroker engine. Indicated here is a wide, beveled area between the top and second ring grooves. This is designed to offer a relief space for possible blow-by pressure from detonation. Damaging ring "flutter" is avoided by allowing excess pressure a place to go if necessary

The TDC volume is the sum of the chamber volume in the head, the volume between the top of the piston and the top of the block (assuming the piston is slightly below the top of the deck), the volume of the valve reliefs (if any) and the volume representing the space between the head and the block surfaces due to the thickness of the head gasket between them.

The compression ratio of your engine is dependent mainly on the piston head and cylinder head designs. Manufacturers will often list the compression ratio of pistons, but are more helpful to customers when they list what the cylinder head chamber volume would need to be to achieve that CR. Often, the manufacturer will list a range of compression ratios that could be achieved on the same engine, depending on chamber volume. Then you would know if your compression with your heads would be higher or lower if you know the chamber volume. The specs will include the actual cc's of the piston top. A negative number, like -21cc, would mean that there is a slight dome on the piston, thus subtracting from chamber volume, while a positive number means there are reliefs cut into the piston top that add volume to the chamber. Some pistons are completely flat on top, which means they have little influence on volume. There are even pistons designed for specific cylinder heads, such as for the unique chambers of the Twisted Wedge heads for small-block Ford engines.

Picking a compression ratio requires some study. The higher the compression, the higher the power output, but this must be tempered by the realities of today's gasoline and your particular application. Higher compression means more possibility of engine-destroying detonation unless

Stock pistons are usually attached to their rods with press-in pins. Most aftermarket performance pistons use full-floating pins, and are used with rods that have honed bushings to accept the pins. The pins are kept in position by inserting spiral-wound snap rings on each side of the pin, fitted to grooves inside the piston's pin-holes. The pin locks are installed by hand with pliers instead of using a press to force them through like a stock rod. The result is reduced friction in the assembly, which translates into a small hp gain

your fuel has enough octane. Pump gas today is lacking in octane rating for our performance purposes, so you have to adjust fuel delivery and ignition timing to compensate. If compression is high, you have to enrich the fuel mix to keep the chambers cooler and/or retard timing under loads to prevent piston damage. On vehicles with electronic ignition and engine management (computer) the task is made simpler by aftermarket electronics (see Chapter 4) that allow you to switch "programs" depending on what fuel is available.

Your driving conditions also play a role in picking a compression ratio. A lightweight car can get away with more compression than a heavy one. Trucks that are actually used for working or towing should have at least a point less CR than passenger cars. With 92-octane, a gasoline additive and a light vehicle, you may get away with 11:1 CR without computer management, but in a truck towing a boat, 9:1 or 10:1 would be safer. Check with experts on your brand of engine for their recommendations, as the chamber design of the head is a factor in the "useable" compression ratio. The large surface-to-volume ratio of the Chrysler Hemi, for instance, allows for higher useable compression than a typical wedge chamber design.

If you plan on using a supercharger or turbocharger, you may have to go mild on compression ratio. With mildly boosted applications of 5-7 psi, the stock compression ratio may be fine, but for truly serious boost levels of 12-18 psi, you'll want some forged pistons with a flat or dished top that keeps static compression to about 8:1.

The other critical factor in choosing pistons is your camshaft profile. You should pick your camshaft and valvetrain components first (see Chapter 8), since this is the heartbeat of a performance build. Once you know what the actual valve lift will be, including any multiplication from aftermarket rocker arms, you can search for a piston that has reliefs big enough to clear the valves with a safe margin. If your engine is already assembled and you are switching cams, you can (and should) check the valve-to-piston clearance by putting a lump of modeling clay on top of one piston, install one head with pushrods only in that hole, and turn the engine over slowly with a breaker bar. If you encounter a hard spot, stop! You may have interference. If the engine turns OK, remove the head and slice the clay with a razor blade, then check with vernier calipers to see the thickness of the clay where the valves made impressions. Your cam manufacturer may have provided the desired clearance in the spec sheet, but for a general guide, the intake valve should clear by 0.080-inch and the hotter exhaust valve by 0.100-inch to be safe. If your measured clearance is less, the valve pockets should be deepened by a machinist.

Engine block

The foundation upon which all your bottom-end components will be based is the engine block itself, and there are a number of ways to release engine power here. A bigger engine can make more power, and the old hot rodders used to say "There's no replacement for displacement!"

More displacement (more cubic inches) is achieved by increasing the bore and/or stroke. The stroke is a function of the crankshaft design (see the *Stroker engines* section later in this Chapter), and the longer the stroke, the more displacement is achieved. The bore is the simplest increase in displacement, and is a routine part of even normal engine rebuilds. As you'll see when ordering new pistons, most are available only for cylinders enlarged by at least 0.030-inches. On a typical 350 Chevy engine, a 30-thousandth overbore results in an additional 5 cubic inches. In a typical rebuild, that much of a bore increase is required to bring tired old cylinders to a straight, true and round bore for the new pistons. On engines with enough meat in the cylinder walls, boring can increase displacement considerably. A 400-cubic-inch engine with a bore increase of 0.125-inch (one-eighth-inch) will wind up with 25 more cubic inches of displacement (most standard modern blocks can't be bored this much). Since the engine build will require some boring and honing of the engine anyway, boring it bigger is only a little more work and expense.

The catch is that most modern engines are designed with thin-wall castings in a quest for lighter weight. Some engines, such as small-block Fords, may only be able to be bored the usual 30 thousandths. To have a bigger bore, you'd have to start with an aftermarket or factory performance block built with thicker cylinder walls. To add to the bore-size dilemma, a slight shift of the cores during casting of a block could result in one or more cylinder being thinner than the rest, sometimes leading to a dangerously thin wall on that cylinder after boring. Another disadvantage of boring on a thin-wall block is that, even if you have enough wall thickness to do it, the thinner walls will now transfer more heat to the engine's coolant and the engine will run hotter.

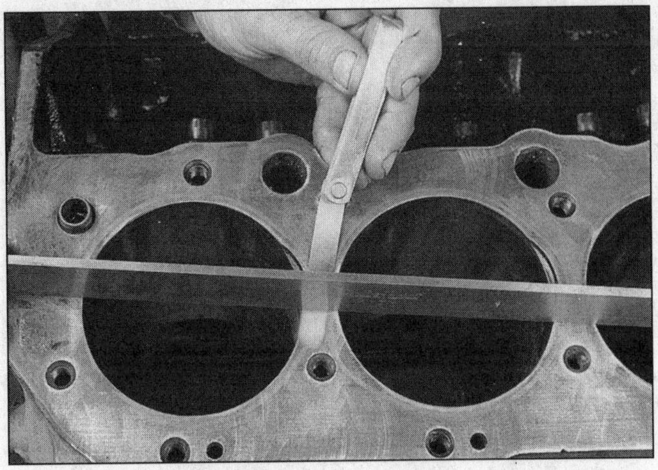

When starting with a used block, there are many checks that need to be made to determine if the block is usable and/or correctable. Most issues (short of a cracked block) can be corrected with precision machine work. Here the deck surface is checked for flatness with a precision straightedge and feeler gauges. If the surface isn't flat within 0.003-inch, it can be easily flattened at the machine shop, a process called "decking" the block, in which the surface is not only made flat, but flat and parallel to the crankshaft centerline, so every cylinder has the same capacity

Careful measurement of the main caps (with bearings in place) tells you if the mains are the right size for your crankshaft. If not, the main caps can be trimmed slightly and the main bores remachined, a process called "line-boring"

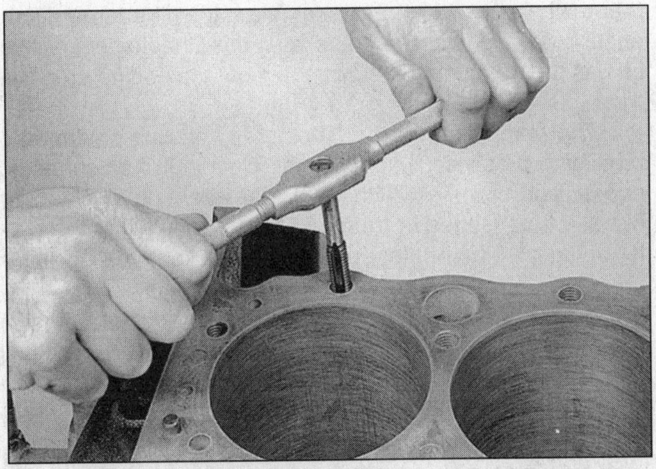

All bolt-holes should be cleaned out first, then further cleaned by running oiled taps through the threads. Any dirt or rust can give false or uneven torque readings when the engine is assembled

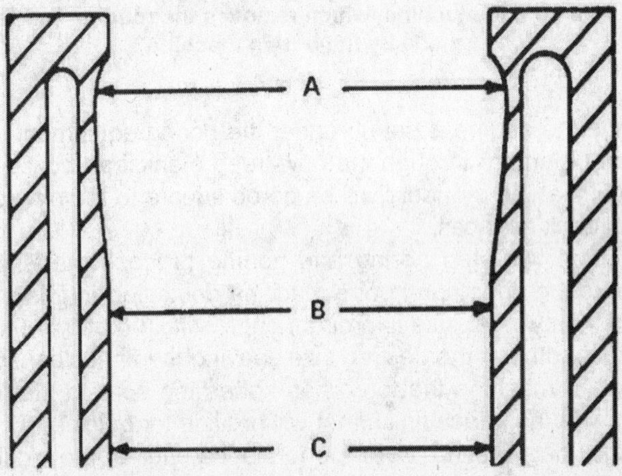

The bore is the other major consideration in a block. The bores must all be round, straight, parallel to each other and perpendicular to the true crankshaft centerline. Careful measurements are taken with a dial-bore gauge at the top (A, just under the wear ridge), at the center (B) and at the bottom (C). A difference between these measurements tells us whether the bores are uneven, which they generally are in a used block. How much machining will be necessary to correct the bores depends on the block. Some thin-wall blocks, if they had a core shift during casting, can't be used because the right amount of boring would cut through into the water jackets of the block

The other paths to power in an engine block are the blueprinting treatments that equalize the cylinders and provide maximum friction reduction by truing surfaces. The crankshaft main bearing bores in the block are usually line-bored, in a similar fashion to the treatment the big-end of connecting rods are trued. A small amount is machined from the bottom of the main caps, then they are torqued in place with the engine in a fixture and a boring bar goes through to slightly recut the main bores (block and caps) to be round and in a straight line. Most of the material removed is from the caps and only a slight amount from the block, since taking much off the block would position the crankshaft closer to the top of the engine, perhaps creating slack in the timing chain.

The deck, or the surface that the cylinder heads bolt to, is also trued at the machine shop. This surface must be exactly parallel to the crankshaft centerline, and the same height at all four corners. Usually this only involves removing a small amount to level the decks. With these two blueprinting steps taken, the cylinders can now be bored and honed.

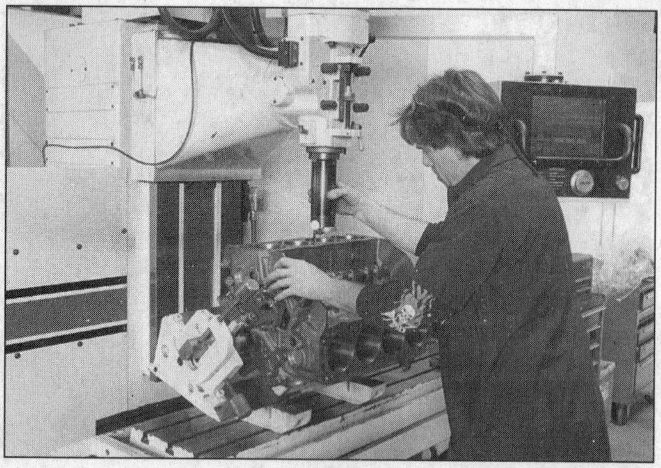

Boring a block is usually done after the mains are line-bored, since a machined bar is placed through the main bores on the boring machine to establish that line when the cylinders are bored. Cylinders are bored to within about 0.003-0.005 thousandths of the desired size, with the final cleanup done on a honing machine, which removes the rougher marks made by the boring machine

The honing machine has precision sensors on each of the stones that detect how smooth the bore is. As the honing proceeds, the readouts on the display tell how close the bore is to desired size and how straight the bore is getting. The speed of the hone going up and down imparts the correct cross-hatching of the bore, ideally with the lines crossed at a 45-degree angle for good ring seating

Since the engine is set up under the boring equipment with a precision bar through the now-trued crankshaft bores, we know that the cylinders will be bored square to the now-parallel deck surfaces.

The two-step boring and honing process starts with the boring operation in one machine dedicated to this step, and the cylinder size is brought out to within 0.003 to 0.005 thousandths of the desired size, leaving the final cleanup to another machine that precision hones the bore to the final size with a surface finish that will provide for quick and consistent ring seating. For a performance engine, the block is often fitted with a thick plate, called a torque plate, that is bolted down with the head bolts before the final honing. The plate simulates the distortion that occurs to the bores when the head bolts are tightened, so that the cylinders will be round when the engine is assembled. It isn't a large difference, but as you have seen so far in this Chapter, every little bit has been proven to help in years of race engine preparation.

The rest of the engine block prep consists of standard rebuilding practices, with thorough cleaning of all surfaces, nooks, and crannies, with particular attention to cleaning out all oil passages in the block, then reinstalling the gallery plugs. All bolt holes, particularly those involving high-

Lubricating and cooling fluid is pumped around the honing stones to keep the bores cool during machining and to flush away the tiny steel particles. If the bore were to heat up, it could change the dimensions and throw off the readings

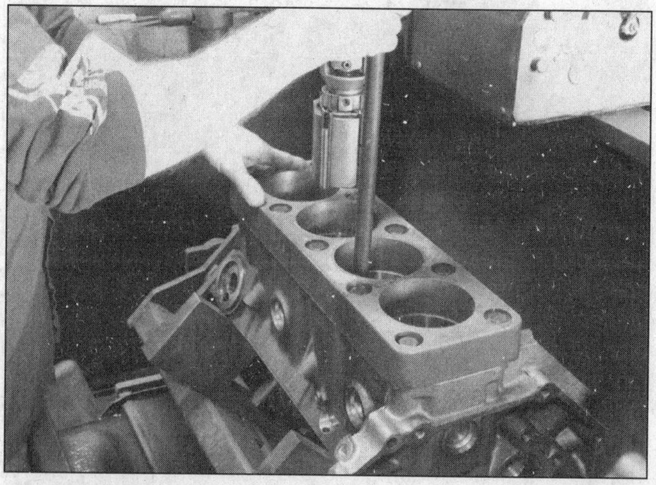

For performance engines, the final few thousandths of honing is done with a torque-plate in place. This thick steel plate is torqued in place to simulate the distortion that occurs when cylinder heads are tightened onto the block, which can subtly alter the bore shape. This blueprinting step was developed by SuperStock drag competitors years ago

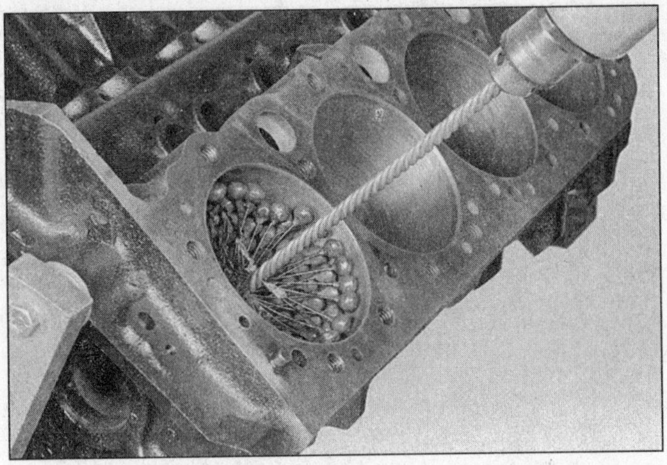

Some engine builders like to finish off a cylinder with a Brush Research Flex-Hone. The balls of abrasive material on the wires do not straighten a bore, but are designed to remove microscopically folded little bits of metal left from using the straight stones

torque fasteners such as head bolts, are thoroughly cleaned with taps, then washed. Any corrosion or dirt in a head bolt holes could change the true torque applied to the bolts during assembly.

Stroker engines

If we can't gain much power through boring our late-model block, we can definitely make a bigger engine by increasing the stroke of the crankshaft. When the rod throws are made further out from the crankshaft centerline, the stroke is longer. This has become one of the most popular paths to power in recent years, especially with the ever-widening marketplace for new crankshafts. Stroker kits have been around in the hot rod world since your grandpa's days souping up flathead Fords, but stroker kits are now available for a wide variety of engines.

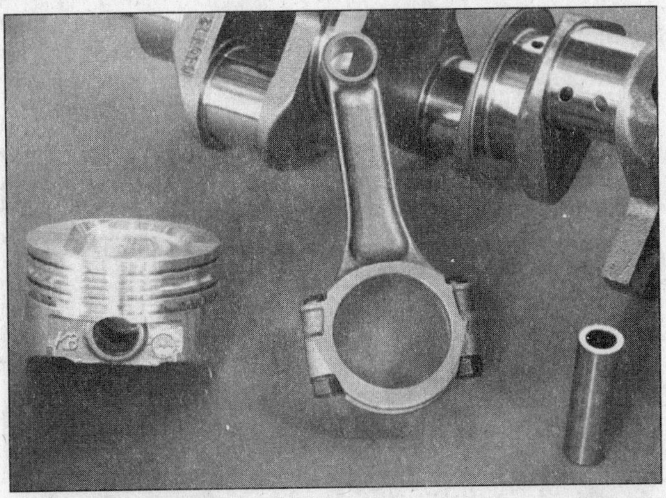

When you're already considering buying a new performance crankshaft, you might consider the greater potential of a stroked crank. "You can't beat cubic inches!" they say. There's more to a stroker engine than just the crankshaft; the rods and pistons have to be selected to match that crank. A number of stroker assemblies are available for popular engines. There's more displacement to be gained with a stroker than boring, and some blocks don't allow much bore increase anyway

If you're shopping for an aftermarket crankshaft for your engine anyway, why not make your engine bigger at the same time? It's not as simple as just swapping in a new crankshaft, as we'll see, but is one of the more rewarding modifications you can make and, unlike top-end power adders like nitrous and blowers, no one can see what you've done inside the block. For some enthusiasts, it's important that observers can't tell how much power the engine might have just by looking at the outside. A stroker assembly will be your (big) secret.

While the crankshaft is the main component to increase your engine's displacement, the rods and pistons will also have to be different. If you lengthen the stroke of your engine and leave the pistons and rods the same, the increased stroke will push the piston right up above the block's deck, which is undesirable to say the least. Short pistons with the pin up high are designed to keep the piston top where it should be, while keeping weight lower.

One of the aspects of achieving a bigger engine through increasing the stroke rather than the bore is that the result yields increased low-end torque, thus stroker kits are ideal for vehicles that tow boats, race cars, horse trailers or anything else. An engine that has the same size bore as it does stroke is considered a "square" design. If the bore is bigger than the stroke, it is called over-square, and is the traditional design for high-revving performance. The stroked engine is designated as an under-square design that tends to build more low-end power than the other types.

There are stroker cranks and complete bottom-end packages that can take a small-block Chevy or Ford V8 and pump it up to as big as 427 cubic inches in the same exter-

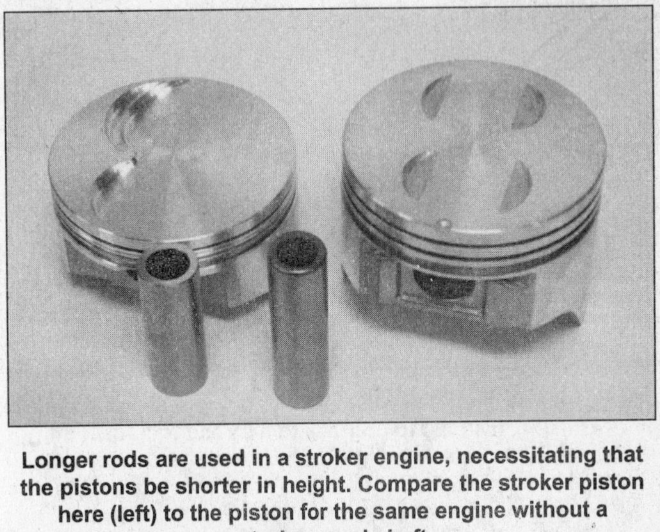

Longer rods are used in a stroker engine, necessitating that the pistons be shorter in height. Compare the stroker piston here (left) to the piston for the same engine without a stroker crankshaft

This selection of small-block Ford rods from left to right, includes a stock 5.0L rod, forged 4340 rod for a 347-cubic-inch stroked 5.0L block, and an even longer forged rod for use in making a little 302 into a mighty 427. The latter will fit any vehicle that is set up for a small-block Ford, and we won't tell anyone you've upgraded

nal package! That's great when you don't have the engine compartment room or the tools and skills to swap a physically larger engine into your vehicle. The engine combo that sparked today's intense marketplace for stroker kits was probably the 383 Chevy. Some enterprising machinist years ago looked carefully at a crankshaft for a 400-cubic-inch Chevy (which was not a performance engine) and determined that by machining the main journals, the longer-stroke crank could be fitted to a popular 350 block, for a 383-inch engine. Lots of companies now make cast and forged aftermarket cranks to do the same thing, and it seems that every older V8 Chevy pickup in the world has a 383 upgrade. The

Because a stroker motor is destined for more action than just cruising, it's best to upgrade to a stronger crankshaft for a serious stroker engine. There are aftermarket cast stroker crankshafts that will live with moderate use, just not with *abuse*. Thus, most stroker cranks are of forged steel construction for extra protection

Generally, an OEM block will require grinding near the bottom of the bores or on the oil pan rail, due to the longer length rods and greater arc of the stroker crank when spinning. Really big stroker motors sometimes even have clearance problems with the camshaft. For those applications, special camshafts are available

parts to build a 383 Chevy cost little more than the parts to rebuild a 350 with stock dimensions. Plus, when you buy a stroker kit, for any engine, you get the benefit of stronger pistons, rods and crankshaft as a bonus.

Even engines that are already big, such as the big-block Chevy and the Chrysler Hemi (old or new), can be made even bigger with a stroker kit. Using stock blocks, the Chevy can be enlarged to 500 inches, and with larger aftermarket blocks can be bigger than 600 cubic inches. A popular size today is a 572-cubic-inch big-block, a buildup of which is in Chapter 13. Small-block strokers range from 383 to 427 for Chevrolets, and for Fords there are displacements of 347,

Destined for a Chevrolet, these Eagle stroker components for an LS motor include a forged crank, forged H-beam rods and forged pistons. The displacement increases to 383 cubic inches

This group of Ford small-block components includes a forged crank for the very popular 347-inch stroker engines, with forged performance rods and forged pistons. As the small-block Ford is an externally balanced engine, these bottom-end parts must all be balanced with the correct damper and flexplate/flywheel

392, 406 and 427. Put one of these big small-blocks in a classic first-generation Camaro or Mustang with a modern five-speed or overdrive automatic and you've got a fine high-performance machine that can still get reasonable fuel economy on the highway.

Installation of a stroker kit is not exactly a drop-in replacement for the stock components. Because the rod throws are further out on a stroker crank, the block will probably need some clearancing, since the rods swing out in a wider circle. For most strokers using a stock factory block, the bottom of the cylinder bores usually must be notched with a coned stone in a grinder so that the connecting rods or their bolts clear the block. Even the aftermarket blocks require some clearancing. On bigger stroker kits, you may have to use a camshaft that's manufactured with a smaller-than-stock base circle so there is no interference there.

A complete stroker assembly usually includes the crank, rods, pistons, bearings and rings. Some kits can be purchased already balanced; other kits will need to be professionally balanced before installation. Another option on some kits is the inclusion of a matching damper and flywheel.

Balancing

The final machining steps before cleaning and assembly of a performance engine should be balancing of the rotating and reciprocating components: the crankshaft, rods and pistons. A stock engine is assembled with components that are very close to each other in weight, but not perfect. For performance engines, you'll want everything exact. Slight amounts of imbalance aren't a problem for stock engines, since they rarely ever see high stress or high rpm, but for our purposes we're attempting to make every cylinder as close to an ideal as possible, with every piston seeing the same compression ratio, the same amount of friction, and imparting the same load on the crankshaft. Balancing the assembly is an important part of this equalizing work.

There are stroker kits for just about every engine out there, including the newer factory performance engines like the GM LS-series engines and the Ford Modular motors. This is an Eagle stroker package for a 4.6L Ford that brings it up to a 5.0L, with enough strength to handle serious modifications such as power-adders

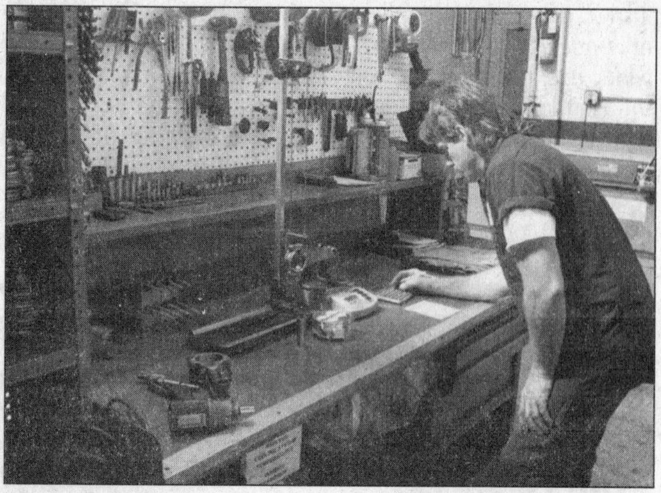

The balancing of an engine's internal components is a time-consuming and precision operation, but essential to any engine that will see high-rpm duty and the stresses of racing or high-performance driving. When the reciprocating parts are weighed, their mass is simulated on the balancing machine and the crank is massaged so loading is equal at all throws

First the rods are all weighed for total weight and compared. You can see that the scale here reads 654 grams. When the lightest rod of the set of eight is found, the other seven must be lightened to match that one. Good aftermarket rods from the same manufacturer seldom vary by much, but everything is checked anyway

If you look at a V8 crankshaft, you can see that the rod throws are offset from the main bearing journals, which are on the centerline of the crankshaft's rotation. It's easy to imagine that if the piston/rod/rings assemblies are of different weights for each cylinder, the loads imposed on the crankshaft throws will be uneven, which can induce undesirable dynamics. The faster you turn the engine, the more the differences in those loads will affect the engine negatively.

The process begins by the machine shop technician precisely weighing the pistons. The piston pins are part of the assembly and are weighed separately. For most quality aftermarket piston pins, their weight is generally the same, so a technician dealing with a brand he knows just weighs one of the pins and records that number on the balancing information sheet he fills out for every engine assembly.

All eight of the pistons are weighed, and there may be some minor variations in their weight, so the balancing technician finds the lightest piston of the eight, then reduces the weight of the other pistons to match that one. Very small amounts of material are removed from the non-critical areas on the underside of the pistons until they all weigh the same, and that weight is recorded. For all intents and purposes, the ring packages for each piston vary only minutely, and only one package is weighed and recorded. Now we have

The rods are then weighed on this fixture, in which only the small-end is on the scale. By subtracting the small-end weight from the total weight of the rod, we determine the weight of the big end. All weights are recorded on a balance sheet

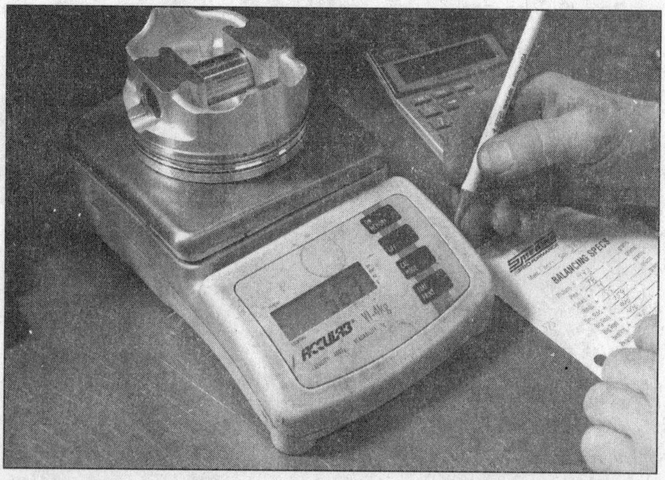

The pistons are weighed and if some are heavier, then they are lightened by machining a small amount from the underside. Obviously, the short skirt of this pistons means it's destined for a stroker assembly. It weighed 563 grams

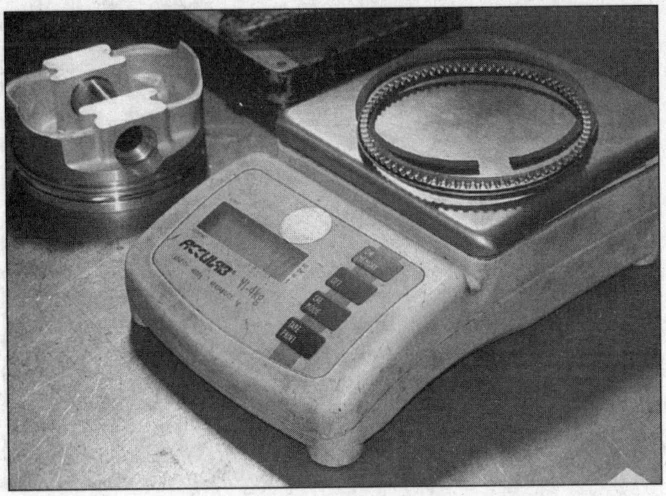

Usually, quality pistons rings vary in such tiny amounts between the sets for each cylinder that just one set of three rings is weighed and recorded on the balance sheet

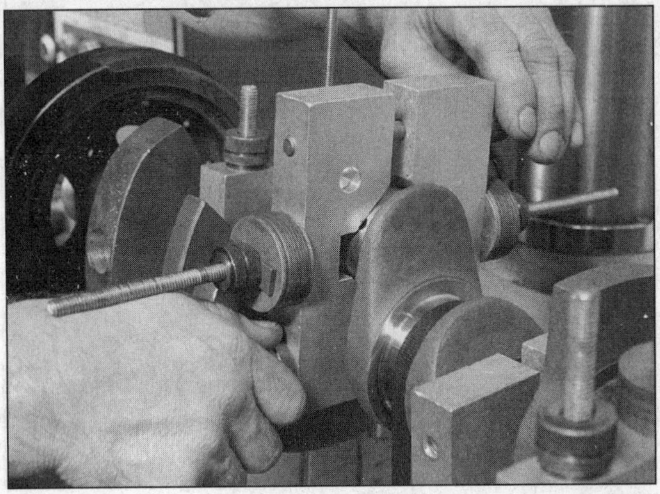

When the total weight for the reciprocating parts (rod, piston, pin and rings) is recorded, the technician attaches weights to each rod throw to simulate the load of the components. The weight is achieved through adding small precision washers to make the correct weight, then the pieces ate tightly clamped to the journals in the straight up position

the upper end of the reciprocating assembly weighed. It should be noted that all of these parts are weighed in grams, a very small measurement. Note too that, on floating piston pins that require lockrings rather than a press-fit in the rods, the lockrings are also included in the weight.

The connecting rods are next. The total weight of each rod is recorded, and if there is any minor difference between them, they are equalized the same way the pistons were treated, lightening all rods to the weight of the lightest one. Again, most quality aftermarket performance rods are practically identical in weight. If you're working with OEM factory rods, you'll see a large projecting pad of metal just above the piston-pin hole. Changing the weight of a stock rod is done by taking a little metal off that pad. Performance rods do not have such pads, since their very design is to be as light as possible while offering superior strength to production rods.

The rods are actually weighed twice. The first measurement is the total weight, and the second is with the rod suspended in a special fixture that allows the technician to weight the big end (crankshaft end) separately. This end of the rod is considered to be part of the rotating mass of the bottom end, while the rest of the rod is considered part of the reciprocating mass, along with the piston/pin/rings. When factory rods are being given a performance rebuild, the big ends are matched in weight to the lightest big end, thus the rods all have the same total weight and big-end weight. Again, quality aftermarket rods seldom require this matching of the big ends.

Now we have all the reciprocating components weighing the same. From here the rest of the balancing procedure is involved with the crankshaft itself. To spin the crankshaft in a balancing machine, weights must be attached to the rod throws to simulate the loads of the reciprocating parts. Obviously, you can't hang the actual parts in place or you'd have a spinning disaster. Aluminum blocks are clamped to each rod journal to make up the bulk of the weight being attached, with the smaller and finer additions of weight in the form of special known-weight washers. The idea is to attach the same amount of weight to each throw as would be representative of the rotating weight of the rods. This is called the bob-weight. Actually, each rod journal is fitted with double the weight of the rod big-end, since each journal is shared by two connecting rods on a V8 engine.

The balancing machine has saddles the crankshaft rests in, and a belt around the center main journal to spin the crankshaft. At several points along the crankshaft, very responsive sensors detect the forces at work while the crank

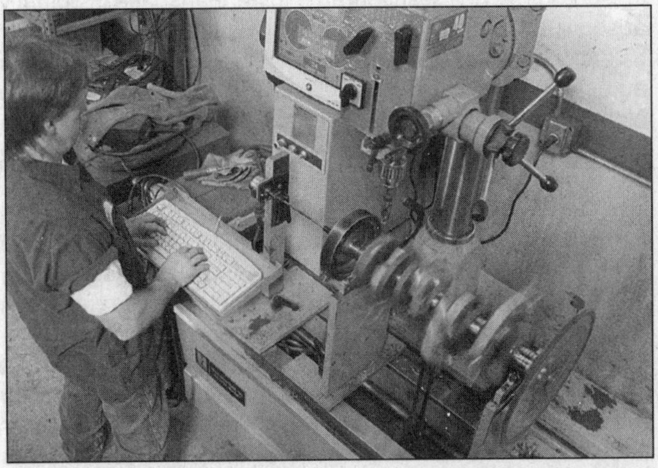

On this Hines balancer, the technician spins the crankshaft for a few seconds, and the computer screen records all the data. Note that this is a Ford engine, which is externally-balanced and must be balanced with the correct damper and flywheel in place

The various views on the computer screen tell the technician the amount of imbalance, the location on the crankshaft and the degree of rotation (out of 360-degrees) where weight should be added or removed from the crank

A special drill press is part of the balancing machine, so the crankshaft does not have to be moved in order to balance the rod throws. The balancing machine tells the operator just how many thousandths down a specific-size drill bit should bore into the counterweight to remove the correct weight. The two holes already on this counterweight are factory, but of course the manufacturer didn't know the exact reciprocating mass you would be using. Good cranks seldom require a lot of drilling unless the rods and pistons are lighter than usual

is spinning, in a similar fashion to the tire/wheel balancing machines you've seen at any tire shop. After a spin of ten seconds or so, the technician stops the spin and watches a computer screen that tells him where and how much the crankshaft is out of balance. While a tire machine measures in ounces, the engine balancer is measuring grams, so we have a much finer scale to work in.

There are two types of balance in an engine's rotating mass. Many engines have external balance, while others have internal balance. In the external-balance type, the crankshaft is matched to offset weights at each end to achieve balance, and these weights are part of the harmonic balancer at the front of the engine and the flywheel at the rear. Putting the wrong flywheel or damper on one of these engines will result in an engine that shakes, violently at some speeds. If you look at the flywheel for an externally balanced engine, you can see a welded weight in place on automatic transmission flexplates (on the side toward the block) and on flywheels for stick-shift applications, you'll see drilled holes around the perimeter and/or an offset weight at the engine side cast into the flywheel.

The internally balanced engine, sometimes called a neutral-balance, has a crankshaft that is balanced by itself. The damper is balanced with no offset and so is the flywheel. On these engines, any neutral-balance damper or flywheel can be used, while on the external-balance engines, you can only use a damper or flywheel with the correct amount of offset balance. For example, late-model small-block Ford engines are externally balanced, and require either a 28-ounce or a 50-ounce imbalance damper, and a flywheel/flexplate designed for the same 28-ounce or 50-ounce imbalance. You must know what the crankshaft requires before replacing either a damper or flywheel. Externally-balanced crankshafts must be balanced on the machine with the damper and flywheel in place.

For extreme performance/racing use, most engines are built using internal or "neutral" balancing. Most of the cast-steel aftermarket crankshafts have the OEM method of balance, either internal or external, while many of the forged aftermarket cranks are internally-balanced, even if the OEM application was external. In high stress applications, the crankshaft should be subject to less harmonic stress with internal balancing, and the offset weights in externally-balanced dampers may create extra loads on the front end of the crankshaft at consistent high rpm levels.

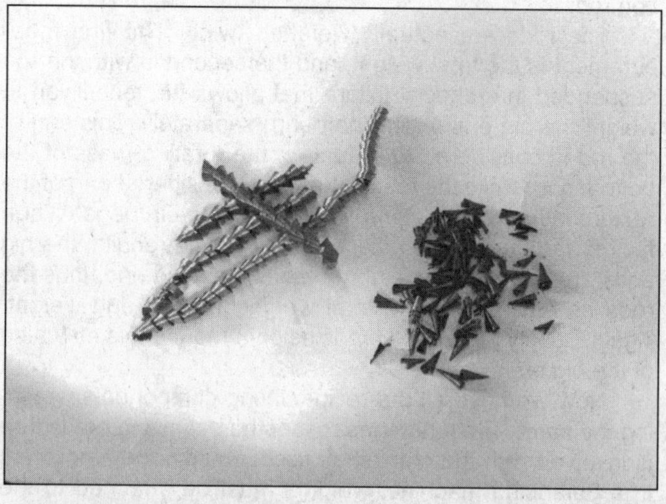

Just to show you what you can learn even from machining chips, the curlycues on the left are from a forged-steel crankshaft, while the little bits at right are from a cast crank

When the technician reads the amount and location of imbalance during the balancing procedure, the balance is achieved by removing weight from the crankshaft counterweights if that area is too heavy, or adding weight where it is needed. The computer screen tells him the exact weight in grams to remove or add. By rotating the crankshaft by hand he can put the counterweight that needs alterations exactly straight-up on the machine. Removing weight is common, and is handled by a special drill-press that is part of the balancer. Holes are drilled to remove weight, and the machine even specifies how deep a hole will remove how many grams. Adding weight is tougher. In the old days, a technician would use a welder to apply some weight to the counterweight, but this was imprecise and time-consuming. Sometimes you just can't add enough metal with this method, so the modern way is to add some "heavy metal." Mallory metal is an expensive alloy that is very dense and heavier than the crankshaft material, so a hole may be drilled in the counterweight and a slug of Mallory metal is pressed in. Thankfully, most cranks require lightening rather that the addition of weight, since the heavy metal is expensive and time-consuming to add to the counterweights.

When the balancing procedure is finished, the crankshaft and other parts can be cleaned and boxed up for later use in assembling the engine. The crankshaft is usually stamped with an ID number or code so that its history can be looked up at any time in the balancing record. If any pistons or rods are replaced someday down the road, the new parts can be balanced to the same specs as on the record sheet at the machine shop, thus avoiding having to rebalance the crankshaft.

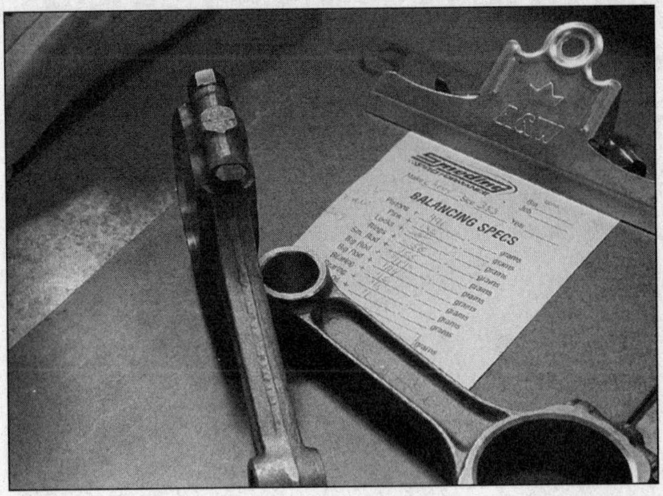

A typical balance sheet at Smeding Performance records all of the data for a complete bottom-end assembly. The customer can have a copy, but the original stays in the shop's files. They number their cranks and engines, so if any component needs to be replaced, they can match the new parts to the balance record, without needing the whole engine

Notes

13 Engine Builds: How the Pros Make Big Power with Reliability

It is said that the devil is in the details, but details are necessary when it comes to building a performance engine. More than just bolting together the proper components, engine building is about the attention to every small aspect of those components, and the pros have fine tuned that attention with their years of experience. What they have learned is that the whole of a performance/racing engine is, in the end, no better than its weakest link. It might not ever cause a problem, but the pros don't want comebacks from unhappy customers, for any reason.

The professional engine builders also know more than the rest of us do regarding the components they install. When builders find suppliers that consistently deliver products they can trust, they keep using those companies. Most engine builders have their favorites, and they particularly like manufacturers who are available for tech concerns and questions. Builders want to be informed if the manufacturer starts making their rods, pistons, cams or head bolts differently, or if there are any different procedures for the products they have used in the past. The good companies also like a close relationship with the pro builders because they get consistent feedback from the builders about what's working, and new ideas or techniques they may not already know about.

Two things you'll find that are different about professional engine shops versus your home garage are tools and organization. You and I may have the basic hand tools, a torque wrench and probably an engine stand, which is fine for building one engine for yourself with no time limit, but the pros have to be efficient in order to make money building engines. In the process of doing an engine swap, a routine repair procedure, or building a performance engine, the weekend mechanic may need to make a few trips to the local hardware and auto parts stores. In the home shop, there never seems to be enough 5/16-inch bolts, washers, RTV or gaskets. Maybe you can't find where you put your ring compressor since the last engine you built four years ago.

In a professional shop, a "clean room" is devoted to assembly work only, where there is no dust or machining chips around to infect the engine components as they go together. By having organized shelves and bins for all the parts they keep on hand, time is saved. Even basic hardware isn't overlooked. The pros have drawers with large quantities of commonly used small items, such as valve stem seals, new plated intake and pan bolts, header bolts, camshaft bolts, Woodruff keys in sizes for the popular engines, rear main and front cover seals, etc. An engine technician can reach up to the shelf, grab a box with the new camshaft and lifters he needs, clean and lube the parts and install them. This isn't to imply that home mechanics can't assemble their own performance engine without a complete redo of the garage. We simply want to illustrate how an engine shop technician can put together an engine every day, once the balanced lower-end parts and cleaned block come to him from the engine machine/balancing department.

As you follow our photo sequences of the engines we're presenting here, note that while every step of the build isn't shown, we do show the important ones. The proper installation of one set of rings, or one rod/piston is much the same as for the other seven cylinders.

The three engines covered here include a cross-section of popular engine combos: a stroker 427 small-block Ford and a BIG big-block Chevy, both built by Smeding Performance of Rancho Cordova, California, and a stroker 383-cubic-inch LS-series GM engine from a 1999 Trans-Am.

13a Building the GM LS1 for extreme street duty

Introduced in the 1997 Corvette, GM's Generation III V8 engine (commonly known by its option code - LS1) revolutionized pushrod V8 engine design. Utilizing the latest computer modeling technologies, GM optimized the LS1 to reduce weight and friction. Design breakthroughs included the engine's 15-degree valve angle and thin-but-tall "cathedral" intake ports. With extensive use of advanced technology, it's no wonder the LS1 produced over one horsepower per cubic inch in its original design. Since 1997, the "LS" series engines continue to impress us with their durability and power output, pushing through 400 and 500 horsepower in stock form.

But what if stock horsepower isn't enough? Is there ever "enough" horsepower? We thought not. Then let's get on with wringing out the true potential of the LS1 engine. And the best way to do that is from the bottom up. We've chosen an ultra-strong Eagle rotating assembly, Comp Cams valvetrain, Airflow Research (AFR) heads and a FAST intake manifold. Our goal was to add 150 horsepower and take 1.5 seconds off our ET while still keeping emissions within the parameters of California smog. Oh yeah, and we wanted our 1999 Trans-Am to retain a decent idle and good low-rpm driveability. Sound like a tall order? Read on!

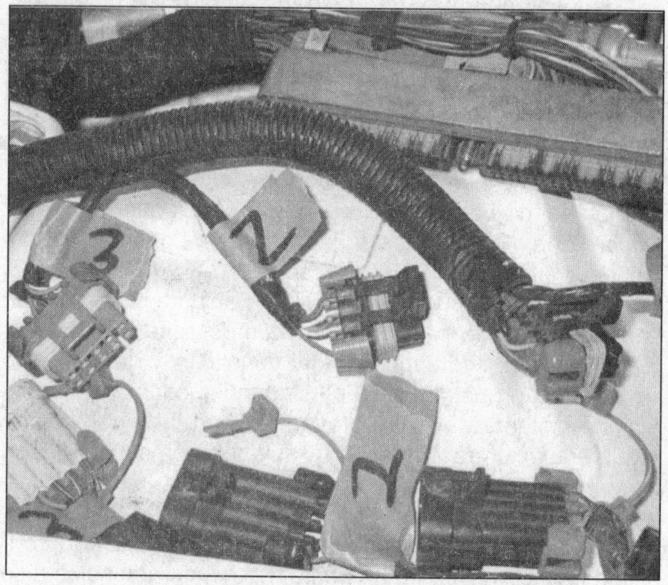

1 Before disconnecting anything, be sure you label the connectors, and take digital photos as you go. When it's time to put the car back together, you'll be glad you took those few extra minutes

2 The details of engine removal vary greatly from model to model, so get a Haynes manual on your particular vehicle for the details. On our Trans-Am, the easiest way to remove the engine was to drop it out from below by separating the subframe from the chassis . . .

3 . . . and lifting the vehicle off the engine/transmission assembly. This, of course, requires a vehicle hoist

4 After the engine is out, it's time to separate it from the transmission and subframe and begin disassembly. Take photos and mark all the parts. Labeled plastic bags work well when you have many similar small bolts or other parts

5 Our machine shop cleaned and honed our block 0.007-inch oversize to the specified 3.905-inch bore. Align-honing was out of the question, since the block is aluminum and the main bearing caps are steel (can you say "egg-shaped?"). As good as this block looks, there's still a lot of cleaning to do, so let's get to it!

6 All bolt holes in the block should be cleaned up for accurate torque. A tap can be used if you're careful, but remember that we're going into aluminum here. Fastener companies make special taps that will reduce thread wear during this process

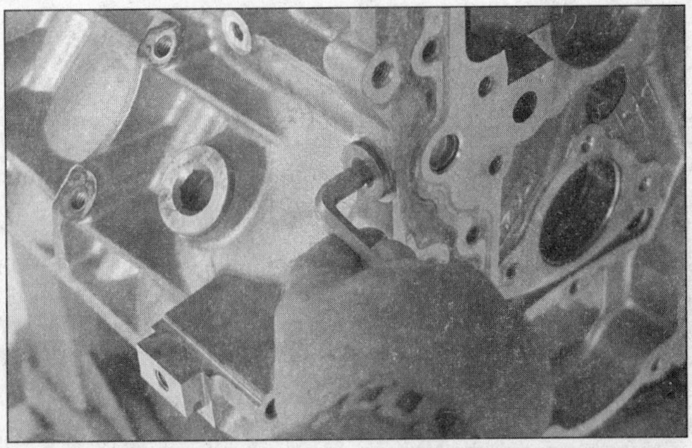

7 Use Allen wrenches to remove all the coolant and oil gallery plugs from the block

8 Many companies make special nylon bristle brushes for cleaning out the oil galleries that run through the engine block. You'll need a set of these brushes and several cans of carburetor cleaner to do the job

9 Scrub out the oil galleries until they're shiny and clean throughout. Use a flashlight to check your work. Because of the aluminum block, DO NOT use rifle-cleaning brushes, since they're usually made from brass and will scratch

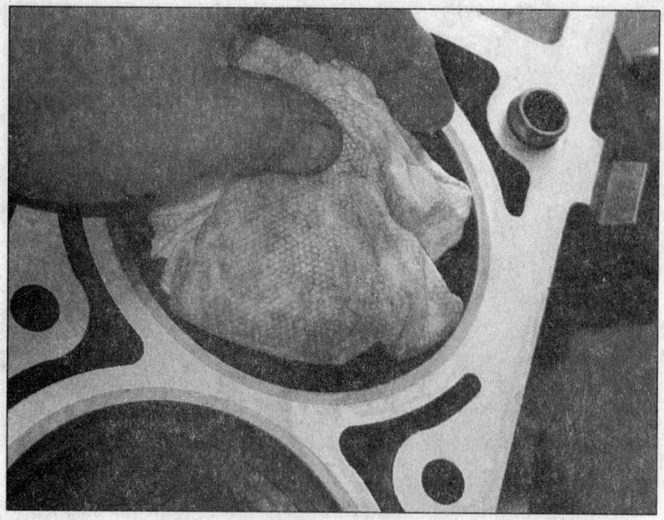

10 Wipe down the cylinder bores with a clean rag soaked in carburetor cleaner or a similar solvent. Our bores appeared clean, but look at all the honing material that came out of this bore. Leaving this in would cause premature wear on the pistons, rings and other engine parts

11 Here's what the cleaned bores should look like. Notice the cross-hatch pattern left by the hone, which should have an angle of about 30-degrees

12 We chose this Eagle rotating assembly with a four-inch stroke to yield 383 cubic inches (about 6.3 liters). This assembly has the strength to easily handle 800 horsepower while maintaining the durability for many thousands of miles of street duty. The difference in price over buying new stock-type components is considerable, but we're gaining strength, horsepower AND torque

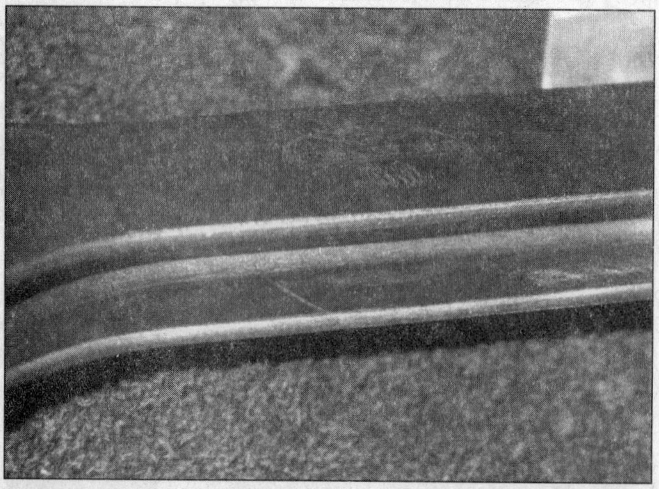

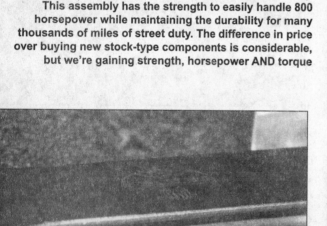

13 Our Eagle "H-Beam" rods are light and strong, due partly to this cavity in each beam edge. Some builders prefer the more-expensive "I-beam" design that does not have a cavity where oil can collect. Either design is a huge improvement over the stock powdered-metal rods, which get questionable near the 500 horsepower mark

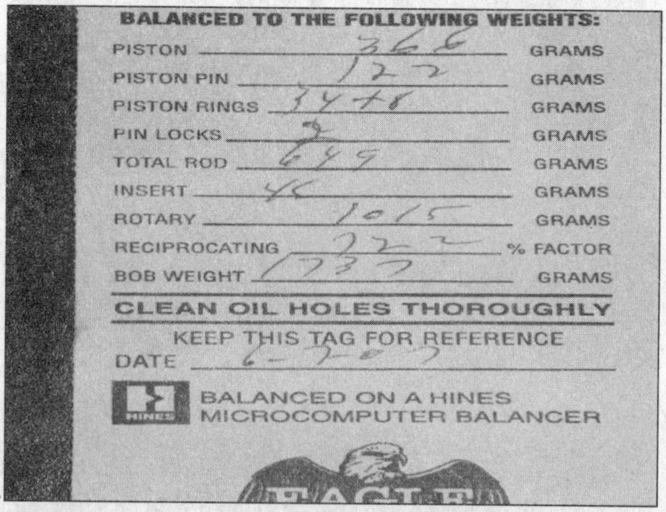

14 Having the rotating assembly balanced at the factory is the way to go. The price is usually reasonable, and you can be sure the assembly is ready to run right out of the box

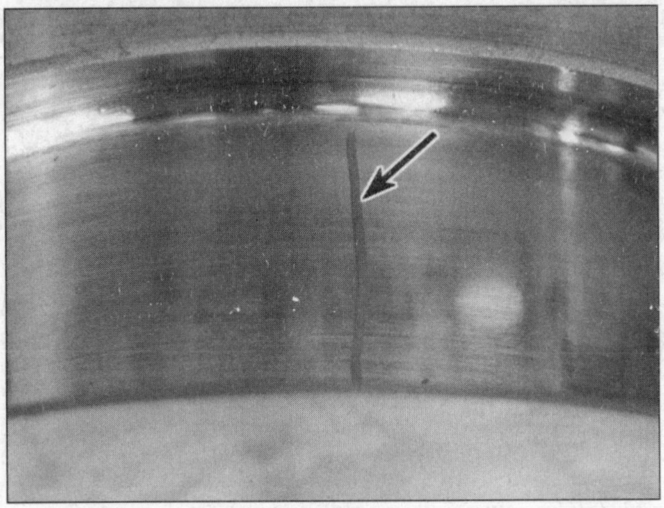

15 With the engine upside-down, carefully put the crankshaft in place on the new main bearings. DO NOT lubricate the bearings yet. Lay a strip of Plastigage (arrow) across each main-bearing journal on the crankshaft and press each bearing cap onto the block (gently!)

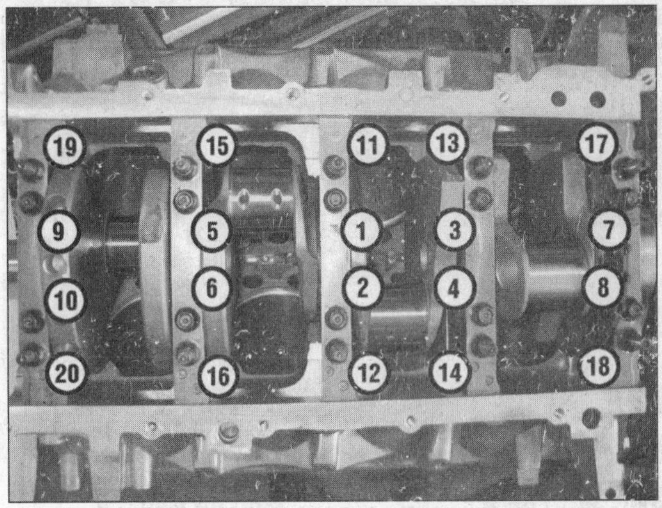

16 Snug up the studs a little at a time, following the correct sequence

17 When the caps are seated against the block, torque them, in sequence, to the final torque. GM uses an angle-torque method for their bolts, but we're using ARP studs that specify 60 Ft-lbs on the inner studs and 50 Ft-lbs on the outer studs. There's no need to install the side bolts at this time

18 After torquing, remove the caps and measure the crushed Plasitigage using the gauge on the envelope. Our oil clearance was about 0.0025, which is right at GM's service limit. Since this is a high-performance engine, the extra clearance (combined with a high-volume oil pump) was what we were looking for

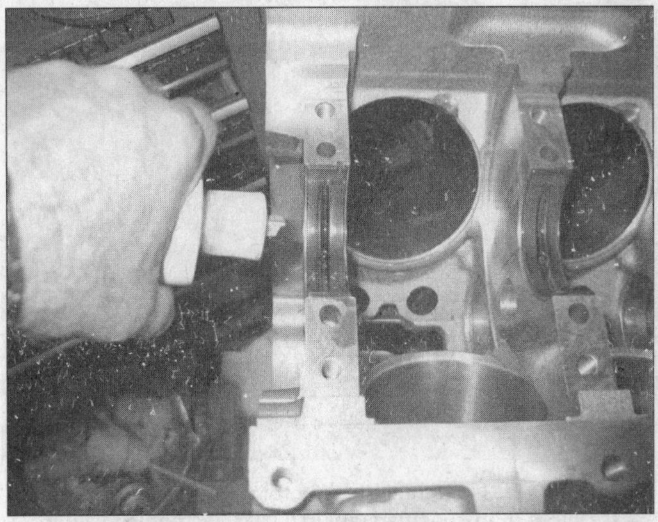

19 Remove the crankshaft again and lube the bearings with a thick engine-assembly lube. Reinstall the crankshaft and main-bearing caps. . .

20 . . . and re-torque the bolts. If you're using aftermarket fasteners, be sure to lube them as recommended. Our ARP main studs required a special lubricant . . .

21 . . . and a 12-point socket

22 After torquing the main studs, install the side bolts. Be sure to use some RTV sealant on the washers and bolt heads to prevent oil leaks

23 After the crankshaft is installed, it should rotate freely with no rough spots or noises. If it's not perfect, stop now and find the problem

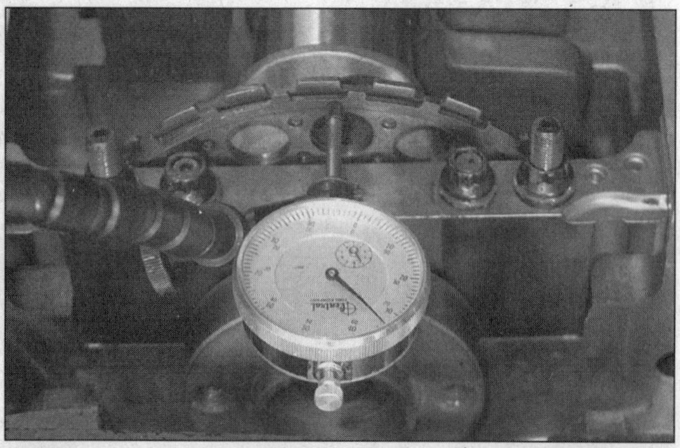

24 On the LS1 engine, the reluctor runout is CRITICAL. If it's more than specified (about 0.017), the engine will not run! Fortunately, it's easy to check. And as long as your dial indicator is set up on the reluctor ring, you can check crankshaft endplay at the same time

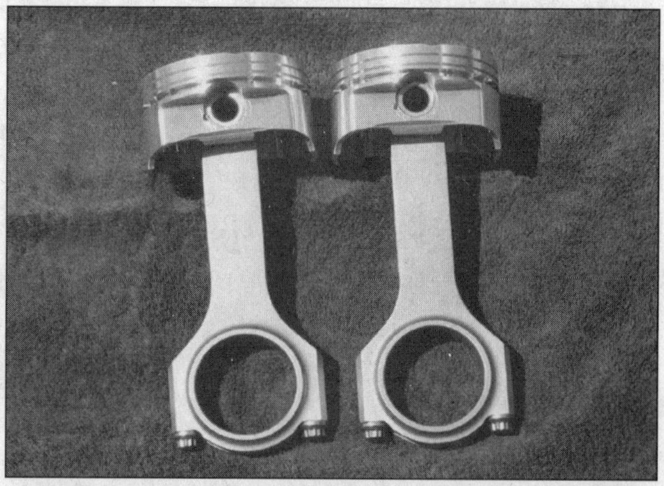

25 Now we're onto the pistons. You'll need to assemble two pistons onto their rods to check rod-to-block clearance. You can leave the rings off for now

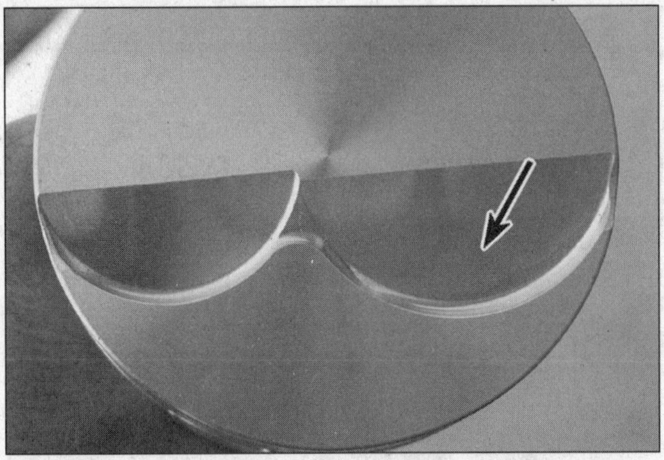

26 Our Arias pistons have different-sized valve pockets that make them easy to index correctly. The larger intake pocket (arrow) should be aligned . . .

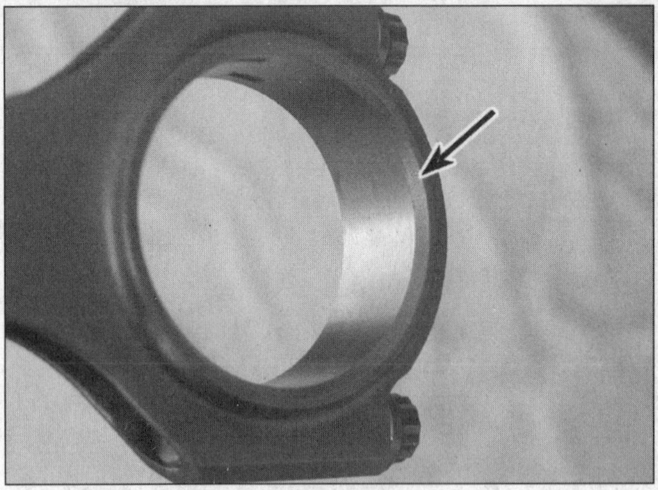

27 . . . with the chamfered side of the connecting rod (arrow)

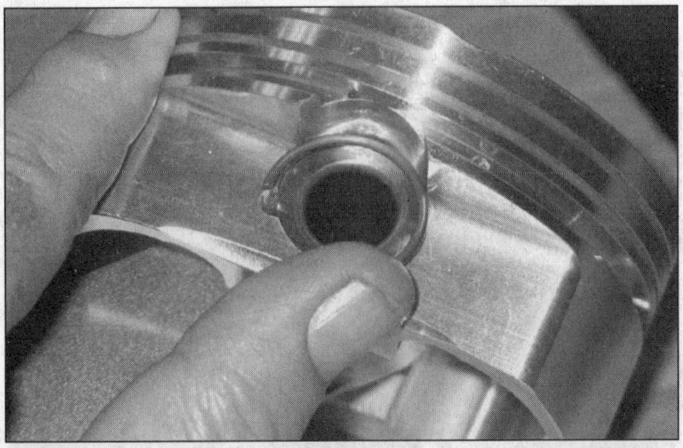

28 Slide the pin through the piston and rod, then install the clips. Our Arias pistons use these simple and durable circlips. Some manufacturers use "spirallocks," which must be "wound" into place

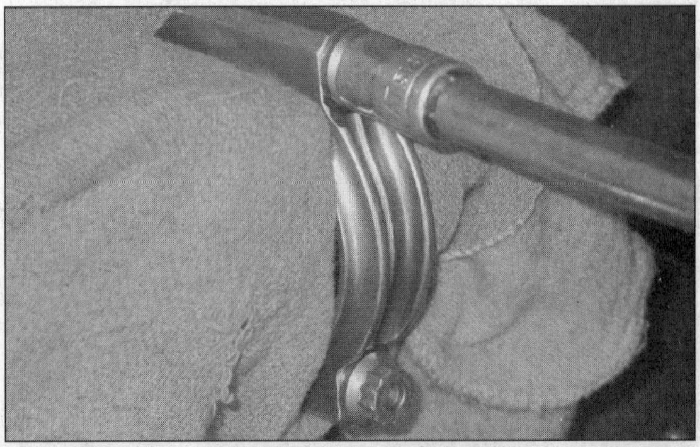

29 As delivered, the connecting rod bolts are very tight. While special vises are available to clamp the rod while loosening the bolts, we used a standard vise with padded jaws. DO NOT use an impact wrench to loosen the bolts, since you could nick the rods, creating stress risers that can lead to cracking

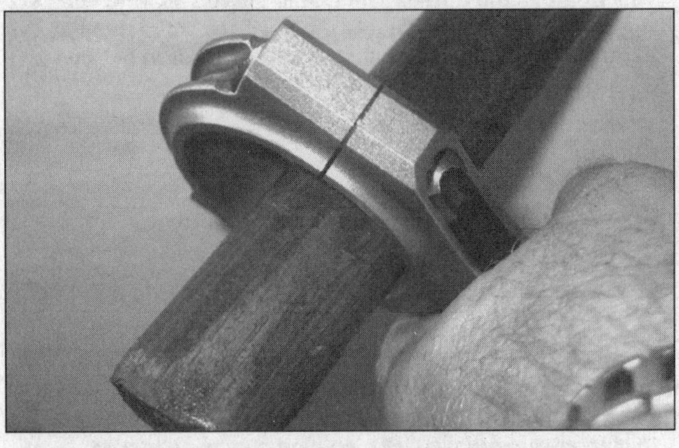

30 The rod bearing caps are also on tight. Do not try to pry them apart. We found that repeated tapping with a wooden hammer handle will eventually loosen the cap. The adage "patience is a virtue" was probably coined by a performance engine builder!

31 You should never mix up your rods and caps, but, if we did, these numbers on our Eagle rods would have saved the day. Each number is unique to the set

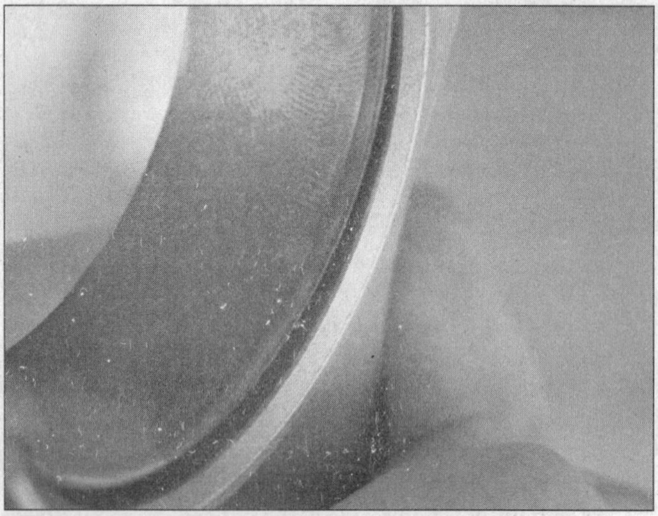

32 When installing the bearings, be sure to match the chamfer on the bearing with the chamfer on the rod . . .

33 . . . and the flat side of the bearing with the flat side of the rod. If you don't match these up correctly, you'll damage your bearings and crankshaft

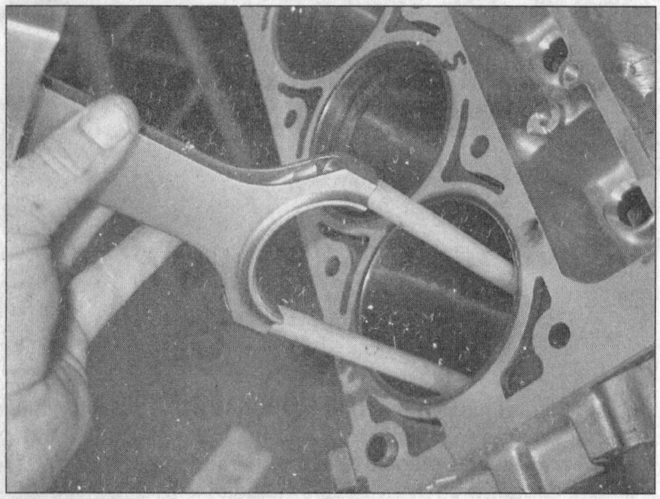

34 Put some oil in the cylinder, as well as on the piston and rod bearings. Carefully install the piston - minus the rings - into the cylinder. We used dowels in the bolt holes to direct the rod onto the crankshaft journal and avoid scratching

35 Remove the dowels and install the rod bearing caps, tightening the bolts snugly (no need to torque them at this time). Now install the companion piston on the opposite side of the block

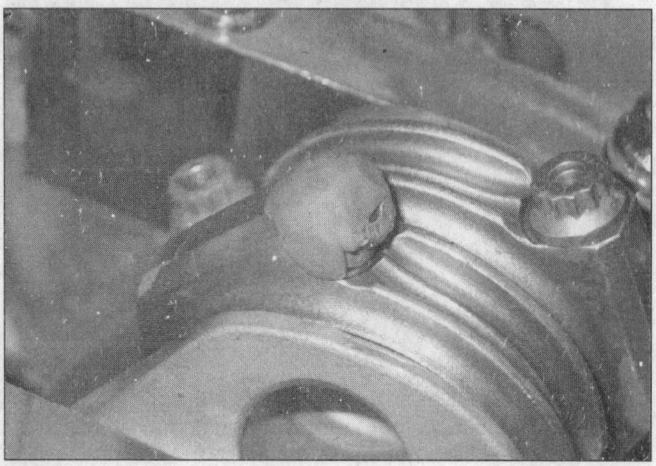

36 If you have a stroker crankshaft, chances are that the rod bolts are not going to clear the bottom of the cylinder bore. If you think you're close to the minimum 0.035 clearance, you can use modeling clay to check. If clearance is inadequate, mark the contact area with a felt-tip pen

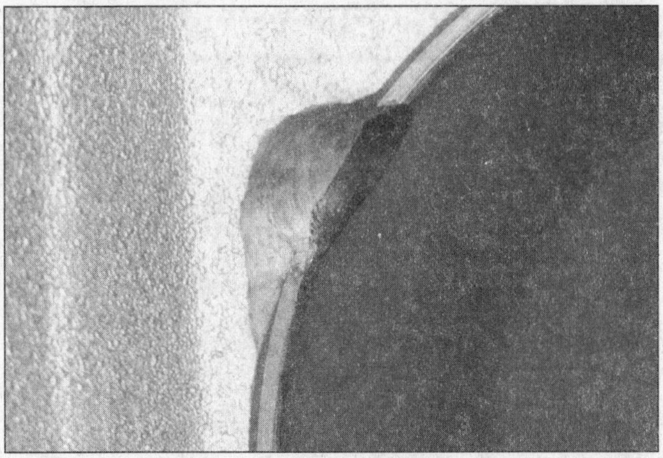

37 After marking the contact areas for all bores, remove the rods/pistons and crank. Use a small, hand-held grinder to remove material from the marked areas. Don't go overboard here - remove only enough material to get the required 0.035-inch

38 Here's what it should look like after clearancing. It's tight at the bottom, but nothing's going to hit. Don't worry about loss of block strength. So long as you've ground a minimum smooth radius, there shouldn't be any significant loss in strength

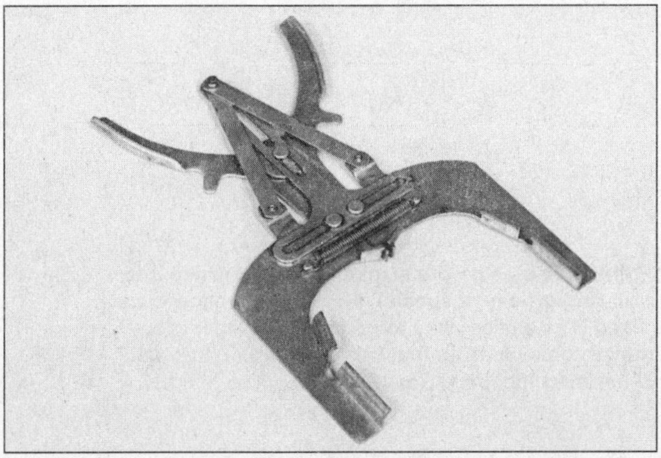

39 Before you install the piston rings, you might want to get a ring installer tool like this. It will make the job easier and might prevent breaking a ring. The tool is only used to install the compression rings (top two rings). The oil-control ring set is installed by hand

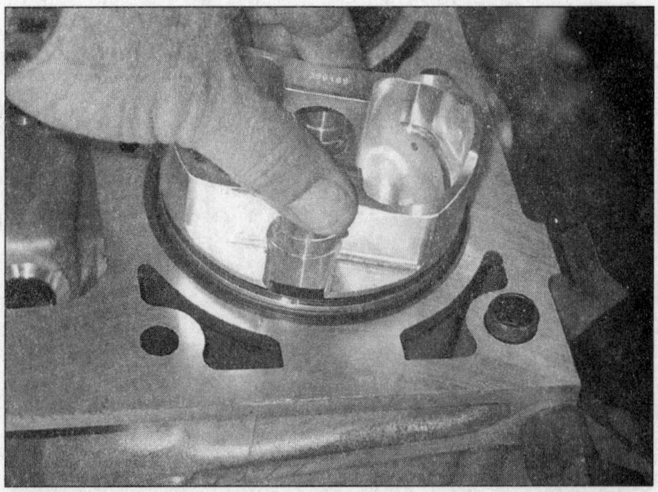

40 We can now prepare our rings for installation. Install a ring in a bore and use a piston to even it up. Installing the second ring on the piston assures that the piston won't be cocked and the ring will be "square" in the bore

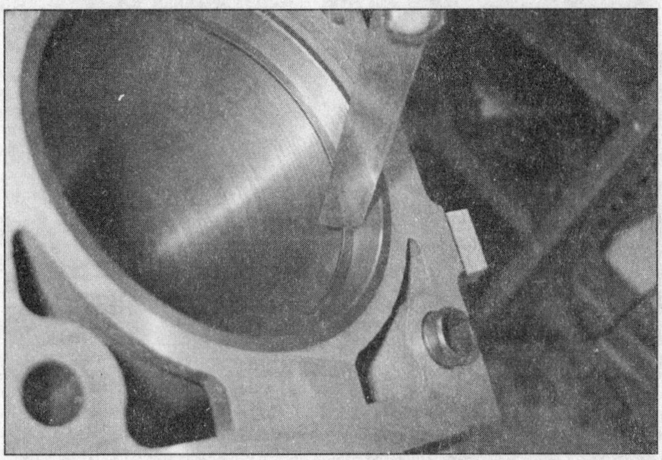

41 Now measure the ring gap with feeler gauges and compare it to the piston-manufacturer's specifications. Arias provides a formula for determining the correct gap, based partly on intended use (nitrous, blower, alcohol, etc.). The gap you use will likely be different than the stock GM specifications - probably larger

42 We're using file-to-fit rings, which means we will, well, file them to fit. Clamp a file in a vise and file each ring a little at a time, from the outside in only, until the ring is exactly at specification

43 After you've fitted a top ring and second ring to a bore, leave them in place. This will keep them organized and allow you to custom-fit each ring set to each bore

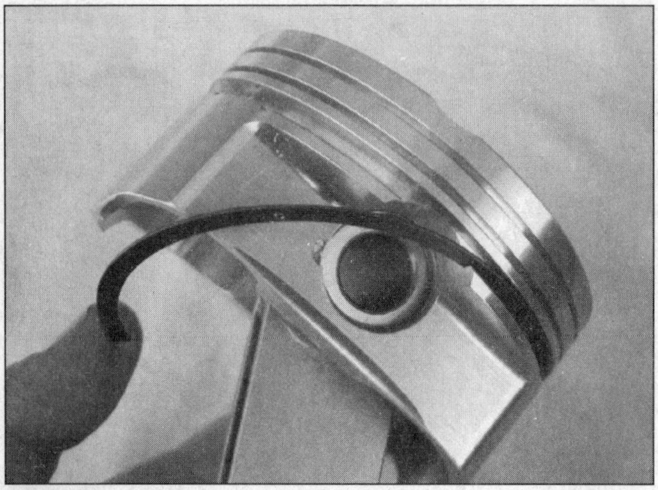

44 Since the pins on our stroker pistons intrude into the oil-ring groove, a special groove-lock spacer must be used. The easiest way to install this spacer is to wind it into place. Note that this spacer also has an end-gap specification. Time for some more filing!

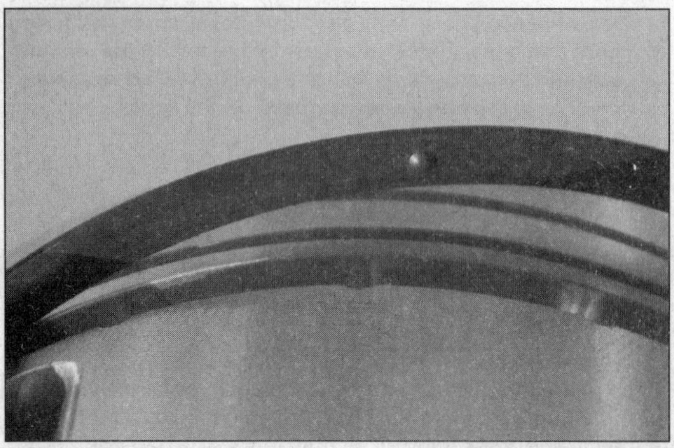

45 The groove-lock spacer has a dimple that must face down and must remain in the open area of the ring groove, near the piston pin

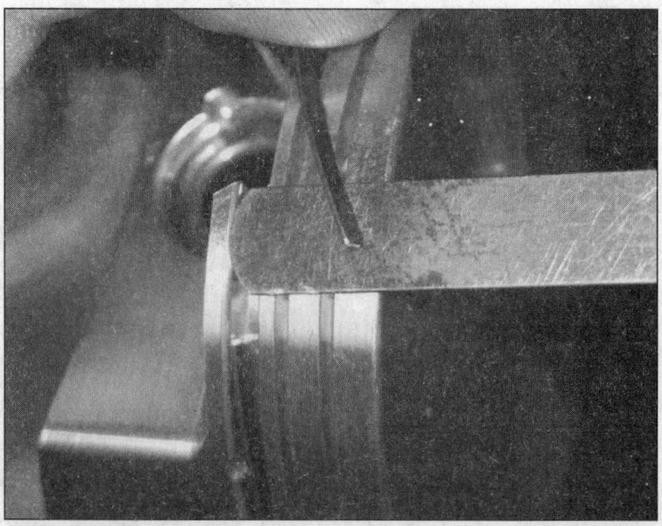

46 The groove-lock spacer fits tightly in the oil-ring groove and is difficult to stretch into place without scratching the piston. We used a thin feeler gauge to protect the piston as we installed the spacer

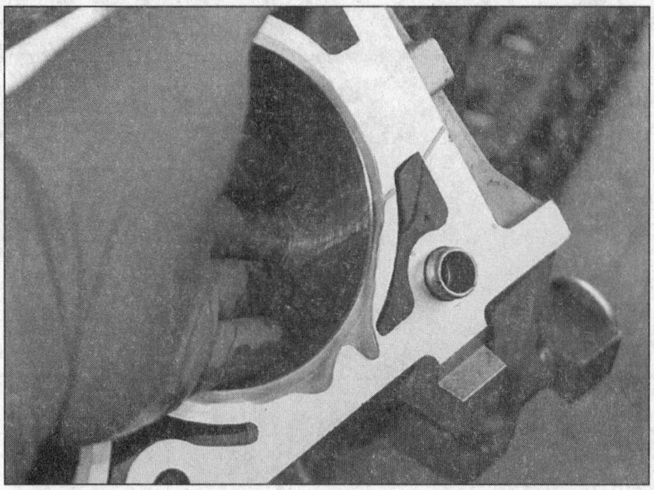

47 Once the rings are in place, it's time to install the pistons. Start by coating the cylinder bore with oil or assembly lube. Also lube the piston and rings. This is a messy process, so wear gloves and old clothes. Make sure the upper bearing half is in the connecting rod

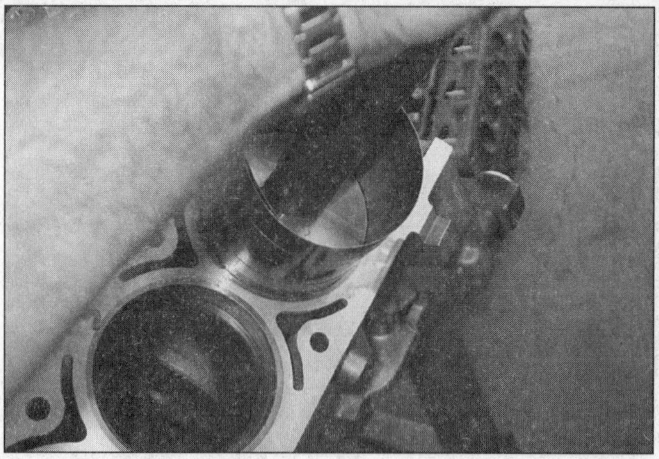

48 When installing the pistons, a ring compressor will be necessary. Tap the piston gently with a plastic or wooden hammer handle. If you feel resistance, stop immediately and check that a ring isn't hanging up

49 Once the piston/rod is in place, it's time to check the rod bearing oil clearance with Plastigage. Use the same procedure as you did for the main bearings. Expect your clearance to be a little greater than factory specification. More clearance - ours was just over 0.002 - provides better oil flow for cooling

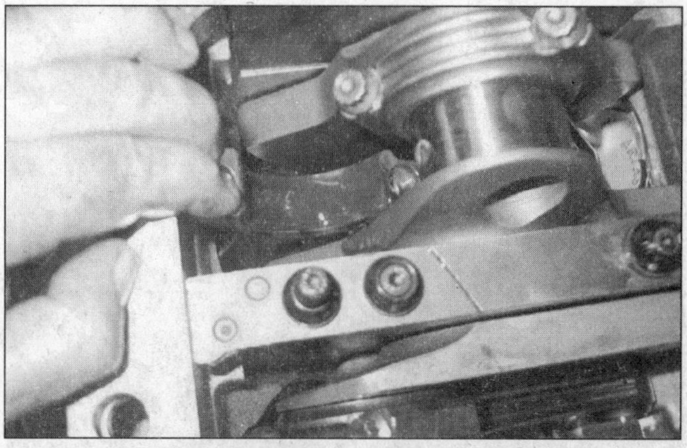

50 After Plastigaging, lube your bearings with engine assembly lube . . .

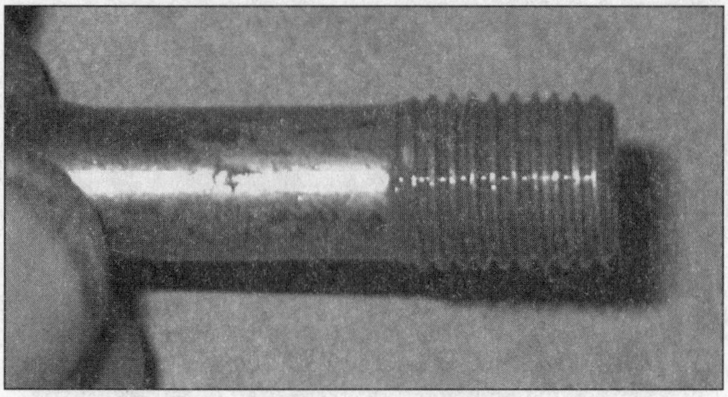

51 . . . and the threads of your rod bolts with the special lubricant provided

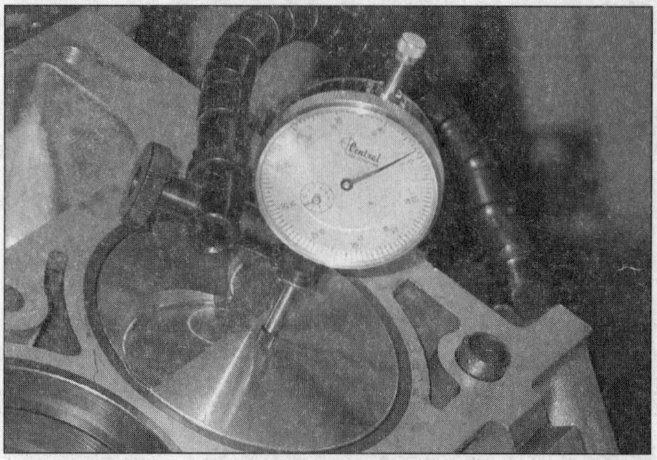

52 Once all the pistons are installed, check the deck height. Our pistons were within a few thousandths of being exactly flush with the deck of the block at TDC. Deck height is an important part of the calculation that determines compression ratio

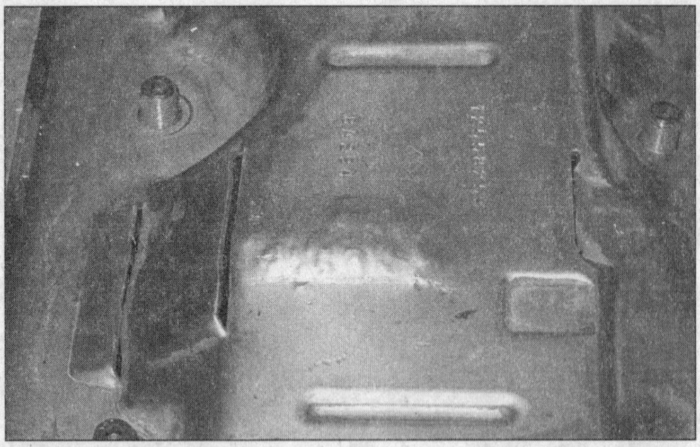

53 Now it's time to install the windage tray. Our factory tray did not have clearance for the longer stroke. This was one of the few times we got to use our hammer in engine assembly! Notice the dented bulge in the tray - it follows the arc of the connecting rod, providing the necessary extra clearance. Not pretty, but it won't show when the engine is assembled

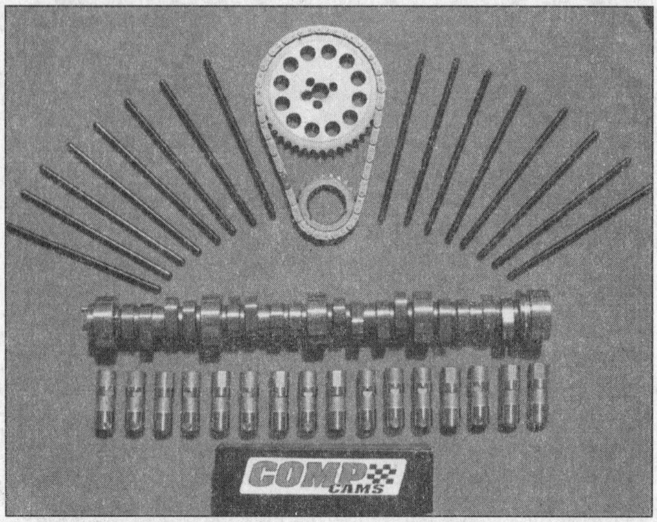

54 We chose Comp Cams for our valvetrain components. It's best to buy all your components from a single reputable manufacturer so you know the components will work together. Our mid-range from Comp's XE-R line works well in our street-driven car, providing good street manners as well as excellent power

55 Since the LS1 camshaft is hollow, you can use a large screwdriver or long 3/8-inch socket extension as a handle during installation. Be sure to lube the lobes and journals. Since this is a roller cam, moly-based lube is not required

56 Our camshaft thrust plate was not worn, but we replaced it due to its integrated oil-gallery seal. Don't take chances when it comes to oil pressure!

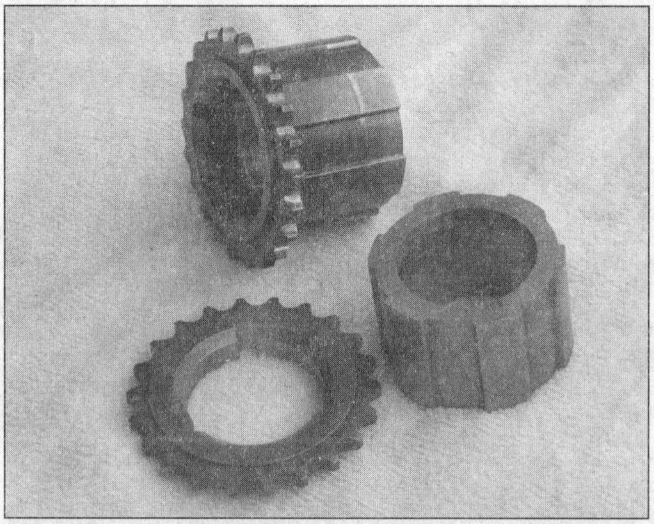

57 The stock crankshaft sprocket/oil pump drive (rear) is one piece, while our Comp Cams replacement (front) splits it into two parts. When installing the crankshaft gear, be sure the marks face out

58 Here's a really cool feature on our Comp camshaft sprocket - you can advance or retard the camshaft several degrees by just loosening the sprocket bolts and turning the adjuster with an Allen wrench. We set our cam to "zero," which is where you'll want to set it unless you know EXACTLY what you're doing!

59 Once the camshaft is installed, it's time to install a set of lifters . . .

60 . . . and a dial indicator so you can degree the cam (see Chapter 8 for details). On our LS1 motor, we were able to install the dial indicator directly on top of the lifter . . .

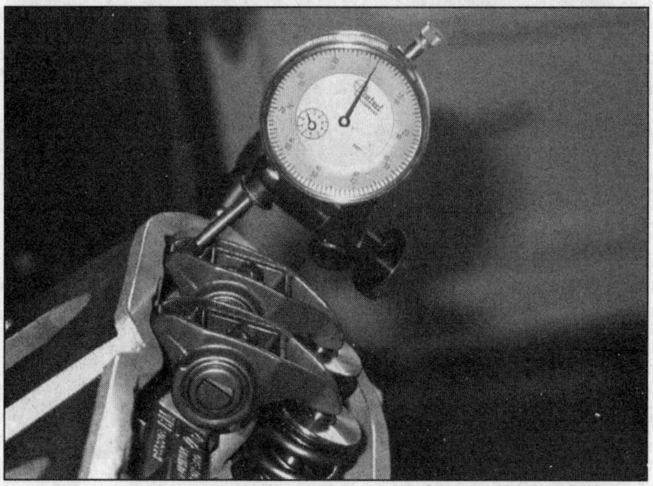

61 . . . or on the rocker arm (after the heads and rockers were in place). Wherever you install the dial indicator, just make sure it is solid and directly in line with the lifter's or pushrod's direction of movement

62 The degree wheel installed easily using our old crankshaft balancer bolt. A piece of coat-hanger wire under one of the front-cover bolts served as a pointer. Although it's rare to find a problem when degreeing a cam, it's good insurance to do the procedure on EVERY installation

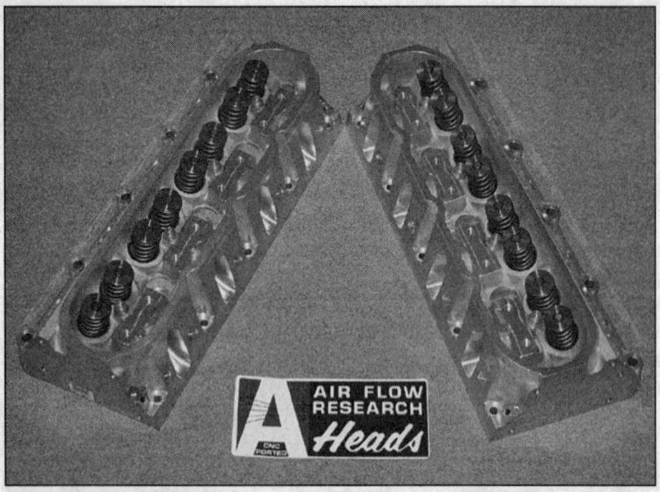

63 Our AFR 205cc heads flowed over 300 cfm at 0.600 lift right out of the box. These heads provide more than enough airflow for a 500 horsepower street engine!

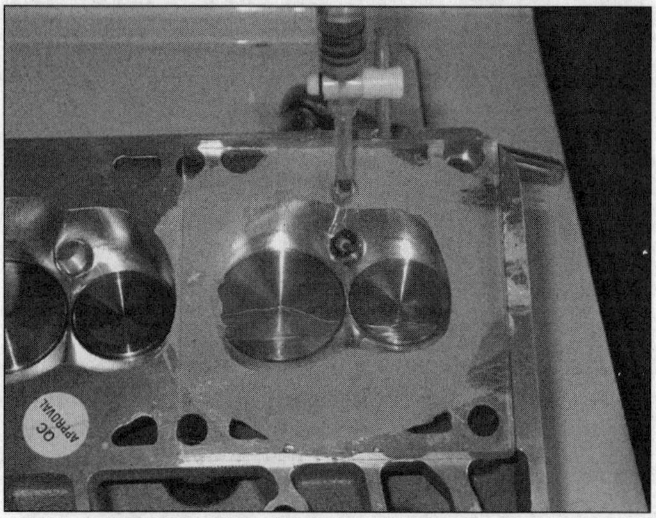

64 Our heads "cc'd" exactly to specifications. Based on advice from AFR's Tony Mamo, we bumped up our compression ratio a full point, to just over 11:1. We haven't noticed any pinging on pump gas - this is due to the two-sided quench designed into the combustion chambers of the AFR heads

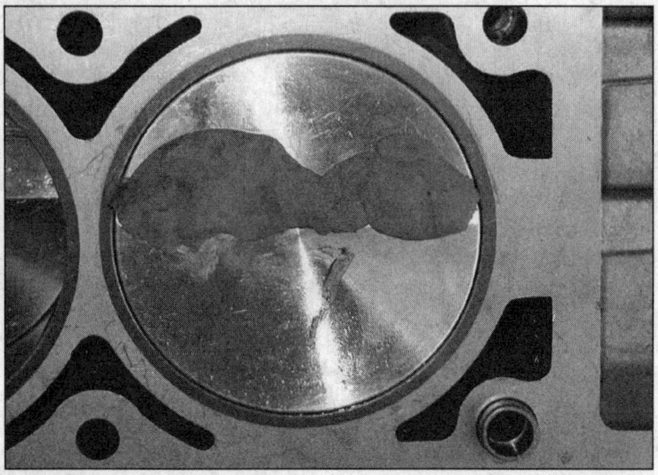

65 Here's an easy way to check for valve-to-piston interference. Put modeling clay in the valve reliefs on the pistons and install the cylinder heads with spacers to simulate gasket thickness (your old gaskets will work, if your new ones are the same thickness). Then install six or so head bolts (don't torque them), rotate the crankshaft through two full revolutions . . .

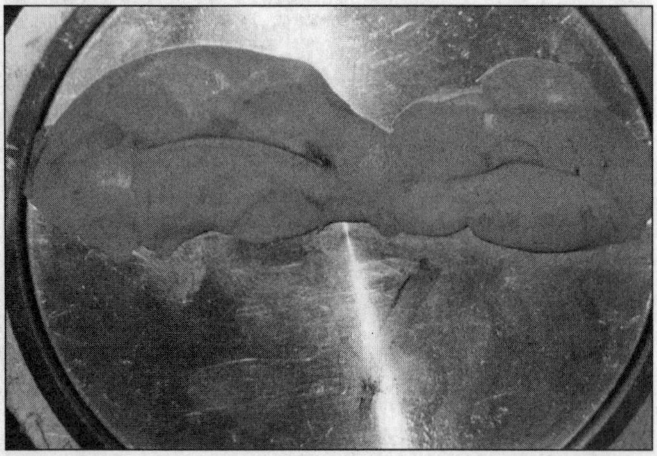

66 . . . take off the head and cut through the clay where the impressions from the valves were left. Measure the thickness of the clay at those points. The minimum thickness of the clay is your valve-to-piston clearance. For best safety, you should have at least 0.100-inch

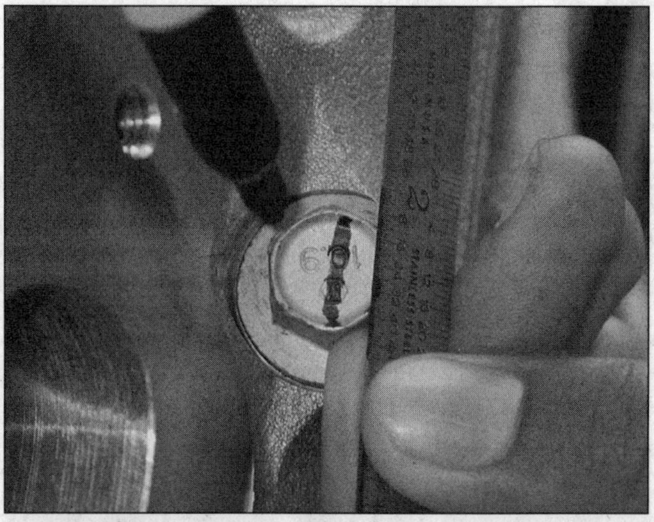

67 Now we're ready to bolt the cylinder heads into place. ARP studs were recommended for our installation, but if you're using stock-type torque-to-yield bolts, mark each bolt head. That way you won't be guessing which bolts have been rotated

68 With factory-style head bolts, the final torquing is done in degrees of rotation. A torque-angle meter is a must. This tool is available inexpensively at auto parts stores

69 Here's a little trick for checking valvetrain geometry. Mark the tip of each valve with a felt-tip pen, then reinstall the rocker arms and rotate the engine through at least two full revolutions. If the geometry is correct . . .

70 . . . the contact pattern will be right across the center of the valve tip. If the pattern is not centered, there's a problem with the geometry that will wear out your valve guides prematurely and cost you horsepower. Work with your machine shop to get your valve and rocker heights correct

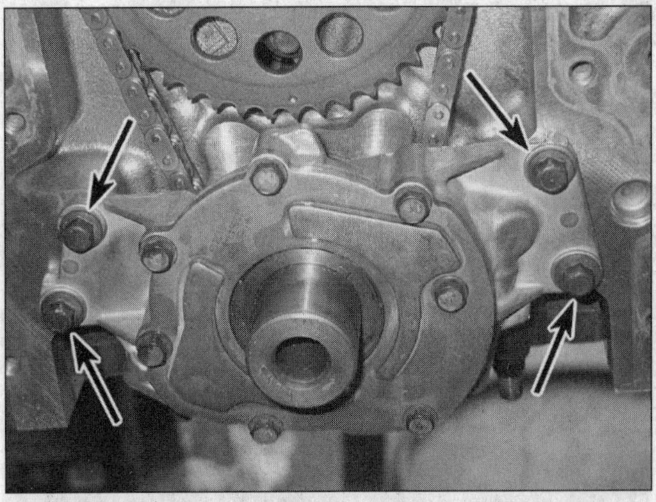

71 The oil pump attaches to the engine with four bolts (arrows), but no gasket or sealant. The oil pump bolts, like all fasteners on the Gen III engine, have precise torque values. ALL fasteners must be torqued to specification - even the ones that don't seem critical

72 Be sure to thoroughly lube all valvetrain components during assembly. This handy spray lube from Comp Cams is perfect for the job

73 Here's a way to check for adequate clearance between the oil pick-up screen and the bottom of the oil pan. Use modeling clay to form a bead around the screen (arrow). Install the oil pan, then remove it and check the thickness of the clay. There is no spec here. You want the pickup very close to the bottom of the pan, but with enough clearance for adequate oil flow

74 Here's our engine, with F.A.S.T. manifold in place, itching to be installed. If you've taken your time and checked everything carefully as you went, the engine should start right up - and make big power!

75 The final step was tuning the engine to optimize the spark timing and air/fuel ratio for the new combo. Having the right tune in your PCM can make a big difference. Rob Barth from Strictly Performance tuned our engine using the latest HP Tuners software. The results were impressive - 418 horsepower at the rear wheels! The numbers are even more impressive when you consider the car has an automatic transmission and a STOCK exhaust system!

13b Pro-building a 427-inch Ford Small-block

1 Experience, organization, attention to detail, and the right parts and equipment are what it takes to consistently build quality performance engines, such as the popular turn-key engines built at Smeding Performance, Rancho Cordova, California

2 This procedure concerns the buildup of an engine that is small-block-Ford in terms of architecture yet big-block in displacement, a 427 stroker motor that will fit anywhere a Windsor small-block could reside. The build starts with a brand new Dart iron block, with beefy cylinder walls and big four-bolt main caps

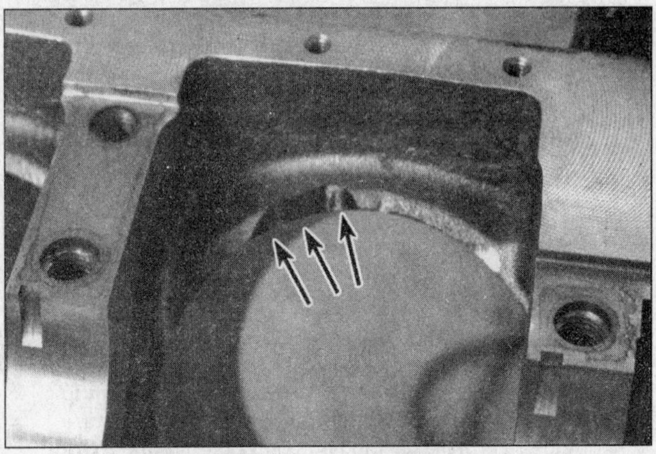

3 Because Smeding is using a long-arm forged stroker crankshaft, the block requires some clearance grinding at the bottom of each bore, to clear the outside corners of the connecting rods

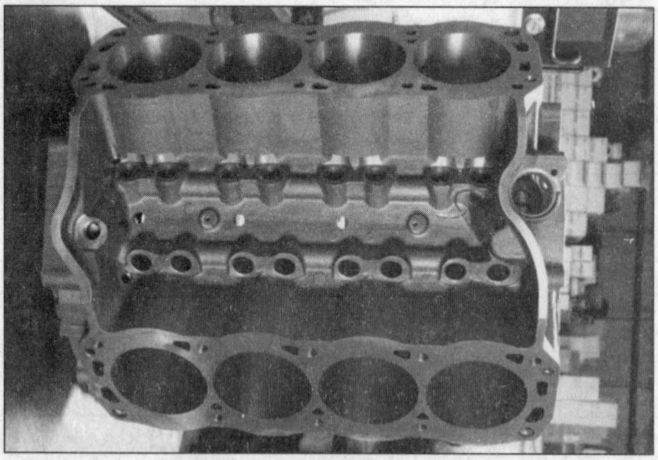

4 Check out the good bore spacing on the cylinders. Ford OEM thin-wall blocks have room only for 0.030-inch overbore, if the block had no core shift. This block is going to be bored to 4.125-inch after final honing with a torque-plate bolted down. The Dart block is roller-cam ready, with the valley set to accept stock Ford lifter retainers and sheetmetal "crab"

5 A speed secret in professional engine assembly is having every part you need on hand and in quantity. No trips to the hardware store mid-build. At Smeding, all parts boxes are labeled as to their engine destination, and drawers have quantities of all the little hardware bits an engine needs

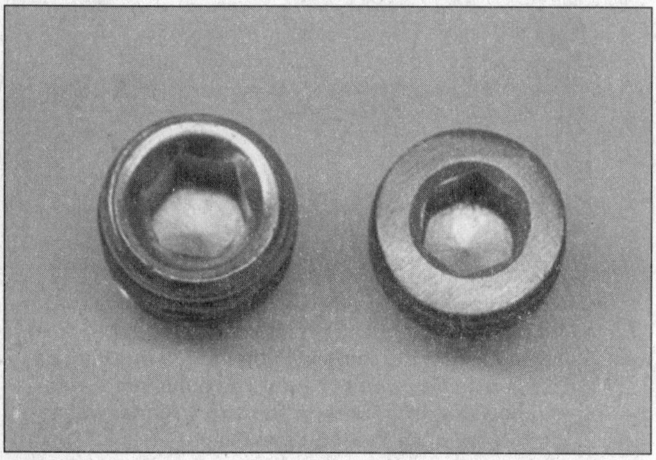

6 The finished and painted block has to be fitted with dowel pins, core plugs and other hardware. These little oil gallery plugs are destined to go next to the camshaft bore in the block. However, sometimes these plugs are actually too tall (left), so Smeding grinds all of his down ahead of time

7 The plugs are pre-coated with sealant and driven in with a small impact tool. Notice how the installed bottom plug is flush with or below the block surface. If the plugs were used the way they came, they would protrude and prevent the camshaft retainer plate from mounting properly

8 Filling the large bores of our 427 will be a set of custom lightweight, forged pistons, swinging on forged 6.2-inch H-beam rods that feature Chevrolet-size big ends and piston pins. Extra displacement and the other performance elements of the engine demand that only the best parts go into the bottom end

9 Smeding's balancing department precisely weighs the rods and pistons, and makes sure each rod or piston weighs the same as the lightest part. This information is recorded on the balance record for each engine

10 With the correct bobweights attached, the stroker crankshaft is spun up on the Hines balancing machine. If weight needs to be removed from the crank throws, the computer locates the exact spot and a specific drill bit is used to remove some metal there, then the assembly is rotated again

11 Whether you're dealing with OEM or quality aftermarket internals for an engine, nothing can be assumed. The crankshaft is measured with a micrometer, and with caps torqued to the block, the internal measurement inside the crank bearings is measured, to arrive at the bearing clearance. Smeding wants to achieve 0.0020 to 0.0022-inch clearance on these thumper 427's

12 Mike Narducci, Sr. installs the new main bearing halves in the block and doses them with assembly lube. The lube he uses is red for easy visibility and it clings well, providing lubrication for startup, even if the engine is going to sit for some time before being used

13 The new one-piece rear seal is oiled and slipped over the rear of the crankshaft. Since the crank hasn't been installed yet, it's easier to install the seal *with* the crank, rather than pressing it in afterwards

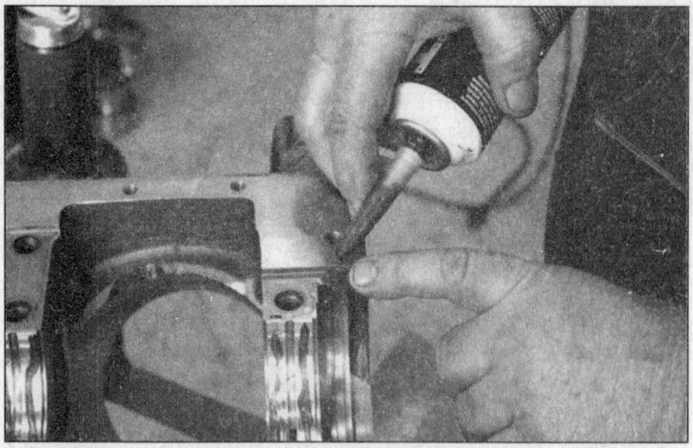

14 A dab of RTV sealant is added to each corner of the rear seal's groove in the block, where the rear main cap, block and seal come together

15 Mike carefully lowers the new stroker crank into the Dart block. The 4340-forged-steel crank features radiused fillets on the mains and rod throws, so bearings are required with a similar chamfer (or radius) on the edges

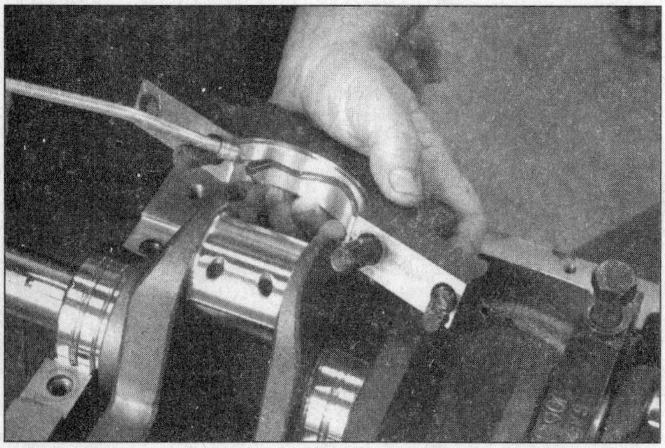

16 Red assembly lube is applied to the upper bearing inserts in the four-bolt main caps to prepare for installation of the caps

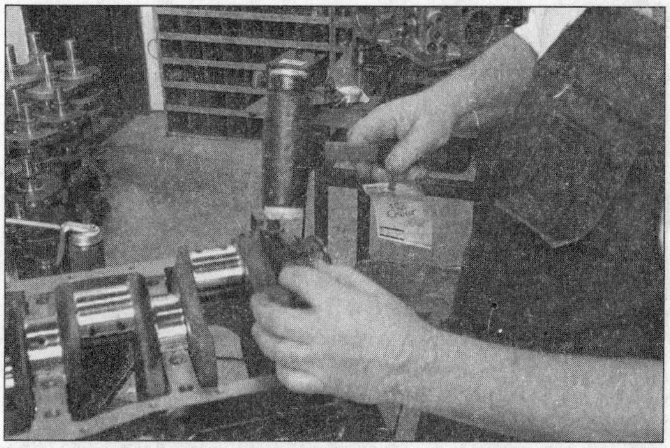

17 The rear main cap is the first to be installed, which should be done before the RTV at the cap/block joints sets up. A few careful taps with a plastic hammer seats the cap into the block

18 With all the caps in place and bolted down (not to final torque), the thrust cap (#3 on most V8s) bolts are kept slightly loose while Mike checks the crankshaft endplay with a dial indicator at the front of the crank. Moving the crank back and forth with a pry tool, he finds the midpoint of crank movement before tightening the rest of the cap bolts. Once the caps are fully torqued, he can check endplay again for the desired 0.005 to 0.007-inch clearance

19 Mike can now torque all the cap bolts to the specifications. He works from the back forward, rotating the crank after each cap is tightened. He's checking for the rotating resistance of the crank. If the crank slows down after one of the caps if torqued, he knows right away it was the last one, and he can recheck the bearing clearance there

20 For performance engines, oversize rings are purchased, so their ring end-gap can be custom-fit to each cylinder. A ring is inserted in a cylinder and pushed down squarely. You can use a piston to do this, but pro builders use a machined tool like this that is square to the bore and always pushes the rings down the same distance

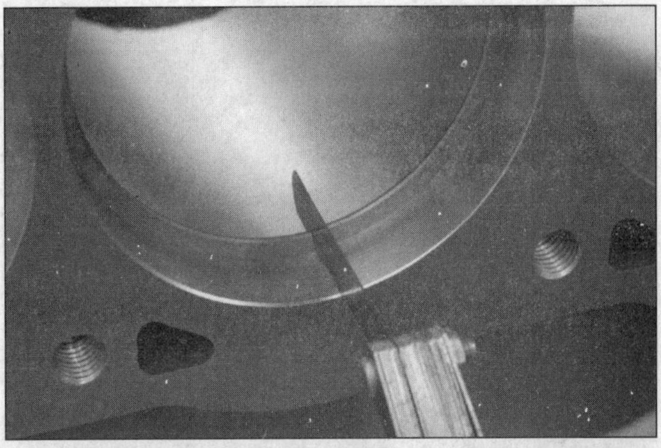

21 Feeler gauges are used to measure the ring end-gap, to determine how much they need to be filed to achieve the desired gap, which is 0.020-inch for the top and second rings on these particular pistons

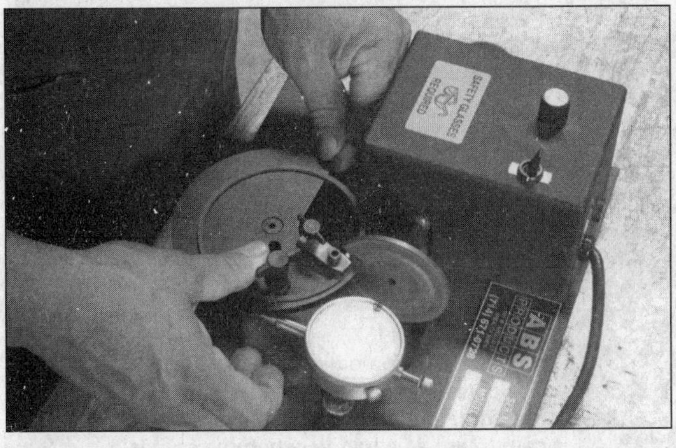

22 Rings can be filed by hand if you're precise and careful, but shops use a machine like this for faster and cleaner work. Experience with the tool is important in working efficiently

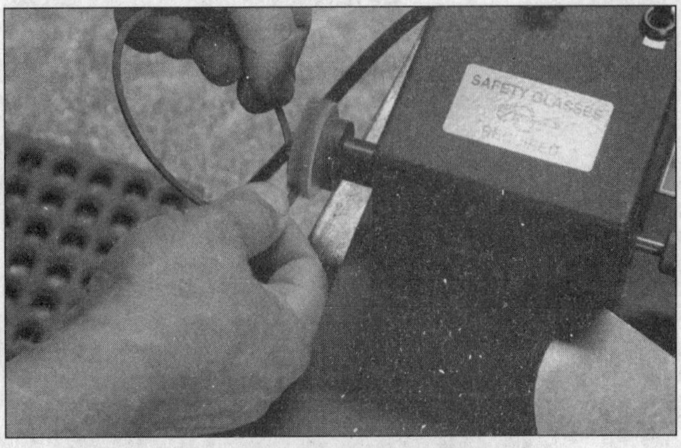

23 After filing a ring, the edges of the filed area must be chamfered to remove any burrs or sharp edges that could scratch a piston or cylinder. A wheel on the other side of the ring-filer burnishes the ring edges

24 All three of the rings for a particular cylinder are installed on the piston designated for that cylinder. The bores are virtually identical in size, but this is a blueprinting step to ensure exactly the same ring gaps in each cylinder

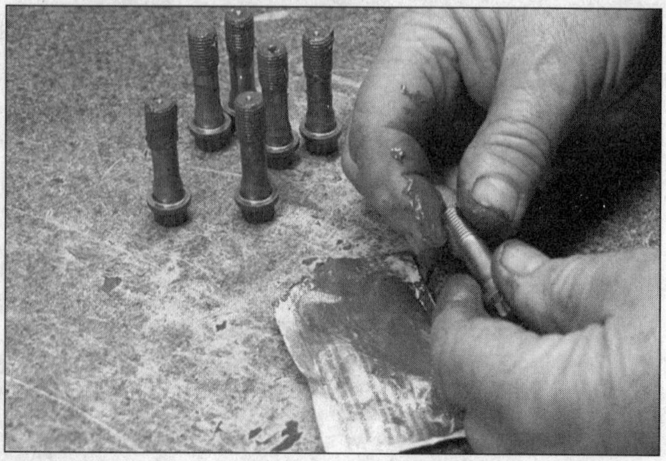

25 High-strength ARP rod bolts are used in the 427's, and they are coated with ARP's own lubricant for installation and uniform torquing

26 After the pistons are assembled to their rods with lock-rings securing the floating piston pins, each rod is put in this padded quick-grip fixture to hold them while the rod bolts are removed

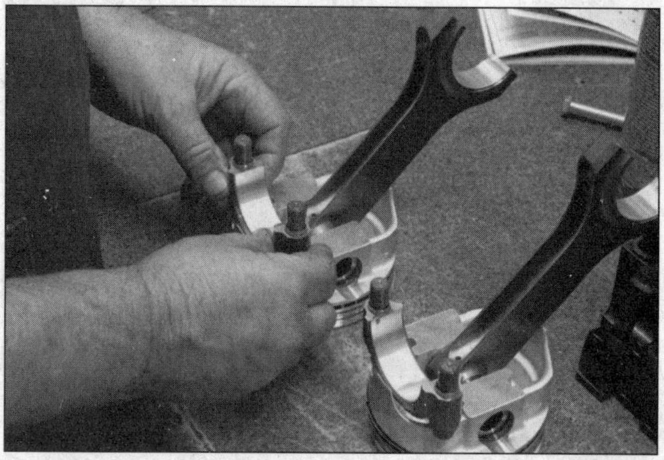

27 Each rod is fitted with the upper bearing shell, while the cap is laid with its rod/piston, lower bearing half in place. When all the rods and pistons are lined up on the bench, further assembly of the engine can take place

28 The 544-lift (573 exhaust) hydraulic roller cam is coated with assembly lube and carefully slipped into the block. A long bolt is threaded into the nose of the cam to act as a handle when the cam is almost all the way in

29 Once the Competition Cams bumpstick is seated home in the block, it's time to bolt on the camshaft retainer plate, which has been lubed on both the front and back surfaces. Duration on the dual-pattern camshaft is 238 degrees (248 exhaust) with the lifter at 0.050-inches lift

30 The timing chain, a double roller performance type, is slipped in place with both gears. It may take a few taps with a plastic hammer to seat the cam gear to the camshaft, and tapping a deep socket to push the crank gear all the way on

31 Our 427 is on a special type of steel cradle Smeding developed. An overhead crane easily repositions the engine for various steps. In this mode, the lubed roller lifters, lifter guides and sheetmetal crab can be installed, and the engine can stay in this same vertical position for piston/rod installation

32 Each cylinder bore is sprayed with brake cleaner and wiped out with white paper towels until nothing shows on the towel, then Mike sprays engine oil on the clean cylinder walls

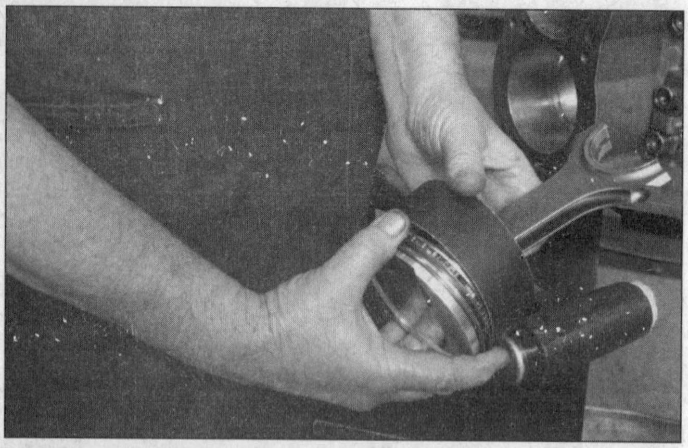

33 Professional engine builders use machined, tapered ring compressors rather than the clamp type - they're positive and they have one for each bore size. Mike will register the bottom of the compressor on the cylinder bore, then tap the piston down with a plastic hammer. There's little chance of a ring breaking when using this type of ring compressor

34 As each piston/rod is installed, the rod and cap are fitted with their bearings and the cap bolts can be torqued

35 The timing chain cover can now be installed. On new engines like these, the cover gasket is usually installed without any sealant

36 Once the cover bolts are torqued, a new razor blade is used to trim off the lower edges of the gasket at the cover/block interface for a flush fit when the oil pan gaskets are installed

37 The new oil pump is bench-primed with engine oil while the driveshaft is turned by hand. A stout aftermarket oil pump driveshaft is used

38 With the oil pump in place on the block, the special pickup tube for the Canton oil pan is bolted to the pump

39 Just as a doublecheck, Ben Smeding lays the oil pan along the pan rail to check for proper clearance between the bottom of the pickup screen and the bottom of the oil pan. Ben looks for about 7/16-inch

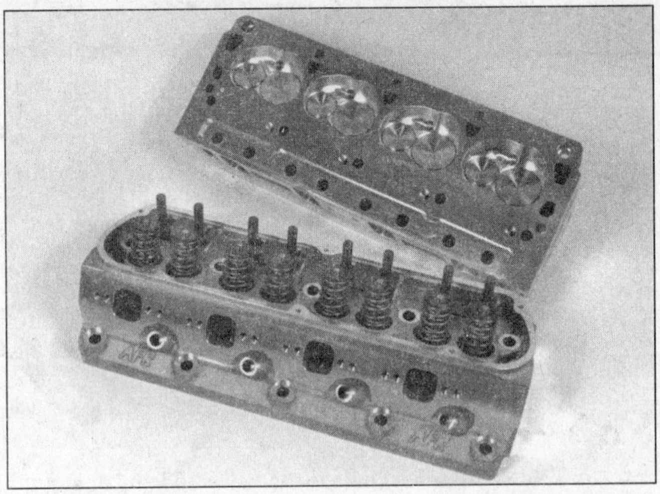

40 The aluminum heads are made for Smeding by Air Flow Research (AFR). These feature stainless valves, CNC porting, 2.08-inch intake valves and 1.60-inch exhausts. Final compression ratio with the pistons used in this engine is 10.25:1

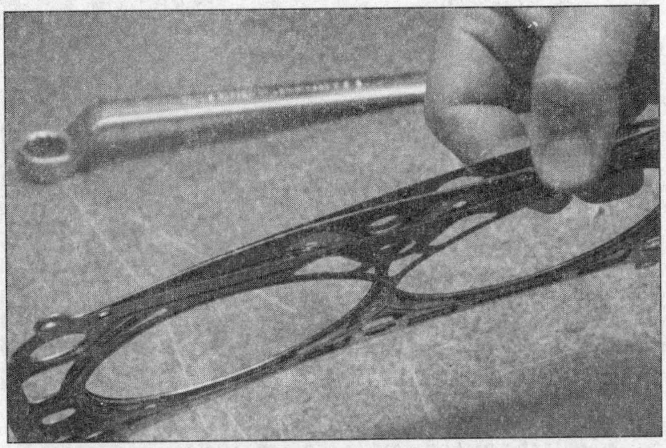

41 These Fel-Pro competition head gaskets are expensive, but their steel center with composite layers on each side really keep things together on hard-pumping engines like the Smeding 427

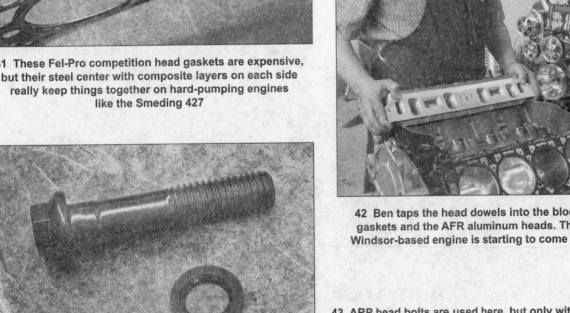

42 Ben taps the head dowels into the block, installs the gaskets and the AFR aluminum heads. The small-is-big Windsor-based engine is starting to come together nicely

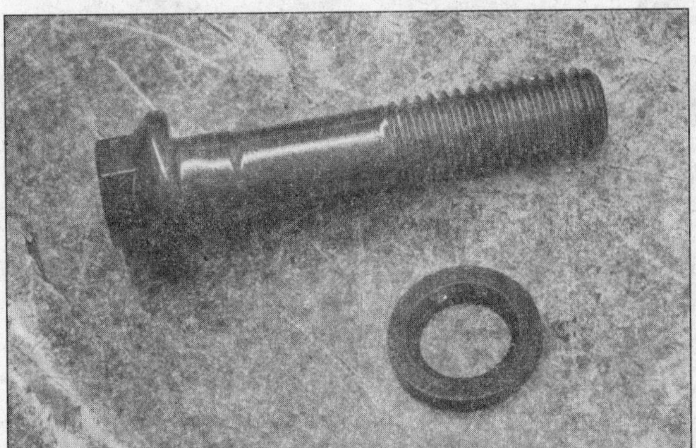

43 ARP head bolts are used here, but only with these chamfered head bolt washers against the softer metal of the aluminum heads

44 Ben applies assembly lube to the valve tips, the tips of the hardened-steel pushrods, and in the notches of the pushrod guide plates in the heads

45 Aluminum roller rocker arms (stock 1.6:1 ratio) provide a sturdy and lightweight portion of the valvetrain. Most aftermarket rockers come with positive-lock-type adjuster nuts

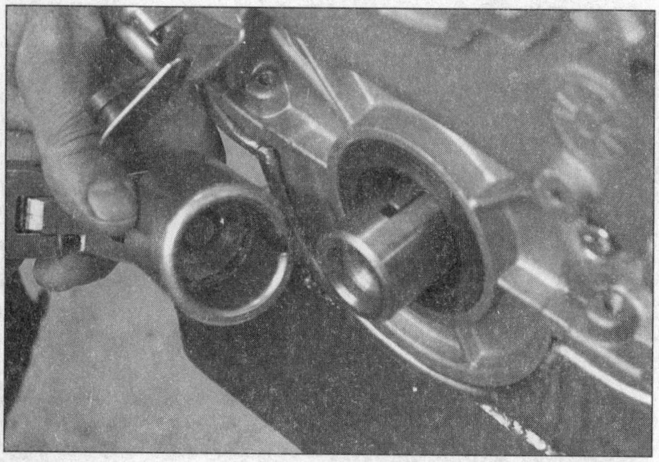

46 This socket has been machined with a groove to fit over the Woodruff keys on the crankshaft, making it easy to rotate the engine with a bar or ratchet

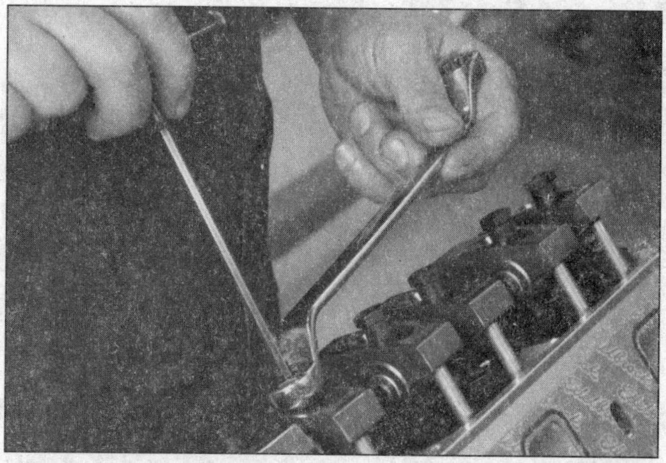

47 As each cylinder is brought to its TDC position, Ben adjusts the rocker arms to the correct clearance for the hydraulic roller lifters. When the clearance is right, the Allen screw in the center of each rocker nut is tightened so the adjustment stays

48 RTV sealant is used instead of cork or other type of end gaskets for the intake manifold mounting, with standard gaskets for the ports, used without sealant, except for a dab of RTV in each of the four corners where the side gaskets meet the front and rear gasket surfaces

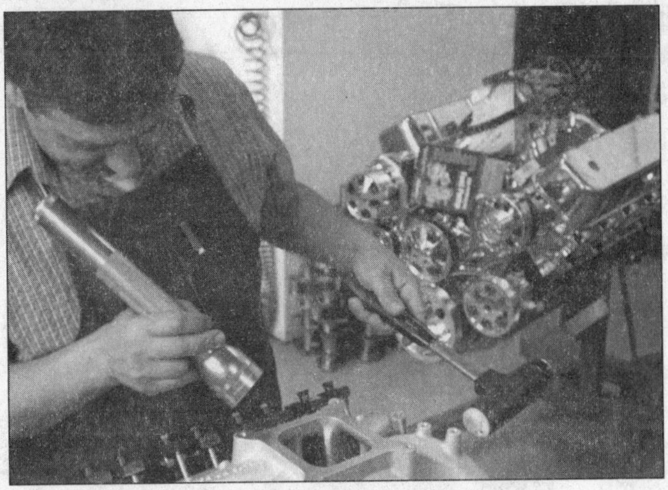

49 Years of experience has taught Ben to look through the intake manifold with a flashlight to see that the ports are aligned to the head, before inserting or tightening any of the intake manifold mounting bolts

50 The engine is turned over until the engraved crank damper indicates the #1 cylinder is eight degrees before TDC, a good starting point for initial timing

51 Ben slips the new distributor down into the block and aligns the rotor tip with a mark he made to indicate where he wants the #1 plug wire to attach to the cap. When the distributor is all the way down, he can attach the hold-down bracket and the engine is pretty close to perfect timing before it even gets to the engine dyno

52 Topping the Edelbrock RPM Air-Gap intake manifold is an 850-cfm Holley double-pumper carburetor, which will be fine-tuned for jetting while on the dyno

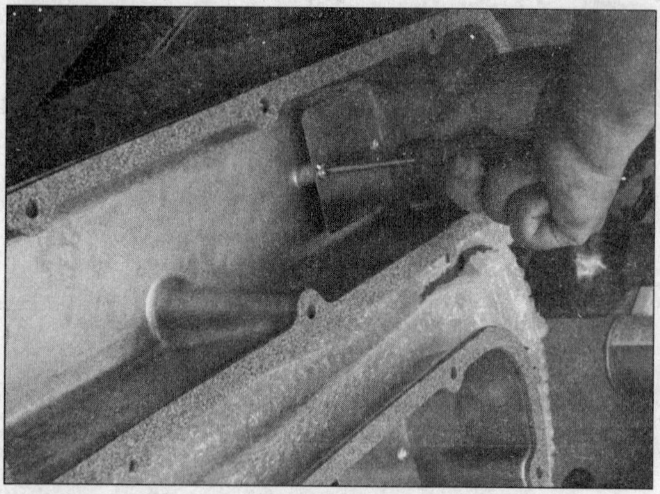

53 Aftermarket valve covers often come with the baffles not installed, so some time is spent chasing the screw holes and driving the screws in to hold the baffles. If you run your covers without these baffles under each breather location, you may suck a lot of oil out of the engine

54 Smeding engines are finished off with water pump, plug wires and other parts so they can be run-in on the engine dyno. When the engine goes off to the customer, everyone knows that it's working, has no leaks or problems and the spec sheet tells the power and torque curves of the engine

13c Blown 572 Big-block Chevrolet Build

1 Ben Smeding builds engines for customers who want all levels of performance, from muscle cars to street rods, boats and fast trucks. One of the more impressive beasts is this blown 572-cubic-inch behemoth that sounds loud even when it's not running!

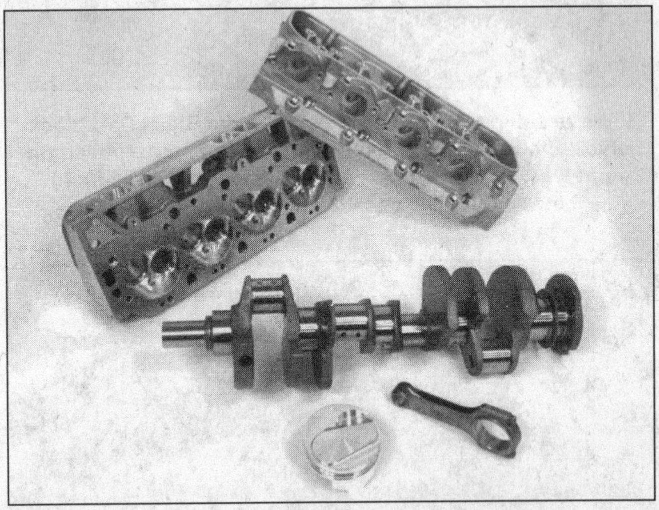

2 Smeding Performance builds turn-key engines using new blocks (factory or aftermarket) and a selection of quality aftermarket components. In the case of this BIG big-block Chevy, nothing but the best would do. All the bottom-end components are forged, from the stroker crank to the H-beam rods and pistons. Actually, the piston shown here is for a normally-aspirated 572, the blower pistons design will be seen later on

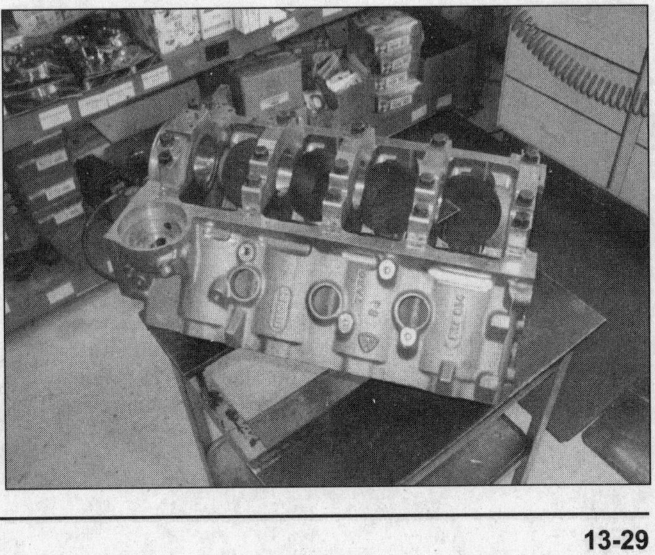

3 The "Big M" Chevy block from Dart Industries is a rugged candidate for building big engine power, with massive four-bolt main caps and big bore spacing. Smeding believes that you can't build a truly high-performance engine with a thin-wall block, because the tolerances can't be kept close enough due to flexing as the engine starts to make serious power

4 We're using the tall-deck version of the Big M Dart block, which allows for bigger displacement and more rod-length choices. Note the difference in deck height (.400-inch) between the low-deck (top) and tall-deck blocks

5 Normally, Smeding Performance has to grind the lower block clearance for connecting rods/bolts using their own templates, but the Big M comes already clearanced from Dart

6 Notice the wall thickness here where the core plug holes are. Ben applies sealant, then drives in new brass core plugs

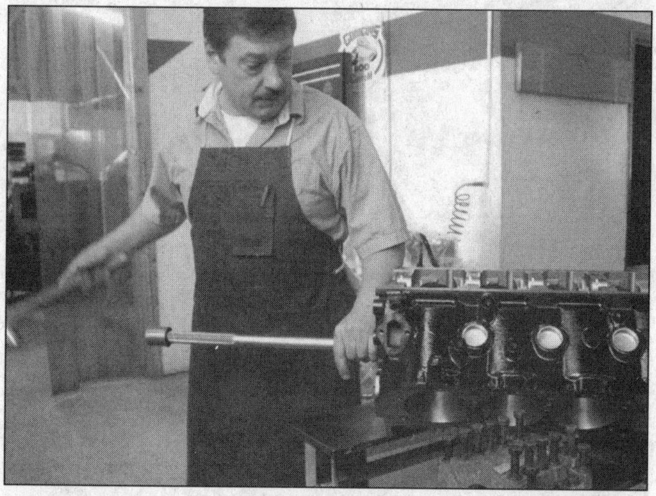

7 The cam bearings are installed first in the freshly-machined, honed, washed and painted block

8 Ben uses a flashlight to look through the oil holes for the cam to ensure that every cam bearing has its oil holes perfectly aligned. The operation is quicker than the common method of poking a welding rod through the oil holes to check

9 The 4340 forged-steel crankshaft has all the good features you'd want when building a powerful engine to live, such as radiused oil holes, radiused journals, pin-drilled throws, and the crank is heat-treated after the drilling. This crank has a healthy 4.375-inch stroke

10 To check the main bearing ID's, Ben torques the main caps with new bearings in place. Note that the front and rear caps have four straight-down bolts, while the center caps feature splayed outer bolts for strength

11 Years of experience using precision measuring tools gives Ben Smeding a "feel" for taking precise measurements. The bearing ID's will be compared to measurements of the crankshaft main journals

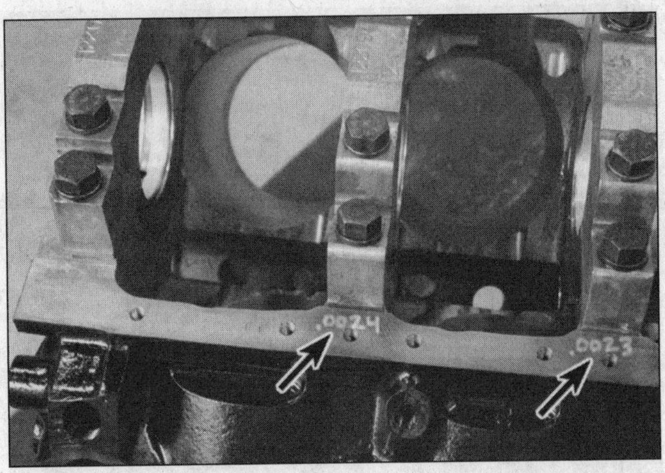

12 As you can see, Smeding paints the recorded main clearances along the pan rail of the engine. This range of .0022 to .0024 is what he likes to see on a serious-power motor like this one

13 The two-piece real main seal is installed with an offset, so the mating edges of the two pieces don't align with the cap-to-block seam. Note the O-ring that must be installed here

14 A cool little trick in the Dart block is the notched slot in the lower part of each main cap. With a couple of screwdrivers, the big caps can easily be levered out of the block

15 Although the clearance measurements were made "dry," Smeding Performance uses a special red pre-lube on all the bottom end components during final assembly

16 With the crank nestled down on the lubed bearings, the big main caps can be installed for the final time. All but the rear (thrust) cap can be torqued in place

17 This is how the offset in the rear main seal pieces will be located before the rear main cap is installed

18 At these points on each side of the block, a small amount of RTV must be applied here just before installing the rear main cap

19 With a dial-indicator to check crankshaft endplay, the crankshaft is forced forward and back to seat the thrust bearing

20 The new Comp Cams Gen VI hydraulic-roller camshaft is lubed and installed. Specs on the cam are 613 gross lift, 315 degrees intake duration (at .006-inch tappet lift), or at .050-inch lift 248 intake and 258 exhaust

21 Instead of a typical performance double-toothed gearset, Ben is using single-tooth cam and crank gears with a massive roller timing chain with two sets of links on every pin

22 The forged 9.5:1 compression pistons that fit the 4.562-inch bores in our engine have a thick area above the top ring to handle the blower boost, plus a "blow-by channel" between the top and second compression rings, designed to reduce ring flutter under boost

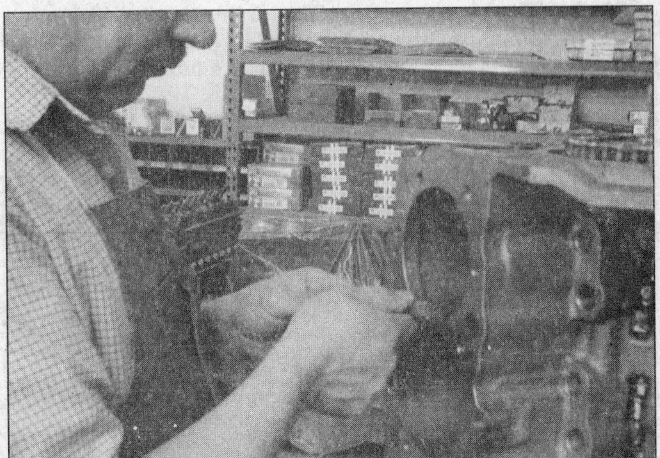

23 With rings in place and squared to the bore, Ben checks the ring end-gap

24 Although he uses an electric ring-filer to achieve the desired gaps, Ben prefers to deburr the ends of the rings by hand with a fine file. A blown engine requires wider gaps due to the extra heat and pressure

25 The Sealed Power (conventional) rings are for a forced-induction engine. The set consists of a 1/16-inch moly-faced top ring, 1/16-inch conventional reverse-taper iron second ring, and 3/16-inch oil ring. When building an engine of this magnitude, it's important to not mix up those compression rings!

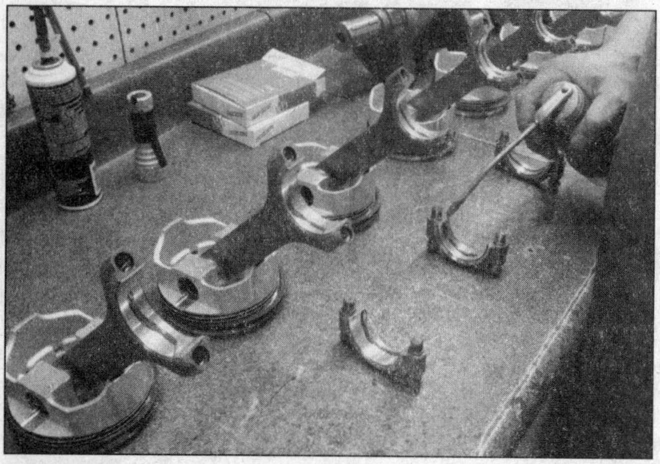

26 Cleanliness and organization are the keys to efficiently build performance engines. All the 572's rods and pistons are lined up on the bench for pre-lubing

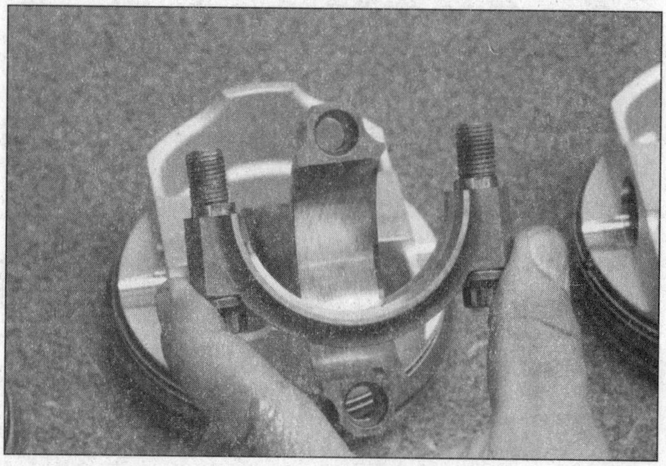

27 The H-beam rods carry big ARP bolts, and the caps are secured with sleeves for alignment

28 The cylinder walls receive a final wash with carb cleaner and shop towels, then they are wiped with clean engine oil prior to piston installation

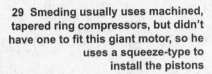

29 Smeding usually uses machined, tapered ring compressors, but didn't have one to fit this giant motor, so he uses a squeeze-type to install the pistons

30 As each rod/piston combo slides through their bore, Ben taps the caps on with a plastic mallet and hand-tightens the bolts

31 One of the engine-building habits Ben has developed is always rotating the bottom-end assembly after each piston is installed. He feels for any signs of unusual drag added with each new piston/ring set installed

32 Our crankshaft features radiused journals, requiring that each rod and rod bearing be installed with their chamfered sides facing the outer edges of the journals, not toward the center

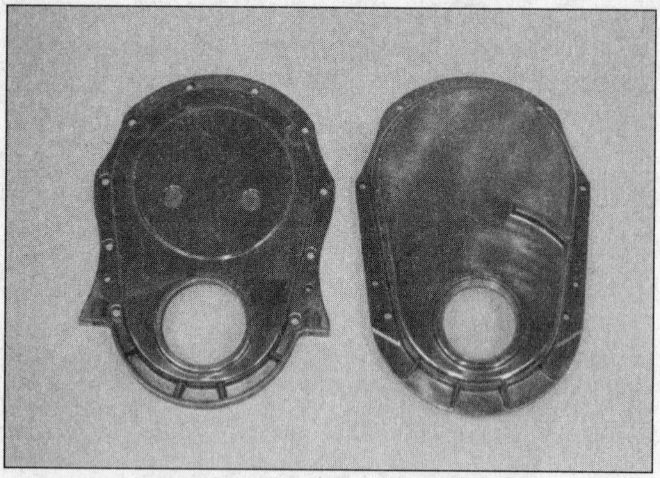

33 There are several timing chain cover designs for big-block Chevys. The one on the left here is for a Gen IV block like our design, while the right is for the Gen VI type. The Gen IV uses a gasket instead of an O-ring, and the two differ in the type of oil pan lip seal

34 This engine, stout as it is, is destined for a Deuce roadster street rod (!), and uses a hydraulic roller cam and lifter (a race motor would have solid lifters). The roller lifter pairs are lubed and slipped into the block

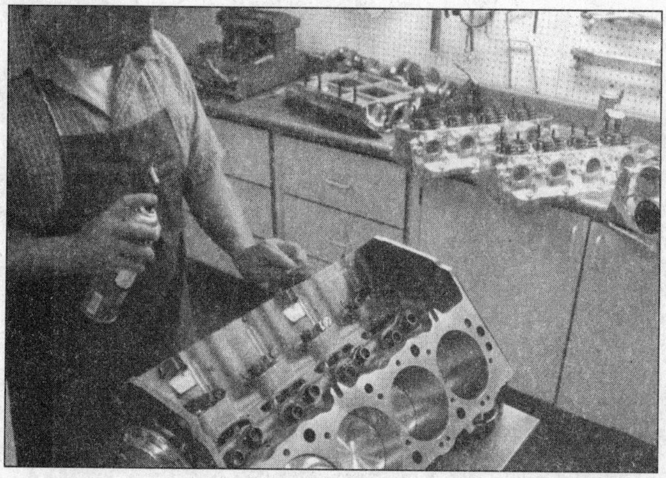

35 Most engine stories don't mention some of the minor details like this, but don't overlook extreme cleanliness of the deck surfaces before installing head gaskets and heads. Ben uses carb cleaner just before installing the gaskets

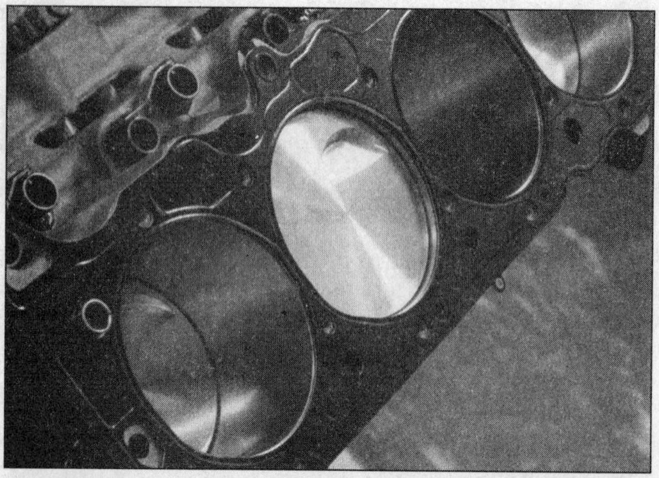

36 The head gaskets have a big job to do on a blown motor like this, and we're using three-layer-sandwich gaskets which have two layers of polymer material with a steel gasket in between. These are expensive but prevent comebacks

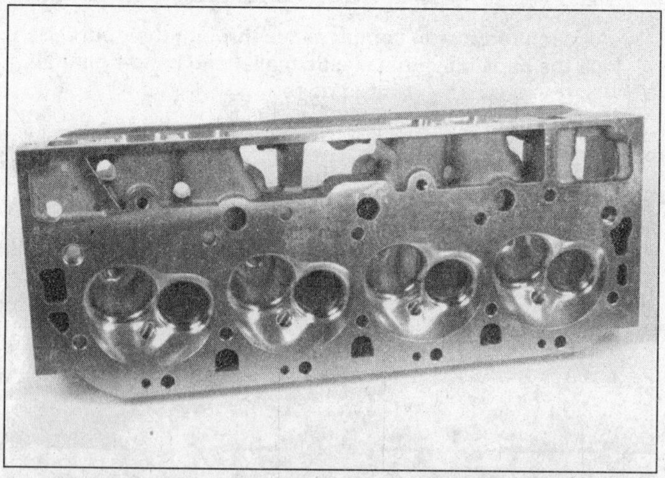

37 The Air Flow Research heads are fully up to the task of handling the output of our cam/displacement/blower combination. Very nice CNC-work at the factory makes them ready to go, big valves and all

38 This engine is designed for show as well as go, so the AFR heads were sent out for polishing! The only procedure Smeding had to perform on the heads was to hone the exhaust stem-to-guide clearance to .002-.0025-inch for a blown or marine engine that will run hotter and expand more. Normal would be .001-.0015-inch, and a marine engine with a blower would require more; .003-inch at least

39 All cleaned and prepped, the new heads can be installed. Heads this big would be hard to handle if they were cast-iron!

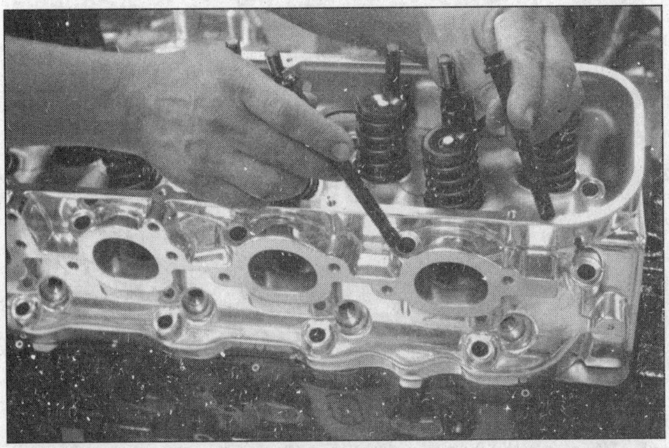

40 With the large, raised exhaust ports on these AFR heads, the center four head bolts on each exhaust side must be longer than the end bolts, which in this case are ARP high-strength

41 The assembled heads for this combo come with longer valves, valve springs and rocker studs

42 Of course, pushrod guide plates are required for any performance pushrod engine, and AFR's are particularly stout. The pushrods are 3/8-inch chrome-moly with .080-inch wall thickness and 210-degree radius on the rocker arm ends (rather than typical 180-degreee radius) due to the big camshaft

43 On big-block Chevys, one rocker arm on each head must have a radiused corner like this where the valve covers have a bolt boss. Our rockers are 1.7:1 billet aluminum

44 The Melling regular big-block oil pump (not a high-volume or high-pressure) is fitted with a pickup that Ben welds to the pump to ensure it can never come loose

45 The pump is carefully fitted on the rear main cap and torqued in place

46 Although the big-block uses a one-piece plastic/rubber oil pan gasket, a small dab of RTV sealant is used at each of the four cap/block corners, front and rear

47 A Canton cad-iridited steel oil pan is fitted to seal up the bottom end and torqued in sequence all around

48 Because of the extra load of the blower pulleys on this engine, the crank was ordered with two keys, 180-degrees apart, and the billet damper also has matching grooves for two keys

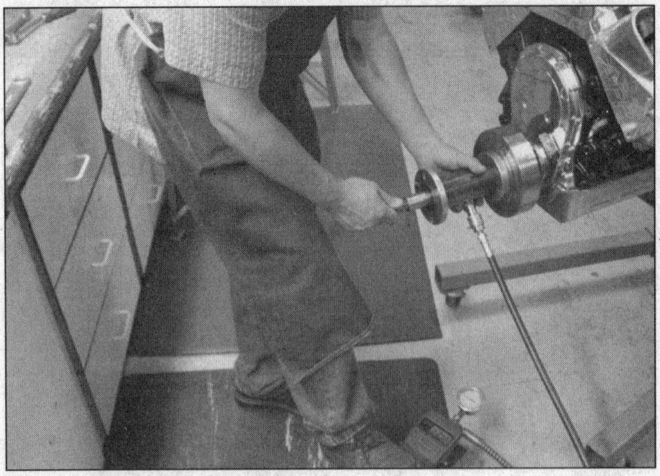

49 Big-block dampers are tighter to install than most engines - you can't just use a bolt to install them easily. Smeding uses this cool air-powered pusher to efficiently install the damper. The foot pedal operates the tool

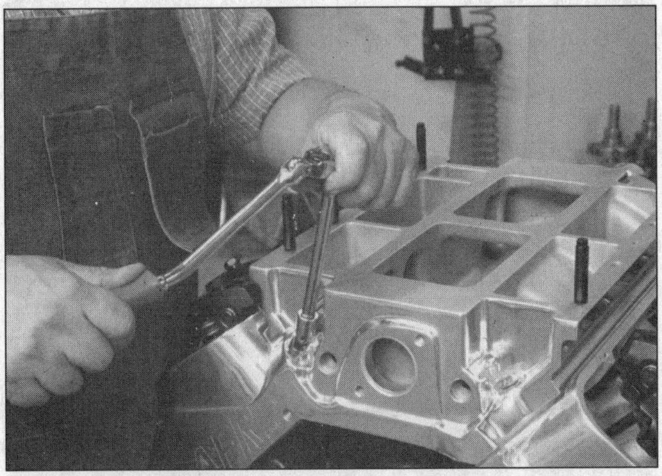

50 The blower and all its related parts are from The Blower Shop, and all the components are polished for this application. This is the blower intake manifold

51 The blower features a billet, CNC-machined case that is hard-anodized, and polished up very nicely. The helical tri-lobe rotors are fitted with Teflon strips along the edges of the lobes

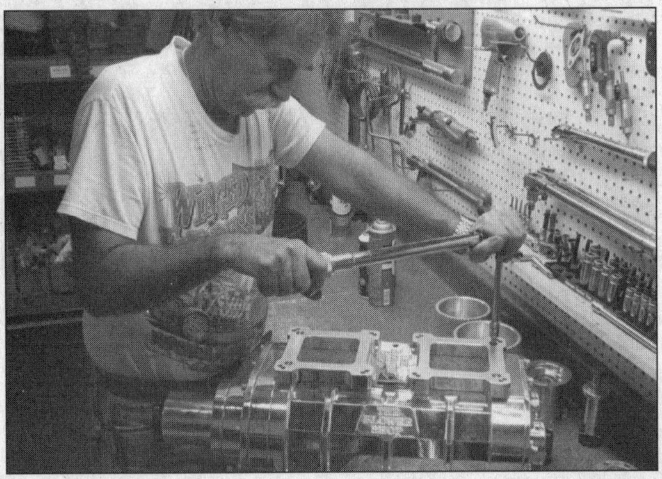

52 Before installing the blower, a special metal screen is installed on top, then the adapter plate for two huge four-barrel carbs is torqued down

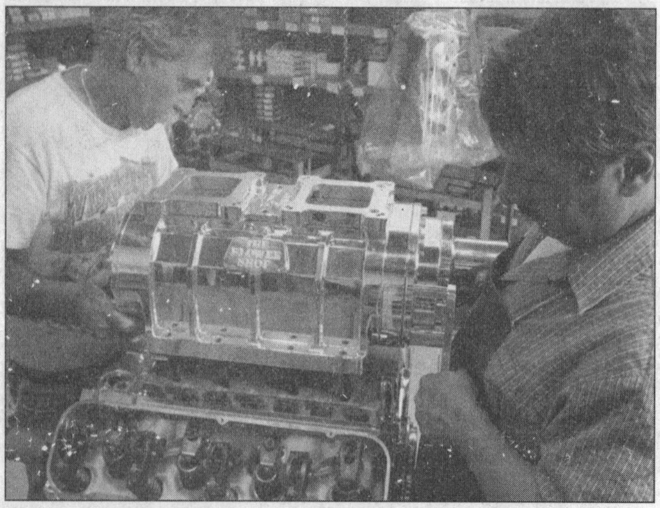

53 Even though it's aluminum, it takes two people to carefully position the blower on the manifold studs

54 The Blower Shop pulleys are installed next and torqued. The bolts that retain the blower to the intake manifold are torqued to only 12 foot pounds, and are of "breakaway" design, so that in the event of a backfire, the blower will lift off instead of being destroyed. And, although some consider them unsightly, it's always a good idea to fit a blower restraint on a motor like this. When one of these pumps lets go under high boost/high rpm, it's like a bomb going off!

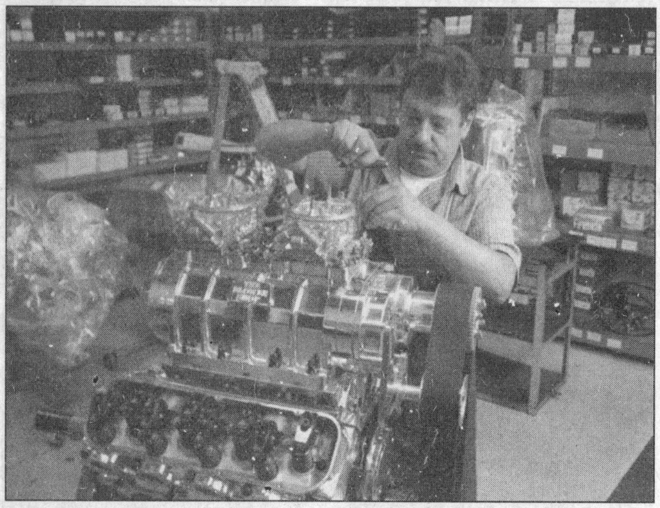

55 The final steps in this blown 572 are installing the two huge Holley carbs, and hooking up the fuel lines and linkage

56 Some engines built for customers turn out so cool that Ben is sad to see them leave the shop! This 572 is tops in both show and go

14 Crates and Swaps

One of the most time-honored paths to "big engine power" has always been the engine swap. Back in the Thirties when there was very little speed equipment available for any engine except the Ford Model T and Model A four-cylinder engines, an enterprising hot rodder could fit his '27 T roadster with a wrecking yard engine from a bigger car, say a Buick straight-eight, and have more horsepower and torque after only a weekend's work. Probably the most popular engine swap of those days, right through until the mid-Fifties, was the Ford flathead V8 fitted to an early Ford roadster. Stripped of its fenders, running boards and often the hood, the lightweight vehicle with a later V8 and a few selected items of speed equipment was "hot stuff" on the streets and racing at the dry lakes in Southern California. The 1932 and later Fords were all set up for the flathead V8, but the less-expensive T's and A's needed some chassis work to make the swap. The expression "A-V8" was the popular designation for this very common engine swap.

Once the new overhead-valve engine designs came out in the early Fifties, the Cadillac and Oldsmobile V8's, plus the famous Chrysler Hemi, the days of the flathead Ford were numbered. Sealing its fate was the introduction in 1955 of the Chevrolet small-block V8, in its original 265-cubic-inch size. Smaller and lighter than the other Fifties V8's, the Chevy could rev well and was adopted by the hot rod community almost from the day it came onto the showroom floors. Speed equipment for all of these overhead-valve V8s was becoming plentiful, and now engine swapping took on new dimensions. Lightweight early Ford bodies were still the favorites of hot rodders everywhere, but now they could choose from a number of more powerful engines to swap in. Motor mount kits were available from Ansen, Hurst, Trans-Dapt and other speed equipment companies.

One of the problems of the flathead era was transmission choice; even a 150-hp hopped up flathead Ford engine could easily break early Ford rear axles and/or deposit the guts of the transmission on the public streets with a hard shift and a pop of the clutch. As the aftermarket equipment for engine swapping became more commercial, you could buy a transmission adapter to put just about any popular V8 in front of most of the modern transmissions, which would last a lot longer than the old Ford boxes. Eventually, the Ford closed-driveline rear axles became the weakest link, and as drag racing developed from the Fifties on, it became common for hot rods to have a powerful OHV engine, a modern three-speed or four-speed Ford or Chevy transmission, and perhaps an Oldsmobile open-drive rear end. Thus was developed the basic idea of street/hot rodding. Older, affordable cars fitted out with modern engines and drivelines were the muscle cars of the day.

Somewhere along the way, Detroit envied the allure of the hot rods and started building cars for that youth market. They were stripped-down versions of their mid-size cars, fitted with engines from the full-size cars, often the biggest in a manufacturer's line. With the right marketing to appeal to the youth market and the beginnings of "easy credit financing," factory muscle cars were the "pre-made hot rods" for that generation of the Sixties.

As that tumultuous decade came to a close, rising insurance costs, the beginnings of vehicle emissions controls and a sharp rise in gasoline prices effectively killed off the Detroit muscle cars, and hot rodding was in a slump. Once the manufacturers had spent a decade or so developing their emissions controls, catalytic converters and electronic fuel injection, the mid-Eighties saw the newer engines with not only improved emissions, but with increases in both economy and power. Technology in the last twenty years has effectively brought back showroom-stock performance cars, with some models today making more power than that of the muscle cars of the glory days. Except for the ever-rising price of gasoline, this is a prime time to be interested in vehicle performance, both from the Detroit manufacturers and the aftermarket.

You have several steps to increased power in your vehicle. One, you can add some performance equipment of the bolt-on variety, as illustrated in a number of Chapters in this book; you can pull the stock engine and make serious internal modifications for greater power; or three, you can pull your stock engine and replace it with one of greater power. The latter is the subject of this Chapter.

There's nothing like the almost-instant gratification of dropping in a new performance engine that's ready to run. No amount of adding power parts one at a time will give the same results. Whether you choose an OEM-built or aftermarket performance engine, you can also have the comfort factor of having a full warranty on all this new power!

Engine swaps are nothing new. When the flathead Ford V8 came out in 1932, it sparked a decades-long affection on the part of hot rodders, who put them in countless hot rods, dragsters, circle-track cars and racing boats. Putting in a "hopped-up" flathead turned many a cheap, lightweight early Ford into powerful combos for the road or track

Crate motors

While any modern or even vintage engine can be rebuilt with performance parts and blueprinted to provide great performance, not everyone is prepared to do that. We all wish we had a fully-equipped shop at home, a rollaway box full of tools, and the experience and knowledge to build our own performance engines, but not all hot rodders are that lucky. All of us are lucky in the fact that today is probably the best time ever in hot rodding to purchase a performance engine already built by experts. If you have a friend with an engine hoist, basic tools and one of you has pulled-and-replaced an engine before, you can do this! For whatever make of car that you're working on, there is a Haynes repair manual for that vehicle that can guide you through the engine replacement procedure, plus provide you with information to help you when working on anything else on your car.

Unless you're installing exhaust headers or some other non-stock exterior components on the new engine, installation of the engine is a basic procedure, with the same steps to follow as in replacing a stock engine.

The term "crate engine" is a modern description of an engine you buy outright, with no trade-in of your old engine. It really should be called a "pallet" engine, since most such new engines are delivered on a pallet instead of in a crate. Crate engines are available from the aftermarket and from the OEM manufacturers. You can buy a basic 350 Chevrolet small-block "Goodwrench" engine from your local dealership parts department that is a stock replacement item, but entirely brand-new and featuring a GM warranty. Ford and Chrysler also have such engines available for stock replacement use.

But hot rodders interested in more-than-stock power and performance have a host of brand-new high-energy engines also available from the OEM manufacturers, and most of these are also delivered with a factory warranty. GM Performance Parts has small-block crate engines with horsepower ratings from 290 to 425, and big-block choices from 425 horsepower all the way to 720 horsepower! They also offer complete LS-series engines with the newest in GM engine technology, ranging from 350 to 505 horsepower. Even vehicles with a worn-out or simply underperforming 3.8L V6 can be pumped up with a GM Performance Parts V6 with 240 or 260 horsepower levels.

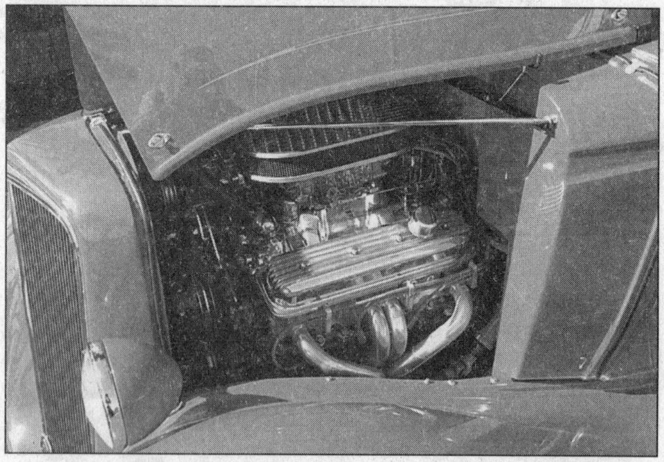

In today's world of hot rodding, everyone is using modern OHV engines, in everything from Thirties cars to old trucks and First Generation muscle cars. This example is a new small-block Chevy powering a 1934 Chevy. The engines are affordable, fit just about any engine compartment, and with headers and a good intake, provide spirited performance in any application

The flathead days may be gone, but Ford V8s are still very popular with the hot rod and engine swap crowd. Though a little longer than a Chevy, they are narrower and tons of factory and aftermarket speed equipment is available for them. This example sports the nostalgic tri-power intake with three two-barrel carbs

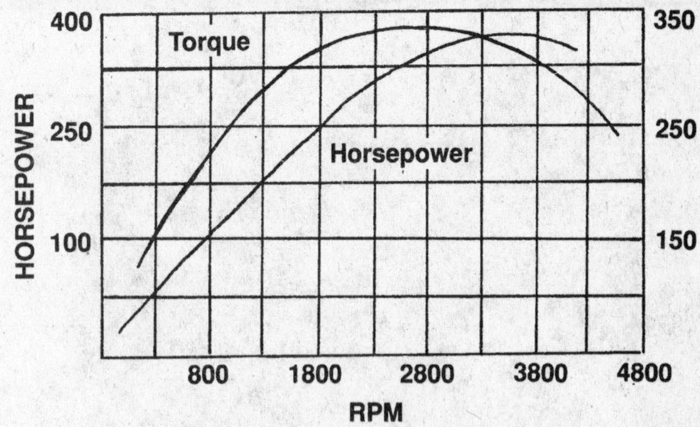

When shopping for a new crate engine, be careful in deciding what your driving needs are. The higher the power output of the engine, the higher up the peak power is generally achieved. An engine with good low and mid-range torque will be more tractable in street driving

In the Ford inventory, there are similarly stimulating options. The basic small block Fords can be ordered in power levels from 340, 360, 390 to 450 horsepower in a package that will fit in any vehicle that was designed for a 5.0L. That's a lot of power in the smallest of the Big Three's small-block V8's! The "347," a popular stroked version of the 5.0L, is available with 415 or 500 horsepower. Going a little bigger in displacement, there are three versions of the 351 Windsor engine, one featuring 385 horses and 377 foot-pounds of torque, to two stroked 392-cubic-inch models pumping out 430 or 475 horsepower, in an engine architecture that is not much bigger than the 5.0L.

Perhaps the best news for small-block Ford fans is the recently introduced "New Boss." This is a new version of a high-winding, free-breathing 302 released in 1969 and 1970 Mustangs, designed for competition in the SCCA Trans-Am

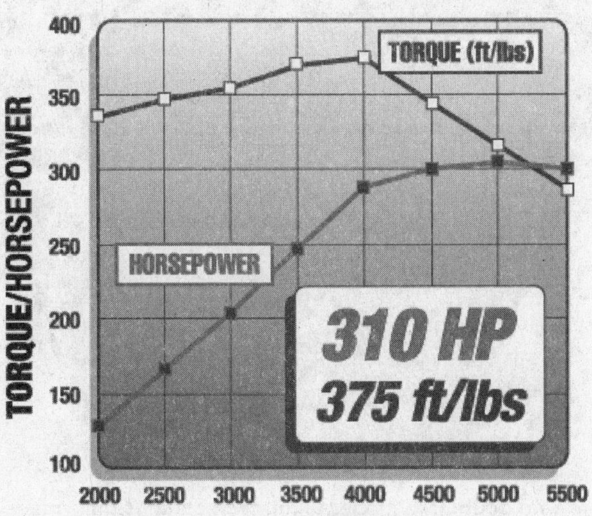

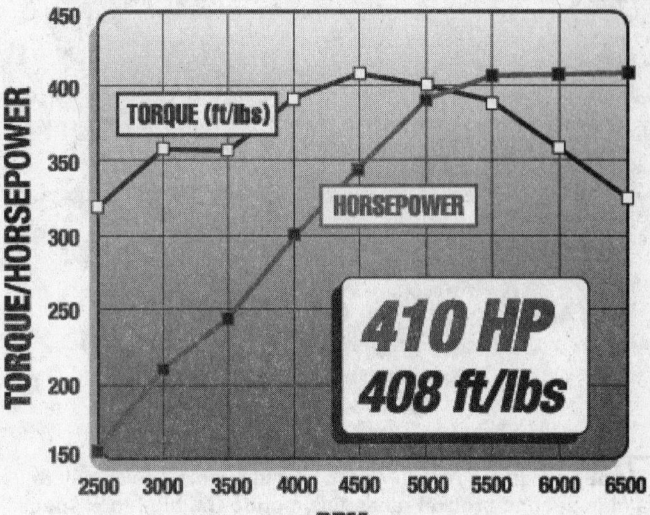

Compare the graphs on these two Edelbrock crate engines. Both are 350-cubic-inch Chevrolets, but the cam, heads, compression ratio and intake are different. Note that the hotter engine has 100 more peak horsepower, but at a higher rpm and with only 33 more foot-pounds of torque. The 310 horse engine makes more torque at a lower rpm, so it would be better for street use and towing. Torque is really what you feel in the seat of your pants when accelerating across an intersection

GM Performance Parts has a plethora of performance-in-a-box small-block engines to choose from, but one of the best buys in OEM crate engines is this Ram-Jet 350 with plug-and-play fuel injection. One horsepower-per-cube and simple to hook up in any pre-emissions vehicle, it has 400 foot-pounds of torque plus excellent driveability and fuel economy. Features include a hydraulic roller cam and Vortec heads. GMPP offers detailed installation/maintenance manuals for most of their crate engines

If you like the plug-and-play aspect and the benefits of EFI, but crave more serious power, the Ram-Jet 502 is GMPP's big-block approach, with that number being the displacement and the horsepower. Forged crank, forged pistons, aluminum heads with huge valves, and high-flow induction add up to an almost flat torque curve with more axle-twisting torque than you can handle, peaking at 565 foot-pounds!

If your needs are for maximum bolt-in engine power, say for a nine-second bracket racer, this mondo GM big-block specs out at 572 cubic inches with all the right internals. The "base" ZZ572 offers 620 hp with a pump-gas 9.6:1 compression ratio and there's a deluxe "R for racing" version with 720 hp and 685 slick-spinning foot pounds. Based on the tall-deck Gen VI, the engine comes with HEI ignition and a 1090-cfm Dominator carb

There's no doubt that modern high-tech engines have made their way into the GMPP parts bins for updating your ride. The amazing LS series (Gen III) small-block Chevrolet engines lead the way, with this LS1 crate motor starting off the lineup. The 5.7L (346 cubic inch) model features six-bolt main caps and a free-breathing EFI top end, providing 350 hp and 365 foot-pounds in a very driveable package

The LS2 engine has 6.0L (364 cubic inches) and can be purchased with factory fuel-injection. Or, in this version with a four-barrel-carb intake, aluminum block and heads, 10.9:1 compression, for an output of 440 hp and 404 foot-pounds

Next up in the hierarchy of the LS engines is the production version that was installed in Cadillac Escalades and the Silverado SS pickups. The 6.0L iron block-and-heads LQ9 engine is the torquey, high-tech motor of choice for trucks, with 345 hp and 380 foot-pounds

Series, where it did very well. The original Boss 302 motors featured four-bolt mains, big cylinder heads and many other performance features. The originals are highly coveted and collectible today, but Ford has just brought it back, in even better form than the original. The old Boss offered 290 horsepower, but equipped with a few pieces from the Ford Performance Parts Book, they made much more. The new Boss block is designed of diesel-grade heat-treated cast-iron, and features ½-inch head bolts, splayed main caps, and thick-walled siamesed bores that allow for enlargement to as big as 4.125-inches. The New Boss is offered as a block, components, or as a complete crate motor. In 302 form, it's available in 340, 345, 360 and 390 horsepower. A bigger version is available at 331 cubic inches that pounds out 500 hp and 400 foot-pounds of torque. The Boss is back!

When the 2004 Corvette came out with this all-aluminum 5.7L LS6 engine, it provided spectacular performance, which you can retro into your older Camaro, Chevelle, Nova or Corvette. The 405 hp and 400 foot-pounds comes in an EFI package that needs only a computer and harness

Ford fans also have bigger engines to choose from. Ford Racing has just come out with their new performance block to fill the needs of 429/460 applications, but with much more potential than the old engines. The hot version sports 521 cubic inches and 575 hp with a low-rise intake and useable cam. The same motor with a tall intake and radical cam delivers 625 hp!

Ford Racing also has complete assembled performance engines based on the 4.6L/5.4L "modular" design. Fans of these cammer engines can now build a big one, because the new block, called "The Aluminator," is capable of handling 700 hp.

Chrysler has its own selection of performance crate engines, even including the famous Hemi. For fans of their "A" engines (small-blocks), Mopar Performance sells a 360 cubic inch motor with 300 horsepower and excellent bottom-end torque of 385 foot-pounds. Another version offers 390 horsepower, and there is a stroker version at 402 cubic inches with 435 horsepower and 457 foot-pounds of torque. The Chrysler "B" engines of 413/426/440 served well in some of the best cars of the muscle car era, plus had the

Every year, more is asked of the GM engineers, and their answer for the 2006-2007 Corvette was this 7.0L (427 cubic inch) all-aluminum LS7. With such race features as dry-sump oiling, titanium rods and valves, it develops 505 hp and 470 foot-pounds. That is enough to make a 'Vette run 11.5s at the drags and yet get 26 mpg with advanced fuel injection

Ford Racing has a complete line of crate engines for both stock replacement and performance needs from mild to wild. The popular small-block V8s are offered in horsepower levels from 340 hp and up, using the new Boss 302 block. The top of that group, the "factory stroker" 347 (M-6007-Z347) puts out 450 hp and 400 foot-pounds thanks to: forged stroker crank, forged rods, hot hydraulic roller cam, 2.02/1.60-valved aluminum heads, MSD ignition, 7-quart oil pan and a Victor Jr (Edelbrock) intake. The factory guys don't recommend this thumper for daily drivers

Though not available as a "crate" engine, Chevrolet does have a new block for enthusiasts who want to build a bigger and better LS-Series engine. The iron LSX block accepts all LS external components, but has been re-engineered inside for maximum potential. The siamesed bores allow boring and stroking (4.25-inch is the recommended max) to achieve displacements up to 482 cubic inches, more than can be done with production LS engines

kind of low-end torque to make them outstanding in other uses, such as trucks and motorhomes. You can still buy a killer Mopar wedge (refers to the combustion chamber shape, which is very different from the Hemi) in the form of a 500 cubic inch engine that delivers 505 horsepower and a stump-pulling 590 foot-pounds of torque.

For a strong runner on the taller-deck 351 block, Ford has this one with 385 hp and 377 foot-pounds, with aluminum heads, 7-quart pan, Victor Jr intake and more

In the big-block selection from Ford racing, this is the brand new block based on the 429/460 "385-series" engines of the past. The heavy-duty block features splayed, 4-bolt caps on mains 2, 3 and 4. In assembled crate engine form, this one is ready to rock-and-roll with roller cam, 9.8:1 compression, Super Cobra-Jet aluminum heads with huge valves, MSD billet distributor and some 625 hp and 600 foot-pounds of torque

Just in case you'd like to answer in the affirmative when some guy pulls up alongside you and asks "Hey, has that thing got a Hemi?" Chrysler does not disappoint. The 5.7L Hemi found in their current cars and trucks can be bought outright in 360/360 (horsepower/torque) form, designed

For some big power in a Ford overhead cam package, Ford Racing has the new "Aluminator" block that can handle 700 horsepower. The engine comes only as a short-block or longblock, but this one has been completed with parts from Ford Racing (including the supercharger) and the regular Ford parts bin. The cool valve covers come with the engine

True-blue-oval Ford guys dream about the legendary Boss 302 of 1969, that made Ford competitive in the pony-car Trans-Am races. It was a great-free-breathing engine with lots of performance features, and the good news is that it's back! Ford is making brand-new Boss 302 engines, with improvements like a stronger block able to be bored more, roller cam/lifter ready valley, siamesed bores, 1/2-inch head bolts, improved coolant passages and splayed, 4-bolt caps on the 2, 3 and 4 mains. In complete engine form, it's available in several power levels. This one is the Boss 331 that makes 500 hp with new CNC-machined Z304 aluminum heads

either for carbureted applications or EFI. As if that lineup of choices wasn't enough, the "Gen II" Hemi is also available as a crate engine. Back in the Fifties, the Chrysler Hemi's first generation made the Dodges, DeSotos and Chryslers kings of the road, and in NASCAR racing and drag racing, when those "Gen I" 354 and 392 engines were the motor of choice for everything from roadsters to Top Fuel dragsters. The early Sixties ushered in the newer-design "Gen II" 426-cubic-inch Hemi that ruled NASCAR (just ask those who raced against Richard Petty) and Super-Stock drag racing.

The crate 426's currently offered by Mopar Performance are strictly for very high-performance applications, with a 426 version at 465 horsepower (486 foot-pounds of torque), a stroker Gen II at 472 inches that checks out at 525 horses, and a behemoth 528-cubic-inch engine with 610 horsepower and 650 foot-pounds of torque! You've probably seen the original Hemi-powered 'Cudas go for a million dollars or more at auction. That may be a little out of your budget, but

Hot rodders have many choices in crate engines, not just those from the "Big Three" automakers. A number of aftermarket engine shops build performance engines using all-new aftermarket parts, most are offered with warranties as well. These engines are awaiting shipment to customers from Smeding Performance, Sacramento, California

In their traditional big-block Mopar line, you can drop this 500-cubic-inch wedge "B" motor into a variety of Chrysler/Dodge/Plymouth vehicles. With 505 hp and 590 foot-pounds of torque, your machine will take on a whole new dimension in performance!

drop one of these 426's into your older Mopar and you could clip the wings of any of those originals for a fraction of the ticket price.

So the Big Three automakers have rekindled the spirit of performance with full catalogs of not only a wide choice of complete performance and racing engines, but all the performance bits and pieces to modify your own existing engine. The main components of their best crate motors are also offered in fully-assembled short-block form, in case you already have some good heads and other ancillary pieces to assemble an engine. Fifteen years ago, no one would have believed that today these companies would be making excellent aluminum performance cylinder heads and selling them over the counter at their dealerships and warehouse outlets. There are even performance parts for some factory four-cylinder and six-cylinder engines.

Some of the crate motors and pieces from Ford, GM and Chrysler are actually for racing, supporting grass-roots amateur Saturday night racing on oval tracks and other venues. They have two-barrel and four-barrel "spec" engines featuring good parts and consistent, quality assembly that give everybody a chance in NASCAR-sanctioned races and other events.

The factories aren't the only ones offering you serious drop-in engine power. There are many experienced engine shops across the country that are building ready-to-run performance engines, most offering a warranty like the OEM programs. These aftermarket crate engines are available in

Mopar also has their share of higher-tech modern crate motors, too. The 5.7L new Hemi is available in complete EFI trim as shown here or as a carbureted version for the traditionalists. This one sports 360 hp and 360 foot-pounds of torque

The Sixties 426-style Hemi is available from your local Mopar dealer in several displacements, including this behemoth 472-incher that is sold as a 465hp/486 torque configuration, or as a much hotter 610/650 version. Those are some serious numbers, at a third of the price of an original Sixties 426!

a good variety of power stages to suit just about every application, whether it's just a better engine for your work truck with more torque for towing, a worry-free mild performance engine for that street rod you're building, or a serious engine for street/strip use or bracket racing.

The aftermarket crate motors are often built from 100% new parts, using brand-new factory blocks, blueprinted, balanced and fitted with quality aftermarket components

Smeding Performance has a full range of Chevrolet engines, all built with brand-new factory blocks and aftermarket internal goodies, with the cams, heads, valves and pistons chosen for a specific power level. Small-block Chevrolet engines are available from 330 horsepower to 530. This impressive piece is their Roots-blown 383 that lays down an impressive 600 horsepower and 580 foot-pounds. It would be worth cutting a hole in your hood to let this show through!

One of the Smeding specialties seems to be stuffing the maximum cubic inches into a "small-block" package. They build a 427 Windsor Ford stroker motor as seen here, as well as a 427 small-block Chevy. They also do 540 and 572-sized engines based on big-block Chevy architecture

The name Edelbrock has been associated with performance engines since the late 1940's, and today they make all their heads and intakes plus sell small-block Chevy crate motors with a two-year warranty!

Edelbrock has all levels of performance available, all built with new blocks and parts. This one is their "Performer RPM 9.5:1", a serious street engine with forged crank, hypereutectic pistons, Crane roller rockers, ZZ 4-bolt block, and Edelbrock aluminum heads and carburetion. The result is 363 pump-gas horsepower and 405 foot-pounds of torque

For a semi-race application with some modern technology added, Edelbrock offers their Performer RPM E-tech engine with 440 horses, 425 foot-pounds, and a fuel injection system with engine management and a 1000-cfm throttle body

For an engine that comes with as much power as it does bragging rights, Pentastar fans need look no further than Keith Black, now offering their all-aluminum 426 Hemi. The first of these crate engines is shown here in the beautiful '62 Chrysler Newport built by One Grand Products. It's as stout as it looks!

Ford offers some great engines, but for something more exotic in the Blue Oval line, Carroll Shelby builds a limited number of all-aluminum big-block (FE style) engines based on the cross-bolted 427 of NASCAR, Cobra and drag racing fame. This example is in Bill Brumley's '63 Galaxy and is 510-cubic inches of brute performance, backed by a Richmond five-speed and Detroit locker. With wide-but-street-legal tires, it runs 11.80's

Another source for a 427 Ford, this time from another well-known name in racing, is this 427R engine from Roush Performance. Based on a new Dart block with aluminum Roush heads and a host of performance goodies such as a 4340 stroker crank and forged H-beam rods, it's ready to go, and delivers 550 hp/535 ft-lbs torque

for durability and performance. Since these builders aren't restricted to the parts in the factory inventory as with OEM crate motors, there is a wider selection of cams, aluminum heads and stroker combinations to suit your application needs. The better shops also take more time in checking dimensions and hand-assembling their motors than an assembly line.

Choosing a crate motor

You'll have to do plenty of research when choosing a crate engine, because of the many options available. Without question, the primary consideration is the power level you really need and can use. The higher the power level, the more compromises in streetability. A radical camshaft profile sounds great with that lumpy idle, but an engine so equipped may not start running hard until 3500 rpm, which makes it more marginal for everyday driving. The bigger the cam, the less vacuum the engine will make, which makes for problems with accessories like power brake boosters, and in automatic transmission applications, you'll have to keep a high idle speed and have an aftermarket, high-stall-speed converter to take advantage of the engine. Such converters

Even more radical performance from Roush is their 588RX motor. Based on the architecture of Ford's biggest V8 family, the 429/460, this one uses a new block from Eliminator Products. With Roush heads and premium internals, its vitals are scary at 630 hp/690 foot-pounds of torque

can be annoying to drive in stop-and-go traffic, create higher transmission fluid temperatures because of the slippage, and of course gas mileage, already low on high-performance engines, will suffer also. If you've driven cars like this before and you know how they behave, it may well be worth your while to get the big engine you've always wanted, knowing the limitations. If your driving needs are not everyday, and this is your weekend toy, go for the level you want.

Your budget is the second consideration. Good performance crate motors can be purchased for $4000 to $6000, while the strokers and higher-tune engines run in the $6000 to $8000 range, and those big, bad-boy engines are $10,000 to $14,000. If your project calls for going through other aspects of the car such as a five-speed manual or performance automatic trans, and upgrades to the brakes and suspension at the same time, don't spend your whole savings on just the engine - only to wind up not finishing the car at all because you're out of cash or credit.

Add up all the various aspects of your project and compare the total to what your expected budget will be. Many hot rodders have learned to build their dream vehicle one step at a time. Do the brakes, suspension and driveline improvements while the car is still roadable, then save up for the engine transplant as the last item. It will take determination to see it through to completion, but that patience will reward you when you start enjoying the finished car, truck or street rod.

The Big Three automakers have excellent catalogs and websites covering their performance parts and crate motors, as do some of the aftermarket engine builders. Read them all very carefully when considering the choices. Compare the various power levels and read all the specifications. The details of the camshaft profile, the valve sizes, the port sizes in the heads, the compression ratio, all these make up the determining factors in the engine's power profile. If you have a computer, there are several software packages that are "virtual dyno" programs. You can put all the specs for an engine you're considering into the program and "run" it on the dyno, charting the horsepower and torque curves. It's fairly easy to learn the programs, and it's fun. It's like daydreaming about engines, but with cool graphics and results you can print out.

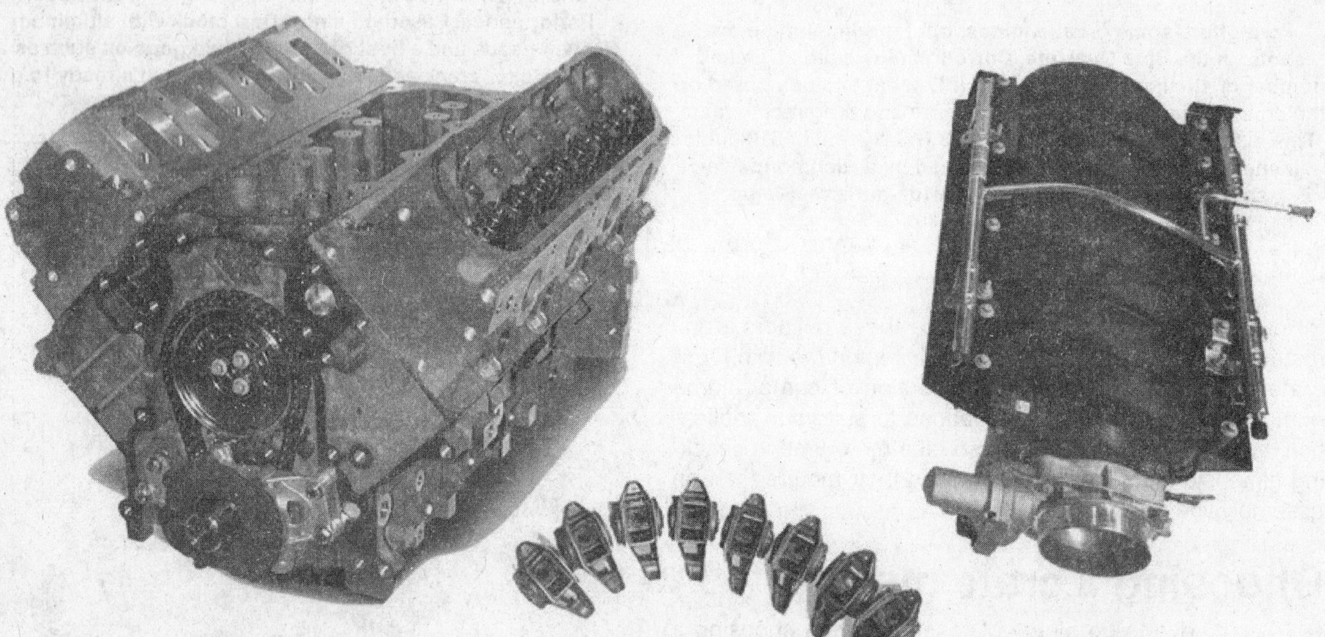

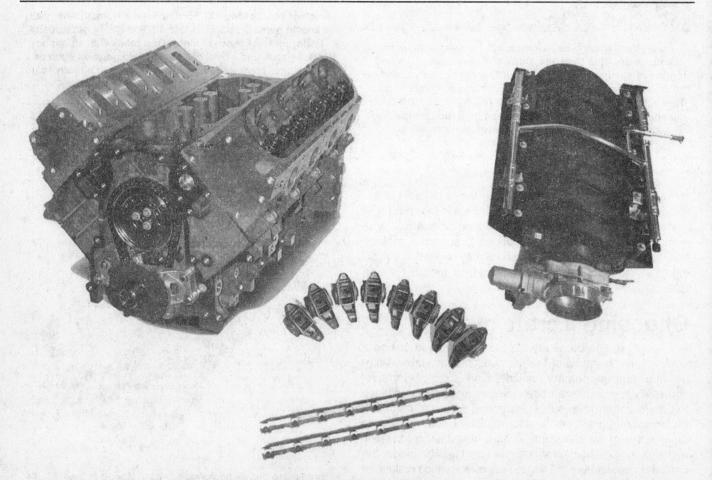

If your taste runs to Chevrolet performance and you want the latest in technology with reliable, driveable horsepower, SLP Performance can set you up with a new LS-series crate motor called the "ZL402." It has an aluminum block and heads, roller rockers, 11:1 compression, SLP heads and cam, Callies forged stroker crank, H-beam rods and forged pistons. Shipped as a long-block assembly (block and heads), it's shown here with SLP's hi-flow EFI

When considering crate engines, pay careful attention to just what is included or not included. Everyone's definition of a "complete" long-block is different. A long-block is generally a full block with heads installed, but does it come with a damper and flywheel, is the water pump included or the oil pan in place? These are the questions you need to answer, since this will affect your budget. You need to know how much other equipment you'll have to buy to make the crate engine actually run.

One of the more popular crate engine choices is a "turnkey" package, which implies that if you hook up power to the starter motor and ignition and add the coolant and engine oil, it will run without adding much else. Of course, these engines are among the most expensive of crate engines, due to all the included new hardware, but it takes the guesswork out of finishing the engine off, and of course, there's the pleasure of immediate gratification in hearing your new engine growl for the first time.

Some of the aftermarket performance engine builders have engine dynamometers in their shop, which allows them to not only finish off the assembly, but run it on the dyno before it is delivered to a customer. This has a number of benefits for both the engine builder and the customer. The engine builder knows that everything is right before the engine leaves the shop, and can offer the customer the actual dyno sheet for his particular engine. The customer also knows that everything is correct, so there's peace of mind for both parties. Engine builders are sometimes faced with newbie customers who send an engine back claiming that something was wrong in the engine, yet when the engine is examined, the builder finds they ran it without oil, installed an incorrect part to complete the engine or some other customer-caused glitch. The dyno runs prove everything was correct on the engine before shipping and also mean that the rings are seated and the camshaft and lifters have had their break-in period.

Back in the day, when the flathead Ford was edged out as the performance favorite, Fifties OHV V8 engines from luxury cars like Chryslers, Oldsmobiles and Buicks spawned a lot of engine swaps for more modern performance. Dropping a big "nailhead" Buick V8 in a little model A Ford like this provided more street performance than available clutches and tires could handle!

Today, hot rodders have a wide variety of engines that can be swapped into popular pre-emissions applications. You can get a late-model engine from a wrecking yard and adapt it with aftermarket parts, or do the same with a brand-new crate motor

Engine swaps

You can take the modern improvements in engines and apply them to just about any vehicle, through a swap to a newer engine. All small-block Chevy V8's, for instance, will fit where one was originally installed, whether it's a '55 Chevy, an old Checker taxicab, a Suburban undergoing restomod, or a First Generation Camaro. This means that your old carbureted engine can easily be replaced with a state-of-the art crate motor such as the turnkey Ram-Jet 350 from GM Performance Parts. This engine makes 350 horsepower and is equipped with electronic fuel injection directed by a computer that's about the size of a wallet. The intake has a plenum designed to look much like the old Ram-Jet mechanical fuel injection used on '57 to '65 Corvettes, which makes for a nostalgic appearance on what is a very modern engine in power and efficiency.

Operation and installation of this engine is very simple. All the factory sensors are in place and the well-marked wiring harness connectors are laid out so that you can hook the whole harness up in a half-hour. There are only three wires to hook to the vehicle and you're ready to run. You get great performance at any altitude, and most users find they can achieve 20 mpg with a Ram-Jet and even more if they

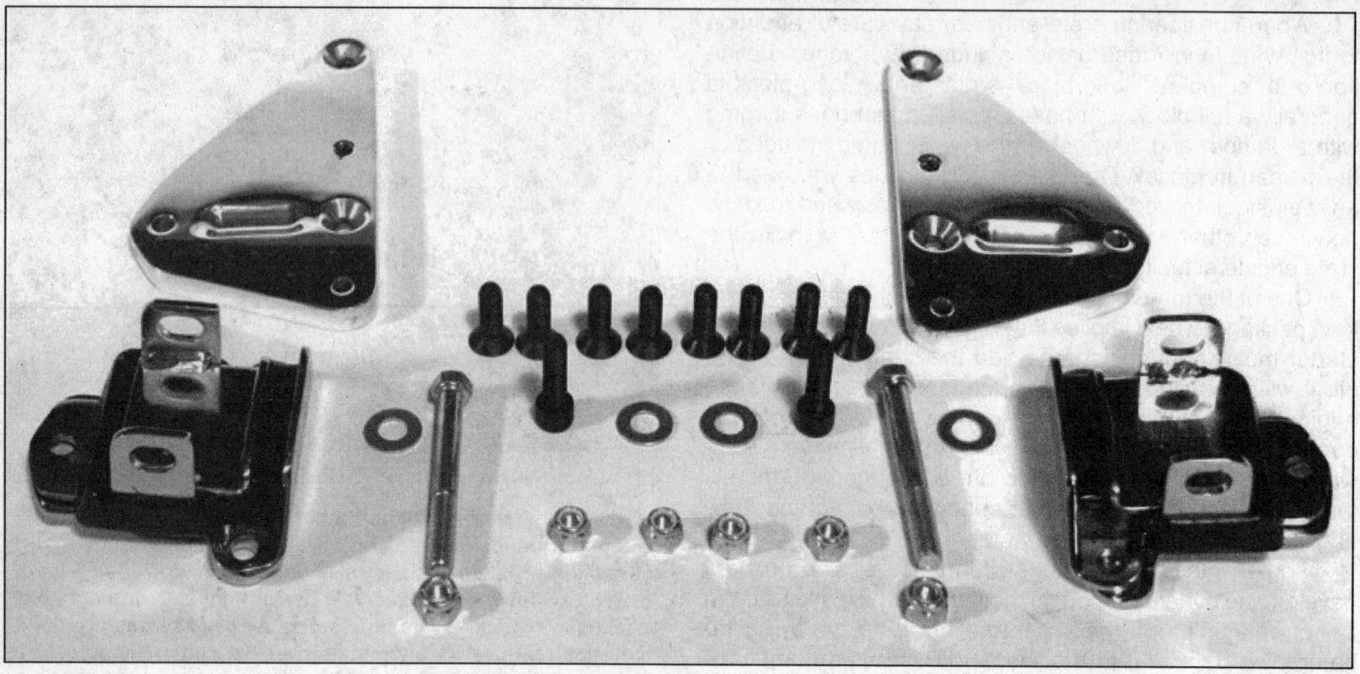

Chevrolet V8 engines have been the most-swapped of all time, being fitted into every imaginable size, make and model of car and truck. While standard 350 small-blocks are the most used, LS-series engines are very popular now. Engine mounts on the LS engines are further back on the block than traditional SBC's, so companies like Total Cost Involved make plates like these that adapt an LS to standard SBC mounts, easing retrofit installations

couple it to a modern overdrive automatic transmission. It comes with a 200-page owners manual and its own code reader for checking trouble codes.

Even the simple swap of a later small-block Chevy for an old one does have some minor details to work out. There are always some wires to add, remove or reroute, the mechanical engine fan may need a short or a long spacer to clear or get close to the radiator (or even a shorter, old-style water pump), there's throttle linkage to modify and you have to find the right radiator hoses for your installation. If you happen to be installing a newer engine into a '55 to '57 Tri-Five Chevy, you will have to change motor mounts, but this is not a big problem. On early V8s, the engine mounts are up front, on either side of the crank damper, while '58 and later engines have mounts on the side of the block. Lots of aftermarket companies have the bolt-in or weld-in mounts to simplify this aspect of new-to-old swap.

The Ford equivalent of a classic update like this would be dropping a modern 5.0L engine into an older Falcon, Comet, Fairlane or Mustang that had originally been equipped with a 221, 260 or 289 engine. Take a look at any of the internet message boards of Mustang or Falcon owners and you'll see every little detail of such swaps discussed, plus advice on disc brake updates and much more. Ford Motorsports even has a special short water pump, available in either "retro" style or modern reverse-rotation flow. If you're swapping in a donor or crate Ford that is fuel injected, aftermarket companies have wiring harnesses made specifically for these very popular engine swaps. No need to sit down with a factory Ford manual and pore over the wiring diagrams.

There are two sources to look to when acquiring an engine to swap. Traditionally, hot rodders would go to a wrecking yard and buy a fairly new engine and trans to swap into their vehicle. Today, many swappers buy a brand new crate motor with a warranty. Either way works, but the donor-vehicle approach is often the most economical.

When swapping a late-model EFI engine into a car with no computer, getting everything hooked up properly can sometimes be a hassle. When good-performing engines started becoming available in wrecking yards, say, engines of the Nineties, your only choice was to buy the engine with its computer and the entire factory harness. The adaptation of all this to the vehicle took determination, but there were hot rodders who broke this ground and pressed on. For those kinds of swaps, it is often an easier and more economical path to buy a complete donor vehicle. Purchase the wrecked Camaro, Mustang or other car at a salvage auction, drag the whole thing home and start examining how it was originally installed and wired. Take photos and notes before pulling everything out and you're miles ahead of the game. The beauty of the donor car is that you don't have to keep going back to the wrecking yard when you need one more piece of the puzzle, like a sensor or bracket you didn't have. After your swap is completed and everything runs as it should, call a wrecking yard and have the remains of the donor car hauled away.

These EFI-motor swaps have been made much easier since the aftermarket companies got involved. With all the requests coming in from non-computer-oriented hot rodders, there is a market for simplified wiring harnesses that don't

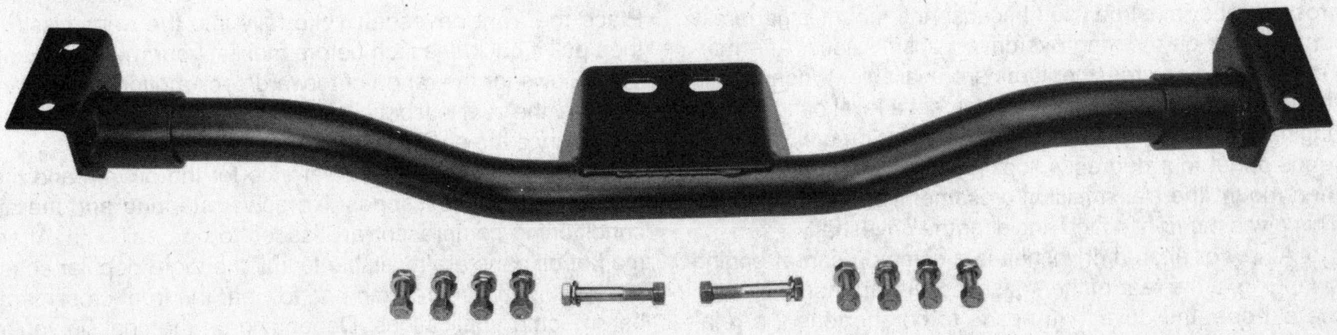

If you're updating an older Chevrolet truck, Classic Performance Products offers these crossmembers to make it easier. The end pieces are bolted to your '47 to '59 Chevy pickup frame rails and the main tube is welded to those ends. Engine mount pads are already on the crossmember. The one on the top is for installing an LS-series engine, and the second crossmember shown is for easy mounting of the LS compatible transmission

require the factory harness as a base. From the donor vehicle, you just need to get the computer that came with your engine, the rest of the hookup is aftermarket. Again, check the internet, searching for info on the swap you intend to make, and you'll find numerous resources.

Generally, the best results for EFI retrofit engines are obtained when the factory computer is sent out for reprogramming to work with the simplified aftermarket wiring harnesses. For compatibility reasons, it's best to have this done by the same company who supplies you with the new harness.

Perhaps the most popular engine swaps today are those that put the latest generation of V8 engines into older vehicles. For Chevrolets and other GM cars, the hot tickets are the Gen III LS-series engines, usually being installed in vehicles that had a traditional small-block. For Fords, there are swaps of 4.6L/5.4L modular engines into older Ford vehicles.

Since it's a popular swap, let's take a look at some of the obstacles in swapping the Gen III engines into a chassis not designed for them. Most swappers are buying low-mileage LS engines (4.8L, 5.4L and 6.0L) in wrecking yards, from 1999 and later GM trucks and SUV's. This is the iron-block version of the engine but is considerably cheaper than the aluminum-block engines, and the main difference is the weight. Buying one of these engines with its matched overdrive automatic like the 4L60-E and the original computer will compare very favorably with building or buying a new small-block and a performance transmission, and the donor vehicles are coming into the wrecking yards more and more.

The LS engine is bigger than a small-block, and the motor mounts are nothing like the old style, but a number of aftermarket companies make adapter plates that bolt to the side of the LS block and accept traditional small-block mounts. Depending on your chassis, you'll have to buy the

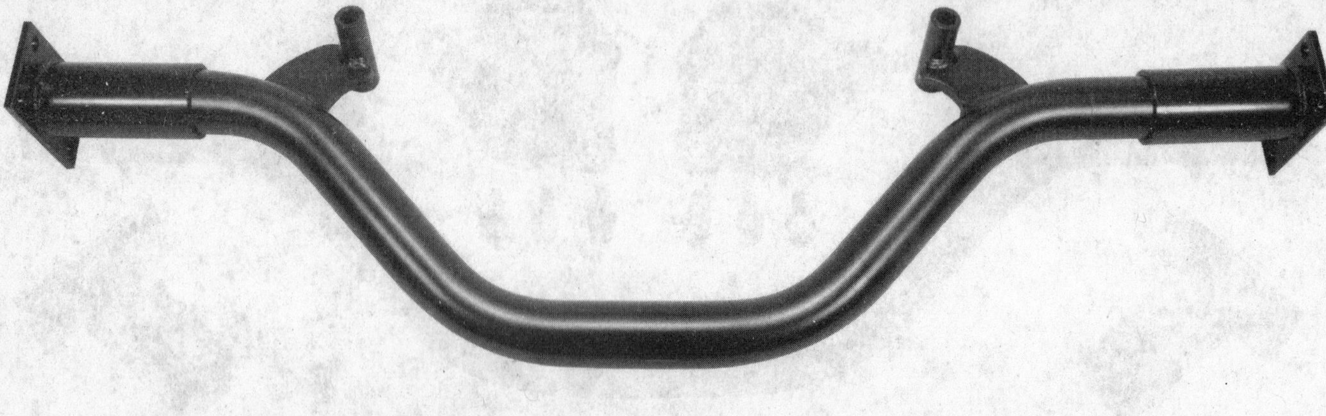

Classic Performance Products also has this engine mount crossmember for installing the perennial favorite swap engine - the small-block Chevy - into the '47 to '59 Chevy trucks

adapters to weld or bolt to the chassis side for the new mount location. At the rear of the drivetrain, a new or modified rear crossmember must be used because the mount is generally further back on the long overdrive transmissions. Aftermarket transmission crossmembers are available. When setting the engine/transmission into the car, set a level on top of the engine and lower the rear of the transmission until the level reads about four degrees, sloping the drivetrain at the rear, then mount the transmission crossmember to the chassis. This gives the right pinion angle for the driveshaft.

A new or altered driveshaft is a common part of engine swapping. If the rear of the transmission is further back than the old one, the driveshaft needs to be shortened, a relatively everyday operation at any good driveline shop. Most shops want you to measure the desired new length from the center of the front U-joint to the center of the rear U-joint. Place the front driveshaft yoke fully into the transmission, then pull it back one inch before making your measurement. This allows for the range of forward/back motion at the front yoke as the rear suspension goes up and down. The shop will balance the shaft for you.

With the LS engines, clearance for the oil pan and the front-mounted accessories like power steering and the air conditioning compressor are issues to be dealt with. Aftermarket oil pans are available to suit the more popular chassis. You need a rear-sump pan to clear the front crossmember in some applications. Depending on the chassis you're working on, the low position of the accessories may require aftermarket mounting brackets; sometimes swapping other GM-application brackets will solve the problem.

Throttle linkage adaptation is part and parcel of any engine swap, but the LS engines have a particular peculiar-

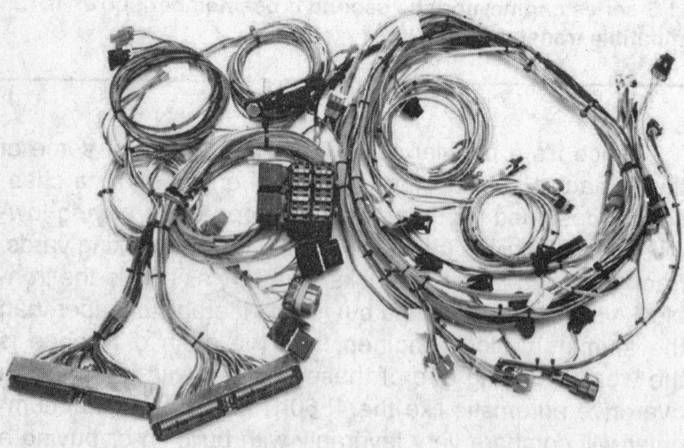

Electronics are as much a part of engine swapping today as the hardware. When you choose that smooth-running late-model fuel-injected engine for your older vehicle, the engine management is critical. Painless Performance is your friend in such cases, offering fully-terminated wiring harnesses to put a late-model donor-car engine into any vehicle. This harness fits LS-1 GM engines, and uses a "VATS bypass" so a stock 1998 Camaro ECM works without reprogramming

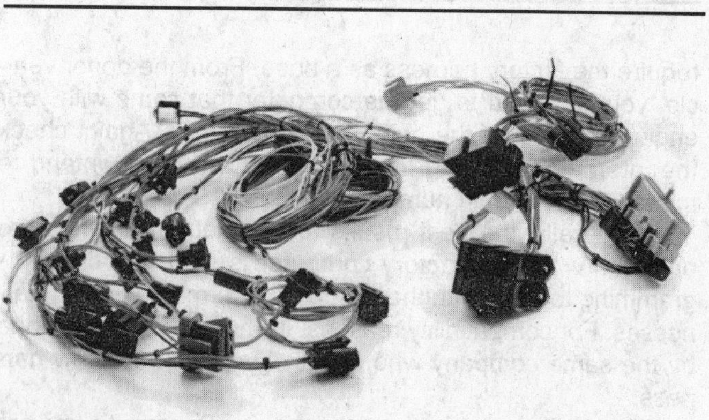

Fords fans love to install the versatile 5.0L EFI V8's in early Mustangs, Falcons, Fairlanes, Rancheros and other Ford Motor Company vehicles for the best of old and new. The Painless harness for these swaps uses your stock ECM from the donor vehicle, which can be mounted at the firewall, under the dash or in the kick panel. Snap the various connectors on the vehicle and engine and you're in business

For a truly plug-and-play installation of an LS-1 GM engine, Painless Performance also has a harness featuring their "Perfect Engine Management System" that includes their own compact, waterproof ECM. The new ECM has been dyno-tuned for each application. All of their harnesses come with detailed instructions, so don't let computer phobia keep you from building the car or truck you want.

ity here. The engines up to 2002 have a throttle cable to operate the throttle body, and these are popular engines to swap because cable throttle linkage is easy to adapt. However, the 2003 and later engines have an electronic "drive-by-wire" system. To use one of these engines, you may have to adapt the accelerator pedal and its APP (accelerator pedal position) switch and its hardware and wiring to your vehicle. Using an aftermarket performance (bigger) throttle body on the drive-by-wire system is trickier.

An engine swap concern for any late-model EFI engine being installed in an older chassis is fuel supply. Fuel injection requires much higher fuel pressure, usually 45-50 psi, and in some cases, a return line from the engine back to the fuel tank. The best place for an electric fuel pump to be mounted is as close to the fuel tank as possible. The OEM approach has always been to put the pump right in the fuel tank, and this is the preferred way. You can install an aftermarket pump in your tank, preferably one that has an extra fitting for the return line from the engine. An older tank can be retrofitted with a late-model pump (another item you can get from your donor vehicle), usually by cutting out the sheetmetal of the newer tank where the pump module attaches. Have your old tank thoroughly cleaned out at a radiator shop, then have a competent welder weld the new section into the top of your tank. This only works if your original tank is deep enough for a late-model fuel pump module. There are some new aftermarket tanks available for the more popular vehicles (Mustangs, Camaros, etc.) that are already fitted with an in-tank EFI pump and feature a sump area to keep fuel around the pickup.

It would take this whole book to describe in detail every step of the popular engine swaps. This Chapter just outlines some of the potential problem areas when you put an engine in a chassis not designed for it. As mentioned before, use your internet research resources and you'll find all the aftermarket sources for parts and information, plus the input from various enthusiast groups, and links to many magazine articles about the swap you're planning. That last word is perhaps the big key to a successful engine swap: planning.

Notes

15 High-performance Cooling Systems

When the air/fuel mixture is ignited, it produces horsepower, and a good deal of heat. In fact, the rapidly expanding gases - the heat - created by ignition are the source of this power. The more power that an engine makes, the greater the heat that it generates. So the majority of this heat makes those pistons move up and down authoritatively, but the rest of it is absorbed by the cylinder head and the block. An engine sheds some heat by simply radiating it into the air passing over its hot surfaces. And it loses more heat (and energy) through the exhaust system (which is why turbochargers make a lot of sense, because they harness this wasted heat and energy). The rest of the engine's heat is managed by recirculating the engine coolant through the radiator and, on many vehicles, by pumping the engine oil through an oil cooler.

Generally speaking, a high-performance engine makes more heat than a stock one, so heavier demands are made on the coolant and engine oil to absorb and shed heat. For example, if you raise the compression ratio, the pressure inside the combustion chambers goes up, and so does the heat. Add a supercharger or turbocharger and the compression pressure - and the heat - inside the combustion chambers goes up. As you increase the power of your engine, you will need to upgrade your cooling systems to manage the additional heat generated by your modifications so that the engine temperature remains within a "survivable" range.

Redline Water Wetter and Justice Brothers Radiator Cooler are two of the more popular coolant additives. Both work well, as do several other brands, including DEI Radiator Relief and Hy-Per Lube Super Coolant

How do you know what an acceptable operating range is? Without getting into complicated formulas, let's just say that if, after some modifications, your coolant temperature gauge indicates that the engine is consistently running hotter than it used to, then it's time to upgrade the cooling system. The actual operating range of engine cooling systems varies. One way to determine the low end of the range is to check the specified opening temperature of the stock thermostat; another is to look at the specified temperature at which the fan switch comes on. High-performance carbureted engines generally require more cooling system upgrades than high-performance fuel-injected engines. Modern engines are designed to run hotter, so you might be able to increase the power by as much as 50 percent before you have to upgrade the cooling system.

Coolant additives

Keep on modifying a high-performance engine and it eventually reaches the point at which the temperature of its cooling system reaches unacceptable levels and does real damage: hoses burst, head gaskets blow, cylinder heads and even the block can warp. So once your engine begins to run a little hot, don't wait - do something! The first thing that you should try is a coolant additive. This is far less expensive than a new radiator or any of the other modifications discussed below. But before we get into additives, bear in mind that this stuff is not a substitute for a leaking hose, a clogged radiator or a worn out water pump. Your cooling system must be in good working order for an additive to do its thing.

What exactly does a coolant additive do? According to the manufacturers who make this stuff, it significantly improves the heat transfer ability of water by reducing the surface tension of the cooling system mixture, which promotes thermal conductivity (heat transfer) through superior penetration of heat-prone metal surfaces. How does it work? Who knows? This isn't a chemistry class! But what we can tell you is that it does work.

The typical coolant additive can lower the operating temperature of the coolant 10 to 15 degrees during extended idling, as much as 15 degrees during cruising, 8 to 15 degrees during no-load high speed cruising (say, 75 mph at 4000 rpm), and 7 to 10 degrees during a brisk uphill climb (say, 5000 rpm). Cylinder head temperatures will be lowered 15 to 20 degrees, and the radiator temperature will drop between 5 and 8 percent. Some coolant additive manufacturers make claims of even more significant reductions in temperature, but the above numbers are based on real world observations. Your actual results will vary with the ambient (outside) temperature and the mixture of ethylene glycol and water that you're using. For best results, automotive manufacturers usually specify a 50/50 mixture of ethylene glycol to water. Some brands of coolant additives are specifically designed to work well with factory recommended ratios and are therefore best suited for improving radiator efficiency on vehicles with minor overheating issues.

Other brands specify mixture ratios that vary somewhat from factory recommendations. Some brands even recommend using straight (distilled) water for best results. Because water is far better at transferring heat than ethylene glycol, water-heavy mixtures are great for racing but not necessarily the hot setup for street use. Some coolant additives do their best work with straight water. At the racetrack you can get good cooling system performance running straight water. But water alone will not work well on the street - particularly if you do a lot of stop-and-go driving in a really hot climate - because water cannot do anything except turn into steam at temperatures above the boiling point. And in cold climates, straight water can freeze, which can cause expensive damage to your engine.

So be sure to read the manufacturer's fine print on the bottle or check out its website before deciding what additive is best for your cooling system. And after visiting the manufacturer's website, do a search for the brand you're considering and check out the results. A number of performance magazines have conducted comparisons of the popular coolant additives, and what they've found is that the additive that works best for your vehicle depends on the driving conditions to which you subject your vehicle. Bottom line: this stuff works, and it's a lot less expensive than your next upgrade - a new radiator.

This beautifully fabricated custom radiator and cooling fan assembly is typical of the kind of quality you can expect from the high-performance aftermarket

Radiators

When you reach the point at which you must think about upgrading your cooling system, there's no better place to start than a bigger or more efficient radiator. The variety of high-performance radiators in the aftermarket is impressive. Most radiator manufacturers offer drop-in clones of your stock unit, albeit with far better performance, as well as a staggering array of highly specialized, custom built units for virtually any application from the Model T to the LS1. Most OEMs also offer their own high-performance radiators.

Radiators are all basically variations on the same theme. Let's look at a basic single-row radiator. Hot coolant enters the radiator at the top end of one of the two tanks (there is a side tank at each end of the radiator, or, in some designs, a top and a bottom tank). The two tanks are connected by a stacked array of tubes equidistant from one another. Hot coolant from the engine is pumped into one tank, then through the tubes to the other tank, from which it exits and travels back to the water pump. The tubes are routed between rows of wafer thin cooling fins. The fins, which are touching the tubing, conduct heat from the hot tubing and radiate it into the air passing through the radiator. That's all there is to it.

Most stock street vehicles usually have a single or double-row radiator, that is, they have either one or two rows of tubing. But the number of rows goes up with horsepower - So does the surface area of the cooling fins because performance radiators have more rows of cooling fins than street units. More rows of tubing and more fins equals better heat dissipation. That is why most high-performance radiators are three or four-row designs. A three-row unit should be good up to about 300 horsepower. Above that, get a four-row unit.

On a high-performance radiator, the tubing itself is usually larger in diameter than the tubing used on OEM radiators. Larger diameter tubing decreases the drag imposed on the coolant being forced through the tubes. This allows the coolant to flow through the radiator more efficiently at

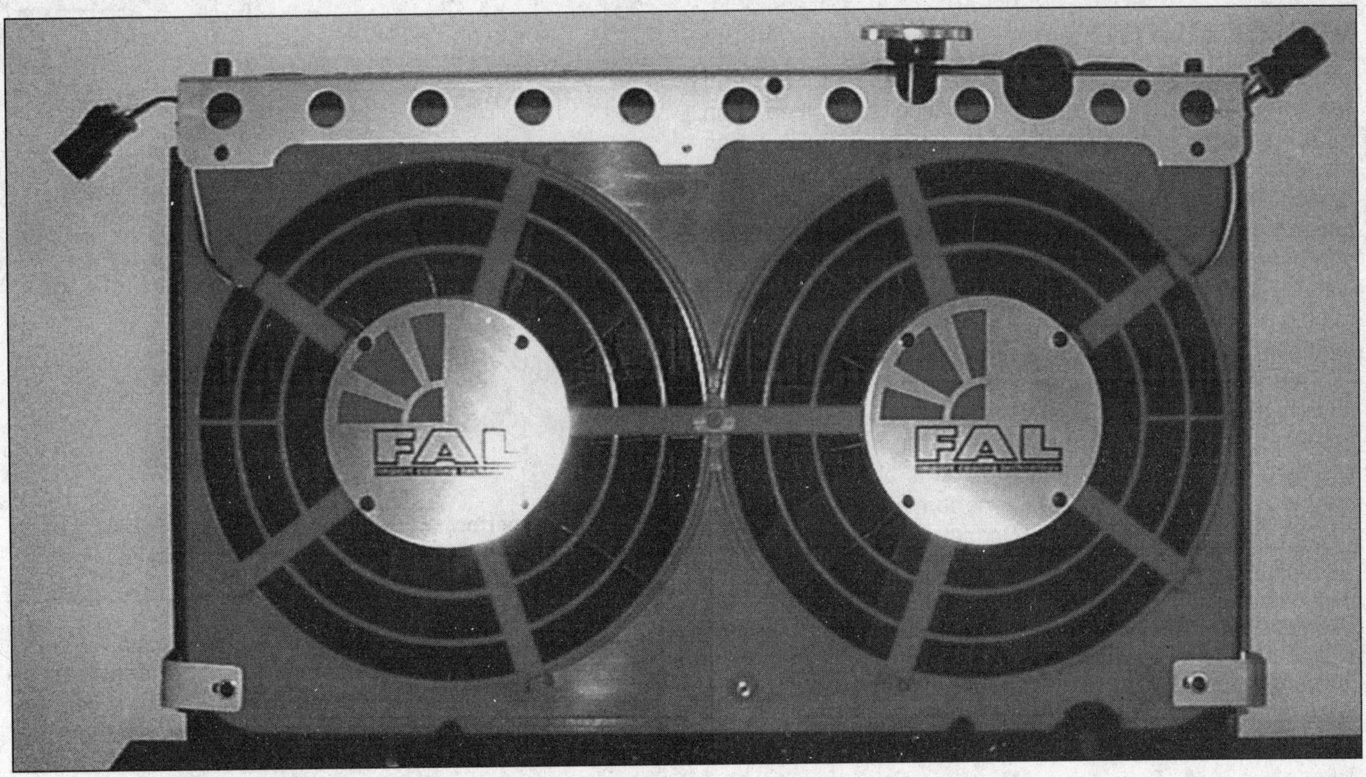

A typical high-performance aftermarket fan assembly

the higher flow rate at which the water pump operates on a high-performance engine. For example, the pump on a stock Ford 5.0L V8 eats an estimated 12 horsepower at 6000 rpm. An aftermarket, freer-flowing radiator would cut down that parasitic loss.

So if you're shopping for a performance radiator, note the size (square inches) of the radiator, the number of rows of tubing, the tubing diameter and the number of fins per inch of tubing. You want the biggest radiator that will fit properly, three or four rows of 1/2-inch or larger diameter tubing and 12 or 14 fins per inch. When comparison shopping, note that a radiator is rated in terms of its "heat rejection" capacity, or BTU (British Thermal Unit) rejection. (A BTU is the quantity of heat required to raise the temperature of one pound of water by one degree Fahrenheit.)

Radiator cooling fans

Even the best radiator needs a little help when the vehicle is stationary or moving slowly in heavy traffic on a hot day. That's why even stock radiators have cooling fans. Many OEM radiators have two cooling fans. One fan is switched on by the fan switch when the coolant reaches a certain temperature. The other fan is switched on when the air conditioning system is turned on, because the condenser, which is located in front of the radiator, sheds its heat into the same airstream moving through the radiator. When you add horsepower to an engine it generates more heat, so the fan's job becomes much more critical. Air conditioning systems and automatic transmissions also add to the heat load imposed on your radiator.

A wide variety of performance radiator fans are available from the high-performance aftermarket. When selecting a new fan, or fans, start by measuring the available area of your high-performance radiator. Then check the manufacturer's specifications for the fan size that will fit; the higher the rated airflow the better. Generally speaking, you want to choose the largest diameter fan that will fit your radiator and your engine compartment. You know the old saying "There's no such thing as too much horsepower?" Well, there's no such thing as too much cooling fan! Typically, you will want a pair of 11-inch or 12-inch diameter fans for a performance V8 engine.

Fans work best when they *pull* air through the radiator, which means that your new fan and shroud assembly must be mounted on the backside of the radiator. There is only so much room between the radiator and the front of the engine, so make sure that you carefully research the dimensions of the fan/shroud assembly and the available space where you're planning to put it.

Cooling fans are available with straight blades and curved blades. The straight blades pull more air through the radiator than curved blades, but they're a little noisier. The curved blades are quieter, but they don't pull as much air through the radiator. You're building a high-performance vehicle, not a luxury car. You know what to do!

Water pumps

People buy high-performance water pumps for different reasons. If all you have is an overheating issue, then shop for a pump that can deliver more coolant more quickly than the stock unit. But be aware that a pump that can push more coolant through the cooling system more quickly will also impose a greater parasitic drag on the engine. So unless you have already upgraded to a high-performance radiator with 1/2-inch or larger tubing, there's no advantage in going too big because the new pump's output will be bogged down by the smaller diameter tubing of the old radiator.

A good high-performance water pump provides a higher flow, higher pressure and equal distribution of the coolant (within one percent) to both sides of the block. The construction of a high-performance pump is also more robust than that of an OE pump. A high-performance pump will, of course, have a larger impeller. On higher quality pumps, the impeller shaft rides on ball and roller bearings and a heavy duty seal prevents leaks. Some good pumps, Edelbrocks for Chevy small blocks, for example, use an O-ring seal instead of a conventional gasket to seal the pump. The best performance pumps also use machined billet pulley hubs for added strength.

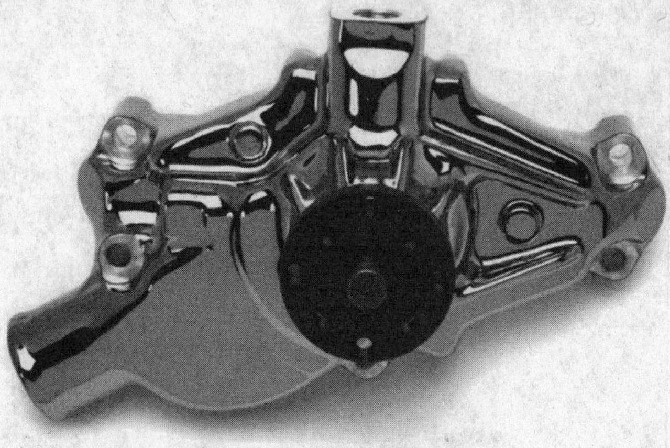

High-performance pumps are available in cast, polished and chromed finishes

Under-drive pulleys

If you want to decrease parasitic drag on the engine, consider an under-drive crankshaft pulley. This pulley is slightly smaller in diameter and therefore turns the accessories a little more slowly than the stock crank pulley, which means less drag on the engine. An under-drive pulley also allows the engine to be revved at higher rpm before the pump "cavitates." Cavitation is the phenomenon that occurs when the pump impeller reaches the rpm at which its centrifugal force produces a cavity, which prevents the pump from circulating coolant, causing the engine to overheat.

Under-drive pulleys are available in various reduction percentages. Make sure that you don't get one that turns so slowly that the alternator and pump can't do their jobs. If your performance vehicle has to work as a daily driver, be forewarned that an under-drive crank pulley might cause the water pump to operate too slowly below 2000 rpm. The alternator output might also be insufficient below 2000 rpm.

On the other hand, when you build up an engine that's going to spin at significantly higher rpms than stock, it's quite possible that the alternator can "overspeed," which could shorten its life span. An underdrive pulley can prevent you from replacing your alternator on a far-too-regular basis.

Electric water pumps

An even better solution to the problem of water pump drag is to eliminate it altogether. An electric water pump imposes almost zero drag on the engine (no energy is free, and an electric water pump will *slightly* impose more load on the alternator, that's why we say "almost zero drag"), which can significantly improve performance under heavy acceleration. Electric pumps also improve fuel economy because of the lessened drag. Another advantage of electric water pumps is that they can be run *after* the engine is shut down to prevent "heat soak." Right after an engine is shut down it continues to heat up for awhile before it starts cooling down. During this period fuel can overheat and vaporize, causing vapor lock when you try to start the engine again. (The phenomenon of heat soak is more likely to occur on carbureted engines than on fuel-injected ones because the fuel is pressurized in fuel-injection systems.)

Deep sump oil pans and engine oil coolers

A high-performance engine transfers a good deal of heat to the oil. Once the oil temperature reaches a certain point, the oil oxidizes, breaks down and loses 50 percent or more of its lubricating properties. Most petroleum-based oils reach this temperature at or below the average temperature of a high-performance engine. So keeping the engine oil temperature within its recommended range is critical to engine survival. Ideally, you want the oil temperature to stay between 220 and 240 degrees F. But on a performance engine with a stock oil pan and no oil cooler, oil can reach 280 degrees F! You have two options: increase the oil volume or install an oil cooler.

Increasing the oil volume is usually achieved by installing a wider aftermarket oil pan with a deep sump. A deep sump oil pan can increase the volume of the oil to seven or eight quarts, which improves heat dissipation. You should be able to achieve a 10 to 15 degree reduction with a deep sump pan. But if that doesn't bring the temperature down sufficiently, you should install an external radiator-type liquid-air oil cooler.

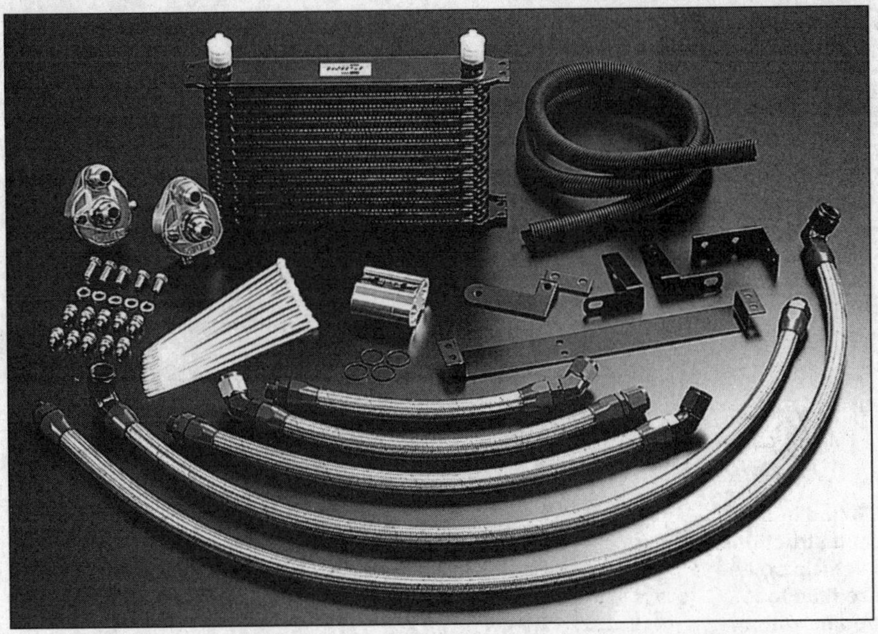

The typical aftermarket engine oil cooler kit includes all the hardware that you'll need

An external oil cooler is relatively inexpensive and fairly easy to install. Look for a location that doesn't block the coolant radiator, the transmission oil cooler or the air conditioning condenser (if equipped). With respect to location, you don't really have any options with radiators and condensers. But an oil cooler, because of its compact size, is easier to locate in a spot that's not competing for the same cooling air with these other heat exchangers.

Transmission oil coolers

This is a modification you should consider if you're using an automatic transmission. It will extend transmission life in almost every application. Consider an auxiliary cooler mandatory for high-performance engines. Slippage in an automatic transmission generates heat, and heat is the greatest enemy of an automatic. It is often said that a 10-percent reduction in transmission heat can double the life of an automatic transmission. Heat causes fluid to break down and lose its lubricating and heat-transfer properties. Heat also causes clutch friction material to varnish, causing still more slippage. Since transmission fluid is in contact with virtually all components within an automatic transmission, cooling the fluid will ultimately cool the transmission. Stock transmission fluid coolers circulate pressurized fluid through lines and hoses to the radiator. A separate transmission fluid chamber within the radiator bottom or side tank is in constant contact with engine coolant. Since normal engine coolant temperature is lower than normal transmission fluid temperature, the transmission fluid chamber transfers heat to the engine coolant, cooling the transmission fluid. This setup works satisfactorily under normal conditions, but if the engine runs hot or overheats, the transmission will likewise run hot or overheat because the stock cooler is unable to shed sufficient heat into the coolant.

An auxiliary transmission cooler will prevent these problems from occurring, and it will extend transmission life by reducing operating temperature. Installing an auxiliary transmission cooler will also relieve the radiator of this additional cooling responsibility and help your engine run cooler when the ambient temperature is high or when it's time to put the pedal to the metal.

There are two basic types of auxiliary coolers available. The first type is an extra-deep transmission pan. The concept behind this modification is that, since a deep pan can hold more transmission fluid, the additional fluid will hold and transfer more heat. Since the pan is deeper, it also exposes more metal surface to the air flowing underneath the chassis. Some deep pans also have longitudinal tubes running the length of the pan that are welded to the front and rear of the pan. This creates holes through the pan that air can flow through and cool the fluid further.

Deep pans have some drawbacks, however. First, they are most effective when the vehicle is moving down the road. When the vehicle is sitting still or moving slowly, they are much less efficient. Second, deep pans reduce ground clearance, so on low-slung vehicles, they're susceptible to damage if they come in contact with the road. And deep pans do not offer nearly the cooling efficiency of a large radiator-type cooler mounted at the front of the vehicle.

Deep sump transmission oil pans, like this one from B & M, is an economical way to reduce transmission fluid temperature

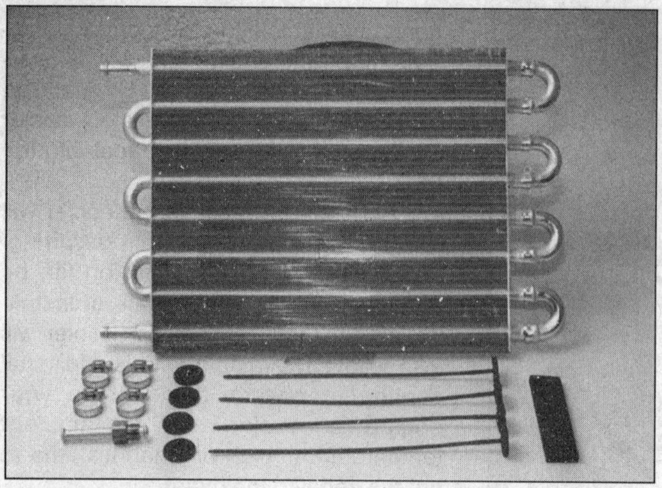

1 This auxiliary cooler is typical of what you'll find in auto parts stores and includes an installation kit and instructions. Before beginning installation, try to park the vehicle so its front end is pointing uphill. This will minimize fluid loss during installation. Read the instructions that come with the kit carefully - they supersede information printed here

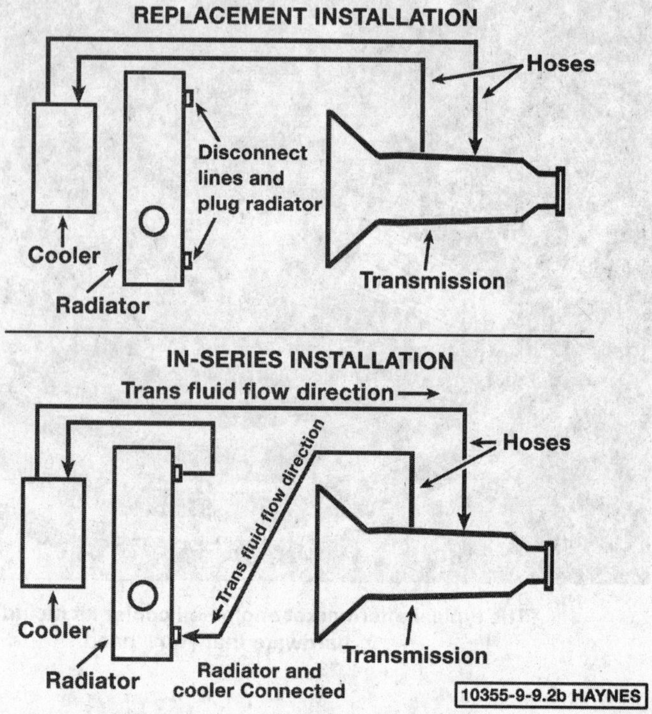

2 Decide if you want to use the auxiliary cooler in conjunction with the existing cooler in the radiator (bottom) or use it by itself (top). Generally, if you live in a cold climate, incorporating the existing cooler is a good idea, since it will allow the transmission to reach operating temperature faster. In a warm climate, it's best to use the auxiliary cooler by itself

Radiator-type transmission coolers are far more effective than deep sump transmission pans. They're available in enough sizes to fit any space on any high-performance vehicle. This type of cooler uses aluminum tubing that runs through heat-dissipating fins. The cooler looks somewhat like a small version of a conventional radiator and installs in front of the vehicle's radiator (or condenser, if the vehicle is air conditioned). When installing the auxiliary cooler, you can either eliminate the stock cooler (which will help the engine's

3 If you'll be using the existing cooler, you'll need to establish which line is the outlet from the cooler. With the engine cold, start the engine and shift the transmission into gear for a moment (no more than 10 seconds). Then feel both lines - the warmer line is the inlet, so cut the other line (don't cut the line now, however - it will be cut in a later step)

4 Attach the hose provided in the kit to the cooler, but don't cut it (leave it in a loop). The hose clamps should be tightened only to the point where the hose rubber is pressed slightly through the slots in the clamp bands and is level with the clamp band. Do not overtighten to the point where rubber is pressed out above the band slots

5 Find a mounting location for the cooler in front of the radiator or condenser (if you have air conditioning). Make sure you've thought out the routing of the hoses so they won't obstruct anything, then mount the cooler with the nylon straps provided. Be sure to stick the adhesive pads to the cooler so they will be sandwiched between the cooler and radiator when the straps are tightened

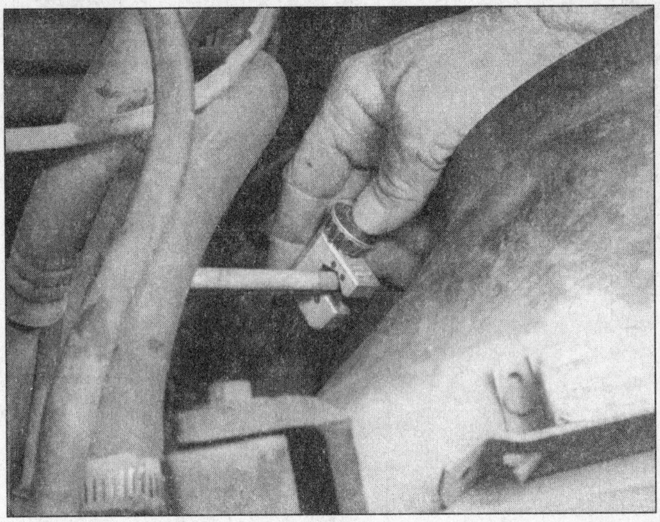

6 Find a convenient location to cut off the steel cooler line(s), as close to the cooler as possible. The miniature tubing cutter shown here is very useful in tight spaces. When the lines are cut, fluid will leak out, so place a container underneath to catch the leakage. If you'll be using the existing cooler in conjunction with the auxiliary cooler (recommended in cold climates), only the return line will need to be cut

cooling system work a little better in warm climates) or install it in-line with the existing cooler (which will speed warm-up in cold climates). If you eliminate the existing cooler, you must make certain the cooler will dissipate enough heat to prevent overheating. Generally, coolers are rated for the Gross Vehicle Weight (GVW) they are capable of cooling for, but bigger is usually better. Get a cooler rated well in excess of the GVW of your vehicle.

The accompanying photographic sequence depicts the installation of a typical auxiliary transmission cooler.

7 Using a flare-nut wrench, unscrew the cut-off ends of the line(s) from the radiator fittings. If you'll be using the existing cooler in conjunction with the auxiliary cooler, install the fitting designed for this purpose - it should be included in the kit

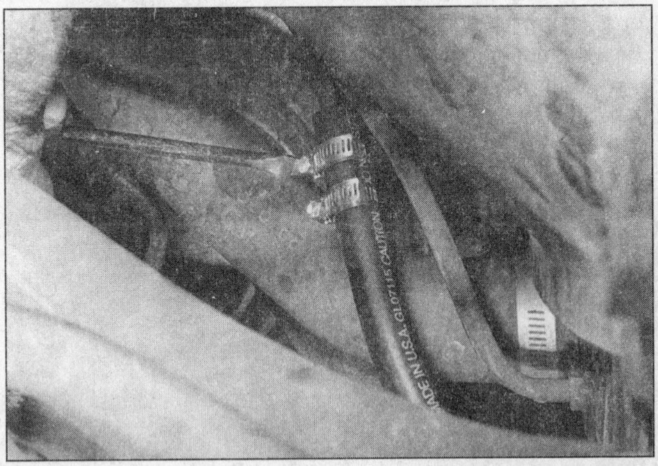

8 Carefully route the hose to the cut-off line(s) (and radiator fitting, if you'll be using the existing cooler). Be careful not to kink the hoses or bend them sharply. Make sure the hoses will not be in contact with any sharp surface or near any hot surfaces that could damage them. If possible, secure the hoses to the chassis or other hoses or lines with nylon tie-straps. Attach the hoses with hose clamps, being careful not to overtighten them. Now start the engine and check carefully for leaks. Check the transmission fluid level and add additional fluid, as necessary. After two weeks or so, recheck all hose clamps for tightness

Notes

16 Monitoring Engine Performance

The gauges in your vehicle are your early warning system. When the coolant temperature gauge needle moves into the red zone or the oil pressure gauge indicates low oil pressure, you pull over and stop before the engine is damaged. A stock street machine is so reliable that such situations are rare, but on a highly modified engine, things can go south in a hurry.

A logical list of gauges for a performance engine includes the tachometer and gauges for coolant temperature, oil pressure, oil temperature and voltage. If your vehicle is turbocharged or supercharged, you'll also want a boost gauge. If you're running nitrous oxide, you'll need a nitrous pressure gauge. That's it, really. More gauges could be a distraction. You have only so much time to look at gauges while you're driving.

But for some enthusiasts the above list is simply the starting point. To these guys, there is no such thing as too much information. They might add a vacuum gauge (indicates intake manifold vacuum), a fuel pressure gauge (supercharged and turbocharged vehicles put a high demand on the fuel pump during hard acceleration) or an air/fuel ratio meter (a handy instrument for tuning, especially on carbureted vehicles). Serious drag racers might want to add a shift light, which can be programmed to illuminate a bright LED when the engine reaches the rpm at which you upshift. And some guys might even want to know the outside air temperature, or the barometric pressure, and so on.

Since your car is probably already equipped with some gauges - perhaps all of the basic gauges listed above - should you simply add the ones you're missing, or replace all of them with a matched set of aftermarket gauges? Let's call the first option the mix-and-match approach. Most of the gauges that you still need aren't that expensive, so why not simply add those gauges to your current array? You might very well end up with different brands, colors and styles of gauges, but this approach costs a lot less than replacing all of the gauges at once, and it still gets the job done. Besides, adding an occasional gauge or two as needed, instead of buying a complete all-new set of gauges, leaves you a bigger budget for performance modifications.

However, for some enthusiasts the above approach is just too visually . . . tacky. If you're part of this crowd, you probably won't be happy with a motley mix of different brands, colors and styles of gauges. Maybe the old gauges are starting to look just a little dated, or it's simply time to upgrade the interior a little. There's nothing like a brand new set of trick matching gauges to give the old dash a new look.

How much will it cost?

Whichever way you go - mix-and-match or all-at-once - do your homework before spending a penny. Even though individual gauges are reasonably priced, a realistic estimate of the total cost of installing one gauge or a dozen of them must also include the cost of any new sending units, switches or sensors, and any gauge mounting plates or pods that you will need to complete the installation. Some gauges will probably work with the existing sending unit (oil pressure or temperature, coolant temperature, for example) and most gauges can be spliced into an existing information sensor circuit, but you still might need to replace the sensor itself if it's old. For example, you will need to buy a new wide-band oxygen (O2) sensor if you're installing an air/fuel ratio meter.

You can usually find a blank spot on the dash to install one or two extra gauges, but to install a larger array you might have to obtain a mounting panel, plate or pod, so remember to include these in your cost estimate.

Up to this point, installing one gauge or all new gauges is basically pretty straightforward. Locating the existing circuits that you'll need to splice into for power, signal, ground, etc. is not a job for people who don't know what they're doing. If you already know your way around automobile wiring harnesses and connectors and know how to make clean splices, then this phase of the installation shouldn't be too intimidating. If, on the other hand, you don't already know all this stuff, then the time and labor you'll spend installing your new gauge(s) could result in an incorrectly operating or non-operative gauge, or could even damage your new gauge or a circuit. So ask yourself: "How difficult is it to wire this gauge or this panel of gauges?" Most retail speed shops and internet based mail-order emporiums will offer general technical support, but don't expect them to provide you with specific instructions for your specific make and model. If you don't already know how to figure out this sort of stuff, find out what it's going to cost to pay a qualified installer to do so and add that to your cost estimate.

When you've added up all the actual costs of installing aftermarket gauges, the numbers themselves should help you decide how deeply you want to get into adding or replacing gauges. Once that's settled, it's time to move on to the next question.

What kind of gauges do you want?

If you're a performance car guy, then you're probably already familiar with the most well known gauge manufacturers. Who makes the "best" gauges? That's not only impossible to answer, it's the wrong question! Instead, ask yourself what size, style, color and type of gauge you want, then compare availability and prices.

Gauge size

When it comes to a choice of gauge sizes, availability is not a problem. Most gauges are available in 2-1/16 inch, 2-5/8 inch, 3-1/8 inch, 3-3/8 inch and 3-3/4 inch diameters. Tachometers are available in 3-3/4 inch and 5 inch diameters. What size you decide to install is largely a matter of how much space is available. Another factor you should consider when determining gauge size is the distance from your eyes to the gauge(s) you plan to install. Ideally, your line of sight should always be directed down the road, not at your gauges, which is why the manufacturer installs the OEM gauges in a cluster right in front of you where they're easy to glance at without taking your eyes off the road for too long. Any gauges you add anywhere else will not be quite as close to your eyes or as easy to read quickly as the stock instrument cluster. So the greater the distance from your eyes to any new gauge(s), the bigger the gauge(s) should be. Bottom line: get the biggest gauges that will fit where you want to put them.

Style and color

Because they must be easy to read, most gauges are simple and stark. One obvious difference between gauge styles is the finish of the bezel (the bezel is the trim ring around the circumference of the gauge face). Some gauge bezels are black, some are brushed aluminum, and some are chrome-plated. All three are attractive, but certain bezel finishes blend in better in some cars than in others. Some cars use a lot of black, aluminum or chrome finishes on the dash and on the bezels of the stock gauges in the instrument cluster. For an installation that looks factory, you'll probably want to stick with a style and finish similar to the OEM gauges.

Of course, you might not want the new gauges to match your car's OEM gauges. Some factory gauges are difficult to read, poorly illuminated or unattractive, so why not upgrade to something you like? Get what *you* want! If an aftermarket gauge installation looks sharp, nobody will ever notice that it doesn't match the originals.

For a long time you could have any color gauge you wanted - as long as it was white numbers on a black face. Then some manufacturers started offering gauges with black numbers and white faces. Nowadays, you can find gauges in a variety of colors. Or, you can simply change the color of your existing gauges by installing replacement faceplates that can be applied right over the stock faceplates. These aftermarket faceplates are available in a wide variety of colors.

Electro-luminescent gauges are another popular option. Using the same technology as luminescent watches, these gauges are equipped with faces that look white in the daytime and emit a soft blue or green glow at night. Or you can change the look of your existing gauges by installing luminescent gauge faceplates. Some electro-luminescent gauges allow you to switch back and forth between different colors!

Mechanical vs. electrical

At one time, most gauges were mechanical. A mechanical gauge actually measures whatever is being measured *at the gauge itself*. For example, if you decide to install a mechanical oil pressure gauge, you must install a tube to carry oil from the sending unit to the backside of your gauge. The advantage of mechanical gauges is that they're simpler than electric gauges, and they're accurate and reliable. The disadvantage is that, if a line comes loose, they're messy! Although you can still find mechanical gauges, they're no longer your only option.

Nowadays, most gauges are electric. An electric gauge uses an electrical sending unit at the source of whatever is being measured. The sender emits an electrical signal in response to the pressure, temperature or number of revolutions, etc. This electrical signal is carried via a wire to a processor inside the gauge that inputs the signal, processes it, then indicates it on the analog or digital face of the gauge.

Where do you put the gauges?

When cars were bigger, so were the dashboards. There was always room for extra gauges. On modern cars, there's not a lot of usable space for extra gauges because there's not a lot of flat space on the dash. The one really flat space for gauges is the existing instrument cluster (the one-piece unit that houses the speedometer, tachometer and a few other gauges such as the fuel level and coolant temperature gauges). So, if you're swapping the old instrument cluster for a new unit, it should be a very straightforward procedure. But if you're planning to install additional gauges, then you might have to be creative.

Gauge "cups" are the traditional strategy for housing gauges that can't be installed in the instrument cluster area. A cup is usually a back metal or plastic canister designed to house one gauge. Each cup is equipped with a mounting bracket that allows you some flexibility in locating the gauge. One drawback of gauge cups is that the wires between the gauge and the sender, voltage source, ground, etc. are exposed between the back of the cup and where they disappear into the dash. On competition or all-out high-performance vehicles, this isn't that big a deal. On street machines, it might be an aesthetic issue for some people. If so, keep reading.

Gauge manufacturers offer pre-cut mounting plates in a variety of sizes and finishes. These plates can be trimmed down for an exact fit in storage recesses or ashtray receptacles in the dashboards of most modern cars. These empty spaces, which are usually located in the center of the dash, just ahead of the center console, were intended for storing small stuff, like sunglasses, cell phones and other items, or for installing aftermarket stereo components such as equalizers or CD players. If your car's dash is equipped with one of these storage areas, consider yourself lucky, because this is an easy way to add some gauges and make it look factory. Gauge plates are available in a wide variety of finishes - brushed aluminum, flat black, etc. - and are equipped with pre-drilled holes for one, two, three, four or more gauges. The holes are drilled in the same diameter as the gauges you intend to use, so when ordering a plate, make sure that you know the number of gauges you intend to install and the outside diameter of each gauge. When you install the gauge(s) in the plate, the bezel (the decorative ring around the outside of the gauge faceplate) covers up any gap between the gauge and the hole.

There are gauge plates designed to fit into the ashtray receptacle of many makes and models. One neat thing about the ashtray is that the electrical lead to the cigarette lighter means that a convenient battery voltage source is already available.

Most of the gauge manufacturers also offer a wide range of "gauge pods," which are plastic housings designed to accept various sizes of gauges. There are pods for just about every vacant area on the dash: above the instrument cluster, to the left or right of the cluster, in the center of the dash, etc. Unlike gauge cups, pods mount flush with the surface of the dash so no wiring is exposed.

One popular variation of the gauge pod is known as a "pillar pod." Pillar pods, which are designed to fit the driver's side A-pillar (the windshield pillar), can house one, two, three or four small gauges. A pillar pod is easy to install and looks as if it was installed at the factory, but be ready to do some drilling in the body and/or the dash to hide all the wires.

Typical gauges

Air/fuel ratio gauge - An air/fuel ratio gauge indicates whether your air/fuel mixture ratio is rich or lean at any given rpm. Although this is not one of your warning gauges, it is a particularly helpful tuning tool because it uses a 5-volt wide-band air/fuel ratio sensor, which, unlike a conventional 2-volt narrow-band oxygen sensor, smoothes out its signal so that you can actually read the air/fuel ratio.

Ammeter - An ammeter tells you how much current your alternator is putting out. Ammeters are not as popular as they once were (most people install a voltmeter instead).

Boost gauge - A boost gauge indicates the boost pressure on a supercharged or turbocharged engine. This is good information to keep track of, since an overboost condition caused by a stuck wastegate can cause serious damage.

Coolant temperature gauge - The coolant temperature gauge indicates the temperature of the engine coolant. You might already have a coolant temperature gauge, so if you're going to replace it, consult the manufacturer to determine whether your new gauge will work with the existing sending unit. If you want to add a coolant temperature gauge - and you don't already have one - you'll also need to install a new sending unit. On many modern vehicles, a single Engine Coolant Temperature (ECT) sensor, which is the information sensor for the engine management computer, also functions as the coolant temperature sending unit for the coolant temperature gauge (see your Haynes manual for verification). If your vehicle is in this category, you might have to install a second sender dedicated to your new coolant temperature gauge.

Cylinder head temperature gauge - The real value of a cylinder head temperature gauge is not that it tells you the temperature of the cylinder head, but that it gives you a good idea of the engine's operating temperature under different conditions. For example, it can indicate whether an engine overheats under full power, or whether it has a tendency to run too cold, just right or too hot over a longer period. You'll need to install a new sender for a cylinder head temperature gauge because this type of gauge is rarely found on cars as original equipment.

Exhaust gas temperature gauge - An exhaust gas temperature gauge tells you the temperature of the exhaust gases as they're exiting the combustion chamber. An exhaust gas temperature of 1100 to 1200 degrees F should result in nice tan-colored spark plug electrodes. A lower reading should produce darker colored plugs, and higher readings should give you gray or white plugs. Once you've identified the "normal" temperature range that produces tan plugs, all you have to do is monitor the exhaust gas temperature gauge and watch for any deviation from normal. An exhaust gas temperature gauge is a useful tuning tool when you're trying to set up the correct mixture ratio. A lean mixture will run hotter than normal, while a rich mixture will run cooler than normal (and will actually make increasingly *less* horsepower as it gets richer). An exhaust gas temperature gauge can also help you identify "hot spots," which can occur when chopping the throttle from a full-throttle situation. The tricky part of installing this setup is that you will need an exhaust gas temperature sensor in *each* exhaust header.

Fuel pressure gauge - A high performance engine, particularly a supercharged or turbocharged engine, makes big demands on the fuel delivery system under acceleration, so you need a heavy-duty fuel pump capable of supplying sufficient fuel. And you need a fuel pressure gauge to make sure that the fuel pressure is adequate under all conditions. A fuel system that fails to deliver sufficient fuel under acceleration or high speed running leans out the air/fuel mixture ratio, which leads to detonation and/or preignition, and it can ruin a motor in seconds! The fuel pressure gauge is primarily used for tuning. One reason for this is that you can't install it inside the car; you wouldn't want high-pressure fuel spraying the inside of the car if a compression fitting came loose!

Nitrous gauge - If you're running nitrous oxide, you need to know how much nitrous is in the tank. Running out of nitrous in the middle of a drag race will cause your air/fuel mixture to turn really rich in a hurry, which could cause big trouble. If you're going to install a nitrous kit, make sure you have a gauge to monitor the level in the tank.

Oil pressure gauge - If you don't have an oil pressure gauge, this is one of the first gauges you should consider installing. An oil pressure gauge can save your engine from some expensive damage. If the engine loses oil pressure because of oil pump failure or a blocked oil passage, oil pressure will drop suddenly; without an oil pressure gauge, you might very well run the engine until it destroys itself. Many aftermarket oil pressure gauges can work with the existing oil pressure sending unit.

Oil temperature gauge - The oil temperature gauge tells you the temperature of the engine oil, which is generally considered a more accurate way of monitoring engine temperature.

Shift light - A shift light is a large, bright LED that can be programmed to come on at a specific, predetermined rpm level. You don't have to take your eyes off the road to watch a shift light; because of its intensity, a shift light can be seen out of the corner of your eye. A shift light can be located on the face of a special aftermarket drag racing tachometer or housed in a separate enclosure mounted on top of the dash.

Tachometer - The tachometer tells you the engine speed in revolutions-per-minute, or rpm. Some aftermarket tachs are also equipped with shift lights, which can be programmed to come on at the desired rpm. And some of the top-of-the-line units even make a recording of each run (or even multiple runs) so that you can analyze the data afterwards.

Voltmeter - The voltmeter tells you the voltage output of your alternator.

G-Tech tuning tools

G-Tech/Pro

One interesting and very helpful product in aftermarket instrumentation is the G-TECH/Pro, which is manufactured by Tesla Electronics of Duarte, California. The G-TECH/Pro uses a silicon accelerometer, which is a sensor that can measure acceleration, or G-force. (One G, which equals 32 ft/sec^2, or 32 feet per second per second, is the rate at which an object falls in the field of gravity.) The G-TECH/Pro measures the speed and distance traveled by integrating acceleration over time. For example, if you know how quickly you are accelerating for a specific period of time, you can calculate how much your speed has changed after that time period. Therefore, if you start at zero mph, then you will know what your speed is at the end of each time period. G-TECH/Pro breaks each run down into a series of 2.5 millisecond intervals, so it's very accurate. Distance is measured the same way: If you know how fast you're going for a specific period of time, you'll be able to calculate the distance traveled during that time period. Using the formula Speed x Acceleration x Weight (of the vehicle), G-TECH/Pro can also measure delivered horsepower (the horsepower at the rear wheels, which is normally 10 to 15 percent less than crankshaft horsepower because of the frictional losses in the drivetrain).

Unlike the other instruments discussed in this Chapter, the G-TECH/Pro is ridiculously easy to install. Simply position the G-TECH/Pro in the middle of the dash (below the rear view mirror), push the rubber suction cup against the inside surface of the windshield, level the G-TECH/Pro and plug it into your cigarette lighter. That's all there is to it. You're ready to go!

The powerful and versatile G-TECH/Pro can measure:

Zero-to-60 mph time
60-to-zero mph braking distance
1/4-mile E.T.
1/4-mile trap speed
Horsepower
Instantaneous Gs
Continuous Gs

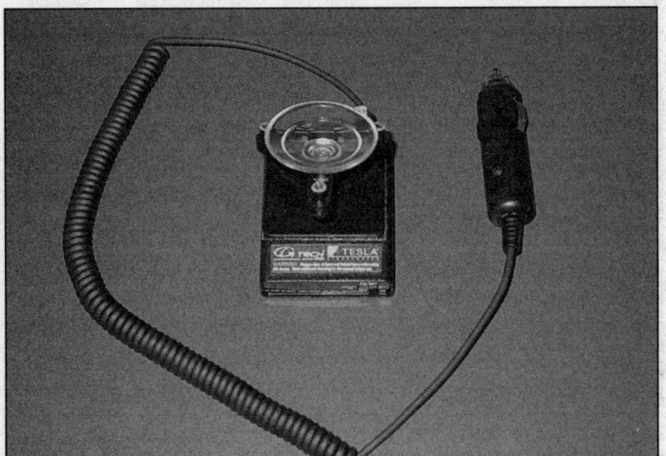

The G-Tech/Pro measures the speed and distance traveled by integrating acceleration over time. For example, if you know how quickly you're accelerating for a specific period of time, you can calculate how much your speed has changed after that time period. Therefore, if you start at zero mph, then you'll know your speed at the end of each time period

The G-Tech/Pro is easy to install: Affix the rubber suction cup to the inside of the windshield, plug in the power lead to the cigarette lighter or a 12V accessory outlet and you're ready to go

G-Tech/Pro COMPETITION

The G-Tech/Pro COMPETITION tuning tool is the more sophisticated successor to the original G-Tech/Pro. The COMPETITION model incorporates several improvements over the original unit. First, it uses three temperature-compensated accelerometers (the G-Tech/Pro only has one accelerometer), which improves its accuracy. Second, it uses a more sophisticated new calibration algorithm. The new unit also has 32 times higher resolution, and new noise-correction algorithms improve overall accuracy. Tesla Electronics claims that these improvements bring accuracy to within 5/100th of a second and consistency (repeatability) within 5/1000th of a second.

The G-Tech/Pro COMPETITION is just as easy to install as the original G-Tech/Pro. And unlike the original unit, the COMPETITION model is self-leveling (you have to make sure that the G-Tech/Pro is level, or it won't produce accurate data).

The G-Tech/Pro COMPETITION model can measure:

1/4-mile E.T. and top speed
1/8-mile E.T. and top speed
1000 foot time
Accelerating and braking Gs
Braking distance
Engine rpm
Engine rpm vs. time graph
Gs vs. time graph
Handling Gs
Horsepower
Horsepower and torque vs. rpm graph
Reaction time
Speed vs. distance graph
Speed vs. time graph
Torque
Zero-to-100 mph
Zero-to-330 feet
Zero-to-60 feet
Zero-to-60 mph

Another advantage of the COMPETITION model is its portability. You can remove it from its mounting bracket to study your tuning data more closely. You can review the results, store logged runs that you want to save and even change the settings before putting the unit back in the car. Or in another car: Specific vehicle data such as weight and shift light settings can be stored and recalled for up to four vehicles.

Scan tools: Spend some quality time with your car's computer

Hand-held scan tools are the most powerful and versatile tools for troubleshooting the engine management systems on modern cars. Think of the scan tool as a way to peek inside your engine's brain. The operating parameters of the information sensors and the output actuators are stored in the computer's "map" (memory). As long as everything operates within its intended range, the system works well. But when a sensor or actuator, or even the PCM itself, begins to operate outside that narrow range - too much or too little voltage, too much or too little resistance, etc. - the computer notes each little out-of-range excursion and stores it for future use. When a sensor or actuator circuit has operated out of range too many times, or even just one time but for too long an interval, the PCM sets a diagnostic trouble code and stores the code in its memory. Then it turns on the Check Engine light, also referred to as the Service Engine Soon light or the Malfunction Indicator Lamp (MIL), on the dash to let you know that something's up.

These Actron and Auto XRay scan tools are typical of the dozens of aftermarket scanners now available at auto parts stores everywhere

On some pre-OBD-II cars (1995 and earlier) you might be able to put the computer into a diagnostic output mode in which it displays the code(s) by flashing the Check Engine light on and off. But on all 1996 and later cars, you'll need a code reader or a scan tool to extract and identify the code(s). And even on earlier vehicles, a scan tool will tell you a lot more information than just the diagnostic code number by itself.

Little engine modifications (upgraded spark plug wires, a less restrictive air filter, etc.) won't have much effect on the serial data being exchanged between the information sensors, the PCM and the actuators. But as the number and complexity of your engine mods increases, sooner or later you will do something that causes a sensor or its circuit to go out of range. A scan tool can help you understand how a recent modification affects the overall operation of your engine because you can look at the data. For example, let's say that you just installed an air/fuel ratio gauge. If you spliced into the signal wire between the oxygen sensor and the PCM (as some aftermarket manufacturers recommend), the addition of the new gauge might slightly alter the small millivolt output of the oxygen sensor that the PCM receives. As long as the tiny voltage signal produced by the oxygen sensor stays within the upper and lower boundaries of its operating range, the PCM will interpret the weaker-than-usual signal as a "leaner-than-normal" but still accurate representation of how much oxygen is actually in the exhaust gases. Then it *enriches* the mixture by turning on the injectors a little longer, even though the air/fuel mixture is actually okay. This will waste fuel, increase emissions and decrease power and mileage. Eventually, by comparing incoming data from other sensors, the PCM will determine that there is something wrong with the oxygen sensor circuit and it will set a diagnostic trouble code. With a scan tool, you can quickly identify the problem circuit and make the necessary repairs before the rich mixture damages the catalytic converter.

A high-end scan tool can also help you diagnose the most maddening intermittent driveability problems by allowing you to retrieve freeze frame data from the memory of the PCM. Freeze frame data is a digital recording of the data that's been transmitted back and forth between the sensors, the PCM and the actuators, for the interval during which a sensor or actuator circuit operated outside its intended range. This ability to look back at the actual circuit voltage values immediately before and after a malfunction occurred is a powerful diagnostic tool. Without a scan tool, the only way to diagnose an intermittent problem is to have the vehicle checked at a dealer service department or other qualified repair shop.

Professional-grade scan tools have all the bells and whistles such as freeze frame, but they're somewhat expensive. Generic aftermarket scan tools, which are much more affordable, are now widely available at auto parts stores. These tools, which are designed for the do-it-yourselfer, are not as powerful or versatile as professional units, but they *can* display all "P-Zero" codes (the non-proprietary codes that can be viewed by someone not working at a dealership). Some of the better units can tell you a little about each code and can indicate whether a circuit is operating inside or outside its intended operating range.

Another recent addition to the growing diagnose-it-yourself market is diagnostic software that turns your laptop into a powerful scan tool. In some ways it is even more user-friendly than a scan tool, since more information can be displayed, graphically, at one time. Scan-tool software kits usually include everything you need to get started with diagnosis, including an interface cable that attaches to your computer and plugs into the diagnostic connector of your vehicle. **Warning:** *When using a laptop computer in the vehicle, keep it off of your lap when driving! If the vehicle is equipped with a passenger-side airbag, keep it off of the passenger's lap, too. In the event of an accident, the last thing you want is a computer being launched into your (or your passenger's) face! Also, when using any scan tool while driving the vehicle, keep your eyes on the road - not the scanner. Most scan tools are capable of recording and storing data, which can be played back after the test drive.*

Laptop too bulky for you? One of the newest developments in hand-held scan tools is software for the Personal Digital Assistant, or PDA. Firms such as Auto Enginuity and IPM Software offer software that turns your PDA into a scan tool! Some of this software rivals the most sophisticated factory scan tools for power and versatility, and costs no more than a generic scan tool.

Installing a Tachometer

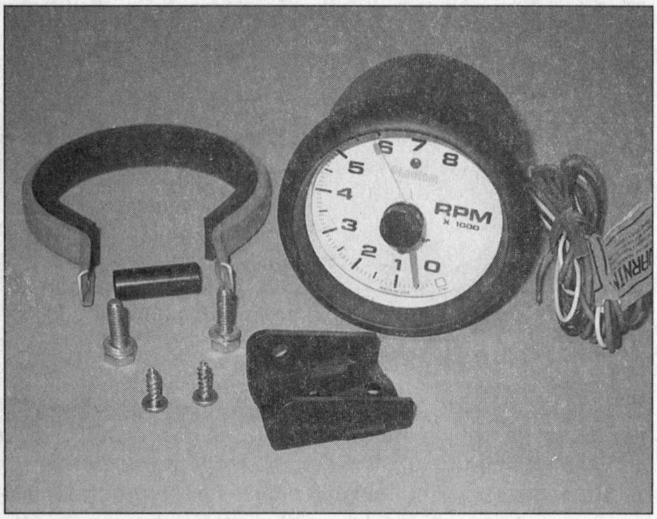

1 Before starting this procedure make sure that everything - tach, mounting bracket, fasteners, wiring, instructions, etc. - is included. Then read the instructions carefully and make sure you understand them before you get going

2 Mount the tach where it will be easy to see without taking your eyes off the road. Make sure that the dash material is substantial enough to support the tach mounting bracket. When you've settled on the right spot, mark the position of the mounting bracket

3 Remove the tach from the mounting bracket and mark the position of the bracket holes for drilling. Make sure that the bracket is angled so that the mounted tach will be facing directly at you

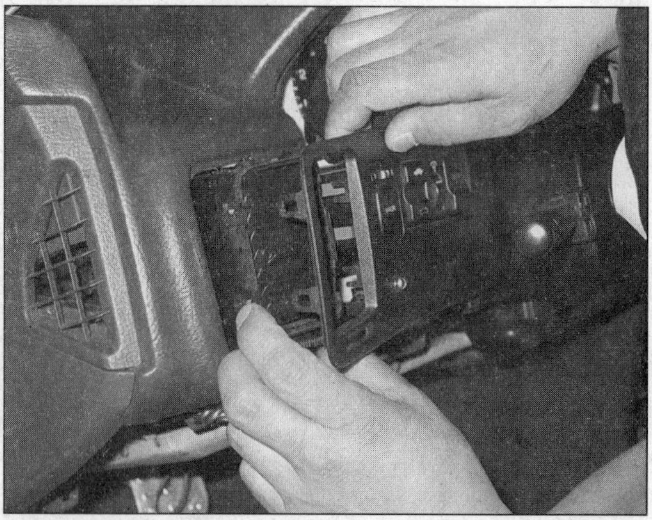

4 Before you drill anything, remove the appropriate switch or trim panel from the dash below the mounting area (refer to the Haynes manual for your car if you don't know how to remove the trim panel) . . .

5 . . . and verify that your drill bit (and mounting screws) won't hit anything important like electrical wiring

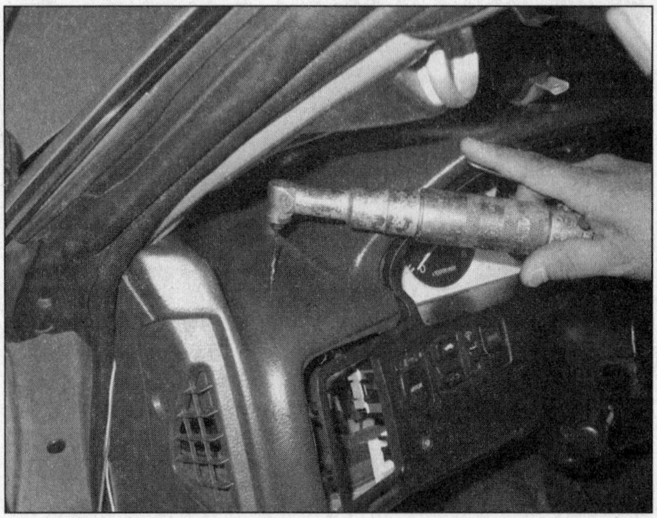

6 Carefully drill the mounting bracket holes

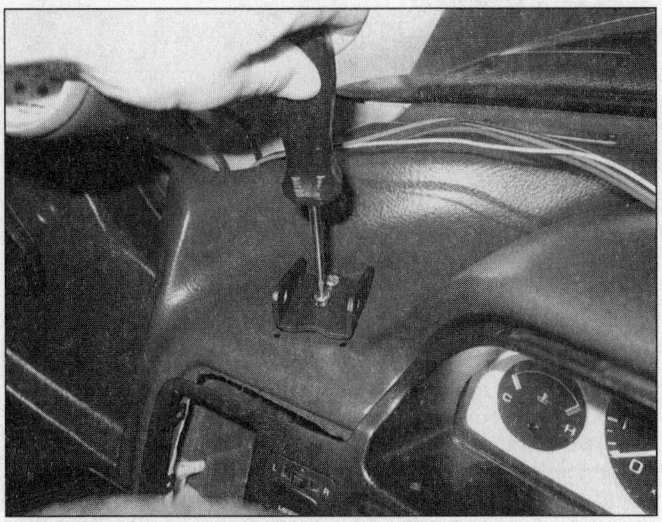

7 Place the tach mounting bracket in position, align it with your marks, install the bracket screws and tighten them securely, but don't overtorque them or you will strip out the dash material

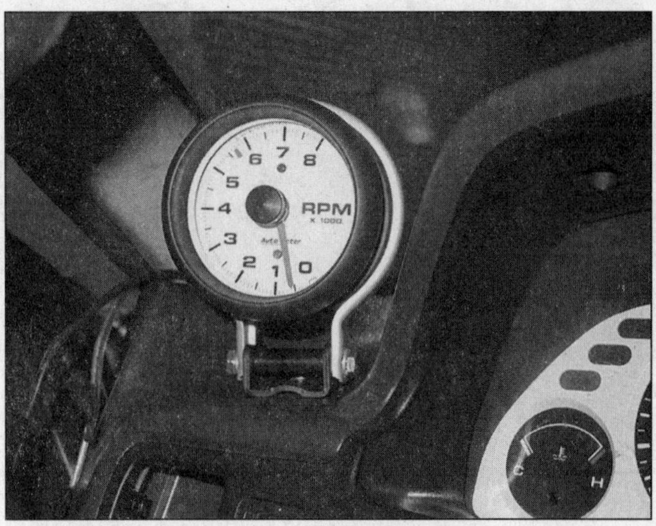

8 Install the tach in its mounting clamp, then bolt the clamp to the mounting bracket. Before tightening the mounting bolt and nut, hop in, adjust the seat to your regular driving position and adjust the angle of the tach so that it's facing directly at you

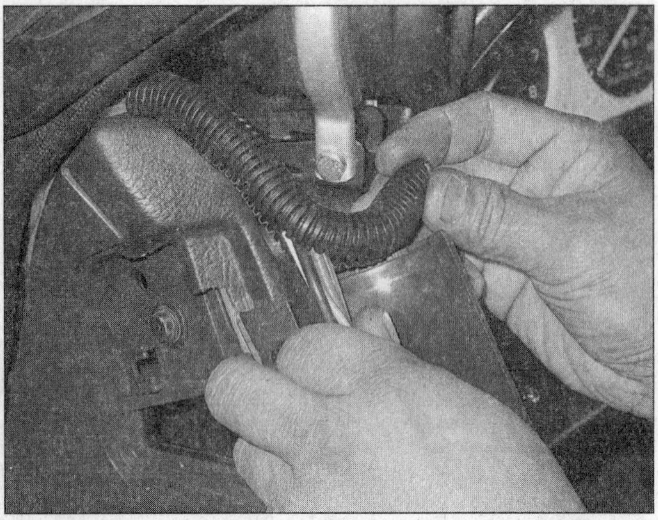

9 Most electrical tachs have four wires: power, ground, illumination and signal. To route the wires so that they're hidden from view, we ran them through a gap between the left end of the dash and the A-pillar trim. Then we covered the short exposed section of wiring between the tach and the pillar with some split loom tubing

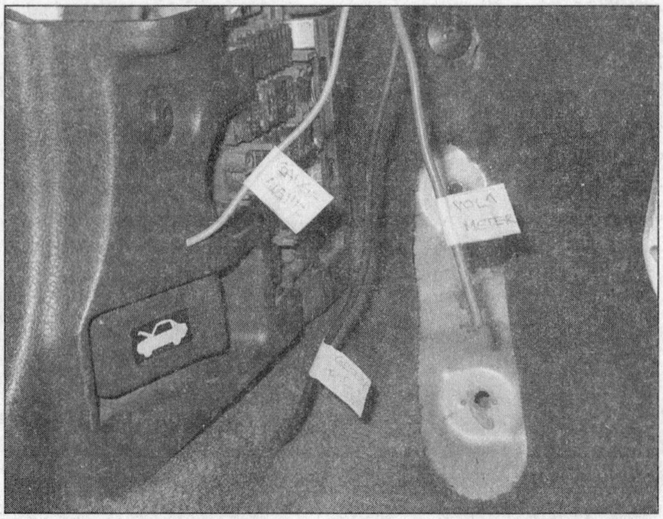

10 Pull the wires down to the interior fuse panel (usually located on the left kick panel, or tucked up under the left end of the dash) and cut off the excess, but leave enough so there's plenty of room to add connectors to the ends. If you're new to wiring, it's a good idea to label the wires so that you don't mix them up

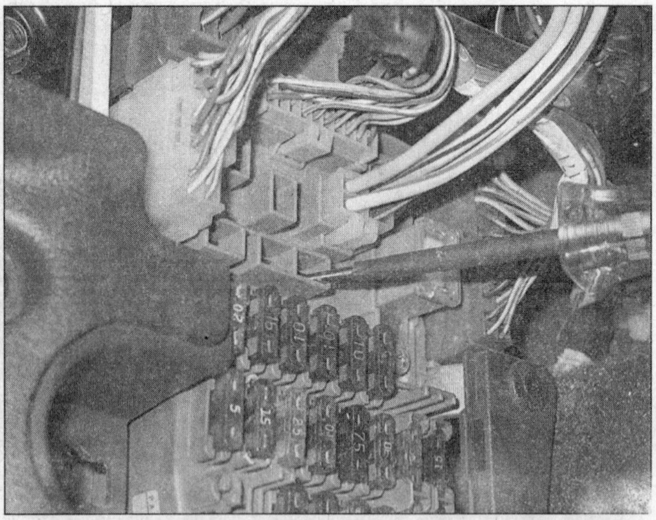

11 Now you're ready to start hooking up the wires. First, using a test light or continuity tester, find a pair of vacant 12-volt terminals on the fuse panel for your power (usually red) and illumination (usually white) wires. You want a switched 12-volt terminal for the power wire, which means that it's an open circuit when the car is turned off, but hot when the ignition key is switched to ON. You'll also need a switched 12-volt terminal for the illumination wire that's open circuit when the lights are turned off, but hot when the parking lights are switched on

12 Strip off about 1/4 to 3/8-inch of insulation from each wire, crimp a connector the same size as the spade terminals you're going to hook up to and connect the power and illumination wires to the fuse panel. Those of you with sharp eyes will notice that these wires are oversize. That's because we plan to use these same wires for the illumination and power leads to the pillar pod gauges and the air/fuel ratio meter that we're also going to install

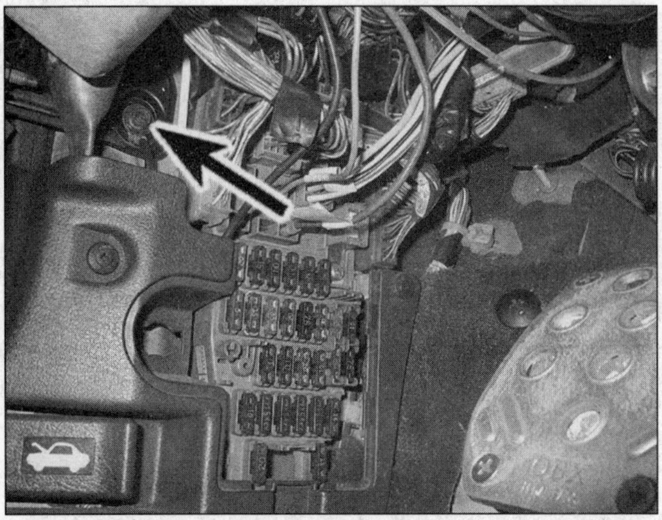

13 Look for a close and convenient fastener to connect the ground wire. Make sure that it grounds the wire to metal. We attached the ground wire to the body at this crossmember brace bolt. If you can't find a fastener nearby, drill a hole into the body and attach the ground wire with a self-tapping sheet metal screw

14 Unlike the other three wires, the signal wire must be routed through the firewall to the engine compartment. Look for a convenient cable grommet (throttle, clutch, hood release, etc.) in the firewall and make a hole in it with an awl. We used the clutch cable grommet because it's big and because it's easy to get to

15 Insert a short length of tubing through the hole in the grommet. The tubing should be just big enough in diameter to insert the signal wire. (If the tubing is too big, seal the outer end with silicone to prevent water from entering the passenger compartment during bad weather.)

16 Insert the signal wire through the plastic tube from under the dash and pull it through from the engine compartment side. Crimp on a suitable connector and connect the signal wire to the negative primary terminal on the ignition coil (standard-type coil) or to the auxiliary terminal meant for a tach wire (aftermarket, high-performance coil). That's it. Done!

Installing pillar pod gauges

If your dash has no room for any more gauges, consider using the driver's side A-pillar, where you can easily install three or four extra gauges. You can install almost any 2-inch or 2-1/16 inch gauge on the A-pillar. The vehicle shown here was already equipped with a water temperature gauge in a single pillar pod. We decided to add an oil pressure gauge and voltmeter to the pillar right above the existing gauge. Why oil pressure and voltage? Because these are the two other functions that should be monitored closely, and because we want to show you how to install a typical mechanical type gauge (oil pressure) and a typical electrical gauge (voltmeter). Although every installation is somewhat specific to the type of gauge(s) being installed and to the make and model of car in which you're installing the gauge(s), the installation procedure shown here is quite similar to the procedure you would follow for any electrical or mechanical gauge. The differences are in the details, which you will find in the instructions for the gauge kit(s) you decide to use.

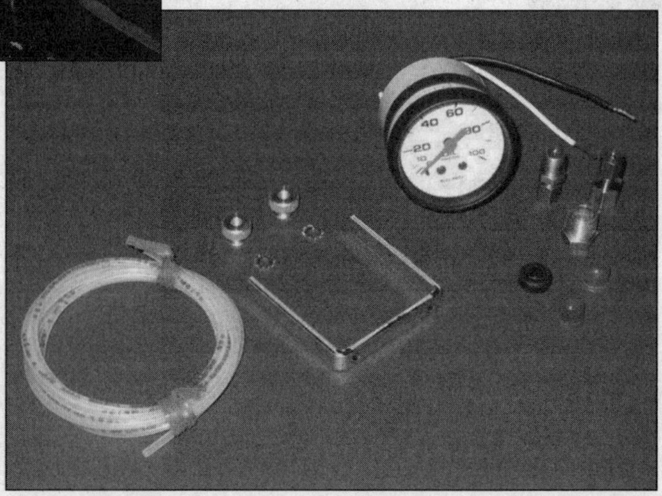

1 Unpack the oil pressure gauge kit and make sure you have everything you'll need to install it. If you're installing a mechanical type oil pressure gauge like this one, you'll need to tap into the hole in the block or cylinder head for the oil pressure sender (or a convenient hole in the block with an oil gallery behind it). So make sure that the kit includes all the adapter fittings you'll need to tee into the existing hole for the oil pressure sender

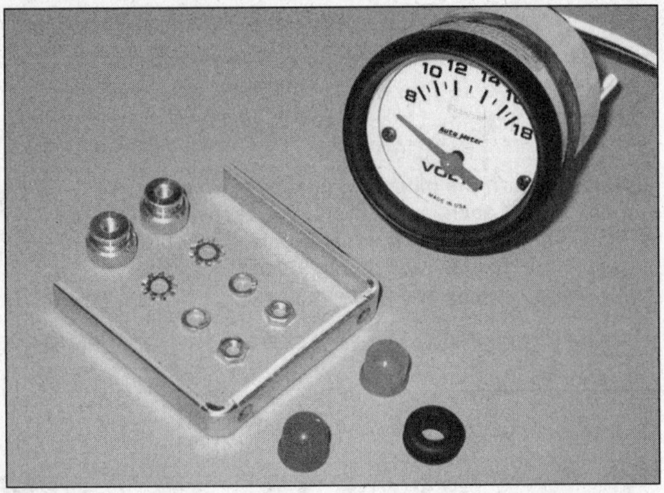

2 Unpack the voltmeter kit and make sure everything is there. Unlike oil pressure gauges, voltmeters are pretty simple to install. Once you've inventoried everything for both kits, push them aside (but keep them separate!) and read the instructions that came with each kit. Pay close attention to all notes, cautions and warnings by the gauge manufacturer. For example, if a manufacturer specifies a certain gauge wire for a 12-volt connection, don't try to skimp by using a smaller wire than specified, or you might see smoke coming from your new gauge!

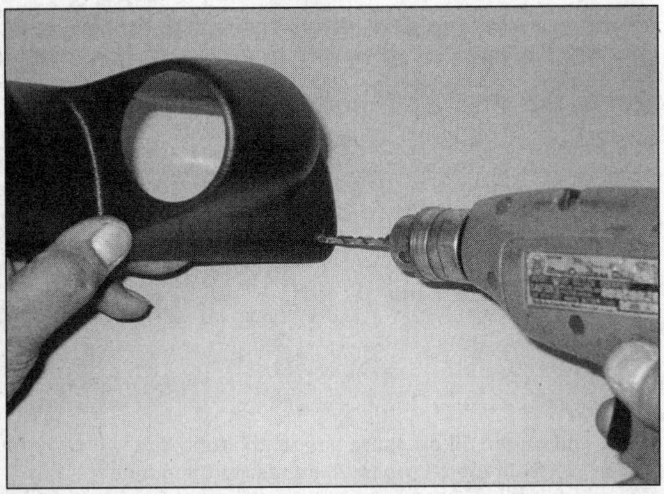

3 Okay, let's get started. Get your pillar pod and dummy it up exactly where you want to put it. Make sure it's a good fit before proceeding. Then, using a 3/16-inch bit, drill a hole at each corner of the pod as shown

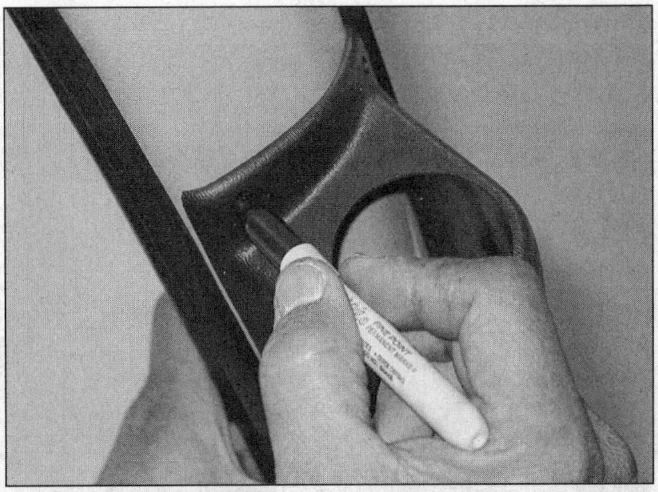

4 Place the pod in position on the pillar and mark the locations of the four holes you're going to drill. Make sure the holes aren't going to be too close to the edges of the pillar

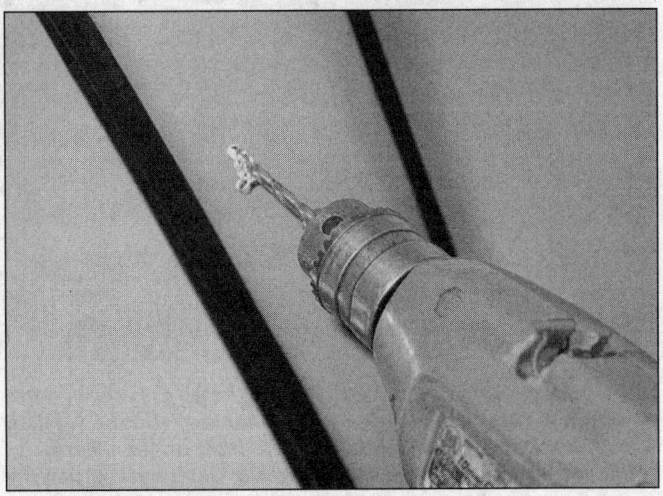

5 Using the same 3/16-inch bit, drill the holes in the pillar

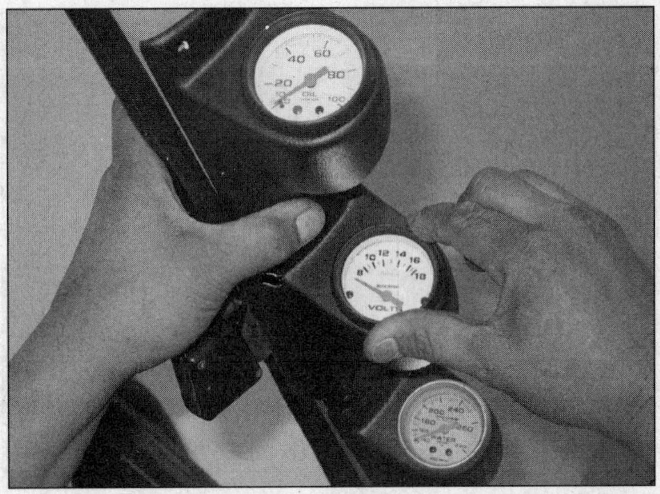

6 Insert the gauges into the pillar pod, place the pod in position on the pillar, then rotate the gauges so the "OIL" and "VOLTS" on the gauge faces are horizontal and parallel to each other

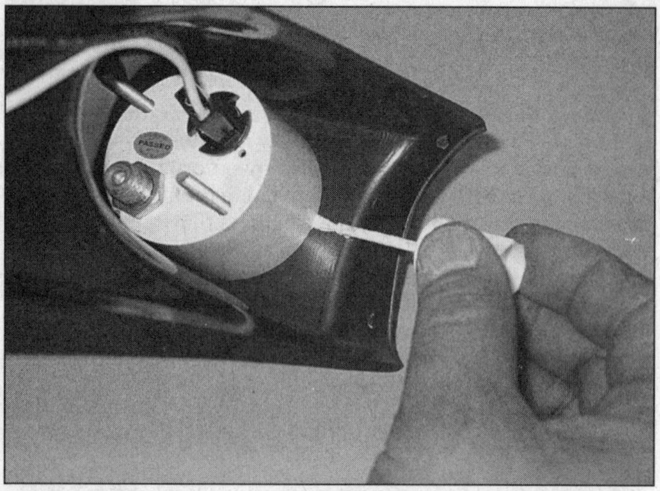

7 Carefully turn the pillar pod upside down and mark the position of each gauge in relation to the pod. (We're using typing correction fluid, available at any office supply store, to make the marks. Its brilliant white color is easy to see, and it doesn't run.)

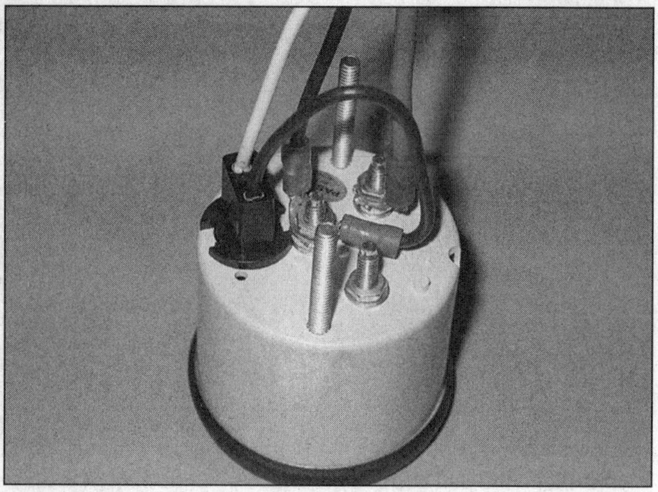

8 Remove the gauges from the pillar pod and connect the wires for power, ground and illumination . . .

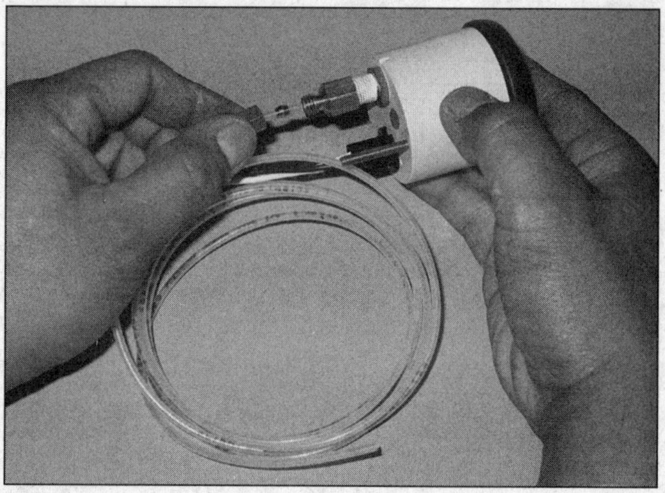

9 . . . and on the oil pressure gauge, the tube that will carry oil from the oil pressure sender to the gauge

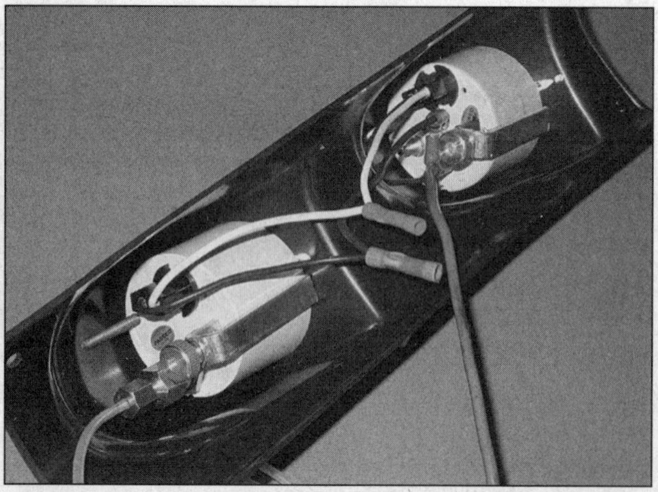

10 Reinstall the gauges in the pillar pod and clamp them into place with the clamps provided by the manufacturer. Note how we spliced the two illumination bulb wires and the two ground wires together

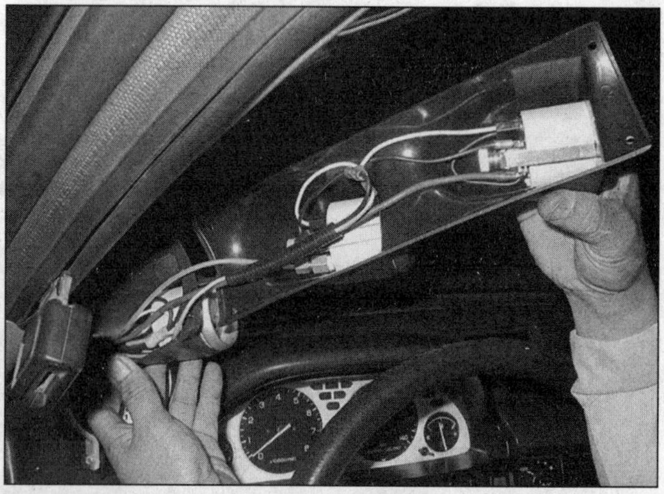

11 Route the wires and the oil line for the oil pressure gauge through the gap between the end of the dash and the A-pillar, then install the pillar pod/gauge assembly on the pillar and attach it with the four mounting screws. Don't overtighten the screws or you'll strip out the holes. When you're done with this phase, hide the wires with some split-loom tubing

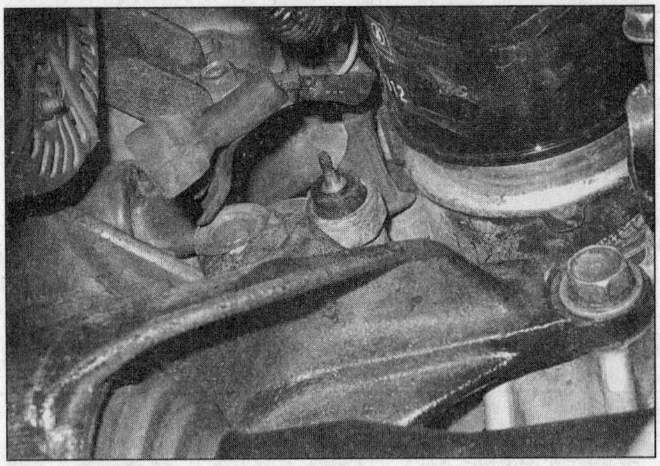

12 We spliced the power, illumination and ground leads from all three pillar pod gauges into the same leads we used for the illumination and ground wires for the tachometer. Then we routed the oil line for the oil pressure gauge through the firewall to the engine compartment using the same tube that we installed in the clutch cable grommet for the signal wire to the tachometer

13 Locate the oil pressure sending unit and disconnect the electrical connector from the sender. The sender is usually - but not always - located somewhere near the oil filter. (Refer to your Haynes manual if you have difficulty finding it.) Be prepared to catch any oil that runs out when you remove the sender. The lower the sensor location on the head or block, the more oil you'll lose when you remove it

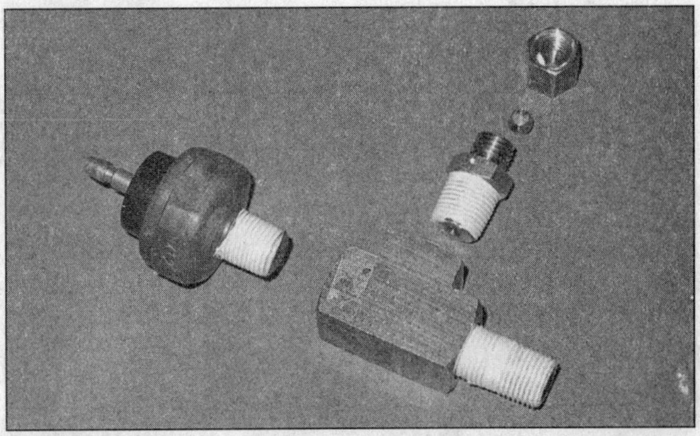

14 Here's our setup for tee-ing into the stock sending unit installation. Before assembling, be sure to wrap the threads of the sender, the adapter fitting and the compression fitting with Teflon tape to prevent leaks

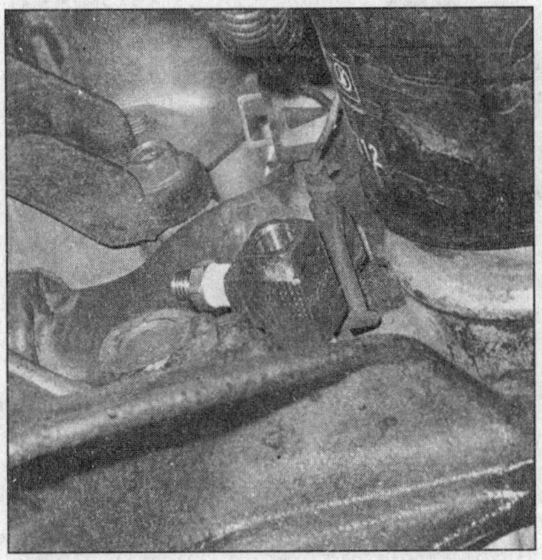

15 Screw the tee-fitting adapter into the block and tighten securely. Make sure that the compression fitting is pointing in a direction that will allow easy connection of the oil pressure gauge line

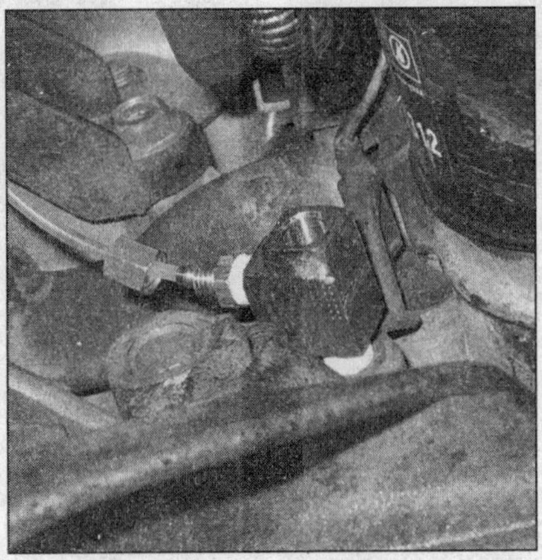

16 Insert the line into the compression fitting, slide the olive down the line until it seats inside the open end of the fitting, thread the nut on and tighten it securely

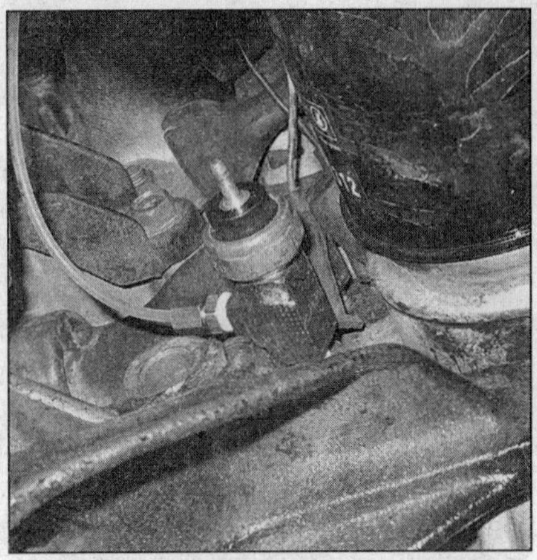

17 Screw on the oil pressure sending unit, tighten it securely, reconnect the electrical connector to the sender and you're done!

Installing a wide-band air/fuel ratio gauge

Is your dashboard getting crowded? How about the area at the forward end of the center console, where most manufacturers put the ashtray? Remove the ashtray and see whether the air/fuel ratio gauge will fit in the ashtray receptacle. Unlike an oil pressure or water temperature gauge, an air/fuel ratio gauge is more of a tuning aid, not part of your early warning system, so it doesn't need to stare you in the face.

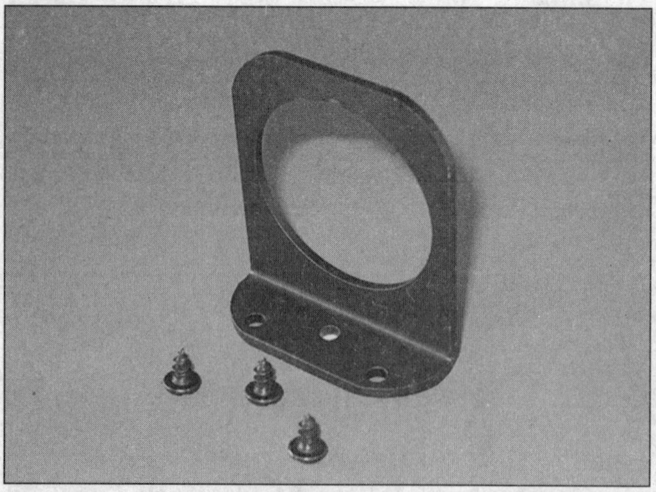

1 Most gauge manufacturers offer a wide variety of mounting solutions for any gauge installation. We purchased this 2-1/16 inch diameter gauge bracket, which was designed for under-dash installations, but works just fine for this job

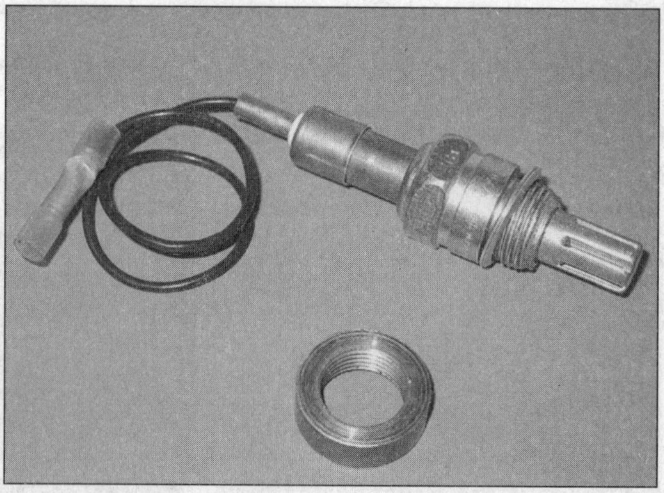

2 You'll also need to purchase a 5-volt wide-band oxygen sensor and a weld-in boss from the manufacturer of the gauge. Don't buy a sensor from the manufacturer of your car. It will cost more money, it will be a 2-volt narrow-band sensor and it won't include the weld-in boss, which you're going to need in order to screw the new sensor into the exhaust pipe

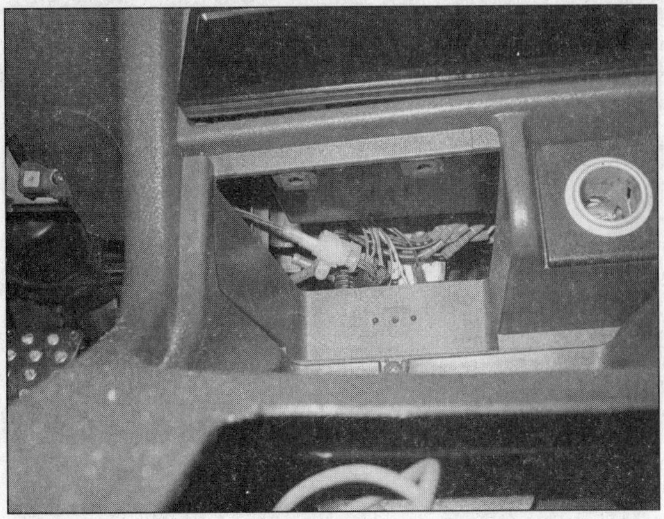

3 After removing the entire ashtray assembly, we discovered a couple of mounting holes that we could use for our under-dash mounting bracket. We also discovered a big hole behind the ashtray receptacle through which we could route the wires (another reason why the ashtray receptacle is a good location for this or any other gauge which you might wish to install in this location)

4 For our installation, we removed the gauge and installed the bracket first, then installed the gauge in the bracket. We routed the power (red), ground (black) and illumination (white) wires over to the fuse panel and spliced them into the same power, illumination and ground connections that we created for the tachometer installation

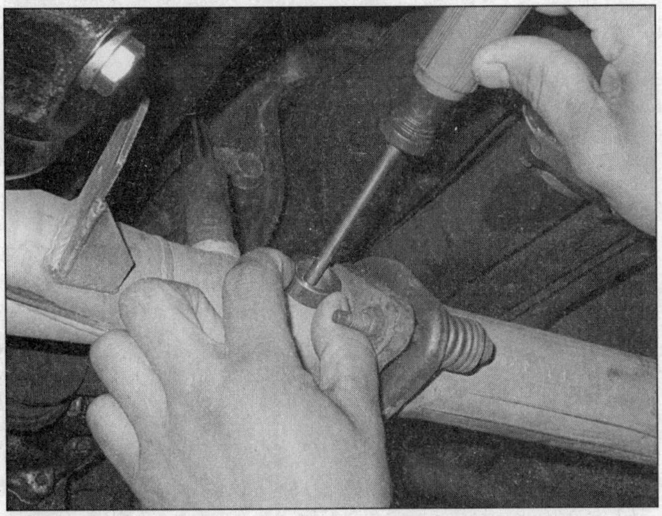

5 Now for the fun part! There's no place to install your new wide-band oxygen sensor, so you're going to have to make one. First, mark the spot with a punch where you want to install the new sensor. For the best accuracy, it should be in the exhaust pipe just ahead of the catalytic converter. On an OBD-II vehicle, this means it will be have to be located near the upstream oxygen sensor for the engine management computer; just make sure that it's not so close that the sensor tips touch

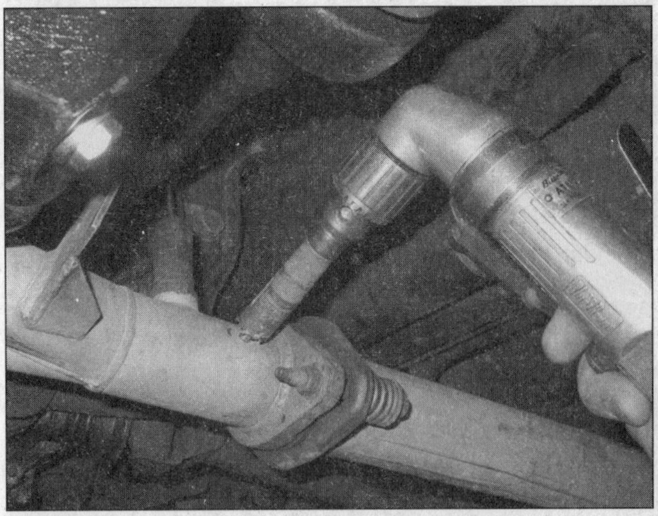

6 Using a hole saw bit, drill a hole in the exhaust, then clean up the edge around the hole with a small grinding tool until it's smooth and clean

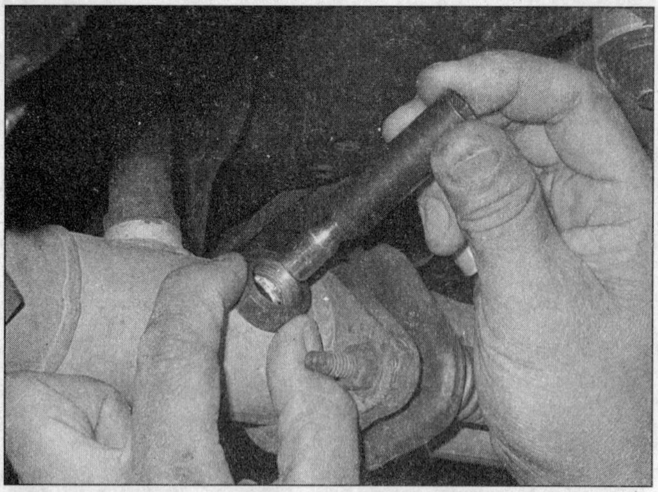

7 Once you've drilled the hole and cleaned it up, place the weld-in boss over the hole, center it with a socket and an extension to keep it exactly in place

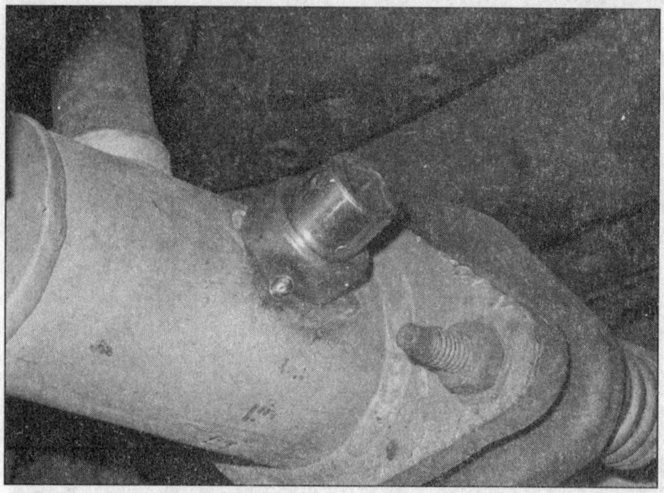

8 Tack the boss into place

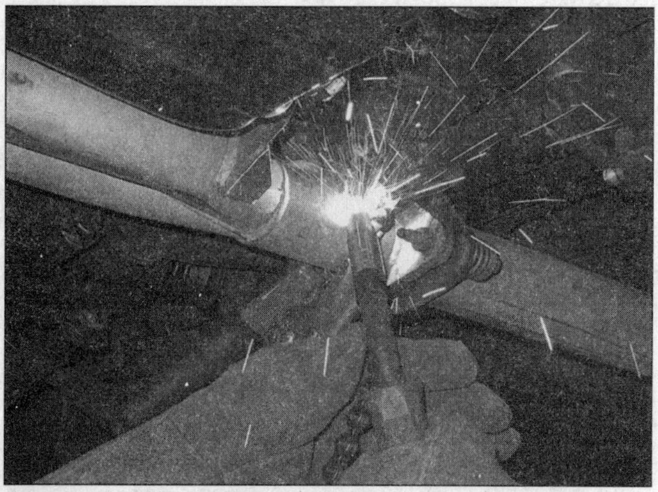

9 With the boss tacked into position, remove the socket/ extension, then weld the boss to the exhaust pipe

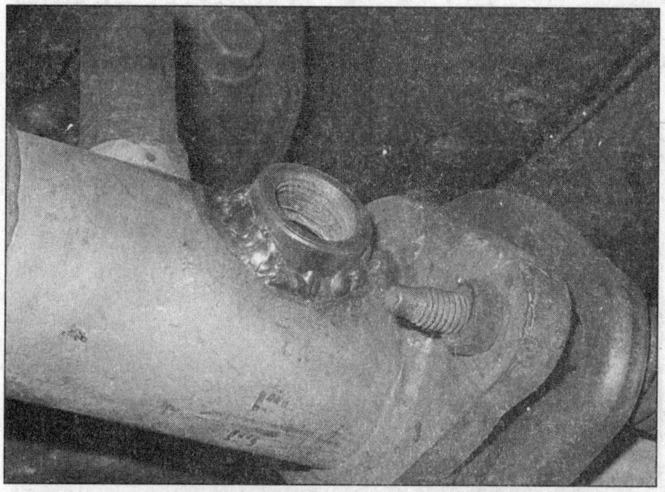

10 Inspect your work and make sure the weld completely surrounds the boss, with no holes. Any holes will allow air into the exhaust system and will cause false readings

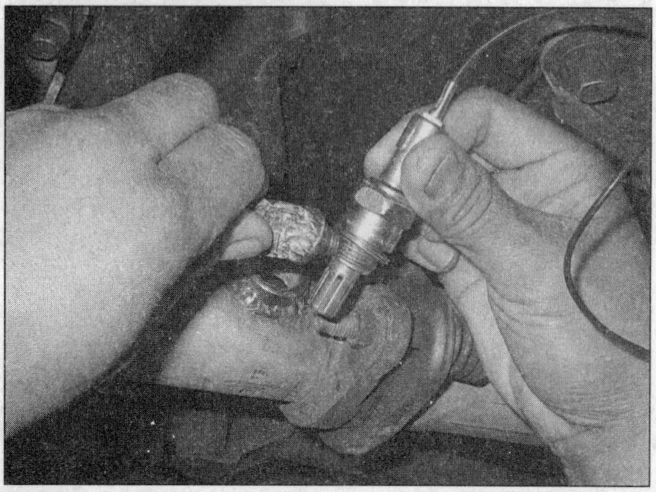

11 Apply a film of anti-seize compound to the threads of the new wide-band sensor . . .

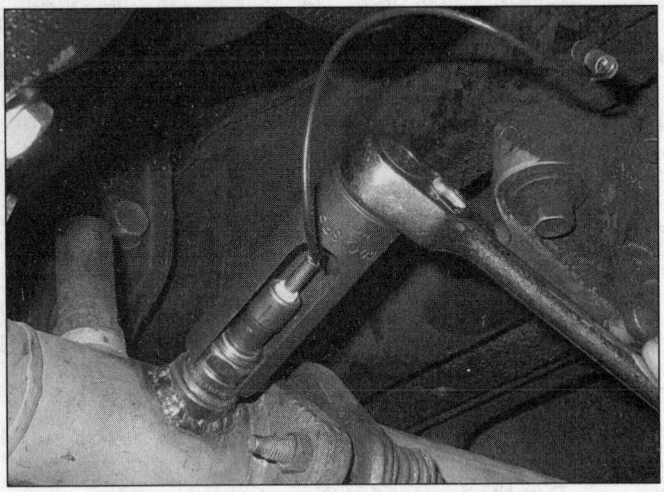

12 . . . then screw the sensor securely into the boss (a special oxygen sensor socket is being used here)

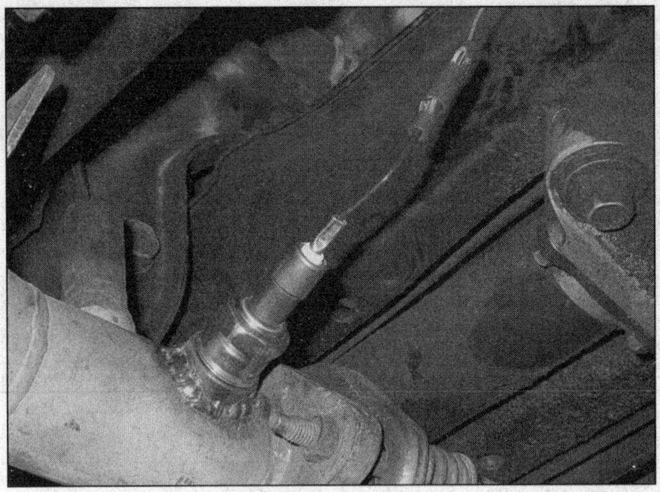

13 Finally, attach the sensor wire to the gauge wire; we used a butt connector here. Now lower the vehicle and test the gauge. Keep in mind that the gauge won't give you an accurate reading until the sensor is fully warmed up

Innovate LM-1 wide-band air/fuel ratio meter

There are several ways to tune high-performance engines. One way is to measure the temperature of the exhaust gases as they exit the cylinder head. The trouble with this method is that not all engines are optimized at the same temperature, meaning that there is a lot of trial and error involved in determining what is the best temperature for your engine. For the professional with an engine dyno and sufficient time, tuning an engine by measuring the temperature of the exhaust gases can produce results. But an amateur enthusiast with limited time and money will quickly run out of both, not to mention patience!

Another time honored tuning method is by examining the spark plugs. But again, even though this can be a valuable tuning tool for the professional with the right know how, it takes a lot of experience before you can extract much useful information from looking at the plugs.

Then there's the wide-band air/fuel ratio meter. With its 0 to 5-volt range, a wide-band air/fuel ratio meter is accurate and its results are easy to decipher. Tuning experts, amateur and professional alike, have known about wide-band air/fuel ratio meters for a decade or more. But until recently, wide-band oxygen sensors were so expensive that nobody but the high-end tuning firms used them. Now Innovate Motorsports makes this technology available at a price that most enthusiasts can afford.

Innovate's digital hand-held unit, the LM-1, is no bigger than a small scan tool, but it packs a big punch. Its digital signal-processing technology samples your engine's exhaust 12 times a second, showing exactly how rich or lean the engine is running at a given rpm. And its self-calibrating circuitry even compensates for changes in altitude and temperature. With the LM-1 you can adjust variables such as carb-jetting or fuel injection tuning in your driveway.

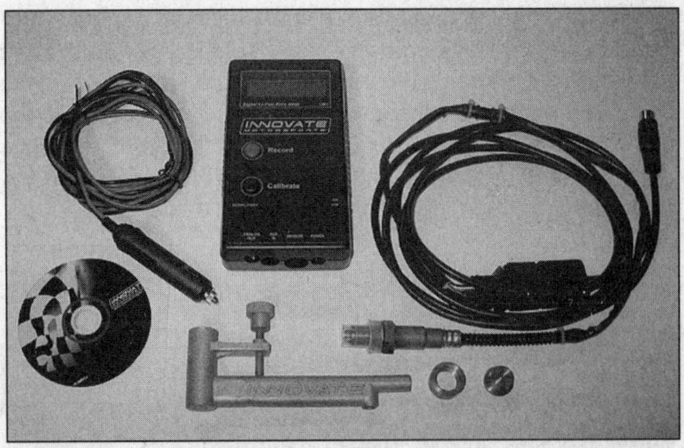

Innovate's fully digital LM-1 wide-band controller kit includes a wide-band Bosch sensor and sensor extension cable, a power cable, a boss that you weld onto the exhaust pipe and a screw-in plug to cap the boss when it's not in use, plus a CD that walks you through all the various diagnostic procedures that this tool can do

Got a desktop or laptop PC? The LM-1 can store up to

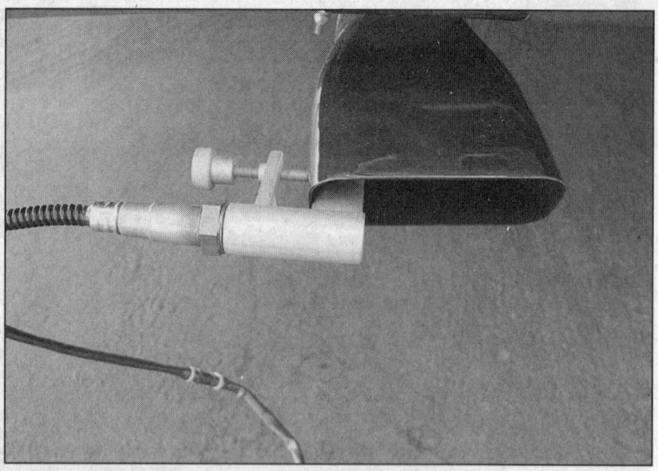

Innovate offers an optional clamp for installing the wide-band sensor in the tailpipe on vehicles without any catalytic converters. Simply insert the clamp into the tailpipe, tighten the clamp screw and screw the sensor into the clamp

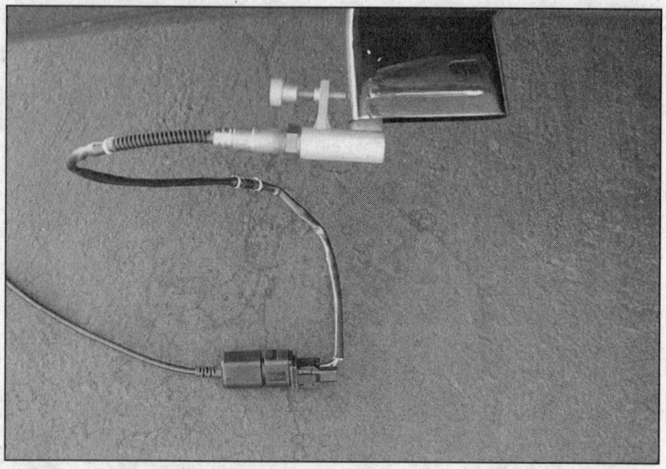

Plug the other end of the sensor lead into the extension cable . . .

44 minutes of data in memory. You can download this data onto your PC or laptop hard drive via a standard serial port and display the data using any standard spreadsheet program, such as Microsoft's Excel. Innovate also offers a wide array of accessories including auxiliary input cables, a battery clip power cable, an AC adapter, an analog display and adjuster cable and even a dash-mounted digital display.

If you're going to be tuning a fuel-injected engine, you'll need to weld a boss onto the exhaust pipe right before the catalytic converter. It's the same procedure you would use to install a wide-band sensor for an air/fuel ratio gauge. Raise the vehicle and place it securely on jackstands. If you have after-hours access to a vehicle hoist at a friend's neighborhood garage or shop, the job will be a lot easier.

Weld the boss onto the exhaust pipe somewhere just upstream in relation to the catalytic converter. If possible, pick a spot on the upper half of the exhaust pipe so that the sensor isn't affected by moisture. Drill an 18 mm hole in the exhaust pipe. Weld on the boss, then screw in the wide-band air/fuel ratio sensor and you're ready to tune!

If you're working on an older vehicle without any catalytic converters, purchase the optional tapped exhaust clamp, which enables you to install the wide-band sensor in any tailpipe. The clamp is a sturdy, well-designed piece. Simply insert the clamp into the tailpipe, tighten the clamp bolt, then screw the sensor into the clamp. The rest of the hook-up procedure is even simpler. Once you're ready to go, all you have to do is follow the instructions in the CD that comes with the kit.

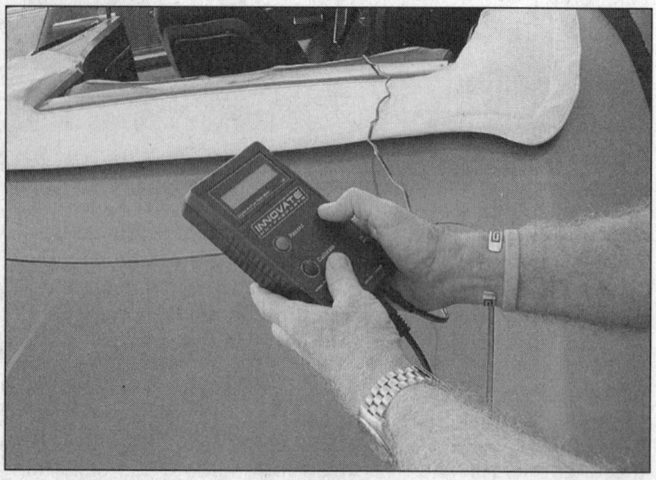

. . . then plug the extension cable into the LM-1 and the power lead into the cigarette lighter. That's all there is to it. You're ready to tune!

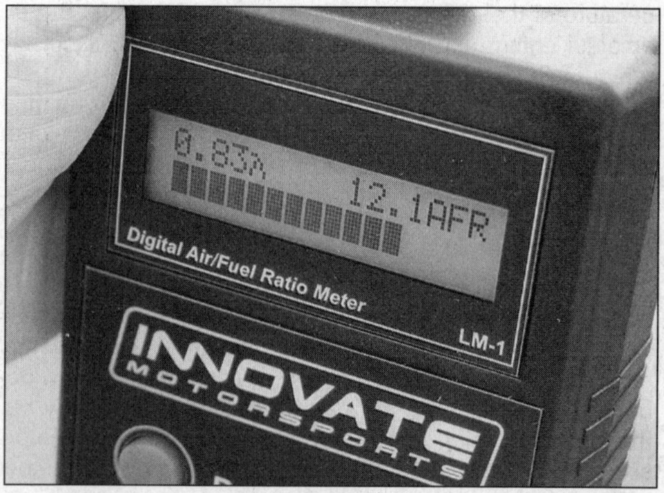

Once the engine is warmed up, turn on the LM-1 and take a reading. This reading (which is being taken on a 500 horsepower 1970 Dodge Coronet 440 punched out to 500 cubic inches) is a little rich

Innovate LMA-3 Multi-sensor Device (AuxBox)

If you're working on a fuel-injected vehicle, you'll want to pick up Innovate's LMA-3 Multi-Sensor Device, or AuxBox. The LMA-3, which was purpose built to work with the LM-1, plugs right in to the LM-1. The LMA-3 has five built-in sensors: Manifold Air Pressure (MAP or boost), Cylinder Heat Temperature (CHT) or Exhaust Gas Temperature (EGT), engine speed (rpm conversion from a tach signal or an inductive clamp), Acceleration (two-axis accelerometer), and injector duty cycle (or dwell). The AuxBox also includes five external inputs for hooking up to the external sensors of your choice instead of using the internal sensors, which allows you to log data from other sensors, like the Throttle Position (TP) sensor.

The LMA-3 is a powerful tool. Of course, it's not quite as elementary as the LM-1, but Innovate goes overboard to provide you with the information that you'll need to get the most out of the LMA-3, including extensive documentation (both an included CD and online), support documentation on everything from the Innovate's Logworks software to every piece of special accessory hardware that the firm sells, online users forums, application notes, and tuner resources.

Innovate's LMA-3 Multi-Sensor Device (AuxBox) connects to the auxiliary input of the LM-1. The AuxBox includes everything that you need to hook up the AuxBox to the LM-1 and to various engine sensors. It also includes mounting hardware

The advantage of the LMA-3 is that it allows you to accurately record and save the operating conditions (engine temperature, rpm, load, etc.) along with the air/fuel readings recorded by the LM-1. When you play back this information using Innovate's Logworks software on your laptop, you can correlate the operating conditions of the engine to the air/fuel ratio, then make your tuning adjustments to the computer to produce more power, more fuel efficiency, or whatever combination of the two that you want. Try THAT on a car without a computer!

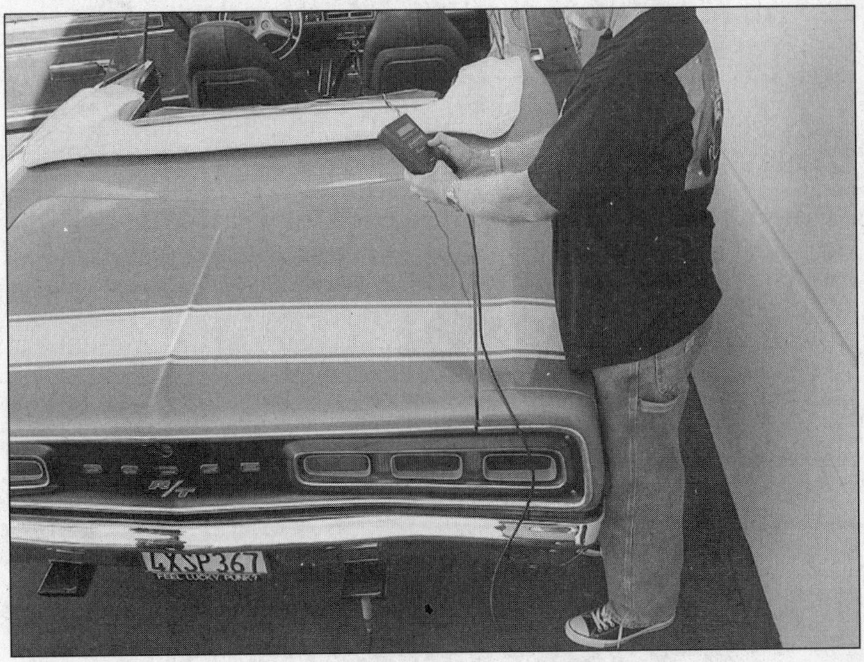

Notes

Glossary

A

ABDC - After Bottom Dead Center.

Acceleration - The time rate of change in velocity; velocity (speed) can be measured in feet-per-second, acceleration in feet-per-second-per-second, or feet-per-second-squared.

Adjustable rocker arm - A type of rocker arm with an adjusting bolt that can be tightened or loosened to adjust valve lash.

Advance - Moving the timing of the camshaft, distributor spark or valve operation ahead so that an event - such as firing of the spark plug or the opening of a valve - occurs earlier in the cycle. This term is also used to describe the mechanism used for accomplishing this.

Air-fuel mixture - The air and fuel traveling to the combustion chamber after being mixed by the carburetor, or after fuel is injected into the airstream by an injector. The mass of air supplied to the engine, divided by the mass of fuel supplied in the same period of time. The *stoichiometric*, or chemically correct, air-fuel ratio (*AFR*, or *A/F ratio*) is the exact ratio necessary to burn all the carbon and hydrogen in the fuel, leaving no other combustion by-products except carbon dioxide and water. See *stoichiometric*.

Air-fuel ratio - The ratio of air to the *weight* of the fuel supplied to the mixture for combustion. See *stoichiometric*.

Air gap - Space between spark plug electrodes, starting motor and generator armatures, field shoes, etc.

Air pressure - Atmospheric pressure (14.7 psi).

Air-to-air intercooler - A heat exchanger, used on a turbocharged engine, which uses ambient air to cool the air coming from the turbo into the intake manifold.

Air-to-water intercooler - A heat exchanger, used on a turbocharged engine, which uses liquid coolant from the radiator to cool the air coming from the turbo into the intake manifold.

ATDC - After Top Dead Center.

B

Babbit bearing - A plain bearing made of babbit. Babbit is the trademark for a soft, silvery antifriction alloy composed of tin with small amounts of copper and antimony.

Backlash - The amount of "play" between two parts. Usually refers to how much one gear can be moved back and forth without moving gear with which it's meshed.

Backpressure - Any resistance to free flow in the exhaust system. For example, catalytic converters and mufflers cause backpressure.

Bank - The portion of a V8 block containing four in-line cylinders.

Base circle - The part of the cam with the smallest diameter from the camshaft center. The area of the cam directly opposite the nose (lobe). No lift is produced by the base circle.

BBDC - Before Bottom Dead Center.

Bearing caps - The caps held in place by nuts or bolts which, in turn, hold the bearing halves in place.

Bearing clearance - The amount of space left between shaft and bearing surface. This space is for lubricating oil to enter.

Bearing crush - The additional height which is purposely manufactured into each bearing half to ensure complete contact of the bearing back with the housing bore when the engine is assembled.

Bearing knock - The noise created by movement of a part in a loose or worn bearing.

Bearing scraper - A small, triangular tool that looks like a file without teeth. Used for deburring and chamfering the edges of camshaft bearings.

Bearing spin - A type of bearing failure in which a lack of lubrication overheats the bearing until it seizes on the shaft, shears its locking lip and rotates in the housing or block.

Bearing spread - A purposely manufactured small extra distance across the parting faces of the bearing half, in excess of the actual diameter of the housing bore.

Bearing tang - A notch or lip on a bearing shell used to correctly locate the bearing during assembly.

Bellhousing (clutch housing) - The metal shroud which covers the flywheel and clutch, or the torque converter assembly.

Big-end bearing - The bearing in the end of the connecting rod that attaches to the crankshaft.

Bleed down - The collapse of a hydraulic lifter as oil drains out.

Block - The lower part of the engine containing the cylinders; the block is the basic framework of the engine.

Block deck - The cylinder head gasket surface.

Blow-by - Leakage of compressed air-fuel mixture and burned gases from the combustion chamber past the piston rings into the crankcase. This leakage results in power loss and oil contamination.

Blow-off valve - A control valve on a turbocharged engine, installed on the intake side of the system, which relieves pressure if it exceeds a predetermined value.

Blueprinting - Dismantling an engine and reassembling it to EXACT specifications.

Bore - An engine cylinder, or any cylindrical hole; also used to describe the process of enlarging or accurately refinishing a hole with a cutting tool, as "to bore an engine cylinder." The bore size is the diameter of the hole.

Bore diameter - Diameter of the cylinders.

Boring - Renewing the cylinders by cutting them out to a specified size. A boring bar is used to make the cut.

Boring bar - An electric-motor powered cutting tool used to machine, or bore, an engine cylinder, thereby removing metal and enlarging the cylinder diameter.

Boss - An extension or strengthened section that holds the end of a pin or a shaft; for example, the projections within a piston for supporting the piston pin or piston-pin bushings.

Bottom end - A term which refers collectively to the engine block, crankshaft, main bearings and the big ends of the connecting rods.

Bounce - A condition in which the valve isn't held tightly closed against its seat, even though the camshaft isn't opening it.

Break-in - The period of operation between installation of new or rebuilt parts and time in which parts are worn to the correct fit. Driving at reduced and varying speed for a specified mileage to permit parts to wear to the correct fit.

Breathing - Air flow into and out of an engine during operation.

BTDC - Before Top Dead Center; any position of the piston between bottom dead center and top dead center, on the upward stroke.

Build date code - A code which tells you what day, month and year the engine was made. Expressed alphanumerically and stamped somewhere on the block.

Burnishing - A sizing process that pushes metal to size by pressure.

Burr - A rough edge or area remaining on metal after it has been cast, cut or drilled.

Bushing - A one-piece sleeve placed in a bore to serve as a bearing surface for shaft, piston pin, etc. Usually replaceable.

Butt - The square ends of a piston ring.

C

Calibrate - To check or correct the initial setting of a test instrument; as in adjusting the needle of a dial gauge to correct zero or load setting.

Caliper - A measuring tool that can be set to measure inside or outside dimensions of an object; used for measuring things like the thickness of a block, the diameter of a shaft or the bore of a hole (inside caliper).

Cam - A rotating lobe or eccentric which, when used with a cam follower, can change rotary motion to reciprocating motion.

Cam follower - A device that follows the cam contour as it rotates. Also called a lifter, valve lifter or tappet.

Cam profile - The shape of the cam lobe.

Camshaft - The shaft in the engine, on which a series of lobes are located for operating the valve mechanisms. The camshaft is driven by gears or sprockets and a timing chain. Usually referred to simply as the cam.

Camshaft gear - The gear used to drive the camshaft.

Carbon - Hard, or soft, black deposits found in combustion chamber, on plugs, under rings, on and under valve heads.

Case-hardened - A piece of steel that has had its outer surface hardened while the inner portion remains relatively soft. Camshaft lobes are often case hardened.

Casting number - The number cast into a block, head or other component when the part is cast. Casting numbers can be helpful when identifying an engine or its parts, but they're not completely accurate, because casting are sometimes machined differently.

Cast iron - An alloy of iron and more than two percent carbon, used for engine blocks and heads because it's relatively inexpensive and easy to mold into complex shapes.

Catalytic converter - A muffler-like device in the exhaust system that catalyzes a chemical reaction which converts certain air pollutants in the exhaust gases into less harmful substances.

Cc'ing - The process of determining the exact volume of a cylinder head combustion chamber by measuring the amount of liquid it takes to fill the chamber. The measurements are generally made in cubic centimeters, or cc's.

Center line - An imaginary line drawn lengthwise through center of an object.

Chamfer - To bevel across (or a bevel on) the sharp edge of an object.

Chase - To repair damaged threads with a tap or die.

CID - Cubic Inch Displacement.

Clearance - The amount of space between two parts. For example, between piston and cylinder, bearing and journal, etc.

Coil binding - Compressing a valve spring to the point at which each coil touches the adjacent coil. See "Solid height."

Cold lash - The valve lash clearance, measured between the rocker arm and valve tip, when the engine is cold.

Collapsed piston - A piston whose skirt diameter has been reduced by heat and the forces imposed upon it during service in engine.

Closed loop fuel control - The normal operating mode for a fuel injection system. Once the engine is warmed up the computer can interpret an analog voltage signal from an exhaust gas oxygen sensor and alter the air/fuel ratio accordingly through the fuel injectors.

Combustion chamber - The space between the piston and the cylinder head, with the piston at top dead center, in which air-fuel mixture is burned.

Combustion chamber volume - The volume of the combustion chamber (space above piston with piston on TDC) measured in cc (cubic centimeters).

Compression height - The distance from the wrist-pin-bore center to the top of the piston.

Compression ratio - The relationship between cylinder volume (clearance volume) when the piston is at top dead center and cylinder volume when the piston is at bottom dead center.

Compression ring - The upper ring, or rings, on a piston, designed to hold the compression in the combustion chamber and prevent blow-by.

Compression stroke - The piston's movement from bottom dead center to top dead center immediately following the intake stroke, during which both the intake and exhaust valves are closed while the air-fuel mixture in the cylinder is compressed.

Connecting rod - The rod that connects the crank on the crankshaft with the piston. Sometimes called a con rod.

Connecting rod bearing - See "Rod bearing."

Connecting rod cap - The part of the connecting rod assembly that attaches the rod to the crankpin.

Core plug - Soft metal plug used to plug the casting holes for the coolant passages in the block.

Counterbalancing - Additional weight placed at the crankshaft vibration damper and/or flywheel to balance the crankshaft.

Counterbore - A concentric machined surface around a hole opening.

Crankcase - The lower part of the engine in which the crankshaft rotates; includes the lower section of the cylinder block and the oil pan.

Crank kit - A reground or reconditioned crankshaft and new main and connecting rod bearings.

Crankpin - The part of a crankshaft to which a connecting rod is attached.

Crankshaft - The main rotating member, or shaft, running the length of the crankcase, with offset "throws" to which the connecting rods are attached; changes the reciprocating motion of the pistons into rotating motion.

Crankshaft gear - The gear on the front of the crankshaft which drives the camshaft gear.

Crankshaft runout - A term used to describe how much a crankshaft is bent.

Crank throw - One crankpin with its two webs.

Crate engine – A performance engine that is completely assembled and ready to be installed. The name comes from the fact that they are usually delivered in a shipping crate.

Creep - When a crankshaft has slightly excessive runout (is slightly bent), it can sometimes be corrected by laying the crank in its saddles, installing the center main bearing cap (with its bearing insert) and leaving it for a day or two. Sometimes the crank will "creep," or bend, enough to put it within the specified runout range.

Cross-bolt - A system of securing the main bearing caps with four bolts per cap by which two bolts support the bearing cap from below, in the conventional way, and two other bolts enter the bearing from the side, passing through the sides of the engine block. The cross-bolts are visible from the outside of the engine. This system of securing the main bearing cap ensures good side-to-side, as well as up-and-down rigidity.

Cross-hatch - The pattern created on the cylinder wall by a hone.

Crush - A slight distortion of the bearing shell that holds it in place as the engine operates.

Cu. In. (C.I.) - Cubic inches.

Cubic inch displacement - The cylinder volume swept out (displaced) by all of the pistons in an engine as the crankshaft makes one complete revolution.

Cycle (four-stroke) - A repetitive sequence of events. In an engine, the term refers to the intake, compression, power and exhaust strokes that take place during each crankshaft revolution.

Cylinder head - The large component above the engine block that contains the valves.

Cylinder sleeve - A replaceable sleeve, or liner, pressed into the cylinder block to form the cylinder bore.

Cylinder surfacing hone - Puts a cross-hatch pattern on the cylinder walls, after they've been bored, to help seat the new rings properly.

D

Damper - See "Vibration damper."

Dead center - A term which refers to the maximum upper or lower piston position when all movement in one direction stops before it reverses direction.

Deburring - Removing the burrs (rough edges or areas) from a bearing.

Decarbonizing - The process of removing carbon from parts during overhaul.

Deck - The flat upper surface of the engine block where the head mounts.

Deck height - The center of the crankshaft main-bearing bores to the block deck surface.

Deglazer - A tool, rotated by an electric motor, used to remove glaze from cylinder walls so a new set of rings will seat.

Degreasing - The process of removing grease from parts.

Degree wheel - A disc divided into 360 equal parts that can be attached to a shaft to measure angle of rotation.

Detonation - In the combustion chamber, an uncontrolled second explosion (after the spark occurs at the spark plug) with spontaneous combustion of the remaining compressed air-fuel mixture, resulting in a pinging noise. Commonly referred to as spark knock or ping.

Dial indicator - A precision measuring instrument that indicates movement to a thousandth of an inch with a needle sweeping around dial face.

Dieseling - The tendency of an engine to continue running after the ignition is turned off. Usually caused by buildup of carbon deposits in the combustion chamber.

Dish - A depression in the top of a piston.

Displacement - The total volume of air-fuel mixture an engine is theoretically capable of drawing into all cylinders during one operating cycle. Also refers to the volume swept out by the piston as it moves from bottom dead center to top dead center.

Dome - See "Pop-up."

Dowel pin - A steel pin pressed into shallow bores in two adjacent parts to provide proper alignment.

Draw file - Smoothing a surface with a file moved sidewise.

Dry manifold - An intake manifold with no integral coolant passages cast into it.

Duty cycle - Many solenoid-operated metering devices cycle on and off. The duty cycle is a measurement of the amount of time a device is energized, or turned on, expressed as a percentage of the complete on-off cycle of that device. In other words, the duty cycle is the ratio of the pulse width to the complete cycle width.

Dwell - The number of degrees that the breaker cam (on the distributor shaft) rotates from the time the breaker points close until they open again.

Dwell meter - A precision electrical instrument used to measure the cam angle, or dwell, or number of degrees the distributor points are closed while the engine is running.

Dykem-type metal bluing - A special dye used to check a valve job. When applied to the valve seat to show up as a dark ring contrasted against the brightly finished top and bottom cuts, making the seat easier to see and measure.

Dynamic balance - The balance of an object when it's in motion. When the center line of weight mass of a revolving object is in the same plane as the center line of the object, that object is in dynamic balance.

Dynamometer (or "Dyno") - A device for measuring the power output, or brake horsepower, of an engine. An engine dynamometer measures the power output at the flywheel.

E

Eccentric - A disk, or offset section (of a shaft, for example) used to convert rotary motion to reciprocating motion. Sometimes called a cam.

Edge-ride - The tendency of crankshaft main bearings to ride up the radius - rather than seat on the journal - when the radius is too large.

Endplay - The amount of lengthwise movement between two parts. As applied to a crankshaft, the distance that the crankshaft can move forward and back in the cylinder block.

Engine tune-up - A procedure for inspecting, testing and adjusting an engine, and replacing any worn parts, to restore the engine to its best performance.

Erode - Wear away by high velocity abrasive materials.

Exhaust manifold - A part with several passages through which exhaust gases leave the engine combustion chamber and enter the exhaust pipe.

Exhaust stroke - The portion of the piston's movement devoted to expelling burned gases from the cylinder. The exhaust stroke lasts from bottom dead center to top dead center, immediately following the power stroke, during which the exhaust valve opens so the exhaust gases can escape from the cylinder to the exhaust manifold.

Exhaust valve - The valve through which the burned air-fuel charge passes on its way from the cylinder to the exhaust manifold during the exhaust stroke.

Externally balanced crankshaft - A crankshaft that requires external balancing weight - usually on the vibration damper or the flywheel - for balance.

F

Face - A machinist's term that refers to removing metal from the end of a shaft or the "face" of a larger part, such as a flywheel.

Fatigue - A breakdown of material through a large number of loading and unloading cycles. The first signs are cracks followed shortly by breaks.

Feeler gauge - A thin strip of hardened steel, ground to an exact thickness, used to check clearances between parts.

Finishing stone - see "Cylinder surfacing hone"

Firing order - The order in which the engine cylinders fire, or deliver their power strokes, beginning with the number one cylinder.

Float - Float occurs when the valve train loses contact with the cam lobe and the parts "float" on air until control is regained.

Flywheel - A heavy metal wheel that's attached to the crankshaft to smooth out firing impulses. It provides inertia to keep crankshaft turning smoothly during periods when no power is being applied. It also serves as part of the clutch and engine cranking systems.

Flywheel ring gear - A gear, fitted to the outer circumference of the flywheel, that's engaged by the teeth on the starter motor pinion (drive gear) to start the engine.

Foot-pound - A unit of measurement for work, equal to lifting one pound one foot.

Foot-pound (tightening) - A unit of measurement for torque, equal to one pound of pull one foot from the center of the object being tightened.

Forging - A process of forming a steel part by repeatedly ramming a hardened-steel form against red-hot steel. Forging produces a uniform grain pattern in steel that makes it more flexible than cast-iron, and less likely to fracture. Forged pistons, connecting rods, rocker arms and crankshafts, although more expensive to produce than similar cast-iron parts, are highly desired in racing and high-performance engines because of their strength.

Four-stroke cycle - The four piston strokes - intake, compression, power and exhaust - that make up the complete cycle of events in the four-stroke cycle engine. Also referred to as four-cycle and four-stroke.

Free height - The unloaded length or height of a spring.

Freeplay - The looseness in a linkage, or an assembly of parts, between the initial application of force and actual movement. Usually perceived as "slop" or slight delay.

Freeze plug - See "Core plug."

Friction horsepower - The amount of power consumed by an engine in driving itself. It includes the power absorbed in mechanical friction and in driving auxiliaries plus, in the case of four-stroke engines, some pumping power.

Fulcrum - The hinge point of a lever. On a fulcrum-type rocker arm, the part on which the rocker arm pivots.

G

Gallery - A large passage in the block that forms a reservoir for engine oil pressure.

Glaze - The very smooth, glassy finish that develops on cylinder walls while an engine is in service.

Glaze breaker - See "Deglazer."

H

Half-round file - A special file that's flat on one side and convex on the other.

Hardened pushrods - Specially treated pushrods designed for use with pushrod-guided rocker arms.

Harmonic balancer - See "Vibration damper."

Head - See "Cylinder head."

Headers - High-performance exhaust manifolds that replace the stock manifold. Designed with smooth flowing lines to prevent back pressure caused by sharp bends, rough castings, etc.

Heat checks - Cracks in the clutch pressure plate.

Heli-Coil - A rethreading device used when threads are worn or damaged. The device is installed in a retapped hole to reduce the thread size to the original size.

Hemi - Short for "hemispherical." Refers to the shape of the combustion chamber in the cylinder head. Generally, hemi heads have the spark plug at the top of the half-sphere combustion chamber. The hemi design is considered superior to many other combustion chamber designs for good flame propagation, resistance to detonation, and ability to produce high-rpm power.

Hone - See "Deglazer."

Horsepower - A measure of mechanical power, or the rate at which work is done. One horsepower equals 33,000 ft-lbs of work per minute. It's the amount of power necessary to raise 33,000 pounds a distance of one foot in one minute.

Hot lash - The valve adjustment on an engine equipped with solid lifters.

Hydraulic valve lifter - Valve lifter that utilizes hydraulic pressure from engine's lubrication system to maintain zero clearance (keep it in constant contact with both camshaft and valve stem). Automatically adjusts to variation in valve stem length. Hydraulic lifters reduce valve noise.

I

Idle speed - The speed, or rpm, at which the engine runs freely with no power or load being transferred when the accelerator pedal is released.

Installed height - The spring's measured length or height, as installed on the cylinder head. Installed height is measured from the spring seat to the underside of the spring retainer.

Intake manifold - A part with several passages through which the air-fuel mixture flows from the carburetor to the port openings in the cylinder head.

Intake stroke - The portion of the piston's movement, between top dead center and bottom dead center, devoted to drawing fuel mixture into engine cylinder. The intake stroke is the stroke immediately following the exhaust stroke, during which the intake valve opens and the cylinder fills with air-fuel mixture from the intake manifold.

Intake valve - The valve through which the air-fuel mixture is admitted to the cylinder.

J

Jam nut - A nut used to lock an adjustment nut, or locknut, in place. For example, a jam nut is employed to keep the adjusting nut on the rocker arm in position.

Journal - The surface of a rotating shaft which turns in a bearing.

K

Keeper - The split lock that holds the valve spring retainer in position on the valve stem.

Key - A small piece of metal inserted into matching grooves machined into two parts fitted together - such as a gear pressed onto a shaft - which prevents slippage between the two parts.

Keyed - Prevented from rotating with a small metal device called a key.

Keyway - A slot cut in a shaft, pulley hub, etc. A square key is placed in the slot and engages a similar keyway in the mating piece.

Knock - The heavy metallic engine sound, produced in the combustion chamber as a result of abnormal combustion - usually detonation. Knock is usually caused by a loose or worn bearing. Also referred to as detonation, pinging and spark knock. Connecting rod or main bearing knocks are created by too much oil clearance or insufficient lubrication.

Knurl - A roughened surface caused by a sharp wheel that displaces metal outward as its sharp edges push into the metal surface.

L

Lands - The portions of metal between the piston ring grooves.

Lapping the valves - Grinding a valve face and its seat together with lapping compound.

Lash - The amount of free motion in a gear train, between gears, or in a mechanical assembly, that occurs before movement can begin. Usually refers to the lash in a valve train.

Lifter - The part that rides against the cam to transfer motion to the rest of the valve train.

Lifter foot - The part of the lifter that contacts the camshaft.

Load at installed height - The specified range of force required to compress a spring to its installed height, usually expressed in terms of so many pounds of force at so many inches.

Lug - To operate an engine with high loads at low speeds.

Lugs - The heavy fastening flanges on parts.

M

Machining - The process of using a machine to remove metal from a metal part.

Main bearings - The plain, or babbit, bearings that support the crankshaft.

Main bearing caps - The cast iron caps, bolted to the bottom of the block, that support the main bearings.

Manifold - A part with several inlet or outlet passages through which a gas or liquid is gathered or distributed. See "Exhaust manifold" and "Intake manifold."

Manifold runners - A single passage in a manifold from one cylinder to the major manifold opening.

Manifold vacuum - The vacuum in the intake manifold that develops as a result of the vacuum in the cylinders on their intake strokes.

Metering orifice - A small hole that restricts the flow of liquid - usually coolant or oil.

Micrometer - A precision measuring instrument which can measure the inside or outside diameter of a part to a ten-thousandth of an inch.

Mike - See "Micrometer."

Mill - To remove metal with a milling machine.

N

Net horsepower - Brake horsepower remaining at flywheel of engine after power required by engine accessories (fan, water pump, alternator, etc.).

Normally-aspirated - An engine which draws its air/fuel mixture into its cylinders solely by piston-crated vacuum, i.e. not supercharged or turbocharged.

Notched rocker arm stud - A rocker arm stud with a notch worn in its side. A notched stud is more likely to break.

O

O.D. - Outside diameter.

OHC - Overhead Cam.

OHV - Overhead Valve.

Oil gallery - A pipe or drilled passageway in the engine used to carry engine oil from one area to another.

Oil pan - The detachable lower part of the engine, made of stamped steel, which encloses the crankcase and acts as an oil reservoir.

Oil pumping - Leakage of oil past the piston rings and into the combustion chamber, usually as a result of defective rings or worn cylinder walls.

Oil ring - The lower ring, or rings, of a piston; designed to prevent excessive amounts of oil from working up the cylinder walls and into the combustion chamber. Also called an oil-control ring.

Oil seal - A seal which keeps oil from leaking out of a compartment. Usually refers to a dynamic seal around a rotating shaft or other moving part.

Oil slinger - A cone-shaped collar that hurls oil back to its source to prevent leakage along a shaft.

Orifice - See "Metering orifice."

O-ring - A type of sealing ring made of a special rubberlike material; in use, the O-ring is compressed into a groove to provide the sealing action.

Out-of-round journal - An oval or egg-shaped bearing journal.

Overhaul - To completely disassemble a unit, clean and inspect all parts, reassemble it with the original or new parts and make all adjustments necessary for proper operation.

P

Pedestal pivot - A semi-cylindrical (half-round) pivot used with pivot-guided rocker arms. A pedestal pivot restricts the rocker arm so it pivots around one axis or in a single plane - the plane of the valve stem and pushrod.

Penetrating oil - Special oil used to free rusted parts so they can be moved.

Phosphate coating - A special coating on camshafts which promotes oil retention.

Pilot - A term which refers to any device used to center a cutting tool or the concentric installation of one part onto another. For example, the valve guide is used as a pilot for centering the grinding stone during a valve job; the pilot bearing is used to center a clutch alignment tool when bolting the clutch disc and pressure plate to the flywheel.

Pilot bearing - A small bearing installed in the center of the flywheel (or the rear end of the crankshaft) to support the front end of the input shaft of the transmission.

Pinning - A procedure for repairing cracks in a cylinder head's combustion chamber using threaded pins.

Pip mark - A little dot or indentation which indicates the top side of a compression ring.

Piston - The cylindrical part, attached to the connecting rod, that moves up and down in the cylinder as the crankshaft rotates. When the fuel charge is fired, the piston transfers the force of the explosion to the connecting rod, then to the crankshaft.

Piston boss - The built-up area around the piston pin hole.

Piston collapse - The reduction in diameter of the piston skirt caused by heat and constant impact stresses.

Piston crown - The portion of the piston above the piston rings.

Piston head - See "Piston crown."

Piston lands - The portion of the piston between the ring grooves.

Piston pin (or wrist pin) - The cylindrical and usually hollow steel pin that passes through the piston. The piston pin fastens the piston to the upper end of the connecting rod.

Piston ring - The split ring fitted to the groove in a piston. The ring contacts the sides of the ring groove and also rubs against the cylinder wall, thus sealing space between piston and wall. There are two types of rings: Compression rings seal the compression pressure in the combustion chamber; oil rings scrape excessive oil off the cylinder wall. Piston ring groove - The slots or grooves cut in piston head to hold piston rings in position.

Piston ring side clearance - The space between the sides of the ring and the ring lands.

Piston skirt - The portion of the piston below the rings and the piston pin hole.

Piston slap - A sound made by a piston with excess skirt clearance as the crankshaft goes across top center.

Plastigage - A thin strip of plastic thread, available in different sizes, used for measuring clearances. For example, a strip of plastigage is laid across a bearing journal and mashed as parts are assembled. Then parts are disassembled and the width of the strip is measured to determine clearance between journal and bearing. Commonly used to measure crankshaft main-bearing and connecting rod bearing clearances.

Pop-up - A raised portion of a piston head.

Port injection - A fuel injection system in which the fuel is sprayed by individual injectors into each intake port, upstream of the intake valve.

Porting - A term which refers to smoothing out, aligning and/or enlarging the intake and exhaust passageways in the cylinder heads to the valves.

Power stroke (firing stroke) - The portion of the piston's movement devoted to transmitting the power of the burning fuel mixture to the crankshaft. The power stroke occurs between top dead center and bottom dead center immediately following the compression stroke, during which both valves are closed and the air-fuel mixture burns, expands and forces the piston down to transmit power to the crankshaft.

Preignition - The ignition of the air-fuel mixture in the combustion chamber by some unwanted means, before the ignition spark occurs at the spark plug.

Preload - The amount of load placed on a bearing before actual operating loads are imposed. Proper preloading requires bearing adjustment and ensures alignment and minimum looseness in the system.

Press-fit - A tight fit between two parts that requires pressure to force the parts together. Also referred to as drive, or force, fit.

Prick punch - A small, sharp punch used to make punch marks on a metal surface.

Prussian blue - A blue pigment; in solution, useful in determining the area of contact between two surfaces. Prussian blue is commonly used to determine the width and location of the contact area between the valve face and the valve seat.

Puller - A special tool designed to remove a bearing, bushing, hub, sleeve, etc. There are many, many types of pullers.

Pushrod - The rod that connects the valve lifter to the rocker arm. The pushrod transmits cam lobe lift.

R

Race (bearing) - The inner or outer ring that provides a contact surface for balls or rollers in bearing.

Ramp - A gradual slope or incline on a cam to take up lash clearance.

Ream - To size, enlarge or smooth a hole by using a round cutting tool with fluted edges.

Rear main bearing seal - The large seal at the rear of the crankshaft that prevents oil from leaking into the bellhousing; there are two types, the rope seal and the rubber lip seal. Lip seals may be one-piece or two-piece.

Reciprocate - Move back and forth.

Retainer - A washer-like device that locks the keepers onto the valve stem and preloads the valve spring.

Ridge - See "Ring ridge."

Ring - See "Piston ring."

Ring gap - The distance between the ends of the piston ring when installed in the cylinder.

Ring ridge - The ridge, formed at the top of the cylinder above the upper limit of ring travel, as the cylinder wall below is worn away. In a worn cylinder, this area is of smaller diameter than the remainder of the cylinder, and will leave a ridge or ledge that must be removed.

Ring side clearance - The clearance between the top or bottom of a piston ring and the roof or floor, respectively, of its corresponding ring groove.

Rocker arm - A lever arm that rocks on a shaft or pivots on a stud as the cam moves the pushrod. The rocker arm converts the upward movement of the pushrod into a downward movement to open a valve.

Rocker arm clips - Clips which fit over the pushrod end of the rocker arm to prevent oil from being thrown off when valves are adjusted at their operating temperature.

Rocker arm pivot - The nut or fulcrum upon which the rocker arm pivots back and forth in a see-saw motion as it's alternately rocked one way by pushrod, then rocked other way by valve as it closes

Rod - See "Connecting rod."

Rod bearing - The bearing in the connecting rod in which a crankpin of the crankshaft rotates. Also called a connecting rod bearing.

Roller rocker arm - A special high-performance rocker arm that pivots on a roller bearing and has a roller tip.

Roller tappets or lifters - Valve lifters that have a roller in the end that contacts the camshaft. This reduces friction between the lobe and lifter. Used when special camshafts and high-tension springs have been installed.

Runout - Wobble. The amount a shaft rotates out-of-true.

S

Saddle - The upper main bearing seat.

Scan Tool - A device that interfaces with and communicates information on a data link. Commonly used to get data from automotive computers.

Scored - Scratched or grooved, as a cylinder wall may be scored by abrasive particles moved up and down by the piston rings.

Scraper ring - On a piston, an oil-control ring designed to scrape excess oil back down the cylinder and into the crankcase.

Scuffing - A type of wear in which there's a transfer of material between parts moving against each other; shows up as pits or grooves in the mating surfaces.

Sealant (gasket) - A thick, tacky compound, usually spread with a brush, which may be used as a gasket or sealant, to seal small openings or surface irregularities.

Seat - The surface upon which another part rests or seats. For example, the valve seat is the matched surface upon which the valve face rests. Also used to refer to wearing into a good fit; for example, piston rings seat after a few miles of driving.

Shimming - Placing a shim or spacer under weak valve springs or springs with a short free height; the shim, which is placed between the spring and the cylinder head, compresses the spring a little more to restore the spring's installed and open loads.

Shim-type head gaskets - A hard, thin, high-performance steel head gasket that raises the compression ratio.

Short block - An engine block complete with crankshaft and piston and, usually, camshaft assemblies.

Side clearance - The clearance between the sides of moving parts that don't serve as load-carrying surfaces.

Silent chain - A special quiet timing chain, usually made quiet through the use of a nylon-coated camshaft timing gear.

Slide hammer - A special puller that screws into or hooks onto the back of the a bearing; a heavy sliding handle on the shaft bottoms against the end of the shaft to knock the bearing free.

Slinger - A ring on a shaft that throws oil from the shaft before it gets to the oil seal.

Slipper skirt - A piston with a lower surface on the thrust surfaces only.

Sludge - An accumulation of water, dirt and oil in the oil pan; sludge is very viscous and tends to reduce lubrication.

Solid height - The height of a coil spring when it's totally compressed to the point at which each coil touches the adjacent coil. See "Coil binding."

Spacer - Another name for a valve spring shim. See "Shimming."

Spark knock - See "Detonation."

Spark tester - A device which indicates whether there's spark at the end of each plug wire. Used for quick check of the ignition system.

Spit hole - See "Spurt hole"

Split-lip-type rear main seal bearing - A two-piece neoprene seal; easier to install and has less friction than a rope-type rear main seal.

Spot-faced - On a connecting rod, a bolt-head seating surface that's machined so it describes a radius on the inboard-side of the bolt head as viewed from the top of the bolt head.

Spurt or squirt hole - A small hole in the connecting rod big end that indexes (aligns) with the oil hole in the crank journal. When the holes index, oil spurts out to lubricate the cylinder walls.

Static balance - The balance of an object while it's stationary.

Step - The wear on the lower portion of a ring land caused by excessive side and back-clearance. The height of the step indicates the ring's extra side clearance and the length of the step projecting from the back wall of the groove represents the ring's back clearance.

Stoichiometric - An air/fuel mixture that is balanced for greatest efficiency.

Stroboscope - See "Timing light."

Stroke - The distance the piston moves when traveling from top dead center to bottom dead center, or from bottom dead center to top dead center.

Stroker crankshaft - A crankshaft, either a special new one or a stock crank that's been reworked, which has the connecting rod throws offset so that the length of their stroke is increased.

Stroker kit - A stroker crankshaft, combined with specially designed pistons and connecting rods to create a complete rotating assembly.

Stud - A metal rod with threads on both ends.

Stud puller - A tool used to remove or install studs.

Sump - The lowest part of the oil pan. The part of oil pan that contains oil.

Supercharger - A mechanically-driven device that pressurizes the intake air, thereby increasing the density of charge air and the consequent power output from a given engine displacement. Superchargers are usually belt-driven by the engine crankshaft pulley.

Swept volume - The volume displaced, or swept, by the piston as it travels from bottom dead center to top dead center.

T

Tang - A lip on the end of a plain bearing used to align the bearing during assembly.

Tap - To cut threads in a hole. Also refers to the fluted tool used to cut threads.

Tap and die set - Set of taps and dies for internal and external threading - usually covers a range of the most popular sizes.

Taper - A gradual reduction in the width of a shaft or hole; in an engine cylinder, taper usually takes the form of uneven wear, more pronounced at the top than at the bottom.

Tapered roller bearing - A bearing utilizing a series of tapered, hardened steel rollers operating between an outer and inner hardened steel race.

Tappet - See "Lifter."

TDC - Top Dead Center.

Threaded insert - A threaded coil that's used to restore the original thread size to a hole with damaged threads; the hole is drilled oversize and tapped, and the insert is threaded into the tapped hole.

Throws - The offset portions of the crankshaft to which the connecting rods are affixed.

Thrust bearing - The main bearing that has thrust faces to prevent excessive endplay, or forward and backward movement of the crankshaft.

Thrust plate - The small plate between the cam sprocket and the block, bolted to the front of the block.

Thrust washer - A bronze or hardened steel washer placed between two moving parts. The washer prevents longitudinal movement and provides a bearing surface for thrust surfaces of parts.

Timing - Delivery of the ignition spark or operation of the valves (in relation to the piston position) for the power stroke.

Timing chain - The chain, driven by a sprocket on the crankshaft, that drives the sprocket on the camshaft.

Timing gear - A gear on the crankshaft that drives the camshaft by meshing with a gear on its end.

Timing light - A stroboscopic light that's hooked up to the secondary ignition circuit to produce flashes of light in unison with the firing of a specific spark plug, usually the plug for the number one cylinder. When these flashes of light are directed on the whirling timing marks, the marks appear to stand still. By adjusting the distributor position, the timing marks can be properly aligned, and the timing is set.

Timing marks (ignition) - Marks, usually located on the vibration damper, used to synchronize the ignition system so the spark plugs will fire at the correct time.

Timing marks (valves) - One tooth on either the camshaft or crankshaft gear will be marked with an indentation or some other mark. Another mark will be found on the other gear between two of the teeth. The two gears must be meshed so that the marked tooth meshes with the marked spot on the other gear.

Tip - See "Valve stem tip."

Toe - The highest point on the cam lobe; the part of the lobe that raises the lifter to its highest point. Also called the nose.

Top dead center - The piston position when the piston has reached the upper limit of its travel in the cylinder and the center line of the connecting rod is parallel to the cylinder walls.

Tolerance - The amount of variation permitted from an exact size of measurement. Actual amount from smallest acceptable dimension to largest acceptable dimension.

Torque - A turning or twisting force, such as the force imparted on a fastener by a torque wrench. Usually expressed in foot-pounds (ft-lbs).

Torque plate - A stout steel plate with four large-diameter holes centered on the engine bores to allow clearance for boring and honing the cylinders, bolted onto the block as a temporary "cylinder head" during machining. Using a torque plate prevents bore distortion while the cylinders are being bored and honed.

Torsional vibration - The rotary motion that causes a twist-untwist action on a vibrating shaft, so that a part of the shaft repeatedly moves ahead of, or lags behind, the remainder of the shaft; for example, the action of a crankshaft responding to the cylinder firing impulses.

Turbocharger - A centrifugal device, driven by exhaust gases, that pressurizes the intake air, thereby increasing the density of the charge air, and therefore the resulting power output, from a given engine displacement.

Twist drill - A metal cutting drill with spiral flutes (grooves) to permit exit of chips while cutting.

U

Umbrella - An oil deflector placed near the valve tip to throw oil from the valve stem area.

Undercut - A machined groove below the normal surface.

Undersize bearings - Smaller diameter bearings used with re-ground crankshaft journals.

V

Valley pan - On big-block V8 engines, the pan-like device, integral with the intake manifold gaskets, that provides an oil seal for the valley area between the two cylinder banks (on big-block Chrysler engines, hot oil never comes in contact with the bottom of the intake manifold).

Valve - A device used to either open or close an opening. Usually used to allow or stop the flow of a liquid or a gas. There are many different types.

Valve clearance - The clearance between the valve tip (the end of the valve stem) and the rocker arm. The valve clearance is measured when the valve is closed.

Valve duration - The length of time, measured in degrees of engine crankshaft rotation, that the valve remains open.

Valve face - The outer lower edge of the valve. The valve face contacts the valve seat in the cylinder head when the valve is closed.

Valve float - The condition which occurs when the valves are forced back open before they've had a chance to seat. Valve float is usually caused by extremely high rpm.

Valve grinder - A special electrically powered grinding machine designed to remove old metal from the valve face.

Valve grinding - Refacing a valve in a valve-refacing machine.

Valve guide - The cast-iron bore that's part of the head, or the bronze or silicon-bronze tube that's pressed into the head, to provide support and lubrication for the valve stem.

Valve keeper - Also referred to as valve key. Small half-cylinder of steel that snaps into a groove in the upper end of valve stem. Two keepers per valve are used. Designed to secure valve spring, valve retainer and valve stem together.

Valve lift - The distance a valve moves from its fully closed to its fully open position.

Valve lifter - A cylindrical device that contacts the end of the cam lobe and the lower end of the pushrod. The lifter rides on the camshaft. When the cam lobe moves it upward, it pushes on the pushrod, which pushes on the lifer and opens the valve. Referred to as a lifter, tappet, valve tappet or cam follower.

Valve lock - See "Valve keeper."

Valve margin - The thickness of the valve head at its outside diameter, between the top of the valve head and the outer edge of the face.

Valve overlap - The number of degrees of crankshaft rotation during which both the intake and the exhaust valve are partially open (the intake is starting to open while the exhaust is not yet closed).

Valve port - An opening, through the cylinder head, from the intake or exhaust manifold to the valve seat.

Valve rotator - The device placed on the end of the valve stem to promote longer valve life. When the valve is opened and closed, the valve will rotate a small amount with each opening and closing.

Valve seat - The surface against which a valve comes to rest to provide a seal against leaking.

Valve seat insert - The hardened, precision ground metal ring pressed into the combustion chamber to provide a sealing surface for the valve face (usually for the exhaust valves) and transfer heat into the head. Inserts are made of special metals able to withstand very high temperatures.

Valve spring - A coil spring designed to close the valve against its seat.

Valve spring squareness - How straight a spring stands on a flat surface, or how much it tilts. The more "square" a spring is, the more evenly it loads the retainer around its full circumference. Uneven retainer loading increases stem and guide wear.

Valve stem - The long, thin, cylindrical bearing surface of the valve that slides up and down in the valve guide.

Valve stem seal - A device placed on or around the valve stem to reduce the amount of oil that can get on the stem and then work its way down into the combustion chamber.

Valve stem tip - The upper end of the valve stem; the tip is the contact point with the rocker arm.

Valve tappet - See "Valve lifter."

Valve timing - The timing of the opening and closing of the valves in relation to the piston position.

Valve tip - The upper end of the valve that contacts the rocker arm.

Valve train - The valve-operating mechanism of an engine; includes all components from the camshaft to the valve.

Valve umbrella - A washer-like unit that's placed over the end of the valve stem to prevent the entry of excess oil between the stem and the guide.

Varnish - The deposits on the interior of the engine caused by engine oil breaking down under prolonged heat and use. Certain constituents of oil deposit themselves in hard coatings of varnish.

Vernier caliper - A precision measuring instrument that measures inside and outside dimensions. Not quite as accurate as a micrometer, but more convenient.

Vibration damper - A cylindrical weight attached to the front of the crankshaft to minimize torsional vibration (the twist-untwist actions of the crankshaft caused by the cylinder firing impulses). Also called a harmonic balancer.

Volumetric efficiency - A comparison between actual volume of fuel mixture drawn in on intake stroke and what would be drawn in if cylinder were to be completely filled.

W

Wastegate - A device which bleeds off exhaust gases before they reach the turbocharger when boost pressure reaches a set limit.

Water jacket - The spaces around the cylinders, between the inner and outer shells of the cylinder block or head, through which coolant circulates.

Web - A supporting structure across a cavity.

Wet manifold - An intake manifold that carries coolant through integral passages. Small-block V8 and 3.9L V6 engines use a wet manifold. Big-block V8 manifolds are dry (no coolant flows through them).

Wet sleeve - A cylinder sleeve whose outside surface is in direct contact with coolant.

Windage tray - On some high-performance engines, another pan within the oil pan, up near the crankshaft, that insulates the crankshaft from the windage phenomenon, which causes oil, in the form of tiny droplets, to become airborne inside the crankcase of an engine running at high rpm. At high rpm, it's possible for as much as two quarts of oil to be airborne within the crankcase. This oil, if it comes in contact with the crankshaft, will cause additional friction and reduce horsepower.

Woodruff key - A key with a radiused backside (viewed from the side).

Wrist pin - See "Piston pin."

Source List

Airflow Research (AFR)
(high-performance cylinder heads and related components)
28611 W. Industry Drive
Valencia, CA 91355
(877) 892-8844
www.airflowresearch.com

Allen Engine
(4.6L Ford blower kits)
(805) 658-8262
www.allenengine.com

Arias Pistons
(custom pistons)
13420 South Normandie Ave.
Gardena, CA 90249
(310) 532-9737
www.ariaspistons.com

ARP, Inc.
(performance fasteners)
1863 Eastman Ave.
Ventura, CA 93003
(800) 826-3045
www.arp-bolts.com

Barry Grant, Inc.
(fuel systems, Demon carburetors, Nitrous Works)
1450 McDonald Road
Dahlonega, GA 30533
(706) 864-8544
www.barrygrant.com

B&M Racing and Performance Parts
(fuel system and many other parts)
9142 Independence Ave.
Chatsworth, CA 91311
(818) 882-6422
www.bmracing.com

Carl's Ford Parts
(Ford intakes and other performance parts)
P.O. Box 38
Homeworth, OH 44634
(330) 525-7291
www.carlsfordparts.com

Carroll Shelby Enterprises
(Ford aluminum blocks, heads, components)
19021 S. Figueroa St.
Gardena, CA 90248
(310) 538-2914
www.carrollshelbyent.com

Competition Cams, Inc.
(cams, valvetrain parts)
3406 Democrat Road
Memphis, TN 38118
(901) 795-2400
(800) 999-0853 (CAM HELP™ line)
www.compcams.com

Crane Cams
(camshafts kits, valvetrain components)
530 Fentress Blvd.
Daytona Beach, FL 32114
(386) 252-1151
www.cranecams.com

Dart Machinery, Ltd.
(race cylinder heads, intakes and blocks)
353 Oliver Street
Troy, MI 48084
(248) 362-1188
www.dartheads.com

Eagle Specialty Products, Inc.
(performance connecting rods, crankshafts, stroker kits, rotating assemblies)
8530 Aaron Lane
Southaven, MS 38671
(662) 796-7373
www.eaglerod.com

Edelbrock Corp.
(intake components, heads, nitrous, crate engines)
2700 California Street
Torrance, CA 90503
(310) 781-2222
www.edelbrock.com

Fuel Air Spark Technology (FAST)
(fuel injection, engine management)
3400 Democrat Road
Memphis, TN 38118
(877) 334-8355
www.fuelairspark.com

Flexalite Consolidated
(electric cooling fans)
7213 45th St., Ct. E
Fife, WA 9424
(253) 922-2700
www.flex-a-lite.com

Flowmaster
(mufflers and exhaust components)
100 Stony Point Rd., Suite 125
Santa Rosa, CA 95401
(707) 544-4761
www.flowmastermufflers.com

Fluidyne
(aluminum radiators)
2605 East Cedar St.
Ontario, CA 91761
(800) 358-4396
www.fluidyne.com

Ford Racing Parts
(Ford crate engines and components)
(see your Ford dealer)
www.fordracingparts.com

GM Performance Parts
(crate engines, components)
(see your GM dealer)
www.gmperformanceparts.com

Holley Performance Products
(Airmass Exhaust, Holley Ignition, intakes, carburetors, NOS, Earl's Plumbing)
1801 Russellville Road, P.O. Box 10360
Bowling Green, KY 42102-7360
(800) Holley-1
www.holley.com

Hooker Headers
(headers and exhaust components)
(see Holley)
www.ilovemyhookerheaders.com

HP Tuners
(tuning software and equipment for computer-controlled vehicles)
P.O. Box 801057
Valencia, Ca 91380-1057
www.hptuners.com

Jacobs Electronics
2519 Dana Drive
Laurinburg, NC 28352
(800) 782-3379
www.jacobselectronics.com

JE Pistons
15312 Connector Lane
Huntington Beach, CA 92649
(714) 898-9763
www.jepistons.com

K&N Engineering
(air filters, cold air intake kits)
P.O. Box 1329
Riverside, CA 92502
(888) 949-1832
www.knfilters.com

Keith Black Racing Engines
(performance engines and components)
11120 Scott Avenue
South Gate, CA 90280
(562) 869-1518
www.keithblack.com

LS1Tech.com
(resource for Generation III and
IV GM V8 engines)
www.ls1tech.com

Magnuson Products, Inc.
(supercharger kits)
1990 Knoll Drive, Suite A
Ventura, CA 93003
(805) 642-8833
www.magnusonproducts.com

Mopar Performance
(crate engines and performance parts)
(see your Dodge, Plymouth, Chrylser dealer)
www.moparperformance.com

MSD Ignition
(ignition products)
1490 Henry Brennan Drive
El Paso, TX 79936
(915) 857-5200
www.msdignition.com

Nitrous Express (NX)
5411 Seymour Highway
Wichita Falls, TX 76301
(940) 767-7695
www.nitrousexpress.com

Nitrous Oxide Systems (NOS)
(see Holley)
www.nosnitrous.com

Painless Performance
(wiring kits, engine swap harnesses)
2501 Ludelle Street
Fort Worth, TX 76105
(817) 244-6212
www.painlessperformance.com

Powerdyne
(supercharger kits)
9145 Deering Avenue
Chatsworth, CA 91311
(818) 993-8400
www.powerdyne.com

Powerhouse Tools
(specialty tools for engine assembly)
3402 Democrat Road
Memphis, TN 38118
(800) 872-7223
www.powerhouseproducts.com

Racing Head Service
(cylinder heads)
(see Competition Cams)
www.racingheadservice.com

Roush Performance Products
(Ford crate engines and components)
28156 Plymouth Road, Suite 2
Livonia, MI 48150
(800) 59-ROUSH
www.roushperformance.com

RPM Motors, Inc.
(GM specialty parts and performance tuning)
6536 Ruether Avenue, Unit 606
Santa Clarita, CA 91350
(888) 755-5391
www.rpm-motors-inc.com

SLP Performance Parts, Inc.
(cylinder heads, intakes, performance
crate engines)
1501 Industrial Way N.
Toms River, NJ 08755
(732) 349-2109
www.slponline.com

Smeding Performance
(performance crate engines)
3340 Sunrise Blvd., #E
Rancho Cordova, CA 95742
(916) 638-0899
www.smedingperformance.com

Strictly Performance Motorsports
(Corvette, Camaro, Firebird specialists)
15703 Saticoy Street
Van Nuys, CA 91406
(818) 342-5693
www.spmotorsports.net

Turbonetics, Inc.
(turbochargers)
2255 Agate Court
Simi Valley, CA 93065
(805) 581-0333
www.turboneticsinc.com

Vortech Engineering
(supercharger kits)
1650 Pacific Avenue
Channel Islands, CA 93033
(805) 247-0226
www.vortechsuperchargers.com

Weiand
(intakes, blower kits)
(see Holley)
www.weiand.com

Whipple Industries, Inc.
(superxchargers and kits)
3292 N. Weber
Fresno, CA 93722
(559) 442-1261
www.whipplesuperchargers.com

ZEX
(nitrous oxide kits)
3418 Democrat Road
Memphis, TN 38118
(888) 817-1008
www.zex.com

Index

A

A brief history of the engine management computer, 4-1
Accelerator Pedal Position Sensor (APPS), 4-2
Accelerator pump(s) and controls, 9-7
Add-on chips and performance upgrades for computers, 4-11
Aftermarket headers, 10-2
Air and coolant temperature sensors, 9-21
Air intakes, short-ram and cold-air, 6-2
Air/fuel ratio meter, 16-19
Ambient temperature sensor, 4-2

B

Backpressure and flow, exhaust, 10-1
Balancing, 12-19
Block, engine, 12-14
Blowers, 11-6
Blowers and turbos, engine management issues, 4-13
Blueprinting
the bottom end, 12-3
the valvetrain, 8-11
Braided steel hose covers, 3-12
Building a 427-inch Ford small-block, 13-17
Building a blown 572 big-block Chevrolet, 13-28
Building the GM LS1 for extreme street duty, 13-2

C

Camshaft Position (CMP) sensor, 4-2
Camshafts, 8-2
Camshafts and Valvetrain, 8-1
blueprinting the valvetrain, 8-11
how to degree a camshaft, 8-8
lifters, 8-6
rocker arms, 8-1
valve springs, 8-9
Carburetor
accelerator pump(s) and controls, 9-7
carburetion setups 6-8
float bowl, 9-7
formula to use in figuring cfm requirement, 9-2
fuel lines and filters, 9-10
heat, 9-9
high-performance fuel pump, 9-11
main body, 9-3
main body and air horn (Rochester carburetors), 9-6
mechanical and vacuum secondaries (Holley), 9-8
metering block (Holley carburetors), 9-5
modification kits, 9-11
modifications, 9-2
secondary circuit, 9-8
selection, 9-1
seven basic operating systems, 9-2
throttle body, 9-3
Cat-back system, installing, 10-6
CDI control module, 5-5
Choosing Speed: Sourcing Performance Equipment and Services, 2-1
Cleaning and detailing your engine compartment, 3-3
Coil bind, valve springs, checking for, 8-12
Coils, ignition, high-performance, 5-1
Cold-air intakes, 6-2
Common mistakes in the quest for power 1-5
Computer, 4-9
add-on chips and performance upgrades, 4-11
engine management, a brief history, 4-1
flashing or replacing chips, 4-12
hand-held programmers, 4-14
piggyback modules, 4-11
Predator Tuning Tool, 4-15
stand-alone aftermarket systems, 4-13
what to expect from piggybacks and reflashed chips, 4-13
Computers and chips, 4-1
Connecting rods, 12-9
Control module and ignition coil, installation locations, 5-2
Cooling systems, high-performance, 15-1
coolant additives, 15-1
cooling fans, 15-3
deep sump oil pans and engine oil coolers, 15-4
electric water pumps, 15-4
radiator cooling fans, 15-3
radiators, 15-2
transmission oil coolers, 15-5
under-drive pulleys, 15-4
water pumps, 15-4

Crankshaft Position (CKP) sensor, 4-3
Crankshaft work, 12-5
Crate motors
choosing, 14-11
general information, 14-2
Crates and Swaps, 14-1
Crossover pipes, exhaust, 10-6
Cylinder Head Temperature (CHT) sensor, 4-4
Cylinder Heads and Valves, 7-1
Cylinder heads, flow bench, 2-7

D

Deep sump oil pans and engine oil coolers, 15-4
Degree-ing a camshaft, 8-8
Dynamometers
chassis, 2-5
engine, 2-4
The Ultimate Tuning Tool, 2-4

E

Electric fuel pump, 9-14
Electric water pumps, 15-4
Electronic Throttle Body, 4-9
Engine block, 12-14
Engine Builds
Building a 427-inch Ford small-block, 13-17
Building a blown 572 big-block Chevrolet, 13-28
Building the GM LS1 for extreme street duty, 13-2
How the Pros Make Big Power with Reliability, 13-1
Engine compartment
cleaning and detailing, 3-3
dressing up a Chevy big-block, 3-10
painting and final details on a Ford small-block, 3-5
washing, 3-4
Engine Coolant Temperature (ECT) sensor, 4-4
Engine dynamometers, 2-4
Engine management
basics, 4-2
computer, a brief history, 4-1
Engine management computer
add-on chips and performance upgrades, 4-11
flashing or replacing chips, 4-12
hand-held programmers, 4-14
Predator Tuning Tool, 4-15
stand-alone aftermarket systems, 4-13
what to expect from piggybacks and reflashed chips, 4-13
Engine oil coolers, 15-4
Engine swaps, 14-13
EVAP canister purge valve, 4-10
EVAP leak detection systems, 4-10
Exhaust Gas Recirculation (EGR) valve, 4-10
Exhaust Gas Recirculation (EGR) valve position sensor, 4-4
Exhaust system
aftermarket headers, 10-2
backpressure and flow, exhaust, 10-1
buying tips, 10-4
component matching, 10-3
conventional or original equipment mufflers, 10-5
crossover pipes, 10-6
header designs, 10-3
headers, disadvantages, 10-4
installing a typical cat-back system, 10-6
length and diameter, header pipes, 10-3
manifolds, 10-1
modifying the exhaust system, 10-2
mufflers, 10-5
pipe diameter, 10-6
stainless steel, 10-6

F

Fans, engine cooling, 15-3
Finding the right carburetor, 9-1
Fire sleeves, 5-4
Flashing or replacing chips, 4-12
Flow bench, 2-7
Fuel filter, 9-16
Fuel hoses and lines, 9-20
Fuel injection systems, 9-12
electric fuel pump, 9-14
fuel injectors, 4-10, 9-17
fuel pressure regulator, 9-19
fuel pulsation damper, 9-17
fuel pump relay, 9-16
fuel rail, 9-17
high-performance fuel pressure regulators and gauges, 9-25
high-performance fuel pumps, 9-27
induction system, 9-14
modifying, 9-25
Multiport electronic fuel injection, 9-13
Throttle body injection (TBI), 9-12
what is fuel injection?, 9-12
why fuel injection?, 9-12
Fuel lines and filters, 9-10
Fuel tank pressure sensor, 4-5

G

Gauges
G-Tech tuning tools, 16-5
G-Tech/Pro, 16-5
G-Tech/Pro COMPETITION, 16-6
installing a Tachometer, 16-8
installing, how much will it cost?, 16-2
mechanical vs. electrical, 16-3
size, 16-2
style and color, 16-2
types, 16-4
what kind of gauges do you want?, 16-2
where to install, 16-3
Glasspack mufflers, 10-5
G-Tech tuning tools
G-Tech/Pro, 16-5
G-Tech/Pro COMPETITION, 16-6

H

Hand-held programmers, 4-14
Header designs, 10-3
Headers, aftermarket, 10-2
High-performance Cooling Systems, 15-1

High-performance fuel pressure regulators and gauges, 9-25
High-performance fuel pumps, 9-27
High-performance ignition coils, 5-1
High-performance Ignition Systems, 5-1
Horsepower vs. torque, 1-4
Hose covers, braided steel, 3-12
How to degree a camshaft, 8-8
Hydraulic lifters, 8-6

I

Idle air control (IAC) valve, 4-10
Ignition system
- CDI control module, 5-5
- control module and ignition coil, installation locations, 5-2
- fire sleeves, 5-4
- high-performance ignition coils, 5-1
- reading the plugs, 5-6
- spark plug wires, performance, 5-4
- spark plugs, 5-6
- timing controls, 5-4

Induction
- carburetion, 6-8
- intake manifolds, 6-5
- Short-ram and cold-air intakes, 6-2
- The Science of Deep Breathing, 6-1
- throttle bodies, 6-4

Induction system, fuel injection, 9-14
Information sensors, 4-2
- Accelerator Pedal Position Sensor (APPS), 4-2
- Ambient temperature sensor, 4-2
- Camshaft Position (CMP) sensor, 4-2
- Crankshaft Position (CKP) sensor, 4-3
- Cylinder Head Temperature (CHT) sensor, 4-4
- Engine Coolant Temperature (ECT) sensor, 4-4
- Exhaust Gas Recirculation (EGR) valve position sensor, 4-4
- Fuel tank pressure sensor, 4-5
- Intake Air Temperature (IAT) sensor, 4-5
- Knock sensor, 4-6
- Manifold Absolute Pressure (MAP) sensor, 4-6
- Mass Airflow (MAF) sensor, 4-6
- Oxygen sensors, 4-6
- Power Steering Pressure (PSP) switch, 4-7
- Throttle Position (TP) sensor, 4-8
- Transmission Range (TR) sensor, 4-8
- Transmission speed sensors, 4-8
- Vehicle Speed Sensor (VSS), 4-9

Injectors, fuel, 9-17
Innovate LM-1 wide-band air/fuel ratio meter, 16-19
Innovate LMA-3 Multi-sensor Device (AuxBox), 16-21
Installed height, valve springs, checking, 8-11
Intake Air Temperature (IAT) sensor, 4-5
Intake manifolds, 6-5

K

Knock sensor, 4-6

L

Lifters, 8-6

M

Manifold Absolute Pressure (MAP) sensor, 4-6, 9-20
Mass Air Flow (MAF) sensor, 9-21
Mass Airflow (MAF) sensor, 4-6
Mechanical and vacuum secondaries (Holley), 9-8
Mistake number one, 1-5
Modifying the exhaust system, 10-2
Monitoring Engine Performance, 16-1
- gauges
  - installing a Tachometer, 16-8
  - installing, how much will it cost?, 16-2
  - mechanical vs. electrical, 16-3
  - pillar pod gauges, installing, 16-12
  - types, 16-4
  - what kind of gauges do you want?, 16-2
  - where to install, 16-3
- G-Tech tuning tools
  - G-Tech/Pro, 16-5
  - G-Tech/Pro COMPETITION, 16-6
- Innovate LM-1 wide-band air/fuel ratio meter, 16-19
- Innovate LMA-3 Multi-sensor Device (AuxBox), 16-21
- scan tools, 16-6
- wide-band air/fuel ratio gauge, installing, 16-16

Mufflers, 10-5
- conventional or original equipment mufflers, 10-5
- glasspack mufflers, 10-5
- turbo mufflers, 10-6

Multiport electronic fuel injection, 9-13

N

Nitrous oxide, 11-2

O

Oil coolers, transmission, 15-5
Output actuators, 4-9
- Electronic Throttle Body, 4-9
- EVAP canister purge valve, 4-10
- EVAP leak detection systems, 4-10
- Exhaust Gas Recirculation (EGR) valve, 4-10
- Fuel injectors, 4-10
- Idle air control (IAC) valve, 4-10

Oxygen sensors, 4-6, 9-22

P

Painting and final details on a Ford small-block engine compartment, 3-5
Painting valve covers, 3-5
Performance plug wires, 5-4
Performance upgrades for computers, 4-11
Performance-oriented automotive machine shops, 2-3
Pick the right speed shop, 2-4
Piggyback modules, 4-11
Pillar pod gauges, installing, 16-12
Port matching, 6-7
Power Adders: Juice and boost, 11-1
Power Planning: Matching goals, budget and driving needs, 1-1

Power Steering Pressure (PSP) switch, 4-7
Pressure regulator, fuel injection, 9-19
Pressure regulators and gauges, high-performance, 9-25
Pressure washing, 3-4
Pro-building a 427-inch Ford small-block, 13-17
Processing: The computer, 9-23
Pulleys, under-drive, 15-4
Pulsation damper, fuel injection, 9-17
Pulse width, fuel injectors, 9-24

R

Racing, street, 1-6
Radiator cooling fans, 15-3
Radiators, 15-2
Reading the plugs, 5-6
Regulator, fuel pressure, 9-19
Relay, fuel pump, 9-16
Retail speed shops, 2-2
Rocker arms, 8-1
Roller lifters, 8-6

S

Scan tools, 16-6
Short-ram and cold-air intakes, 6-2
Spark plug wires, performance, 5-4
Spark plugs, 5-6
Spark plugs, reading, 5-6
Speed shops
  is the shop affordable?, 2-8
  performance-oriented machine shops, 2-3
  pick the right people, 2-6
  retail, 2-2
  tuning shops, 2-5
  what IS a speed shop, 2-2
  why you need help, 2-1
Springs, valve, 8-9
Street racing, 1-6
Stroker engines, 12-17
Superchargers and turbos, engine management issues, 4-13
Supercharging, 11-7

T

The Bottom End: Building it to Last, 12-1
The Flow Bench: The Tuner's Wind Tunnel, 2-7
The Fuel System, 9-1
The Look of Speed, 3-1
Throttle bodies, 6-4
Throttle body injection (TBI), 9-12
Throttle position (TP) sensor, 4-8, 9-23
Timing controls, ignition system, 5-4
Timing the injection system, 9-23
Torque vs. horsepower, 1-4
Transmission oil coolers, 15-5
Transmission Range (TR) sensor, 4-8
Transmission speed sensors, 4-8
Tuning shops, 2-5
Tuning Tool Test, 4-15
Turbo mufflers, 10-6
Turbocharging, 11-15
Turbos and blowers, engine management issues, 4-13

U

Under-drive pulleys, 15-4

V

Valve covers, detailing, 3-5
Valve job, description, 7-7
Valve lifters, 8-6
Valve springs, 8-9
Valvetrain and camshafts, 8-1
Valvetrain blueprinting, 8-11
Vehicle Speed Sensor (VSS), 4-9
Volumetric efficiency, 9-2

W

Water pumps, 15-4
What IS a speed shop?, 2-2
What to expect from piggybacks and reflashed chips, 4-13
Why you need help, 2-1
Wide-band air/fuel ratio gauge, installing, 16-16

Haynes Automotive Manuals

NOTE: If you do not see a listing for your vehicle, consult your local Haynes dealer for the latest product information.

HAYNES XTREME CUSTOMIZING
11101 Sport Compact Customizing
11102 Sport Compact Performance
11110 In-car Entertainment
11150 Sport Utility Vehicle Customizing
11213 Acura
11255 GM Full-size Pick-ups
11314 Ford Focus
11315 Full-size Ford Pick-ups
11373 Honda Civic

ACURA
12020 Integra '86 thru '89 & Legend '86 thru '90
12021 Integra '90 thru '93 & Legend '91 thru '95

AMC
Jeep CJ - *see JEEP (50020)*
14020 Mid-size models '70 thru '83
14025 (Renault) Alliance & Encore '83 thru '87

AUDI
15020 4000 all models '80 thru '87
15025 5000 all models '77 thru '83
15026 5000 all models '84 thru '88

AUSTIN-HEALEY
Sprite - *see MG Midget (66015)*

BMW
18020 3/5 Series not including diesel or all-wheel drive models '82 thru '92
18021 3-Series incl. Z3 models '92 thru '98
18022 3-Series, E46 chassis '99 thru '05, Z4 models '03 thru '05
18025 320i all 4 cyl models '75 thru '83
18050 1500 thru 2002 except Turbo '59 thru '77

BUICK
19010 Buick Century '97 thru '05
Century (front-wheel drive) - *see GM (38005)*
19020 Buick, Oldsmobile & Pontiac Full-size (Front-wheel drive) '85 thru '05
Buick Electra, LeSabre and Park Avenue; Oldsmobile Delta 88 Royale, Ninety Eight and Regency; Pontiac Bonneville
19025 Buick Oldsmobile & Pontiac Full-size (Rear wheel drive)
Buick Estate '70 thru '90, Electra'70 thru '84, LeSabre '70 thru '85, Limited '74 thru '79
Oldsmobile Custom Cruiser '70 thru '90, Delta 88 '70 thru '85,Ninety-eight '70 thru '84
Pontiac Bonneville '70 thru '81, Catalina '70 thru '81, Grandville '70 thru '75, Parisienne '83 thru '86
19030 Mid-size Regal & Century all rear-drive models with V6, V8 and Turbo '74 thru '87
Regal - *see GENERAL MOTORS (38010)*
Riviera - *see GENERAL MOTORS (38030)*
Roadmaster - *see CHEVROLET (24046)*
Skyhawk - *see GENERAL MOTORS (38015)*
Skylark - *see GM (38020, 38025)*
Somerset - *see GENERAL MOTORS (38025)*

CADILLAC
21030 Cadillac Rear Wheel Drive all gasoline models '70 thru '93
Cimarron - *see GENERAL MOTORS (38015)*
DeVille - *see GM (38031 & 38032)*
Eldorado - *see GM (38030 & 38031)*
Fleetwood - *see GM (38031)*
Seville - *see GM (38030, 38031 & 38032)*

CHEVROLET
24010 Astro & GMC Safari Mini-vans '85 thru '03
24015 Camaro V8 all models '70 thru '81
24016 Camaro all models '82 thru '92
24017 Camaro & Firebird '93 thru '02
Cavalier - *see GENERAL MOTORS (38016)*
Celebrity - *see GENERAL MOTORS (38005)*
24020 Chevelle, Malibu & El Camino '69 thru '87
24024 Chevette & Pontiac T1000 '76 thru '87
Citation - *see GENERAL MOTORS (38020)*
24027 Colorado & GMC Canyon '04 thru '06
24032 Corsica/Beretta all models '87 thru '96
24040 Corvette all V8 models '68 thru '82
24041 Corvette all models '84 thru '96
10305 Chevrolet Engine Overhaul Manual
24045 Full-size Sedans Caprice, Impala, Biscayne, Bel Air & Wagons '69 thru '90
24046 Impala SS & Caprice and Buick Roadmaster '91 thru '96
Impala - *see LUMINA (24048)*
Lumina '90 thru '94 - *see GM (38010)*
24048 Lumina & Monte Carlo '95 thru '05
Lumina APV - *see GM (38035)*
24050 Luv Pick-up all 2WD & 4WD '72 thru '82
Malibu '97 thru '00 - *see GM (38026)*
24055 Monte Carlo all models '70 thru '88
Monte Carlo '95 thru '01 - *see LUMINA (24048)*
24059 Nova all V8 models '69 thru '79
24060 Nova and Geo Prizm '85 thru '92
24064 Pick-ups '67 thru '87 - Chevrolet & GMC, all V8 & in-line 6 cyl, 2WD & 4WD '67 thru '87; Suburbans, Blazers & Jimmys '67 thru '91
24065 Pick-ups '88 thru '98 - Chevrolet & GMC, full-size pick-ups '88 thru '98, C/K Classic '99 & '00, Blazer & Jimmy '92 thru '94; Suburban '92 thru '99; Tahoe & Yukon '95 thru '99
24066 Pick-ups '99 thru '06 - Chevrolet Silverado & GMC Sierra '99 thru '06, Suburban/Tahoe/ Yukon/Yukon XL/Avalanche '00 thru '06
24070 S-10 & S-15 Pick-ups '82 thru '93, Blazer & Jimmy '83 thru '94,
24071 S-10 & Sonoma Pick-ups '94 thru '04, Blazer & Jimmy '95 thru '04, Hombre '96 thru '01
24072 Chevrolet TrailBlazer & TrailBlazer EXT, GMC Envoy & Envoy XL, Oldsmobile Bravada '02 thru '06
24075 Sprint '85 thru '88 & Geo Metro '89 thru '01
24080 Vans - Chevrolet & GMC '68 thru '96
24081 Chevrolet Express & GMC Savana Full-size Vans '96 thru '05

CHRYSLER
25015 Chrysler Cirrus, Dodge Stratus, Plymouth Breeze '95 thru '00
10310 Chrysler Engine Overhaul Manual
25020 Full-size Front-Wheel Drive '88 thru '93
K-Cars - *see DODGE Aries (30008)*
Laser - *see DODGE Daytona (30030)*
25025 Chrysler LHS, Concorde, New Yorker, Dodge Intrepid, Eagle Vision, '93 thru '97
25026 Chrysler LHS, Concorde, 300M, Dodge Intrepid, '98 thru '03
25027 Chrysler 300, Dodge Charger & Magnum '05 thru '07
25030 Chrysler & Plymouth Mid-size front wheel drive '82 thru '95
Rear-wheel Drive - *see Dodge (30050)*
25035 PT Cruiser all models '01 thru '03
25040 Chrysler Sebring, Dodge Avenger '95 thru '05
Dodge Stratus '01 thru 05

DATSUN
28005 200SX all models '80 thru '83
28007 B-210 all models '73 thru '78
28009 210 all models '79 thru '82
28012 240Z, 260Z & 280Z Coupe '70 thru '78
28014 280ZX Coupe & 2+2 '79 thru '83
300ZX - *see NISSAN (72010)*
28018 510 & PL521 Pick-up '68 thru '73
28020 510 all models '78 thru '81
28022 620 Series Pick-up all models '73 thru '79
720 Series Pick-up - *see NISSAN (72030)*
28025 810/Maxima all gasoline models, '77 thru '84

DODGE
400 & 600 - *see CHRYSLER (25030)*
30008 Aries & Plymouth Reliant '81 thru '89
30010 Caravan & Plymouth Voyager '84 thru '95
30011 Caravan & Plymouth Voyager '96 thru '02
30012 Challenger/Plymouth Saporro '78 thru '83
30013 Caravan, Chrysler Voyager, Town & Country '03 thru '06
30016 Colt & Plymouth Champ '78 thru '87
30020 Dakota Pick-ups all models '87 thru '96
30021 Durango '98 & '99, Dakota '97 thru '99
30022 Dodge Durango models '00 thru '03
Dodge Dakota models '00 thru '04
30023 Dodge Durango '04 thru '06, Dakota '05 and '06
30025 Dart, Demon, Plymouth Barracuda, Duster & Valiant 6 cyl models '67 thru '76
30030 Daytona & Chrysler Laser '84 thru '89
Intrepid - *see CHRYSLER (25025, 25026)*
30034 Neon all models '95 thru '99
30035 Omni & Plymouth Horizon '78 thru '90
30036 Dodge and Plymouth Neon '00 thru'05
30040 Pick-ups all full-size models '74 thru '93
30041 Pick-ups all full-size models '94 thru '01
30042 Dodge Full-size Pick-ups '02 thru '05
30045 Ram 50/D50 Pick-ups & Raider and Plymouth Arrow Pick-ups '79 thru '93
30050 Dodge/Plymouth/Chrysler RWD '71 thru '89
30055 Shadow & Plymouth Sundance '87 thru '94
30060 Spirit & Plymouth Acclaim '89 thru '95
30065 Vans - Dodge & Plymouth '71 thru '03

EAGLE
Talon - *see MITSUBISHI (68030, 68031)*
Vision - *see CHRYSLER (25025)*

FIAT
34010 124 Sport Coupe & Spider '68 thru '78
34025 X1/9 all models '74 thru '80

FORD
10355 Ford Automatic Transmission Overhaul
36004 Aerostar Mini-vans all models '86 thru '97
36006 Contour & Mercury Mystique '95 thru '00
36008 Courier Pick-up all models '72 thru '82
36012 Crown Victoria & Mercury Grand Marquis '88 thru '06
10320 Ford Engine Overhaul Manual
36016 Escort/Mercury Lynx all models '81 thru '90
36020 Escort/Mercury Tracer '91 thru '00
36022 Ford Escape & Mazda Tribute '01 thru '03
36024 Explorer & Mazda Navajo '91 thru '01
36025 Ford Explorer & Mercury Mountaineer '02 thru '06
36028 Fairmont & Mercury Zephyr '78 thru '83
36030 Festiva & Aspire '88 thru '97
36032 Fiesta all models '77 thru '80
36034 Focus all models '00 thru '05
36036 Ford & Mercury Full-size '75 thru '87
36044 Ford & Mercury Mid-size '75 thru '86
36048 Mustang V8 all models '64-1/2 thru '73
36049 Mustang II 4 cyl, V6 & V8 models '74 thru '78
36050 Mustang & Mercury Capri all models Mustang, '79 thru '93; Capri, '79 thru '86
36051 Mustang all models '94 thru '04
36052 Mustang '05 thru '07
36054 Pick-ups & Bronco '73 thru '79
36058 Pick-ups & Bronco '80 thru '96
36059 F-150 & Expedition '97 thru '03, F-250 '97 thru '99 & Lincoln Navigator '98 thru '02
36060 Super Duty Pick-ups, Excursion '99 thru '06
36061 F-150 full-size '04 thru '06
36062 Pinto & Mercury Bobcat '75 thru '80
36066 Probe all models '89 thru '92
36070 Ranger/Bronco II gasoline models '83 thru '92
36071 Ranger '93 thru '05 & Mazda Pick-ups '94 thru '05
36074 Taurus & Mercury Sable '86 thru '95
36075 Taurus & Mercury Sable '96 thru '05
36078 Tempo & Mercury Topaz '84 thru '94
36082 Thunderbird/Mercury Cougar '83 thru '88
36086 Thunderbird/Mercury Cougar '89 and '97
36090 Vans all V8 Econoline models '69 thru '91
36094 Vans full size '92 thru '05
36097 Windstar Mini-van '95 thru '03

GENERAL MOTORS
10360 GM Automatic Transmission Overhaul
38005 Buick Century, Chevrolet Celebrity, Oldsmobile Cutlass Ciera & Pontiac 6000 all models '82 thru '96
38010 Buick Regal, Chevrolet Lumina, Oldsmobile Cutlass Supreme & Pontiac Grand Prix (FWD) '88 thru '05
38015 Buick Skyhawk, Cadillac Cimarron, Chevrolet Cavalier, Oldsmobile Firenza & Pontiac J-2000 & Sunbird '82 thru '94
38016 Chevrolet Cavalier & Pontiac Sunfire '95 thru '04
38017 Chevrolet Cobalt & Pontiac G5 '05 thru '07
38020 Buick Skylark, Chevrolet Citation, Olds Omega, Pontiac Phoenix '80 thru '85
38025 Buick Skylark & Somerset, Oldsmobile Achieva & Calais and Pontiac Grand Am all models '85 thru '98
38026 Chevrolet Malibu, Olds Alero & Cutlass, Pontiac Grand Am '97 thru '03
38027 Chevrolet Malibu '04 thru '07
38030 Cadillac Eldorado '71 thru '85, Seville '80 thru '85, Oldsmobile Toronado '71 thru '85, Buick Riviera '79 thru '85
38031 Cadillac Eldorado & Seville '86 thru '91, DeVille '86 thru '93, Fleetwood & Olds Toronado '86 thru '92, Buick Riviera '86 thru '93
38032 Cadillac DeVille '94 thru '05 & Seville '92 thru '04
38035 Chevrolet Lumina APV, Olds Silhouette & Pontiac Trans Sport all models '90 thru '96
38036 Chevrolet Venture, Olds Silhouette, Pontiac Trans Sport & Montana '97 thru '05
General Motors Full-size Rear-wheel Drive - see BUICK (19025)

GEO
Metro - *see CHEVROLET Sprint (24075)*
Prizm - *'85 thru '92 see CHEVY (24060), '93 thru '02 see TOYOTA Corolla (92036)*

(Continued on other side)

Haynes Automotive Manuals (continued)

NOTE: If you do not see a listing for your vehicle, consult your local Haynes dealer for the latest product information.

40030 **Storm** all models '90 thru '93
Tracker - *see SUZUKI Samurai (90010)*

GMC
Vans & Pick-ups - *see CHEVROLET*

HONDA
42010 **Accord CVCC** all models '76 thru '83
42011 **Accord** all models '84 thru '89
42012 **Accord** all models '90 thru '93
42013 **Accord** all models '94 thru '97
42014 **Accord** all models '98 thru '02
42015 **Honda Accord** models '03 thru '05
42020 **Civic 1200** all models '73 thru '79
42021 **Civic 1300 & 1500 CVCC** '80 thru '83
42022 **Civic 1500 CVCC** all models '75 thru '79
42023 **Civic** all models '84 thru '91
42024 **Civic & del Sol** '92 thru '95
42025 **Civic** '96 thru '00, **CR-V** '97 thru '01, **Acura Integra** '94 thru '00
42026 **Civic** '01 thru '04, **CR-V** '02 thru '04
42035 **Honda Odyssey** all models '99 thru '04
42037 **Honda Pilot** '03 thru '07, **Acura MDX** '01 thru '07
42040 **Prelude CVCC** all models '79 thru '89

HYUNDAI
43010 **Elantra** all models '96 thru '01
43015 **Excel & Accent** all models '86 thru '98

ISUZU
Hombre - *see CHEVROLET S-10 (24071)*
47017 **Rodeo** '91 thru '02; **Amigo** '89 thru '94 and '98 thru '02; **Honda Passport** '95 thru '02
47020 **Trooper & Pick-up** '81 thru '93

JAGUAR
49010 **XJ6** all 6 cyl models '68 thru '86
49011 **XJ6** all models '88 thru '94
49015 **XJ12 & XJS** all 12 cyl models '72 thru '85

JEEP
50010 **Cherokee, Comanche & Wagoneer Limited** all models '84 thru '01
50020 **CJ** all models '49 thru '86
50025 **Grand Cherokee** all models '93 thru '04
50029 **Grand Wagoneer & Pick-up** '72 thru '91 Grand Wagoneer '84 thru '91, Cherokee & Wagoneer '72 thru '83, Pick-up '72 thru '88
50030 **Wrangler** all models '87 thru '03
50035 **Liberty** '02 thru '04

KIA
54070 **Sephia** '94 thru '01, **Spectra** '00 thru '04

LEXUS
ES 300 - *see TOYOTA Camry (92007)*

LINCOLN
Navigator - *see FORD Pick-up (36059)*
59010 **Rear-Wheel Drive** all models '70 thru '05

MAZDA
61010 **GLC Hatchback (rear-wheel drive)** '77 thru '83
61011 **GLC (front-wheel drive)** '81 thru '85
61015 **323 & Protogé** '90 thru '00
61016 **MX-5 Miata** '90 thru '97
61020 **MPV** all models '89 thru '94
Navajo - *see Ford Explorer (36024)*
61030 **Pick-ups** '72 thru '93
Pick-ups '94 thru '00 - *see Ford Ranger (36071)*
61035 **RX-7** all models '79 thru '85
61036 **RX-7** all models '86 thru '91
61040 **626** (rear-wheel drive) all models '79 thru '82
61041 **626/MX-6 (front-wheel drive)** '83 thru '92
61042 **626** '93 thru '01, **MX-6/Ford Probe** '93 thru '01

MERCEDES-BENZ
63012 **123 Series Diesel** '76 thru '85
63015 **190 Series** four-cyl gas models, '84 thru '88
63020 **230/250/280** 6 cyl sohc models '68 thru '72
63025 **280 123 Series** gasoline models '77 thru '81
63030 **350 & 450** all models '71 thru '80

MERCURY
64200 **Villager & Nissan Quest** '93 thru '01
All other titles, see FORD Listing.

MG
66010 **MGB** Roadster & GT Coupe '62 thru '80
66015 **MG Midget, Austin Healey Sprite** '58 thru '80

MITSUBISHI
68020 **Cordia, Tredia, Galant, Precis & Mirage** '83 thru '93
68030 **Eclipse, Eagle Talon & Ply. Laser** '90 thru '94
68031 **Eclipse** '95 thru '01, **Eagle Talon** '95 thru '98
68035 **Mitsubishi Galant** '94 thru '03
68040 **Pick-up** '83 thru '96 **& Montero** '83 thru '93

NISSAN
72010 **300ZX** all models including Turbo '84 thru '89
72015 **Altima** all models '93 thru '04
72020 **Maxima** all models '85 thru '92
72021 **Maxima** all models '93 thru '04
72030 **Pick-ups** '80 thru '97 **Pathfinder** '87 thru '95
72031 **Frontier Pick-up** '98 thru '04, **Xterra** '00 thru '04, **Pathfinder** '96 thru '04
72040 **Pulsar** all models '83 thru '86
Quest - *see MERCURY Villager (64200)*
72050 **Sentra** all models '82 thru '94
72051 **Sentra & 200SX** all models '95 thru '04
72060 **Stanza** all models '82 thru '90

OLDSMOBILE
73015 **Cutlass** V6 & V8 gas models '74 thru '88
For other OLDSMOBILE titles, see BUICK, CHEVROLET or GENERAL MOTORS listing.

PLYMOUTH
For PLYMOUTH titles, see DODGE listing.

PONTIAC
79008 **Fiero** all models '84 thru '88
79018 **Firebird** V8 models except Turbo '70 thru '81
79019 **Firebird** all models '82 thru '92
79040 **Mid-size Rear-wheel Drive** '70 thru '87
For other PONTIAC titles, see BUICK, CHEVROLET or GENERAL MOTORS listing.

PORSCHE
80020 **911** except Turbo & Carrera 4 '65 thru '89
80025 **914** all 4 cyl models '69 thru '76
80030 **924** all models including Turbo '76 thru '82
80035 **944** all models including Turbo '83 thru '89

RENAULT
Alliance & Encore - *see AMC (14020)*

SAAB
84010 **900** all models including Turbo '79 thru '88

SATURN
87010 **Saturn** all models '91 thru '02
87011 **Saturn Ion** '03 thru '07
87020 **Saturn** all L-series models '00 thru '04

SUBARU
89002 **1100, 1300, 1400 & 1600** '71 thru '79
89003 **1600 & 1800** 2WD & 4WD '80 thru '94
89100 **Legacy** all models '90 thru '99
89101 **Legacy & Forester** '00 thru '06

SUZUKI
90010 **Samurai/Sidekick & Geo Tracker** '86 thru '01

TOYOTA
92005 **Camry** all models '83 thru '91
92006 **Camry** all models '92 thru '96
92007 **Camry, Avalon, Solara, Lexus ES 300** '97 thru '01
92008 **Toyota Camry, Avalon and Solara and Lexus ES 300/330** all models '02 thru '05
92015 **Celica Rear Wheel Drive** '71 thru '85
92020 **Celica Front Wheel Drive** '86 thru '99
92025 **Celica Supra** all models '79 thru '92
92030 **Corolla** all models '75 thru '79
92032 **Corolla** all rear wheel drive models '80 thru '87
92035 **Corolla** all front wheel drive models '84 thru '92
92036 **Corolla & Geo Prizm** '93 thru '02
92037 **Corolla** models '03 thru '05
92040 **Corolla Tercel** all models '80 thru '82
92045 **Corona** all models '74 thru '82
92050 **Cressida** all models '78 thru '82
92055 **Land Cruiser** FJ40, 43, 45, 55 '68 thru '82
92056 **Land Cruiser** FJ60, 62, 80, FZJ80 '80 thru '96
92065 **MR2** all models '85 thru '87
92070 **Pick-up** all models '69 thru '78
92075 **Pick-up** all models '79 thru '95
92076 **Tacoma** '95 thru '04, **4Runner** '96 thru '02, **& T100** '93 thru '98
92078 **Tundra** '00 thru '05 **& Sequoia** '01 thru '05
92080 **Previa** all models '91 thru '95
92081 **Prius** all models '01 thru '08
92082 **RAV4** all models '96 thru '05
92085 **Tercel** all models '87 thru '94
92090 **Toyota Sienna** all models '98 thru '02
92095 **Highlander & Lexus RX-330** '99 thru '06

TRIUMPH
94007 **Spitfire** all models '62 thru '81
94010 **TR7** all models '75 thru '81

VW
96008 **Beetle & Karmann Ghia** '54 thru '79
96009 **New Beetle** '98 thru '05
96016 **Rabbit, Jetta, Scirocco & Pick-up** gas models '75 thru '92 & Convertible '80 thru '92
96017 **Golf, GTI & Jetta** '93 thru '98 **& Cabrio** '95 thru '98
96018 **Golf, GTI, Jetta & Cabrio** '99 thru '02
96020 **Rabbit, Jetta & Pick-up** diesel '77 thru '84
96023 **Passat** '98 thru '01, **Audi A4** '96 thru '01
96030 **Transporter 1600** all models '68 thru '79
96035 **Transporter 1700, 1800 & 2000** '72 thru '79
96040 **Type 3 1500 & 1600** all models '63 thru '73
96045 **Vanagon** all air-cooled models '80 thru '83

VOLVO
97010 **120, 130 Series & 1800 Sports** '61 thru '73
97015 **140 Series** all models '66 thru '74
97020 **240 Series** all models '76 thru '93
97040 **740 & 760 Series** all models '82 thru '88
97050 **850 Series** all models '93 thru '97

TECHBOOK MANUALS
10205 **Automotive Computer Codes**
10206 **OBD-II & Electronic Engine Management Systems**
10210 **Automotive Emissions Control Manual**
10215 **Fuel Injection Manual, 1978 thru 1985**
10220 **Fuel Injection Manual, 1986 thru 1999**
10225 **Holley Carburetor Manual**
10230 **Rochester Carburetor Manual**
10240 **Weber/Zenith/Stromberg/SU Carburetors**
10305 **Chevrolet Engine Overhaul Manual**
10310 **Chrysler Engine Overhaul Manual**
10320 **Ford Engine Overhaul Manual**
10330 **GM and Ford Diesel Engine Repair Manual**
10333 **Building Engine Power Manual**
10340 **Small Engine Repair Manual,** 5 HP & Less
10341 **Small Engine Repair Manual,** 5.5 - 20 HP
10345 **Suspension, Steering & Driveline Manual**
10355 **Ford Automatic Transmission Overhaul**
10360 **GM Automatic Transmission Overhaul**
10405 **Automotive Body Repair & Painting**
10410 **Automotive Brake Manual**
10411 **Automotive Anti-lock Brake (ABS) Systems**
10415 **Automotive Detaiing Manual**
10420 **Automotive Electrical Manual**
10425 **Automotive Heating & Air Conditioning**
10430 **Automotive Reference Manual & Dictionary**
10435 **Automotive Tools Manual**
10440 **Used Car Buying Guide**
10445 **Welding Manual**
10450 **ATV Basics**
10452 **Scooters, Automatic Transmission 50cc to 250cc**

SPANISH MANUALS
98903 **Reparación de Carrocería & Pintura**
98904 **Carburadores para los modelos Holley & Rochester**
98905 **Códigos Automotrices de la Computadora**
98910 **Frenos Automotriz**
98913 **Electricidad Automotriz**
98915 **Inyección de Combustible 1986 al 1999**
99040 **Chevrolet & GMC Camionetas** '67 al '87 Incluye Suburban, Blazer & Jimmy '67 al '91
99041 **Chevrolet & GMC Camionetas** '88 al '98 Incluye Suburban '92 al '98, Blazer & Jimmy '92 al '94, Tahoe y Yukon '95 al '98
99042 **Chevrolet & GMC Camionetas Cerradas** '68 al '95
99055 **Dodge Caravan & Plymouth Voyager** '84 al '95
99075 **Ford Camionetas y Bronco** '80 al '94
99077 **Ford Camionetas Cerradas** '69 al '91
99088 **Ford Modelos de Tamaño Mediano** '75 al '86
99091 **Ford Taurus & Mercury Sable** '86 al '95
99095 **GM Modelos de Tamaño Grande** '70 al '90
99100 **GM Modelos de Tamaño Mediano** '70 al '88
99106 **Jeep Cherokee, Wagoneer & Comanche** '84 al '00
99110 **Nissan Camioneta** '80 al '96, **Pathfinder** '87 al '95
99118 **Nissan Sentra** '82 al '94
99125 **Toyota Camionetas y 4Runner** '79 al '95

Over 100 Haynes motorcycle manuals also available

10-07